DATE DUE

#45220 Highsmith Inc. 1-800-558-2110

A REFERENCE GUIDE TO THE UNITED STATES SUPREME COURT

A REFERENCE GUIDE TO THE UNITED STATES SUPREME COURT

ADVISORS

RICHARD S. KAY, *School of Law, University of Connecticut*

ROBERT C. KHAYAT, *School of Law, University of Mississippi*

JAMES W. ZIRKLE, *Marshall-Wythe School of Law, College of William and Mary*

GENERAL EDITOR

STEPHEN P. ELLIOTT

Facts On File Publications
New York, New York ● Oxford, England

A REFERENCE GUIDE TO THE UNITED STATES SUPREME COURT

Copyright © 1986 by Sachem Publishing Associates, Inc.

Library of Congress Cataloging-in-Publication Data
Main entry under title:

A Reference Guide to the United States Supreme Court.

   Bibliography: p.
   Includes index.
   1. United States.   Supreme Court.   I. Kay, Richard S.
II. Khayat, Robert C.   III. Zirkle, James W.
IV. Elliott, Stephen P.
KF8742.R45   1985   347.73'26   85-20464
ISBN 0-8160-1018-8   347.30735

Printed in the United States of America

10 9 8 7 6 5 4 3 2 1

Contents

Introduction

The Supreme Court of the United States, in making definitive judgments on crucial social and economic problems, has been at the center of the most vexing controversies in American life: general issues such as the responsibilities of the branches of the federal government, the sharing of power by the federal and state governments, and the rights of individuals, as well as more specific questions such as slavery, business trusts, the rights of labor unions, voting, school segregation, abortion, and capital punishment. The Court's decisions have been both praised and criticized, and its members have been characterized as too old, too young, too conservative, and too liberal. Considering the volatile questions before it and the passions generated by its decisions, the Supreme Court has done well to retain the respect of the American people and to see its reputation grow for nearly two centuries.

This reference guide to the Supreme Court provides both an account of the major issues confronted by the Court and easily-accessible summaries of the cases and of the careers of the justices—the people who formulated the decisions that have shaped so much of U.S. history. These text sections are supported by *Appendixes* with tabular data on the justices and their decisions, a comprehensive *Bibliography*, and the *Index*.

The Role of the Supreme Court section discusses the origins of the Court in the deliberations of the Constitutional Convention of 1787, the key role of *The Federalist Papers* in shaping the national leaders' perceptions of the judiciary, and the importance of the Constitution, the document that emerged from the Convention. The section also describes the Court's schedule and procedures, as well as its relationship with the lower federal courts and its place as a court of appeal. Throughout its history, the Court has had to base its decisions on a constitution that is flexible and open to varying interpretations. As the balance of the section shows, the Supreme Court has had a major impact, through its interpretation of the Constitution, in helping to establish federal power and in maintaining an equilibrium between federal and state powers.

The section on *The Constitutional Powers of the Branches of the Federal Government* examines the various rights and obligations accorded the legislative, executive, and judicial branches by the Constitution and the Supreme Court's rulings on issues affecting their powers. One of the primary strengths of the modern Court is its power of judicial review, the ability to determine the validity of actions by other branches of government. Since this function was not expressly stated in the Constitution, the Court itself had to establish its authority for judicial review. Chief Justice John Marshall's paramount role in this process, beginning with *Marbury v. Madison* in 1803, is explored in detail in the section, which in addition deals with the Court's authority to review state court judgments. The section also discusses the Court's relationships with its co-equal branches of government, the legislative and the executive, and how these relationships have evolved since the Constitution was adopted. In this role the Court has frequently had to resolve conflicts of authority between the executive and legislative branches.

The ongoing tension between the federal and state authorities is the subject of *Division of Power: The Federal Government and the States*. As the section shows, the tension exists not only because the Constitution explicitly reserves some powers for the federal government and others for the state governments, but also because of the implied powers given to Congress and the federal government. The Supreme Court's interpretation of the Constitution's intent in these gray areas has occupied a large part of the Court's time, particularly regarding the commerce power. A broader interpretation by the Court of the commerce power permitted a more aggressive enforcement at the beginning of the 20th century of the Sherman Antitrust Act, had a substantial effect on the Court's acceptance of New Deal legislation, and from 1964 was used to combat racial discrimination.

During recent decades, cases involving the rights of individual citizens have been the most prominent decisions made by the Court. The *Individual Rights* section traces the Court's thinking on an amendment-by-amendment basis, showing how the Court's reading of the Constitution's guarantees of such rights as free speech and practice of religious belief have evolved. At different times in the nation's history, different individual rights have gone through periods in which they have been tested before the Court. Some amendments, such as the 14th, were originally designed for one purpose, such as guaranteeing the civil rights of former slaves, and are now used in arguments to obtain and protect other rights, such as abortion.

The *Landmark Cases* section contains alphabetically-arranged summaries of more than 325 of the Supreme Court's key decisions. Each summary outlines the issues in dispute, explains the Court's decision, and, when useful, gives the conflicting views of the Court's members. These decisions are often cited in the preceding text sections and in the *Biographies of the Justices* section that follows, so reference guide users should consult *Landmark Cases* whenever full details of a case, including its citation number, are needed.

Individual personalities always play an important role in the actions of a group, and the *Biographies of the Justices* section allows users of the reference guide to examine both the influences on and the thinking of the individual justices and how individuals interacted with each other and with the prevailing mood of the Court. Arranged alphabetically, the biographies detail a justice's background and career before reaching the Supreme Court, the justice's philosophy and key decisions while sitting on the Court, and any significant activities after leaving the bench.

The *Appendixes* enable users of the reference guide to scan quickly data about individual justices and cases and to relate items to each other within a chronological framework. The chart of Sitting Courts shows when justices served together on the Court. The full text of the *Constitution* follows the *Appendixes*, and there is a comprehensive *Bibliography* divided into two sections: general works about the Supreme Court and works about or by the justices.

The *Index* contains both subject listings that permit users to research the treatment of specific topics and a complete listing of all cases cited in the guide. Case names appear in italics in the *Index*. The multi-level *Index* is intended as a research tool; users of the reference guide can consult it to approach a topic in several ways. The reader can look for page references under a subject heading (such as School desegregation), a case name (*Brown v. Board of Education of Topeka*), or the name of a justice involved with the issue (Warren, Earl). At each point of entry, the reader will find references to the overall subject, to cases pertaining to the issue, and to the justices involved with the decision.

The Role
of the
Supreme Court

The Role of the Supreme Court

When the Constitutional Convention met in Philadelphia in 1787, its initial task was to correct the principal defects of the Articles of Confederation, among which was the absence of a national government sufficiently powerful to conduct foreign relations and to regulate interstate trade and commerce. The separate states (having been unified by the Revolutionary War) were free under the Articles to regulate commerce without regard to the interests of adjoining states. Coastal states imposed tariffs on goods moving through their ports to interior states, taxes were laid on goods moving in interstate commerce, and in general the welfare of the individual state was placed ahead of the welfare of the nation. The Articles of Confederation essentially provided for a joining of relatively independent states. It was against this background of increasing Balkanization that the delegates met in secret session in Philadelphia in May 1787. Out of that convention, however, came the Constitution of the United States, a document very different from the Articles of Confederation. The Constitution provides for national powers to regulate foreign relations and commerce, as well as a host of other activities that are attributes of sovereignty. Lest there be any doubt that the drafters intended to create a new nation, they specifically provided that the "Constitution, and the laws of the United States which shall be made in Pursuance thereof; and all Treaties made, or which shall be made, under the Authority of the United States, shall be the supreme law of the land."

Defining The Court's Role

Article I provides for the Congress, Article II for the Executive. Article III, the judiciary article of the Constitution, establishes the judicial power and vests it in "one Supreme Court, and in such inferior courts as the Congress may, from time to time, ordain and establish." Congress acted quickly in exercising its authority under Article III. In 1789, in the first Judiciary Act, Congress provided for a chief justice of the United States and five associate justices of the Supreme Court, and, in what must be regarded as one of the most important acts ever passed by Congress, provided for the establishment of lower federal courts. In 1807, Congress raised the number of justices to seven, including the chief justice. In 1837, Congress raised the total to nine justices, including the chief justice. With the exception of some adjustments during the Civil War years, the size of the Supreme Court has remained unchanged, with eight associate justices plus the chief justice, all appointed with life tenure by the president, with the advice and final approval of the Senate. The makeup of the Court, however, has not been without controversy. The most famous instance was Pres. Franklin D. Roosevelt's unsuccessful attempt to enlarge or "pack" the Supreme Court in the 1930s in order to reverse a pattern of decisions of the Court striking down a number of progressive legislative programs enacted by Congress in response to the Great Depression that began with the stock market crash of 1929. Prior to its change of direction in 1937, the Supreme Court had invalidated a number of Roosevelt's programs on the ground that they violated the constitutional guarantees of due process and exceeded the power of Congress.

The judicial power defines and limits the types of cases that may be brought before the federal courts. Article III, Section 2 defines the judicial power in two broad categories. The first, and most important, deals with federal questions, that is, questions arising under the Constitution, treaties, and laws of the United States, as well as admiralty and maritime jurisdiction. The second category of cases to which the judicial power extends is defined in terms of the parties to the dispute. In diversity cases, numerically the most significant type within this category, there are usually no federal questions involved, that is, no questions of federal law, constitutional or statutory, are raised in the dispute between the parties. Diversity jurisdiction was designed as a type of protective jurisdiction created to protect a litigant from possible discrimination resulting from an appearance in an out-of-state court in a suit against a citizen of that state.

The first Judiciary Act of 1789, broadly speaking, provided jurisdiction to the lower federal courts to hear civil litigation between citizens of different states, admiralty jurisdiction, federal criminal cases, and cases in which the United States was the plaintiff. The Judiciary Act did not vest in the federal courts all of the jurisdiction in diversity cases that could have been granted under the Constitution, nor, more importantly, did the act give the lower federal courts jurisdiction to hear civil cases presenting claims under the Constitution or laws of the United States. This latter jurisdiction, of considerable importance today, was not given the lower courts until 1875. Jurisdiction to hear all cases potentially arising within the judicial power has never been granted to the federal courts.

Just as the United States took its language from the English, so did it adopt the English system of laws. The United States employs the English common law system, as distinguished from the civil or Napoleonic Code system found in continental Europe. The common law model can be traced to the reign of Henry II, in the twelfth century, when measures were first undertaken to develop a centralized court system, to administer legal remedies that would apply to all of England. This common law was distinct from local law. In a common law system the rule of law may be traceable more directly to judicial decisions rather than statutory codes promulgated by a legislature or sovereign. Thus, the common law system depends much more on so-called judge-made law, and legal norms are developed out of litigation between interested parties. In the American system, truth is sought through the adversarial process in which, at least in theory, parties to a controversy fully and vigorously present all aspects of their case. In this system, the role of the court is at once greater and lesser than that of a European court. It is lesser in that, unlike the civil law model, the court is not the inquisitor but instead allows the evidence to be developed by the adversarial process. It is greater in that ultimately the court itself plays a major role in the evaluation of new legal norms.

It was out of this English common law system that the legal systems of the original colonies developed. And it was against this background that the Constitutional Convention convened in May of 1787.

The Federalist Papers. Alexander Hamilton, James Madison, and John Jay, three of the Constitution's greatest proponents, published a series of eighty-five essays in New York newspapers under the pseudonym Publius. The combined papers, called *The Federalist Papers,* purport to

The Supreme Court remains impressive even at night.

explain the nature of our government at its inception. These essays defend the new federal Constitution and call for a republican form of government. They are one of the best contemporary sources of constitutional theory and provide a useful background for subsequent developments in the role of the judiciary and the courts, especially the Supreme Court, under the Constitution.

Number 78 of *The Federalist* stressed the role of the judiciary, the importance of its independence from the other branches of government, and the interrelationships of the judiciary, legislature, and executive.

Whoever attentively considers the different departments of power must perceive, that, in a Government in which they are separated from each other, the Judiciary, from the nature of its functions, will always be the least dangerous to the political rights of the Constitution; because it will be least in a capacity to annoy or injure them. The Executive not only dispenses the honors, but holds the sword of the community. The Legislature not only commands the purse, but prescribes the rules by which the duties and rights of every citizen are to be regulated. The Judiciary, on the contrary, has no influence over either the sword or the purse; no direction either of the strength or of the wealth of the society; and can take no active resolution whatever. It may truly be said to have neither FORCE nor WILL, but merely judgment; and must ultimately depend upon the aid of the Executive arm even for the efficacy of its judgments.

This simple view of the matter suggests several important consequences. It proves incontestably, that the Judiciary is beyond comparison the weakest of the three departments of power; that it can never attack with success either of the other two; and that all possible care is requisite to enable it to defend itself against their attacks. It equally proves, that though individual oppression may now and then proceed from the courts of justice, the general liberty of the People can never be endangered from that quarter: I mean so long as the Judiciary remains truly distinct from both the Legislature and Executive....

The complete independence of the Courts of justice is peculiarly essential in a limited Constitution. By a limited Constitution, I understand one which contains certain specified exceptions to the Legislative authority; such, for instance, as that it shall pass no bills of attainder, no *ex post facto* laws, and the like. Limitations of this kind can be preserved in practice no other way than through the medium of the Courts of justice; whose duty it must be to declare all Acts contrary to the manifest tenor of the Constitution void. Without this, all the reservations of particular rights or privileges would amount to nothing.

Some perplexity respecting the rights of the Courts to pronounce Legislative acts void, because contrary to the Constitution, has arisen from an imagination that the doctrine would imply a superiority of the Judiciary to the Legislative power. It is urged that the authority which can declare the acts of another void, must necessarily be superior to the one whose acts may be declared void. As this doctrine is of great importance in all the American Constitutions, a brief discussion of the ground on which it rests cannot be unacceptable.

There is no position which depends on clearer principles, than that every act of a delegated authority, contrary to the tenor of the commission under which it is exercised, is void. No Legislative act, therefore, contrary to the Constitution, can be valid. To deny this, would be to affirm, that the deputy is greater than his principal; that the servant is above his master; that the Representatives of the People are superior to the People themselves; that men acting by virtue of powers, may do not only what their powers do not authorize, but what they forbid.

If it be said that the Legislative body are themselves the constitutional judges of their own powers, and that the construction they put upon them is conclusive upon the other departments, it may be answered, that this cannot be the natural presumption, where it is not to be collected from any particular provisions in the Constitution. It is not otherwise to be supposed, that the Constitution could intend to enable the Representatives of the People to substitute their *will* to that of their constituents. It is far more rational to suppose, that the Courts were designed to be an intermediate body between the People and the Legislature, in order, among other things, to keep the latter within the limits assigned to their authority. The interpretation of the laws is the proper and peculiar province of the Courts. A Constitution is, in fact, and must be regarded by the Judges, as a fundamental law....

Nor does this conclusion by any means suppose a superiority of the Judicial to the Legislative power. It only supposes that the power of the People is superior to both; and that where the will of the Legislature, declared in its statutes, stands in opposition to that of the People, declared in the Constitution, the Judges ought to be governed by the latter rather than the former. They ought to regulate their decisions by the fundamental laws, rather than by those which are not fundamental.

. . .

If then the Courts of justice are to be considered as the bulwarks of a limited Constitution, against Legislative encroachments, this consideration will afford a strong argument for the permanent tenure of Judicial offices, since nothing will contribute so much as this to that independent spirit in the Judges, which must be essential to the faithful performance of so arduous a duty.

This independence of the Judges is equally requisite to guard the Constitution and the rights of individuals, from the effects of those ill humors, which the arts of designing men, or the influence of particular conjunctures, sometimes disseminate among the People themselves, and which, though they speedily give place to better information, and more deliberate reflection, have a tendency, in the mean time, to occasion dangerous innovations in the Government, and serious oppressions of the minor party in the community.

In Number 80 of *The Federalist*, addressed to the people of New York state, the specific roles of the judiciary were discussed in detail.

One of the primary writers of **The Federalist**, *Alexander Hamilton played a key role in developing support for the concept of a supreme court for the United States.*

Having thus laid down and discussed the principles which ought to regulate the constitution of the Federal Judiciary, we will proceed to test, by these principles, the particular powers of which, according to the plan of the Convention, it is to be composed. It is to comprehend "all cases in law and equity arising under the Constitution, the laws of the United States, and treaties made, or which shall be made, under their authority; to all cases affecting Ambassadors, other public Ministers, and Consuls; to all cases of admiralty and maritime jurisdiction; to controversies to which the United States shall be a party; to controversies between two or more States; between a State and citizens of another State; between citizens of different States; between citizens of the same State, claiming lands under grants of different States; and between a State or the citizens thereof, and foreign States, citizens, and subjects." This constitutes the entire mass of the Judicial authority of the Union. Let us now review it in detail. It is then to extend,

First. To all cases in law and equity, *arising under the Constitution and laws of the United States.* This corresponds with the two first classes of causes, which have been enumerated, as proper for the jurisdiction of the United States. It has been asked, what is meant by "cases arising under the Constitution," in contradistinction from those "arising under the laws of the United States?" The difference has been already explained. All the restrictions upon the authority of the State Legislatures furnish examples of it. They are not, for instance, to emit paper money; but the interdiction results from the Constitution, and will have no connection with any law of the United States. Should paper money, notwithstanding, be emitted, the controversies concerning it would be cases arising upon the Constitution and not the laws of the United States, in the ordinary signification of the terms. This may serve as a sample of the whole.

It has also been asked, What need of the word "equity?" What equitable causes can grow out of the Constitution and laws of the United States? There is hardly a subject of litigation between individuals, which may not involve those ingredients of *fraud, accident, trust,* or *hardship,* which would render the matter an object of equitable, rather than of legal jurisdiction, as the distinction is known and established in several of the States. . . . In such cases, where foreigners were concerned on either side, it would be impossible for the Federal judicatories to do justice without an equitable as well as a legal jurisdiction. Agreements to convey lands claimed under the grants of different States, may afford another example of the necessity of an equitable jurisdiction in the Federal Courts. This reasoning may not be so palpable in those States where the formal and technical distinction between LAW and EQUITY is not maintained, as in this State, where it is exemplified by every day's practice.

Number 80 went on to detail the constitutional authority of the judiciary to deal with issues arising out of treaties and from admiralty and maritime law and to decide cases in which the United States, different states, or citizens of different states as well as foreigners, were involved.

Also addressed to the people of New York, Number 81

examined the structure of the court system and the relations between the different types of courts.

That there ought to be one Court of supreme and final jurisdiction, is a proposition which is not likely to be contested. The reasons for it have been assigned in another place, and are too obvious to need repetition. The only question that seems to have been raised concerning it, is, whether it ought to be a distinct body, or a branch of the Legislature. The same contradiction is observable in regard to this matter, which has been remarked in several other cases. The very men who object to the Senate as a Court of Impeachments, on the ground of an improper intermixture of powers, advocate, by implication at least, the propriety of vesting the ultimate decision of all causes, in the whole or in a part of the Legislative body.

. . .

In the first place, there is not a syllable in the plan under consideration which *directly* empowers the National Courts to construe the laws according to the spirit of the Constitution, or which gives them any greater latitude in this respect than may be claimed by the Courts of every State. I admit, however, that the Constitution ought to be the standard of construction for the laws, and that wherever there is an evident opposition, the laws ought to give place to the Constitution. But this doctrine is not deducible from any circumstance peculiar to the plan of the Convention; but from the general theory of a limited Constitution; and as far as it is true, is equally applicable to most, if not to all the State Governments. There can be no objection, therefore, on this account, to the Federal judicature, which will not lie against the local judicatures in general, and which will not serve to condemn every Constitution that attempts to set bounds to Legislative discretion.

But perhaps the force of the objection may be thought to consist in the particular organization of the Supreme Court: in its being composed of a distinct body of magistrates instead of being one of the branches of the Legislature, as in the Government of Great Britain and that of this State. . . . From a body which had even a partial agency in passing bad laws, we could rarely expect a disposition to temper and moderate them in the application. The same spirit which had operated in making them would be too apt in interpreting them; still less could it be expected, that men who had infringed the Constitution, in the character of Legislators, would be disposed to repair the breach in the character of Judges. Nor is this all; every reason which recommends the tenure of good behavior for Judicial offices, militates against placing the Judiciary power, in the last resort, in a body composed of men chosen for a limited period. . . . The members of the Legislature will rarely be chosen with a view to those qualifications which fit men for the stations of Judges; and as, on this account, there will be great reason to apprehend all the ill consequences of defective information, so, on account of the natural propensity of such bodies to party divisions, there will be no less reason to fear, that the pestilential breath of faction may poison the fountains of justice. The habit of being continually marshalled on opposite sides, will be too apt to stifle the voice both of law and of equity.

. . .

Having now examined, and, I trust, removed the objections to the distinct and independent organization of the Supreme Court, I proceed to consider the propriety of the power of constituting inferior Courts, and the relations which will subsist between these and the former.

The power of constituting inferior Courts, is evidently calculated to obviate the necessity of having recourse to the Supreme Court in every case of Federal cognizance. It is intended to enable the National Government to institute or *authorize,* in each State or district of the United States, a tribunal competent to the determination of matters of National jurisdiction within its limits.

But why, it is asked, might not the same purpose have been accomplished by the instrumentality of the State Courts? This admits of different answers. Though the fitness and competency of those Courts should be allowed in the utmost latitude, yet the substance of the power in question may still be regarded as a necessary part of the plan, if it were only to empower the National Legislature to commit to them the cognizance of causes arising out of the National Constitution.

. . .

These reasons seem sufficient to satisfy a candid mind, that the want of such a power would have been a great defect in the plan. Let us now examine, in what manner the Judicial authority is to be distributed between the Supreme and the inferior Courts of the Union.

The Supreme Court is to be invested with original jurisdiction, only "in cases affecting Ambassadors, other public Ministers, and Consuls, and those in which A STATE shall be a party.". . . [I]t is both expedient and proper, that such questions should be submitted in the first instance to the highest judicatory of the Nation. Though Consuls have not in strictness a diplomatic

New York City's Old Royal Exchange Building, at the foot of Broad Street, was used in 1790 for the Court's first sessions.

The Court shifted to Philadelphia after the city was made the nation's capital in 1790. The Court's sessions were held in the Old City Hall from 1791 to 1800.

character, yet as they are the public agents of the Nations to which they belong, the same observation is in a great measure applicable to them. In cases in which a State might happen to be a party, it would ill suit its dignity to be turned over to any inferior tribunal.

. . .

Let us resume the train of our observations. We have seen, that the original jurisdiction of the Supreme Court would be confined to two classes of causes, and those of a nature rarely to occur. In all other cases of Federal cognizance, the original jurisdiction would appertain to the inferior tribunals; and the Supreme Court would have nothing more than an appellate jurisdiction, "with such *exception,* and under such *regulations,* as the Congress shall make."

The amount of the observations hitherto made on the authority of the Judicial department is this: that it has been carefully restricted to those causes which are manifestly proper for the cognizance of the National Judicature; that in the partition of this authority, a very small portion of original jurisdiction has been reserved to the Supreme Court, and the rest consigned to the subordinate tribunals; that the Supreme Court will possess an appellate jurisdiction both as to law and fact, in all the cases referred to them, but subject to any *exceptions* and *regulations* which may be thought advisable; that this appellate jurisdiction does, in no case, *abolish* the trial by jury; and that an ordinary degree of prudence and integrity in the National Councils, will insure us solid advantages from the establishment of the proposed Judiciary, without exposing us to any of the inconveniences which have been predicted from that source.

There is little discussion of the judiciary in the records of the Constitutional Convention. The resolution of Governor Randolph of Virginia that "a national judiciary be established" was agreed to without fanfare on June 4. While the fundamental question of whether there should be a national judiciary was accepted with relatively little discussion, probably from an understanding that a judiciary was an essential component of a national government, the precise form and function of that judiciary took more time to establish. The method of appointment of the judges engendered considerable discussion and was not resolved until the end of the convention when, on September 7, as part of a general agreement on appointments, the convention agreed that appointment would be by the executive with the advice and consent of the Senate. There was also some discussion within the convention of the assignment of extrajudicial functions to the federal judiciary. Governor Randolph's proposal to create a National Council of Revision to be composed of the Chief Executive and "a convenient number of national judiciary" to review acts of Congress to determine their constitutionality was finally rejected.

Supreme Court Procedures

The Supreme Court is the only federal court established by the Constitution itself rather than by act of Congress. In the early days of the Republic the Supreme Court of the United States sat in what is now the old Supreme Court Chamber in the U.S. Capitol, having first met in February 1790 in New York City, which at that time was the nation's capital. It moved to Philadelphia the next year, when that city became the temporary capital. In 1801, the Court moved to the District of Columbia, where it has remained.

The present Supreme Court building is located in Washington, D.C., across the street from the Capitol and adjacent to the Library of Congress. It was completed in 1935. In addition to the actual courtroom, the Supreme Court building contains the offices of the chief justice and associate justices; their law clerks, law libraries, and administrative staffs; a large central law library; the Supreme Court clerk's office; and various related administrative offices. The Supreme Court's annual term begins on the first Monday in October and usually concludes in late June. Six justices now constitute a quorum, and there have been a small number of cases in which the Court was unable to act because a quorum could not be obtained.

Rule 4(1) of the Supreme Court Rules provides that the Court, on scheduled days, sits to hear arguments "from ten until noon, recesses until one, and adjourns for the day at three." The current practice of the Court is to hear oral arguments only on Monday, Tuesday, or Wednesday. The new regular term formally commences on the first Monday in October, and the Court typically schedules about fourteen

The Court held its first session in Washington, D.C., in 1801. Several locations were used during the early years, including some 1809 sessions in Long's Tavern, the far left section of Carroll Row, now the site of the Library of Congress.

After years of cramped quarters, the Court moved to the old Senate chamber in the Capitol. The room was used until the current Supreme Court building was completed in 1935.

weeks of oral argument, beginning with the first week of the term, and ending in late April or early May. Usually, two consecutive weeks of oral argument are scheduled, with intervals of two weeks or longer between the biweekly argument sessions. The Court customarily reserves the Friday of each week during which arguments are held as its major conference day, when the justices meet to consider cases argued during the preceding week. The Court also usually schedules Wednesday afternoon, after oral argument, for the same purpose. Justice Rehnquist has described the conferences as follows:

> As soon as we come off of the bench Wednesday afternoon around three o'clock, we go into private "conference" in a room adjoining the chambers of the Chief Justice. At our Wednesday afternoon meeting, we deliberate and vote on the four cases which we heard argued the preceding Monday. The Chief Justice begins the discussion of each case with a summary of the facts, his analysis of the law, and an announcement of his proposed vote (that is, whether to affirm, reverse, modify, etc.). The discussion then passes to the Senior Associate Justice, presently Mr. Justice Brennan, who does likewise. It then goes on down the line to the Junior Associate Justice. When the discussion of one case is concluded, the discussion of the next one is immediately taken up, until all the argued cases on the agenda for that particular Conference have been disposed of.

On Thursday during the week of oral argument we have neither oral arguments nor Conference scheduled, but on the Friday of that week we begin a Conference at 9:30 in the morning, go until 12:30 in the afternoon, take forty-five minutes for lunch, and return to continue our deliberations until the middle or late part of the afternoon. At this Conference we dispose of the eight cases which we heard argued on the preceding Tuesday and Wednesday. We likewise dispose of all the petitions for certiorari and appeals which are before us that particular week.

At the beginning of the week following the two-week session's oral argument, the Chief Justice circulates to the other members of the Court an Assignment List, in which he assigns for the writing of the Court opinion all the cases in which he voted with the conference majority. Where the Chief Justice was in the minority, the Senior Associate Justice voting with the majority assigns the case.

The Lower Federal Courts

The United States Court of Appeals was created in 1891 and was known at that time as the Circuit Courts of Appeals. There are now thirteen courts of appeals, one each for the eleven judicial circuits, one for the District of Columbia, and the recently created Court of Appeals for the Federal Circuit. The number of judges varies among the various courts of appeals, the largest being the 9th Circuit, which encompasses the West Coast states. The courts of appeals hear appeals coming from the United States district courts within their particular circuit, as well as orders of administrative agencies. Cases are usually heard by a panel or division of the court consisting of three judges. Appeals may be taken from the decision of the panel to the entire court of appeals sitting *en banc*. The decision of whether to review *en banc* is within the discretion of the court. By statute, a majority of the circuit judges currently in active service is required for a hearing or re-hearing *en banc*.

The system of federal district courts, the usual court of original jurisdiction in the U.S. federal system, originated in the Judiciary Act of 1789. Actually the Judiciary Act created a system containing two sets of trial courts, the district courts and what were then called circuit courts. The states then in the Union were divided into districts along state lines, with separate districts being established in those parts of Massachusetts and Virginia that were to become Maine and Kentucky. Thus was established the precedent followed with only one very minor exception of establishing judicial districts within state boundaries. Eleven of the thirteen original districts (excluding the territories that were to become Maine and Kentucky) were divided into three circuits. These circuit courts, not to be confused with the late Circuit Courts of Appeal, were invested with some original jurisdiction in addition to the power to review certain civil and admiralty cases tried in the district courts. Unlike the district courts, which had judges appointed to those courts, the circuit courts

consisted of a three-judge panel made up of one district judge and two Supreme Court justices sitting on circuit. The burden imposed on the justices of the Supreme Court by having to ride circuit was readily apparent from the beginning, and the statute was amended in 1793 to require only one justice per circuit, thereby reducing, but not eliminating, this time-consuming burden. With the rapid expansion and development of the United States, additional district and circuit courts were established, thereby putting additional stress on the justices and, as might have been expected, ultimately on the circuit courts themselves. In 1802, in creating additional circuit courts, Congress attempted to reduce the burden imposed on the Supreme Court justices by reducing the number of Supreme Court sessions to one a year, while authorizing a single district judge to sit on circuit. This led to the embarrassing result that district court judges found themselves in the position of reviewing, at the circuit court level, their own decisions below. But it was not until 1891 that Congress, in the Circuit Court of Appeals Act (the Evarts Act), established what was to become the modern system, by creating for each of the nine existing circuits a circuit court of appeals. The old system of circuit courts, however, was not abolished until 1911, although the Evarts Act did eliminate their appellate jurisdiction over the district courts.

Today the United States, including the District of Columbia and Puerto Rico, is divided into ninety-one judi-

Chief Justice William Howard Taft (**center**) *speaks at the 1922 rededication of the Philadelphia Supreme Court building. Taft spearheaded the drive for a separate building for the Court in Washington.*

cial districts, each containing a district court. Current statutes authorize five hundred seven district judges, with the largest district being the Southern District of New York, consisting of twenty-seven judges. In 1968, Congress enacted the Federal Magistrates Act. Magistrates assist the district courts in a variety of ways, including supervision of pretrial procedures and arraignment of defendants in criminal cases.

There are several specialized courts within the federal system. Some, which exercise the judicial power, were created under Article III, while others were created under Article I of the Constitution. The district courts in United States territories in the Virgin Islands, Guam, and the Northern Mariana Islands exercise, with some exceptions, both the federal judicial power of United States district courts and the more general jurisdictional powers of state courts. The District Court for the District of Puerto Rico is also a specialized court in the sense that it exercises some jurisdictional powers in excess of those generally found in district courts. There are two sets of courts within the District of Columbia. The Superior Court and the District of Columbia Court of Appeals, both general jurisdiction courts, are similar to state courts, exercising jurisdiction over both criminal and civil matters of a local nature. Decisions involving a substantial federal question may be appealed to the United States Supreme Court from the District of Columbia Court of Appeals, just as decisions from a state supreme court would be appealable. The second system of courts within the District of Columbia, the District Court for the District of Columbia and the United States Court of Appeals for the District of Columbia Circuit, are Article III courts with essentially the same jurisdiction as other district courts and courts of appeal.

In 1982 another specialized court, the Court of Appeals for the Federal Circuit, was created through the merger of the Court of Customs and Patent Appeals and the Court of Claims. The original jurisdiction formerly exercised by the Court of Claims was vested in a new trial court, the United States Claims Court.

The United States Tax Court is an Article I court that hears certain types of tax disputes. Article I is also the constitutional source for the system of military courts. Offenses under the Uniform Code of Military Justice, a part of the United States Code, are tried by Courts Martial, with automatic review by the Court of Military Review for that individual's branch of service. Final review rests in the Court of Military Appeals. Military courts normally have jurisdiction only over members of the armed services charged with military offenses or offenses arising on a military reservation. Members of the armed forces who commit nonmilitary crimes on civilian property are normally brought to trial in a state or federal district court.

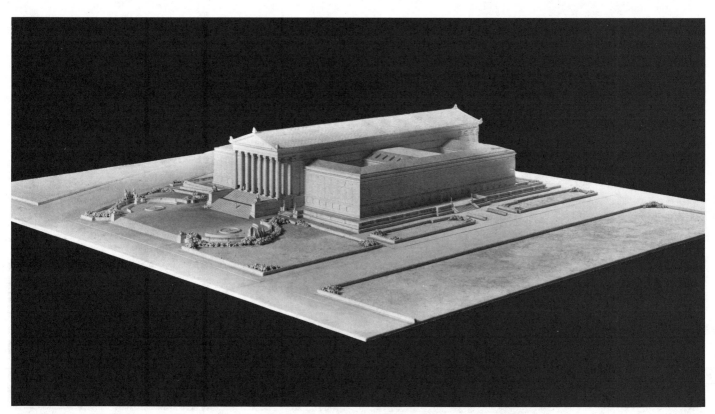

Architect's model of the current Supreme Court, authorized by Congress in 1929 and completed in 1935.

Chief Justice Charles Evans Hughes lays the cornerstone of the Supreme Court Building, October 1932.

The Supreme Court's Appellate Jurisdiction

The preponderance of the work of the Supreme Court consists of the review of cases arising on appeal from lower federal courts or from a state supreme court. The statute defining the Supreme Court's appellate jurisdiction provides for appeals in certain cases from the highest court of a state capable of rendering a decision. In normal practice, the highest court is the supreme court or, as it is called in some states such as New York, the court of appeals. There are some instances, however, when appeals from lower state courts have been taken by the Supreme Court. Perhaps the best known of these unusual cases is Justice Black's opinion for the Court in *Thompson v. Louisville* (1960), involving an appeal from a Kentucky municipal court. The United States Supreme Court reversed a conviction for loitering and disor-

derly conduct on the ground that the charges "were so totally devoid of evidentiary support as to render the conviction unconstitutional under the due process clause of the fourteenth amendment." It should be noted that in appeals from state courts to the United States Supreme Court, the Court has jurisdiction to consider only those appeals involving "substantial federal questions." Thus, not all decisions of state courts are appealable to the Supreme Court, even though a losing party may feel that the state court has incorrectly decided one or more issues in the case. Even if a particular case contains a substantial federal question, the United States Supreme Court may still be without jurisdiction to consider the appeal. If there is an "adequate and independent state ground" on which the state court decision can be based, the United States Supreme Court lacks juris-

The Supreme Court Building under construction in the early 1930s.

diction to consider the appeal. This means that the Supreme Court cannot review a state decision resting on both state and federal law if the decision on the federal question was unnecessary in light of the disposition of the state law question.

Disputes in litigation typically involve a mix of questions of law and fact. Factual issues are usually decided by the trial court and are normally not reviewed by an appellate court so long as the record of trial indicates some evidence on which the court might have based its decision. Thus, it is usually questions of law, not questions of fact, that are appealed. The Constitution does not expressly provide for Supreme Court review of state court decisions. It does, however, in Article III, authorize Congress to provide for appellate review of federal questions, and Congress, by statute, has provided for appellate review of federal questions arising in a state court system.

The Supreme Court, however, will not review all cases in which a federal question is raised. The federal question must be "substantial," that is, not frivolous or expressly foreclosed by a previous decision. Further, the federal question must have been raised in a proper and timely manner during the course of the proceedings in the state courts. What constitutes proper and timely is usually determined by the procedural rules of the state. An experienced litigator will normally raise a federal question at every opportunity permitted by state procedure. There is one notable exception,

however, to the requirement for timely presentation of a federal question. If the highest court of a state in which a decision could be obtained actually decides a federal question, whether or not it was raised below, it is reviewable by the Supreme Court. This is not to say that the Supreme Court must take such a case, only that it may. The state court decision, however, must be a final judgment or decree. The question of what constitutes a final judgment or decree is left to the Supreme Court itself. The practice of the Court has been to consider a judgment final for purposes of review if any acts remaining are merely ministerial. In recent years the Court has become more willing to create narrow exceptions to this finality rule, particularly in those situations where the federal question is conclusive, or the outcome of further proceedings is preordained, notwithstanding the fact that, technically, further proceedings are yet to occur (*Cox Broadcasting Corp. v. Cohn,* 1975). In order to bring a case to the Supreme Court, it is necessary to make timely application to the Court in accordance with the Supreme Court Rules.

The federal statute that provides for review of state court decisions by the Supreme Court, 28 U.S.C. Section 1257, provides for two mechanisms by which state court decisions may be reviewed. A writ of certiorari may be granted at the discretion of the Supreme Court in any case falling within the terms of the statute–essentially any case involving a federal question where review is sought of a final judgment or decree. In a more narrow range of cases, review may be by appeal, which in theory is a matter of right and not within the discretion of the Supreme Court. In practice, however, both modes of review are now, for all practical purposes, within the Court's discretion. A writ of certiorari is an order from a higher court to a lower court to send up the record below so that it may be reviewed by the higher court. The practice of the Supreme Court is to issue a writ of certiorari in response to a petition for certiorari from below when at least four justices vote to grant the writ. A denial of certiorari however is not a decision on the merits, but simply a recognition that the minimum number of four justices could not be persuaded to grant the writ. A denial of certiorari leaves the lower court decision intact and does not have any precedential value in other cases raising the same legal questions.

In a more narrow range of cases, as defined by the statute, review may be sought by appeal. Review by appeal may be obtained where a state court has held a federal statute or treaty invalid or has upheld a state statute against a claim that it is repugnant to the Constitution, treaties, or laws of the United States. In practice, both modes of review are essentially discretionary, although the likelihood of review by appeal is greater than by a writ of certiorari, and for this reason, lawyers normally prefer to seek review by this method. Under current statutory law the Supreme Court has the power to consider an appeal that has been improvidently taken as if it were a petition for certiorari. Thus the Court, on occasion, will dismiss an appeal while simultaneously granting certiorari in the same case. Supreme Court review of decisions of the Court of Appeals are authorized by 28 U.S.C. Section 1254, while 28 U.S.C. Section 1257 authorizes review of state court decisions.

Section 1254. Courts of appeals; certiorari; appeal; certified questions

Cases in the courts of appeals may be reviewed by the Supreme Court by the following methods:

(1) By writ of certiorari granted upon the petition of any party to any civil or criminal case, before or after rendition of judgment or decree;

(2) By appeal by a party relying on a State statute held by a court of appeals to be invalid as repugnant to the Constitution, treaties or laws of the United States, but such appeal shall preclude review by writ of certiorari at the instance of such appellant, and the review on appeal shall be restricted to the Federal questions presented;

(3) By certification at any time by a court of appeals of any question of law in any civil or criminal case as to which instructions are desired, and upon such certification the Supreme Court may give binding instructions or require the entire record to be sent up for decision of the entire matter in controversy.

Section 1257. State courts; appeal; certiorari

Final judgments or decrees rendered by the highest court of a State in which a decision could be had, may be reviewed by the Supreme Court as follows:

(1) By appeal, where is drawn in question the validity of a treaty or statute of the United States and the decision is against its validity;

(2) By appeal, where is drawn in question the validity of a statute of any state on the ground of its being repugnant to the Constitution, treaties or laws of the United States, and the decision is in favor of its validity;

(3) By writ of certiorari, where the validity of a treaty or statute of the United States is drawn in question or where the validity of a State statute is drawn in question on the ground of its being repugnant to the Constitution, treaties or laws of the United States, or where any title, right, privilege or immunity is specially set up or claimed under the Constitution, treaties or statutes of, or commission held or authority exercised under, the United States.

The National Government

The Constitution of the United States establishes a federal government while simultaneously placing limitations on some of the powers that the federal government may exercise, thereby reserving to the states most of the powers formerly exercised by individual states prior to the ratifying of the Constitution. The Constitution contains few absolutes and reflects in its terms the compromises that were the result of the competing philosophies and interests of the leaders of the Convention and the states that those individuals represented. The three branches of government–the executive, legislative, and judicial–exercise only those powers permitted by the Constitution. The federal government thus created is a government of limited powers. There must be a constitutional basis of power supporting the exercise of governmental authority. In some areas the power of the federal government is exclusive, while in other areas it may be exercised concurrently with that of the states. Only the federal government, for example, may engage in the conduct of foreign relations or mint coins, while both the federal and state governments may, within constitutional limitations, regulate commerce within and among the various states. One of the more interesting aspects of the U.S. constitutional system has been its adaptability to the dramatic changes that have occurred since the late eighteenth century. Differing schools of constitutional interpretation debate whether the United States continues to operate from a Constitution that was created in 1787 or whether it has, through judicial interpretation, modified the original document in response to the dramatic change in society, while arguably maintaining the philosophy of the original document. One of the most obvious examples of this evolution is found in the

The courtroom of the Supreme Court.

judicial interpretations of the commerce power, the power of Congress to regulate commerce among the states.

One of the principal shortcomings of the Articles of Confederation was the lack of a central government with sufficient powers to regulate interstate commerce. The result was that the newly independent states began, as might be expected, a process of Balkanization, enacting laws and tariffs that favored their own economic interests. There was little incentive, and no effective mechanism, to protect the greater goal of encouraging the development of interstate business and trade. Interestingly, when the delegates met to consider revisions to the Articles of Confederation in the first and only constitutional convention, a new form of government emerged. It is less than clear whether a modern constitutional convention, called to enact narrow amendments, might in fact be so limited once the convention has been convened. It is not difficult to imagine, for example, that in a constitutional convention called to modify the Constitution to require a balanced budget, there would be voices raised seeking other, perhaps even more drastic, amendments.

In the Constitution that emerged from the Constitutional Convention a central government was created. But the document also reflected the framers' concerns that the central government not become overly powerful. Thus, the Constitution makes clear that governmental power is allocated between the federal government and the states, with the powers of the federal government being divided among the three branches. This allocation of power between the nation and the states was reaffirmed in the 10th Amendment, which provides that powers not vested in the federal government are to be "reserved to the states respectively, or to the people."

Extent of Federal Power. It was inevitable that questions should arise concerning the extent of the federal power, particularly that allocated to Congress in Article I of the Constitution. Was the Congress to be limited to those powers and activities specifically enumerated in the Constitution, or was the grant of constitutional authority broader, encompassing all of those powers "necessary and proper" to the carrying out of those powers specifically enumerated? In 1819 the U.S. Supreme Court was presented with an opportunity to define further both the scope of the national powers and the extent to which the states themselves might regulate activities otherwise within the orbit of the national government as an incident to their acknowledged power over local activities. In writing the opinion of the Court in *McCulloch v. Maryland* (1819), Chief Justice John Marshall not only developed an expansive reading of the implied powers of the federal government but also, in justifying that interpretation, eloquently established an approach to constitutional interpretation that has, with some lapses, persisted to this day.

In *McCulloch*, the Court was called upon to consider whether Congress could constitutionally charter a national bank and, if so, whether the state of Maryland could constitutionally impose a tax on the Maryland branch. Congress had chartered the Second Bank of the United States in 1816 in response to pressures to exercise control over the national economy in the wake of problems arising during and after the War of 1812. Rather than restraining the economy, however, the bank at first encouraged the use of credit, providing loans to both state banks and private individuals. In a foreshadowing of future economic cycles, the boom economy soon became a bust, with a financial depression developing in 1818. This created for the bank a lack of reserves, forcing it to call in some of its outstanding loans, much to the anger and chagrin of local authorities. In 1818, Maryland attempted to impose a tax on all banks or branches operating within the state. When the Bank of the United States refused to pay, an action was brought against the chief cashier of the Baltimore branch, James McCulloch, who, in addition to the pursuit of his authorized activities, had also secretly, and unbeknownst to his superiors, been engaging with some of his associates in a substantial embezzlement plan.

The Constitution contains no express provision authorizing Congress to charter a bank. And it was to the question of the constitutionality of this statute that Marshall first turned his attention.

If any one proposition could command the universal assent of mankind, we might expect it would be this–that the government of the union, though limited in its powers, is supreme within its sphere of action. This would seem to result necessarily from its nature. It is a government of all; its powers are delegated by all; it represents all, and acts for all. Though any one state may be willing to control its operations, no state is willing to allow others to control them. The nation, on those subjects on which it can act, must necessarily bind its component parts. But this question is not left to mere reasons; the people have, in express terms, decided it by saying, "this constitution, and the laws of the United States, which shall be made in pursuance thereof," "shall be the supreme law of the land," and by requiring that the members of the state legislatures, and the officers of the executive and judicial departments of the states shall take the oath of fidelity to it.

The government of the United States, then, though limited in its powers, is supreme; and its laws, when made in pursuance of the constitution, form the supreme law of land, "anything in the constitution or laws of any state to the contrary notwithstanding."

Among the enumerated powers, we do not find that of establishing a bank or creating a corporation. But there is no phrase in the instrument which, like the articles of confederation, excludes incidental or implied powers; and which requires that everything granted shall be expressly and minutely described. . . .

Although, among the enumerated powers of govern-

Marble figures symbolizing the law and its power flank the broad steps leading to the Supreme Court Building, the female figure to the left, the male to the right.

ment, we do not find the word "bank" or "incorporation," we find the great powers to lay and collect taxes; to borrow money; to regulate commerce; to declare and conduct a war; and to raise and support armies and navies. The sword and the purse, all the external relations, and no inconsiderable portion of the industry of the nation, are entrusted to its government. It can never be pretended that these vast powers draw after them others of inferior importance, merely because they are inferior. Such an idea can never be advanced. But it may with great reason be contended, that a government, entrusted with such ample powers, on the due execution of which the happiness and prosperity of the nation so vitally depends, must also be entrusted with ample means for their execution. The power being given, it is the interest of the nation to facilitate its execution. It can never be their interest, and cannot be presumed to have been their intention, to clog and embarrass its execution by withholding the most appropriate means....The power of creating a corporation, is one appertaining to sovereignty, and is not expressly conferred on Congress. This is true. But all legislative powers appertain to sovereignty. The original power of giving the law in any subject whatever, is a sovereign power; and if the government of the Union is restrained from creating a corporation, as a means for performing its functions, on the single reason that the creation of a corporation is an act of sovereignty; if the sufficiency of this reason be acknowledged, there would be some difficulty in sustaining the authority of Congress to pass other laws for the accomplishment of the same objects.

The government which has a duty to do an act, and has

imposed on it the duty of performing that act, must, according to the dictates of reason, be allowed to select the means; and those who contend that it may not select any appropriate means, that one particular mode of effecting the object is accepted, take upon themselves the burden of establishing that exception.

. . .

The power of creating a corporation is never used for its own sake, but for the purpose of effecting something else. No sufficient reason is, therefore, perceived, why it may not pass as incidental to those powers which are expressly given, if it be a direct mode of executing them.

But the constitution of the United States has not left the right of Congress to employ the necessary means for the execution of the powers conferred on the government to general reasoning. To its enumeration of powers is added that of making all laws which shall be necessary and proper, for carrying into execution the foregoing powers, and all other powers vested by this constitution, in the government of the United States, or in any department thereof."

. . .

We admit, as all must admit, that the powers of the government are limited, and that its limits are not to be transcended. But we think the sound construction of the constitution must allow to the national legislature that discretion, with respect to the means by which the powers it confers are

John Marshall's opinion in **McCulloch v. Maryland** *(1819) helped to establish the regulatory power of the federal government.*

to be carried into execution, which will enable that body to perform the high duties assigned to it, in the manner most beneficial to the people. Let the end be legitimate, let it be within the scope of the constitution, and all means which are appropriate, which are plainly adapted to that end, which are not prohibited, but consist of the letter and spirit of the constitution, are constitutional.

As in *McCulloch,* it fell to Chief Justice Marshall in other cases to interpret the Constitution in deciding important legal issues of the new country. In carrying out this task, Marshall made clear that the Constitution of the United States was to be applied by the courts both with flexibility and sensitivity to the nature of the particular problem before the court, not in a narrow or dogmatic fashion by limiting the power to the precise and express words of the document, as one might do with a statute.

John Marshall's role in shaping the new nation was substantial, but the difficulties of constitutional interpretation have not diminished. The decision in *McCulloch v. Maryland* gave an expansive reading to the necessary and proper clause of Article I. It did not and could not answer all the questions that would arise in interpreting the Constitution. But it was a grand beginning. The Constitution should, Marshall indicated, be interpreted through a contextual analysis of the problem presented to the Court. And the trends of decision are evolutionary. For example, Congress

has the power to regulate interstate commerce. Yet that commerce obviously takes place within individual states (or the District of Columbia). The Supreme Court, in a line of decisions stretching over almost two centuries, has undertaken to define the scope of this power and the extent to which the federal government may regulate otherwise local activities within a particular state in furtherance of the regulation of interstate commerce.

The Commerce Power

In a long series of decisions, sometimes with conflicting rationales and results, the Supreme Court gradually evolved a view of the commerce power that required courts to determine how directly the regulated activities affected commerce. If there was a "direct" effect on interstate commerce, such as in the establishment of rail rates, Congress could, if it chose, occupy or regulate the area, including the regulation of intrastate as well as interstate rates. If, however, the activities were essentially local and not directly connected with interstate commerce, the states were permitted to regulate. Because the federal powers are enumerated and because the Supreme Court until 1937 had for the most part applied a narrow definition of the commerce power, the Court was deemed to be without the constitutional power to regulate what were regarded as local activities. Thus in 1918, in *Hammer v. Dagenhart,* the Court was called upon to decide the constitutionality of an act of Congress prohibiting the movement in interstate commerce of goods produced in factories that employed children under the age of fourteen. In holding the law unconstitutional the Court, employing a view of the Constitution that emphasized protection for private enterprise, found that the "act in its effect does not regulate transportation among the states, but aims to standardize the ages at which children may be employed in mining and manufacturing within the states. The goods shipped are of themselves harmless...when offered for shipment, and before transportation begins, the labor of the production is over, and the mere fact that they were intended for interstate commerce transportation does make their production subject to federal control under the commerce power." It was an era when property rights were exalted over personal liberty and when the welfare of children was left to the discretion of the states. And the states that might otherwise have acted to forbid the exploitation of children were faced with the unhappy prospect of placing their own manufacturing concerns at an economic disadvantage in competition with out-of-state manufacturers that were permitted in their respective states to take advantage of the low wages paid children. This was an era when the Supreme Court struck down progressive legislation favoring the rights of individuals in favor of the protection of property rights of private individuals and corporations. It was not that the Court was unaware of the difficulties of individual states in

The storm of protest over President Roosevelt's 1937 plan to pack the Supreme Court helped to defeat FDR's effort to change the Court's composition.

addressing problems that were, by their nature, national in scope. It was rather a failure by the Court to respond adequately to changes in society brought about by industrialization.

New Deal Decisions. It was not until 1937, in *National Labor Relations Board v. Jones & Laughlin Steel Corp.*, that the Supreme Court began to articulate an interpretation of the commerce clause and the necessary and proper clause that permitted the United States to regulate in a broad fashion local activities associated with the national economy. The economic collapse of 1929 and the subsequent Great Depression, including severe droughts in the Midwest, cre-

ated conditions that were devastating to the American economy and morale. The policies of the Hoover administration were blamed, probably unjustly, for the economic problems if not the weather. Franklin Delano Roosevelt was elected president in 1932 on a promise that he would do something about it. And he did.

He immediately proposed, and Congress passed, a number of legislative programs designed to stabilize and stimulate the economy. But "the nine old men," as Roosevelt referred to the Supreme Court, struck down a number of these programs, finding that Congress had exceeded its constitutional authority. The principal difficulty was that the

Court was applying reactionary interpretations of the Constitution to invalidate federal efforts to regulate a national economy that was clearly beyond the power of the individual states to control adequately. Unable, of course, to fire the justices and replace them with what he regarded as more progressive jurists, Roosevelt seized upon his famous plan to "pack" the Supreme Court by increasing the number of justices to create a new majority on the Court. In 1937, in the midst of this controversy, Justice Roberts began to vote with the younger members of the Court, thereby creating a new majority that was prepared to support broader federal powers to regulate commerce. It was assumed at the time that Justice Roberts had been influenced by the Court packing plan, but the best evidence now suggests that he had in fact formed his views prior to the push by the President to pack the Court. In any event, the decision in *Jones & Laughlin* is the seminal decision for the modern interpretation of the commerce power. At issue in that case was the constitutionality of the National Labor Relations Act of 1935. In administrative proceedings initiated by a labor union, the N.L.R.B. had found that Jones & Laughlin was guilty of "unfair labor practice" by unlawfully discharging employees for engaging in union activities, and the board ordered the company to cease such activities. Jones & Laughlin failed to comply and the board sought judicial enforcement of its order. In finding the N.L.R.A. constitutional, Chief Justice Hughes, speaking for the Court, stated that:

> [t]he fundamental principle is that the power to regulate commerce is the power to enact "all appropriate legislation" for "its protection and advancement"; to adopt measures "to promote its growth and ensure its safety"; "to foster, protect, control and restrain." That power is plenary and may be exerted to protect interstate commerce "no matter what the source of the dangers which threaten it." Although activities may be intrastate in character when separately considered, if they have such a close and substantial relation to interstate commerce that their control is essential or appropriate to protect that commerce from burdens and obstructions, Congress cannot be denied the power to exercise that control.

From this expansive reading of the commerce powers, the Court subsequently upheld the Agricultural Adjustment Act of 1938, which regulated the wheat commodities market through the establishment of quotas for individual farms, in *Wickard v. Filburn* (1942). And it was the commerce power, in part, that was relied upon by Congress as the constitutional basis of authority for the enactment of Title 2 of the Civil Rights Act of 1964, which prohibits racial discrimination in places of public accommodation. The objectives of this act were upheld in *Heart of Atlanta Motel v. United States* (1964) and *Katzenbach v. McClung* (1964).

The changing interpretations of the commerce power demonstrate the necessity for and problems associated with

The first step in a Supreme Court justice's career is nomination. Here, Senator Hugo Black (right), nominated in August 1937, is congratulated by Vice President Garner.

interpreting the Constitution. How can the intent of the framers be applied to modern problems unknown in the eighteenth century, while affirming the fundamental premise that the Constitution creates a national government with enumerated and limited powers? Some powers, such as the commerce power, are now viewed as extremely broad, which should not be surprising given the developments that have occurred in transportation and communication since the Industrial Revolution. In a sense, American society has become both more complex and more fragile. Some of the practical questions posed today, in fact, go not so much to the necessity of solving problems at the national level but at the international level. The Constitution, as Chief Justice Marshall pointed out in *McCulloch,* is not an inflexible document.

Jurisdiction: Article III Limitations

The Constitution is both a source of and a limitation on the powers of the federal government. Congress and the president are limited to those powers that are specifically enumerated in Articles I and II of the Constitution and to those powers necessary to accomplish those purposes not specifically enumerated in the document but nevertheless found within one of the specific grants. In the same sense, the federal courts are also limited in power. They derive their constitutional authority from the judicial article, Article III,

William O. Douglas (second from right) at Senate confirmation hearings following his nomination in 1939.

and are limited by the judicial power as defined in that article. There is a fundamental distinction between the jurisdiction exercised by federal courts and by state courts. With the exception of the relatively narrow original jurisdiction of the Supreme Court, which is set forth in Article III, the appellate jurisdiction of the Supreme Court and all of the jurisdiction of the lower federal courts are defined by statute pursuant to the authority contained in Article III. The federal courts are thus courts of limited jurisdiction and in this sense are different from the courts of the various states, which for the most part are courts of general jurisdiction. The distinction is an important one; a state may authorize its courts to hear any type of suit brought before them. The usual presumption is that they possess this authority, although state law may provide that certain types of suits will be brought in specified courts. The federal courts, on the other hand, are constitutionally limited to those types of cases that are to be found within the judicial power defined in Article III. Congress does not have the power to confer upon Article III courts any jurisdiction not contained within the judicial power. And it is well settled in federal practice that one seeking to invoke the jurisdiction of a federal court must affirmatively show that the case is within the jurisdiction of the court.

Article III, Section 2 defines the judicial power:

The judicial power shall extend to all cases in law and equity arising under this Constitution; the laws of the United States

and treaties made, or which shall be made, under their authority; to all cases affecting ambassadors, other public ministers and consuls; to all cases of admiralty and maritime jurisdiction; to controversies to which the United States shall be a party; to controversies between two or more states, between a state and citizens of another state, between citizens of different states, between citizens of the same state claiming lands under grants of different states, and between the state or the citizens thereof, and foreign states, citizens or subjects. In all cases affecting ambassadors, other public ministers and consuls, and those in which a state shall be party, the Supreme Court shall have original jurisdiction. In all the other cases before-mentioned, the Supreme Court shall have appellate jurisdiction, both as to law and fact, with such exceptions and under such regulations as Congress shall make.

The judicial power thus defines two broad categories of cases that may be brought before a court exercising Article III powers. Federal question jurisdiction encompasses those cases arising under the Constitution, laws, or treaties of the United States. Diversity jurisdiction, on the other hand, depends upon the citizenship of the parties, involving suits between citizens of different states or between a citizen of a state and an alien. The federal courts also have jurisdiction over admiralty matters.

All of these cases, of course, could be brought in state courts unless Congress has provided for exclusive federal jurisdiction, since state courts are courts of general jurisdiction. And there have been substantial efforts made in recent

After his 1925 nomination to the Court, Harlan Fiske Stone (left) visits retiring Justice McKenna, whom Stone replaced.

years to remove diversity jurisdiction from the federal courts, thereby requiring these cases to be brought in state court. Diversity jurisdiction is a form of protective jurisdiction. It was established out of a concern that out-of-state litigants might be disadvantaged. This view has been increasingly challenged in recent years. Whatever the view of the continuing need for diversity jurisdiction in the federal courts, this category of jurisdiction constitutes a significant portion of the district court's business. And with American society becoming ever more litigious, proposals to reduce the workload of the federal courts by requiring that these cases be tried in state court may become increasingly attractive.

There are exceptions to the rule that state courts are assumed to have concurrent jurisdiction with the federal courts in both federal question and diversity cases, especially when Congress places jurisdiction over a particular category of federal claims exclusively in the federal courts. Diversity jurisdiction, on the other hand, does not involve federal claims, so these cases may be brought in either state or federal court. It is a well-settled doctrine that state courts may not decline to hear federal questions properly brought in state court if the state court hears similar types of claims arising under state law, and a refusal to entertain the federal claim would operate, in effect, to discriminate against those parties seeking to vindicate federally portected interests.

Cause of Action. In order to act, a court must not only have jurisdiction (broadly speaking, the power to decide a case) to rule on the particular type of controversy in question,

but must also have jurisdiction over the parties or things in controversy. For example, in a suit for damages arising from an automobile accident between two private persons, citizens of the same state, a federal court would lack jurisdiction because such a dispute is outside the scope of the judicial power as defined in Article III.

Jurisdiction, however, does not by itself create rights that may be vindicated in court. This is done through the creation of a cause of action. A precise definition of a cause of action is not easy to arrive at. In the hypothetical automobile accident, state law would provide that individuals injured through the negligence of others in the operation of their motor vehicle could sue in court to recover damages for their injuries. Federal statutes, or in a limited number of cases the Constitution itself, may provide causes of action to redress various types of injury. For example, if an individual is arrested or otherwise restrained from expressing views on a controversial subject, the 1st Amendment guarantees of free speech may provide a basis for going into court to obtain relief from the allegedly unconstitutional restriction.

The distinction between jurisdiction and cause of action becomes important in an examination of the diversity jurisdiction of the federal courts. Unlike federal question cases, where the dispute concerns issues of federal law and the law of the case is to be found in the corpus of federal jurisprudence, in diversity cases the cause of action is a matter of state law, and the law applied by the federal district courts in diversity cases has been, since *Erie Railroad Co. v.*

Tompkins (1938), a matter of state law. To say that in diversity cases the rule of decision is to be state law rather than federal law, as *Erie Railroad Co. v. Tompkins* requires, does not, of course, settle the problem of what shall be the choice of law in the diversity case. By definition, a case in diversity involves citizens of more than one state or country. Often the question of which law shall apply is itself a complicated legal issue. For that matter, even in federal question cases state law may also be involved. In a question of federal tax law, for example, whether or not a type of property is subject to taxation may depend upon how the law of that particular state defines the property interest, assuming that federal law does not supply the needed definition. Choice of law questions are particularly difficult in complex civil litigation. A major airline accident may easily involve persons and corporations of dozens of different states, and in some cases, the determination of which rule of law will apply also determines who will win and lose the lawsuit.

Cases and Controversies. Article III also provides that the judicial power of the United States is limited to cases or controversies. This definition of the judicial power, in terms of cases or controversies, has been seen from the beginning as a limitation on the jurisdiction of the federal courts. A precise definition of what constitutes a case or controversy is not easy. It is possible, however, to describe this requirement in general terms. Since the judicial system is adversarial in nature, the case or controversy requirement serves to limit the types of disputes that the federal courts can entertain to those that are not hypothetical or abstract. But not all adversarial cases are susceptible of judicial resolution. There is a narrow category of cases that, though adversarial in nature, are nevertheless not decided by federal courts because the nature of the controversy is more properly left to one or both of the other branches of government. This latter category of cases, presenting what are known as political questions, are usually characterized as being nonjusticiable, requiring the court to dismiss the action. Problems of justiciability normally do not arise in litigation between private parties but are usually found in suits against high government officials questioning decisions made in the political process or otherwise raising questions of broad public policy.

The requirement of a case or controversy also prevents a federal court from rendering an advisory opinion as well as from performing a nonjudicial function. In 1793, President Washington, acting through Secretary of State Jefferson, inquired whether the Supreme Court would be willing to provide advice to the President on questions of international law and treaty interpretation, particularly concerning American obligations under treaties with France, which at that time was at war in Europe. After considering the request, the Court declined to provide the requested advice on the ground that to do so would involve them unconstitutionally in the business of a coordinate branch and might complicate

Members of the Waite Court listen to arguments in the Court's chambers in the Capitol in 1888.

The Supreme Court's case load was a major concern of Chief Justice Burger in the mid-1980s, but even a century earlier the Court felt overburdened.

their role should a judicial case involving these questions subsequently arise.

A more specific example of the dangers of one branch of government unconstitutionally intruding into another's area of responsibility was presented the year before, in 1792, in *Hayburns Case*. In this instance Congress by statute attempted to provide that the federal courts would act in an administrative capacity to determine which veterans of the Revolutionary War, as a result of their wounds in combat, should be placed on the pension list for the period of time in which they were disabled. The act provided for submission of certificates from the military commanders as well as affidavits from citizens attesting to the disability and required the circuit court, upon proper receipt of this evidence, to determine whether the individual had a service-related disability that would qualify him for the pension list. The recommendation of the circuit court was to go to the secretary of War who, under the terms of the act, would have the authority to overturn the decision of the court. The Supreme Court held that the lack of finality, that is, the power of the executive branch to review and revise the decisions of the federal courts, was unconstitutional.

There is an obvious point of contact between this case and the situation presented by President Washington's letter to the Court requesting advice on matters of international law. In both instances, any decision of the Court would be advisory and hypothetical. In neither instance did it appear

that an actual case or controversy existed. To have approved either plan would have meant placing the Article III courts in a position where they would be providing advice to the executive branch, a nonjudicial function. The case or controversy requirement has thus from the very beginnings of the republic been firmly established as a basic requirement to the exercise of Article III jurisdiction. It permits courts to decide only those issues in which opposing parties are prepared to argue fully their respective positions and thereby, at least in theory, provide the court with the maximum amount of information and insight into the legal issues presented by the suit.

Standing To Sue

If the Constitution requires concrete cases or controversies as a prerequisite to judicial involvement, the obvious question is what types of parties are necessary in order to create the necessary adversity? That is, if a proper suit is to be brought in federal court, who must bring it? These questions are addressed in the doctrine of standing. These questions typically do not arise in controversies between private parties. If one alleges that another has negligently injured him, his standing to sue is clear. The difficulty more often arises when an individual attempts to reverse a decision of public policy through intervention by the judicial system.

The doctrine of standing is complicated. The Supreme

Court made reference to it in *Baker v. Carr* (1962), noting that "the gist of the question of standing" is whether a party seeking judicial redress has alleged "such a personal stake in the outcome of the controversy as to assure the concrete adverseness which sharpens the presentation of issues upon which the court so largely depends for illumination of difficult constitutional questions." To have standing a plaintiff must have been "injured in fact." He must be asserting rights protected by a statute or the Constitution. And he must in most cases be asserting rights that are personal to him. With few exceptions, the courts have declined to permit standing where an individual seeks to raise the rights of others. In recent years, however, there has been an increased willingness on the part of the Supreme Court to permit individuals to raise *jus tertii*, the rights of others, in certain types of 1st Amendment cases and in situations where persons are involved in professional or business relationships that are subject to governmental regulation. For example, the Court has allowed physicians to assert the rights of their patients who are being subjected to a statute that unconstitutionally limits the right to abortion (*Singleton v. Wulff*, 1976).

Political Questions

Certain types of suits are held to be nonjusticiable under the so-called political question doctrine. This doctrine is premised on the belief that there are a relatively narrow range of questions that are concerned with political issues and judgments more properly left to the legislative or executive branches. The modern doctrine is traceable to the legislative reapportionment decision concerning unequal representation in the Tennessee state legislature that reached the Supreme Court in *Baker v. Carr*. In the Court's opinion Justice Brennan emphasized that the political question doctrine is based on the idea of separation of powers within the tripartite federal government. He defined political questions as follows:

> Prominent on the surface of any case held to involve a political question is found a textually demonstrable constitutional commitment of the issue to a coordinate political department; or a lack of judicially discoverable and manageable standards for resolving it; or the impossibility of deciding, without an initial policy determination, of a kind clearly for non-judicial discretion; or the impossibility of a court's undertaking independent resolution without expressing lack of the respect due coordinate branches of government; or an unusual need for unquestioning adherence to a political decision already made; or the potentiality of embarrassment from multifarious pronouncements by various departments on one question.

It is not the case, however, that all questions involving the political process are susceptible of characterization as political questions. The right of an individual to register to vote

*Relations between the Supreme Court and the President are usually formal and correct. Chief Justice Taft (**right**) and the associate justices call on President Harding at the White House.*

Chief Justice and Mrs. Warren (right) stand with President and Mrs. Kennedy at a 1963 White House dinner for sitting and retired justices.

and participate in the elective process free from racial discrimination is beyond question. Since the decision in *Baker v. Carr*, the federal courts have been more willing to entertain questions that might previously have been declined. But the doctrine is still viable. It was used frequently during the Vietnam War by courts that consistently found that attempted challenges to American involvement in that war raised nonjusticiable issues.

The Judiciary Act

Article III of the Constitution, the Judiciary Article, was not self-executing, and it remained for Congress to enact the necessary legislation to establish the federal court system. This Congress did when, on September 24, 1789, it passed "An Act to establish the Judicial Courts of the United States." This act, as noted earlier, provided for the size of the Supreme Court, which was to consist of a chief justice and five associate justices. The language of Article III would appear to have required nothing less, providing that "the judicial power of the United States shall be vested in one Supreme Court." But Congress, also in the first Judiciary Act, went further and exercised its constitutional option of establishing a federal court system, which was to consist of circuit and district courts. Congress also established the jurisdiction of these lower courts as well as the appellate jurisdiction of the Supreme Court. Congress also undertook

in the first Judiciary Act to define the original jurisdiction of the Supreme Court, a definition that for all practical purposes corresponds to the constitutional definition in Article III. Also, the Supreme Court's original jurisdiction is specifically defined in the Constitution, and the Supreme Court on many occasions has said that it can be exercised without further statutory authority from Congress. It has long been settled, however, that Congress has the power to make the Supreme Court's original jurisdiction concurrent with the jurisdiction of the lower federal courts (*Bors v. Preston*, 1884; *Ames v. Kansas*, 1884).

In *Bors v. Preston*, the Supreme Court quoted an observation of Chief Justice Taney on circuit concerning the necessity of making a portion of the Supreme Court's original jurisdiction concurrent with that of a lower court.

> . . . It could hardly have been the contention of the statesmen who framed our Constitution to require that one of our citizens who had a petty claim of even less than five dollars against another citizen, who had been clothed by some foreign government with a consular office, should be compelled to go into the Supreme Court to have a jury summoned, in order to enable him to recover it; nor could it have been intended, that the time of that Court, with all its high duties to perform, should be taken up with the trial of every petty offense that might be committed by a consul in any part of the United States; that consul, too, being often one of our own citizens.

In addition to establishing a system of lower federal courts, the first Judiciary Act also defined the appellate jurisdiction of the Supreme Court. The system of federal courts is a system of tribunals of limited jurisdiction, and the inferior federal courts, and the Supreme Court in its appellate jurisdiction, exercise that jurisdiction established by statute consistent with the Article III definition of the judicial power. Unlike the Supreme Court's original jurisdiction, its appellate jurisdiction is left to Congress. Article III provides that "[i]n all the other Cases before mentioned, the supreme Court shall have Appellate Jurisdiction, both as to Law and Fact, with such Exceptions, and under such Regulations as the Congress shall make."

The United States Supreme Court had occasion, in 1850, to review the question of whether Congress might constitutionally decline to convey upon a federal court all of the judicial power as defined in Article III. In *Sheldon v. Sill* (1850), the Supreme Court was asked to determine the constitutionality of a restriction in the Judiciary Act that required that in cases of diversity involving an assignment, jurisdiction would lie only if the suit might have been brought by the original parties before the assignment was made. In this case, diversity was created only by the assignment of a debt by a citizen of Michigan to a citizen of New York. The circuit court had taken jurisdiction of the case notwithstanding the statutory restriction, presumably upon the assumption that since Article III provides that the judicial power shall extend to "controversies between citizens of different states," Congress had been acting without constitutional authority in restricting jurisdiction to those cases where diversity existed prior to the assignment. The Supreme Court reversed the lower court, holding that Congress need not confer upon the federal courts the whole of the judicial power.

Justice Grier, writing for the Court, observed:

It must be admitted, that if the Constitution had ordained and established the inferior courts, and distributed to them their respective powers, they could not be restricted or divested by Congress. But as it has made no such distribution, one of two consequences must result,–either that each inferior court created by Congress must exercise all the judicial powers not given to the Supreme Court, or that Congress, having the power to establish the courts, must define their respective jurisdictions. The first of these inferences has never been asserted, and could not be defended with any show of reason, and if not, the latter would seem to follow as a necessary consequence. And it would seem to follow, also, that, having a right to prescribe, Congress may withhold from any court of its creation jurisdiction of any of the enumerated controversies. Courts created by statute can have no jurisdiction but such as the statute confers. No one of them can assert a just claim to jurisdiction exclusively conferred on another, or withheld from all.

The Constitution has defined the limits of the judicial

Following Chief Justice Stone's death in 1946, his seat was draped in black.

*The duties of the Chief Justice can include swearing in the President. Chief Justice Stone (**hand raised**) administers the oath of office to Harry Truman in 1945.*

power of the United States, but has not prescribed how much of it shall be exercised by the Circuit Court; consequently, the statute, which does prescribe the limits of their jurisdiction, cannot be in conflict with the Constitution, unless it confers powers not enumerated therein. Such has been the doctrine held by this court since its first establishment. To enumerate all the cases in which it has been either directly advanced or tacitly assumed would be tedious and unnecessary.

Congress And Jurisdiction

The Supreme Court's decision in *Sheldon v. Sill* is undoubtedly correct, so far as it goes, and has since been reconfirmed many times. But the question that was not presented in *Sheldon v. Sill* and has rarely presented itself elsewhere, is to what extent Congress may, under its authority to establish the jurisdiction of the federal courts, withdraw jurisdiction previously granted in order to prevent a court from enforcing a constitutional right. The question is particularly important where the appellate jurisdiction of the Supreme Court is at issue since that Court also reviews decisions from the state courts. The language of Article III is less than clear, providing that "...the Supreme court shall have appellate Jurisdiction ...with such Exceptions, and under Regulations as the Congress shall make."

There have been a few attempts in recent years in the Congress to pass statutes that would have restricted the Supreme Court's appellate jurisdiction in cases where mem-

bers of Congress disagreed with the Court's interpretation of the Constitution, particularly in areas such as school prayer and civil rights. None of these efforts has been successful. No statutes have been passed limiting the authority of the Supreme Court to consider certain types of controversial cases appealed from lower federal or state courts. But there is a substantial constitutional question presented by this type of limiting legislation, and there is a substantial amount of scholarly discussion to be found on this subject. It was precisely this question that led the late Professor Henry Hart, a distinguished commentator in this field, to observe that the ultimate judicial bulwark in this area against the infringement of constitutional rights may be the state courts, rather than the federal courts with their limited jurisdiction.

Reconstruction Cases. The Supreme Court has seldom had occasion to review the power of Congress to withdraw jurisdiction from the Supreme Court. The only case in which the matter has been squarely addressed arose in the aftermath of the Civil War. In *Ex parte McCardle* (1869), the Supreme Court was petitioned for a writ of habeas corpus for release from military custody by a newspaper editor who was being held by military authorities as a result of his severe criticism in his Vicksburg, Mississippi, newspaper of the military occupation in that state resulting from Reconstruction. McCardle had applied to the circuit court for the southern district of Mississippi for a writ of habeas corpus pursuant to the Habeas Corpus Act of 1867, which authorized the grant of such writs "in all cases where any person may be restrained of his or her liberty in violation of the Constitution, or of any treaty or law of the United States." The law had been enacted by Congress as a means of protecting the rights of blacks in the Southern states. As is sometimes the case, however, the statute was invoked by the Mississippi editor challenging his confinement by the military authorities pending trial for publication of articles in his newspaper that were alleged to be libelous and incendiary.

The appeal was argued in the Supreme Court, but before the Court could hand down a decision, Congress, fearful that the Court would use the *McCardle* case as a vehicle for holding portions of Reconstruction unconstitutional, passed the Act of March 27, 1868, which provided:

And be it further enacted, that so much of the Act approved February 5, 1867, entitled "An act to amend, an act to establish, the judicial courts of the United States, approved September 24, 1789," has authorized an appeal from the judgment of the circuit court to the Supreme Court of the United States, or the exercise of any such jurisdiction by said Supreme Court, on appeals which have been, or may hereafter be taken, be, and the same is hereby repealed.

The repealing act, which withdrew the appellate jurisdiction of the Supreme Court to hear appeals for denial of the writ

of habeas corpus under the 1867 act, was passed over the veto of President Andrew Johnson.

The Court, after considering argument on the effect of the repealing act, recognized the broad (but not necessarily unlimited) congressional power to withdraw jurisdiction previously granted. The Court recognized this power in a case that had already been brought before the Court and argued prior to the congressional action. The Court noted:

We are not at liberty to inquire into the motives of the legislature. We can only examine into its power under the Constitution; and the power to make exceptions to the appellate jurisdiction of this Court is given by express words.

What, then, is the effect of the Repealing Act upon the case before us? We cannot doubt as to this: without jurisdiction the Court cannot proceed at all in any case. Jurisdiction is power to declare the law, and when it ceases to exist, the only function remaining to the Court is that of announcing the fact and dismissing the cause. And this is not less clear upon authority than upon principle...

It is quite clear, therefore, that this Court cannot proceed to pronounce judgment in this case for it has no longer jurisdiction of the appeal; and judicial duty is not less fitly performed by declining ungranted jurisdiction than in exercising firmly that which the Constitution and the laws confer.

Counsel seem to have supposed, if effect be given to the Repealing Act in question, that the whole appellate power of the Court, in cases of habeas corpus, is denied. But this [is

The Chief Justice is sometimes asked to head special boards. Chief Justice Warren delivers the Warren Commission Report on President Kennedy's assassination to President Johnson in 1964.

*Justices occasionally retire from the Court to accept other positions. Justice Goldberg (**center**) retired to accept President Johnson's (**left**) nomination of him as ambassador to the UN. Justice Black congratulates Goldberg on his new appointment.*

in] error. The Act of 1868 does not except from that jurisdiction any cases but appeals from circuit courts under the Act of 1867. It does not affect the jurisdiction which was previously exercised.

The appeal of the petitioner in this case must be dismissed for want of jurisdiction.

Thus Congress was successful, at least for a time, in preventing the Court from examining and perhaps holding unconstitutional the military occupation provisions of the Reconstruction legislation. But the possibility that the Supreme Court might yet have an opportunity to consider the question was soon presented in *Ex parte Yerger* (1868), when the Court held that the 1868 act left intact courts' appellate jurisdiction to review denial of the writ under another provision of the Judiciary Act. Once again, however, a decision on the merits was avoided, this time by the release of Yerger from military custody.

The Supreme Court never considered the constitutionality of the Reconstruction acts. The importance of the Court's decision in *Ex parte McCardle,* though, is obviously not limited to that particular situation. Can the Congress, if it disagrees with the constitutional interpretation of the Supreme Court, withdraw from the Court the appellate jurisdiction necessary to adjudicate in that area? It is not clear what interpretation should be given today to the *McCardle* opinion. Would a modern court acquiesce to the

same degree that the Reconstruction era Court did? In *United States v. Kline* (1872), another case from Reconstruction, the Supreme Court held that a statute purporting to withdraw jurisdiction from the Court in any pending claims based upon a presidential pardon was unconstitutional under the doctrine of separation of powers. This case arose out of a suit in the Court of Claims by the administrator of a deceased property owner whose property had been seized by federal forces during the Civil War and sold pursuant to act of Congress authorizing the sale of property held by those engaged in the rebellion. If a property owner was found to be loyal to the Union, however, his property would, of course, not be eligible for confiscation. Also, the Supreme Court had previously held that evidence of a presidential pardon was sufficient proof to establish loyalty. Congress, by statute, then provided that a pardon would not be admissible as proof of loyalty, and further, that acceptance of such a pardon without protest or disclaimer by the recipient would be conclusive evidence of the recipient's disloyalty.

The Court, in holding the Act of Congress unconstitutional, found that Congress in attempting to legislate the effect to be given to this evidence, had intruded into the judicial function in violation of the separation of powers doctrine. The Court further found that Congress had encroached upon the executive function by attempting to impair the effect of a presidential pardon, also in violation of the separation of powers doctrine.

Later Opinions. It is not clear how the Supreme Court today might handle a withdrawal of jurisdiction question similar to that presented in *McCardle*. Justice Douglas, in a footnote to his dissenting opinion in *Glidden Co. v. Zadnok* (1962), stated:

> [The majority opinion of Justice Harlan] cites with approval *Ex parte McCardle,* . . . in which Congress withdrew jurisdiction of this Court to review a habeas corpus case that was *sub judice,* and then apparently draws a distinction between that case and *United States v. Kline,* . . . where such withdrawal was not permitted in a property claim. *There is a serious question whether the McCardle case could command the majority view today.* Certainly the distinction between liberty and property (which emanates from this portion of my brother Harlan's opinion) has no vitality even in terms of the due process clause. . . . [emphasis added]

The ability of Congress to limit the appellate jurisdiction of the Supreme Court under such circumstances may depend in part upon a question of available remedies. That is, the Constitution may require only that a forum be available in which one may vindicate constitutionally protected rights. That forum, so the argument goes, need not necessarily be a federal one. Thus, in a sense, the state courts may be the ultimate guarantors of federally guaranteed rights. There are, however, some circumstances under which a state court must entertain federal claims. In *Testa v. Katt* (1947), the Supreme Court, in an opinion by Justice Black, held that the state of Rhode Island was constitutionally required to permit an action for violation of the act to be maintained in the state courts.

> For the purposes of this case, we assume, without deciding, that [Section] 205(e) is a penal statute in the "public international," "private international," or any other sense. So far as the question of whether the Rhode Island courts properly declined to try this action, it makes no difference into which of these categories the Rhode Island court chose to place the statute which Congress has passed. For we cannot accept the basic premise on which the Rhode Island Supreme Court held that it has no more obligation to enforce a valid penal law of the United States than it has to enforce a penal law of another state or foreign country. Such a broad assumption flies in the face of the fact that the states of the Union constitute a nation. It disregards the purpose and effect of Article VI, [Section] 2 of the Constitution which provides: "This Constitution, and the Laws of the United States which shall be made in Pursuance thereof; and all Treaties made, or which shall be made, under the Authority of the United States, shall be the supreme law of the Land; and the Judges in every State, shall be bound thereby, any Thing in the Constitution or Laws of any State to the Contrary notwithstanding." . . .
>
> The Rhode Island Court and its *Robinson* decision on which it relies, cites cases of this Court which have held that states are not required by the full faith and credit clause of the Constitution to enforce judgments of the courts of other states based on claims arising out of penal statutes. But those holdings have no relevance here, for this case raises no full faith and credit question. Nor need we consider in this case prior decisions to the effect that federal courts are not required to enforce state penal laws.
>
> For whatever consideration they may be entitled to in the field in which they are relevant, those decisions did not bring before us our incident problem of the effect of the supremacy clause on the relation of federal laws to state courts. Our question concerns only the right of a state to deny enforcement to claims growing out of a valid federal law.
>
> It is conceded that this same type of claim arising under Rhode Island law would be enforced by the State's courts. Its courts have enforced claims for double damages growing out of the Fair Labor Standards Act. Thus the Rhode Island courts have jurisdiction adequate and appropriate under established local law to adjudicate this action. Under these circumstances, the State courts are not free to refuse enforcement of petitioner's claim. . . .

It is unlikely that the Supreme Court would hold constitutional the congressional withdrawal of appellate jurisdiction if the effect of such a withdrawal were to be a denial of a constitutionally created or guaranteed right, where it cannot be clearly demonstrated that another remedy would be effective to protect the federal claim. Modern attempts by individual members of Congress to circumvent Supreme Court decisions through attempts to limit the jurisdiction of the Supreme Court for these purposes raise substantial constitutional issues. It is not clear whether there would be a legal difference between removing all of the Supreme Court's appellate jurisdiction, which would be politically unthinkable, and removing a small portion related to a specific controversial issue. These proposed bills have never been adopted, nor do any successful attempts appear likely in the foreseeable future.

The independence of the federal judiciary is a bulwark of the American system. The Constitution was amended by the Bill of Rights to make clear that majority rule is not always appropriate in the constitutional system. Certain rights are fundamental and protected from the actions of a tyrannical majority. It is the singular role of the federal judiciary to define and protect these constitutional rights.

The legislative and executive branches of our government were essentially established in Articles I and II of the Constitution. The powers and obligations of the Congress and the president are set forth in some detail. As a result, these two institutions were, for all practical purposes, established by the Constitution itself, although two hundred years of history and judicial interpretation continue to define the outer boundaries of the two branches. The judicial branch, however, was provided for, but, with the exception of the Supreme Court and the Court's original jurisdiction, was

Modern justices are infrequently captured in informal activities as Justices Joseph McKenna (left) and John Clarke were on the golf course around 1920.

not per se established by the Constitution. Instead provision was made that a national court system could be established through the legislative process. And this was done, beginning with the Judiciary Act of 1789.

Judicial Review

It fell to the Supreme Court itself to define, through the judicial process, the role of the Supreme Court and the federal judiciary as a coequal branch of a tripartite government. The great Chief Justice John Marshall, the fourth man to occupy that position, was presented with and seized the opportunity to establish this system of constitutionalism. It was through judicial review of questions presented to the courts in litigation that this process took, and takes, place. Judicial review is the linchpin of the U.S. constitutional process, and as such it raises fundamental questions concerning the proper role of the judiciary and of the democratic system of government. Federal judges are not elected by the people. They are appointed by the President with the advice and consent of the Senate. They serve for life, and their salaries may not be diminished during their term of office. Federal judges may be removed from office only through the process of impeachment for "Treason, Bribery, or other high Crimes and Misdemeanors." The United States thus has an institution singularly insulated from political pressure,

one that, through judicial review, determines the constitutionality of acts of Congress and actions of the executive. The Constitution itself, however, makes clear, particularly in the Bill of Rights, that the will of the majority is not always to control. There are some fundamental rights that are to be protected against a tyrannical majority, and the concept of judicial review was well established at the time of the Constitutional Convention in 1787.

Marbury v. Madison. It was in the case of *Marbury v. Madison* (1803) that Chief Justice Marshall, writing for the Court, established the doctrine of judicial review, and it is not by accident that in the private dining room of the justices at the Supreme Court the portraits of William Marbury and James Madison are to be found side by side. In the last days of the administration of President John Adams, a Federalist, the Federalist Congress, in an effort to seize and maintain control of one branch of government, attempted to reorganize the federal judiciary. Congress passed and the President signed the Circuit Court Act of February 13, 1801, which permitted President Adams to appoint sixteen new federal judges, the so-called midnight judges. In the Organic Act of the District of Columbia, which was passed on February 27, 1801, less than a week before the end of President Adams's term, the President was presented with the opportunity to name forty-two justices of the peace for the District of Columbia. The commissions of

William Marbury and the other petitioners in the *Marbury* case were signed by President Adams on his last day in office as well as by John Marshall himself, who was acting secretary of State and who received the commissions from the President, but for some reason did not or could not deliver them prior to the expiration of Adams's term at the end of the day. Marbury and the other petitioners brought suit in the Supreme Court, seeking a writ of mandamus to compel the new secretary of State, James Madison, to deliver the previously signed and sealed commissions. John Marshall, who had been secretary of State in the Adams administration, was nominated by President Adams in January 1801, near the close of his administration, to be chief justice of the United States. He was confirmed by the Senate and took the oath of office on February 4, 1801. He continued to serve, however, as acting secretary of State until the close of the Adams administration on March 3, 1801. Thus Marshall was well aware of the facts in the *Marbury* lawsuit and, in fact, might well have excused himself from hearing the case because of his personal involvement.

Chief Justice Marshall's opinion in *Marbury v. Madison* marks the beginnings of the U.S. system of constitutionalism. Its importance cannot be underestimated, and it is the beginning point of most courses in constitutional law taught in American law schools. The opinion itself is a political and judicial masterpiece. Marshall concluded that Marbury and the others were entitled to their commissions but also held that the Supreme Court had no jurisdiction to order Secretary of State Madison to deliver them because the act of Congress that purported to give the Court jurisdiction to decide such a case was itself unconstitutional. "Thus," in the words of Professor Alexander Bickel, "did Marshall assume for his Court what is nowhere made explicit in the Constitution–the ultimate power to apply the Constitution, acts of Congress to the contrary notwithstanding." Marshall's opinion in *Marbury v. Madison* established the principle of judicial review. Through the exercise of this power, the Court has shaped the American constitutional form of government and thereby shaped U.S. society.

Hunter's Lessee. The second major decision of the Marshall era Court in defining the federal judicial authority was *Martin v. Hunter's Lessee* (1816). The opportunity for this decision arose from the refusal of the Virginia Court of Appeals to obey the Supreme Court mandate in *Fairfax's Devisee v. Hunter's Lessee* (1813). The ruling in *Fairfax* was the result of land litigation that had commenced two decades earlier, in 1791. The land in question was the vast holding of Lord Fairfax, which Virginia claimed it had properly seized subsequent to the Revolutionary War under its authority to confiscate the lands of British Loyalists. Virginia, in turn, had sold some of the land to some of its own citizens, and Hunter based his interest in the land in question upon a grant from the state of Virginia. Martin, on the other hand, based his claim upon a devise from Lord Fairfax and insisted that the lands were protected from seizure by the state under provisions of the peace treaty of 1783 and the Jay Treaty of 1794. Martin's claim, therefore, was based upon a federal question, namely the interpretation and application of treaties to which the United States was a party.

The Supreme Court ruling in *Fairfax's Devisee v. Hunter's Lessee* upheld the contention put forward by Martin that the land had been protected from seizure and had therefore never vested in Virginia. The Virginia Court of Appeals had refused to obey the Supreme Court's mandate, claiming that the Supreme Court had exceeded its constitutional authority. The basis of Virginia's refusal to obey the Supreme Court's mandate was essentially that Congress had exceeded its authority by providing in Section 25 of the Judiciary Act of 1789 for Supreme Court review on federal questions of decisions of the highest state court. Virginia contended that, as a sovereign state, it could not be subjected to judicial review by courts of another sovereign, including the Supreme Court of the United States. Not surprisingly, the Supreme Court rejected this view in its second opinion on the Fairfax lands, *Martin v. Hunter's Lessee*, and asserted the authority of the Supreme Court to review state court decisions.

In **Marbury v. Madison** *new Secretary of State James Madison became a central figure in a case that established the principle of judicial review.*

Members of the conservative Court that struck down a labor law limiting working hours in **Lochner v. New York.** *The members of the Court were* (rear) *Justices Holmes, Peckham, McKenna, Day;* (front) *Brown, Harlan, Chief Justice Fuller, Justices Brewer and White.*

Later Decisions. In 1821, five years after the Supreme Court asserted its authority to review state court decisions pursuant to Section 25, it held in *Cohens v. Virginia* that the Judiciary Act also authorized, and the Constitution permitted, Supreme Court review of state court decisions in criminal cases where federal issues were properly presented. *Cohens* arose from a conviction in state court for selling District of Columbia lottery tickets in violation of Virginia laws. The defendants claimed that since the lottery tickets had been authorized by Congress, they were protected under the supremacy clause from prosecution under state laws. Unlike *Martin v. Hunter's Lessee,* which was a civil case, this presented a question of criminal law. Further, in *Cohens,* Virginia was a party in the case.

John Marshall, having been forced to sit out the *Martin v. Hunter's Lessee* case because of his own involvement as well as that of his brother in the land transaction, reaffirmed in *Cohens* the Court's earlier decision holding that the Supreme Court was constitutionally and statutorily empowered to review cases, criminal as well as civil, arising in the state courts, providing that those cases were within the Article III definition of the judicial power. The fact that Virginia was a party to the case would not serve to deny the Court jurisdiction.

Thus it was the so-called Marshall Court that established the principle of judicial review and that extended that review to decisions of the state courts. The Marshall Court also established the authority of the Congress, through the commerce power and the necessary and proper clause, to regulate interstate transactions, thereby forging a nation from what had previously been a network of separate states. One of the major failures of the Articles of Confederation had been the lack of power in the central government to regulate commerce among the states. In *McCulloch v. Maryland* (1819), involving the Second Bank of the United States, Marshall affirmed the American system of federalism and held that Maryland could not constitutionally impose a tax on the Bank of the United States even though a branch of that bank was located in Baltimore. It was national sovereignty that prevented that tax, and it was national sovereignty, the constitutional power of Congress to regulate interstate transactions, that was at issue in *Gibbons v. Ogden* (1824). In *Gibbons* the issue was whether Congress, in licensing "vessels employed in the coasting trade," might supersede a New York law granting a monopoly to operate steamboats in New York waters. In upholding the power of Congress to regulate interstate commerce in this manner, Chief Justice Marshall wrote a broad and sweeping opinion on the powers of the national government to regulate in those areas enumerated in the Constitution. It has been this commerce power, amplified by the necessary and proper clause, that has been the source both of much litigation and much of the governmental power on which many present-day regulatory mechanisms are based.

Regulating Commerce

The tides of judicial interpretation were to ebb and flow in interpreting the national power to regulate commerce during the following century. The rise of industrialization and the building of interstate transportation facilities, primarily the railroads, presented the courts with questions of interpretation that were not always addressed with the vision and resourcefulness of a John Marshall. For example, in *Lochner v. New York* (1905), a reactionary Supreme Court struck down a New York labor law limiting the working hours of bakery employees to ten hours a day or sixty hours a week. The Court, in a notorious example of judicial activism, overturned the New York statute, which had been designed to protect the health and welfare of employees, on the ground that the state had violated the due process clause of the 14th Amendment. "[The] general right to make a contract in relation to his business is part of the liberty of the individual protected by the fourteenth amendment." One of the difficulties of an active judiciary, of course, is that such a judiciary may be active in the wrong direction. That is what happened in *Lochner* and the result in Lochner is often cited by proponents of a more restrained judiciary.

Lochner involved a state statute, not an effort by Congress to regulate the economy through an exercise of the commerce power. But the same judicial philosophy that struck down the New York statute was also employed in a number of cases growing out of efforts by President Roosevelt's administration and Congress to enact progressive, some said radical, legislative efforts to address the problems of the Great Depression. *Schecter Poultry Corp. v. United States* (1935) involved the National Industrial Recovery Act, and *Carter v. Carter Coal Co.* (1936) concerned the Bituminous Coal Conservation Act of 1935. Frustrated, Roosevelt developed his now infamous plan to "pack" the Supreme Court with younger and presumably more progressive justices. The plan failed, but, as Roosevelt claimed, while he lost the battle he won the war.

In 1937 the Supreme Court reversed itself on the scope of the national powers to regulate in *National Labor Relations Board v. Jones & Laughlin Steel Corp.*, which was a very substantial case questioning the constitutionality of the recently enacted National Labor Relations Act of 1935. The Supreme Court upheld the power of Congress to regulate labor practices in those industries affecting interstate commerce and in so doing articulated a broad view of the federal commerce power, which was to permit Congress to exercise enormously greater powers in regulating the national economy. The areas affected included those aspects of local commerce that were intrastate in form but that could be shown to affect in some meaningful way the national economy or a national regulatory structure. The Court's holding in *Jones & Laughlin,* incidentally, was not necessarily contrary to the earlier pronouncements by Chief Justice Marshall more than a century earlier.

In 1942 the Supreme Court upheld in *Wickert v. Filburn* the marketing quotas established by the Agricultural Adjustment Act of 1938, which was designed to stabilize and regulate the national wheat market. Filburn was a farmer in Ohio who owned and operated a small wheat farm. His practice was to sell a portion of his crop while using the rest to feed his poultry and livestock, to make flour for home consumption, or to keep for seeding the following year. Even though the impact of Filburn on the national market would have been infinitesimal, such small farmers taken in the aggregate would have, in the Court's view, an impact on interstate commerce and thus could be regulated by Congress.

In *United States v. Darby* (1941), a Georgia lumber manufacturer had been charged with violating the Fair Labor Standards Act of 1938. The district court had held the act unconstitutional because it attempted to regulate hours and wages of employees engaged in local manufacturing activities. The Supreme Court reversed the district court and upheld the constitutionality of the act. As it was to do in *Wickert v. Filburn* a year later, the Supreme Court upheld the power of Congress to create a comprehensive legislative scheme designed to regulate a given industry. In *Darby,* the Supreme Court permitted Congress to exercise broad regulatory powers under the commerce clause and the necessary and proper clause in order to prevent the shipment in interstate commerce of goods that had been manufactured locally in plants not in conformity with the Fair Labor Standards Act. These cases and their progeny are important because they recognize a broad national power to regulate in what has become a complicated and interconnected economic unit.

Civil Rights Effects. The commerce power was evoked in the passage of the Civil Rights Act of 1964, which prohibits, among other things, discrimination in places of public accommodation. The difficulties faced by blacks in interstate travel because of segregated facilities were well known. The commerce power provided a ready instrument to strike at long established patterns of racial discrimination, particularly in the South. The constitutionality of the Civil Rights Act was upheld in *Heart of Atlanta Motel v. United States* (1964) and *Katzenbach v. McClung* (1964).

The role of the Supreme Court in defining the scope of the federal commerce power is one of the more obvious examples of the impact of the Supreme Court on American society. It is by no means, however, the only example. The decision interpreting the 14th Amendment in *Brown v. Board of Education* in 1954 effected enormous social changes, particularly in the South. And the Court's decisions in cases involving the rights of criminal defendants have reshaped the American system of justice. The Supreme Court of the United States is a powerful institution, yet, it is also a fragile one. Much of its jurisdiction is dependent upon statutes enacted by Congress and signed by the president. In such a system, it is necessary that the Court as an institution retain the respect of a substantial portion of the American people. If the Court moves too far ahead of the body politic, it risks constitutional confrontations that might ultimately undermine its institutional integrity. The full potential for the congressional regulation of the jurisdiction of the federal courts, touched upon in *Ex parte McCardle,* has never been fully exercised. Whatever its applicability in a major confrontation today between the Congress and the judiciary, it remains a reminder of the interdependency of our three branches of government.

The Constitutional Powers of the Branches of the Federal Government

The Constitutional Powers of the Branches of the Federal Government

The U.S. Constitution is "the supreme law of the land." However, a reading of the document, including its twenty-six amendments, yields little or nothing of its meaning. This is so because the body of American constitutional law is composed mainly of decisions of the U.S. Supreme Court. The judicial gloss placed upon the Constitution has brought it to life.

The problems dealt with in American constitutional law consist primarily of the federal government's ability to rule its citizens and its obligation to curb itself. The Constitution grants and limits governmental powers, both explicitly and implicitly. The first two articles of the Constitution delineate the powers of the legislative and executive branches, respectively, while Article III invests judicial power in the U.S. Supreme Court, as well as in other courts as set up by Congress.

The Constitution specifically lists certain constraints placed on government. For example, Congress is expressly forbidden to pass an *ex post facto* law (a law passed after the commission of an act that retrospectively changes the act's legal consequences) or a bill of attainder (a legislative act that applies to an identifiable group in a manner that inflicts punishment without the benefit of a trial). Further, Congress may not suspend the writ of *habeas corpus*, a writ designed to test the legality of a detention or imprisonment of an individual. However, most of the Constitution's limiting principles are not defined explicitly. The Bill of Rights, composed of the first ten amendments, enumerates other limitations on the power of the federal government, the boundaries of which are more obscure.

The Constitution's structure implies other fundamental theories of government, including those of federalism, the separation of powers, and the doctrine of judicial review.

The Doctrine Of Judicial Review

The concept of judicial review is one method by which government is kept tethered. The power of the Supreme Court to determine the constitutionality and validity of actions of the other branches of government is now firmly entrenched as a basic component of the U.S. system of government. This doctrine, however, was not always so readily accepted. An examination of the Court's history will unveil an ongoing effort to establish and nurture this judicial power to review.

The historical basis for judicial review is unclear; it is not explicitly proscribed by the Constitution. No final conclusion has emerged as to whether the framers of the Constitution envisioned the Supreme Court as the final interpreter of the Constitution. Although some evidence does exist that indicates that the concept, at least in part, was endorsed by some of the states before the enunciation of the doctrine in the *Marbury v. Madison* decision of 1803, legal scholars have engaged in endless debate as to the historical roots of judicial review. There is little factual basis for judicial review in the English judicial system. However, the American colonists may have understood the system to encompass some

In **The Federalist Paper No. 78,** *Alexander Hamilton argued for a strong Supreme Court with the authority to review the constitutionality of acts of Congress.*

form of judicial review, since the English government was empowered to void acts of the colonial legislature that were considered in violation of their charters or of English law. This practice was limited in scope, however, and was not readily accepted by many colonies. The importance of this examination, though, lies in the perception of the colonists of judicial review as a valid check on legislative power, rather than in the factually correct view of the practice.

A more fruitful source of the concept of judicial review is the Constitutional Convention and the literature surrounding the ratification of the Constitution. Although the framers made the Constitution "the supreme law of the land," they neglected to identify who was to maintain this supremacy. Several suggestions were posed in the Philadelphia Convention debates of 1787. One was to allow Congress to solicit the Court's opinion as to the validity of federal legislation. Another urged that a council of revision be established, composed of the judiciary and executive branches, that would have veto power over congressional legislation. Members of the Convention opposed to any form of judicial review argued that it would violate the principle of the separation of powers. Finally, although the debates indicate that the framers intended to establish some form of judicial review, the exact nature of the concept was left undefined.

Federalist Paper No. 78. During the ratification process, Alexander Hamilton's *The Federalist Paper No. 78* (1788) endorsed a strong, independent Supreme Court, whose justices were empowered as "faithful guardians of the Constitution." Hamilton gave special attention to the argument against judicial review that investing the Court with the authority to void an act of the legislative branch would give the Court superiority over the legislature.

He described the judiciary as "the least dangerous to the political rights of the Constitution," in comparison with the executive and legislative branches. Unlike the other two branches, the Court holds neither the sword nor the purse and can therefore take no action to injure either the strength or the wealth of society. Furthermore, the judiciary is the weakest of the three branches and is unable successfully to attack the other two. Therefore, "liberty can have nothing to fear from the judiciary alone, but would have everything to fear from its union with either of the other departments."

Hamilton described the Constitution as "a fundamental law" of the people that was to be interpreted and protected by the Court. If a conflict should arise between the Constitution and a legislative act, the judiciary has the duty to uphold the Constitution, since the Constitution has the "superior obligation and validity." He then reasoned that this conclusion does not make the judicial branch superior to the legislature. "The power of the people is superior to both,

When President John Adams appointed some justices of the peace whose commissions were not delivered before he left office, he inadvertently created the controversy that led to the **Marbury v. Madison** *decision.*

and that where the will of the legislature, declared in its statutes, stands in opposition to that of the people, declared in the Constitution, the judges ought to be governed by the latter rather than the former."

Hamilton argued for an appointed and life-tenured judiciary, since independence is essential to the difficult task of protecting a Constitution from legislative infringement. The Court must be independent enough to withstand a challenge to the Constitution that may arise from the majority. Elected representatives, however, would be powerless "whenever a momentary inclination happens to lay hold of a majority of their constituents incompatible with the provisions in the existing Constitution...."

The Importance Of Marbury v. Madison

Many of these same arguments were made fifteen years later by Chief Justice John Marshall in *Marbury v. Madison* (1803). This landmark case was the first decision by the Supreme Court to hold a federal statute unconstitutional and was the only case to do so until *Dred Scott* in 1857. *Marbury* marked the establishment of the the the doctrine of judicial review that rested on the argument that the Constitution is law and that law belongs especially to the courts to interpret.

Background to Marbury. The historical setting of *Marbury* provides an essential insight into the facts of the case. The end of the eighteenth century marked a period of intense political rivalry, with the Federalist Party in control of the national government. In 1800, the Federalists lost power for several reasons, one of which was their use of the Sedition Act to silence those who opposed President Adams or the Federalist Congress.

Jefferson was elected as the next president. Before he and the Democratic-Republicans took office, however, Adams nominated John Marshall as the fourth chief justice for the U.S. Supreme Court. Marshall, a leading Federalist and Adams's secretary of State, was confirmed by the Senate. Adams and the Federalists sought to maintain their control through an expanded federal judiciary. The Circuit Court Act was passed, which reduced the number of justices on the Supreme Court and abolished the system of holding court in the circuits. They also created sixteen new circuit courts and federal judgeships that they filled with Federalist appointees. Since these appointees were confirmed only two days before Jefferson took office, they have been called the "midnight judges." The *Marbury* litigation, however, centered around even later appointments.

The day before the Democratic-Republicans came into power, the Senate confirmed forty-two appointed justices of the peace who had been named by Adams, only five days earlier, to serve in the District of Columbia and Alexandria. Marshall, who had remained secretary of State until the end of Adams's term, was unable to deliver all forty-two commissions that night. When Jefferson took office, the new President refused to deliver the remaining commissions to the Federalist appointees.

The Supreme Court Case. William Marbury was among the justices of the peace who had failed to receive his commission. He brought suit against the new secretary of State, James Madison, for delivery of his commission by filing an original action in the Supreme Court. He sought an order of *mandamus* to Madison to compel the delivery. Marbury could legally file suit directly to the Supreme Court under one of Congress's first acts, the Judiciary Act of 1789, Section 13, which established U.S. courts and authorized the Supreme Court to issue writs of *mandamus* to public officers.

Jefferson believed that such an action could not be ordered by a court. The Court then issued a rule to show cause, which required Secretary Madison to show why the *mandamus* should not issue, and set the case for argument in its 1802 term. The new anti-Federalist Congress was in the process of repealing the Federalist Circuit Court Act, and it eliminated part of the 1802 term of the Supreme Court. Thus, when the Court began its 1803 term, it intended to resolve the issue of judicial power in relation to the executive and legislative branches of government.

Chief Justice Marshall's Opinion. Marshall's opinion was skillfully written so as to establish the claim to judicial authority without provoking political reprisals against the Court. It ruled that the Court had no jurisdiction to hear Marbury's claim, but it also asserted the power of the Supreme Court to review the constitutionality of both legislative and executive actions.

In the opinion, the Supreme Court held that the facts clearly demonstrated a case for *mandamus*; Marbury had a right to his judicial commission. This ruling subjected the executive to constitutional restraints that could be enforced by the Court. A writ of *mandamus* could issue only from the Court under the authority granted it by Section 13 of the Judiciary Act of 1789. The Court ruled, however, that it had no jurisdiction to dispense this remedy in an original action as it was not within the powers invested in it by Article III of the Constitution. Since the Judiciary Act of 1789, as it was interpreted, placed this case under the Court's jurisdiction, it was in conflict with the Constitution. Marshall concluded with the finding that the Supreme Court was empowered to invalidate this law as a violation of the Constitution.

Marshall's opinion framed the case in three issues: first, did Marbury have a right to his commission? Second, was a remedy for the deprivation of that right established by law? Third, could the Supreme Court issue a writ of *mandamus* in an original action?

With respect to the first issue, the Court ruled that Marbury had a vested right to his commission. Although the commission had never been delivered, Marbury's right became irrevocable after the execution of the commission.

After finding that Marbury thus had a vested legal

Chief Justice Marshall's 1803 opinion in **Marbury v. Madison** *remains historically important for its assertion that the Supreme Court had the authority to review executive and legislative actions.*

right, the Court ruled that a legal remedy was required to correct a legal wrong. Marshall relied on the "essence of civil liberty," which compelled the protection of an individual's vested legal rights. He then pointedly noted that a judicial remedy would not correct a wrong that was political, and not legal, in nature. Such a wrong would have to be left to the political process, as its remedy was up to the discretion of the executive.

The last issue then became the question upon which the case turned. Marbury had a right to his commission and deserved a remedy. However, was he entitled to the remedy that he sought from the Supreme Court? This issue was further subdivided into two questions regarding the issuance of a writ of *mandamus* from the Supreme Court.

Marshall examined the nature of the writ of *mandamus* and concluded that the judiciary possessed the power to review the actions of the executive branch, where the actions were not political and therefore not within the executive's sole discretion. Where the Constitution or federal law established a duty of the executive, however, the Court could enforce that duty. Marshall thus established the basis for finding not only that the judiciary could review executive action under Constitution and federal law, but also that

the executive could be compelled to comply with those principles.

After this analysis, the final question remained: could the Court issue a writ of *mandamus* against the executive in this specific case? In his consideration of this issue, Marshall found a conflict between the statutory jurisdiction given to the Court by the Judiciary Act of 1789 and its original jurisdiction prescribed by Article III of the Constitution.

According to his interpretation, the statutory jurisdiction enabled the Court to hear original actions for writs of *mandamus* to federal officers, such as the *Marbury* action. However, Marshall's reading of the Court's Article III jurisdiction excluded such actions. This conflict between the federal statute and the Constitution led to the issues of whether such a statute could be valid and, if not, whether the Supreme Court was empowered to invalidate such a law.

Marshall found that a statute in conflict with the Constitution was inherently invalid. This ruling was premised on the superiority of the Constitution, which was evidenced by the fact that the Constitution was written and established by the people with the intent to create fundamental principles that would be eternally binding on all levels of government. Therefore, since a written constitution is the "fundamental and paramount law of the nation...an act of the legislative, repugnant to the constitution, is void."

Marshall then discussed whether the Court was bound to follow the legislative act, despite its conflict with the Constitution. In a seemingly simple argument, he asserted the basis for judicial review of the federal legislative under the Constitution. His primary contention was that "it is emphatically the province and duty of the judicial department to say what the law is." Since he had already declared the Constitution to be the paramount law of the land, it was only logical that the ultimate authority on matters of constitutional interpretation lay with the judiciary. It is precisely this notion of the superiority of the Constitution and the responsibility of the Court to interpret the law that forms the basis for judicial review.

Marshall then found that since the Constitution was supreme, the Court was bound to follow it rather than any inconsistent pieces of federal legislation. Thus, Marbury was denied his commission since the Court held that it had no jurisdiction to hear such an original action under Article III of the Constitution. To the extent that the Judiciary Act of 1789 was incompatible with the Article III jurisdiction of the Court, it was unconstitutional and invalid.

The Impact of Marbury. The significance of *Marbury* extends far beyond the initial question of whether a justice of the peace should be granted his commission. Most important, the decision established the doctrine of judicial review over the acts of the legislature under the Constitution. Marshall's politically skillful writing of the ruling protected it from an attack by the executive. The denial of *mandamus* avoided an imminent confrontation with Jefferson and shielded the assertion and exercise of judicial review over federal statutes. As described by Robert McCloskey in *The American Supreme Court* (1960), "The decision is a master work of indirection, a brilliant example of Marshall's capacity to sidestep danger while seeming to court it, to advance in one direction while his opponents are looking in another."

The decision further established the principle that the executive, when not acting within his political or discretionary powers, is subject to the law as interpreted and enforced by the Court. When legal issues are involved, the Court has the authority to direct the actions of the other branches of government.

Finally, while *Marbury* clearly established the foundation of judicial review, it did not do so without limitations. The Court may not invalidate an act of the legislature merely because it conflicts with the Constitution. Such a ruling must be triggered by the existence of a suit properly before the Court. Furthermore, the suit must require a determination that a statute is unconstitutional.

The Legitimacy Of Judicial Review

The historic *Marbury v. Madison* opinion has sparked considerable controversy ever since 1803. Marshall's critics claim that the case could have been decided on alternate grounds. The Court could merely have ruled that it lacked jurisdiction, thereby avoiding the statements concerning remedies against executive illegality, which some consider unnecessary and inappropriate.

Other critics believe that Marshall could have sidestepped the discussion of judicial review had he decided some of the initial issues differently. He might have found that, in order to perfect Marbury's appointment, more than a signing and sealing of the commission was necessary. The end result of the case would not have been altered, yet the assertion of judicial review might have been avoided.

The legitimacy of judicial review itself has been challenged by critics of the *Marbury* decision. The authority of the Court to invalidate a federal statute has been called a usurpation of power. Proponents of this view claim that Marshall's argument is unsupported and flawed. The Constitution nowhere explicitly authorizes such extraordinary power, and the theories of the Constitutional Convention were too obscure to provide legitimation.

Marshall derived the notion of judicial review from the fact that the Constitution was written and had as its major purpose the assurance of limited government. Yet Marshall's attackers claim that judicial review is not a natural result of constitutionalism; a constitution can exist without judicial review. That a government may not exceed its constitutional authority does not imply who may decide whether a conflict with the constitution exists. The perception of the constitution as "law," then, provides the crucial link between constitutionalism and the power of the Court to administer constitutional issues. This link, while vital to the foundation of judicial review, was not a unanimous view when Marshall wrote the *Marbury* opinion.

Justice Gibson's Position. Almost a quarter of a century later, the dissent of the Pennsylvania Supreme Court's Justice Gibson in *Eakin v. Raub* (Pa. 1825) represented a strong judicial disagreement with Marshall's reasoning in *Marbury*. The opinion of this state supreme court justice is generally recognized as the most effective answer to Marshall's arguments in support of judicial review. Gibson denied that the highest Pennsylvania court was authorized to consider the constitutionality of acts of the state legislature.

Although Gibson conceded that a legislative act must give way to a constitution should the two collide, he questioned whether this collision was a legitimate subject for judicial determination. He feared that such extraordinary power would place the judiciary above the other branches of government. It might lead to such undesired results as the calling for election returns by the court, or the examination of legislators' credentials. Gibson argued that every officer of a government, not only a judge, has the duty to uphold a constitution. This duty, however, extends only as far as his official duty. "The enactment of a law and the interpretation of it are not concurrent acts, and as the judiciary is not

In 1957, President Dwight D. Eisenhower ordered federal troops into Little Rock, Arkansas, to protect black students attending previously white-only schools and thereby upheld the legitimacy of the Supreme Court's decision in **Brown v. Board of Education.**

required to concur in the enactment, neither is it in the breach of the constitution which may be the consequence of the enactment, the fault is imputable to the legislature and on it the responsibility exclusively rests...." The judiciary's business, according to Gibson, is to interpret the law and not to question the authority of the legislature.

Twenty years after his dissent in *Eakin*, however, Justice Gibson recanted. In *Norris v. Clymer* (Pa. 1845), he accepted the concept of judicial review out of necessity, if not historical accuracy.

Hand-Wechsler Debate. This tension between a fear of undemocratic rule by the Court, a nonelected entity, and a desire for checks and balances on the federal system of government persists to this day. The debate between Judge Learned Hand and Professor Herbert Wechsler in the 1950's illustrates the continuing concern over the standards of judicial review and the relation of these standards to the American democratic system.

According to Judge Hand, since there is no solid basis in the text or history of the Constitution for judicial review, the power of the Court to invalidate acts of the executive or legislature must be exercised only rarely. This absolute necessity arises only when democracy seeks to overturn a supreme constitutional principle.

However, if one believes that judicial review rests on a more solid historical basis, then there is greater leeway within which to use this power. Professor Wechsler found a greater role for judicial review since he claimed that the framers of the Constitution envisioned such powers for the Court. This did not assume that the judiciary might invalidate any acts of the government with which it disagreed. Professor Wechsler instead propounded that the Court should intervene against democracy only when a "neutral" principle was endangered, one that was independent of the Court's own views of the policies behind a government act. This idea of a legitimate but limited judicial review is the foundation of the legal philosophy of "judicial restraint" espoused by, among others, Associate Justice Felix Frankfurter.

Authoritativeness Of The Courts' Interpretations

The question of whether the Supreme Court is the ultimate interpreter of the Constitution continued. A modern school desegregation case, *Cooper v. Aaron* (1958), provided the major judicial support for a view widely held by the American public: that the interpretation of the Constitution by the Court is supreme and final.

The case arose when Arkansas Governor Faubus and other state officials opposed the desegregation of the Little Rock public schools. They claimed they were not bound by the Court's desegregation holding in *Brown v. Board of Education* (1954). Although Arkansas was not a party in the *Brown* decision, a lower court had later directed a Little Rock school board to desegregate. Governor Faubus attempted to prevent the school board from complying with the desegregation order. He called out the National Guard and prevented black students from approaching Little Rock High School. When a trial court issued an injunction against the governor, the National Guard was withdrawn, and black students attended school under the protection of federal troops. The school board requested and received from the U.S. district court a postponement of the desegregation program. The Court of Appeals reversed, however, and this decision was affirmed by the Supreme Court.

Cooper v. Aaron's Significance. In its decision, the Supreme Court could have limited itself to the rationale that state officials lacked the authority to invalidate a federal court order. The holding went further, however, and the Court, in its *dicta*, reasserted the principles of judicial review as set forth in *Marbury v. Madison.*

The opinion reiterated the supremacy of the Constitution and the duty of the judiciary to interpret the Constitution. It then extended the reasoning of *Marbury* and stated that the judiciary was supreme in its interpretation of the Constitution and that this supremacy was an "indispensable feature of our constitutional system." Therefore, the Court held, its interpretation of the 14th Amendment in *Brown* was "the supreme law of the land" and, as such, was binding on the states.

The *Cooper v. Aaron* opinion declared that the Court's powers of judicial review were already settled doctrine. However, the notion of judicial exclusiveness to interpret the Constitution was not firmly staked out in *Marbury.* Marshall had left open the possibility that the other branches of government could also declare the constitutionality of laws.

The authoritativeness of the Court's interpretation of the Constitution was reinforced in *Cooper.* It was made clear that the states have neither the power nor the right to disregard the Constitution or its administration by the Court. However, the constitutional decisions made by the federal judiciary are often very difficult to enforce.

Enforcement Problems. Unlike the executive and legislative branches, the Court has no independent mechanism at its disposal to enforce its decisions. By Article I, Section 8 of the Constitution, Congress is empowered to declare war; to raise and support armies; and to provide for organizing, arming, disciplining, and calling forth the militia. The president is the commander-in-chief of the Army, Navy, and state militias as prescribed by Article II, Section 2. The Supreme Court, however, was delegated no such authority. To enforce its decisions, therefore, it must rely on subtler measures, such as respect by the public, the American tradition of constitutionalism, and ultimately, obedience to the law.

In certain situations, however, such as school desegregation and legislative reapportionment, the Court depends on the other branches of government for the efficacy of its rulings. For example, when the University of Mississippi, the all-white state university at Oxford, Mississippi, rejected James Meredith, a black man, for academic reasons, he filed suit in federal district court charging racial discrimination. After much frustration in the lower courts, Supreme Court Justice Hugo Black ordered the university to admit Meredith at once. Mississippi Governor Ross Barnett refused to comply with the court order and prevented Meredith from registering. The executive, President Kennedy, had to involve himself in this case to ensure that the Court's ruling would be carried out and used much the same approach as had President Eisenhower in the Little Rock situation. He, through Attorney General Robert Kennedy, eventually enrolled Meredith at the university. However, it was only after days of threats, negotiation, and the use of federal troops that the court order was enforced. Without aid from the executive branch, Justice Black's directive might never have been implemented.

The difficulty the Court had in enforcing its *Brown v. Board of Education* school desegregation decision carries over to most instances of judicial review of state action. This lack of enforcement power probably influences the Court to exercise judicial review only when it is reasonably certain that its decision will be followed.

Authority To Review State Court Judgments

Thirteen years after *Marbury,* the Supreme Court defended the legitimacy of judicial review of state court judgments resting on interpretations of federal law. Justice Story's opinion in *Martin v. Hunter's Lessee* (1816) is second to *Marbury* among the important decisions of the Marshall era that

Attorney General Robert Kennedy played a key role in enforcing Associate Justice Hugo Black's order that James Meredith be admitted to the all-white University of Mississippi. As in Little Rock, Arkansas, federal troops were needed to enforce integration.

enunciated the limits of federal judicial authority. The Court held that it had the jurisdiction and power to review all state acts under the Constitution, laws, and treaties of the United States. It rejected the highest Virginia court's challenge to the constitutionality of Section 25 of the Judiciary Act of 1789, which provision essentially provided for Supreme Court review of state courts' final decisions that spurred claims resting on federal law.

Martin v. Hunter's Lessee concerned conflicting claims to land located in northern Virginia. This particular plot had once been part of the vast holdings of Lord Fairfax, a former British national who had become a Virginia citizen before his death. He had willed the property to his English nephew, Denny Martin, in 1781. Virginia later passed acts enabling it to appropriate all land held by British loyalists during the Revolutionary War. The Fairfax land was among those holdings that Virginia claimed was properly seized. Virginia then granted part of the property to David Hunter.

Litigation ensued between the representatives of Martin and Hunter over title to the land. Martin's claim stemmed from the devise from Lord Fairfax. He asserted that the land was improperly seized by Virginia since it was protected by the Peace Treaty of 1783 and the Jay Treaty of 1794. Since title had passed to him under the 1781 will and did not vest in Virginia before 1793, it was thereafter protected from

seizure by the treaty provisions. Hunter's claim, by contrast, was based on several Virginia statutes relating to the forfeiture of land owned by British subjects to the state.

Negotiations over the disputed claim continued for almost twenty years before it reached the Court. These negotiations involved future Chief Justice John Marshall, who, acting on behalf of the British representatives, had arranged a compromise and personally purchased a large share of the land from the Fairfax heirs. Due to these financial interests, Marshall later excused himself from participating in the decision.

The Virginia Court of Appeals, the state's highest court, held for Hunter in 1810 and upheld the seizure of the property under state law. The Supreme Court reversed that decision in 1813 and found that the treaties secured title in Martin. Since state law is subordinate to federal law under the supremacy clause (Article VI, Clause 2), which declares the Constitution "the supreme law of the land," the case was returned to the Virginia court with an order for the entry of judgment for Martin's representatives and successors. The Virginia Court of Appeals refused to follow this order for several reasons. First, it found that the case should have been decided differently on the basis of state law. More important, though, was Virginia's contention that the United States Supreme Court could not constitutionally exercise jurisdiction over a state's highest court.

Had this state decision been allowed to stand, Section 25 of the Judiciary Act of 1789 would have been void. This challenge to the constitutionality of Section 25 constituted an attack on the authority of the national government and, particularly, on the power of the Supreme Court.

Justice Story and Martin v. Hunter's Lessee. Justice Story upheld the constitutionality of Section 25 and found that the Judiciary Act properly recognized the existence of appellate jurisdiction in the Supreme Court over state court actions. He rested his analysis on the assumption that Article III of the Constitution left considerable discretion to Congress regarding the allocation of jurisdiction to the federal courts. The supremacy clause of Article VI indicates that the framers recognized that federal issues might arise in state cases. The grant of jurisdiction to the Supreme Court in Article III over all cases within the power of the federal judiciary, therefore, had to encompass such decisions.

In response to Virginia's contention that it was a sovereign, and was therefore not bound to adhere to Supreme Court rulings, Justice Story asserted that the people had elected to curtail state sovereignty when they established the Constitution of which Article I restricts state acts in various ways. Since the supremacy clause required state courts to follow federal law, there was no reason to exempt the state judiciary from these constitutional restrictions that would not further hinder state court functions. To hold otherwise would be to nullify the intent of the supremacy clause.

In his conclusion, Story emphasized the Supreme

Court's power and duty as the single, final arbiter of the Constitution and federal law. A centralized government must include a sole entity to interpret its laws. Furthermore, Story reasoned that state courts had to follow the decisions of the Supreme Court in federal issues in order to maintain a uniform interpretation and application of federal laws, treaties, and the Constitution.

Cohens v. Virginia Chief Justice Marshall had his chance to address the Supreme Court's authority to review state court judgments in *Cohens v. Virginia* (1821). Although Story's forceful opinion in *Martin v. Hunter's Lessee* had affirmed the constitutionality of Section 25 of the Judiciary Act, the controversy over the provision's justifiability was not quieted. Instead, the Martin dispute triggered a wave of attacks by the states on Section 25.

Cohens v. Virginia concerned the Supreme Court's power to review state criminal cases. The Supreme Court upheld the state prosecution of interstate sellers of lottery tickets, but in so doing, asserted its authority to oversee state criminal proceedings.

The case involved the conviction of the Cohen brothers in a Norfolk, Virginia, court for selling District of Columbia lottery tickets in Virginia in violation of state laws. The defendants claimed that, since a federal statute authorized a lottery in the District of Columbia, they were immune from state law under the supremacy clause. The Court decided against them and held that the federal act conferred no such immunity on them.

The main issue in the case, however, was whether the Supreme Court had constitutional authority to review state criminal judgments. Counsel for Virginia reiterated the arguments presented in *Martin v. Hunter's Lessee* and added several others. They claimed that, unlike *Martin*, the state was a named party in this case. The constitutional grant of original jurisdiction to the Supreme Court over cases in which a state was a named party excluded the exercise of appellate jurisdiction in such cases. Additionally, they contended that the Constitution did not confer federal jurisdiction over disputes between a state and its own citizens.

Marshall rejected the constitutional attack on Section 25 and struck down the jurisdictional challenge. The identity of the parties, he found, did not affect the jurisdiction conferred on the Court by the Constitution. The power of judicial review over state court judgments rests not on the nature of the parties but upon that of the issues involved. He found an unambiguous textual basis for jurisdiction in the Constitution and in federal statutes to review federal issues adjudicated in state courts. This jurisdiction was not withdrawn by the 11th Amendment in cases where the suit was brought by the state itself against a citizen. The 11th Amendment provides that the federal judiciary's power does not extend to a suit brought against a state by a citizen.

Most significantly, Marshall emphasized the control exerted by the Constitution over state actions. He found the Constitution to be distinct from and superior to the notion of state sovereignty since it was an original act of all the people. The Constitution was established as a paramount and enduring law that required support from outside challenges. Marshall believed that the role of constitutional protector fell to the federal courts. He expressed concern over the reliability of state court judges. Reasoning that they relied on their state legislatures for their office and salary, he doubted their competence to uphold the Constitution and federal law against state challenges.

Congressional Power Of Curtailment

The Supreme Court is the only federal court established directly by the text of the Constitution. The language of

Associate Justice Joseph Story asserted the power of the Supreme Court—and therefore of the federal government—over state sovereignty in **Martin v. Hunter's Lessee.**

Article III vested the judicial power in "one Supreme Court." Inferior federal courts were delegated judicial power only as the Congress "may from time to time ordain and establish" such lower courts.

Article III sets out the limits of federal court jurisdiction, beyond which it cannot be expanded. Federal courts may hear matters "arising under" the Constitution, federal laws, and treaties, and other cases that involve special classes of parties, such as ambassadors, citizens of different states, the states themselves, and the United States itself. The maximum Article III powers need not be conferred on the lower federal courts by Congress; in fact, it has never done so. For instance, while federal courts are empowered to hear diversity cases, cases in which the parties are citizens of different states, Congress has imposed a limitation on this exercise of Article III jurisdiction: the amount that is being disputed must exceed $10,000.

Article III, Clause 2 states that the Supreme Court will have original jurisdiction over cases involving ambassadors or other such public officials and over cases in which a state is a named party. This grant of jurisdiction cannot be constitutionally enlarged. Article III also confers appellate jurisdiction on the Supreme Court over all the other types of cases within Article III's limited jurisdiction. This appellate jurisdiction, however, is granted subject to "such exceptions, and under such Regulations as the Congress shall make."

Ex parte McCardle. The scope of congressional power over the Court's appellate jurisdiction was broadly defined in *Ex parte McCardle* (1869). In that case, Congress imposed military governments on a number of former Confederate states under the post-Civil War Reconstruction Acts. McCardle was a Mississippi newspaper editor imprisoned by the military on charges of publishing inflammatory and libelous articles. He brought a *habeas corpus* action under the February 5, 1867 Reconstruction Act of Congress that authorized federal courts to grant *habeas corpus* to those held in violation of the Constitution and that also provided for appeals to the Supreme Court. When the circuit court denied McCardle's *habeas* petition, he appealed to the Supreme Court.

After the Court recognized jurisdiction of the appeal and after arguments were heard on the merits, but before a decision was rendered, Congress passed the Reconstruction Act of March 27, 1868. This law had the function of withdrawing the statutory right to an appeal provided by the 1867 act. The purpose of Congress in so doing was to avoid a Supreme Court determination that the Reconstruction legislation, under which McCardle was imprisoned, was unconstitutional. The Court complied with the 1868 act and dismissed McCardle's action for lack of jurisdiction. In its dismissal, the Court relied on the power conferred upon Congress by Article III to regulate and define its appellate jurisdiction. It did not purport to question the motives of Congress, since the Constitution clearly gave the legislature

such authority. The Court, then, had no choice but to dismiss the case. It has also been suggested that the Court may have acquiesced to Congress's control so readily because the Court did not want to jeopardize the validity of the government's Reconstruction program.

The *McCardle* decision has been read broadly and has been used to bolster unsuccessful attempts by the legislature to control substantive results of Supreme Court decisions in areas such as school busing and reapportionment by the assertion of power over the Court's jurisdiction. This broad reading is not necessarily implied by the *McCardle* opinion, however. The limits of the statutory jurisdictional withdrawal were recognized by the Court. Chief Justice Chase noted that the 1868 act excepts only those cases for which jurisdiction arose under the act of 1867. The Court's other jurisdictional powers, such as that to hear cases on writs of *certiorari*, were unaffected by the 1868 act. Essentially, Congress withdrew only one of several possible avenues of appeal to the Supreme Court.

Restriction of McCardle. The limitations of the *McCardle* opinion were evident in a case decided only months later. In *Ex parte Yerger* (1869), the Court found that the identical statute at issue in McCardle did not affect its *certiorari* jurisdiction. The Court took jurisdiction of another *habeas corpus* action by a petitioner in military detention in Mississippi. Like McCardle, Yerger was denied *habeas* in a lower federal court. However, Yerger's appeal to the Supreme Court was not premised on the 1867 act. Therefore, the 1868 act withdrawing such appellate jurisdiction was inapplicable. The Court averted a ruling on the constitutionality of the Reconstruction Acts, however, since Yerger was released before the merits of the case could be heard.

The historical background of the Article III clause granting Congress the authority to regulate the Court's appellate jurisdiction supports the view that the power be limited to procedural matters. It has been argued that the framers did not intend to give Congress the power to control the results of particular cases through the exception clause. Therefore, the legislature may not utilize this authority to direct the outcome of specific Court decisions.

An implication of Article III that was not challenged by the *McCardle* holding is that the assurance of an independent federal judiciary restricts the legislature in its use of control over federal court jurisdiction. The Court's decision in *United States v. Klein* (1871) bolsters this principle. In it, the Court held that Congress may not eliminate a path of appeal through legislation for the purpose of directing the results of particular cases.

Klein sought an indemnification of property captured during the Civil War, relying on an 1863 statute that allowed recovery if the claimant could prove he had not participated in the rebellion. The Court of Claims opinion that granted Klein's request rested on an earlier Supreme Court decision holding that an award of amnesty from the President fulfilled a claimant's eligibility requirement. While the government's appeal was pending, Congress enacted a new law, which provided that a presidential pardon not only did not support a claim for captured property but also proved precisely that the pardon recipient *had* assisted the rebellion. Further, Congress mandated that when the Court of Claims based its judgment on such a presidential pardon, the Supreme Court lacked appellate jurisdiction.

The Court's opinion in *Klein* declared this restriction on jurisdiction unconstitutional. It held that, while the exception clause of Article III enabled Congress to limit the federal judiciary's appellate jurisdiction, that power was restricted by those Article III provisions calling for a judicial branch that was independent of the legislative and executive branches. Congress's exercise of that control in this instance was not simply a denial of appeal in certain types of cases, but rather a means to deny to presidential pardons the meaning the Court had previously ruled them to have.

A dismissal of the appeal would effectively allow Congress to prescribe a rule for the Court in the decision of its cases. Congress had therefore overstepped its authority to limit appellate jurisdiction and had violated the separation of powers principle required by the Constitution. The *Klein* decision mandates that Congress must exercise its control over appellate jurisdiction so as not to eclipse the independence of the federal judiciary. Any use of this power must be neutral, in that it must not be merely a pretense for controlling the results of a particular case.

Limitations On Congressional Control

Since the congressional power to limit appellate jurisdiction was a potential weapon for use by the Court's critics, advocates of the Court had developed arguments to curtail its use. Professor Henry M. Hart, Jr., articulated a limit on Congress's Article III power to limit the jurisdiction of federal courts, contending that the exercise of this legislative power must not impair the Court's "essential role" as intended by the Constitution. This role, as he saw it, had two strands: to maintain the supremacy of federal law and to provide resolution of any conflicting interpretations of federal law made by state and federal courts. Another noted constitutional law scholar, Herbert Wechsler, has argued that Article III cannot be convincingly read so as to curtail legislative power.

The due process clause of the 5th Amendment works to limit further Congress's Article III powers over federal court jurisdiction. The legislature is prohibited from exercising this power with the purpose of depriving a party of rights secured by the Constitution. For example, since the equal protection guarantee of the due process clause of the 5th Amendment forbids discrimination on the basis of gender, Congress could not pass a law that would deny jurisdiction over actions brought by women. The Court will not uphold a statutory limitation on jurisdiction if the Court determines that the objective of the statute is to infringe on a constitutional right.

The "portal-to-portal" series of cases illustrates the limitation of the due process clause on Congress's Article III control over federal court jurisdiction. In the 1940's the Supreme Court held that any time spent by workers in incidental activities, such as underground travel in mines, was part of their work week and therefore compensable under the Fair Labor Standards Act. This decision created huge liabilities for many businesses, which now owed their employees for hours spent on previously noncompensable activities. Congress then passed the Portal-to-Portal Act, which explicitly amended the statute to make such work noncompensable, in an attempt to alleviate this immense liability. The new legislation also removed jurisdiction from the courts to hear any cases brought under the old statute.

The Court of Appeals for the 2nd Circuit considered the constitutional problems of Congress's removal of jurisdiction in *Battaglia v. General Motors Corp.* (1948). It found that the amendment eliminated the plaintiff's claim for overtime pay under the Fair Labor Standards Act, and, since no rights accrued in the plaintiffs, the amendment did not amount to a taking of property in violation of the due process clause. The restriction on jurisdiction was, therefore, valid. It held that Congress had not exercised its Article III power to deprive any person of life, liberty, or property without just compensation. The consideration of this constitutional claim indicated that the congressional power over federal court jurisdiction is limited by the due process clause of the Constitution.

Advisory Opinions And Declaratory Judgments

The framework that governs the exercise of Supreme Court authority is provided by Article III of the Constitution. On the sparse language of this provision, however, a complex set of rules and practices has been erected.

Article III, Section 2 provides the most complicated elements of the judicial ground rules. This provision states that federal court jurisdiction shall be limited to certain specific "cases" and "controversies." The definition of this requirement is a significant example of the self-imposed constraints on judicial review. The hotly litigated topic of what constitutes a "case" or "controversy" has instigated constitutional meanings, as well as nonconstitutional concepts of judicial self-restraint.

The "case" or "controversy" requirement has been interpreted as a ban on the rendering of advisory opinions, opinions rendered at the request of the government or an interested party indicating how the Court would rule on a matter should adversary litigation develop. An advisory opinion, is therefore, an interpretation of the law that has no binding effect.

While serving as the first Chief Justice, John Jay opposed the practice of judges issuing advisory opinions and worked to establish judicial independence.

John Jay's Position. The framers of the Constitution never provided for the issuance of advisory opinions by the Court. The practice began quite early in the Court's history, as the justices often submitted letters containing legal opinions to the executive and to legislators. In 1790, for example, Chief Justice John Jay offered his opinion in response to President Washington's letter of request regarding the constitutionality of their duty to ride circuit. This apparently had no legal effect on the issue, for when the practice was actually challenged in litigation, ten years later, the Court upheld it, disregarding Jay's opinion. The decision relied on historical precedent, and no reference was made to the earlier correspondence.

Hayburn's Case (1792) is one of the most famous instances of letters to the president regarding the constitutionality of a federal statute. Two circuit courts objected on constitutional grounds to the provisions of a statute that authorized the courts to certify eligible pension claimants. The objections took the form of letters to the President, which were footnoted in the opinion. The judges refused to undertake the duties assigned them by the statute for they feared that such judicial actions would be altered and controlled by representatives of the legislative and executive branches. Such revision of judicial decision was considered to be inconsistent with an independent judiciary.

The idea that it was vital that federal court decisions be

final and not subject to revision by the other branches of government was voiced the following year by the Supreme Court justices. In what has been called the 1793 refusal, Chief Justice John Jay denied President Washington's request to render an advisory opinion concerning the legal issues involved in America's neutrality in the ongoing war between England and France. Secretary of State Thomas Jefferson, on the President's behalf, had written to the justices for an opinion on the interpretation of various treaties and trade agreements with the two warring countries. The President wished to elicit the Court's opinion as to the correct posture the United States should assume in order to avoid becoming embroiled in the dispute.

Jay and the associate justices refused to render an advisory opinion to the President and relied on the separation of powers principle mandated by the Constitution. The federal system of government was set up with three separate branches, each of which possessed certain unique powers. As the Chief Justice continued, these being "in certain respects checks upon each other, and our being judges of a court in the last resort, are considerations which afford strong arguments against the propriety of our extra judicially deciding the questions alluded to, especially as the power given by the Constitution to the President, of calling on the heads of departments for opinions, seems to have been *purposely* as well as expressly united to the *executive* departments." The Court refused to render an advisory opinion as it feared the practice would lead to collusion among the three departments of government, thereby undermining the basic theory behind the adversary system.

Constitutional Interpretations. Jay referred to the Supreme Court as a "court in the last resort." This language indicates that the justices believed that it was essential that they be the ultimate arbiters of a case, rather than the creators of a tentative decision subject to review by the other two branches of government. According to the Constitution, the Court alone bore the powers of adjudication. Any revision of its rulings by the executive or the legislature would be unconstitutional since an independent judiciary is mandated by Article III. Therefore, advisory opinions, which had no binding legal effect on the party that solicited them, would run afoul of the Constitution.

The language of Article III further illustrates the framers' intent that the Court refrain from rendering advisory opinions. The provision explicitly limits the Supreme Court adjudicatory powers to "cases" and "controversies," which implies a requirement of adverse parties and their presentation of opposing arguments before the Court. A genuine dispute must exist, with a specific set of facts and circumstances. The Court cannot render a complex, constitutional decision on a purely hypothetical situation. Its rulings must be based on the narrow grounds of an actual controversy.

The framers' rejection of the advisory opinion is further evident in the fact that they declined to adopt Madison's proposal of having the justices sit on a Council of Revision. This idea would have joined the justices with the president in the veto process. The framers' rejection of Madison's suggestion rested partly on the opposition to having the Supreme Court give its opinion on public policy measures. Moreover, a provision that would have enabled Congress and the president to procure advisory opinions from the Court on questions of law was also rejected at the Constitutional Convention.

Additionally, institutional considerations preclude the rendering of advisory opinions by the Court. First, the Court is too busy deciding actual cases to dispense advice that may not necessarily be heeded. Second, the Court is not competent to give advice, but merely to decide specific issues that arise from a given set of facts. Finally, the Court needs a concrete factual context in order to interpret the law with sufficient understanding. An abstract question does not emerge concisely framed since it has not stemmed from a conflict of adversarial arguments.

Declaratory Judgments

Similar concerns formed the basis for the ban on the rendering of declaratory judgments, a ban that was not removed until 1934. A declaratory judgment can be likened to an advisory opinion in that it is a remedy for the determination of a controversy where the plaintiff is doubtful about his or her legal rights. However, in order to pronounce a declaratory judgment, an actual "case" or "controversy" must be before the Court. The judgment is then legally binding and is conclusive in a subsequent action between the parties with respect to the matters declared.

Prior to the authorization of declaratory judgments by the Federal Declaratory Judgment Act of 1934, the Court believed that such a judgment would run afoul of the ban on advisory opinions. The *dicta* of Justice Brandeis in *Willing v. Chicago Auditorium Association* (1928) evidences those fears. In this case, the association desired to tear down the auditorium it had erected on a leased parcel of land and to build a new one. One of the lessors had informally remarked that the lease did not authorize such action without the consent of the lessors and bondholders. The association then brought a federal action against the lessors and bondholders to establish its right to raze the old building.

Brandeis refused to grant relief to the association and held that the suit did not present a "case" or "controversy" as required by Article III. No actual dispute existed since no defendant had wronged or threatened to wrong the plaintiff; no one had infringed upon its right to tear down the building. The plaintiff merely wanted a declaratory judgment rendered by the Court. Brandeis held that such relief was beyond the federal judiciary's power.

Five years later, some of the fears surrounding declara-

In 1793, President George Washington asked the Supreme Court to advise the executive on a neutrality issue. The Court's refusal to do so strengthened the principle of separation of powers.

tory judgments had dissipated. In *Nashville, Chattanooga & St. Louis Railway v. Wallace* (1933), the Court found no Article III obstacle to the review of a declaratory judgment rendered by a state court. The case concerned a company that had been threatened with an income tax it alleged was unconstitutional. It sought a ruling that the tax unconstitutionally burdened interstate commerce. Since the action was concrete enough to be adjudicated in a traditional injunction action, the Court held, there was no reason to find it less so because the complainant was able to bring it before the state courts without requesting an injunction. The opinion reiterated the necessary criteria for Supreme Court review of a state court declaratory judgment of a federal question: the case must be a true adversarial action, involving a genuine controversy.

The 1933 Supreme Court, led by Chief Justice Charles Evans Hughes (front, center), was more sympathetic to declaratory judgments—similar to advisory opinions—than Associate Justice Brandeis (front, far left) had been in 1928.

The *Nashville* case facilitated passage of the Declaratory Judgment Act the following year. That act's constitutionality was upheld in *Aetna Life Insurance Co. v. Haworth* (1937). Justice Hughes's opinion held that a declaratory judgment can be rendered by a federal court only where an Article III "case" exists but, even then, a court may withhold relief according to its discretion.

Requirement Of Standing

The requirement of standing to litigate is one of the most important limitations on judicial review. When a person has standing to sue, it means that the person possesses a sufficient stake in a judiciable controversy to obtain adjudication of that controversy. The plaintiff must have a legally protectable and direct interest in the litigation. Standing is a jurisdictional issue and concerns the federal courts' power to hear and decide cases. The substantive merits of the claims are not involved or affected.

The criterion essential to the standing requirement is that the litigant has a sufficient personal interest in the relief sought, or that the litigant is an appropriate representative of an interested third party to warrant giving the litigant relief, if the litigant can substantiate the alleged illegality. These questions are easily answered in tort cases, for example, in which the plaintiff has sustained some physical injury for which redress is sought. In contract law, too, standing is

rarely at issue. A party who has suffered economic harm through breach of a contract will have a sufficiently personal stake in the litigation to fulfill the standing requirement. In constitutional law, however, the injuries sustained and the parties that have suffered the loss are frequently not so clear. May a student bring suit for the infringement of the 1st Amendment right to free expression when a school has prevented the student from wearing a black armband in protest of the Vietnam War? Is this injury sufficient? Or, may a taxpayer file an action for what the taxpayer believes is the unconstitutional spending of public funds? Has the taxpayer sustained any damages?

Questions such as these have been the subject of considerable litigation and changing trends in the Supreme Court. The modern approach to the standing requirement was enunciated by Justice Douglas in *Association of Data Processing Service Organizations v. Camp* (1970). In order to have standing to litigate, the complainant must meet a two-part test. First, the plaintiff must allege "that the challenged action has caused him injury in fact, economic or otherwise." Secondly, the "question is whether the interest sought to be protected by the complainant is arguably within the zone of interests to be protected or regulated by the statute or constitutional guarantee in question."

This opinion explicitly rejected an earlier test that required that the right infringed upon be a "legal right." Additionally, the injury now is not limited to economic damages, but may be aesthetic or conservational or may involve a conceptual stake in free speech.

The Court's later opinion in *Sierra Club v. Morton* (1972) strengthens its intent not to limit the required injury to an economic injury. In this case, the Sierra Club filed suit to contest a proposed ski resort development in the Mineral King Valley on the grounds that the plan would decrease the area's aesthetic and recreational values. Although the Sierra Club did not have standing to litigate, since it did not allege that it was among the injured, the Court found that environmental interests, as well as economic interests, are deserving of protection by the judiciary.

Frothingham Decision. The question of who may allege an injury has always been a hotly debated issue for the Court. A taxpayer's status as a possible plaintiff, in particular, has generated a plethora of cases. The first important statement regarding taxpayer standing was made in *Frothingham v. Mellon* (1923). Justice Sutherland's opinion in this case has become the general rule of federal taxpayer standing to litigate.

Mrs. Frothingham, as a federal taxpayer, filed suit against Secretary of the Treasury Mellon to enjoin him from making any expenditures of public funds under the Maternity Act of 1921. This act provided for appropriations to state programs implemented to reduce maternal and infant mortality rates. The plaintiff argued that the act was a usur-

Secretary of the Treasury Andrew Mellon was sued by a citizen who alleged standing on a basis of being a federal taxpayer who would be injured by Mellon's expenditure of funds.

pation of power by the Congress over and above that granted to it by the Constitution and that Congress had invaded the states' self-government powers as reserved to them by the 10th Amendment. She further alleged that an expenditure of public funds under the act would injure her by the increase in her tax liability and result in a "taking" of her property without due process of law in contravention of the 5th Amendment.

The Supreme Court was not persuaded by the allegation of injury and held that the federal taxpayer did not have standing under either the 10th Amendment or the due process clause of the 5th Amendment to enjoin the federal grant of public funds to the states under the Maternity Act. Mrs. Frothingham's injury as a taxpayer was not direct and immediate. Her interest was "comparatively minute and indeterminable," and the effect upon future taxation was too speculative and remote to confer standing to sue. Justice Sutherland also expressed the fear that if standing were granted to a federal taxpayer, then virtually anyone would be able to attack any federal law whose administration required the expenditure of public funds. The Court refused to question Congress's judgment in the passage of the act and to consider its constitutionality unless the plaintiff could demonstrate "not only that the statute is invalid but that he has sustained or is immediately in danger of sustaining some direct injury as the result of its enforcement, and not merely

In a 1970 decision, Associate Justice William O. Douglas set out a modern approach, consisting of a two-part test, for a requirement of standing before the Supreme Court.

that he suffers in some indefinite way in common with people generally."

Taxpayer suits such as *Frothingham* are challenges to the *spending* power of Congress, not to its taxing power. Mrs. Frothingham did not object to the fact that she was taxed, but to the purpose to which some of her taxes were directed. If she were successful in her suit, her tax burden would not have been even slightly decreased. The money would only have been applied elsewhere. However, even under Frothingham, a taxpayer may challenge a tax that is earmarked for a specific purpose.

In *Bailey v. Drexel Furniture Co.* (1922) a taxpayer's attack on the payment of a child labor tax was upheld. The taxpayer had contended that the purposes for which the tax was earmarked were unconstitutional. A successful suit of this type results in direct relief to the taxpayer, unlike in *Frothingham*, since the tax burden is alleviated.

The *Frothingham* result has been attacked as going too far in the limitation of taxpayer suits. In the mid-1960's proposals were made in Congress for a statutory revision of the *Frothingham* rule. Proponents of the modification contended that decision was based primarily on the policy of judicial self-restraint rather than on the Article III "case" or "controversy" requirement.

Reconsideration in Flast Decision. With these considerations in mind, the Supreme Court reexamined federal taxpayer standing in *Flast v. Cohen* (1968). In *Flast*, a group of federal taxpayers challenged the expenditure of federal aid to religious schools, under the Elementary and Secondary Education Act of 1965, which was used to finance the teaching of reading, math, and other subjects. Such an expenditure, they claimed, was in violation of the establishment clause of the 1st Amendment to the Constitution, which provision prohibits the federal government from passing laws that aid one or more religions. The lower court dismissed their suit because of the insurmountable obstacle to taxpayer standing erected in *Frothingham*.

The Supreme Court reversed the lower court's decision and held that taxpayer standing could be granted when the statute challenged is alleged to violate the establishment and free exercise clauses of the 1st Amendment. The *Flast* decision did not, then, overrule *Frothingham*, but was merely a limited exception to the general rule of taxpayer standing.

Chief Justice Warren reexamined the *Frothingham* rule of standing and concluded that it was based on principles of judicial self-restraint, not on the requirements of the Constitution. There was nothing in Article III that absolutely prevented suits brought by federal taxpayers to challenge allegedly unconstitutional exercises of the federal taxing and spending powers.

The opinion then set out two criteria that a taxpayer must meet in order to qualify for standing. First, there must be a "logical nexus" between the taxpayer status and the type of legislation challenged. Second, the taxpayer must establish a nexus between the taxpayer status and the precise nature of the constitutional infringement alleged.

Under the first requirement, the taxpayer status is appropriate only to challenge those legislative enactments passed under the congressional taxing and spending powers conferred in Article I, Section 8 of the Constitution. This nexus was clearly established by both Mrs. Frothingham and the *Flast* plaintiff. Both complained of the congressional use of its spending power, and both claims involved more than "an incidental expenditure of tax funds in the administration of an essentially regulatory statute."

However, only the *Flast* taxpayer met the second criterion: that there be a logical link between the taxpayer status and the exact nature of the alleged constitutional violation. The Court considered the history of the establishment clause and concluded that its purpose was to prevent the exercise of the spending power to encourage one religion over another. Therefore, the challenged act overstepped a precise limitation that had been imposed on Congress's taxing and spending powers. By contrast, Mrs. Frothingham's challenge rested on a general assertion that the taxing and spending were beyond Congress's power. Unlike the establishment clause relied on in *Flast*, the 10th Amendment, upon which the *Frothingham* claim was based, is not a specific limit on the taxing and spending powers of the legislative branch.

Implications of Flast. The implication of the *Flast* opinion is that there are very few Article III constraints on standing. The question of whether or not to grant standing is to be decided primarily on principles of judicial self-restraint. Justice Harlan expressed fears about such an exercise of judicial discretion in his lone dissent to the *Flast* opinion. The filing of taxpayer suits that challenge federal legislation, he claimed, "strain[s] the judicial function and press[es] to the limit judicial authority." Harlan believed that the Congress, not the Court, should have the task of granting standing to taxpayer litigation through legislation.

The *Flast* decision rested on narrow grounds. Its wide limitations became evident in later cases in which the Supreme Court denied standing to taxpayers to challenge the constitutionality of federal actions. The *Flast* majority mentioned no examples, other than the establishment clause, of the types of constitutional provisions that were specific limitations on the taxing and spending power and that could be used to satisfy the second nexus of the Flast test.

Restricting Taxpayer Standing. Thus a divided Court held, in *United States v. Richardson* (1974), that a federal taxpayer did not have standing to challenge a federal statute for allegedly violating Article I, Section 9, Clause 7 of the Constitution. This provision requires that "a regular Statement of Account of the Receipts and Expenditures of all public Money shall be published from time to time." This constitutional provision was not a specific limitation on the congressional taxing and spending powers. Therefore, the plaintiff did not meet the second part of the *Flast* test. There was no logical link between the taxpayer status and the exact nature of the constitutional violation alleged.

The taxpayer claimed that the Central Intelligence Agency Act of 1949, which provides that CIA expenditures be kept from the public, was a violation of Article I, Section 9, Clause 7. The act enabled the CIA director to avoid publicly reporting the agency's expenditures of public funds, as required by the Constitution.

Chief Justice Burger's majority opinion found that there was no logical nexus established between the taxpayer status and alleged failure of Congress to elicit more specific records of CIA expenditures. The plaintiff did not claim that public funds were being spent in a manner that violated the taxing and spending powers. Rather, he sought a directive from the Court to Congress to disclose information regarding how the CIA spends its appropriations.

Like the *Frothingham* case, this claim was merely a general grievance; the impact on the complainant was common to all taxpayers. He did not allege that, as a taxpayer, he was threatened by a direct and concrete injury as a result of the challenged federal statute. The Court emphasized that, rather than through the judiciary system, the plaintiff should seek redress through the electoral process. When citizens are dissatisfied with the behavior of their elected officials, they would do best to get relief in the political arena and at the polls.

Noneconomic Issues And Standing. The question of standing is largely whether a party has "alleged such a personal stake in the outcome of the controversy as to assure that concrete adverseness which sharpens the presentation of issues," as set out by the Supreme Court in *Baker v. Carr* (1962). In the taxpayer quests for standing, the Court's task was to determine whether the taxpayer status conferred such a personal stake upon the litigant. In nontaxpayer actions, the requirement is a showing of "injury in fact."

As established by *Sierra Club v. Morton*, the Court does not limit "injury in fact" to economic injury. The *Sierra Club* decision recognized that the injury may be aesthetic or recreational, as well as economic. Although the Court denied standing, since the Sierra Club did not allege injury to itself, the case broadened the criteria used in granting personal standing to litigate. As opposed to the requirement for taxpayer standing, that the injury must be unique to the taxpayer and not a general grievance, the Court in *Sierra Club* emphasized that the fact that "environmental interests are shared by the many rather than by the few does not make them less deserving of legal protection through the judicial process." Thus, as the opinion indicated in a footnote, the Sierra Club would qualify for standing if it amended its complaint to allege a threat of injury to its members by the development of Mineral King Valley.

SCRAP Decision. The Supreme Court's increasingly liberal view of standing was evident in its opinion in *United States v. Students Challenging Regulatory Agency Procedures* (1973), also known as the SCRAP case. The Court applied a less stringent requirement for personal standing when it granted SCRAP standing to challenge an Interstate Commerce Commission (ICC) freight surcharge.

SCRAP was composed of several law students who were concerned with the quality of the environment. SCRAP's action concerned the ICC's failure to repeal a 242 percent surcharge on freight rates. The surcharge, it claimed, was responsible for the aesthetic, recreational, and economic injuries sustained by its members since it had a detrimental effect on the quality of the environment.

The alleged injuries to SCRAP's members were multifaceted. First, SCRAP argued that its members were forced to pay higher prices for finished products due to the rate structure. Second, the surcharge had an adverse impact on recycling as it encouraged the use of nonrecyclable commodities. The members' use of the forests, rivers, and streams would thereby be impaired by the surcharge. Moreover, the quality of the air would be adversely affected by the ICC rate structure. Finally, SCRAP alleged that its members had to pay higher taxes because of the public funds required to dispose of otherwise reusable waste materials. The surcharge was illegal, SCRAP argued, because the ICC had neglected to file a detailed environmental impact statement, which must be done whenever a major federal action significantly affects the quality of the environment.

A majority of the Court found standing and emphasized that they were not dissuaded by the fact that the types of harm alleged by the SCRAP members were suffered by the public at large. They refused to deny standing merely because the injury claimed by the environmental group was not limited to its members. The Court further relaxed its requirements for personal standing when it held that standing was not restricted to those substantially affected by agency action. All the plaintiff must demonstrate is an "identifiable trifle" of injury in order to qualify for standing.

Third Party Standing. In the cases previously discussed, the recurrent issue regarding standing was whether a potential plaintiff has a sufficient personal stake in the litigation to justify access to the courts. However, in the case of third party standing, standing to assert the rights of others not before the Court, a different question is posed. Although the litigant's access to court to assert a personal interest is clear, the issue is whether the plaintiff may assert the interests of others, as well as his or her own.

As a general rule, the Court will not grant third party standing. In order to get relief, the individual whose interest is at stake must be before the Court. However, the Court has carved out several narrow exceptions to this rule that enable a third party's rights to be asserted.

In justification of these exceptions to the third party standing barrier, the Court has enunciated three factual

The members of the 1973 Supreme Court took a more liberal view of the requirements for personal standing in **United States v. Students Challenging Regulatory Agency Procedures,** *holding that substantial injury was not necessary to qualify for standing. Chief Justice Burger is at center front.*

considerations. However, all three need not be present for the Court to grant third party standing. Indeed, the Court applied these justifications in a somewhat incoherent pattern.

First, there must be a substantial relationship between the claimant and the third party. For instance, in *NAACP v. Alabama* (1958), the NAACP was granted third party standing to assert the rights of its members. The Court found that its nexus with them was sufficiently close to allow it to act as their representative in litigation.

Second, the Court must find that the third party's ability to assert its own rights has been impaired or blocked. Although some justices prefer a showing of impossibility, in *Singleton v. Wulff (1976)*, one of the post-*Roe v. Wade* abortion cases, a showing of "genuine obstacle," or a substantial barrier to the assertion of his rights, was sufficient to allow a doctor, injured in fact by an anti-abortion statute, to defend the interests of his patients as well.

Finally, the Court considers the danger that the third party's rights will be diluted unless the party present is permitted to litigate his claims. Therefore, in *Eisenstadt v. Baird* (1972), the Court granted third party standing to a doctor convicted of violating a statute that prohibited the distribution of contraceptives to unmarried persons. The doctor was permitted to assert the rights of his unmarried patients, in addition to his own interests, since the patients' rights could not be litigated any other way. The law prohib-

ited the distribution, not use, of contraceptives, so the patients themselves could not be prosecuted for its violation, although they were adversely affected by its enforcement. Had the doctor been denied a forum to assert the patients' claims, their rights would have been diluted.

Showing of Inquiry. In addition to these three factual considerations, there must be a strong showing of injury to the potential litigant in order to get third party standing. A strict application of the standing requirements was enforced by the Court in *Warth v. Seldin* (1975). In this case, the Court refused third party standing to certain plaintiffs challenging a town's zoning regulations.

Various organizations and individual residents of the Rochester, New York, area filed suit against the neighboring town of Penfield and its zoning board. They contended that Penfield's zoning requirements regarding lot size, setback, and floor area unconstitutionally prevented low-income persons from settling there. The litigants refused third party standing were Rochester taxpayers who claimed specifically that Penfield's restriction on low-income housing raised their taxes because their own town provided more such housing than it otherwise would.

The Court found that these litigants suffered no "distinct and palpable injury" because they were not subject to Penfield's ordinances. The only basis for standing that the Court found was that the Penfield zoning regulation infringed upon the rights of third parties, persons with low incomes who were excluded from living in Penfield. However, the taxpayer litigants did not qualify for third party standing. First, no relationship existed between the taxpayers and that class of persons excluded from Penfield. At most, they may have had a coincidental overlapping of interests. Second, the taxpayers did not indicate that the low-income persons who were actually excluded from Penfield were impeded from asserting their own rights. Since they could protect their own interests in proper litigation, their rights are in no danger of being diluted by a refusal of access to the courts to the Rochester taxpayers. Therefore, the Court withheld third party standing from the taxpayer litigants.

Duke Power Case. In recent years, the Court has broadened the requirements for personal standing outside of the taxpayer connection. The more relaxed criteria for personal standing were set out in *Duke Power Co. v. Carolina Environmental Study Group, Inc.* (1978). In *Duke Power*, the plaintiffs, comprising forty individuals who lived near the planned power plants, an environmental group, and a labor organization, were granted standing to challenge the Price-Anderson Act. They claimed that the act violated due process since it limited aggregate liability for a nuclear power accident to $560,000,000. The act had been passed in order to induce the development of nuclear power by private companies. The plaintiffs argued that the act's unconstitutionality arose from the lack of assurance of sufficient compensation to potential victims of a nuclear accident. The plaintiffs asserted that they qualified for standing since they were threatened with environmental and aesthetic injuries originating from the nuclear power plants.

Through a reexamination and modification of the "personal stake in the outcome" doctrine, the Court held that a two-part test must be met before standing will be conferred. First, the plaintiff must demonstrate a "direct and palpable injury." Second, there must be a "'fairly traceable' causal connection between the claimed injury and the challenged conduct." The second strand of this test may be met by a showing of a "substantial likelihood" that the remedy sought will relieve the claimed injury.

The Court found the two-pronged test satisfied by the *Duke Power* plaintiffs and granted them personal standing to challenge the act's constitutionality. The first part of the test was met by a demonstration that environmental harm caused by nuclear power plants, such as thermal pollution of nearby lakes and emission of radiation into the atmosphere, was adequate to constitute "a direct and present injury." Furthermore, the Court accepted the lower court's finding that a significant likelihood existed that the defendant would not be able to complete and maintain its nuclear plants without the protection offered by the Price-Anderson Act. Thus, the second half of the test was satisfied, and the plaintiffs were deemed to have a sufficiently personal stake in the outcome to qualify for standing.

In *Duke*, the Court rejected the *Flast* nexus test, which required a showing of a logical link between the injury claimed and the constitutional right asserted. This criterion was limited to taxpayer suits and was not necessary to qualify for personal standing. The Court, if it wished to avoid reaching the merits of this case, could have denied standing to the *Duke* plaintiffs on this ground. The plaintiffs' injuries may not have fallen within the zone of interest that the due process clause, the constitutional right allegedly violated by the act, was designed to protect. That the Supreme Court rejected such a showing indicates a possible phasing-out of the nexus doctrine.

The Mootness Obstacle

Related to the problems of standing and advisory opinions is the mootness obstacle to the adjudication of a constitutional claim. In general, a case is considered moot when it no longer presents a justiciable controversy because the issues involved are either academic or dead. Although the litigants may have clearly had an Article III "case" or "controversy" when the action arose, events subsequent to the filing have deprived the plaintiffs of their stake in the outcome. In other words, the dispute, for some reason, no longer exists.

At times the Supreme Court has considered the mootness barrier to have its origins in the Constitution. Since Article III grants jurisdiction to the Court only over "cases" and "controversies," the Court may not decide a moot issue since it lacks the requisite concreteness and adversity. If the case is moot, there is no real and substantial subject matter that the Court's decision can affect. However, the Court has demonstrated its willingness to relax the mootness barrier in order to review the merits of an important constitutional issue. The Court has found several exceptions to the mootness doctrine, in spite of the constitutional basis for the barrier. For this reason, mootness is considered to stem both from the constitutional limitations on the Court's jurisdictional powers and from the Court's own principles of judicial self-restraint, which are frequently relaxed by the Court.

Reasons for Mootness. There are many reasons why a case may become moot. A party may die during the course of litigation, or may no longer be affected by a challenged statute that is applicable only to minors. Perhaps the defendant has paid the sum owed the plaintiff, or the law has changed since the filing of the suit. In any event, if the controversy ceases to exist during any stage of litigation, the case has become moot.

The Court has created several exceptions to the mootness doctrine, one of which was designed to prevent either party from formulating a "technical mootness" as a pretense to deprive the Court of jurisdiction. For instance, a defendant may cease the offending conduct just long enough to make the plaintiff's action moot. Unless the defendant can prove that the illegal activity can never be resumed, the Court will overcome the mootness barrier and reach the merits of the case.

Another exception was created for situations in which collateral consequences of a judgment present the possibility of another suit, even after the original issue has been satisfied. As an example, in *Powell v. McCormack* (1969) the Court heard Congressman Powell's complaint (naming Speaker of the House McCormack) regarding his exclusion from the House of Representatives despite the fact that he had been seated by the time his case reached the Supreme Court. Although the original issue was moot, a collateral issue still remained: the question of Powell's back pay. Since the possibility of another suit was still present, the Court heard the case.

The Court has further mitigated the mootness barrier with respect to class action suits. In *Sosna v. Iowa* (1975), the Court heard the plaintiff's complaint even though a live controversy no longer existed by the time the case came up for review. The Court reasoned that, although this particular plaintiff did not have an active dispute, the case was not moot so long as a live controversy still existed between the defendant and a member of the plaintiff's class.

Finally, the last exception to the mootness doctrine is a case "capable of repetition yet evading review." That is, if the issue is likely to recur and would become moot each time, then the Court may hear the case. Commonly falling into this category are cases whose factual settings appear to make the issue moot by the time it is reviewed on appeal. A noted example of this exception is the string of anti-abortion statute cases headed by *Roe v. Wade* (1973). Jane Roe, using a pseudonym, filed a suit in 1970, challenging the constitutionality of a Texas anti-abortion law. At the time, she was pregnant, was unmarried, and wanted an abortion. She included in her suit all women in similar situations. By the time the case was heard in the district court, there was no evidence that she was still pregnant.

When the case reached the Supreme Court, almost three years after the initial filing, the appellee contended that the case be mooted since neither Roe nor any of the women she represented were subject to any 1970 pregnancy. However, the Court refused to dismiss the case and relied on the "repetition" exception to the mootness barrier. It reasoned that in any actions concerning pregnancy, the normal nine-month gestation period will usually be terminated before the case comes up for review. If the mootness rule were rigidly maintained, then no case in which pregnancy was an issue could ever survive the trial stage of litigation. Since pregnancy can occur more than once in the same woman, it is clearly "capable of repetition yet evading review." Therefore, dismissal for mootness was denied.

The Ripeness Doctrine

Just as a case may be brought too late and be dismissed for mootness, a case brought too early, before the issues are ripe for adjudication, may also be nonjusticiable. The ripeness doctrine is another technical restraint on judicial review that has frequently been litigated before the Supreme Court. The concerns about concrete factual records and premature intervention lie at the core of this concept. As in the context of advisory opinions, the courts will not hear a case unless the dispute has jelled and the issues are well defined. The controversy must be as fully developed as it can be.

The basis for the ripeness requirement of adjudication is rooted in the text of the Constitution as well as in judicial discretion. The Article III "case" or "controversy" concerns have compelled the Court to ascertain whether a concrete and specific dispute exists before the case may be adjudicated. When a case is not yet ripe as, for example, when a plaintiff files suit to obtain a ruling on the legality of an action that she fears may be taken against her, the relationship between the parties is still in flux. It is sheer speculation to predict what action the parties may take in the future. Since the controversy has not yet jelled, Article III considerations preclude the adjudication of the case.

The ripeness rule is just as firmly anchored in the discretionary policies of judicial self-restraint. Various policy concerns may dissuade a judge from taking a case should the issues be yet unripe for a hearing on the merits. It is more difficult for the Court to weigh the practical merits of each party if the case is too abstract. For example, when the constitutional claims of both parties are very close, the Court may demand a more detailed factual record. It needs to know concrete facts about actual practices, something the hypothetical case of an unenforced statute will not reveal. Further, the Court may require a concrete fact pattern in order to decide a case on its narrow set of facts, thereby avoiding a controversial constitutional question. Or, perhaps the specific circumstances behind the legislation and enforcement of a statute, for instance, will justify a narrow application of its scope and quell a challenge to its constitutionality.

Standards on Ripeness. In order to overcome the ripeness barrier, the litigant must bring clearly defined, unambiguous issues before the Court. The controversy must be realistically grounded on actual facts; a hypothetical situation will not merit the Court's attention. The case must be capable of being decided upon a fully developed record. Since, unlike the legislature, the judiciary has no fact finding mechanisms to employ, it relies solely on the adversarial parties to bring to it all the details of the case.

These standards were used by the Court in *United Public Workers v. Mitchell* (1947), in which it held that the ripeness doctrine precluded the plaintiffs from attacking the constitutionality of a provision of the Hatch Act. The plaintiffs sought declaratory relief and an injunction against the members of the U.S. Civil Service Commission to prevent enforcement of the provision that prohibited an employee of the federal executive branch from political activities.

As to the plaintiffs who had not violated the act, the Court refused to adjudicate their claims. It failed to find a

The seizure of steel mills by President Harry Truman during the Korean War triggered a storm of public protest and led to the Supreme Court holding in **Youngstown Street and Tube Co. v. Sawyer** *that the President's action was illegal.*

justiciable case or controversy in the "general threat of possible interference" with their civil rights should they violate the act. A hypothetical threat was insufficient to satisfy the jurisdictional requirement.

Similarly, the Court found that an action was not ripe when a union and several of its alien members filed suit to enjoin the enforcement of an immigration law that would result in aliens domiciled in the United States being treated as first-time aliens when they return from temporary jobs in Alaska. If considered newly-arrived aliens, they may be deported for reasons less justifiable than if they were resident aliens. In *International Longshoreman's and Warehouseman's Union 37 v. Boyd* (1954), the Court held that the mere potential enforcement of a statute was not concrete enough to merit adjudication. The situation had not yet arisen in which the law could be enforced, and, conse-

quently, no injury had been suffered. Furthermore, it was not even definite that the immigration law would be enforced should the occasion arise.

Implicit in the Court's analysis in cases such as *Mitchell* and *Boyd* is the balancing of the interests and policies involved. It weighs the party's need for judicial protection of his or her constitutional rights versus whether the passage of time will eliminate the need for judicial review. For example, in *Mitchell*, as in *Boyd*, the constitutional interests of the litigants did not present such an urgent problem. No infringement of their rights had yet occurred; they had sustained no injuries. Further, there were no obvious threats that their rights would be violated if the Court refused to entertain their claims. On the other hand, the odds were in favor of the dissipation of any need for adjudication should the Court merely wait to see what the future would bring.

There was no certainty that the plaintiffs would sustain the constitutional rights violations they feared. In all probability, the actual controversies would never arise and the Court could avoid consideration of the issues entirely.

The Political Question Doctrine

The political question doctrine is another restraint on the Court's judicial powers. This concept holds that certain matters are nonjusticiable due to their political nature and are best resolved by the body politic. If the Court finds that this doctrine is applicable to an issue, it will withhold judicial review. However, unlike the other restrictions on judicial review, such as standing, ripeness, and mootness, the political question doctrine can never be "cured" by a change in factual circumstances. A holding of nonjusticiability due to a question's political ramifications is absolute in its foreclosure of judicial examination.

Some constitutional law scholars have held that the political question doctrine is actually a misnomer. Although many issues that are nonjusticiable under this concept are political in nature, the Court has heard and decided other cases despite their political origins. For example, the Court rendered an opinion in the steel seizure case and did not withhold judicial scrutiny due to the political issues involved. The *Youngstown Sheet and Tube Co.* case held that President Truman's seizure of steel mills during the Korean War was unconstitutional. As Justice Jackson has noted, however, political consequences are found in all constitutional interpretations. Perhaps a more accurate definition of the political question doctrine, then, is the nonjusticiability of any matters that are simply inappropriate for judicial consideration.

Standards For Political Questions. Issues are included in this broad category at the Court's discretion, although such determination is not without some standards. However, the components of the political question doctrine have been the subject of considerable litigation. At least three strands to the concept have emerged and are followed by the Court. The first, which is perhaps the most legitimate, is the "constitutional commitment" rationale. This strand holds that if the Constitution has explicitly delegated the authority to resolve a matter to another branch of government, then the case is inappropriate for judicial review and the political question doctrine of justiciability precludes judicial consideration. This rationale rests on the separation of powers principle and reflects the Court's concern to avoid interference with another government agency's prescribed authority.

A second element of the political question concept emphasizes the lack of judicial competence. The Court may rely on this doctrine if the case cannot be resolved by "judicially manageable standards." Unlike the legislative branch, for example, the judiciary possesses no fact-finding mechanisms of its own. If the Court cannot resolve the case on the basis of data available to it, the matter is considered nonjusticiable as a political question.

An even more ambiguous part of the doctrine is a problem of judicial discretion. The Court must consider whether it will decide an issue whose resolution will result either in a policy inappropriate for judicial determination, or in embarrassment to another governmental agency due to inconsistent decisions from different departments.

Baker v. Carr. One of the most significant developments of the political question doctrine emerged in *Baker v. Carr* (1962), which upheld the justiciability of legislative reapportionment. Prior to this decision, legislative districting controversies were considered nonjusticiable, due to their political nature. In *Baker v. Carr*, however, the Court ruled that a constitutional challenge to legislative reapportionment was justiciable when based upon the equal protection clause of the 14th Amendment. The opinion expressed the belief that judicially manageable standards could be found with which to resolve such an issue.

The appellants argued that the districting of the Tennessee General Assembly violated their equal protection rights by the dilution of their votes. The assembly had not been reapportioned since 1901, despite the fact that the Tennessee Constitution required representation according to population. The appellants sought an injunction against further elections under the present districting system and requested the fed-

Associate Justice William Brennan wrote the Court's decision in **Baker v. Carr,** *which established several tests for the political question doctrine.*

During the Pullman Strike of 1894, one of the most violent American labor disputes, President Cleveland ordered federal troops to keep the railroad running, an order upheld by the Supreme Court.

eral trial court to decree a reapportionment. The lower court denied relief.

The Supreme Court heard the case and held that no nonjusticiable political question was present. In its reasoning, it outlined a general theory of the political question doctrine and propounded several tests for use in its determination. The Court ruled that a political question controversy arises only out of the relationship between the judiciary and the other branches of the federal government, rather than that between the federal judiciary and the states. Since such a relationship did not give rise to the *Baker v. Carr* case, no political question existed, and the case was proper for judicial scrutiny.

The Court then enumerated several situations that indicate the presence of a political question. Among the tests mentioned in the opinion were the existence of a constitutional commitment of the issue to another branch of government, the lack of judicially manageable standards for

resolution of the matter, and the possibility of the making of an initial policy determination that would be better left to the body politic. Since none of these situations was found by the Court, *Baker v. Carr* was held to be properly subject to judicial review.

The Authority To Make National Policy

The Supreme Court must often resolve conflicts of authority that develop between the executive and legislative branches. Although the framers of the Constitution deliberately provided specific delegations of power to each of the three branches of government, this separation of powers is not total or absolute. The powers are not wholly discrete; they tend to overlap and intertwine. This is evident in, for example, the presidential veto power over the legislature and in the congressional power of impeachment. Beyond the constitutionally explicit boundaries and overlaps of powers, however, are ambiguous and indistinct areas of authority that have caused considerable competition among the different branches of government. Most often, such conflicts were resolved through a test of political strength. Judicial determinations of the separation of powers principle are relatively few, and the controversies have usually been left to political resolution.

Domestic Affairs. The competition that exists between the executive and legislative branches is evident in the area of domestic affairs. Conflicts over the authority to make national policy have arisen with great frequency, although no clear and authoritative lines have yet emerged. The basic issue involved is the extent to which Article II of the Constitution empowers the executive to fashion national policy in the absence of, or in conflict with, congressional decision making. May the president of the United States regulate private conduct in a national emergency? Does the president have the explicit or implicit power to create national policy when Congress has failed to do so? May the executive ever exert his powers to supersede a congressional directive? Issues such as these have not met with decisive resolutions. Instead, each particular case has been practically adjusted to accommodate the situation.

Article II of the Constitution assigns specific powers to the president; among them is the duty to execute faithfully the laws of the United States. The restraints on this particular power have not been enunciated. However, in *In re Debs* (1895), the Supreme Court upheld President Cleveland's deployment of troops to maintain operation of the railroad during the Pullman Strike of 1894. The Court based its reasoning on the executive authority to assure the execution of the laws that relate to the free flow of interstate commerce. This is but one example of an interpretation of the executive power over national policy that was designed to suit the factual circumstances.

The Court has been reluctant, however, to imbue the Constitution with a stringent definition of executive power. Such a restricted view of constitutional authority, the Court fears, may impair the system of checks and balances between the executive and legislative branches. For this reason, the Court has interpreted the executive implied powers to regulate the national economy quite narrowly.

Significance Of Youngstown Sheet And Tube. For example, in *Youngstown Sheet and Tube Co. v. Sawyer* (1952), the Court ruled that President Truman's seizure of the steel mills in order to avert a strike during the Korean War was an unconstitutional use of his executive power. Such economic regulation was not authorized by the executive power as commander-in-chief nor by any other constitutional provision.

During the Korean War, President Truman issued an executive order that authorized Secretary of Commerce Sawyer to seize many of this country's steel mills. He feared that an impending steelworkers' strike would threaten national security. Truman relied on constitutional and statutory provisions that endowed him with powers of the executive and commander-in-chief. The mills were seized and instructed to operate in accordance with Department of Commerce regulations. Truman informed Congress of these events, but, despite the fact that Congress had already provided methods for dealing with this type of situation, the legislature took no action and did not condone the government seizure of private property.

On an appeal by the steel companies, the Supreme Court declared the executive order invalid. The Court found that no express or implied statutory provision authorized the President's seizure order and rejected the argument that the order should be upheld as a valid exercise of the President's power as commander-in-chief. Justice Black, the author of the Court's opinion, concluded that such an action was more properly in the legislative domain.

In a concurring opinion, Justice Jackson propounded a three-part analysis to the exercise of executive authority. He stated that the executive power is at its peak when it is justified by an express congressional authorization. If Congress had directed the seizure of the steel mills, the executive order would have been upheld. The second situation is one in which the president acts in the absence of a congressional directive. This is a "zone of twilight" in which the distribution of powers is uncertain. The last situation, where the executive power is at its weakest, is one in which the president acts contrary to the express or implied will of Congress. Jackson concluded that the steel seizure fell into this last category. He considered that the seizure was contrary to the will of Congress, and, therefore, the executive order could be valid only if the Constitution supported such authority. Since no constitutional support existed, the executive order could not stand.

The *Youngstown* decision has been interpreted as a set of guidelines for the exercise of executive power during a national emergency. Although the president's emergency powers were not completely diluted by the decision, they were severely limited in times of domestic emergencies, at which time the president may act only within the restrictions imposed by Congress. When Congress has voiced its opposition to the executive action, the executive action will be invalidated if not authorized by the Constitution.

Impoundment Controversy. Another issue that has sparked considerable controversy between the executive and legislative branches is the impoundment of funds. The Congress's power to provide funds for its programs is an established constitutional right. However, in certain circumstances, the president may impound funds appropriated by Congress for a particular purpose. The extent to which Congress may restrict the executive control over the appropriation process has given rise to jealousy and competition between the two branches of government.

The presidential impoundment power stems from an

inherent executive authority to administer the national budget. This authority has its roots in Article II, Section 3 of the Constitution, which obligates the president to "take care that the laws be faithfully executed." Proponents of the executive power to oversee the budget contend that this inherent power is necessary to ensure that the expenditure of funds remains in keeping with the Constitution. However, the impoundment power is not limitless. Rather, it is a form of the presidential veto, and, as such, it can be overridden by Congress and is much less restrictive than an absolute power to impound funds.

Controversies stemming from the impoundment of funds have usually been settled through political rather than judicial processes. The Court has avoided adjudicating such matters due to the absence of specific constitutional provisions authorizing this power. It is reluctant to define the scope of legislative and executive power spheres in an area that lacks explicit constitutional definitions. Unless no other resolution is possible, the Court declines to hear such cases under the political question restraint on judicial review.

Foreign Affairs. Unlike the limited executive powers in domestic matters, the presidential authority in foreign affairs has been more broadly defined. The president was bestowed with the ultimate responsibility for conducting the country's foreign relations in *United States v. Curtiss-Wright Export Corp.* (1936). In this leading case, Associate Justice Sutherland deemed the president "the sole organ of the nation in its external relations, and its sole representative with foreign nations."

This controversy arose out of an embargo proclamation issued by the President in 1934, which prohibited the sale of arms to countries involved in the Chaco conflict in South America. A joint congressional declaration passed on the same day authorized the executive embargo. The defendants were indicted for conspiring to sell arms to Bolivia (one of the countries in conflict), and they challenged the executive embargo proclamation as an unconstitutional delegation of power. On appeal to the Supreme Court, however, the proclamation was considered a valid exercise of executive authority.

Justice Sutherland's opinion emphasized the primary responsibility that the president possesses in international affairs, as opposed to the more limited role he plays in internal matters. Although the justice noted that President Roosevelt had acted pursuant to a joint resolution of Congress, he concluded that the broad executive power stemmed from the presidential role as the sole representative of the country in foreign affairs. The Court recognized that such authority was independent, in that it need not be based on an act of the legislature. However, the opinion also stressed that the power must be exercised in accordance with any limits imposed by the Constitution.

The broad executive authority in foreign affairs that was recognized in *Curtiss-Wright* does not extend to the

Senator Barry Goldwater was among a group of senators who unsuccessfully challenged presidential authority to abrogate a treaty in **Goldwater v. Carter**, *which concerned President Carter's decision to terminate a treaty with Taiwan.*

president's ability to conduct domestic wiretapping without a court order for the purpose of foreign intelligence. In the Keith case, *United States v. U.S. District Court* (1972), the Court rejected the executive's claim that warrantless electronic surveillance in domestic security cases was an inherent presidential power. Although the monitoring of the activities of foreign nations was the alleged objective, the Court stressed the domestic aspects of national security and invalidated the executive action.

Congressional Role. The president possesses special powers in foreign affairs due to the need for decisive action and a uniform policy with regard to sensitive foreign relations. Congress, however, retains certain controls over foreign affairs, which include the powers to declare war, appropriate funds, and ratify treaties. Although the executive is the sole negotiator of a treaty, it must receive the consent of two-thirds of the Senate before it becomes the law of the land. Once the treaty is passed, it may then be the basis of enforcement legislation that would otherwise be beyond congressional authority. Additionally, Congress may alter or negate the effect a treaty has on domestic law through the implementation of a statute.

An issue that has been the focus of some dispute is whether the president has the unilateral authority to abrogate treaties once they have become the law of the land. Although this question has arisen before the Court, no limits have been set nor have the issues been reviewed. In *Goldwater v. Carter* (1979), President Carter notified the Congress of his intent to abrogate a treaty with Taiwan in order to recognize the Peking government. Several individual senators sued to enjoin termination of the treaty without a two-thirds vote of the Senate. Although the Court dismissed the complaint, it did not issue any guidelines for the treatment of such a controversy. No majority opinion was rendered; however, a concurring opinion held that the case presented a political question and was therefore inappropriate for judicial review.

Power And The Armed Forces. The power of the federal government over the nation's armed forces is yet another source of controversy, since this power is divided between the executive and legislative branches. Article II of the Constitution designates the president as commander-in-chief of the military, but Congress has been delegated the authority to declare war. The conflict between these two spheres has increased greatly in recent years due to the mounting controversy about U.S. military involvement in Southeast Asia. Although there was no formal declaration of war by Congress, presidential justification of American participation claimed an autonomous authority over the military forces under the executive constitutional powers.

Many questions about U.S. involvement in Vietnam lie unresolved, such as whether there was a legal justification for the presence of U.S. military forces without a formal declaration of war. The reason for the persistence of this conflict is the refusal of the Supreme Court to hear cases relating to the participation of U.S. armed forces in Vietnam. For example, the Court denied *certiorari* to *Mora v. McNamara* (1967). In this case, a group of army draftees challenged the legality of U.S. military activities in Vietnam. The lower federal courts dismissed their action and the Supreme Court refused to hear their appeal. Only Justice Stewart, in a lone dissent, conceded that many troubling questions existed about the legality of the involvement of U.S. armed forces without a declaration of war. He alone recognized that these problems would not simply disappear by the Court's refusal to entertain the appeal.

The Legislative And Executive Branches

Article I, Section 6 of the Constitution, which is known as the "speech or debate" clause, concedes the need for legislative independence in a government that rests on the separation of powers principle. It states that members of Congress "shall not be questioned in any other place" for "any Speech or Debate in either House." The clause protects speech in Congress by making legislators' conduct during congressional business immune from civil or criminal suit. This clause has not come to mean that representatives' conduct is absolutely unrestrained. In recent years, the privileges of the clause have been narrowly interpreted by the Supreme Court.

The Legislative Branch. In *United States v. Brewster* (1972), the Court held that Article I, Section 6 did not bar the prosecution of a former senator for accepting a bribe relating to his actions on postage rate legislation. The opinion distinguished between legislative acts that are "clearly a part of the legislative process--the due functioning of the process," and other activities that are essentially political in nature. Any conduct that is only peripherally related to the legislative process was unprotected by the speech or debate clause and was therefore properly subject to review.

Another restrictive application of the clause was set out in *Powell v. McCormack* (1969). In this case, the Court refused to extend protection to activities of legislative employees who acted under the direction of Congress. The Court decided the merits of a charge by Congressman Pow-

Vice-President Spiro Agnew tried to claim immunity from prosecution under Article I, Section 3 of the Constitution, but the Justice Department decided that only the president enjoyed this privilege while in office.

The Supreme Court, in an opinion by Chief Justice Burger, held that President Nixon's claim of executive privilege did not apply to tape recordings of White House meetings and that they could not be withheld from a special prosecutor.

ell that he was unlawfully excluded from being seated in Congress. Although the action was dismissed, the Court held that the speech or debate clause did not provide immunity to House of Representatives employees who were acting under orders from members of Congress.

The Executive Branch. Unlike the legislative branch, executive officials are not given any express immunity from judicial process in the Constitution. Instead, the history of cases suggests the rejection of even an implied immunity under the doctrine of separation of powers principles. As early as 1803, the *Marbury v. Madison* decision subjected executive officials to writs of *mandamus*. Although in this particular case the Court found that it had no jurisdiction, Chief Justice Marshall declared that the Supreme Court could properly exercise its power to compel Secretary Madison to perform his ministerial duty.

In cases of criminal liability, it is unclear whether the executive official must first be impeached before being tried for a crime. The question arises from the language of Article I, Section 3 of the Constitution, which states that any

party convicted of impeachment "shall...be liable and subject to Indictment, Trial, Judgment, and Punishment according to law." Vice-President Agnew raised this defense while he was subjected to grand jury proceedings while still in office. The Justice Department responded that only the president was immune from criminal prosecution while still holding his office.

Presidential Immunity. Presidential immunity, then, appears to raise unique problems of amenability to judicial process, even though the president, like other executive officials, is protected by no explicit grant of privilege in the Constitution. The difficult issue of executive privilege was discussed at length in the litigation over the Watergate tapes.

In *United States v. Nixon* (1974), the Supreme Court held that executive immunity did not give the president an absolute, unqualified general privilege of immunity from judicial process under all circumstances. Although the Court had already established its power of judicial review over the conduct of executive officials, never before had process issued directly against the president.

After seven members of President Nixon's staff had been indicted for conspiracy to defraud the United States to obstruct justice, the same grand jury named the President as an unindicted co-conspirator. A special prosecutor then issued a subpoena that required President Nixon to produce certain tapes of meetings between him and his staff. The President's counsel moved to quash the subpoena on grounds of executive privilege, which motion was denied by a lower court. On appeal to the Supreme Court, the denial was affirmed, and the Court ordered the President to produce the requested tapes.

After finding the case justiciable, Chief Justice Burger addressed the main issue of executive privilege. Although he agreed that the President had a privilege to protect the confidentiality of internal communications, he emphasized that such a privilege was neither absolute nor unrestrained. When either the prosecution or defense, in a criminal proceeding, demonstrates a need for the evidence, the privilege is superseded by the judicial process. The Court used a balancing test to decide this case and determined that, unless a need to protect military, diplomatic, or sensitive national security interests exists, the examination of presidential communications does not significantly damage the president's confidentiality under these narrow circumstances and that legitimate judicial needs outweigh the need for a blanket executive privilege.

The results of the *Nixon* decision are clear, but by no means does the case answer all questions pertaining to executive privilege. The Court stressed the fact that, although presidential communications are presumptively privileged, the president himself is not wholly immune from the judicial process. However, the Court did not discuss the role of executive privilege in civil litigation, as opposed to criminal proceedings. Nor did the opinion mention how a congressional subpoena would affect the executive privilege. Lastly, the question of the president's interest in preserving state secrets was also left unresolved.

There is little in *Nixon* to indicate how further litigation of the executive privilege will proceed. Perhaps the Supreme Court considers itself to be the final arbiter of any contro- versy among the branches of the federal government that pertains to this issue. The Supreme Court's power of judi- cial review is increasingly being taken for granted. Justice Marshall's words in *Marbury v. Madison* carry more truth today than in 1803: "[I]t is, emphatically, the province and duty of the judicial department, to say what the law is."

Division of Power:
The Federal Government and the States

Division of Power: The Federal Government and the States

In the United States the sovereign authority of each of the several states operates within the overriding authority of the national government. Throughout the nation's history, the primary issues raised by this federalist system relate to how power is divided between the national and state governments. On the one hand, the framers of the Constitution recognized the need to have a central government sufficiently powerful to maintain a unified nation despite state and regional differences. On the other hand, the framers also recognized the dangers of centralizing too much authority in one government at the expense of state sovereignty.

The Constitution established a limited national government that was without authority to act outside of the specific enumerated powers delegated to it by the Constitution. The states retained plenary (full, or absolute) authority subject only to the limitations established in the Constitution. The constitutional history of federal-state relations has revolved around interpreting the scope of the national government's enumerated powers and determining how the existence of these powers has affected the plenary authority of the states. The express and implied powers delegated by the Constitution to the U.S. Congress have been one of the major areas of constitutional interpretation. Another important area has been the development of the broadest congressional power "to regulate commerce. . .among the several states," including the doctrines that have been developed to resolve issues that arise when the Congress's "commerce power" overlaps with the states' "police power" to regulate their welfare.

Enumerated Powers Of The Congress

Article I, Section 8 of the Constitution enumerates the powers of Congress. These powers fall into several major categories, which reflect the intent of the Constitution's framers to assure sufficient power in the national government to act in areas in which the individual states were incompetent to act in the national interest.

In the area of finances, Congress is granted the power to raise taxes; levy duties, imposts, and excises; coin money and fix its value; borrow money on the credit of the United States; protect against counterfeit coin and securities; repay government debts; and "provide for the common defense and general welfare of the United States." This latter power is the basis of Congress's spending power, which has allowed Congress to achieve federal control by making the states' receipt of federal funds conditional on compliance with federal regulations. The spending power has also been a source of federal-state dispute.

The most substantial area of congressional power is in commerce and trade. Congress is delegated the power to regulate commerce with foreign nations and with Indian tribes, establish laws on bankruptcies, establish a mechanism for patents and copyrights, and fix weights and measures. Most significantly, Congress has the power to "regulate commerce. . .among the several states." The commerce clause has become a very broad source of congressional power, and the substantial case law surrounding the interpretation of the commerce power forms a large and important part of the history of federal-state relations.

The Constitution also delegates power to Congress in the areas of foreign policy and the military. Although most authority in these areas resides in the executive branch, Congress retains control over finances and appropriations. Thus, Congress has the authority to provide for the common defense, raise and support armies, establish and regulate a navy, issue letters of marque and reprisal (defined by a combination of treaty and traditional practice, these permit the seizure of the national and commercial property of nations or parties that deny justice for Americans abroad), and establish a uniform rule of naturalization.

Congress also has considerable control over the federal judiciary. Pursuant to this authority, Congress established the federal court system and retains substantial power to determine the jurisdiction of the lower federal courts and the appellate jurisdiction of the U.S. Supreme Court.

The last congressional power enumerated in Article I, Section 8, delegates the authority to "make all laws which shall be necessary and proper for carrying into Execution the foregoing Powers. . . ." The broad interpretation given this phrase early in the nation's constitutional history has had the greatest impact on federal power.

Position Of The States. In contrast, nothing in the federal Constitution enumerates the powers of the states; their power is presumed to be plenary. Thus, the 10th Amendment provides that "[the] powers not delegated to the United States by the Constitution, nor prohibited by it to the States, are reserved to the States respectively, or to the people." This amendment was adopted partly in response to the arguments of states' rights advocates that too much control would be removed from the states by the new Constitution. Nevertheless, the amendment has often been interpreted as a truism; it merely states explicitly what would otherwise be implied by the absence of enumerated state powers.

As the language of the 10th Amendment indicates, however, the Constitution does limit state authority in certain specified areas. Article I, Section 10 of the Constitution expressly forbids states from levying import or export duties; coining money; emitting bills of credit; passing bills of attainder, *ex post facto* laws, or laws that impair the obligation of contracts; making a foreign policy; raising armies for foreign use; or granting letters of marque and reprisal.

These express limitations on state authority primarily address areas in which the framers foresaw that the states would be incompetent to act. Two other articles of the Constitution that limit state authority have raised more controversial problems in federal-state relations. First, the 14th Amendment, ratified soon after the Civil War, prohibits states from abridging the rights of citizens to due process of law and equal protection of the laws. The 14th Amendment has had considerable impact over state authority in the areas of criminal procedure and civil rights and its controversial

history is discussed in more detail in Chapter 4. Second, the supremacy clause in Article VI, Section 2 of the Constitution provides that the laws and the treaties of the United States "shall be the supreme law of the land and the judges in every State shall be bound therebye, anything in the constitution or the laws of any State to the contrary notwithstanding." The supremacy clause underlies the resolution of every issue involving federal and state authority. This clause is the backbone of federal-state relations.

National Supremacy And Implied Powers

The landmark case of *McCulloch v. Maryland* (1819) decided two issues critical in determining the scope of federal authority: first, how broad was Congress's power to determine the means by which it would carry out its enumerated powers and second, what, if any, power did the states have to interfere with congressional actions.

Background To McCulloch. McCulloch v. Maryland involved the Second Bank of the United States, established in 1816 by an act of Congress for the purpose of establishing credit, raising money, issuing bank notes, and regulating the monetary system. The new bank, however, was beset with charges of corruption and with speculation. Investors lost millions of dollars, which caused innumerable banking and business failures. Popularly, the bank was blamed for the nation's period of financial depression.

Noted orator Daniel Webster argued for the Bank of the United States before Chief Justice Marshall in **McCulloch v. Maryland.**

Several states, primarily those in the South and West, where the Bank of the United States was especially unpopular, acted to restrict or prevent the operation of its branches within their borders. They took two approaches: direct prohibition in state constitutions or burdensome taxation. Maryland chose the taxation approach, and its legislature levied a heavy tax on every note the bank issued. McCulloch, cashier at the Baltimore branch, issued notes without paying the tax. The state of Maryland brought action against McCulloch in a state court for the statutory penalty. The Maryland courts upheld the validity of the state law, and the bank appealed its case to the U.S. Supreme Court.

The Court's Decision. Some of the greatest lawyers in the country argued the case, including Daniel Webster and William Pinkney for the bank, who were opposed by Luther Martin and Joseph Hopkinson for Maryland. Three days after the close of argument, Chief Justice Marshall handed down the unanimous decision of the Court, which upheld the constitutional power of Congress to charter the bank and to have exclusive control over it, denied the right of Maryland to interfere with the federal government by taxing its agencies, and declared the Maryland tax unconstitutional.

In holding that Congress had the constitutional authority to incorporate a bank, Marshall rejected the argument that because the states had ratified the Constitution, the national government's power was derived from the states and therefore was subordinate to them. He reasoned that power under the Constitution was derived not from the states but from the people represented by popularly-elected delegates who ratified the Constitution at conventions in each state. The states, by submitting the proposed Constitution to the people, had assented to be bound by it.

Implied Powers Established. In *McCulloch*, Marshall established the doctrine of "implied powers." Marshall compared the Constitution to the document it superseded, the Articles of Confederation, which had included the phrase, "Each state retains. . .every power. . .not. . .expressly delegated." In contrast, the 10th Amendment did not include the word "expressly." It merely stated that powers "not delegated to the United States nor prohibited to the States, are reserved to the States or to the people." Marshall reasoned that the failure to use the word "expressly" meant that the federal government's power should be determined by looking at the instrument as a whole.

Thus, although the Constitution had not expressly granted to the United States the right to create or establish a bank, by the very nature of the authority delegated to the government by the Constitution, the government must have the right to select appropriate means to carry out its powers. Had the framers attempted to foresee and enumerate the future occasions for the exercise of federal power, the Constitution "would partake of the prolixity of a legal code, and could scarcely be embraced by the human mind." Implied in the Constitution, therefore, was the authority of Congress

to use means not expressly enumerated to execute the powers that were expressly enumerated.

Marshall agreed that Congress did not have unlimited power to select these means. He rejected the argument that the clause empowering Congress "to make all laws necessary and proper for carrying into execution the foregoing powers" limited Congress to selecting "necessary" or indispensable means "without which the power would be nugatory." Marshall liberally construed the term "necessary" and noted that the clause had been placed in the section of the Constitution that expanded congressional power, not in the section that limited it. He expounded on the need for Congress to have discretion to select its means, emphasizing again that the Constitution was "intended to endure for ages to come, and, consequently, to be adapted to the various crises of human affairs."

Marshall established the test for determining the constitutionality of an implied power: "Let the end be legitimate, let it be within the scope of the constitution, and all means which are appropriate, which are plainly adapted to that end, which are not prohibited, but consist with the letter and spirit of the constitution, are constitutional." A bank was a proper means to several enumerated powers in the same way that the power of establishing post offices and post roads included the right to regulate the roads and punish those who steal the mail.

The second part of Marshall's opinion held that under the doctrine of national supremacy the Maryland law taxing the bank was unconstitutional. Marshall noted again that the federal power was derived from the people who were represented in Congress. He pointed to the supremacy clause and held that when state law conflicted with national law, the latter must prevail. The "power to tax is the power to destroy," and if federal agencies could be taxed by the several states, their continuance would be dependent upon the will of the states rather than that of the national government. The bank was a lawful instrument of federal authority; thus the state did not have the right to attempt to destroy it.

Impact Of McCulloch. The doctrines of implied powers and national supremacy articulated by Marshall in *McCulloch v. Maryland* are as alive today as they were in 1819. The opinion, widely considered to be one of Marshall's greatest, provided Congress with broad authority while still limiting it to action necessary to achieve the enumerated powers. Similarly, while striking a state law that interfered with a federal agency, the opinion simultaneously reaffirmed the states' sovereign authority to act where it did not interfere with federal power.

The significance of *McCulloch* was recognized immediately. Reprinted by many of the newspapers of the day, it became the focal point of a move to amend the Constitution, led by ex-Presidents Madison and Jefferson. The movement died when only five of the fourteen states sent a request to Congress to reverse the effect of the *McCulloch* decision.

New York financier Robert Livingston originally held the steamboat monopoly that was the genesis of the **Gibbons v. Ogden** *decision.*

The Commerce Power Established

No provision of the Constitution has been a more fertile source of federal power than the grant of authority to Congress to regulate "commerce among the several states." The framers had sought to replace the confused condition of foreign and interstate commercial relations prevailing under the Articles of Confederation with an orderly system.

Gibbons v. Ogden. In *Gibbons v. Ogden* (1824), the first Supreme Court case arising under the commerce clause, Chief Justice Marshall gave a broad interpretation of the national commerce power. *Gibbons* originated in the attempts of several states to grant "exclusive privileges" over their state waters to steamboat interests. New York State had granted the exclusive right to operate steamboats on the state's waters to Robert Fulton and Robert Livingston. Aaron Ogden secured from this monopoly a license to navigate by steam across the Hudson River between New York and New Jersey. When Thomas Gibbons, Ogden's competitor, began navigating the same route, Ogden sued, requesting an injunction to restrain Gibbons's competition. Gibbons claimed the right to navigate the route under a license

granted to him by the federal government. The New York courts granted the injunction, holding that the case did not present a conflict between federal and state authority. Gibbons appealed to the U.S. Supreme Court.

As he had in *McCulloch v. Maryland*, Chief Justice Marshall rejected the arguments of strict constuctionists in *Gibbons* and construed each term of the commerce clause to give Congress broad commerce powers. Defining the term "commerce," Marshall rejected the argument that the term was limited to the buying and selling of goods and did not include navigation. Rather, the term "commerce" encompasses both transportation and transactions. "Commerce" meant "commercial intercourse" and regulating navigation was part of regulating commerce.

Marshall next defined the term "among the several states" to extend Congress's power to commercial intercourse that affects more than one state. Thus, commerce completely internal to a state is beyond the power of Congress. However, Marshall refused to hold that because the monopoly in *Gibbons* extended only to New York waters, it was beyond the commerce power of Congress. The commerce power would be useless if it "stop[ped] at the external boundary of each state." To regulate interstate

Steamboat inventor Robert Fulton held a monopoly with Robert Livingston on steamboat navigation in New York waters, a condition that led to a broad interpretation of the commerce clause by John Marshall in **Gibbons v. Ogden.**

By the late 19th century, the American public was alarmed at the economic power of trusts and other powerful business combinations, a situation that led to several key Supreme Court decisions.

commerce, federal power must be able to operate within state boundaries.

Finally, Marshall defined the type of power delegated to Congress: the power to regulate. He stated that this power "may be exercised to its utmost extent, and acknowledges no limitations, other than are prescribed in the Constitution."

Marshall refrained from deciding whether the states had authority to regulate commerce concurrently with Congress. Rather, he decided only that the New York law granting Fulton and Livingston's monopoly was in conflict with the act of Congress authorizing coasting licenses and that the state law must therefore give way.

Because the broad construction of interstate commerce applied to the unpopular steamboat monopolies, it gained more adherents than detractors. The nascent railroads, encouraged by the freedom from parochial state prohibitions mandated by *Gibbons*, developed and expanded. However, the broader significance of *Gibbons* became apparent only with the passage of time.

Later Interpretations. In *Brown v. Maryland* (1827), Marshall formulated the "original package" doctrine. The state of Maryland required, by statute, wholesalers of imported goods to secure a special license from the state. The Constitution specifically forbade the imposting of duties upon foreign goods. Marshall's first point in this case was

that although one could reasonably argue that in the stream of intrastate commerce, articles from foreign countries became "mixed up with the mass of property in the country" and thus became subject to the state's taxing power, as long as goods were in the importer's warehouse, a tax upon such goods at that time constituted an unconstitutional duty. Second, Marshall argued that under the commerce clause, Congress, not the states, had the right to authorize the importer to sell his goods. The states could not use their power to tax to obstruct "the free course of a power given to Congress." Just so the states would not think that the Court distinguished between domestic and foreign articles, Marshall reiterated the supremacy of Congress in interstate commerce.

In *Willson v. Black Bird Creek Marsh Co.* (1829), the Court drew some boundaries around the powers of Congress. The state of Delaware authorized a company owning marshy lands along Black Bird Creek to dam and bank the creek in an attempt to improve its lands. The creek, which was navigable, flowed into the Delaware River. The owners of a sloop, licensed and enrolled under the Coastal Trade Act, the same act cited in *Gibbons*, broke the dam in order to secure passage. The company sued for the resulting damage, and the defendants claimed the law violated the commerce clause of the Constitution.

Marshall, writing for another unanimous Court, upheld the Delaware law on the ground that in the absence of federal legislation on the regulation "over those small navigable creeks into which the tide flows, and which abound throughout the lower country of the middle and southern States," the state laws stood. Although this seems a retrenchment, Marshall succeeded, in effect, in establishing the policy of federal judicial determination of whether a challenged state law was a valid exercise of its police power or was an unconstitutional infringement upon the federal power to regulate foreign and interstate commerce.

National Economic Regulation

While the interpretation of the commerce clause in *Gibbons* was expansive, neither Chief Justice Marshall nor the framers of the Constitution could have foreseen the enormous impact the Industrial Revolution would have on the impetus to regulate commerce.

Until the late 19th century, the potential authority over commercial life had been only sporadically exercised. In a few situations, the authority of the states to regulate commerce had been recognized. Most federal regulation of commerce involved matters of foreign commerce or waterborne activity, having relatively little effect on the scope of the commerce power. The move for national economic regulation came largely in response to the growth of trusts or combinations in the oil and railroad industries. The states were deemed incapable of regulating these industries, which had become vast and, in some instances, nationwide.

In 1882, Standard Oil was formed from a combination of thirty-nine companies doing business in every state in the union, refining oil in a half-dozen states, digging wells in others, and transacting business across four continents. Other huge combinations existed in sugar, steel, and tobacco. By 1892, the American Sugar Refining Company controlled the production of most of the sugar in the country. Independent steel companies were selling out to a trust that in 1901 would become United States Steel. The trusts bought out the small companies, had the power to make or break cities and towns almost overnight, and replaced the idealized free market system with a monopolistic one. Although many states passed antitrust laws, they proved to be ineffective against the magnitude of the trusts. In response to the need for national regulation of the vast businesses, in 1890 Congress passed the Sherman Antitrust Act, which declared illegal contracts, combinations, trusts, and conspiracies in restraint of "trade or commerce among the several states."

The Knight Case. However, the Supreme Court interpreted congressional power under the commerce clause more narrowly than Congress had perceived its power in enacting the Sherman Antitrust Act. In *United States v. E. C. Knight* (1895), the Supreme Court, reasoning that manufacturing was not part of interstate commerce, held that to construe

the Sherman Act to fall within the commerce power, the act could not prohibit combinations in businesses involved in the production or manufacturing of goods. In *E. C. Knight*, the government contended that the American Sugar Refining Company was a trust constituting a substantial restraint of interstate commerce. The company had gained control of more than 90 percent of the manufacturing of all refined sugar in the United States. The government moved to invalidate the contracts upon which the trust rested and requested an injunction restraining the defendants from any further violations of the act.

The Supreme Court affirmed a trial court decision dismissing the suit. In his opinion, Chief Justice Fuller distinguished between manufacturing and commerce. "Commerce succeeds to manufacture and is not a part of it." Manufacturing was part of the state's internal business, and Justice Fuller found that the power to protect citizens from the "burden of monopoly" had been left by the Constitution to the states. The Sherman Antitrust Act was directed only against combinations in interstate commerce and could not be construed as invalidating such combinations in production. The Court relied on precedents such as *Coe v. Errol* (1886), which held that goods collected for shipment but not yet delivered are subject to state but not federal taxation and *Kidd v. Pearson* (1888), which held that Iowa had the

Under Chief Justice Fuller, the Supreme Court often took a narrow view of the power of Congress under the Constitution's commerce clause, notably in **United States v. E.C. Knight,** *in which the Court dismissed a federal suit against the sugar monopoly.*

Still under Chief Justice Fuller, the 1897 Supreme Court began to apply the Sherman Antitrust Act, finding a rate-fixing combination of western railroads in violation of the act.

power to prohibit the manufacture of spirits sold entirely out of the state because such prohibition did not fall within the definition of interstate commerce. In *Kidd*, Justice Lamar's majority opinion made a distinction between manufacturing and commerce that was to supply the precedent for the *E. C. Knight* decision.

> No distinction is more popular to the common mind, or more clearly expressed in economic and political literature, than that between manufacturing and commerce. Manufacturing is transformation–the fashioning of raw materials into a change of form for use. The functions of commerce are different.

In a prescient comment, Justice Lamar added:

> If it be held that the term includes the regulation of all such manufactures as are intended to be the subject of commerical transactions in the future, it is impossible to deny that it would also include all productive industries that contemplate the same thing. The result would be that Congress would be invested, to the exclusion of the States, with the power to regulate, not only manufactures, but also agriculture, horticulture, stock raising, domestic fisheries, mining–in short, every branch of human industry.

In distinguishing between manufacturing and commerce, the *E. C. Knight* Court found that manufacturing had only an indirect effect on commerce. It rejected the federal government's argument that, however indirect, manufacturing ultimately had a substantial effect on interstate commerce. It drew a sharp distinction between "direct" and "indirect" effects upon commerce. Only trusts or monopolies having a direct effect on commerce were subject to federal regulation. "Contracts, combinations, or conspiracies to control domestic enterprise in manufacture, agriculture, mining, production in all its forms, or to raise or lower prices or wages, might unquestionably tend to restrain external as well as domestic trade; but the restraint would be an indirect result, however inevitable and whatever its extent."

Aftermath Of Knight. For almost a decade following the *E. C. Knight* case the Court retained the direct/indirect effects distinction but it did find constitutional applications of the Sherman Act. In *United States v. Trans-Missouri Freight Association* (1897), the Court held that an "association" formed by several western railroads to fix rates violated the act. In *Addyston Pipe and Steel Co. v. United States* (1899), the Court held that the act could apply to a conspiracy among iron pipe companies to divide sales territory and arrange for noncompetitive bidding. The Court distinguished *Addyston* from *Knight* because the *Addyston* agreement directly restrained the purchase, sale, or exchange of the pipe as well as its manufacture. Finally, in *Northern Securities Co. v. United States* (1904), the Court held that the act could be applied to break up joint control of competing railroads by a holding company that "directly or necessarily" operated in restraint of trade.

Northern Securities expanded the commerce power

under the direct effects test and reflected the Court's response to a new way of thinking about federal power. Theodore Roosevelt had campaigned with William McKinley as the "Trust Buster," and with McKinley's assassination, Roosevelt became president in 1901. He searched for potential Supreme Court appointees who would interpret the commerce power of the federal government more broadly. He appointed Oliver Wendell Holmes to the Court in 1902 and William R. Day in 1903.

Broadening the Commerce Definition. With the broadening of the definition of commerce covered under the Sherman Act in *Northern Securities*, other victories for the government followed. The most notable of these was *Swift & Co. v. United States* (1905), in which the Court formulated the "stream of commerce" doctrine. The government

After the election of President William McKinley in 1896, the Court gradually broadened its application of the Sherman Antitrust Act.

sought to enjoin a number of large meat packing houses from conspiring to manipulate and control the flow and price of livestock that were transported to slaughterhouses and then shipped out of state as meat. In speaking for the Court, Justice Holmes found that the purportedly local transaction affected interstate commerce. Holmes saw the yards as only an "interruption" in the "stream of commerce" because "commerce among the states is not a technical legal conception, but a practical one, drawn from the course of business." The stream of commerce provided a logical basis for a later decision that regulation of manufacturing was within the commerce power.

Just as Congress's power under the Sherman Act had been hotly disputed, congressional authority under the Interstate Commerce Act of 1887 also produced substantial litigation. The act had been passed in response to the vast expansion of railroads. Railroad practices that favored some parts of the nation over others and that often fixed rates oppressive to producers made attempts by the states to regulate them relatively ineffective. In response, the Interstate Commerce Act established the Interstate Commerce Commission (ICC) and authorized the commission to regulate railroad rates. After over a decade of dispute over Congress's power under the act, the Supreme Court upheld Congress's authority under the act and, more significantly, removed the limitations on the commerce power that had been established in *E. C. Knight*.

In the *Shreveport Rate Cases* (1914), the Court sustained the ICC's authority to regulate intrastate rail rates where the rates had a "close and substantial relation" to interstate commerce. The Houston, East & West Railway and its affiliates brought an action to have set aside an ICC order requiring the railroads to charge rates that did not discriminate against interstate freight by charging more for freight from points in Texas going east to Shreveport, Louisiana, than for intrastate freight covering the same distance from eastern to western Texas. The lower intrastate rates arose because the Texas Railroad Commission's fixed rates for Texas were lower than the ICC's standard rates. The railroads claimed that the interstate commerce power did not extend to the regulation of intrastate rates.

The Court upheld the validity of the commission's order, even when interpreted as invalidating a purely intrastate rate. Justice Hughes, in his opinion for the Court, cited *Gibbons v. Ogden* and recalled that the purpose of the commerce power is to ensure national commercial unity by preventing local impediments to interstate commercial traffic. The Court reasoned that in order to protect the freedom of interstate commercial intercourse, Congress's power "necessarily embraces the right to control interstate carriers in all matters having such a close and substantial relation to interstate traffic that the control is essential or appropriate to the security of that traffic . . . ." Thus, although preventing discrimination against interstate commerce meant federal

An activist "trust buster," President The-odore Roosevelt appointed Supreme Court justices, such as Oliver Wendell Holmes and William R. Day, who took a broader view of the Constitution's commerce clause.

control over wholly intrastate rates, Congress had the author-ity under the commerce clause to control those rates. The *Shreveport Rate Cases* appeared to abolish *E. C. Knight*'s distinction between direct and indirect effects on commerce by recognizing federal authority over activity that had a "substantial," even if indirect, effect on interstate commerce.

The Development Of A National "Police Power"

The Industrial Revolution produced social problems of a magnitude and type that the nation had never before faced. The resulting reform movements attempted to prevent indi-viduals from engaging in immoral or undesirable activities and to attack the conditions that created those problems. Many demanded federal legislation to address such prob-lems as crime, immorality, the white slave trade, and child labor. However, these were areas of social, not commercial, legislation, which, as constitutional history had established,

fell uniquely to the province of state, not federal, legislation. The broad commerce power established in *Gibbons* and later cases extended federal authority to legislate for com-mercial purposes, and the precedents were inadequate to uphold national authority to legislate to alleviate social evils.

Champion v. Ames. One exceptional early case, *Champion v. Ames* (1903), provided Congress with the authority to prohibit from shipment in interstate commerce morally objectionable items and signaled the beginning of congressional attempts to exercise a national police power. In *Champion v. Ames* the Court upheld an act of commerce that forbade the shipment of lottery tickets in interstate commerce. Justice Harlan, writing for the five-member majority, established that the plenary power to regulate com-merce under *Gibbons* included the power to prohibit items from interstate commerce. In response to the argument that the suppression of social evils was within the police power

Associate Justice John Marshall Harlan wrote the Court's opinion in **Champion** v. Ames, *which upheld the right of Congress to bar items from interstate commerce.*

reserved to the states by the 10th Amendment, Justice Harlan reasoned that just as the states could control such "evils" within their own borders, the federal government could control them among the several states. Harlan found that Congress was not interfering with the wholly internal affairs of a state. Congress was supplementing the police power of the states, not supplanting it.

The dissenting opinion, written by Chief Justice Fuller, focused on the purpose of the law. It argued that because the real purpose of the statute was to suppress lotteries and not to regulate interstate commerce, the power Congress was attempting to exercise was a police power belonging exclusively to the states under the 10th Amendment. Quoting *E. C. Knight*, the dissent maintained that the distinction between the federal commerce power and the state's police power is essential to preserving state autonomy within the federalist system. In addition, the majority's recognition of this form of national police power usurped state authority.

Champion v. Ames permitted Congress to enact several more statutes over the next 15 years under the commerce power that attempted to remedy social problems. Among the more important were the Pure Food and Drug Act (1906), the Meat Inspection Acts (1906, 1907), and the White Slave Traffic Act (1910). During this same period, however, all but two of the justices on the Court had retired and been replaced.

Restricting The Police Power. Elements of the minority view in *Ames* resurfaced in the majority opinion in *Hammer v. Dagenhart* (1918), which held the Child Labor Act of 1916 unconstitutional and halted the expansion of the federal commerce power.

The Child Labor Act prohibited shipment in interstate commerce of products from any mine or quarry in which children under sixteen had been employed or products from any factory, cannery, or like workshop where either children under fourteen were employed or children between fourteen and sixteen were employed for more than eight hours a day, six days a week. By a five to four majority the Court in *Hammer v. Dagenhart* invalidated the act as beyond the commerce power of Congress.

The Court, in an opinion by Justice Day, held that the power to regulate interstate commerce did not provide Congress with the power to forbid the interstate movement of commodities. The decision distinguished *Champion v. Ames* and similar cases by noting that in those cases the harmful character of the particular subjects was such that "the use of interstate transportation was necessary to the accomplishment of harmful results." Thus, the only way to regulate the interstate transportation was by "prohibiting the use of interstate facilities to effect the evil intended."

In contrasting these cases with *Hammer*, Justice Day looked to the purpose of the law and found that the "act in effect does not regulate transportation among the states, but aims to standardize the ages at which children may be employed in manufacturing and mining within the states." Drawing the familiar distinction between commerce and manufacturing, he stated that the purpose of the commerce clause was to regulate interstate commerce and "not to give it authority to control the states in their exercise of the police power over local trade and manufacture." Further, the authority of the federal government was "not intended to deny the local power always existing and carefully reserved to the states in the 10th Amendment to the Constitution." To the argument that this law would equalize the ability of states to compete for industry while still protecting children, Justice Day answered that the commerce clause was "not intended to give Congress a general authority to equalize such conditions." He concluded by saying that to sustain this statute "would sanction an invasion by the federal power of the control of a matter purely local in its character and over which no authority has been delegated to Congress in conferring the power to regulate commerce among the states."

In his dissent, Justice Holmes was joined by Justices Brandeis, McKenna, and Clarke. At the outset, Holmes conceded that as to methods of production the states should be free of "direct intermeddling" by Congress. However, he argued that *Champion v. Ames* and subsequent cases established clearly that Congress had the power to prohibit items from interstate commerce.

Thus, the statute in its "immediate operation" was

within the commerce power of Congress. The issue for the dissent was whether an otherwise constitutional act of Congress under the commerce power could be made unconstitutional because it indirectly interfered in matters of state authority. To Justice Holmes, the resolution of this issue was obvious: "I should have thought that the most conspicuous decisions of this Court had made it clear that the power to regulate commerce. . .could not be cut down or qualified by the fact that it might interfere with carrying out of the domestic policy of any state."

Hammer v. Dagenhart's restrictive view of the commerce power, which distinguished between manufacturing and commerce, placed the regulation of interstate commerce for social purposes out of the reach of the commerce power. This remained the law in the years leading up to the Depression. That law would ultimately prove inadequate to weather the approaching economic crisis.

New Deal Legislation And Decisions

The economic collapse of the 1930's led to sweeping economic and social legislation. The controversy over the constitutionality of this legislation caused upheaval on the Court and threatened President Roosevelt's New Deal. In 1933, President Roosevelt was elected amid economic disaster. Unemployment reached unprecedented heights, and total wages fell to below half of what they had been in pre-Depression years. Farm mortgage foreclosures, business failures, and consequent bank failures were rampant.

After Roosevelt's inauguration Congress passed a flurry

Designed to protect children from harsh and dangerous work such as mining, the Child Labor Act of 1916 was found unconstitutional in **Hammer v. Dagenhart.**

of new legislation that regulated economic life as never before. Among other measures, the government imposed regulations on wages, hours, and working conditions; instituted methods for refinancing farm and home mortgages; established social security and unemployment programs; and began intensified regulation of the banking and securities industries. However, the Supreme Court was not prepared to expand its view of the government's constitutional authority to enact such sweeping laws. In a series of controversial decisions, the Court invalidated much of the central New Deal legislation.

Schechter Poultry Case. In *Schechter Poultry Corp. v. United States* (1935) a unanimous Court invalidated the National Industrial Recovery Act of 1933 (NIRA). Heralded as one of the most important pieces of New Deal legislation, the act authorized the president to approve "codes of fair competition" developed by trade or industry associations that would proscribe unfair or wasteful trade practices and establish minimum wages, maximum hours, and collec-

Associate Justice Holmes dissented in **Hammer v. Dagenhart,** *arguing that the Court's ability to regulate interstate commerce had been established in* **Champion v. Ames.**

tive bargaining. The Schechter Poultry Corporation was charged with violating a poultry business code that established a maximum forty-hour week and a minimum fifty-cent per hour wage, prohibited child labor, set the minimum number of employees based on sales volume, and prohibited certain "unfair methods of competition." Schechter Poultry ran wholesale slaughterhouse markets that sold only within New York City. Ninety-six percent of the live poultry sold in New York City came from other states. Schechter successfully argued that the NIRA was an unconstitutional delegation of legislative power to the president and that it attempted to regulate intrastate transactions beyond the authority of Congress's commerce power.

In an opinion by Chief Justice Charles Evans Hughes, the Court noted that "extraordinary conditions do not create or enlarge constitutional power. . . .Such assertions of extraconstitutional authority were anticipated and precluded by the explicit terms of the Tenth Amendment." The Court responded to the argument that the poultry in *Schechter* was part of the "stream of commerce" and thus subject to Congress's power under *Swift & Co. v. United States.* The Court distinguished *Swift,* in which the slaughterhouses were a mere interruption of interstate commerce, from Schechter, in which the poultry reached a "permanent rest" in New York City. Thus the poultry in question were not part of interstate commerce, and the federal government had acted beyond its commerce power. Further, despite its citation of the *Shreveport Rate Cases,* the Court held that "In determining how far the federal government may go in controlling intrastate transactions on the ground that they 'affect' interstate commerce, there is a necessary and well-established distinction between direct and indirect effects." The Court found that the effect the wages and hours of Schechter poultry workers might ultimately have on the price and quality of poultry in interstate commerce was an indirect effect that did not bring Schechter within Congress's commerce power. Chief Justice Hughes concluded, "[if] the commerce clause were construed to reach all enterprises and transactions which could be said to have an indirect effect upon interstate commerce, the federal authority would embrace practically all the activities of the people and the authority of the state over its domestic concerns would exist only by sufferance of the federal government." Thus, under *Schechter* the direct/indirect effects test was revived and the stream of commerce test was limited.

Following *Schechter,* the businesses that had objected to the NIRA flooded the federal courts seeking injunctions. Over 1,600 injunctions were filed against the act and other New Deal legislation. Under the terms of the NIRA, Congress had to renew its authority to issue codes and the rollover date was set for three weeks after the *Schechter* decision. As a direct result of *Schechter,* the code structure collapsed. Roosevelt told the press that America was "back to the horse and buggy days" and implied that he would be

President Franklin Roosevelt enjoyed popular and Congressional support for his New Deal programs, but the Supreme Court invalidated many of them during the mid-1930s.

pleased to accept the challenge of constitutional reform that the Court had issued. *Schechter* made it clear that the direct effects test would be applied to New Deal legislation. The case also established that commodities that have "come to rest" are no longer part of the stream of commerce subject to congressional authority.

Court Action Against Prices And Labor Practices. *Carter v. Carter Coal Co.* (1936) took both these holdings a step further. In *Carter*, the Court invalidated the Bituminous Coal Conservation Act of 1935 (commonly called the Guffey Coal Act), which imposed an excise tax of 15 percent on the sale of bituminous coal. If producers agreed to comply with a code establishing minimum prices for mines by their geographical areas and minimum wages and maximum hours for workers in the mines, then they could obtain a 90 percent reduction of the tax. In addition, the act authorized the President to appoint a labor board that would enforce

collective bargaining between mine workers and their employers. Section 1 of the act indicated that Congress perceived its authority as grounded in the commerce clause: "the production and distribution by producers of such coal bear upon and directly affect interstate commerce, and render regulation of production and distribution imperative for the protection of such commerce. . . ."

James Carter, the president of Carter Coal Company, attempted to enjoin the company from complying with the act in a stockholder's suit, a commonly-used device in attacking such legislation. The trial court upheld the act but the Supreme Court reversed and, by a six to three vote, held the act unconstitutional.

In the majority opinion, Sutherland relied on *E. C. Knight* and *Schechter*. He held that, because coal production was not within the stream of commerce and because coal production had only an indirect effect on interstate

The Court held the Agricultural Adjustment Act unconstitutional in 1936, by which time the press already portrayed the Court as old men resisting progressive legislation.

commerce, the Guffey Coal Act was not within Congress's authority under the commerce clause. He restated the distinction between production and commerce, noting that "the effect of the labor provisions of the act. . .primarily falls upon production and not upon commerce." Because "production is a purely local activity," it does not have a direct effect on interstate commerce. Even though every item in interstate commerce may have had a local origin and without such local production commerce would "practically disappear," the "question is not–What is the *extent* of the. . . effect produced upon interstate commerce?, but–what is the *relation* between the activity or condition and the effect?" The Court found only an indirect relation between coal production and interstate commerce because production was not within the stream of commerce. Just as the poultry in *Schechter* had "come to rest" and were no longer part of the stream of commerce, the coal in *Carter* had not yet entered

the stream of commerce and was also not within Congress's power to regulate.

In addition to invalidating the Guffey Coal Act and the NIRA, the Supreme Court also invalidated other key New Deal legislation, including the Agriculture Adjustment Act of 1933, which was intended to raise farm prices and reduce crop surplus, and the Railroad Retirement Act of 1934, which established a retirement and pension system for railroad employees. Amid the controversy surrounding the decisions, some charged that the Court had not ruled on the constitutional issues presented by the New Deal legislation but on the basis of its own economic philosophy.

Court Packing And Its Aftermath. Infuriated by the judicial blows to the New Deal, in February 1937 President Roosevelt proposed legislation to Congress to "reorganize the judicial branch." More commonly known as Roosevelt's "court-packing plan," the proposal would have required that wherever a federal judge serving ten years or more failed to retire within six months after his seventieth birthday, the president might appoint an additional judge to the court on which he served. As six of the justices on the Supreme Court were over the age of seventy, the plan would have permitted Roosevelt the number of new appointments necessary to produce a majority sympathetic to the New Deal. The message accompanying the President's proposal pointed out that a "lowered mental or physical vigor leads men to avoid an examination of complicated and changed conditions. Little by little, new facts become blurred through old glasses fitted, as it were, for the needs of another generation; older men, assuming the scene is the same as it was in the past, cease to . . . inquire into the present or the future."

As it became obvious that the President's purpose was to change the attitude on the Supreme Court, hostility toward the plan grew, and the Senate Judiciary Committee killed the bill. Shortly thereafter, the Court reversed its long-standing opposition to New Deal legislation. Some speculate that, in reaction to the plan, Justices Hughes and Roberts shifted their position so as to form a majority that would uphold the New Deal legislation. Further, Roosevelt's plan may have contributed to the decisions of conservative Justices Van Devanter and Sutherland to retire in 1937 and 1938. In addition to the court-packing plan, another significant factor in the Court's shift may have been Congress's passage of the retirement plan for justices. From 1937 to 1941, President Roosevelt appointed seven members of the Court, and there was a substantial shift in the judicial philosophy of the Court.

The immediate and dramatic change on the Court in 1937 was evidenced by *National Labor Relations Board v. Jones & Laughlin Steel Corp.* (1937), in which the Court gave the New Deal a major victory. In this case, the National Labor Relations Board (NLRB), established by the National Labor Relations Act of 1935, had found that Jones & Laughlin Steel committed unfair labor practices in dismissing employees in an iron and steel manufacturing plant for union-organizing activities. The NLRB ordered reinstatement as well as other relief.

Jones & Laughlin Steel relied on *Schechter* and *Carter* and argued that the NLRB's order was beyond the range of the federal commerce power because the employees in question were in manufacturing, which was not a part of interstate commerce. Jones & Laughlin Steel was one of the largest steel companies in the nation and was "vertically integrated," owning everything from the mines to the facilities that distributed their products. The government argued that labor strife in manufacturing would disrupt the flow of commerce so that even under present doctrine the NLRB's order was within the commerce power. It also argued that under the *Shreveport Rate Cases* the disruption caused by labor strife would have such a substantial effect on interstate commerce that Congress had the power to protect it.

By 1937, the Supreme Court already showed the effects of President Roosevelt's court-packing plan. Decisions became more favorable to New Deal programs and Hugo Black (**rear, far right**) *replaced the conservative Willis Van Devanter.*

By 1941, Roosevelt's appointments had remade the Court, which was decidedly more sympathetic to the President's aims than the "nine old men" of the mid-1930s.

Justice Hughes, writing for a five to four majority, cast aside the *Carter* and *Schechter* precedents and adopted the premise of the *Shreveport Rate Cases* that congressional authority under the commerce clause depends on the degree to which an activity affects interstate commerce, not on whether the relationship was "direct" or "indirect." Hughes distinguished this case from *Schechter*, where the tie between poultry workers and interstate commerce was too remote, and *Carter*, where the Guffey Coal Act's invalidity could have rested entirely on the unconstitutional delegation of federal power. Finding that labor disputes in the steel industry could have far-reaching consequences to interstate commerce, the Court held that Congress had the power to protect interstate commerce by regulating labor relations in steel manufacturing plants.

Thus, the Court laid to rest the "direct effects" test and adopted the "close and substantial relationship" test enunciated in the *Shreveport Rate Cases*. The extent of an activity's effect on interstate commerce would henceforth be the primary issue in determining Congress's power under the commerce clause.

The Commerce Power Expanded

The effect of the Jones & Laughlin Steel decision was electrifying. It had been the only decision announced that day. For the second time in two weeks the Court had upheld New Deal legislation, reversing itself on decisions held just one year earlier. (The first had been *West Coast Hotel Co. v. Parrish*, in which the Chief Justice held that a Washington state statute setting a minimum wage for women was within the police powers of the state and did not violate the due process clause.) It seemed clear that the Court had for one reason or another decided to expand the scope of the commerce power.

The *Jones & Laughlin* ruling rekindled the "affecting commerce" rationale. This view justified the federal regulation of intrastate activities due to their effect on interstate commerce. This rationale continued to dominate cases decided under the commerce power. During the next few years, the Court upheld laws that regulated employment relationships and single state production activities.

Effects On Small Companies. For example, in *NLRB v. Fainblatt* (1939), the Court broadened the federal commerce power to encompass a small production enterprise. In *Fainblatt*, a small-scale garment processor challenged the constitutionality of the National Labor Relations Act. The Court upheld the application of the act to this manufacturer, even though he sold his entire output within one state. The company regulated in *Jones & Laughlin* contrasts greatly with this producer. The Jones & Laughlin company was a vertically integrated operation that was active in many states. Its effect on interstate commerce was obvious. The results of *Fainblatt* and its companion cases indicate that it was no longer necessary to demonstrate a stream of commerce or a large volume of business to justify federal regulation under the commerce power.

The Court elaborated on the "affecting commerce" rationale in *Wickard v. Filburn* (1942), in which it explicitly recognized a plenary commerce power based on economic theory. A unanimous Court held that particular intrastate activities, conducted on a small scale, could be federally regulated if they might affect interstate commerce when combined with similar small-scale operations.

In *Wickard*, the Court found that a marketing quota applied to a wheat farmer, even though most of his small crop was consumed on his farm. This lone farmer's activities would not noticeably affect interstate affairs. The Court easily found that this farmer could be regulated because, if many farmers followed his example and raised wheat mainly for home consumption, they would affect the flow of interstate commerce. This trend would affect both the supply of wheat for interstate commerce and the demand for the product, since these two variables affect the price of wheat on the national market. The Court had little difficulty in reaching the individual farmer with such regulation because the marketing quotas at issue were designed to control wheat prices. In the *Wickard* decision, the Court returned to the broad view of the federal commerce power that had existed for most of this country's history.

Another expansive interpretation of the commerce power is found in *United States v. Darby* (1941). The Court emphasized that economic impact on the national market justified the exercise of the commerce power. It deferred to Congress to prescribe the conditions under which products destined for multistate transactions were produced. The Fair Labor Standards Act of 1936 regulated hours, wages, and other working conditions, such as child labor. Darby, a Georgia manufacturer, was indicted for violating the act and moved to quash the indictment on the grounds of unconstitutionality. The district court sustained Darby because it found that the act controlled local production and was therefore not within the scope of the commerce power. The government moved directly to the Supreme Court. Wages in the Southern lumber industry varied from ten to twenty-seven cents per hour; the average annual wage was approximately $389. Justice Stone, speaking for a unanimous Court, sustained the government and the act, after a careful examination of the facts and issues before it.

According to Justice Stone, the intent of the act was clear: to exclude goods produced for interstate commerce and to prevent their production "under conditions detrimental to the maintenance of the minimum standards of living necessary for health and general well-being." The use of the commerce power in this context would prevent the "spreading and perpetuating of substandard labor conditions among the workers of the several states." The decision held that the powers of the federal government over interstate commerce did not differ "in extent or character" from those retained by the states over intrastate commerce. The Court declared that *Hammer v. Dagenhart* had been a departure from established principles and was overruled. Citing *Shreveport*, the Court re-emphasized that the regulation of intrastate transactions is necessary to control interstate commerce effectively, because both types of activity are closely linked.

In addition to the "affecting commerce" rationale applied in *Wickard*, the Court used a "commerce-prohibiting" analysis to regulate the intrastate operation in *Darby*. The regulatory scheme included a ban on interstate shipments if the production standards were not met. The Court sustained the wage and hour regulations of production activities as "means reasonably adapted to the attainment of the permitted end" of "excluding from interstate commerce all goods produced" under nonconforming conditions. Thus, this means-end justification was sufficient to uphold the regulation, independent of the effect that the intrastate activities might have on interstate commerce.

The 10th Amendment. The commerce power has retained its broad scope since the early 1940's. However, this expansive power is not unrestricted. The commerce power is limited by the Bill of Rights and by other fundamental constitutional guarantees, as are all federal powers. However, the Court did not believe that the 10th Amendment contained a guarantee specific enough to restrict the

Chief Justice Stone wrote the Court's opinion in 1941 in **United States v. Darby**, *which took an expansive view of the commerce clause and overruled* **Hammer v. Dagenhart.**

commerce power. The amendment reads as follows: "The powers not delegated to the United States by the Constitution, nor prohibited by it to the States, are reserved to the States respectively, or to the people." The language of the amendment vaguely suggests that it may in fact place some checks on federal power. However, the Court could find no neutral principle embodied in the 10th Amendment that would support judicial power to restrict the broad scope of the commerce clause.

This theoretical foundation for the judicial hesitation to enforce the amendment appeared unassailable during this forty-year period. In 1976, however, the 10th Amendment was rejuvenated as the Court declared it a specific check upon Congress's power to regulate the operation of state and local governments.

Until 1968, the Court had not yet considered the application of federal regulation to the employees of state governmental agencies although it had already upheld federal statutes that regulated the employees of state-owned railroads. In *Maryland v. Wirtz* (1968), the Court sustained the application of federal minimum-wage laws to employees of state institutions, such as schools and hospitals. There was no question that the working conditions of laborers affected interstate commerce and therefore fell within Congress's power. The debate in the Court focused on the possibility that an exemption for state and local employment practices may have been created by the Constitution. A majority of the justices held that no such exemption existed. The Congress could act within its enumerated powers even if, in so doing, it overrode important state interests.

The Usery Decision. Eight years later, the Court overruled the *Wirtz* decision. In *National League of Cities v. Usery* (1976), the Court held that the minimum wage and overtime pay provisions of the Fair Labor Standards Act (FLSA) could not be applied to state government employees. It dismissed as "wrong" all earlier statements that disallowed the states this exemption from the federal commerce power. However, it did not disturb the modern commerce clause scope in any other respect.

The Court accomplished this result by finding that the federal commerce power did indeed reach the activities of such enterprises. The Court emphasized that the wages and hours of state employees affected interstate commerce. However, it then reasoned that the 10th Amendment invalidated the application of this power to the employees of state and local governments.

Significantly, the five to four decision denied that the 10th Amendment would function to reserve areas of commerce for state regulation. The federal commerce power extended to the activities of nongovernmental entities and employees and was not restricted by the 10th Amendment. Congress could still regulate activities of local importance; they were still subject to federal sovereignty.

Additionally, the decision noted that the exemption carved out by the 10th Amendment extended only to purely government activities, to the operation of "states *qua* states." It implied that the federal commerce power over state-owned businesses in the private sector remained undisturbed. In order to come within the 10th Amendment exemption, the activity not only had to relate to the state's sovereign existence but also had to impair the essential activities of the state. As Justice Rehnquist stated:

> [the] dispositive factor is that Congress has attempted to exercise its Commerce Clause authority to prescribe minimum wages and maximum hours to be paid by the States in their capacities as sovereign governments...
>
> [I]nsofar as the challenged amendments operate to directly displace the States' freedom to structure integral operations in areas of traditional governmental functions, they are not within the authority granted Congress. . .

Subsequent decisions have clarified the 10th Amendment exemption to the federal commerce clause as it was stated in *Usery*, although it remains a narrow obstacle to federal regulation. In *Hodel v. Virginia Surface Mining and Reclamation Association* (1981), the Court upheld a federal statute that controlled surface mining and replaced state control over the mining conditions. The federal act at issue empowered the Department of the Interior to set standards for surface coal mining within each state. Once such standards were established, the states could assume control over mining operations if they adopted the regulations approved by the secretary of the Interior. This federal action effectively removed an element of state sovereignty by taking over the regulation of an activity within states' jurisdiction.

However, the Court ruled that this type of federal infringement of state sovereignty was not prohibited by the 10th Amendment. The Court applied the previously established standard for compatibility with the commerce clause. When the Congress has determined that an activity affects interstate commerce, the judiciary needs only inquire as to whether the finding is rational.

The majority opinion held that three requirements must be met for judicial invalidation of congressional commerce-power legislation. First, the federal statute must regulate "States as States." Second, the statute must regulate "matters that are indisputably attributes of state sovereignty." Third, the regulation must impair the state's ability "to structure integral operations in areas of traditional functions."

In *Hodel*, the regulated activity did not meet these criteria and therefore did not require judicial scrutiny under the 10th Amendment. Legislation that regulated nongovernmental enterprises, such as this, needed only to be tested under the rational basis test used in previous commerce decisions. As a result of this decision, the 10th Amendment remains a check on the federal commerce power; however, it will be employed in those few situations that meet all three parts of the test. For example, in *Equal Employment*

Opportunity Commission v. Wyoming (1983), the Court upheld federal regulation of state game wardens. In applying the *Usery* criteria, the Court found that providing game wardens was not an "essential state function" and that regulation of this activity did not merit judicial scrutiny under the 10th Amendment.

Usery Reversed. However, the standards enunciated in *National League of Cities* were short-lived. In *Garcia v. San Antonio Metropolitan Transit Authority (SAMTA)* (1985), the Court rejected the *Usery* definition of a traditional governmental function when it upheld the application of the Fair Labor Standards Act (FLSA) to mass transit.

SAMTA is a public mass transit authority that provides most of the transportation in the metropolitan area of San Antonio, Texas. It received a substantial amount of federal funding under the Urban Mass Transportation Act of 1964. In 1979, the Department of Labor issued an opinion that SAMTA was not immune from the FLSA under the *Usery* decision. SAMTA filed for declaratory relief in federal district court, which exempted SAMTA from the FLSA obligations. It held that the operation of a mass transit system is a traditional governmental function and therefore, under *National League of Cities v. Usery*, is beyond the reach of the FLSA.

Justice Blackmun, the author of the five-to-four majority opinion, held that Congress violated no limit on its commerce power when it afforded SAMTA employees the protection of the FLSA wage and hour provisions. He rejected the *Usery* standards of state immunity from federal regulations. The unworkability of the definition of a traditional governmental function and the inconsistency with which it has been applied persuaded the Court to overrule *National League of Cities v. Usery*.

The Court reasoned that the sovereign definition of states can be protected without the *Usery* rule through the political process. States' interests "as States" are adequately preserved and represented in Congress. In SAMTA's case, Congress has been financially generous and cannot be said to have imposed a financial burden by making it comply with the FLSA.

Thus, *Garcia* has effectively expanded Congress's power to regulate state activity under the commerce clause. Whether the 10th Amendment poses a genuine obstacle to this federal power and, if so, what form this obstacle will take remains to be seen.

The Commerce Power And Civil Rights

After extraordinary pressure, coming in part from the executive branch, Congress in 1964 passed a Civil Rights Act, invoking the commerce power with the objective of banning racial discrimination in public accommodations. Title II of that act provided for injunctive relief against the denial of or coercive interference with the rights of any person attempting to use a public accommodation. The act defined those as (1) any inn, hotel, or motel, or other establishment providing lodging to transient guests; (2) any restaurant, cafeteria, lunch counter, soda fountain, or other facility engaged in selling food for consumption on the premises; (3) any motion picture house, theater, concert hall, sports arena, or stadium; and (4) any establishment that is physically located in any of the above.

Although hotels and inns affect interstate commerce by the very nature of the services, the act then stated that the other listed establishments affected interstate commerce if a "substantial portion" of travelers, food sold, or services provided "moves in commerce" between the several states. "Bona fide private clubs" were exempted from the act except to the extent that those facilities were used by patrons traveling interstate. The reliance of Congress on the commerce power to pass legislation with a non-economic purpose gave rise to a new strand of judicial analysis.

Consideration of the 1964 act produced lengthy debates on the floors of both houses of Congress. In particular, they discussed the constitutional issues triggered by this piece of proposed legislation. When the administration bill was originally sent to Congress, it relied almost totally on the commerce clause as its basis in the Constitution. The bill referred to the equal protection clause of the 14th Amendment almost as an afterthought. The Congress's findings dealt almost entirely with the commerce clause emphases of the civil rights bill. Congress concluded that the "burdens on and obstructions to commerce which are described above can best be removed by invoking the powers of Congress under the 14th Amendment and the commerce clause of the Constitution."

Title II of the Civil Rights Act of 1964 imposed penalties on anyone who deprived another of equal enjoyment of public accommodation on the basis of race, color, religion, or national origin. As a result of its basis in the commerce clause, the act covered a broad spectrum of public establishments. The act reached all but the smallest roominghouses, restaurants, and other retail enterprises that used products that had moved in or otherwise affected interstate commerce.

Title II Upheld. The Supreme Court upheld Title II's application to hotels in *Heart of Atlanta Motel v. United States* (1964). The owner of a motel brought a declaratory judgment action, challenging the constitutionality of Title II. A three-judge court sustained the act and enjoined its further violation by the motel. An appeal was taken to the Supreme Court, which unanimously affirmed the act's constitutionality.

Justice Clark delivered the opinion of the Court. First, the "determinative test of the exercise of power. . .is simply whether the activity sought to be regulated is 'commerce which concerns more than one state' and has a real and substantial relation to the national interest." Noting that the power of Congress to regulate interstate travel was established as early as 1849, he added that it was irrelevant whether the purpose of the travel was commercial. Next, Clark moved to the basis for congressional action, finding that discrimination against black travelers created "a qualitative as well as quantitative effect on interstate travel" and that the evidence was "overwhelming" that there was discrimination based on race.

The Heart of Atlanta Motel was located near the intersection of two major interstate highways. It maintained over fifty billboards and highway signs "soliciting patronage," accepted convention trade from outside the state of Georgia, and served predominantly an out-of-state clientele. The motel refused to rent to blacks and stated that it had no intention of doing so in the future. After the first issue before the Court, the constitutionality of Title II, was settled in favor of the act, the only remaining question was whether the act applied to the motel. The Court found that a motel that concededly served interstate commerce was reached by

the act. Therefore, the motel was ordered to stop its discriminatory practices.

Extending Title II. In *Katzenbach v. McClung* (1964), the Court upheld Title II's application to a restaurant that served no interstate travelers. The restaurant, Ollie's Barbeque, was a family-owned restaurant in Birmingham, Alabama, and was located over a mile away from an interstate highway or major line of transportation. The restaurant noted that it was a small business, not a major motel, and that most of its business was local. Although it served no interstate travelers, the meat it served was purchased from a supplier who acquired it from out-of-state sources. The opinion found that this fact brought the restaurant under the act and sustained the exercise of the commerce clause over it.

Justice Clark again delivered the opinion of the Court. He reasoned that the commerce power "extends to activities of retail establishments, including restaurants, which directly or indirectly burden or obstruct interstate commerce." The

Associate Justice Tom Clark wrote the Court's opinion in **Heart Atlanta Motel,** *a case that used the powers of the commerce clause to halt racially discriminatory practices.*

opinion also noted that no congressional testimony established a connection between discrimination in such an establishment and interstate commerce. However, a search for such information would not conform to the Court's role in examining commerce power legislation. There was no dispute with the rationality of the theory that restricting the availability of food and public accommodation to people of minority races had an inhibitive effect on their ability to travel interstate. The Court could inquire no further into Congress's objectives because the question was simply whether Congress had a rational basis for finding a regulatory plan necessary to protect commerce.

It did not matter that Ollie's Barbeque was a small business. The Court reiterated the *Wickard* principle that Congress could regulate seemingly trivial activities if they contributed to the flow of commerce.

Use Of The Commerce Power. The commerce power has been used by the federal government as a means to expand its authority into areas not touched by the states or into areas in which states have refused to legislate. In the civil rights cases, it used the commerce power as a tool for creating a national policy on the issue of equal rights and equal access. The scope of the commerce power has been broadened as a source of national authority to regulate local activities. When faced with a constitutional challenge to legislation premised on the commerce power, the Court's only inquiry is whether any rational basis exists for Congress's action. As a result of the Court's decisions, Congress has almost unlimited commerce clause power.

State Regulation And The National Economy

Just as restrictions have been placed on national powers by local concerns, there are limitations on state powers that emanate from national concerns. However, the essential issue remains the same: the origins and the sufficiency of constitutional restrictions. Do these constraints arise from the text of the Constitution, from history, or from inferences based upon the structure of the Constitution? There is no explicit constitutional provision that limits state legislation. Therefore, the recurrent problem is the adequacy of the interpretation and implementation of constitutional values. The grant of enumerated powers to the federal government and the exercise of these powers effectively curtail state authority.

The limitations on state legislation that originate in the national commerce power arise in two types of situations, which often overlap. In the first situation, Congress has been silent in that it has not taken any action that indicates its policy regarding a specific subject matter. In this case, the barrier to state authority lies in the "dormant" commerce clause, on the unexercised power itself. The second type of situation arises when Congress has acted pursuant to the commerce power and has demonstrated its policy on a given topic. The challenge to state action rests on "supreme" national legislation, which preempts inconsistent state authority by virtue of the supremacy clause of Article VI, as well as through the exercise of the federal commerce power.

Source And Scope Of The Commerce Power. The constitutional framers clearly intended to enable a national market to develop. Under the Articles of Confederation, markets had been chaotic and the duties imposed by different states had created a totally balkanized economy. In the Constitution, the framers wanted to avoid past mistakes and so must have meant to prohibit the states from entertaining divisive actions. As situations arose concerning the legislation of the several states, the Court developed a pattern of certain implied restrictions, delineating areas beyond which the states could not move and thereby touching on the conduct of interstate commerce.

The Search For Judicial Standards

In *Gibbons v. Ogden* (1824), Chief Justice Marshall examined the scope of both federal and state powers under the commerce clause. In this case, the state of New York had granted a steamboat monopoly to a private company, which transferred this monopoly to Ogden. When Gibbons began a competing steamboat service, Ogden sued Gibbons for encroachment on the monopoly. Gibbons's defense was that the state, by granting the monopoly to Ogden, had violated the commerce clause.

The opinion did not define the scope of state powers under the commerce clause. Instead, it declared the monopoly invalid because it conflicted with a valid federal statute that governed the licensing of ships engaging in coastal trade. The state law was invalid because it was inconsistent with the supreme law of the land.

Marshall interpreted the federal commerce power quite broadly. He defined commerce as "intercourse" and recognized that it extended into every state. Congress was empowered to regulate commerce concerning more than one state wherever it existed. Therefore, Congress could exercise its commerce clause authority even within a state's borders.

Marshall would not place any limits on the federal commerce power other than those prescribed in the Constitution. However, he did state that some "internal" commerce fell within a state's police power and would be beyond Congress's reach. Notwithstanding this statement, Marshall did not intend to restrict Congress's power in order to preserve the powers of individual states. He characterized Congress's commerce power as the possession of unqualified authority by a supreme sovereign. He denied that the states' very existence effectively restricted such authority.

However, five years later, the Court upheld a Delaware law that authorized construction of a dam across a creek. Although this dam blocked the passage of ships, including those holding federal licenses, the Court found the statute consistent with the federal commerce clause.

In *Willson v. Black Bird Creek Marsh Co.* (1829) Chief Justice Marshall stated that he believed that the statute was within the state's police power. The states retained this internal authority even after the ratification of the federal commerce clause because it was a valid means of protecting the public welfare. Marshall also found that Congress did not intend to exercise its authority over such creeks. Therefore, the state statute did not conflict with the federal commerce power. However, Marshall did not indicate that he would restrict Congress's commerce powers to act on this matter even though it was within a state's internal police powers.

Balancing Interpretations. The conflict between the supremacy of the federal commerce power and the states' local police powers continued to rage for several decades. In subsequent cases, the Court seemed to rely on one or some combination of the two views. These conflicts within the Court were somewhat reconciled in *Cooley v. Board of Wardens* (1851), which formulated the doctrine of "selective exclusiveness." This doctrine constituted a more restrained view of state authority than the one previously espoused by the Court. The case arose from an 1803 Pennsylvania statute that required vessels entering or leaving the port of Philadelphia to accept local pilots for pilotage through the Delaware River. Cooley, the consignee of two vessels that sailed from Philadelphia to New York without taking on the local pilot, was brought before the state courts. In defense, Cooley replied that the statute was in direct violation of the congressional power to regulate interstate commerce.

Benjamin Curtis, just recently appointed an associate justice by President Fillmore, delivered the opinion of the Court. He affirmed the Pennsylvania law that required the retainer of a local pilot. The Court sustained this statute on the basis of a distinction between those subjects of commerce that necessitate a uniform national law and those that allow for diversity of treatment to fill local needs. The opinion explicitly rejected both extreme interpretations of the commerce clause. The Congress's commerce powers were not exclusive nor could state regulation in the absence of federal action go unchecked.

According to the *Cooley* doctrine, the nature of the subject to be regulated determines the validity of the challenged regulation. If the subject requires a uniform national policy, then Congress's power is exclusive. However, concurrent state regulation is authorized if the subject matter involves a particularly local concern even though it is within the Congress's commerce powers.

The search for a reasoned and reasonable approach to the question of state authority in regulation lay dormant for

The decision of the 1890 Court, headed by Chief Justice Fuller (front, center), *in* **Minnesota v. Barber** *set the style for subsequent decisions in regulating trade and transportation.*

several decades, overshadowed by the crises of the Civil War era. The issue arose again in the late 1880's with the attempts of states to regulate railroads, the new corporations, production, and trade. A number of cases reached the courts in the health inspection and quarantine fields as well.

Inspection And Quarantine Cases. In one of these, *Hannibal & St. Joseph Railway Co. v. Husen* (1877), the question was the validity of a Missouri statute that provided that no Texan, Mexican, or Indian cattle should be transported into Missouri between March 1 and November 1 of any given year. The rationale for the act was a cattle disease known as Texas or Mexican fever. The Court invalidated the statute on the grounds that it was not a legitimate inspection or quarantine law and was thus an unwarranted interference with interstate commerce. At the same time the Court upheld the states' authority to pass such proper legislation.

In *Minnesota v. Barber* (1890) a state statute requiring that meat be inspected within twenty-four hours before slaughter was held to be an improper restriction of interstate commerce because, in order to have meat inspected twenty-four hours before slaughter, it seemed necessary that the meat be slaughtered in that state. Since the law prevented the importation of pre-slaughtered meat, it restricted trade and was thus unconstitutional.

The issues and the arguments set forth in these cases laid the basis for future court decisions in the areas of transportation, regulation of incoming trade, and environmental protection. The Court was often faced with the problem of balancing the interference with interstate commerce with the exercise of the legitimate police power of the state. Often the decisions turned on the nature of the specific case before the Court rather than on the issue of the particular state law. What became clear was that a state could not predict with certainty whether its statute would be found constitutional by the Court.

State Regulation Of Transportation

During the 19th century the Court sought to identify the situations in which the commerce clause precluded state regulation of the subjects of interstate commerce. With the creation of the Interstate Commerce Commission in 1887, the federal government assumed responsibility for many aspects of railroad travel. In 1893 the Federal Safety Appliance Act was adopted, which covered some aspects of safety. Not until 1935 did Congress adopt the Federal Motor Carrier Act. Since the states also had extensive railroad regulations, the Court had many opportunities to examine the limits of state power over business matters connected to interstate commerce.

During this same period, the Court moved from a deferential stance regarding the authority of the states to a more activist approach as it moved from a "means and ends" test to one of actually balancing the factors of each

situation as those factors came before the Court in individual cases. Thus, the extent of the impact upon interstate commerce, the burden on such commerce, and the rules and regulations of the various states came under scrutiny.

An early example of the deferential approach was the decision in the *Minnesota Rate Cases* (1913). The Minnesota Warehouse Commission issued an order fixing intrastate railroad rates; these were conceded to affect interstate rates by both the commission and the railroads. The Court upheld the validity of the regulation on the grounds that this particular area was one in which the federal government had not yet acted. Therefore, the option to act was left to the state. Chief Justice Hughes relied on the *Cooley* rationale for this decision.

In *Port of Richmond and Bergen Point Ferry Co. v. Board of Chosen Freeholders* (1914), the Court again upheld a locally-based regulation that could be said to affect interstate commerce on the grounds that Congress had not yet acted on this particular subject. However, in this decision, the Court also laid the groundwork for moving in more activist directions. Although one could claim that "the mere fact that interstate transportation is involved is sufficient to defeat the local regulation of rates. . .this would not be deemed a sufficient ground for invalidating the local action without considering the nature of the regulation and the special subject to which it relates." Again, the seeds of future change were planted.

Permissible State Regulation. In subsequent decisions, the Court continued to recognize the states' concurrent power to regulate commerce. Congress's exclusive commerce powers were well entrenched, but the question regarding the extent of permissible state regulation remained. The Court was unsuccessful in its attempts to formulate predictable standards of permitted and invalid state regulation.

However, one principle consistently arose in the Court's reasoning: a legitimate exercise of state regulatory power that burdened interstate commerce would not stand unless the extent of that burden was outweighed by a valid state objective. It was imperative that the local objective be unreachable by a less burdensome alternative. The Court was willing to defer to the judgment of state governments if those burdened by the regulation were represented by that government. For example, a state regulation that treats local residents and nonresidents equally is more likely to be sustained than one that favors local citizens and burdens noncitizens. While discrimination against interstate commerce was an important factor, it did not solve the Court's problem in formulating a consistent standard.

In the midst of the Court's dilemma, noted law professor Noel T. Dowling published an article in the *Virginia Law Review* that provided the Court with a practical solution. In "Interstate Commerce and State Power" (1940), Dowling described a structure that presumed congressional disapproval of any state regulation that unreasonably interfered with national interests. This state action would fail unless Congress rebutted this negative presumption. However, if state regulation did not interfere with national concerns, it would remain until superseded by congressional action.

The basis for this theory is that Congress's will is controlling. The Court's function is to weigh the local benefits of the challenged state statute against the competing national interests in light of Congress's power under the dormant commerce clause. If the Court sustains the state law as not burdening interstate commerce, no congressional action is necessary. If Congress disagrees with the state regulation, it may terminate its silence and legislate its will under the commerce clause.

Applying The Balancing Test. An analytical pattern emerged in the Court decisions of balancing the regulation against its effect on interstate commerce. In *Buck v. Kuykendall* (1925), for instance, the Court invalidated a Washington statute after an analysis of its effect on carriers on the Pacific Highway, which carried interstate traffic exclusively. On the other hand, in *Bradley v. Public Utilities Commission* (1933), the Court affirmed the right of the state of Ohio to refuse a license to a common carrier to use a particular state highway as a valid exercise of its police power. It denied the carrier's contention that such refusal precluded him from operating interstate. With the passage of the Federal Motor Carrier Act in 1935, the states were more restricted in their right to regulate transportation within their states. Such rights, however, were not totally eroded.

In *South Carolina State Highway Department v. Barnwell Bros.* (1938), the Court upheld a South Carolina statute prohibiting the use on state highways of motor trucks and "semi-trailer" trucks whose width exceeded ninety inches and whose weight including load exceeded 20,000 pounds. The district court enjoined the enforcement of the weight provision after hearing evidence that indicated, among other factors, that (1) 85 to 90 percent of the trucks used in interstate traffic were ninety-six inches in width; (2) only four other states prescribed weight limits as low as 20,000 pounds; and that (3) the critical issue for highway maintenance was not weight but the distribution of the weight among the axles.

The Court again, as in the past, stated its principles of decision-making and included the factual evidence as part of a "balancing test" without specifically stating that it was doing so. There was no question, said the Court, that there was, indeed, a burden on interstate commerce, "But so long as the state action does not discriminate, the burden is one which the Constitution permits because it is an inseparable incident of the exercise of a legislative authority, which, under the Constitution, has been left to the states." The Court pointed out that the "nature of the authority of the state over its own highways" had often been sustained by the Court in the past.

In reiterating its stand, the Court noted that in general "courts do not sit as Legislatures. . .and cannot act as Congress does when, after weighing all the conflicting interests, state and national, it determines when and how much the state regulatory power shall yield to the larger interests of a national commerce. And in reviewing a state highway regulation where Congress has not acted, a court is not called upon, as are state legislatures, to determine what, in its judgment, is the most suitable restriction to be applied of those that are possible...."

Just seven years later, however, the Court began to narrow the scope of state regulation on matters affecting interstate commerce. In *Southern Pacific Co. v. Arizona* (1945), the Court found that the specific regulations of Arizona limiting train lengths to no more than fourteen passenger and seventy freight cars was unreasonable and did not match the legislation and regulation of other states. "The record shows here that the enforcement of the Arizona statute results in freight trains being broken up and reformed at the California border, and in New Mexico, some distance from the Arizona line." Because of railyard locations, this Arizona law affected rail traffic all the way to Los Angeles.

The trial court had overturned the statute, finding it had no reasonable relation to safety. The purpose of the law was not being served by the law, the Court decided. Moreover, it substantially impeded interstate commerce, more than the limits placed on trucks in South Carolina. "An examination of the relevant factors make it plain state interest is outweighed by the interest of the nation in an adequate, economical, and efficient railway transportation service, which must prevail." Thus, the United States Supreme Court reversed the Arizona Supreme Court, which had reversed the trial court, and held the statute unconstitutional.

The Court began by stating the constitutional basis of state regulation authority in transportation issues affecting interstate commerce. Then the Court shifted gears: "But ever since *Gibbons v. Ogden.* . .the states have not been deemed to have authority to impede substantially the free flow of commerce from state to state. . .upon the presumed intention of Congress where Congress has not spoken." Citing the statistics indicating that 93 percent of the freight and 95 percent of the passenger traffic affected by the law is interstate, the Court reserved to itself the right to make a finding on the facts.

Recent Balancing Tests. A similar balancing test was applied in *Raymond Motor Transportation, Inc. v. Rice* (1978). The Court invalidated a Wisconsin law that barred trucks longer than fifty-five feet from its highways. Wisconsin's sole justification for this regulation was highway safety.

The Court's opinion, written by Justice Powell, weighed the law's safety benefits against the degree of interference with interstate commerce. The trucking company, which challenged the statute, presented an array of evidence proving not only that the regulation did not contribute to

The opinions of Associate Justice William O. Douglas on interstate transportation regulation evolved into a more liberal interpretation of the Court's powers between the **Southern Pacific** *decision in 1945 and* **Biff v. Navajo Freight** *in 1959.*

highway safety but also that the state routinely allowed other types of vehicles to use its highways even though their lengths exceeded fifty-five feet. The state failed to rebut this evidence in its presentation.

The Court found that this statute substantially interfered with interstate commerce in that it slowed and increased the cost of the movement of goods in the national market. Since the state of Wisconsin failed to make "even a colorable showing" that the law contributed to highway safety, the result of the Court's balancing test mandated the statute's invalidation.

Justice William O. Douglas, who dissented in *Southern Pacific*, wrote the majority opinion in *Bibb v. Navajo Freight Lines* (1959), which invalidated an Illinois statute requiring the use of a certain type of rear fender mudguard on trucks and trailers using Illinois highways. The justices had now begun analyzing the information and determining whether or not the state regulation was required on balance against the interests of a national economy and its transportation.

The Court found that trucks equipped with the required mud flaps threw no less mud than trucks without such flaps. Additionally, this mud guard was legal in forty-five other states and was itself illegal in the state of Arkansas. For this reason, the Illinois statute interfered with the practice of interlining, that is, of shifting trailers from one cab to another, a practice particularly connected with the shipment of perishables. The Court determined that this interference constituted substantial interference with interstate commerce and thus overturned the statute. "This is one of those cases–few in number–where local safety measures that are nondiscriminatory place an unconstitutional burden on interstate commerce," Douglas commented.

In *Bibb*, the Court also mentioned that if the only issue were the cost of adjustment to this new safety regulation, the measure would be sustained. Instead, the Court based its decision on the lack of evidence supporting the safety rationale of the regulation. Therefore, the onerous burdens on interstate commerce outweighed the alleged safety benefits.

State Barriers To Incoming Trade

In most of the preceding cases, the impact of the challenged state regulation fell on an interstate transportation facility. The state's usual objective was the protection of local health and safety. In the following cases, the impact falls on interstate trade or on an interstate buyer or seller. The state's objective shifts from health and safety to economic purposes. In both types of cases, the Court frequently balances the state's interest in achieving its legitimate objectives against the burdens imposed on interstate commerce. However, the opinions indicate that state objectives become more questionable when they are economic in nature. Although one of the main features of the federal commerce clause is to discourage the states from legislating a competitive advantage to local economic interests, the questions remain of whether this justifies judicial suspicion of all states with an economic objective and of which state justifications will be recognized as legitimate.

Court Tests. Baldwin v. G.A.F. Seelig (1935) was an early challenge to state economic barriers. The 1933 New York Milk Control Act established minimum prices to be paid by dealers to producers. The act prohibited the sale of milk produced from outside the state at a lower price than that produced within the state. Seelig, a New York milk dealer, purchased Vermont milk, shipped it into New York and sold 90 percent of the milk in its original containers. When the state of New York refused to license Seelig's business, he sought to enjoin the enforcement of the statute. A federal district court did enjoin enforcement as applied to milk sold from the original containers but did not for milk sold in bottles.

The Court, in a decision written by Justice Cardozo, treated the state law as discrimination against out-of-state milk. Cardozo stated flatly that one state could not discriminate against the imports of another state. Moreover, it was irrelevant to the Court whether milk was in forty-quart cans or had been rebottled; milk was milk and the state could not create artificial barriers to trade. Clearly the state had a right to regulate the *quality* of milk entering the state but not the *price* of the milk.

Referring to the "original package" theory in *Brown v. Maryland*, the Court noted that it was not an "ultimate principle" but the "illustration of a principle," a "convenient boundary." "What is ultimate is the principle that one state in its dealings with another may not place itself in a position of economic isolation." Discriminatory pricing was akin to establishing impost and duties, which were expressly prohibited by the Constitution to the states.

In *Dean Milk Co. v. City of Madison* (1954), the Court invalidated a local ordinance prohibiting the sale of milk in the city of Madison, Wisconsin, which had not been pasteurized within a five-mile radius of that city. This ostensible health ordinance was found by the Court to be an ordinance of economic discrimination "protecting local industry against competition from without the State" and was untenable because there were "reasonable and adequate alternatives" available if health and safety were concerns in this situation.

Hunt v. Washington Apple Advertising Committee (1977) involved a North Carolina law that prohibited state grades on apple containers. All containers sold or shipped within the state could be marked only with federal grades or marked "not graded." This statute was found to be discriminatory against the state of Washington, a major apple producer, because the law prohibited the display of the more stringent Washington state grade. The North Carolina statute was therefore held violative of the commerce clause by burdening the interstate sale of Washington apples and was hence invalid.

State Barriers To Outgoing Trade

Just as states are prohibited from enacting regulations that discriminate against incoming products, they are not allowed to create local economic advantage by the restriction of the entry of home commodities into the national market. State laws that burden the exportation of local goods are *per se* repugnant to the common market philosophy. However, the Court has engaged in a balancing approach in order to determine whether such statutes may stand. In order to be sustained, the regulation must represent the least burdensome alternative for achieving a necessary goal. The Court considered such laws nondiscriminatory, and therefore allowed them to remain if they operated equally on domestic and foreign consumers.

Milk Control Statutes. State restrictions on outgoing trade have produced several types of cases before the Court. One type of case arose out of the milk regulation laws passed to secure steady milk supplies in the wake of the Depression. The financial instability and the fact that milk producers often found themselves paid less than the price of production induced them to slaughter their cows for the meat prices. Recognizing the need for a stable supply of fresh milk, state governments began to pass milk control statutes. New York led the way in 1933 with a statute declaring that the milk industry was "a business affecting the public health and interest," establishing a milk control board with general supervisory powers over the industry, and requiring producers to secure licenses revocable for violations of the law.

The state of Pennsylvania passed a milk control statute in 1935 that was similar to the New York statute. The state law required the licensing of milk dealers and compelled them to pay a minimum price to producers within the state. The State Milk Control Board sought to enjoin a milk producer named Eisenberg from operating his business in violation of its statute. Eisenberg operated a receiving plant for milk from local farmers in which he cooled down the milk, tested and weighed it, and readied it for shipment to New York. Both the trial court and the Pennsylvania Supreme Court held that the application of the law to Eisenberg violated the commerce clause.

In *Milk Control Board v. Eisenberg Farm Products* (1939), the Court, in an opinion by Justice Roberts, reversed the lower court rulings and held the law constitutional. Using a balancing test, the Court stated that the question of state regulation in the areas of prohibitions, price controls, licensing, and bonding could be answered only "by weighing the nature of the respondent's [Eisenberg] activities, and the propriety of local regulation of them, as disclosed by the record." Since such a small percentage of the total milk production of Pennsylvania was shipped out of state, the Court found that the law equally burdened local and out-of-state consumers and was, therefore, nondiscriminatory. Additionally, considerations affecting health and safety were deemed necessary by the state, "in the absence of regulation by Congress"; therefore the statute was held to be a valid exercise of the police power.

The significance of a discriminatory impact was emphasized in *H. P. Hood & Sons v. DuMond* (1949). The Court reversed the denial of a license to a Massachusetts firm seeking to establish a fourth New York milk receiving plant to increase the milk supply to the Boston area, which obtained about 90 percent of its milk from out of state. The New York Agriculture and Markets Law provided that no license should be issued "unless the commissioner [of agriculture] is satisfied that. . .issuance of the license will not tend to a destructive competition in a market already adequately served, and that issuance of the license is in the public interest." Hood was denied the license although it met all other requirements under the law.

In his opinion, Justice Jackson, speaking for the Court, stated: "The present controversy begins where the Eisenberg decision left off." The health and safety aspects of the law were not being challenged but "only additional restrictions, imposed for the avowed purpose and with the practical effect of curtailing the volume of interstate commerce to aid local economic interests." Unlike the regulatory schemes that the Court had sustained earlier, such as the statute in *Eisenberg*, this licensing law discriminated against interstate commerce because the New York regulation burdened only nonresidents. Moreover, the nature of this discrimination indicated that those affected were not represented in the state political process that created the burden. This was the type of trade barrier that the commerce clause was meant to eliminate. In these circumstances, the Court consistently invoked the national market doctrine that prohibited a local embargo.

"The Commerce Clause is one of the most prolific sources of national power," Jackson declared, "and an equally prolific source of conflict with legislation of the state." The Constitution did not specifically say what the states may or may not do in the absence of congressional action or what is not commerce between them. The Court has "advanced the solidarity and prosperity of the Nation by the meaning it has given to these great silences of the Constitution." Quoting a precedent from several decades before that had not permitted states to keep articles or products within its boundaries once they are a "subject of commerce," Jackson went on to say, "The principle that our economic unit is the Nation, which alone has the gamut of powers necessary to control the economy, including the vital power of erecting customs barriers against foreign competition has as its corollary that the states are not separable economic units." Quoting *Baldwin*, Jackson continued, "The Court has not only recognized this disability of the state to isolate its own economy as a basis for striking down parochial legislative policies designed to do so, but it has recognized the incapacity of the state to protect its own inhabitants from competition as a reason for sustaining particular exercises of the commerce power of Congress to reach matters in which states were so disabled." He then pointed to the consequences of local control of local resources: "We need only consider the consequences if each of the few states that produce copper, lead, high-grade iron ore, timber, cotton, oil or gas should decree that industries located in that state shall have priority. What fantastic rivalries and dislocations and reprisals would ensue if such practices were begun!" Jackson's essay on the nature of the commerce clause closed with the following:

> Our system, fostered by the Commerce Clause, is that every farmer and every craftsman shall be encouraged to produce by the certainty that he will have free access to every market in the Nation, that no home embargoes will withhold his export, and no foreign state will by customs duties or regulations exclude them. Likewise, every consumer may look to the free competition from every producing area in the Nation to protect him from exploitation by any. Such was the vision of the Founders; such has been the doctrine of this Court which has given it reality.

Other Court Tests. The *Hood* decision raised a number of questions concerning the power of the states to protect local interests. The Court did not apply the "balancing test" in *Hood*. Earlier, in *Parker v. Brown* (1943), a California case in which local producers were required to turn over a portion of their crop to a regulatory body to eliminate destructive competition, the Court applied the "mechanical test" to determine whether interstate commerce was even involved. This analysis consisted of the determination of whether or not the state regulation was imposed before or after the articles entered interstate commerce. On the whole, establishing a cooperative marketing system was found not to violate interstate commerce since the effect of that system was to aid the products rather than hinder their commerce out of state. One year after *Hood*, the Court did permit minimum price regulation in natural gas supply because of the state's interest in "preventing rapid and uneconomic dissipation" of its resources. Facing the commerce clause issue squarely in *Cities Service Gas Co. v. Peerless Oil & Gas Co.* (1950), the Court concluded that state regulation in this case reflected the national interest in conservation, that there was no regulation that was discriminatory, and that it was therefore constitutional.

The *Cities Service* case suggests the broader issue that the purpose of local regulation is not to protect narrow economic interests but to preserve local resources. An early case, *Geer v. Connecticut* (1896), concerned a state statute forbidding the killing of woodcock, ruffed grouse, or quail for the purpose of transportation out of state. In sustaining the statute, the Court relied on the theory that the state has an ownership interest in wildlife. This special state interest in certain commodities removed these restrictions from the ordinary rules about commerce regulation.

In another early case, *Hudson County Water Co. v. McCarter* (1908), the Court sustained a New Jersey statute forbidding any person to transport "the waters of any fresh water, lake, pond, brook, creek, river or stream" into any other state. This was applied to a contract that imported fresh water to Staten Island from a New Jersey river. Justice Holmes, writing for the Court, stated, "few public interests are more obvious, indisputable and independent of particular theory than the interest of the public of a State to maintain the rivers that are wholly within it substantially undiminished, except by such drafts upon them as the guardian of the public welfare may permit for the purpose of turning them into a more perfect use."

The premise upon which these rulings rested, however, began to change during the 1920's and 1930's. In *Pennsylvania v. West Virginia* (1923), the Court invalidated a statute requiring that the needs of West Virginia gas users be satisfied before any natural gas could be exported. The Court declared that the state did not have this particular interest in natural gas. Rather, gas was a "commodity," belonging to the owner of the land; it was his property and subject to his control. The West Virginia law was therefore declared to be unduly burdensome to interstate commerce.

Finally, in 1979, *Geer* was specifically overruled. In writing for a seven to two Court, Justice Brennan commented, "Time has revealed the error of the result reached in *Geer*." The concept of "state" property had changed, and it was now reflected in *Hughes v. Oklahoma* (1979). The Oklahoma statute in question prohibited the transfer out of state of minnows from state waters; that statute had been defended upon the basis that animals and other creatures in the wild were under state ownership. Citing the *Hood* decision, the Court held that *any* action a state takes to conserve its natural resources must be taken in accordance with the principle that "our economic unit is the Nation" and that once an item becomes an item of commerce, such as the minnows fished from state waters, there could be no restrictions that unduly burdened interstate commerce. Conservation, a worthy goal, could not be discriminatory in its nature, and the measures taken to ensure it must be consistent with the goals of national unity.

During this same time, the Court recognized the expansion of both federal and local powers to deal with new problems faced in a rapidly expanding economy, such as environmental pollution. Local and state ordinances on air and water pollution were often upheld in the courts. However, as the nation as a unit became increasingly aware of the scope of the problem, the demand for national legislation grew. Both the Clean Air Act and the Clean Water Act were, in part, responses to both the jurisdictional and constitutional inadequacies of local and state environmental statutes. As Congress asserted its legislative prerogative in these areas, states could act only in the manner in which specifically granted authority to do so. Some of the legislation set minimal standards below which states could not go and simultaneously allowed state flexibility in determining whether standards should be more stringent. Other legislation made standards nationwide and uniform.

Federal Preemption Of State Law

When Congress exercises a granted power, concurrent conflicting state legislation may be challenged by the preemption doctrine. The supremacy clause of Article VI, Clause 2 of the Constitution mandates that federal law supersedes any inconsistent state law when the two cannot coexist. For example, a federal statute that prohibits an act that is required under state law would override that state law. Unfortunately, preemption questions are seldom as clear.

The Court has borne the responsibility of discovering Congress's intent to preempt and, if necessary, of invalidating state statutes that are superseded because they impermissibly interfere with federal objectives. However, Congress can reverse such decisions if it does not intend to preempt the field. There is no simplistic constitutional standard for defining the limits of preemption, however, and the difficulty of finding any uniform standards arises because of the diversity of preemption problems. Despite this diversity, the constitutional principles are designed with a common purpose: to avoid conflicting exercise of authority by various bodies of power that might have some degree of control over the same subject matter.

Preemption Decisions. There are several examples of the Court's traditional methods of analysis. In *Hines v. Davidowitz* (1941), the Court held that the Federal Alien Registration Act of 1940 superseded Pennsylvania's Alien Registration Act of 1939. The opinion emphasized the supremacy of federal power in the field of foreign policy, as well as the sensitivity of the relationship between the processing of aliens and the conduct of foreign affairs. The Court concluded that the Congress's enactment of uniform immigration regulation preempted any state regulation in the field. Although no rigid formula was enunciated, the test used was whether, under the specific circumstances, the state law "stands as an obstacle to the accomplishment and execution of the full purposes and objectives of Congress."

Fifteen years later, the Court elaborated on this test in *Pennsylvania v. Nelson* (1956). In this case, the Court affirmed the Pennsylvania Supreme Court's decision that federal anti-communist legislation superseded the state's Sedition Act. The opinion stressed that the need for national predominance indicated that Congress intended to "occupy" the field.

Chief Justice Warren used a three-pronged analysis to ascertain whether federal preemption was necessary. First, he examined the pervasiveness of the federal regulatory scheme. Second, he questioned whether the need for national uniformity called for federal occupation of the field. Last, he discussed the danger of conflict between state law and the federal legislation. Under this analysis, the Pennsylvania statute was preempted by the federal regulation of seditious conduct.

In making such a case-by-case assessment, the balancing of interests is similar to the Court's approach to defining unconstitutional burdens on interstate commerce. The Court accorded greater deference to local legislation when the state measures' objectives are the protection of health and safety. However, the decision in each case turns on its particular set of facts.

Given this reliance on the specific facts of each situation, different results may occur even within the same statutory scheme. In *Maurer v. Hamilton* (1940), the Court sustained a Pennsylvania statute that prohibited the carrying of cars over truck cabs. The statute was considered a weight and height regulation and, therefore, not barred by the Interstate Commerce Commission's authority to regulate safety. The opinion noted deference to state legislation that involved public safety and health.

In a later case, the Court struck down an Illinois law that revoked an interstate carrier's right to use state highways for violations of Illinois truck weight limits. In *Castle v. Hayes Freight Lines* (1954), the Court distinguished *Maurer*, although it did not overrule it, on the grounds that the Interstate Commerce Commission had exclusive authority to regulate *which* motor carriers could operate in interstate commerce. The Court concluded that the form of state regulation in *Castle* was not within the powers reserved to the states.

In recent cases, the traditional approach to preemption, judicial second-guessing of congressional intent, has been rejected. The Court will not invalidate state legislation unless preemption was "the clear and manifest purpose of Congress." If no clear congressional intent to preempt exists, the Court will hold in favor of the state regulation's validity.

New York State Department of Social Service v. Dublino (1973) exemplifies this new approach. In this case, the Court upheld New York work rules that conditioned an individual's receipt of federal assistance upon the fulfillment of an additional state requirement: the acceptance of employment. Justice Powell failed to find that the New York legislation was preempted due to the pervasiveness of federal regulation in the field. Instead, he emphasized the presumption of the state law's validity absent congressional intent of preemption. Had Congress intended preemption, Powell reasoned, it would have provided for it.

State Taxes And The Commerce Power

In the wake of the Depression many states enacted legislation that structured state taxes in such a way as to favor local business and to discriminate against out-of-state business. Some economic theorists termed this the "Balkanization" of the nation. The Court invariably declared the discriminatory forms of tax legislation unconstitutional. Since the *Black Bird Creek Marsh* and *Cooley* decisions, the Court has generally sustained state legislation passed in many areas in which Congress has not acted. However, it has also maintained that legislation could not discriminate in favor of one state or against any other state.

In *Ingels v. Morf* (1937), the Court invalidated a California tax on automobile "caravans." The $15 fee on each vehicle brought into the state for resale was far above the actual administrative costs of the state. The state lowered the tax to $7.50 per vehicle, and in *Clark v. Paul Gray, Inc.* (1939), the statute was declared constitutional because fees were more in line with the actual costs created by the out-of-state vehicles. Both these decisions used the "balancing test" within the context of the commerce clause and the prerogative of the state.

Other states levied taxes against items such as cement, coal, and mail-order sales. Taxes that clearly discriminated against particular goods when shipped in from out of state were usually invalidated. However, in *Nelson v. Sears Roebuck & Co.* (1941), the Court sustained an Iowa use tax (a form of sales tax) on any out-of-state item ordered through a catalog and shipped to persons within Iowa. Such a tax was deemed to do no more than put the out-of-state goods on an equal footing with local goods.

Intergovernmental Immunities

The first discussion of the intergovernmental immunity doctrine is *McCulloch v. Maryland* (1819), in which Chief Justice Marshall declared that the federal government is free from all state taxes, even nondiscriminatory ones. In that case, the tax on the Bank of the United States constituted an interference by the state of Maryland with a federal function and thus was declared unconstitutional. This immunity of the United States was extended to property to which it held title and to the property of the United States to which individuals held legal title (U.S. Bonds). In *Van Brocklin v. Tennessee* (1886), the Court held that a state could not impose its general *ad valorem* property tax, saying, "The States have no power, by taxation or otherwise, to retard, impede, burden or in any manner control the operations of the constitutional laws enacted by Congress to carry into execution the powers vested in the General Government." The Court earlier had extended this immunity to bonds. In *Weston v. Charleston* (1829), the Court said, "The tax on government stock is thought by this court to be a tax on the contract, a tax on the power to borrow money on the credit of the United States, and consequently repugnant to the Constitution."

The State Immunity Question. In 1871 the Court applied the same immunity from infringements by federal taxation to state governments when it declared the national income tax did not apply to a state judge in *Collector v. Day.* From this period until the late 1930's, the Court gradually expanded the immunity, usually in specific cases of individuals having some sort of relationship with either a state or the federal government.

During the late 1930's, courts began to limit these immunities, in part because such immunity had grown out of proportion to its usefulness and in part due to the need for income. In *James v. Dravo Contracting Co.* (1937), the Court upheld a state gross receipts tax imposed on a contractor's receipts from federal contract work. The major case before the Court that signaled the changed view of intergovernmental immunities was *Helvering v. Gebhardt* (1938). The United States had decided to tax the salaried income of employees of the Port of New York Authority, a bi-state corporation created by the states of New York and New Jersey. The Court cast its shifting view in the following manner: "With the steady expansion of the activity of state governments into new fields they have undertaken the performance of functions not known to the states when the Constitution was adopted, and have taken over the management of business enterprises once conducted exclusively by private individuals subject to the national taxing power. . .if every federal tax which is laid on some new form of state activity, or whose economic burden reaches in some measure the state or those who serve it, were to be set aside as an infringement of state sovereignty, it is evident that a restriction upon national power, devised only as a shield to protect the states from curtailment of the essential operations of government which they have exercised from the beginning, would become a shady means for striking down the taxing power of the nation. . . ."

The next year the converse was sustained. The state of New York attempted to tax an attorney for a corporation created by an act of Congress. In *Graves v. New York ex rel. O'Keefe* (1939), the Court stated that a state tax on the income of a federally owned entity was constitutional. The Court had clearly reversed its stand: "The theory, which once won a qualified approval, that a tax on income is legally or economically a tax on its source, is no longer tenable, and the only possible basis for implying a constitutional immunity from state income tax of the salary of an employee of the national government or a governmental agency is that the economic burden of the tax is in some way passed on. . . ." *Collection v. Day* was explicitly overruled. The tax did, however, need to be nondiscriminatory to be constitutional.

Although *McCulloch* flatly said that the states could not tax the federal government, it did not say the reverse was

the case; in fact, in the doctrine of national supremacy enunciated by Marshall, *McCulloch* implied that the federal government had the power to tax the states. In *New York v. United States* (1946), the Court accepted the implications of *McCulloch* and applied the national supremacy doctrine to extend the power of the federal government to tax the states directly. The state of New York operated a health resort and recreational facility in Saratoga Springs. The state also bottled and sold mineral waters at a profit. The United States imposed a tax on mineral waters and secured a judgment against New York in the district court, which was affirmed by the court of appeals. Justice Frankfurter delivered the opinion of the Court. Forty-five other states had joined New York in *amicus curiae* to argue for state immunity.

"The federal government is the government of all the States, and all the States share in the legislative process by which a tax of general applicability is laid," the opinion began. Pointing out that the reason this problem did not emerge before the 20th century was because of the limited scope of federal taxation. Justice Frankfurter quoted an earlier case: "When a state enters the market place seeking customers it divests itself of its quasi sovereignty pro tanto, and takes on the character of a trader, so far, at least, as the taxing power of the federal government is concerned." (From *Ohio v. Helvering*, in which the Court held the

Associate Justice Felix Frankfurter wrote the Supreme Court's opinion in **New York v. United States,** *which applied the national supremacy doctrine to permit the federal government to tax the states directly.*

imposition of a sales tax on a state-run liquor monopoly to be constitutional.) He concluded with a comment defining the limits of the decision delivered: "The process of Constitutional adjudication does not thrive on conjuring up horrible possibilities that never happen in the real world and devising doctrines sufficiently comprehensive in detail to cover the remotest contingency. . .we decide enough when we reject limitation upon the taxing power of Congress derived from such untenable criteria as 'proprietary' against 'governmental' activities of the States, or historically sanctioned activities of Government or activities conducted merely for profit, and find no restriction upon Congress to include the States in levying a tax exacted equally from private persons upon the same subject matter."

Limiting Federal Regulation. The limits of federal regulation, as opposed to taxation, of state and local governmental units were addressed in *National League of Cities v. Usery* (1976), which concerned the 1974 amendments to the National Fair Labor Standards Act of 1938, which specified minimum wage and maximum hours rules. The original act had specifically excluded the states and their political subdivisions (counties and cities) from its coverage. In the 1974 amendments Congress extended the minimum wage and maximum hour provisions to almost all the public employees in the nation. The National League of Cities, joined by the National Governors' Conference and individual cities and states, brought an action in the district court for the District of Columbia asserting that the congressional action violated an implicit constitutional rule allowing states to be run as states to preserve their basic sovereignty. The argument was not that the conditions of the employees were beyond the scope of Congress but that, with respect to state employees, the amendments violated an additional limit on federal power.

In the five to four decision, which overturned the statute, Justice Rehnquist stated: "The Court has never doubted that there are limits upon the power of Congress to override state sovereignty, even when exercising its otherwise plenary powers to tax or to regulate commerce. . .In [an earlier case], for example, the Court took care to assure the appellants that it had ample power to prevent. . .'the utter destruction of the State as a sovereign political entity' which they feared." The Court agreed that the 10th Amendment had often been called a "truism"; however it "expressly declares the constitutional policy that Congress may not exercise power in a fashion that impairs the States' integrity or their ability to function effectively in a federal system."

Interstate Relations. Article II, Section 2 of the Constitution states that "The Citizens of each State shall be entitled to all Privileges and Immunities of Citizens in the several States." This provision and its antecedent in the Articles of Confederation were prompted by the questions of how a federal system of government would actually function in terms of persons being citizens of a state and simultaneously citizens of the United States. It was intended to forbid a state from discriminating against residents of other states while within the first state's jurisdiction. The framers wanted to protect U.S. citizens as they crossed state lines, whether for business and commerce or for other reasons. The issue first arose before a justice of the Court on circuit in *Corfield v. Corywell* (1829), in which a Pennsylvania citizen was charged with violating a New Jersey statute while in New Jersey. The state of New Jersey had limited clamming, oystering, and fishing in its own waters to New Jersey citizens only. Justice Washington stated that the phrase "privileges and immunities in the several states" with respect to which equal treatment was demanded should be confined to "those privileges and immunities which are, in their nature, fundamental" and "which belong, of right, to citizens of all free governments." What was "fundamental" was clear, stated the opinion, and what they actually constituted "would be more tedious than difficult to enumerate," although they could be listed under a number of general categories: the right to travel, practice one's profession, *habeas corpus*, protection by the government, and the "enjoyment of life and liberty, with the right to acquire and possess property of every kind." It did not, however, include all those that might be the "exclusive right" of citizens of a particular state such as the use of "common property" of that particular state. Clamming and oystering came within this second, non-fundamental and therefore unprotected, class of rights.

This line of reasoning was continued throughout the rest of the century, although after the adoption of the 14th Amendment, it became more difficult to distinguish between residence and state citizenship since the amendment provides that "All persons born or naturalized in the United States, and subject to the jurisdiction thereof, are citizens of the United States and of the State wherein they reside." The Court did, however, continue to separate "essential rights" from those kinds of preferential treatments for residents deemed to be part of a state's prerogative. Thus, in *Blake v. McClung* (1898), it was not within the power of a state "when establishing regulations for the conduct of private business of a particular kind, to give its own citizens essential privileges connected with that business which it denies to citizens of other states."

States were allowed to discriminate against out-of-state visitors in areas such as differential fees for use of state facilities on the theory that state citizens paid for the use of such facilities through their taxes. Thus in *Baldwin v. Montana Fish and Game Commission* (1978), access to state recreational facilities was not to be considered fundamental in terms of the privileges and immunities clause and restricted access to non-residents was held valid.

Preferential treatment in hiring state residents, however, was invalid under that clause. In *Hicklin v. Orbeck* (1978), Justice Brennan, writing for a unanimous Court, stated that privileges and immunities "does not preclude disparity of treatment in the many situations where there are perfectly valid reasons for it." The Constitution does forbid discrimination against citizens of other states "where there is no reason for discrimination beyond the mere fact that they are citizens of other states." The commerce clause forbade this form of discrimination as interfering with the free flow of commerce throughout the nation. Unemployment could not be used as an excuse, moreover, since one could not prove that unemployment was directly attributable to persons entering Alaska from out of state to work on pipelines.

Individual Rights

Individual Rights

The individual rights of Americans are derived from the Constitution of the United States and its amendments, particularly the Bill of Rights. The other amendments that have been particularly important to the development of the Supreme Court's view of individual rights are the 13th, 14th, 19th, and 24th. These documents limit governmental power over citizens, ensuring that certain essential liberties are not sacrificed merely to maintain a federal government. The constitutional amendments enumerate rights that citizens and lawmakers found necessary to individual freedom both immediately after the Constitution's ratification and in the nearly two hundred years following.

Originally the guarantees of the Bill of Rights–the first ten amendments to the Constitution–were enforceable only against the federal government. Through time and the 14th Amendment due process clause, however, nearly all these guarantees are now enforceable against the states as well. Since the 14th Amendment was adopted, the Bill of Rights guarantees have slowly been incorporated within it; nearly every right derived from the constitutional amendments is derived, in part, from the 14th Amendment.

Many individual rights may be traced to several constitutional amendments, in addition to the 14th Amendment. An individual's right to personal privacy is probably guaranteed by more amendments than any other right, although each amendment addresses a different aspect of privacy. The lst Amendment protects individuals from publication of intimate facts of their lives. Privacy in the home and office are protected by the 3rd and 4th Amendments, which prohibit quartering of troops without the homeowner's consent and unreasonable searches, respectively. The 5th Amendment protection from self-incrimination guarantees that an individual need not reveal damaging facts. The 9th Amendment broadly protects many human rights, including that of personal privacy.

The right to vote, fundamental in the United States, is guaranteed in its various aspects by the 15th, 19th, and 24th Amendments. The 15th Amendment, which grants suffrage to black citizens where all other citizens have the right to vote, was enacted along with the 13th and 14th Amendments, immediately following the Civil War, to protect the newly freed slaves' rights.

The familial rights to use birth control or have an abortion, although not spelled out anywhere in the Constitution, are derived from several amendments. The lst, 3rd, 4th, 5th, and 9th Amendment guarantees of privacy, in particular, have been used to interpret a constitutional right to privacy in family matters.

Criminal defendants' rights and the conduct of criminal proceedings are subject to much constitutional control. The 4th Amendment prohibits unreasonable searches and seizures by any government agent and creates several requirements for valid search warrants. It restricts searches in homes and offices, as well as eavesdropping. Evidence obtained in violation of the 4th Amendment is inadmissible in criminal trials. Besides permitting criminal defendants to "take the fifth," or not testify at their own trials, the 5th Amendment guarantees individuals a grand jury indictment for federal felonies, which requires both a reasonable likelihood that the defendant committed the offense charged and that he knows what crime is charged. The 5th Amendment also guarantees that no person is tried twice for the same crime, unless a mistrial occurs, an appeal is granted, or a separate court system (such as a federal rather than a state court) conducts the subsequent trial. That no one be deprived of life, liberty, or property without due process of the law is also guaranteed.

The 6th Amendment guarantees that criminal defendants have speedy, public trials, to prevent prolonged and unnecessary incarceration before trial. An impartial jury consisting of community members from the crime's location is also guaranteed, as is the right to be informed of the crime alleged. The accused is entitled to confront all opposing witnesses, generally done by his attorney at or before trial, and to compel the attendance of favorable witnesses, permitting his attorney to prepare the best defense possible. The right to obtain legal counsel in a criminal defense is likely the most significant guarantee of the 6th Amendment, as it helps ensure a fair trial. The freedom of the press, specifically considered solely in the 1st Amendment, is complemented by the 6th Amendment guarantee of public criminal trials. That bail not be excessive for the crime charged is guaranteed by the 8th Amendment, which also proscribes excessive fines and cruel or unusual punishment. Sentences must be appropriate to the crime, and punishment must not violate an individual's dignity nor inflict unnecessary pain. In civil, as opposed to criminal, actions, a jury trial is also guaranteed, but only when at least one party desires it and there are factual issues to be decided.

The 10th Amendment reserves all powers not delegated to the federal government for the state governments, permitting states to function effectively within the federal system. States are free to structure their own governments, run their court systems, and control laws concerning taxes, contracts, hunting, agriculture, and marriage. The 5th Amendment, however, permits neither federal nor state governments to take private property for public use without giving the owner fair compensation for the property. That is, the government must pay an individual for his land before building a highway through it.

Doctrine of State Action

Most of the rights that the amendments to the Constitution bestow upon individuals are rights that may be exercised as against the federal or state governments only. Most of the amendments do not confer rights upon individuals as against other private individuals, groups, or legal entities. For this reason, an individual (or individuals) can claim an infringement of his constitutional rights only when some government has contributed to the deprivation of his free exercise of those rights. When a government does so, then and only then does "state action" exist. The right the 13th Amendment bestows regarding slavery is the only one not requiring state action for its enforcement.

State action exists in two situations. First, state action exists when a government empowers a private individual (or group) to the extent that he becomes an agent of that government and the actions are actually those of the state. This type of state action corresponds to the "public function"

doctrine of state action. Second, state action exists when a government has sufficient contacts (or nexus) with an individual or group directly impairing or infringing upon constitutional rights. This type of state action corresponds to the "nexus" doctrine of state action.

Under the public function doctrine, state action exists in several situations. First, state action exists when, for example, the state allows a private entity or political party to assume a public function such as conducting a political primary, part of the electoral process. For this reason, a "whites-only primary" excluding black participation and conducted under the aegis of a political party violates the 15th Amendment right-to-vote provisions. Second, state action may exist, for example, when a legal entity operates a company town or a shopping center. Such operation under certain circumstances may be deemed a public function.

But the public function doctrine requires, first, that the public function assumed by the private entity be one traditionally the exclusive prerogative of the state and, second, that a statute or state constitution requires the state to perform that function.

Under the nexus doctrine, in contrast to the public function doctrine, state action exists only when a certain character attaches to the conduct and activity of the *government*, rather than that of the private actor. The relevant conduct is that of the government, not that of the private actor. Under this branch of the doctrine of state action, state action exists in four situtaions. First, state action exists when the state commands a private actor to adopt certain behavior. Second, state action exists when the state encourages the private actor to adopt certain behavior. For example, a state's repeal of civil rights laws may be held to be encouragement of racial discrimination (*Reitman v. Mulkey*, 1967). Third, state action exists when the state and a private actor have a mutually beneficial relationship whereby each benefits from the conduct of the other. Fourth, state action exists when the state's conduct becomes entangled with that of the private actor. This entanglement may arise, for example, from state funding of the private actor's conduct or the cooperation of a government official with the conduct of a private actor. However, under the nexus theory, the government action does not rise to the level of state action if the government involved only acquiesces in the private actor's conduct or tolerates it.

Recently, the Supreme Court has perhaps narrowed the doctrine of state action. In *Lugar v. Edmondson Oil Co.* (1982), the Court held that private conduct could be attributed to a state only when a private actor whose conduct is complained of is acting in accordance with a state created right or privilege or a rule of conduct imposed by a state or a person for whom a state is responsible.

1st Amendment

Congress shall make no law respecting an establishment of religion, or prohibiting the free exercise thereof; or abridging

After World War I, with free-expression supporters such as Justices Brandeis (**rear, far left**) *and Holmes* (**front, second from right**)*, the Court under Chief Justice White* (**front, center**) *permitted claims of 1st Amendment rights in cases it heard.*

the freedom of speech, or of the press; or the right of the people peaceably to assemble, and to petition the Government for a redress of grievances.

The 1st Amendment for all practices lay dormant until after World War I. Prior to World War I, Supreme Court decisions were hostile to the value of freedom of expression and often made no mention of the 1st Amendment at all. The Court rejected any such 1st Amendment claims when directly confronted with them.

After World War I, enforcement of the Espionage Act of 1917 and the Sedition Act of 1918 led the Supreme Court for the first time to consider the issue of free expression. In the postwar period, authorities suppressed forms of expression that allegedly threatened to result in dangerous or illegal acts, such as the violent overthrow of the government. The Supreme Court eventually determined that speech must present a "clear and present danger" to a substantial governmental interest before it can be suppressed.

The Supreme Court has interpreted the 1st Amendment to give it a meaning broader than its literal one. For example, the amendment states that "*Congress* shall make no law," but the amendment governs state as well as federal action, and judicial and executive as well as legislative action. For these reasons, the president, state governors, state legislatures, and state and federal judges must all conform to 1st Amendment strictures even though the text of the amendment itself

mentions only Congress. Even local and municipal governments must obey the amendment's strictures.

Today, the right to free expression is a source of frequent controversy. This right encompasses the areas of free press, belief, political persuasion, travel, and religion. The right is upheld to a more limited extent when the speech involved falls into the categories of fighting words or symbolic speech.

Freedom of the Press. Formerly, the Supreme Court held that 1st Amendment protection of speech did not extend at all to certain forms of speech, such as libelous, obscene, or commercial speech, fighting words, and incitement to riot. Today, however, 1st Amendment protection extends more fully to some of these categories. Libelous speech receives limited constitutional protection. A court must first determine whether a statement is libelous and, if so, whether it is protected libel. A libelous statement must be false, and it must be a misstatement of fact. Statements of opinion are never libelous.

When is libelous speech protected? In *New York Times Co. v. Sullivan* (1964), the Court held that defamatory falsehoods concerning public officials are protected unless the party suing can prove "actual malice," that is, that the defendant made his statement with the knowledge that it was false or with reckless disregard of whether it was false. In short, the party suing must prove that the defendant acted intentionally or recklessly; proof that the defendant acted negligently is insufficient.

In Time, Inc. v. Firestone, *the 1976 Court clarified its definition of public figures and of what constituted a "public controversy."*

Public figures are subject to the same standard as public officials, but mere wealth does not place someone in that category (*Time Inc. v. Firestone,* 1976), nor does involvement in a public issue (*Gertz v. Robert Welch, Inc.,* 1974). In the *Gertz* decision the Court defined public figures as those who have notorious or famous achievements or who have vigorously and successfully sought public attention:

> In some instances an individual may achieve such pervasive fame or notoriety that he becomes a public figure for all purposes and in all contexts. More commonly, an individual voluntarily injects himself or is drawn into a particular public controversy and thereby becomes a public figure for a limited range of issues. In either case such persons assume special prominence in the resolution of public questions.

In *Firestone,* Mary Firestone sued the publisher of *Time* magazine for libel. *Time* had erroneously reported the statements of the judge deciding the divorce case involving Firestone and her former husband, Russell Firestone. The divorce trial attracted considerable public attention, and Mary Firestone even held press conferences while it was pending. In holding that Firestone was not a public figure despite the attention that she had received and the press conferences she had convoked, the Court stated:

> [Time Inc.] contends that because the Firestone divorce was characterized by the Florida Supreme Court as a "cause célèbre," it must have been a public controversy and

[Firestone] must be considered a public figure. But in so doing [Time Inc.] seeks to equate "public controversy" with all controversies of interest to the public. Were we to accept this reasoning, we would reinstate the doctrine...that the *New York Times* privilege should be extended to falsehoods defamatory of private persons whenever the statements concern matters of general or public interest. In *Gertz,* however, the Court repudiated this position.

In *New York Times,* civil rights activists had published a full-page advertisement in *The New York Times.* The advertisement, in decrying racial discrimination and the denial of equal rights to blacks in the South, allegedly defamed Sullivan, a city commissioner in Montgomery, Alabama. While finding that the advertisement did contain some misstatements of fact, the Supreme Court held that those particular misstatements were immaterial. The Court also stated:

> Authoritative interpretations of the First Amendment guarantees have consistently refused to recognize an exception for any test of truth– whether administered by judges, juries, or administrative officials–and especially one that puts the burden of proving truth on the speaker...The constitutional protection does not turn upon "the truth, popularity, or social utility of the ideas and beliefs which are offered."

The Court then held that neither factual error nor defamatory content, nor both of them in combination, sufficed to remove the constitutional shield from criticism of official conduct. To remove the shield from such criticism, actual malice is required. Moreover, a state libel law allowing a defendant to escape liability only by proving the truth of his statements does not pass constitutional muster under these circumstances because there must be an allowance for "erroneous statements honestly made." The Court wrote:

> A rule compelling the critic of official conduct to guarantee the truth of all his factual assertions –and to do so on pain of libel judgments virtually unlimited in amount–leads to a comparable "self-censorship." Allowance of the defense of truth, with the burden of proving it on the defendant, does not mean that only false speech will be deterred. Even courts accepting this defense as an adequate safeguard have recognized the difficulties of adducing legal proofs that the alleged libel was true in all its factual particulars.

Then the Court stated the standard to be used in libel cases involving public figures and public officials:

> The constitutional guarantees require, we think, a federal rule that prohibits a public official from recovering damages for a defamatory falsehood relating to his official conduct unless he proves that the statement was made with "actual malice" –that is, with knowledge that it was false or with reckless disregard of whether it was false or not.

In *Gertz*, the Court had opportunity to explain and expand on its reasoning in *New York Times*. In *Gertz*, the Court wrote:

> Under the First Amendment there is no such thing as a false idea. However pernicious an opinion may seem, we depend for its correction not on the conscience of judges and juries but on the competition of other ideas. But there is no constitutional value in false statements of fact. Neither the intentional lie nor the careless error materially advances society's interest in "uninhibited, robust, and wide-open" debate on public issues…They belong to that category of utterances which are no essential part of any exposition of ideas, and are of such slight social value as a step to truth that any benefit that may be derived from them is clearly outweighed by the social interest in order and morality.

When the party suing is neither a public official nor a public figure, free speech considerations are not as strong because he is more susceptible to injury. Moreover, private individuals may lack "effective opportunities for rebuttal." Additionally, the *Gertz* opinion said that:

> the communications media are entitled to act on the assumption that public officials and public figures have·voluntarily exposed themselves to increased risk of injury from defamatory falsehood concerning them. No such assumption is justified with respect to a private individual. He has not accepted public office or assumed an "influential role in ordering society." He has relinquished no part of his interest in the

protection of his own good name, and consequently he has a more compelling call on the courts for redress of injury inflicted by defamatory falsehood. Thus, private individuals are not only more vulnerable to injury than public officials and public figures; they are also more deserving of recovery.

Accordingly, when the party suing is neither a public official nor a public figure, he may, for example, be required to prove only that the defendant made his statement with negligent (rather than reckless) disregard of whether it was false. Whether the party suing will be required to prove recklessness or merely negligence will depend on the libel laws of the state that the party suing seeks to have enforced. Some states may require that the party suing prove only that the defendant made his statement negligently.

The Supreme Court has decided only that the *New York Times* standard applies to news media defendants. It has never ruled on whether a non–news media defendant may be held liable on a lesser, easier to meet standard.

Punitive damages may be awarded a private party suing under a negligence standard only if the defendant makes his statement with knowledge of its falsity or with reckless disregard of whether it is false. Otherwise, the party suing may recover only for actual injury; he may recover only compensatory damages.

Public Interest Issues. Matters of public interest may usually be discussed without liability for invasion of privacy. There are four types of invasion of privacy. Only two receive any measure of 1st Amendment protection. Both involve the invasion of the privacy of a private party by another party, rather than by a government, federal or state. (The right to privacy from a government is not explicitly provided for by any one constitutional amendment, being found implicitly in several of them. It is different from the right to privacy from private parties.)

The first of these two may be called "publicity-of-private-life" invasion, and the second "false light" invasion. The first occurs when someone publicizes details of another's private life and such publicizing would be highly offensive to a reasonable person. The publicizing of facts that are available to the public by virtue of, say, existence on the public records, is not an invasion of privacy. For this reason, the publicizing of the identity of a rape victim is not an invasion of privacy when that identity is a matter of public record even where state law prohibits such publicizing, the Court held in *Cox Broadcasting Corp. v. Cohn* (1975). The 1st Amendment protects the publication of such information.

"False light" invasion occurs when someone places another before the public eye in a false light and when this false light would be highly offensive to a reasonable person. In *Time Inc. v. Hill* (1967), the Supreme Court held that Time Inc. was not liable for having published material that placed a party before the public eye in a false light. *Time* erroneously stated that the party suing had suffered certain violent traumatic experiences. The Court held that *Time* was not liable because it had not published its statements with knowledge of their falsity or with reckless disregard of whether they were false. In short, in false light cases, the defendant is not liable unless the party suing can prove that the defendant made his statement with knowledge of its falsity or with reckless disregard of whether it was false. (Note the similarity between this standard of liability and the standard used in cases involving the alleged libel of public figures or officials.) The 1st Amendment does not protect the publication of known falsehoods that are highly offensive to a reasonable person (*Cantrell v. Forest City Publishing Co.*, 1974). Aspects of personal privacy including searches, self-incrimination, and other natural rights are addressed in the 4th, 5th, and 9th amendments.

Obscenity Tests. Obscene publications are not protected by the guarantees of free speech or free press; federal and state governments may prohibit such forms of expression. Obscenity, however, is a term that has proved difficult to define in actual cases. Generally, obscene publications are those that appeal to "prurient" interests only. Material that appeals to prurient interests is material that "turns you on" physically. It *is* sex, not just a description of sex.

The Supreme Court was divided upon which test to apply to determine what constitutes obscene material; it is difficult to separate obscenity from sexually-oriented constitutionally protected speech. The portrayal of an idea cannot be limited simply because the idea is "immoral" (*Kingsley Int'l Pictures Corp. v. Regents of the University of the State of New York,* 1959). Although obscenity distribution laws are allowed, the *private* possession of obscene matter cannot be made criminal because there can be no infringement upon the flow of ideas in private (*United States v. Reidel*, 1971; *Stanley v. Georgia*, 1969).

In weighing social interest against the limitation upon free speech, the Supreme Court created a test for obscenity in *Roth v. United States* (1957). This original test asks whether the average person would see the dominant theme of the material, taken as a whole, as appealing to prurient interests and devoid of redeeming social value. If so, the material is obscene and unprotected by the 1st Amendment.

The *Roth* test has since been expanded to a three-part test. This modern standard for defining obscene material was laid out in *Miller v. California* (1973). The test that the Court followed was:

(1) Whether the average person, applying contemporary community standards, would find that the work, taken as a whole, appeals to the prurient interest.

(2) Whether the work depicts or describes, in a patently offensive way, sexual conduct specifically defined by the applicable state law.

(3) Whether the work, taken as a whole, lacks serious literary, artistic, political, or scientific value.

Thus, states may prohibit commercial exhibition of obscene films even to consenting adults where the theater has notice that its films fall within the state regulation and the *Miller* test is satisfied. Also, a state may use the exhibition of sexually explicit adult movies to statutorily classify theaters, but a state cannot totally ban a form of expression, such as nude dancing. However, the Supreme Court has been especially reluctant to find that child pornography is constitutionally protected speech. It has adopted doctrines giving states additional power to regulate child pornography, power additional to that given to them under the Court's other obscenity decisions.

Commercial Speech. Commercial speech, such as price advertising, is entitled to 1st Amendment protection, although it is subject to more regulation than is permissible for non-commercial speech. If speech is intended and tailored primarily to sell something, or if it proposes a commercial transaction, or if it relates solely to the economic interests of the speaker and his audience, then it is commercial speech. Not all paid advertisements are commercial speech, since some have a political content only. To determine the degree of protection, courts weigh the free speech interest in the contents of the speech against the public interest served by the governmental regulation.

In *Virginia State Board of Pharmacy v. Virginia Citizens Consumer Council, Inc.* (1976), the Supreme Court determined that consumers and society in general have a vital interest in the free flow of commercial information; the danger of misuse of price advertising is outweighed by the danger of suppressing such information. Commercial advertising is not disqualified from protection merely because it is economically motivated, but it is subject to proper restrictions. Such restrictions include time, place, and manner restrictions; false and misleading advertisement prohibitions; and prohibitions against advertising illegal transactions.

The important idea in the commercial speech area is the free flow of information to consumers. Such prohibitions as the placing of "for sale" signs on real estate to prevent "white flight" are invalid because this inhibits the free flow of information, according to *Linmark Associates, Inc. v. Township of Willingboro* (1977). However, a state may regulate advertising by attorneys where such advertising is shown to be misleading or economically undesirable or to have an adverse effect on professionalism, the quality of legal services, or the administration of justice (*Bates v. State Bar of Arizona*, 1977). A state may also discipline lawyers for in-person solicitation of clients for personal gain under circumstances likely to lead to misrepresentation, overreaching, and invasion of privacy. States may also prohibit practice under a trade name, a name adopted for the purpose of doing business. This type of commercial speech has no value to the public, for it conveys no information about price or service. The value of protection is thus outweighed by the state interest in protecting the public from misleading names.

A more rigorous approach to commercial speech was developed in *Central Hudson Gas & Electric Corp. v. Public Service Commission* (1980). The Supreme Court used a four-part test to determine if the prohibition of commercial speech violates the lst Amendment.

(1) Determine whether the expression is protected. If it is lawful activity and not misleading, then it is protected.
(2) Determine whether the asserted governmental interest is substantial.
(3) If so, then determine whether the regulation directly advances the governmental interest and does so in the least restrictive manner possible.
(4) Determine whether the regulation is more extensive than necessary. If it is overbroad, the regulation will not be upheld.

This test was applied in *Bolger v. Youngs Drug Products Corp.* (1983). The Court determined that the mailing of unsolicited advertisements for contraception was commercial speech protected under the lst Amendment.

The Federal Communications Commission (FCC) has a fairness doctrine that requires radio and television stations to present discussion of public issues with fair coverage of each side. Also, individuals attacked on the air must be given reply time. In *Red Lion Broadcasting Co. v. FCC* (1969), the Supreme Court declared that such a requirement is a valid regulation of speech. It allows a right of access to the broadcasting media, which enhances freedom of speech and press. Such access to the broadcasting media is limited, however. The FCC allows broadcasters to refuse all editorial advertisements. Broadcasters have a right to control the content of their programs as long as they meet a "public interest" standard, and such advertisements are not conducted to further the public interest (*Columbia Broadcasting System v. Democratic National Committee*, 1973).

Prior Restraint. In general, governments cannot regulate in advance what expressions may be published or uttered, even if those expressions would be unprotected by the Constitution once made. Such regulation would be censorship. In *Near v. Minnesota* (1931), the Supreme Court applied this principle to defamatory publications and declared that the only permissible restraint upon the publication of defamatory material is the deterrent effect of subsequent suits.

The limitation upon prior restraint is applied broadly. In *New York Times Co. v. United States* (the Pentagon Papers case, 1971), the Supreme Court held that the government cannot prevent the publication of information even when its release might threaten to cause grave injury to the public interest. One exception occurs when such publication threatens national security. However, the government must meet a heavy burden to justify any such prior restraint. Such a burden is met, for instance, when the government shows that publication of the information will affect its ability to

In 1931, Chief Justice Hughes wrote the Court's opinion in **Near v. Minnesota,** *which established narrow criteria for restraining the publication of defamatory statements.*

wage war successfully, or will cause direct irreparable harm to the United States. The latter instance is illustrated in *United States v. Progressives, Inc.* (1979), where a district court exercised prior restraint over the publication of technical material on hydrogen bomb design. The court found that national security outweighs the right to publish in such circumstances. This is the only instance where a federal court has ever enjoined the press. The government eventually declined to pursue the appeal of the lower court decision because of the particular difficulties in containing the dissemination of this information.

There are other exceptions to the limitation on prior restraint. For example, a prohibition against the publishing in newspapers of sex-designated "help wanted" ads may be permitted. The purpose of the prior restraint rule is to prevent the suppression of a communication before there can be an adequate determination of whether the lst Amendment protects that communication. Where a communication has been repeated often enough and long enough for prior determination that the lst Amendment does not protect it (as when the communication is obscene), then the communication may be enjoined (*Pittsburgh Press Co. v. Pittsburgh Commission on Human Relations,* 1973). Another exception to the prior restraint rule involves a technical field of legal procedure known as discovery. Discovery occurs under the aegis of a court and is done in preparation for a trial. It occurs when opposing parties to a lawsuit gather evidence from one another by asking and answering questions. The limitation on prior restraint does not apply when one of the parties to a lawsuit attempts to publish information gathered in the discovery process if that information might subject the other party to harassment or harm. However, the party that seeks to publish may do so if it obtains that information by some means other than the discovery process, the Court held in *Seattle Times Co. v. Rhinehart* (1984).

Prior restraint on pretrial publicity to ensure the fairness of a criminal trial is subject to the same review as prior restraint generally. Because prior restraint on speech and publication is the least tolerable infringement on 1st Amendment rights, the restraint may be imposed only where the gravity of the evil and its probability justifies such an invasion. In trial publicity cases, the issue involves the conflict between a fair trial and a public trial. The court must find that pretrial publicity would actually threaten a fair trial, that there are no alternative measures available, and that prior restraint would actually protect the accused, a very difficult test to meet (*Nebraska Press Association v. Stuart,* 1976). If these elements are found, then prior restraint of pretrial publicity will be allowed.

Tangential to such prior restraint is the right of access to press sources. In *Branzburg v. Hayes* (1972), the Court held that the 1st Amendment does not grant a special privilege to reporters to protect them from being forced to divulge confidential information to a grand jury. But a majority of states have enacted press shield laws to allow the press some degree of special protection. Nor does the press have full constitutional protection from exclusion from a pretrial hearing on suppression of evidence, when all parties to the case agree to close the hearing to assure a fair trial. In that instance, the 1st Amendment access interest may be outweighed by the defendant's right to a fair trial (*Gannett Co. v. De Pasquale,* 1979). However, when the defendant wants the pretrial hearing opened, it must be opened, especially when the public has a strong interest in having the hearing opened and the judge's order closing the hearing is too broad or fails to give specific reasons for the closing (*Waller v. Georgia,* 1984). Waller has substantially limited the Court's holding in *De Pasquale.* Trials, even more than pretrial hearings, cannot be closed to the public and the press unless there is an overriding interest with no sufficient alternatives; the Constitution guarantees the public right of access to criminal trials (*Richmond Newspapers Inc. v. Virginia,* 1980). Moreover, jury selection may not be closed to the public.

Limitations on prior restraint do not apply to commercial

Justice Oliver Wendell Holmes, an advocate of 1st Amendment freedoms, enunciated the Court's "clear and present danger" test during the World War I era, when public sentiment often condemned any criticism of the American war effort.

speech cases. A state may, for example, prevent the promulgation of information that would advertise an illegal transaction or would advertise misleadingly. A state in some circumstances may also require that the information be submitted for governmental review before publication.

Freedom Of Speech

The Constitution protects the freedoms of belief and political expression, and the right to organize into groups for religious, political, and social purposes has long been recognized. This freedom of association became controversial during and after World War I, when the Supreme Court first considered the validity of statutory restriction of political radicals.

Early Clear and Present Danger Test. The Espionage Act of 1917 and the Sedition Act of 1918 prohibited false statements that interfered with the military or aided U.S. enemies. The acts were aimed at socialists, communists, and pro-Germans, among others, who were considered to be dangerous by the United States government. The acts were established to prevent any erosion of the country's war position.

Although 1st Amendment protections are important, the courts have established that freedom of expression is not absolute; there must be a balancing between the government interest in regulating expression and the interests upon which the right is based. During World War I, the courts allowed Congress freely to suppress speech when it appeared that such speech might present danger to an important governmental interest, such as military recruitment. A test of requiring clear and present danger (resulting from the speech) before speech could be suppressed was proposed, but as implemented it provided little protection for political speech. The clear and present danger test requires two elements before speech can be prohibited: the speech must present an obvious, definite danger to a substantial government interest, and that danger must be immediate. The test as originally applied did not protect most speech because congressional legislation was presumed to be a valid identifier of a substantial and immediate danger.

There are several areas in which the early clear and present danger test was applied during World War I to allow government regulation of speech and association. Circulars declaring conscription to be unconstitutional were not protected speech due to their perceived threat to the draft, as established in *Schenck v. United States* (1919). Newspaper articles were found to present a clear and present danger when they attacked the U.S. position in wartime, because they could affect troop recruitment and the war effort (*Frohwerk v. United States*, 1919). Public speeches denouncing public policy and advocating socialism could be prohib-

The conviction of Socialist Eugene Debs for public opposition to the role of the United States in World War I was upheld by the Court under the clear and present danger test.

ited due to the clear and present danger posed to recruitment in wartime (*Debs v. United States,* 1919). In *Abrams v. United States* (1919), a majority of the Supreme Court concurred with the holding that publications to hinder production of war materials also could be prohibited under the clear and present danger test. However, the "clear and present danger" test that the majority of the Supreme Court used in *Abrams* was much different from the "clear and imminent danger" test that Justice Holmes applied in his dissenting opinion. The two tests were similar in name and title only; they produced entirely different results when applied to the same facts.

Holmes vigorously dissented from the majority opinion in *Abrams*. In that case, the defendants published leaflets decrying the American invasion of Bolshevik Russia and urging a general strike of munitions workers for the purpose of curtailing the production of munitions. The leaflets were intended to arouse dissatisfaction with the government's conduct of military operations against Russia, a previous co-combatant with the United States against Germany, and to arouse Americans to halt those operations. The majority held that the defendants, young Russian expatriates, had violated the Espionage Act of 1917 and that the 1st Amendment did not protect their political expression. The defendants received lengthy prison sentences and substantial fines even though there was no evidence that they had even approached achieving their goal of impairing the government's military operations against Russia or that they had in any way tangibly harmed American interests.

Holmes's dissenting opinion was eventually to carry the day, for the Supreme Court later incorporated his test for determining when the government could enjoin advocacy of illegal or violent conduct into its own such test. Holmes, who originally articulated the clear and present danger test in *Schenck,* wrote that the United States may constitutionally punish speech that "produces or is intended to produce a clear and imminent danger that will bring about forthwith certain substantive evils that the United States constitutionally may seek to prevent" for the same reasons that would justify punishing persuasion to murder. He went on to state that the government's power to punish such speech "undoubtedly is greater in time of war than in time of peace because war opens dangers that do not exist at other times." Then Holmes wrote:

> But as against dangers peculiar to war, as against others, the principle of the right to free speech is always the same. It is only the present danger of immediate evil or an intent to bring it about that warrants Congress in settling a limit to the expression of opinions where private rights are not concerned.
>
> . . .

In this case sentences of twenty years' imprisonment have been imposed for the publishing of two leaflets that I believe the defendants had as much right to publish as the govern-

The members of the Supreme Court call at the White House to inform President Coolidge that the Court is in session in 1925, when **Gitlow v. New York** *was decided.*

ment has to publish the Constitution of the United States now vainly invoked by them....

Persecution for the expression of opinions seems to me perfectly logical. If you have no doubt of your premises or your power and want a certain result with all your heart you naturally express your wishes in law and sweep away all opposition. To allow opposition by speech seems to indicate that you think the speech impotent, as when a man says that he has squared the circle, or that you do not care wholeheartedly for the result, or that you doubt either your power or your premises. But when men have realized that time has upset many fighting faiths, they may come to believe even more than they believe the very foundations of their own conduct that the ultimate good desired is better reached by free trade in ideas,–that the best test of truth is the power of the thought to get itself accepted in the competition of the market; and that truth is the only ground upon which their wishes safely can be carried out. That, at any rate, is the theory of our Constitution. It is an experiment, as all life is an experiment.... While that experiment is part of our system I think that we should be eternally vigilant against attempts to check the expression of opinions that we loathe and believe to be fraught with death, unless they so imminently threaten immediate interference with the lawful and pressing purposes of the law that an immediate check is required to save the country.... Only the emergency that makes it immediately dangerous to leave the correction of evil counsels to time warrants making any exception to the sweeping command, "Congress shall make no law abridging the freedom of speech." Of course I am speaking only of expressions of opinion and exhortations, which were all that were uttered

here; but I regret that I cannot put into more impressive words my belief that in their conviction upon this indictment the defendants were deprived of their rights under the Constitution of the United States.

In the period between the wars, the Supreme Court continued to give great deference to legislative decisions to regulate speech. There was no requirement that there be any actual harmful result or incitement flowing from the speech before it could be prohibited. In *Gitlow v. New York* (1925), the Court held that language of direct incitement, such as advocacy of criminal anarchy, could be prohibited. States could determine that such language was inimical to the general welfare, and if the statute prohibiting such language was not arbitrary or unreasonable, it would be valid, even if there were no actual harmful results caused by the language. In other words, the Supreme Court required only that there be a sufficient likelihood or tendency to cause harm to justify suppression of speech.

Not only could states prohibit language advocating criminal conduct, they could outlaw organizations that the government believed endangered the peace and welfare of the state. Thus, someone who joined an organization such as the Socialist Party was not protected by the lst Amendment from punishment; that person could be punished for mere membership even if they disagreed with some of the tenets of the party (*Whitney v. California*, 1927). Justice Brandeis, eloquently writing in what in substance was a dissent in *Whitney*, developed a theory of the lst Amendment protec-

When Justice Brandeis joined the Court in 1916, he was characterized as a liberal who would oppose entrenched interests. His eloquent defense of free speech, as in **Whitney v. California,** *and other 1st Amendment freedoms, confirmed his liberal reputation during his long tenure on the Court.*

tions for speech that in later years would become the accepted standard.

Those who won our independence believed that the final end of the state was to make men free to develop their faculties; and that in its government the deliberate forces should prevail over the arbitrary. They valued liberty both as an end and as a means. They believed liberty to be the secret of liberty. They believed that freedom to think as you will and to speak as you think are means indispensable to the discovery and spread of political truth; that without free speech and assembly discussion affords ordinarily adequate protection against the dissemination of noxious doctrine; that the greatest menace to freedom is an inert people; that public discussion is a political duty; and that this should be a fundamental principle of the American government. They recognized the risks to which all human institutions are subject. But they knew that order cannot be secured merely through fear of punishment for its infraction; that it is hazardous to discourage thought, hope and imagination; that fear breeds repression; that repression breeds hate; that hate menaces stable government; that the path of safety lies in the opportunity to discuss freely supposed grievances and proposed remedies; and that the fitting remedy for evil counsels is good ones. Believing in the power of reason as applied through public discussion, they eschewed silence coerced by law–the argument of force in its worst form. Recognizing the occasional tyrannies of governing majorities, they amended the Constitution so that free speech and assembly should be guaranteed.

Fear of serious injury cannot alone justify suppression of free speech and assembly. Men feared witches and burned women. It is the function of speech to free men from the bondage of irrational fears. To justify suppression of free speech there must be reasonable ground to fear that serious evil will result if free speech is practiced. There must be reasonable ground to believe that the danger apprehended is imminent. There must be reasonable ground to believe that the evil to be prevented is a serious one. . . .

Those who won our independence by revolution were not cowards. They did not fear political change. They did not exalt order at the cost of liberty. To courageous, self-reliant men, with confidence in the power of free and fearless reasoning applied through the processes of popular government, no danger flowing from speech can be deemed clear and present, unless the incidence of the evil apprehended is so imminent that it may befall before there is opportunity for full discussion. . . . It is, therefore, always open to Americans to challenge a law abridging free speech and assembly by showing that there was no emergency justifying it.

Moreover, even imminent danger cannot justify resort to prohibition of these functions essential to effective democracy, unless the evil apprehended is relatively serious. Prohibition of free speech and assembly is a measure so stringent that it would be inappropriate as the means for averting a relatively trivial harm to society. . . . But it is hardly conceivable that this court would hold constitutional a statute which punished as a felony the mere voluntary assembly with a society formed to teach that pedestrians had the moral right to cross unenclosed, unposted, waste lands and to advocate their doing so, even if there was imminent danger that advocacy would lead to a trespass. The fact that speech is likely to result in some

violence or in destruction of property is not enough to justify its suppression. There must be the probability of serious injury to the state. Among freemen, the deterrents ordinarily to be applied to prevent crime are education and punishment for violations of the law, not abridgement of the rights of free speech and assembly.

However, two subsequent decisions established that a person could not be punished where there was no evidence that the organization advocated crime or violence, nor when he simply helped to conduct an otherwise lawful meeting held under the auspices of a banned organization (*Fiske v. Kansas,* 1927; *De Jonge v. Oregon,* 1937).

Modern Clear and Present Danger Test. Eventually, the modern clear and present danger test was evolved as a means to protect some categories of expression. The Supreme Court now requires that the substantive harm caused by the speech be extremely serious and the degree of imminence be extremely high before speech may be curtailed. Due to the stricter test, the government is required to demonstrate that a clear and present danger exists before it can regulate expression. Relevant evidence includes: (1) evidence of any substantial effect from the expression; (2) the type of language used; (3) circumstances in which the words were spoken; and (4) the intent of the speaker.

Thus, when the government showed that a speech was given in front of two thousand angry protesters and used

The 1927 Court, led by Chief Justice Taft, (front, center), *was as a whole less liberal in its interpretation of the 1st Amendment than Justice Brandeis* (front, far right).

Justice Harold Burton (**right**) *receives congratulations from President Truman after joining the Court in 1945. Burton voted with the majority in* **Dennis v. United States,** *which upheld the anti-Communist Smith Act.*

virulent language with the intent of causing a riot, the clear and present danger test will be satisfied, and the speech may be prohibited (*Terminiello v. Chicago,* 1949). However, where a statute is found to be too broad because the description of the prohibited speech or the actor's intent is too sweeping, there can be no prohibition of the speech. Under such a statute the standard of guilt will not be sufficiently definite and any conviction will be an unconstitutional infringement upon freedom of speech and association. For example, in *Herndon v. Lowry* (1937), mere membership in the Communist Party and the solicitation of a few members did not show an attempt to incite others to insurrection. No specified conduct or utterance was made an offense.

Post-World War II prosecutions of Communist Party leaders were attempted under the Smith Act of 1940. The act punished any persons who knowingly or willfully advocated overthrowing any government in the United States through force or violence, as well as those who attempted such acts or became members of an organization with knowledge that it was involved in such acts. The validity of the act was upheld in *Dennis v. United States* (1951), in which the Supreme Court declared that Congress may protect the government from violent overthrow by prohibiting expression aimed at inciting such a result. The Court held that the gravity of the evil must be discounted by the improbability of its occurrence in determining whether there is sufficient danger to prohibit speech. This test is viewed by many as a restatement of the clear and present danger test.

The Smith Act does not prohibit mere advocacy or teaching of forcible overthrow as an abstract principle. There

In the late 1950's, the Supreme Court led by Chief Justice Warren (front, second from right), *appointed by President Eisenhower* (third from right), *made decisions that weakened the Smith Act and strengthened 1st Amendment freedoms.*

must be an effort to instigate action to that end before the government may regulate the speech (*Yates v. United States,* 1957). When punishing someone under the membership claim of the Smith Act the government must establish active and knowing membership (*Scales v. United States,* 1961). With the decisions in *Yates* and *Scales* prosecutions under the Smith Act collapsed. The 1st Amendment protection for the individual was advanced.

The Supreme Court became more protective of speech following World War II. The government tried to require the registration of certain organizations in order to impose sanctions upon their members, but those registration provisions have never been successfully implemented. Although such registration requirements were declared valid in *Communist Party v. Subversive Activities Control Board* (1961), the government was required to meet strict criteria: the statutes must deal with a demonstrated substantial danger, the means of regulating the danger must be reasonable, and the regulations must be narrowly drawn.

The Supreme Court has found most of the attempted sanctions unconstitutional. Registration requirements for Communist Party members were found to violate the privilege against self-incrimination in *Albertson v. Subversive Activities Control Board* (1965). Criminal sanctions for the issuance of passports to members of organizations required to register as Communist organizations were declared overbroad and thus unconstitutional in *Aptheker v. Secretary*

of State (1964). The sanctions were overbroad because they applied to people who may not have been aware of their organization's registration requirement and because they were applied without regard to the individual's degree of activity in the organization, or purposes and areas of travel. Employment restrictions prohibiting members of Communist organizations from working in defense facilities were also held unconstitutional. They infringed upon the right of association because they applied to all members regardless of whether or not those members were aware of the registration requirement or agreed with the organization's unlawful aims (*United States v. Robel,* 1967).

The Supreme Court has severely limited the government's ability to prohibit speech that advocates criminal doctrines. In contrast to the holding in *Whitney v. California,* now overruled, the Supreme Court has since held that a state law may not prohibit advocacy of civil disruption without distinguishing mere advocacy from actual incitement to lawless acts. *Brandenburg v. Ohio* (1969) held that a state cannot prohibit advocacy unless the advocacy is directed at inciting lawless conduct and is likely imminently to produce such action. The Supreme Court has moved away from applying the clear and present danger test for this category of speech and now looks at intent and words of incitement on the face of the speech.

Many of the cases in this period deal with the freedom of political expression or association. Political expression has been given much constitutional protection in the areas of state and federal employment. For instance, a state may not prevent the appointment or retention of a "subversive" in state employment by a plan based on vague definitions of offenses. Statutes that bar all members of listed organizations without considering whether the members know of or agree with the organization's unlawful aims are invalid the Court held in *United States v. Robel* and *Keyishian v. Board of Regents* (1967).

There are some very narrow limitations permitted. For the practice of law, for example, states may require applicants for admission to the bar to take an oath to support the federal and state constitutions (*Law Student Research Council v. Wadmond,* 1971). The justification for these requirements is the direct connection between the requirements and the practice of law.

Furthermore, a government may place limits on the right to express political beliefs when those limits are established in an attempt to further that government's legitimate ends. An example of a government's legitimate end would be a city's promotion of its aesthetic character. For instance, a city may enact an ordinance requiring the routine, indiscriminate removal of all posters attached to utility poles and similar objects in order to prevent visual clutter and promote its aesthetic character even when some of the posters removed under the ordinance express political views. However, as established in *Members of the City Council of the City of Los Angeles v. Taxpayers for Vincent* (1984), the ordinance may not favor some viewpoints at the expense of others. This suppression of unpopular speech per se is never a legitimate end without a showing of clear and present danger or incitement.

Right To Travel

Although the right to travel is not specifically granted by the Constitution, it is recognized as a basic federal right that Congress has the authority to protect. Some of that authority comes from the commerce clause of Article I, Section 8 of the Constitution, which grants Congress the power to regulate commerce with foreign nations and among the states. The right to travel is also protected, however, when its restriction infringes upon free speech. This occurs most often in international travel, when the government attempts to keep individuals out of the United States because of their political beliefs or affiliations.

If an individual is denied a passport for failing to provide information on whether or not one is a Communist, then it is an unconstitutional restriction of freedom to travel (*Kent v. Dulles,* 1958). If the denial is based solely on membership in an organization required to register with the government (because of suspected subversive activities), the Court held in *Aptheker v. Secretary of State* that the restriction is unconstitutional.

Some restrictions upon travel are allowed. The secretary of State has the power to revoke passports when he determines that the citizens' activities abroad are likely to cause serious damage to United States foreign policy or national security. This right was upheld in *Haig v. Agee* (1981). The Supreme Court allows this type of restriction because freedom to travel outside the United States is not the same as the right to travel within the United States. Also, protection of national security can be a compelling government interest.

In addition to revoking passports, the secretary of State has the power to adopt area restrictions when issuing passports, as in *Zemel v. Rusk* (1965). Also, refusing to grant alien visas that would allow foreign Communists to enter the United States is a valid exercise of Congress's traditional plenary power over the exclusion of aliens (*Kleindienst v. Mandel,* 1972).

Symbolic Speech

Symbolic speech consists of conduct in place of or in addition to pure speech. Conduct qualifying as symbolic speech may contain both "speech" (expressive) and "nonspeech" (nonexpressive) elements. For example, the burning of a draft card to express symbolically opposition to war or to the draft may constitute symbolic speech.

The distinction between conduct and speech is important. When expression involves only speech elements and no conduct elements, then any government attempt at regulat-

Secretary of State John Foster Dulles was named in **Kent v. Dulles,** *a decision that struck down some restrictions on the freedom to travel.*

ing that expression will receive strict judicial scrutiny and will usually be declared unconstitutional. But when conduct and speech are combined in the same expression, a sufficiently important government interest in regulating the nonspeech element may justify incidental limitations on 1st Amendment freedoms. The government interest, however, in regulating the nonspeech element must be substantial and compelling, the Court held in *United States v. O'Brien* (1968), which involved the protest burning of draft cards. Additionally, the government interest must be unrelated to the suppression of free expression. Moreover, the incidental restriction on alleged 1st Amendment freedom cannot be greater than is essential to the furtherance of that interest; the restriction cannot be overbroad. Finally, the government regulation must be within the constitutional power of the government.

Suppose that high school students wear black armbands to a public school to protest a war. Because this action might seem to contain only "speech" elements, any government attempt to regulate it might seem unconstitutional. However, it may nevertheless involve nonspeech elements if, for example, the wearing of the armbands causes a disturbance or a disorderly argument that interferes with the work and purpose of the school. As the Court held in *Tinker v. Des Moines Independent School District* (1969), only if the armbands actually cause such disturbance may school officials ban or otherwise regulate the wearing of those armbands, at least where other types of buttons and slogans are permitted.

In *O'Brien,* the Supreme Court stated that it would not strike down as unconstitutional an otherwise constitutional statute "on the basis of an alleged illicit legislative motive." The Court's position was that the congressional motivation and purpose in passing a statute was irrelevant to whether the statute unconstitutionally suppressed symbolic speech. However, in later cases, including *Washington v. Davis* (1976), the Court indicated that legislative motivation and purpose may be relevant to a statute's constitutionality. But because those later cases did not involve symbolic speech, it is uncertain whether the *O'Brien* rule regarding legislative motive still stands.

Freedom Of Religion

In the United States, there has traditionally been a separation between church and state. The 1st Amendment contains two references to religion: the "establishment" clause, which forbids laws respecting the establishment of religion, and the "free exercise" clause, which forbids laws prohibiting the free exercise of religion. Together, they protect the individual's freedom of religious belief and practices.

The establishment clause requires that states be neutral in their treatment of and relations with groups of religious believers and nonbelievers. Supreme Court decisions have focused on the intrusion of religious matter into govern-

mental activities and on governmental aid to religious organizations.

Three theories of government action have been advocated. The "no aid" theory prohibits the government from doing anything at all that supports religion or is favorable to the cultivation of religious impact. Under this theory, even legislation with an incidental impact upon religion is suspect. The "neutrality" theory requires the government to be neutral with respect to religious matters; it cannot favor or hinder religion. According to the "balancing test" theory, the government may or must act to accommodate its laws to further religious freedom in order to meet the free exercise guarantee. Freedom of religion guarantees are balanced against establishment clause prohibitions. The balancing test is the most prevalent view because it is often impossible for the government to preclude all aid to religion or to be totally neutral.

The three theories have been applied in many different instances, and the results have varied. In general, where the government action is generalized and neutral in purpose, it is presumptively valid. For instance, a state may use public funds to provide student transportation to parochial as well as public schools because it is held to be a neutral act, aiding education. There is no violation of the establishment clause when governments permit religious institutions to share the social benefits derived from neutral government programs, the Court held in *Everson v. Board of Education* (1947).

Other Court decisions along the same lines have established that a state may require school districts to purchase and loan textbooks to students at parochial and private schools as well as public schools (*Board of Education v. Allen,* 1968; *Wolman v. Walter,* 1977). Under *Zorach v. Clausen* (1952), a state may also grant students permission to leave school grounds during school hours in order to receive religious instruction elsewhere.

Although release time programs are valid, government acts that have a religious purpose or motivation are invalid. Decisions in this area have been particularly controversial. In *Engle v. Vitale* (1962), the Court held that a state may not require daily recitation of prayers in public schools, even where the prayers are nondenominational. States may not include reading and recitation from the Bible in public school activities per the decision in *Abington School District v. Schempp* (1963). Also, states cannot prohibit the teaching of evolution in state-supported schools (*Epperson v. Arkansas,* 1969).

There must be a secular purpose and a neutral effect for legislation to be valid. Sunday closing laws have been held valid because they further the secular purpose of providing a mandatory and uniform day of rest for employees (*McGowan v. Maryland,* 1961). Real property tax exemptions to religious organizations are valid because such organizations contribute to the community in nonreligious ways, as do

The decision of the 1983 Supreme Court in **Bob Jones University v. United States** *reflected the Court's opposition to racial segregation and segregation's continued presence in American society.*

other nonprofit organizations, the Court held in *Walz v. Tax Commission* (1970). A state may also financially assist a religious institution to perform secular state-required tasks, such as testing or record-keeping (*Committee for Public Education & Religious Liberty v. Regan,* 1980).

Government funding for institutions of higher education has been a source of controversy under the establishment clause. In general, no aid or tax exemption may be given by a state to an educational institution that discriminates on the basis of race (*Bob Jones University v. United States,* 1983). However, religious colleges may receive government funds in at least two instances. In two cases, *Tilton v. Richardson* (1971) and *Hunt v. McNair* (1973), the Court held that federal funds may be provided under specified restrictions for the construction of colleges, including church-related institutions, because of the high degree of academic freedom provided. A subsequent case, *Roemer v. Board of Public Works of Maryland* (1976), held that annual grants to colleges, including church-related colleges, are valid. In neither instance, however, may the public funds be applied directly to the furtherance of religious purposes.

The constitutional guarantee of free exercise of religion is often difficult for governments to accommodate. Often, a general, neutral regulation (such as college exams given only on Saturdays and Sundays) interferes with behavior dictated by religious beliefs or compels conduct forbidden by religious beliefs. Thus, free exercise is restricted. However,

limits are placed upon exemptions for religious believers from general regulations by the establishment clause. To avoid this problem, the Supreme Court has distinguished between belief and action. The free exercise clause absolutely prohibits any infringement on freedom to believe but does not absolutely prohibit infringement on action taken upon religious beliefs. Such action may be regulated by the government where there is an important or compelling state interest.

Generally, dissemination of religious beliefs, observance of religious practices, and equality of religions are protected. Sunday closing laws are upheld because they do not directly promote one religious belief over another. The state obviously may not punish someone for worshipping on a day other than Sunday, however (*Braunfield v. Brown,* 1961; *Sherbert v. Verner,* 1963). The state also may not condition receipt of benefits upon conduct proscribed by a religious belief. For instance, a Jehovah's Witness cannot be denied unemployment compensation after leaving a factory job requiring him to produce weapons (*Thomas v. Review Bd. Ind. Empl. Sec. Div.,* 1981). In addition, the Court held in *Wisconsin v. Yoder* (1972) that a state must make provisions in its mandatory education laws for students whose religious beliefs prevent them from attending secondary school.

The government may impose certain "burdens" upon religion that are not unconstitutional if the state can show an overriding governmental interest. Such a burden would be

The decision of the 1939 Supreme Court under Chief Justice Hughes (front, center) *in* United States v. Miller *remains the major statement on the right to bear arms. The Court was then in transition between the conservative Court of the early 1930's and the more liberal one of the 1940's.*

payment and receipt of social security benefits, which are forbidden by the Amish faith. The social security system may be uniformly applied to all, the Court held in *United States v. Lee* (1982).

In recent years there has been much litigation concerning conscientious objectors. Since the decision in the *Selective Draft Law Cases* (1918), it has been established that there is no constitutional right to be a conscientious objector. However, conscientious objectors may be exempted from wartime obligations if they are opposed to all wars in any form (*Gillette v. United States,* 1971). Finally, according to *Johnson v. Robinson* (1974), the government may grant educational benefits to veterans but deny them to conscientious objectors because the resulting incidental burden on free exercise of religion is justified by the government interest served.

2nd Amendment

A well regulated Militia, being necessary to the security of a free State, the right of the people to keep and bear Arms, shall not be infringed.

The 2nd Amendment has not been invoked very often to protect personal liberties. Although many states have questioned the amendment's meaning in the context of gun control, the Supreme Court has dealt with the issue of 2nd Amendment guarantees in only one major case.

In *United States v. Miller* (1939), the Supreme Court held that the purpose of the amendment was to preserve the effectiveness and the continuation of a well-regulated militia. The Court has found no personal right to have, keep, or use firearms guaranteed under the 2nd Amendment. There is also no absolute barrier to governmental regulation of firearms. Many state cases have followed the *Miller* reasoning to allow regulation of the right to bear arms when the possession is unrelated to a government militia.

3rd Amendment

No Soldier shall, in time of peace be quartered in any house, without the consent of the Owner, nor in time of war, but in a manner to be prescribed by law.

The 3rd Amendment has not received much use, although it was designed to assure a fundamental right of privacy, one that had been abused during the colonial period. The first and major federal case to question the meaning of the 3rd Amendment was *Engblom v. Carey,* a decision in 1982 on the Court of Appeals for the 2nd Circuit.

Engblom involved the question of whether the peacetime quartering of troops in any house without the consent of the owner violates the 3rd Amendment. The court of appeals decided that national guardsmen are soldiers within the meaning of the amendment, that the amendment has been incorporated into the 14th Amendment to apply to the states, and that the protection applies to any case where the "owner" has a lawful occupation or possession of the property with the legal right to exclude others. Thus, the 3rd Amendment protects even a tenant from the quartering of troops during peacetime without his consent.

4th Amendment

The right of the people to be secure in their persons, houses, papers, and effects, against unreasonable searches and seizures, shall not be violated, and no Warrants shall issue, but upon probable cause, supported by Oath or affirmation, and particularly describing the place to be searched, and the persons or things to be seized.

The 4th Amendment operates to limit the government's ability to invade an individual's privacy. The amendment prohibits unreasonable searches and seizures and limits the validity of search warrants through numerous requirements. The 4th Amendment requires state action and applies only to unreasonable searches conducted or encouraged by the government, however; private searches are not affected, the Court held in *Burdeau v. McDowell* (1921). Privacy is also protected by the lst, 5th, and 9th Amendments. Many of the criminal law and procedure issues addressed by the 4th Amendment are tangentially considered in the 5th and 6th Amendments.

Historically, the Supreme Court determined the constitu-tionality of a search by the type of property interest involved. If the search invaded a tangible property interest such as the person or his home, the search constituted a physical invasion. If the search invaded an intangible property interest, such as someone's telephone lines, the search was not a physical invasion. Thus, in *Olmstead v. United States* (1928), wire-tapping initially was not seen as an invasion of property rights. This property interest analysis has since been rejected by the Supreme Court. The Court now looks at an individ-ual's expectations of privacy; the 4th Amendment protects people rather than places, so seizures of oral statements as well as tangible items are covered, the Court held in *Katz v. United States* (1967).

The Government stresses the fact that the telephone booth from which the petitioner made his calls was constructed partly of glass, so that he was as visible after he entered it as he would have been if he had remained outside. But what he sought to exclude when he entered the booth was not the intruding eye–it was the uninvited ear. He did not shed his right to do so simply because he made his calls from a place where he might be seen. No less than an individual in a business office, in a friend's apartment, or in a taxicab, a person in a telephone booth may rely upon the protection of the Fourth Amendment. One who occupies it, shuts the door behind him, and pays the toll that permits him to place a call is surely entitled to assume that the words he utters into the mouthpiece will not be broadcast to the world. To read the

Soon after he became chief justice, the Court under William Howard Taft (front, center) *held in* **Burdean v. McDowell** *(1921) that there was a distinction between public and private searches.*

Chief Justice Taft **(left)** *and Justice Oliver Wendell Holmes both sat on the 1928 Court that heard* **Olmstead v. United States,** *the first case to involve wiretapping.*

Constitution more narrowly is to ignore the vital role that the public telephone has come to play in private communication ...The Government's activities in electronically listening to and recording the petitioner's words violated the privacy upon which he justifiably relied while using the telephone booth and thus constituted a "search and seizure" within the meaning of the Fourth Amendment. The fact that the electronic device employed to achieve that end did not happen to penetrate the wall of the booth can have no constitutional significance.

Thus, the 4th Amendment as well as the 1st Amendment protect certain rights to privacy.

With the recognition that privacy interests are protected under the 4th Amendment, the Supreme Court has begun to scrutinize wiretapping techniques. In response, Congress passed legislation in 1980 that established a comprehensive scheme for judicial approval of electronic surveillance. Thus, most of the Court's decisions in this area now involve statutory rather than constitutional interpretation.

Search and Seizure. In general, a search is an examination or probing of someone's belongings with the intent to find contraband or evidence of criminal conduct. Not all searches are searches for 4th Amendment purposes, however. Open fields are not considered to be included under 4th Amendment protections because there is little expectation of privacy in open fields, the Court held in *Hester v. United States* (1924). Dog "sniffs" are not 4th Amendment searches, either (*United States v. Place,* 1983). Also, plain view is a substitute for a search and does not violate the 4th Amendment, a position established by *Coolidge v. New Hampshire* (1971).

> It is well established that under certain circumstances the police may seize evidence in plain view without a warrant. But it is important to keep in mind that, in the vast majority of cases, any evidence seized by the police will be in plain view, at least at the moment of seizure. The problem with the "plain view" doctrine has been to identify the circumstances in which plain view has legal significance rather than being simply the normal concomitant of any search, legal or illegal.

A seizure is forcible dispossession of an object from its owner, or the deprivation of an individual's freedom by taking him into custody. Not all seizures are 4th Amendment seizures. Law enforcement officials cannot randomly stop and search vehicles without cause, but such stops are permissible at roadblocks or fixed checkpoints, such as state or national borders. The random, suspicionless stopping and boarding of vessels in waters accessible to the open sea, however, does not violate the 4th Amendment.

> The nature of waterborne commerce in waters providing ready access to the open sea is sufficiently different from the nature of vehicular traffic on highways as to make possible alternatives to... [the boarding of vessels where there is no articulable suspicion] ...less likely to accomplish the obviously essential governmental purposes involved. The system of prescribed outward markings used by States for vehicle registration is also significantly different than the system of external markings on vessels, and the extent and type of documentation required by federal law is a good deal more variable and more complex than are the state vehicle registration laws. The nature of the governmental interest in assuring compliance with documentation requirements, particularly in waters where the need to deter or apprehend smugglers is great, are substantial.

Warrants. The 4th Amendment protects people against extensive searches by forbidding general warrants. The requirements set forth in the amendment act as built-in safeguards, forcing warrants to be specific in order to be valid. The warrants must describe the particular place to be searched, the persons to be arrested, and the property to be seized. They may be issued only upon probable cause so there must be a reasonable belief that the material sought is where the government wants to search. If a search warrant is too general, the search conducted under it may be invalid.

In addition to the above restrictions, a search warrant may be issued only by a neutral magistrate, as established in *Shadwick v. City of Tampa* (1972) and *Lo-Ti Sales, Inc. v. New York* (1979). Thus, an independent magistrate must evaluate the persuasiveness of the government's contentions regarding the search and, if approved, must word the warrant narrowly to make the search reasonable. When evaluat-

ing probable cause, the magistrate must look to the facts in each instance, the Court held in *United States v. Harris* (1971).

One issue that the Supreme Court often addresses in the area of probable cause is the extent to which a magistrate may rely upon the affidavits of informers. The Court originally used a two-prong test that focused on the reliability of the informer and his basis of knowledge or accuracy (*Aguilar v. Texas,* 1964). Recently, the Court adopted in *Illinois v. Gates* (1983) a "totality of the circumstances" test to evaluate informers' tips.

> This totality of the circumstances approach is far more consistent with our prior treatment of probable cause than is any rigid demand that specific "tests" be satisfied by every informant's tip. Perhaps the central teaching of our decisions bearing on the probable cause standard is that it is a "practical, nontechnical conception"...In dealing with probable cause,... as the very name implies, we deal with probabilities. These are not technical; they are the factual and practical considerations of everyday life on which reasonable and prudent men, not legal technicians, act.

Although the magistrate determines whether probable cause exists, parties may, of course, challenge the evidence upon which probable cause is based, according to the Court's decision in *Franks v. Delaware* (1978).

Searches Without Warrants. Warrantless searches are generally unreasonable under the 4th Amendment. However, the Supreme Court has recognized several types of warrantless searches that are reasonable and constitutional when based upon probable cause. These exceptions include consent searches, searches incident to a lawful arrest, stop and frisk searches, border searches, inventory searches, administrative inspections, and exigent circumstances.

To pass the reasonableness test, warrantless consent searches must be voluntary; that is, the consent must not be a result of coercion or duress. While a warning to the suspect that he has the right to refuse to consent is not required, the nature of the suspect must be examined to determine voluntariness. The Court looks at the suspect's education, intelligence, and the lack of any effective warnings to decide whether his consent was voluntary (*Schneckloth v. Bustamonte,* 1973). The government must establish that consent was voluntary, by at least a preponderance of the evidence, according to *United States v. Matlock* (1974). Consent may be limited by the person granting it.

The warrant exception allowed for searches incident to a lawful arrest is more limited today than it was in the past. This type of search is allowed so that police may locate any concealed weapons in the detained person's immediate vicinity, as determined by *Chimel v. California* (1969).

> When an arrest is made, it is reasonable for the arresting officer to search the person arrested in order to remove any

weapons that the latter might seek to use in order to resist arrest or effect his escape. Otherwise, the officer's safety might well be endangered, and the arrest itself frustrated. In addition, it is entirely reasonable for the arresting officer to search for and seize any evidence on the arrestee's person in order to prevent its concealment or destruction. And the area into which an arrestee might reach to grab a weapon or evidentiary items must, of course, be governed by a like rule. A gun on a table or in a drawer in front of one who is arrested can be as dangerous to the arresting officer as one concealed in the clothing of the person arrested. There is ample justification, therefore, for a search of the arrestee's person and the area "within his immediate control"– construing that phrase to mean the area from within which he might gain possession of a weapon or destructible evidence.

Earlier decisions had established that this search is permitted only where the crime has been committed in the officer's presence and that the items must be observable without any type of intrusion or rummaging. Because the 4th Amendment protects privacy interests, any item in plain view is seizable. In other words, any seizable item that is observable by a police officer who has a lawful right to be where he is may be seized. Great deference is given to the privacy of the arrested person, and an arrest outside a house does not justify search of the house, the Court held in *Vale v. Louisiana* (1970).

The stop and frisk exception is a protection provided to police officers. Upon probable cause under *Terry v. Ohio* (1968), a police officer may stop a suspect and frisk him on the street while questioning the individual. The stop may be based on any reasonable suspicion of criminal activity or an informant's information (*Adams v. Williams,* 1972). A primary concern of the Court is preventing undue harassment of citizens by legislation subjecting them to random scrutinization by law enforcement officials. While invalidating a state law in 1983, the Court said in *Kolender v. Lawson* that "[The state is] unconstitutionally vague on its face because it encourages arbitrary enforcement by failing to describe with sufficient particularity what a suspect must do in order to satisfy the statute."

Warrantless border searches are allowed because every sovereign government has the right to bar dangerous items from entering its country, as established in *Carroll v. United States* (1925). There are few constitutional limitations upon border and harbor inspections. Roving patrols near the border may stop vehicles if there is a reasonable suspicion of criminal activity, and mail may be opened on crossing the border.

Inventory searches and administrative inspections are permitted for public safety reasons. The general test for such inspections has been one of reasonableness; the degree of intrusiveness is weighed against the public interest served. Before 1981, when the regulation was a pervasive one of long standing, a warrantless inspection was generally allowed.

If not a pervasive regulation of long standing, the public interest had to outweigh the invasion of privacy for the warrantless inspection to be valid. Since its decision in *Donovan v. Dewey* (1981), the Court has looked at the pervasiveness and regularity of such regulations to determine whether a warrant is necessary for inspections.

The final exceptions to the warrant requirement are searches under exigent circumstances. These exceptions occur where the delay to obtain a warrant would result in the removal or destruction of the property sought, or where an emergency search is necessary to save a life. Searches of moveable vehicles without a warrant are valid both because the vehicle may be moved and because there is less expectation of privacy in a vehicle. Thus, a car can be searched for contraband upon probable cause even though there has been no warrant issued for the search under the Court's decisions in *United States v. Ross* (1982) and *Michigan v. Thomas* (1982).

Exclusionary Rule. The exclusionary rule, first recognized by the Supreme Court in *Weeks v. United States* (1914), bars evidence from trial that was obtained in violation of a defendant's 4th Amendment rights. In *Mapp v. Ohio* (1961), the Court extended this rule to state court proceedings, to eliminate the use of illegally seized evidence at a trial in a jurisdiction different from where it was seized. The purpose of the exclusionary rule is to deter law enforcement personnel from violating individuals' constitutional rights as well as to maintain judicial integrity. There are exceptions to what evidence is to be excluded from particular forums. Thus, while evidence may not be admitted at trial, it may be admitted in other proceedings, such as grand jury hearing or in civil tax litigation, as the Court held in *United States v. Calandra* (1974) and *United States v. Janis* (1976). The Supreme Court has been limiting the use of the exclusionary rule to the case-in-chief at trial.

In a recent opinion on the exclusionary rule, *Nix v. Williams* (1984), the Court added a new exception that allows the admission of illegally obtained evidence "if the prosecution can establish by a preponderance of the evidence that the information ultimately or inevitably would have been discovered by lawful means." The illegally obtained evidence in *Nix* was the body of a ten-year-old girl murdered on Christmas Eve. A police detective, knowing the suspected murderer to be deeply religious, pointed out to the suspect that snow was expected and might hide the body, denying the parents "a Christian burial for the little girl who was snatched away from them on Christmas Eve and murdered." The suspect led police to the body, but this evidence was obtained illegally and excluded because there was no attorney present during the conversation leading to the discovery of the body. The Court felt, however, that the body would have been discovered eventually because a massive search for it was being conducted as the conversation took place. This new exception applies only where police did not intentionally violate a suspect's rights, where they acted in good faith, and where there is no doubt that the evidence would have eventually been available.

5th Amendment

No person shall be held to answer for a capital, or otherwise infamous crime, unless on a presentment or indictment of a Grand Jury, except in cases arising in the land or naval forces, or in the Militia, when in actual service in time of War or public danger; nor shall any person be subject for the same offence to be twice put in jeopardy of life or limb; nor shall be compelled in any criminal case to be a witness against himself, nor be deprived of life, liberty, or property, without due process of law; nor shall private property be taken for public use, without just compensation.

The 5th Amendment, like the 4th and 6th, provides several protections for individuals in the areas of criminal prosecutions and property rights. It also adds to the protection of personal privacy provided by the 1st, 4th, and 9th Amendments. It may be divided into five distinct parts or guarantees: the right to an indictment by a grand jury, the right against double jeopardy, the right against self-incrimination, the right to due process of law, and the right to just compensation for private property taken. Although the amendment as a whole, because of its multiple parts, has not received extensive judicial analysis, each component has been the subject of much litigation.

Grand Jury Indictment. The 5th Amendment guarantees an individual a right to a grand jury indictment in federal felony proceedings. The reasoning behind this 5th Amendment right is that a person should not be prosecuted for a felony unless some fact-finding body finds it likely that he committed the offense charged. The indictment also assures that the defendant knows what crime he is being charged with, allowing him to prepare an adequate defense.

The 5th Amendment indictment guarantee is not as strong a protection as one might think, for two reasons. First, the requirement for a grand jury indictment has never been applied to the states, per *Hurtado v. California* (1884). Second, there has been a trend toward simplifying procedures. As a result, the technicalities of the indictment procedure are less strictly applied and are rarely fatal to judicial proceedings.

Double Jeopardy. The double jeopardy principle embodies the concept that no person should be tried twice for the same crime. Double jeopardy has a long history in common law, and the common law rules were adopted by the 5th Amendment. As established by *Whalen v. United States* (1980), there are three situations in which those rules may be applied: in a retrial for the same offense after acquittal, in a retrial for the same offense after conviction, and for multiple punishments for the same offense after one conviction.

The double jeopardy rule has been applied to the states. To assert double jeopardy, one must determine when "jeopardy" occurs. The Supreme Court has found that jeopardy attaches when the jury is sworn in in a jury trial, and when the judge begins to hear evidence in a bench trial (*Crist v. Bretz*, 1978).

The application of the double jeopardy rule is not entirely clear-cut. Although a verdict of "not guilty" shields a defendant from the retrial of that offense, if the offense violates several criminal statutes (as will often happen), and the government fails to gain a conviction under one statute, it can retry a defendant under another. If the government successfully convicts on a lesser included offense, however, it cannot attempt to try the defendant on the greater offense later (*Brown v. Ohio*, 1977). Also, the rule does not restrict the government from pursuing a civil case against an individual acquitted in a criminal case.

In recent years the Supreme Court has viewed the double jeopardy rule as a bar to multiple prosecutions of an acquitted defendant. It does not necessarily apply to defendants in other situations. For instance, if a mistrial occurs, there may be another trial allowed for the same offense, the Court held in *United States v. Perez* (1824), although a retrial is not always allowed. The Court generally follows the "manifest necessity" doctrine, which permits retrial after a mistrial when it was a "manifest necessity" to discontinue the original trial. "Manifest necessity" may occur because of jury bias, wartime, a hung jury, or any emergency circumstance that forces the judge to declare a mistrial.

There may also be a retrial allowed when the mistrial is based on the prosecution's error (*Gori v. United States*, 1961). The rule the Supreme Court seemed to follow was one of negligence; retrial would not be allowed if there was a less drastic way to cure the negligent mistake, the Court held in *United States v. Jorn* (1971). The Court tends to balance this test in favor of the public good, to allow retrial. Recently, a new test has developed concerning the prosecution's intent. If the prosecution intended to force the defendant into declaring a mistrial, the double jeopardy rule bars another trial. However, the prosecution's intent is extremely difficult to prove, as shown in *Oregon v. Kennedy* (1982). Retrial is allowed when a mistrial is due to the defense's misconduct.

A mistrial is not the only area in which the double jeopardy rule may not apply. Cases involving dismissals and appeals may be retried in some instances. The double jeopardy clause prohibits retrial after a dismissal if the dismissal is equivalent to an acquittal (*United States v. Martin Linen Supply Co.*, 1977). However, where the dismissal is not based on the merits of the case there may be problems. At one time, under *United States v. Jenkins* (1975), the Supreme Court barred retrial after a dismissal when the retrial would require further findings of fact, regardless of whether the decision was based upon the merits or not. *Jenkins* was overruled because the Court could find no difference between a dismissal not on the merits and a mistrial. Thus, where a defendant successfully obtains a dismissal without demanding a factual determination of his guilt or innocence, he may be retried, as held in *United States v. Scott* (1978).

All states allow defendants to appeal. The government is not barred from retrying a defendant who has won an appeal when the new trial concerns the conviction that he appealed. The Supreme Court reasons that whether or not the defendant waived his plea of jeopardy when he appealed, the original jeopardy is continued because the first conviction is not final. Thus, there is no double jeopardy problem (*Green v. United States*, 1957). There is one exception: the government cannot retry a conviction where the appellate court has found that the prosecution has produced insufficient evidence. This has been upheld in *Burks v. United States* (1978) and *Hudson v. Louisiana* (1981).

Where the original trial involves a greater offense, such as first-degree murder, but the defendant is convicted only of a lesser offense, such as second-degree murder, the defendant is considered acquitted of the greater offense. Thus, if the defendant appeals the lower offense conviction, and wins the appeal, the government cannot retry him on the greater offense, the Court decided in *Green*. This rule applies only if jeopardy attaches for the greater offense. If an inferior court tries a defendant on a lesser charge that is part of a greater state offense, the inferior trial bars state action on the greater offense, unless an essential element of the greater offense develops after the prosecution.

Double jeopardy itself does not preclude the issuance of harsher sentences. However, a sentence cannot be increased when the original sentencing proceeding resembled a trial

JUSTICE BRADLEY.　　JUSTICE MILLER.　　CHIEF JUSTICE WAITE.　　JUSTICE FIELDS.　　JUSTICE MATHEWS.

JUSTICE WOOD.　　JUSTICE GRAY.　　JUSTICE HARLAN.　　JUSTICE BLATCHFORD.

SUPREME COURT OF THE U. S.

States are not required to have a grand jury indictment in felony cases, the 1884 Court held in **Hurtado v. California.**

on guilt or innocence (*Bullington v. Missouri,* 1981). Also, when there is a possibility of vindictiveness involved in sentencing, a harsher sentence is allowed only when the judge gives a reason and factual data supporting the increase in sentence. The data must consist of identifiable conduct occurring after the original sentencing, the Court held in *North Carolina v. Pearce* (1969):

> Due process of law, then, requires that vindictiveness against a defendant for having successfully attacked his first conviction must play no part in the sentence he receives after a new trial. And since the fear of such vindictiveness may unconstitutionally deter a defendant's exercise of the right to appeal or collaterally attack his first conviction, due process also requires that a defendant be freed of apprehension of such a retaliatory motivation on the part of the sentencing judge.
>
> In order to assure the absence of such a motivation, we have concluded that whenever a judge imposes a more severe sentence upon a defendant after a new trial, the reasons for his doing so must affirmatively appear. Those reasons must be based upon objective information concerning identifiable conduct on the part of the defendant occurring after the time of the original sentencing proceeding. And the factual data upon which the increased sentence is based must be made part of the record, so that the constitutional legitimacy of the increased sentence may be fully reviewed on appeal.

The prosecution can appeal pretrial rulings because jeopardy has not attached at that point, so there is no double jeopardy problem. Appeals of nonacquittal dismissals after jeopardy attaches can be made, and if won the defendant can be retried.

The double jeopardy clause applies only to reprosecution for the same offense. The Supreme Court uses two tests to determine when two trials deal with the same offense. They are the "same evidence" test and the "same transaction" test. Under the same evidence test, a conviction or acquittal in a trial bars a subsequent trial if the evidence required to support a conviction in the second trial would have been sufficient to support a conviction in the first. This test limits the double jeopardy protection, for a single act may result in several offenses, leaving the defendant open to multiple prosecutions. However, once convicted of an offense, the defendant cannot be tried on a greater or lesser offense. There are three exceptions to this rule. When the defendant requests separate trials for the greater and lesser offenses, double jeopardy does not bar successive prosecutions. There is no double jeopardy problem when an essential element to a greater offense develops after the prosecution of the lesser offense (*Jeffers v. United States,* 1977). Finally, where the prosecutions are by separate sovereigns, the rule does not apply (*United States, v. Wheeler,* 1978).

Under the same transaction test, as established in *Sanabria v. United States* (1978), all behavior of the defendant that leads to his arrest and conviction must be brought to issue at one trial. While this test does not lead to multiple prosecutions as the same evidence test does, it does not provide a very clear definition of what constitutes a same offense.

An entity may reprosecute a defendant, even if he has already been convicted for the same offense, as long as that entity is a separate sovereign from the one obtaining first prosecution. Thus, both the state and federal governments may convict a single defendant for the same crime, an approach established in *United States v. Lanza* (1922), and reaffirmed in *Bartkus v. Illinois* (1959). However, states and their municipalities are not considered separate sovereignties for double jeopardy purposes (*Waller v. Florida,* 1970). This rule goes against the theory behind the double jeopardy doctrine. The Supreme Court has limited multiple prosecutions by state and federal governments through preemption or liberal construction theories.

Self-incrimination. The 5th Amendment declares that no person should be compelled to be a witness against himself in a criminal case. This guarantee has become very important and controversial in criminal trials. The right is necessary not only to protect the accused but to ensure the integrity of the judicial system as well. The self-incrimination provision is made binding upon the states to further these goals (*Malloy v. Hogan,* 1964).

The protection against self-incrimination extends beyond the trial courtroom and applies to extrajudicial events also. The privilege may be asserted in any governmental inquiry, such as a grand jury hearing or a police questioning. Difficulties often occur, however, when applying the privilege to pretrial discovery and court-ordered psychiatric exams. Privileges against self-incrimination cause problems in pretrial discovery when the prosecution requests the defense to reveal information relevant to the pending case, information that probably came from the defendant. Rules requiring such disclosure are valid if the prosecution has the same discovery obligation.

Similarly, the privilege may cause problems for the admittance of psychiatric exams because the defendant answered questions bearing upon the offense. The general rule in this area assumes that the defendant made a partial waiver of the privilege when he claimed insanity as a defense. This waiver permits the psychiatric inquiry. However, the examining doctor's testimony is limited to his overall conclusions on the sanity issue, and the defendant's actual statement is not included. The self-incrimination privilege bars the use, during the sentencing phase of a capital murder case, of evidence obtained from state-initiated psychiatric exam if the defendant was not warned of his right to remain silent (*Estelle v. Smith,* 1981).

People may assert the privilege against self-incrimination, and this privilege is personal; it may be asserted only by the person to be questioned. Thus, attorneys and accountants cannot claim the privilege on behalf of a client. Ordinarily, a person must affirmatively claim the privilege or it will be waived. The defendant automatically asserts the privilege because the prosecution cannot call him to the stand. A claim of the privilege must be honored unless it is clear that the witness's answers will not be incriminating. Thus, the 5th Amendment is applied broadly to allow a witness to refuse to answer any question that might produce an incriminating answer (*Hoffman v. United States,* 1951). The privilege may be asserted for the first time on cross-examination and cannot be used to infer guilt. When the possibility of self-incrimination remains after conviction, the 5th Amendment often continues to apply. The failure of a defendant to take the witness stand at trial cannot be used as evidence of guilt, the Court held in *Carter v. Kentucky* (1981).

> The freedom of a defendant in a criminal trial to remain silent "unless he chooses to speak in the unfettered exercise of his own will" is guaranteed by the Fifth Amendment and made applicable to state criminal proceedings through the Fourteenth . . . And the Constitution further guarantees that no adverse inferences are to be drawn from the exercise of that privilege . . . Just as adverse comment on a defendant's silence "cuts down on the privilege by making its assertion costly,". . . the failure to limit the juror's speculation on the meaning of that silence, when the defendant makes a timely request that a prophylactic instruction be given, exacts an impermissible toll on the full and free exercise of that privilege. Accordingly, we hold that a state trial judge has the constitutional obligation, upon proper request, to minimize the danger that the jury will give evidentiary weight to a defendant's failure to testify.

The purpose of the 5th Amendment right is to protect against incrimination. If there is no possibility of incrimination from an answer, the 5th Amendment protection does not apply. This situation occurs if the government offers the witness immunity from prosecution, or if the statute of limitations has run on the underlying offense. Statements from immunized testimony can be used against witnesses only in a subsequent perjury trial.

Although the 5th Amendment attempts to protect individuals against incrimination, it does not protect them against every incriminating statement made; the right only bars the use of those statements obtained through coercion or compulsion. The test to determine whether compulsion exists is whether under the circumstances the witness could not exercise free will (*United States v. Washington,* 1977). Records required to be kept by statute are not protected by the 5th Amendment. However, possibly incriminating information required to be disclosed under statutes directed at a select group in an area permeated by criminal statutes is protected, the Court held in *Marchetti v. United States* (1968). Such statutes include registration and occupational tax laws applying only to gamblers. Compulsion does not extend to a person other than the one against whom the evidence is to be used.

Miranda and Its Successors. Compulsion in connection

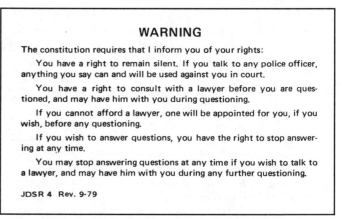

WARNING

The constitution requires that I inform you of your rights:

You have a right to remain silent. If you talk to any police officer, anything you say can and will be used against you in court.

You have a right to consult with a lawyer before you are questioned, and may have him with you during questioning.

If you cannot afford a lawyer, one will be appointed for you, if you wish, before any questioning.

If you wish to answer questions, you have the right to stop answering at any time.

You may stop answering questions at any time if you wish to talk to a lawyer, and may have him with you during any further questioning.

JDSR 4   Rev. 9-79

The standard warning read by police to suspected criminals is known as a "Miranda warning" and is used as a result of the Court's decision in **Miranda v. Arizona** *(1966).*

with pretrial investigations will invoke the 5th Amendment protection. The Supreme Court has determined that there must be an affirmative waiver of that protection against self-incrimination whenever someone is being interrogated by law enforcement officials. The decision in *Miranda v. Arizona* (1966) has been a source of controversy and has been criticized as hampering the efforts of law enforcement officers. Thus, for a statement made under interrogation to be admissible, a set of warnings must be given to the accused informing him of his right to remain silent.

> He must be warned prior to any questioning that he has the right to remain silent, that anything he says can be used against him in a court of law, that he has the right to the presence of an attorney, and that if he cannot afford an attorney one will be appointed for him prior to any questioning if he so desires. Opportunity to exercise these rights must be afforded to him throughout the interrogation. After such warnings have been given, and such opportunity afforded him, the individual may knowingly and intelligently waive these rights and agree to answer questions or make a statement. But unless and until such warnings and waiver are demonstrated by the prosecution at trial, no evidence obtained as a result of interrogation can be used against him.

Failure to give what have became known as Miranda warnings can lead to the exclusion of incriminating evidence even if the information is volunteered.

The Court recently established the first exception to the requirement to give Miranda warnings before interrogation, that being for "overriding considerations of public safety." In *New York v. Quarles* (1984), a woman informed two police officers that she had just been raped by a gunman and that he was inside a nearby supermarket. The officers located the suspect, noticed his empty gun holster, and asked for the location of the gun–which he gave them–without first reading him the Miranda warnings. The Court held that the threat of a loaded gun in a public place was paramount to the suspect's rights. The Court does "not believe that the doctrinal underpinnings of *Miranda* require that it be applied in all its rigor to a situation in which police officers ask questions reasonably prompted by a concern for the public safety."

Although a written waiver is not required, any waiver of 5th Amendment protection must be voluntary and intelligent, according to *North Carolina v. Butler* (1979). Silence after the Miranda warnings is not a valid waiver. However, a witness's admission of an incriminating fact does constitute a waiver with respect to details associated with the admission, unless they present a real danger to further incrimination. In many courts, a waiver made in grand jury proceedings extends to trial, even though generally a waiver in one proceeding does not extend to a later proceeding. An otherwise valid confession is admissible in court if not coerced, and the state need only prove voluntariness by a preponderance of the evidence to have a confession admitted at trial.

In addition to the incrimination and compulsion requirement, application of the 5th Amendment protection against self-incrimination requires that the information be testimonial. In other words, individuals are protected from compelled information of a testimonial or communicative nature only. In *Schmerber v. California* (1966), the Court held that:

> It could not be denied that in requiring petitioner to submit to the withdrawal and chemical analysis of his blood the State compelled him to submit to an attempt to discover evidence that might be used to prosecute him for a criminal offense. He submitted only after the police officer rejected his objection and directed the physician to proceed. The officer's direction to the physician to administer the test over petitioner's objection constituted compulsion for the purposes of the privilege. The critical question, then, is whether petitioner was thus compelled "to be a witness against himself."
>
> ...Not even a shadow of testimonial compulsion upon or enforced communication by the accused was involved either in the extraction or in the chemical analysis. Petitioner's testimonial capacities were in no way implicated; indeed, his participation, except as a donor, was irrelevant to the results of the test, which depend on chemical analysis and on that alone. Since the blood test evidence, although an incriminating product of compulsion, was neither petitioner's testimony nor evidence relating to some communicative act or writing by the petitioner, it was not inadmissible on privilege grounds.

Thus, blood samples, handwriting samples, voice samples, fingerprints, measurements, photographs, and compulsion to appear in a lineup, stand, walk, or gesture in court are not normally subject to 5th Amendment protection.

Written documents may pose a problem here because they are not as clearly testimonial as are verbal statements. Originally, private books and papers were considered protected under the 5th Amendment (*Boyd v. United States,* 1886), but today such protection is almost nonexistent. Per-

sonal business papers are not protected, and the privilege does not extend to the preparation of the papers. Thus, documents voluntarily prepared are not protected.

Due Process. The 5th Amendment guarantees that no one will be deprived of life, liberty, or property without due process of law. This guarantee, which originally applied only against the federal government, was extended to the states by the 14th Amendment. The protection under the 5th Amendment is the same as that under the 14th. Due process guarantees are discussed more fully under the 14th Amendment.

Taking Property. Under the 5th Amendment, neither the federal nor state governments can take private property for public use without giving the owner just compensation for the property. Although this power of eminent domain is essential to the conduct of government, this amendment limits that power. The government cannot single out individuals' property to sacrifice for the public good when, in all fairness, the burden should be borne by the public as a whole, the Court held in *Armstrong v. United States* (1960).

To apply the 5th Amendment protection, there must be a taking by the federal or a state government. A taking technically occurs when the owner is deprived of the use of his property, either through physical takeover or destruction of value.

Destruction of value may occur, for example, when a government regulates property use in such a way that the property's owner may not fully use the property. Occasionally, zoning ordinances are struck down as being a taking without compensation for this reason, for such ordinances sometimes significantly reduce property values. However, not all governmental actions that reduce property values are takings. They may instead be only regulations not severe enough to amount to takings. As a general, empirical rule, regulations relating to land use (zoning), environmental protection, and landmark preservation are held to be takings only in rare instances.

The taking must be for a public use. A government may not use its power of eminent domain to transfer property from one private party to another, regardless of the amount of compensation. A government may use that power only to acquire property that it then puts to a public use. Damages resulting from a loss of business due to a taking of land are not recoverable as part of the compensation, the Court held in *Mitchell v. United States* (1925).

If the taking is justified by the owner's use of the property to injure others, such as polluting, compensation is not required. Just compensation is the fair market value of the property at the time it was taken, the full monetary equivalent of the property taken (*United States v. Reynolds,* 1970). Lost investment profits are ignored; only the diminution of property value is relevant to determining whether a taking has occurred and the amount of compensation that must be paid.

6th Amendment

In all criminal prosecutions, the accused shall enjoy the right to a speedy and public trial, by an impartial jury of the State and district wherein the crime shall have been committed, which district shall have been previously ascertained by law, and to be informed of the natures and cause of the accusation; to be confronted with the witnesses against him; to have compulsory process for obtaining Witnesses in his favor, and to have the Assistance of Counsel for his defence.

The 6th Amendment protects the defendant in a criminal trial, allowing him a fair opportunity to prepare his case. The guarantees under this amendment are constantly exercised in criminal proceedings today. The 6th Amendment adds to the protection provided for criminal defendants by the 4th and 5th Amendments.

Speedy, Public Trial. The 6th Amendment provides for speedy and public trials in criminal cases. Speedy trials protect the accused from prolonged detention prior to trial, as well as from anxiety about the charges made and public suspicion. This protection is important because it is thought to be in the accused's best interest to litigate before evidence disappears or memories fade. As the Court said in *Dickey v. Florida* (1970):

The right to a speedy trial is not a theoretical or abstract right but one rooted in hard reality in the need to have charges promptly exposed. If the case for the prosecution calls on the accused to meet charges rather than rest on the infirmities of the prosecution's case, as is the defendant's right, the time to meet them is when the case is fresh. Stale claims have never been favored by the law, and far less so in criminal cases. Although a great many accused persons seek to put off the confrontation as long as possible, the right to a prompt inquiry into criminal charges is fundamental and the duty of the charging authority is to provide a prompt trial. This is brought sharply into focus when, as here, the accused presses for an early confrontation with his accusers and with the State. Crowded dockets, the lack of judges or lawyers, and other factors no doubt make some delays inevitable. Here, however, no valid reason for the delay existed; it was exclusively for the convenience of the State. On this record the delay with its consequent prejudice is intolerable as a matter of fact and impermissible as a matter of law.

The right to trial by jury in criminal cases was recognized by the common law. The 6th Amendment embodied this common law right, which has since been extended to the states in *Duncan v. Louisiana* (1968). The Supreme Court considers the jury's function to be fundamental to the administration of criminal justice; the jury functions as a buffer between the accused and the government. The 6th Amendment does not require a specific number of jurors or a particular make-up for a jury; juries can be structured in any way as long as they remain effective. However, juries of fewer than six members would unconstitutionally impair the purpose and functioning of the jury, the Court held in *Ballew v. Georgia* (1978). There is also no requirement that the jury verdict be unanimous where the jury has more than six members, while six-member juries must make unanimous decisions to convict defendants.

The 6th Amendment guarantees that the jury will be impartial and take its members from the community where the crime occurred. Jury members must also represent a fair cross-section of the community, the Court held as early as 1879 in *Strauder v. West Virginia.* Intentional, systematic exclusion of minorities from juries is unconstitutional. The defendant need only show systematic exclusion of a "significant discrete" group to prove unconstitutional underrepresentation (*Taylor v. Louisiana,* 1975).

We accept the fair-cross-section requirement as fundamental to the jury trial guaranteed by the Sixth Amendment and are convinced that the requirement has solid foundation. The purpose of the jury is to guard against the exercise of arbitrary power–to make available the commonsense judgment of the community as a hedge against the overzealous or mistaken prosecutor and in preference to the professional or perhaps overconditioned or biased response of a judge...This prophylactic vehicle is not provided if the jury pool is made up of only special segments of the populace or if large, distinctive groups are excluded from the pool. Community participation in the administration of the criminal law, moreover, is not only consistent with our democratic heritage but is also critical to public confidence in the fairness of the criminal justice system. Restricting jury service to only special groups or excluding identifiable segments playing major roles in the community cannot be squared with the constitutional concept of jury trial.

The prosecution may not use its challenges to create a jury that will return a verdict of death nor prevent questioning about racial prejudice if racial issues are involved in the trial. Otherwise, the guarantee of an impartial jury would be violated.

Although the 6th Amendment guarantees the accused a trial by an impartial jury, the guarantee does not apply to all criminal cases. The crime charged must be "serious" before the 6th Amendment may be invoked, and "serious" means that the crime may be punished with imprisonment for more than six months. Jury trials are not required in the adjudicatory phases of state juvenile court proceedings because they would impair the purpose of juvenile courts by making the proceedings indistinguishable from criminal trials. Jury trials are also not required where the sentence is probation, no matter how long. Finally, jury trials are not required where there are multiple violations involved, each with its own sentence of less than six months.

The accused has the option of waiving his right to a jury trial in any criminal case. The judge must determine that the waiver is express and intelligent (*Patton v. United States,* 1930). In addition, the waiver must be authorized by the prosecution and the court (*Singer v. United States,* 1965). As established by *Gannett Co., Inc. v. DePasquale* (1979),

Associate Justice Hugo Black (right) *swears in future justice Thurgood Marshall* (center) *as solicitor general as President Johnson observes. Black wrote the Court's majority opinion in* **Pointer v. Texas.**

the accused also has the option of having pretrial suppression hearings closed to the public, if all other parties agree. However, closing a trial or any courtroom proceeding to the public is hardly possible: it is only in the extraordinary case that the media may be excluded from the courtroom. It is not clear whether the 6th Amendment guarantees the right to a public trial to benefit the defendant or the public.

The right to a speedy trial is extended to the states through the 14th Amendment (*Klopfer v. North Carolina,* 1967). The sole remedy for the violation of this right is dismissal, because failure to provide a speedy trial cannot be cured by a new trial. The speedy trial guarantee applies only after a person has been accused of a crime, although the due process clause provides some protection in the case of preaccusation delay.

In *Barker v. Wingo* (1972), the Supreme Court balanced four factors to determine whether a speedy trial has been denied a defendant: the length of the delay, the reason for the delay, the time that the defendant first asserted his right, and whether any actual prejudice to the defendant resulted. These factors must be applied after trial has been completed. In addition to the *Barker* test, there is statutory law, the Federal Speedy Trial Act, that enforces specific deadlines for different stages of criminal proceedings. Despite the protection for this privilege, the right to a speedy trial is seldom asserted.

Informed of the Charge. The 6th Amendment requires that a person accused of a crime be informed of the nature and the cause of the charge against him. This right allows the accused to prepare an adequate defense. If not informed of the charge against him, he could not meet the requirement that proof and allegations correspond. This guarantee has not received much litigation at the Supreme Court level. The Supreme Court held in *Logan v. United States* (1982), however, that a reading of the indictment to the accused is sufficient to show that the accused was informed of the accusations against him.

Confront Witnesses. Under the 6th Amendment, the accused has the right to confront all witnesses against him in any criminal prosecution. There has been little major litigation involving this right, although it has been applied to the states in *Pointer v. Texas* (1965). Although this right ensures that the jury will have an opportunity to evaluate the credibility of the plaintiff's witnesses, basic evidence law has been modernized to assure fair trials. Because evidence rules allow defendants to produce and examine evidence, there is little need to raise confrontation claims.

The right of a defendant to confront the witnesses against him is determined by the same standards, regardless of whether the proceeding is state or federal (*Smith v. Illinois,* 1968). This confrontation guarantee is not absolute; if a witness is unavailable, his testimony is still admissible if the government has made a good faith effort to secure his presence, according to *Barber v. Page* (1968). Also, when crucial witnesses die between a trial overturning a conviction and the retrial, a transcript of the testimony the deceased witness had given at the earlier trial is admissible. The admission of the testimony of an unavailable witness is based upon its reliability or trustworthiness.

In addition to the right to confront witnesses against the defendant, the confrontation clause, per *Pointer,* guarantees the defendant the right to cross-examine such witnesses. Originally, the Supreme Court suggested that this privilege is not waived when the defendant fails to cross-examine witnesses in a preliminary hearing. The right of confrontation was considered a trial right, so even if a defendant did not cross-examine a witness in a preliminary hearing, he would still have the right to confront that witness at trial.

More recently, in *California v. Green* (1970) and *Ohio v. Roberts* (1980), the Court has considered that the opportunity to cross-examine a witness at a preliminary hearing satisfies the confrontation clause. However, when a codefendant's confession is introduced at trial, the defendant's confrontation right is violated even if there is a jury instruction limiting the evidence to the codefendant. The admission causes prejudicial error. If the codefendant takes the stand, there is no 6th Amendment problem. Cross-examination may include any relevant matter.

Under the 6th Amendment the accused has the right to be present in the courtroom at all stages of his trial. This privilege may be lost by consent or extreme misconduct in the courtroom and may be reinstated upon the resumption of good conduct. The Supreme Court determined in *Illinois v. Allen* (1970) three ways for a judge to deal with an unruly defendant that satisfy the confirmation privileges: bind and gag him, cite him for contempt, or remove him until he promises to behave.

Compulsory Process. The 6th Amendment guarantees the accused the privilege of compulsory process for obtaining witnesses. In the seventeenth century, the accused was allowed to call favorable witnesses but not to compel their attendance. The compulsory process clause eliminated this inhibition on the accused, constitutionalizing his right to present the evidence necessary for an effective defense. This privilege has been construed broadly to cover letters and papers, guaranteeing the right of process at an early enough stage to give the accused adequate time to prepare a defense.

The compulsory process clause has been applied to the states in *Washington v. Texas* (1967). States may not violate compulsory process privileges by enforcing laws that exclude certain classes of people from testifying on behalf of the defendant. The Supreme Court interprets the 6th Amendment as guaranteeing a defendant the right to put his witnesses on the stand.

> The right to offer the testimony of witnesses, and to compel their attendance, if necessary, is in plain terms the right to present a defense, the right to present the defendant's version of the facts as well as the prosecution's to the jury so it may decide where the truth lies. Just as an accused has the right to confront the prosecution's witnesses for the purpose of challenging their testimony, he has the right to present his own witnesses to establish a defense. This right is a fundamental element of due process of law.

He should have the same advantage as the government does in presenting his case. If the government can subpoena certain witnesses or put them on the stand, the principle of evenhandedness will bar any prohibition of the accused's rights in these respects.

The 6th Amendment guarantees will be violated by unfair treatment of the defendant in presenting his case. If a judge harshly admonishes the defense witnesses and no others, compulsory process has been violated, the Court held in *Webb v. Texas* (1972).

> The trial judge gratuitously singled out this one witness for a lengthy admonition on the dangers of perjury. But the judge did not stop at warning the witness of his right to refuse to testify and of the necessity to tell the truth. Instead, the judge implied that he expected Mills to lie, and went on to assure him that if he lied, he would be prosecuted and probably convicted for perjury, that the sentence for that conviction would be added on to his present sentence, and that the result would be to impair his chances for parole. At least some of these threats may have been beyond the power of this judge to carry out. Yet, in light of the great disparity between the posture of the presiding judge and that of a witness in these circumstances, the unnecessarily strong terms used by the judge could well have exerted such duress on the witness' mind as to preclude him from making a free and voluntary choice whether or not to testify.
>
> ... In the circumstances of this case, we conclude that the judge's threatening remarks, directed only at the single witness for the defense, effectively drove that witness off the stand, and thus deprived the petitioner of due process of law under the Fourteenth Amendment.

If the jury is instructed to evaluate defense witnesses' testimony on a stricter standard than for other witnesses, compulsory process has also been violated. Even the presidential withholding of evidence can violate compulsory process, despite the interest in confidentiality, a position established in *United States v. Nixon* (1974).

While evenhandedness and equal access are the major measures for compliance with compulsory process privileges, the Supreme Court has recently invoked a "harmlessness" test. Under this test, in *United States v. Valenzuela-Bernal* (1982), the defendant must make some showing that the excluded evidence would be relevant, material, and useful to his case. This test applies when the evidence or witness is excluded in furtherance of a substantial governmental policy. Thus, there must be some reason to believe that the exclusion hurt the defendant's case before a 6th Amendment violation will be declared.

DIVISION OF CORRECTIONS
CORRESPONDENCE REGULATIONS

MAIL WILL NOT BE DELIVERED WHICH DOES NOT CONFORM WITH THESE RULES

No. 1 -- Only 2 letters each week, not to exceed 2 sheets letter-size 8 1/2 x 11" and written *on one side only,* and if ruled paper, do not write between lines. *Your complete name* must be signed at the close of your letter. *Clippings, stamps, letters* from other people, *stationery* or *cash* must not be enclosed in your letters.

No. 2 -- All *letters* must be addressed in the *complete prison name* of the inmate. *Cell number,* where applicable, and *prison number* must be placed in lower left corner of envelope, with your complete name and address in the upper left corner.

No. 3 -- *Do not send any packages without a Package Permit.* Unauthorized *packages* will be destroyed.

No. 4 -- *Letters* must be written in English only.

No. 5 -- *Books, magazines, pamphlets,* and *newspapers* of reputable character will be delivered *only if* mailed direct from the publisher.

No. 6 -- *Money* must be sent in the form of *Postal Money Orders* only, in the inmate's complete prison name and prison number.

INSTITUTION _____/_____ CELL NUMBER _____

NAME _____ NUMBER _____

In The Supreme Court of The United States
Washington D.C.
Clarence Earl Gideon
Petitioner | *Petition for a writ*
vs. | *of Certiorari directed*
H.G. Cochran, Jr, as | *to The Supreme Court*
Director, Divisions | *State of Florida.*
of corrections State | No. **890** Misc.
of Florida | OCT. TERM 1961
U.S. Supreme Court

To: The Honorable Earl Warren, Chief
Justice of the United States
Comes now The petitioner, Clarence
Earl Gideon, a citizen of The United states
of America, in proper person and appearing
as his own counsel. Who petitions this
Honorable Court for a Writ of Certiorari
directed to The Supreme Court of The State
of Florida. To review the order and Judge-
ment of the court below denying The
petitioner a writ of Habeus Corpus.
Petitioner submits That The Supreme
Court of The United States has The authority
and jurisdiction to review the final Judge-
ment of The Supreme Court of The State
of Florida the highest court of The State

Clarence Earl Gideon's petition to the Supreme Court, handwritten in a Florida prison, resulted in increased legal protection for indigent defendants unable to afford counsel.

Right to Counsel. Probably the most important right protected by the 6th Amendment is the right to have the assistance of legal counsel in a criminal defense. This right is aimed at securing the defendant a fair trial by protecting him from a conviction due to his ignorance of the law, as established in *United States v. Wade* (1967). The *Miranda* decision also guarantees the defendant a right to counsel, but the 6th Amendment right is broader. While the Miranda rule applies only to custodial interrogations, the 6th Amendment does not require custody; it applies to undercover work as well.

Today, the right to counsel is considered necessary for fundamental fairness. Thus, indigents must be provided with counsel. This right to counsel for indigents is applied to the states through the 14th Amendment. In the landmark case of *Gideon v. Wainwright* (1963), the Supreme Court unanimously decreed that all criminal defendants have a right to legal counsel regardless of whether they are tried in federal or state court. Before *Gideon,* defendants had no constitutional right to legal counsel when tried in state court. But in *Gideon* the Supreme Court held that the right to be provided

with counsel was "fundamental and essential to fair trials." The Court pointed out that "[g]overnments, both state and federal, quite properly spend vast sums of money to establish machinery to try defendants" and that "few defendants...fail to hire the best lawyers they can get to prepare and present their defense. That government hires lawyers to prosecute and defendants who have the money hire lawyers to defend are the strongest indications of the widespread belief that lawyers in criminal courts are necessities, not luxuries." Additionally, the Court reasoned, "[f]rom the very beginning, our state and national constitutions and laws have laid great emphasis on procedural and substantive safeguards designed to assure fair trials before impartial tribunals in which every defendant stands equal before the law. This noble ideal cannot be realized if the poor man charged with crime has to face his accusers without a lawyer to assist him." The Court then quoted with approval a former Supreme Court justice, who had written that "[t]he right to be heard would be, in many cases, of little avail if it did not comprehend the right to be heard by counsel."

Originally limited to capital cases, the scope of the right to counsel has been expanded to include all felony cases and even misdemeanors where the defendant receives a jail term of any length. The right to counsel also exists in any civil proceeding that results in institutional commitment (*In re Gault,* 1967). In both instances there must be an actual confinement for the right to apply.

Where the accused does have a right to counsel, restrictions on the counsel's ability to represent his client at trial may be unconstitutional. For instance, a defendant cannot be prevented from consulting with his attorney during a recess between direct and cross-examination, and statutes cannot require the defendant to testify before any other defense testimony can be heard. Such regulations unconstitutionally infringe upon the client's right to counsel.

The Supreme Court has clearly determined that the right to counsel is applicable at trial. The Court is now concerned with whether this right applies to pretrial and post-trial proceedings. Applying an equal protection analysis (an analysis based on the equal protection clause of the 14th Amendment) of the issue, the Court determined in *Griffin v. Illinois* (1956) that where state appellate review depends on the availability of a transcript of trial proceedings, a transcript must be provided for indigent defendants. Also, indigent defendants have a right to appointed counsel in appeals as of right, but that right does not extend to discretionary appeals.

Under a different analysis of this issue, an indigent defendant has the right to counsel in every "critical stage" in the prosecution against him. This analysis is the one used most frequently by the Supreme Court. A "critical stage" is some adversarial judicial proceeding in which the rights of the accused could be affected and an attorney's presence would help avoid any prejudice. Thus, a preliminary hearing to determine whether there is probable cause to send a case to the grand jury is a critical stage requiring a right to counsel. Per *Miranda,* the category of critical stage in a criminal prosecution also includes custodial interrogations.

Recently, the Supreme Court has limited the critical stage theory to the time after the formal charge or indictment; arrest alone will not trigger the right to counsel (*Kirby v. Illinois,* 1972). In general, indictments, formal charges, preliminary hearings, arraignments, sentencing, and parole revocation proceedings all invoke the right to counsel privilege. Thus, noncustodial interrogations after indictment, such as obtaining statements from the defendant by hidden radio transmitters, violate the right to counsel when the defendant already has a lawyer, and postindictment identification proceedings such as lineups are also subject to the right to counsel.

Because the Supreme Court dislikes the broadness of the critical stage test, it has developed two new tests to assess right to counsel violations. One test examines the challenged event to see if it is a trial-like confrontation. If the accused needs a counsel's help to deal with legal problems or the prosecutor, the event is a trial-like confrontation and invokes the right to counsel privilege. Thus, counsel is not required at pretrial photo identification sessions for witnesses.

The second test the Supreme Court has recently begun to use is a case-by-case test. Under this test, the Court evaluates each claim by its facts to determine whether a right to counsel exists. Although parole and probation revocation proceedings have traditionally required the presence of counsel, that privilege is applied on a case-by-case basis. The privilege to counsel at summary courts-martial of enlisted Marines has also been denied based on the case-by-case test. The Court appears to consider whether or not the accused claims either that he did not commit the alleged offenses or that there are complex mitigating factors involved. If the accused appears to have difficulty speaking for himself, the Court will be more likely to grant the 6th Amendment privilege.

Like preconviction stages of criminal proceedings, postconviction stages may invoke a right to counsel. There is no general right to counsel for prisoners who seek postconviction relief. However, a state cannot prohibit inmates from helping each other prepare habeas corpus petitions without providing alternative assistance.

Denial of the right to counsel results in a reversal of any judgment obtained against a defendant without counsel. The right to counsel may be waived by the accused if the waiver is voluntary and intelligent, according to *Johnson v. Zerbst* (1938). However, courts generally will rule in favor of application of the privilege when there is doubt about the validity of a waiver. Waiver cannot be presumed from a silent record; it must be explicit.

In deciding whether a defendant's waiver is voluntary and intelligent, courts consider the defendant's age, edu-

cation, mental condition, experience, and surrounding circumstances, including the way the right to counsel was explained. Although courts have an automatic presumption against waivers of this right, the defendant's wish to represent himself will be recognized. In fact, the Supreme Court has held, in *Faretta v. California* (1975), that a criminal defendant has a constitutional right to defend himself without the assistance of counsel.

The right to counsel would be useless if the counsel did not adequately represent his client. When counsel is inadequate, the conviction resulting from the ineffective assistance will be reversed. Ineffective assistance claims have risen dramatically in recent years, probably due to limitations placed on habeas corpus actions and the increase in young public defenders.

Originally, most courts required an extremely high level of incompetency before an attorney's performance could be considered ineffective. The standard was extremely vague and difficult to apply, placing a tremendous burden of proof upon the defendant. Recently, the standard has been redefined by several courts. A malpractice-type standard has been applied by the Supreme Court, in *McMann v. Richardson* (1970), analyzing a counsel's assistance according to whether it was within the normal and customary degree of skill possessed by attorneys in similar cases. In most jurisdictions the defendant still has the burden to prove that the counsel was incompetent and that the incompetence was prejudicial to his case. A minority of courts have shifted the burden to the prosecution to show lack of prejudice once the incompetence has been established.

There are several areas in which ineffective assistance will be found. One such area is the preparation for trial. Consulting a client for the first time five minutes before trial, failure to interview key witnesses, and failure to check for a prior record all constitute ineffective counsel. Other areas include preparation of defense, state interference in the attorney-client privilege, the counsel's knowledge of the law, and conflict of interest. A 1984 Supreme Court ruling on effective counsel, *Strickland v. Washington,* established the most specific guidelines yet. A criminal defender will have been denied effective counsel if his attorney's performance falls below "prevailing professional norms" and "there is a reasonable probability that, but for counsel's unprofessional errors, the result of the proceeding would have been different."

7th Amendment

> In suits at common law, where the value in controversy shall exceed twenty dollars, the right of trial by jury shall be preserved, and no fact tried by a jury, shall be otherwise reexamined in any Court of the United States, than according to the rules of the common law.

The 7th Amendment provides a right to a jury trial in civil suits, a guarantee so important to the judicial system that any curtailment of the right to a jury trial has been examined closely by the Court. The 7th is similar to the 6th Amendment in this respect, but does not apply in criminal cases, and the guarantee applies to federal but not to state courts. This right also protects private litigants from the oppression of judges.

Originally, the 7th Amendment privilege was applied according to the "historical" test: courts looked at the English system to determine which types of claims were legal and which were equitable. Under the common law, there was a right to a jury trial when the case involved a legal remedy. However, when a case involved both legal and equitable claims, courts of equity applied the "clean up doctrine" and heard the entire suit in equity, without a jury. The legal-equitable distinction has become less recognizable because law and equity have merged in the United States. Today, when a civil claim involves both legal and equitable issues, the right to a jury trial exists. The suit need not be primarily legal; the privilege applies even when the only legal issue is found in a counterclaim.

According to the Supreme Court in *Dairy Queen Inc. v. Wood* (1962), the right to a jury trial attaches to every legal issue. Thus, when money damages are sought, when the cause of action is analogous to a tort at common law, or when the action involves rights and remedies traditionally enforced in legal actions, a jury trial is guaranteed. There is no right to a jury trial when there are no issues of fact to be tried, however.

A new test for the application of the 7th Amendment has developed recently. Courts weigh three factors to determine whether the case is legal or equitable. They look at premerger custom, the remedy sought, and the practical abilities and limitations of the jury (*Ross v. Bernhard*, 1970). Many state courts have applied the jury limitation factor to deny a jury trial when the case is complex. The Supreme Court has several times rejected the complexity exception, using the nature of the issues involved to determine whether the 7th Amendment applies.

8th Amendment

> Excessive bail shall not be required, nor excessive fines imposed, nor cruel and unusual punishments inflicted.

The 8th Amendment provides protection for defendants in all cases. It deals with the processes of setting bail and sentencing. While the excessive bail prohibition has not been explicitly applied to the states, the cruel and unusual punishment clause has been under *Stack v. Boyle* (1951) and *Robinson v. California* (1962).

The 8th Amendment stipulates that bail shall not be excessive. The amendment is unclear as to whether there is a constitutional right to bail, or only a prohibition against excessive bail when bail is granted. The Supreme Court has never directly addressed this interpretation problem, for federal statutes have always guaranteed that privilege in all noncapital cases.

Bail furthers the presumption of innocence until guilt is proven. Without bail, the accused would essentially be punished for a crime for which he has not been proven guilty. Excessive bail has the same effect. The idea behind bail is to ensure the appearance of the accused at trial. Excessive bail is bail set at a higher amount than would reasonably be needed to accomplish that goal. Bail is usually not set for an amount greater than the maximum monetary sentence for the crime charged.

What constitutes "excessive" depends upon the facts of the individual case. The nature of the crime is often the determining factor. For instance, the right to bail is normally denied in capital cases because a person accused of a crime for which he may be put to death is very likely to flee if let out of confinement. The Supreme Court has indicated that an individual's attachment to the community, his prior criminal record, and his physical condition may be considered in setting bail (*Chambers v. Mississippi*, 1972).

In addition to pretrial guarantees, the 8th Amendment may prohibit excessive bail after conviction. Not all jurisdictions allow postconviction bail for an accused who is appealing his case. However, the Supreme Court has stated that bail should not be denied after conviction except for strong reasons. There are stricter standards for postconviction bail; courts consider the likelihood of reversal, the seriousness of the conviction, the length of the sentence given, and the threat to the community.

The most widely known aspect of the 8th Amendment is its prohibition against cruel and unusual punishment. The standard for "cruel and unusual" is a fluctuating one because it evolves from social values and standards. However, some generalizations are clear. Cruel and unusual punishment is perceived as punishment that causes an unnecessary and wanton infliction of pain (*Gregg v. Georgia*, 1976). Punishment cannot be grossly out of proportion to the severity of the crime charged, nor can it violate the convicted individual's dignity (*Rummell v. Estelle*, 1980). A proportionality analysis considers such factors as the gravity of the offense and the harshness of the penalty, the sentences imposed on other criminals in the same jurisdiction, and the sentences imposed for commission of the same crime in other jurisdictions.

In the area of noncapital offenses, the Supreme Court has been unwilling to set aside sentences that are seemingly disproportionate, deferring to the states in such decisions, unless the sentence is preposterously excessive. Thus, the Court declared in *Solem v. Helm* (1983) that a life sentence with no possibility of parole constitutes cruel and unusual punishment when imposed as a result of a seventh nonviolent felony. Such declarations by the Court are rare.

The Death Penalty. The Court has been far more active in regard to capital punishment. The 8th Amendment has been used to declare the death penalty invalid in a number of cases. Mandatory death sentences violate the 8th Amendment, as established in *Roberts v. Louisiana* (1976) and *Woodson v. North Carolina* (1976). Arbitrary death sentences with no established criteria for application also violate the 8th Amendment, according to *Furman v. Georgia* (1972). Mandatory and arbitrary death sentences must be replaced by legislative schemes that provide objective standards for judges and juries. For example, a statute that provides for two trials, one to determine guilt and one for sentencing, enables juries to review evidence pertinent to sentencing and that is inadmissible in a criminal trial. Under *Gregg v. Georgia,* this type of standard is not cruel and unusual punishment.

The Supreme Court looks at contemporary standards concerning punishments, as well as social values, history, and jury determinations when considering the constitutionality of a death penalty. To avoid 8th Amendment problems, juries must review all mitigating and aggravating circumstances when sentencing, according to *Jurek v. Texas* (1976). Such circumstances include any aspect of the defendant's character or record. Thus, a conviction for drunkenness is not necessarily cruel and unusual, and neither is paddling school children to keep discipline in class. However, there can be no death penalty imposed on a defendant who merely aided in a felony that resulted in a killing by another, where the defendant had no intent to kill (*Edmund v. Florida,* 1982). Nor can the death penalty be imposed for a rape (*Coker v. Georgia,* 1977).

9th Amendment

The enumeration in the Constitution, of certain rights, shall not be construed to deny or disparage others retained by the people.

The 9th Amendment was enacted to protect inherent natural rights not enumerated in the Constitution from legislative encroachment. Although the amendment protects personal and not public rights, it is seldom used to protect those rights. There has been no direct Supreme Court judicial construction of the amendment, although the Court has distinguished this amendment from the first eight, which deal with limitations rather than rights. One of the most important rights protected by the 9th Amendment is personal privacy, also protected by the 1st, 4th, and 5th Amendments.

Originally, under *Fox v. Ohio* (1847), the first eight amendments were applicable to the states, whereas the 9th Amendment was restricted to the federal government. Today, however, the 9th Amendment guarantees are applied to state governments. For example, states cannot deprive citizens of their right to retain property by taxing citizens to support private industry (*Savings and Loan Association v. Topeka,* 1875). Also, states are prohibited from interfering with a citizen's right to privacy (which is also protected by the 14th Amendment). In essence, then, the 9th Amendment protects any person from the deprivation of any right that is

The 1875 Court, under Chief Justice Waite (center), *established 9th Amendment rights for private citizens in* **Savings and Loan Association v. Topeka.**

inherent to human nature, when the deprivation occurs by a governmental act, at either the national or state level.

10th Amendment

The powers not delegated to the United States by the Constitution, nor prohibited by it to the States, are reserved to the States respectively or to the people.

The 10th Amendment is basically a truism, stating that all the powers not surrendered to the federal government are retained by the states, a position upheld in *United States v. Darby* (1941). The amendment protects states from federal intrusions that might threaten their separate and independent existence. According to the Supreme Court in *Fry v. United States* (1975), Congress cannot exercise its powers in a way that would impair a state's ability to function effectively in the federal system. Thus, any federal act that eliminates a state's ability to structure its vital governmental functions is unconstitutional.

There is a three-prong test, developed in *National League of Cities v. Usery* (1976), that must be met for an act to be unconstitutional under the 10th Amendment. First, the act must regulate the states as states. Second, it must deal with matters indisputably attributable to the state. Third, and most important, the state's compliance must directly impair its ability to structure its integral functions. This test will not apply if the exercised power has been expressly delegated to the federal government. Nor will it apply if the exercised power can be implied from an expressly delegated power (*United States v. Butler,* 1936). In both cases, there is no question of an infringement upon a 10th Amendment guarantee because the power *was* delegated to the federal government by the Constitution.

To determine when a federal act violates the three-prong test, the Supreme Court must first decide whether the issue concerns an unreserved power left to the states. There are certain functions over which states have traditionally presided. States have the power to structure their own internal governments. Taxation, laws concerning gaming, and contracts are considered to be within state powers as well as the exercise of power over state courts. Regulation of agricultural production and the production of oil, gas, and petroleum within a state is also considered to be reserved to the states.

In addition to the above powers, states have exclusive jurisdiction to regulate or control marriages and divorces within their borders. Under *Standard Oil Co. v. New Jersey* (1951), states may dispose of property within their borders when owners remain unknown after efforts are made to find them. States also have broad powers to determine voting requirements and conditions under which voting rights may be exercised (*Evans v. Cornman,* 1970).

The Supreme Court has used the three-prong test to limit federal regulation of state powers. Even though the federal government's power to regulate commerce is very broad, it cannot, under *Usery,* force states to apply federal minimum wage and maximum hour requirements to state employees; such requirements displace a state's ability to structure employer-employee relationships that are vital to its government. However, federal regulation of labor relations in state-owned railroads does not impair a state's ability to carry out a sovereign function. Also, the application of the Age Discrimination in Employment Act of 1967 to state and local government practices is a valid exercise of commerce clause power, the Court held in *Equal Employment Opportunity Commission v. Wyoming* (1983). In addition, Congress *can* exclude articles from interstate commerce when their use could reasonably be expected to injure public health, morals, or welfare, or when their use would contravene the destination state's policy. Finally, the government can impose liability upon a state for misusing funds from federal education grants without violating the 10th Amendment (*Bell v. New Jersey,* 1983).

Although the federal government has the authority to use all appropriate means to exercise a granted power, there are some limitations. Federal courts must apply state law where to do otherwise would result in discrimination by the noncitizen against a citizen, or the lack of uniform administration of state law. The government cannot impose cumulative penalties greater than those specified by state law for violations of state criminal codes by state citizens, and the government cannot force federal drug control laws on states if they fall within state police powers.

In general, any government effort to control or prevent activities constitutionally subject to state regulation cannot be achieved by broad, sweeping means that invade areas of protected freedoms. However, the federal government can use delegated powers to override countervailing state interests in economic activities validly regulated by the government when engaged in by private persons (*Maryland v. Wirtz,* 1968). For instance, businesses are subject to both federal and state law. Where federal and state laws and regulations of particular businesses conflict, federal law prevails. Where a state regulates a particular economic activity that Congress could regulate exclusively if it so chose, Congress may constitutionally pass legislation forcing states to regulate that activity in certain ways.

13th Amendment

SECTION 1. Neither slavery nor involuntary servitude, except as a punishment for crime whereof the party shall have been duly convicted, shall exist within the United States, or any place subject to their jurisdiction.

SECTION 2. Congress shall have power to enforce this article by appropriate legislation.

In 1914, the Court's decision in **United States v. Reynolds** *reaffirmed the 13th Amendment's guarantee against involuntary servitude. The 1914 Court included such noted associate justices as Charles Evans Hughes, a future chief justice* (**front, right**), *and Oliver Wendell Holmes* (**front, second from right**).

The 13th Amendment, adopted in December 1865 in the aftermath of the Civil War, is divided into two parts. The first part essentially abolishes slavery. The amendment is aimed at creating and maintaining a system of free and voluntary labor, according to *Pollock v. Williams* (1944), while slavery and involuntary servitude are conditions of enforced compulsory service of one to another. Thus, peonage, or the practice of holding people in servitude or partial slavery to work off debts, is invalid under the Constitution.

The 13th Amendment not only prohibits governments from establishing involuntary servitude; it prohibits slavery on the private, individual level in order to establish freedom for everyone. Although the amendment was aimed at blacks, it can be used by others to guarantee freedom from slavery, the Court held in the *Slaughter-house Cases* (1872).

Several different types of laws have been questioned on the basis of whether they create involuntary servitude. Plaintiffs must show that a compulsion to work exists. Statutes requiring every healthy male between certain ages to either work on roads and bridges for six days per year, provide a substitute, or instead pay the overseer three dollars do not impose involuntary service under the 13th Amendment, although they would probably today violate the due process clause; they are not compulsory (*Butler v. Perru,* 1916). Conscription requirements for military

service also do not impose involuntary servitude. However, the Supreme Court has decided that no type of indebtedness validates a suspension of the right to be free from compulsory service.

There are many decisions that apply the 13th Amendment to situations of indebtedness and contractual relations. Statutes that use the failure or refusal to perform or refund money gotten under a contract with an employer as prima facie evidence of an interest to injure or defraud are invalid under this amendment, per *Bailey v. Alabama* (1911). This amendment may also be violated when a contract to work off indebtedness is created as the result of a criminal conviction. The 13th Amendment *allows* compulsory service as punishment for a crime, as in a criminal sentence of hard labor. Such a sentence, however, is a public penalty; any other form of compulsory labor is considered involuntary servitude and, thus, unconstitutional. Involuntary servitude was found to exist unconstitutionally in *United States v. Reynolds* (1914), where a convict "comes into court with a surety, and confesses judgement in the amount of fine and costs, and agrees with the surety, in consideration of the payment of that fine and costs, to perform service for surety." Although this appears to be a valid contract exchanging labor for the payment of a legal fine, in fact, "[c]ompulsion of such service by the constant fear of imprisonment under the criminal laws renders the work compulsory, as much so as authority to arrest and hold his person would be if the law authorized that to be done." Additionally, such a contract may result in compulsory service greater than that which the state would have required, had the sentence been hard labor rather than a fine. In *Reynolds,* the convict would have been sentenced to ten days of hard labor had he failed to pay his fine, plus fifty-eight days for court costs; in contrast, his surety demanded nine months and twenty-four days to pay off the same debt, and he was subject to rearrest for failure to perform this service.

In addition to these contractual cases, the Supreme Court applies the 13th Amendment to race discrimination claims. In *Heart of Atlanta Motel v. United States* (1964), the Court held that public accommodation provisions requiring unwilling motel operators to give blacks rooms do not constitute involuntary servitude. Also, closing city streets commonly traversed by blacks through white residential neighborhoods does not violate the 13th Amendment when there is no discriminatory motive to outweigh interests of child safety (*City of Memphis v. Greene,* 1981).

The varieties of private conduct that Congress can regulate under the 13th Amendment today extend beyond the actual imposition of slavery or involuntary servitude. For instance, the Supreme Court in *Flood v. Kuhn* (1972) declared professional baseball's reserve system for players lawful under the 13th Amendment. In another decision, an act that made unlawful the coercion of a licensee to employ more employees than those needed to conduct a radio broadcast, was held constitutional under the 13th Amendment. Legislation that classifies employee strike activity as an unfair labor practice unless the employee leaves the premise in an orderly manner to go on strike also complies with 13th Amendment limitations (*International Union Local 232 v. Wisconsin Employment Relations Board,* 1949).

Now that claims arising under the 13th Amendment have moved away from strict slavery or involuntary servitude questions, recent cases brought before the Supreme Court tend to rely less on the 13th Amendment and more on other amendments dealing with civil rights and equal protection. For instance, the 13th Amendment does not protect the individual rights of blacks, so it does not directly apply to claims concerning the validity of deed covenants prohibiting transfer of property to blacks. In contrast, the 14th Amendment does apply to such claims. The difference is that the 13th Amendment concerns slavery, not race, color, or class, whereas the 14th Amendment deals with the latter types of classifications (*Civil Rights Cases,* 1883). Thus, decisions concerning race, such as equal representation in voting and private conspiracies to discriminate in employment contexts, all involve the 14th Amendment, as well as the

13th. The 13th Amendment remains a back-up for civil rights litigation.

14th Amendment

SECTION 1. All persons born or naturalized in the United States, and subject to the jurisdiction thereof, are citizens of the United States and of the State wherein they reside. No State shall make or enforce any law which shall abridge the privileges or immunities of citizens of the United States; nor shall any State deprive any person of life, liberty, or property, without due process of law; nor deny to any person within its jurisdiction the equal protection of the laws.

SECTION 2. Representatives shall be apportioned among the several States according to their respective numbers, counting the whole number of persons in each State, excluding Indians not taxed. But when the right to vote at any election for the choice of electors for President and Vice President of the United States, Representatives in Congress, the Executive and Judicial officers of a State, or the members of the Legislature thereof, is denied to any of the male inhabitants of such State, being twenty-one years of age, and citizens of the United States, or in any way abridged, except for participation in rebellion, or other crime, the basis of representation therein shall be reduced in the proportion which the number of such male citizens shall bear to the whole number of male citizens twenty-one years of age in such State.

SECTION 3. No person shall be a Senator or Representative in Congress, or elector of President and Vice President, or hold any office, civil or military, under the United States, or under any State, who, having previously taken an oath, as a member of Congress, or as an officer of the United States, or as a member of any State legislature, or as an executive or judicial officer of any State, to support the Constitution of the United States, shall have engaged in insurrection or rebellion against the same, or given aid or comfort to the enemies thereof. But Congress may by a vote of two-thirds of each House, remove such disability.

SECTION 4. The validity of the public debt of the United States, authorized by law, including debts incurred for payment of pensions and bounties for services in suppressing insurrection or rebellion, shall not be questioned. But neither the United States nor any State shall assume or pay any debt or obligation, incurred in aid of insurrection or rebellion against the United States, or any claim for the loss or emancipation of any slave; but all such debts, obligations and claims shall be held illegal and void.

SECTION 5. The Congress shall have power to enforce, by appropriate legislation, the provisions of this article.

The 14th Amendment was adopted in 1868 in the Reconstruction period following the Civil War. The first and fifth sections were adopted to help the Civil Rights Bill of 1866 protect the freedom and citizenship of the newly-freed slaves. The second, third, and fourth sections of the amendment represented the desire of the North to punish the South and its citizens and no longer have any true significance.

Prior to the Civil War, the guarantees of the Bill of Rights protected individuals from federal interference but were not enforceable against the states (*Barron v. Mayor and City Council of Baltimore,* 1833). The 14th Amendment is interpreted as applying most of the Bill of Rights guarantees to state citizens, as, indeed, it appears many of the amendment's drafters intended. It took decades, however, for this interpretation to evolve. The Court held in *The Slaughterhouse Cases* (1873), one of the first decisions reached by the Supreme Court on the 14th Amendment, that its clause protecting citizens from state infringement on their privileges and immunities applied only to their rights of national citizenship, not to the rights guaranteed by their state citizenship. This restrictive interpretation is still valid; most of the rights that today are credited to the 14th Amendment come from its clauses, particularly the first section, guaranteeing all persons equal protection of the laws and due process, or fairness, in the application of those laws.

As individual rights became incorporated within the two significant 14th Amendment clauses and were thereby made binding upon the states, a debate grew as to whether the Bill of Rights should be incorporated totally or selectively. Selective rights that are fundamental principles of liberty are to be incorporated. In fact, the proponents of total incorporation have won, as nearly the entire Bill of Rights has been incorporated, item by item, in the century since the 14th Amendment was adopted. In *Palko v. Connecticut* (1937), the Court defined the fundamental principles of liberty that are to be selectively incorporated into the 14th Amendment as those that are implicit in the concept of ordered liberty. The Court held that the 5th Amendment prohibition against double jeopardy was not sufficiently fundamental as to warrant its application to the states. This opinion has since been overruled.

In the early 1960's, the Warren Court took a broader approach to selective incorporation and relaxed the *Palko* test. Today, any guarantee that is fundamental to the states' judicial processes would be incorporated. In fact, every important Bill of Rights guarantee has been incorporated into the 14th Amendment except for 5th Amendment grand jury indictment provisions and the 7th Amendment's right to jury trials.

Most of the better known incorporation cases involve criminal procedural guarantees, such as the right to counsel in *Gideon v. Wainwright* (1963) and *Powell v. Alabama* (1932); the option for six-member juries and nonunanimous jury verdicts in *Williams v. Florida* (1970) and *Apodaca v. Oregon* (1972), respectively; and the exclusion of illegally-obtained evidence from criminal trials in *Mapp v. Ohio* (1961).

Substantive Due Process

Initial review and application of the 14th Amendment due process clause focused on the fairness of the states' legal *procedures.* In fact, it is the *substantive* reasonableness of state legislation that eventually became of prime importance in 14th Amendment interpretation. Rather than concentrating on whether state regulation was equitably applied, the Supreme Court shifted its focus to the substantive contents of state regulation, determining whether a regulation deprived states' citizens of a fundamental right unfairly or without due process of law.

Economic Rights. The Supreme Court's first extended use of 14th Amendment substantive due process concerned economic rights and was nearly always applied to decrease government interference in the economic sphere. *Allgeyer v. Louisiana* (1897) was the first case in which a state statute was struck down on substantive due process grounds. In holding that a state could not prevent its citizens from obtaining insurance from out-of-state companies, the Court stated that the 14th Amendment guarantees all citizens freedom to work in any legal employment and to enter into any contracts relevant to that employment.

The most significant of the many economic substantive due process cases decided in the early 1900's was *Lochner v. New York* (1905). The *Lochner* case marked an era, now greatly criticized and looked upon as a time when the Supreme Court lost its perspective on American priorities and fundamental rights, when economic rights were valued and protected by the Court above almost all others. In *Lochner,* the Court struck down a statute limiting bakery employees' hours to ten per day and sixty per week as violative of the liberty to contract. The purposes of protecting a labor force that might have decreased bargaining power and of protecting the public safety and health were found to be valid but not sufficiently important to warrant infringing what the Court then believed to be the much more significant interest in the freedom to contract. The Court articulated in *Lochner* a test of very strict scrutiny whenever economic rights were restricted in favor of public health, safety, welfare, or morals. Infringement of economic rights required that the restriction imposed, or the means, be very closely related to an important and legitimate purpose or end, and the close means-ends nexus was not found in *Lochner.*

The *Lochner* philosophy of closely scrutinizing all economic regulation was pervasive in Supreme Court decisions until the late 1930's. During this period, the Court struck down minimum wage laws and anti–yellow dog contract laws (laws prohibiting employers from conditioning employment on promises to not join a union), but upheld laws aimed at groups the Court found to need special protection, such as women.

In the years following *Lochner,* the decision was widely

President Theodore Roosevelt's appointments helped to liberalize the Court's consideration of individual rights. A conservative majority, however, still controlled the Court in 1905 when it held unconstitutional, in Lochner v. New York, *a state law limiting working hours.*

criticized, and the Court began to lessen its scrutiny of economic regulation, deferring more and more to legislative judgment. *Nebbia v. New York* (1934) signaled a departure from *Lochner,* where the Court upheld a state regulation on milk-industry prices, deferring to the state legislature's economic policy. The *Lochner* era is considered to have been officially ended, however, when the Court upheld a state minimum wage law, *West Coast Hotel v. Parrish* (1937), because of the need to equalize the bargaining power of disadvantaged workers. Following *West Coast Hotel,* in the wake of the realization of the harms inflicted by the Court during the *Lochner* era, less and less scrutiny has been used on cases involving economic regulation. In *U.S. v. Carolene Products* (1938), the Court abandoned nearly all scrutiny for a presumption of constitutionality for legislative economic

regulation. Finally, *Williamson v. Lee Optical Co.* (1955) established the modern test of minimal rationality for economic legislation, that is, that the legislation will be upheld if the Court can find that it has some rational basis.

Privacy and Family Relations. While the Court now gives almost no substantive due process review to economic rights, nearly always deferring to legislative judgment, substantive due process has recently become important for such noneconomic rights as privacy, autonomy, and family relations, which are considered to be fundamental rights, although they are not enumerated within the Constitution. These fundamental rights are protected from infringing legislation by a strict standard that scrutinizes legislation and requires that the state have a compelling purpose for the law and that the means adopted be necessary to achieve that end. Where a right is found to be nonfundamental, such as an economic right, the Court uses the minimal rationality scrutiny of *Williamson v. Lee Optical,* which amounts to virtually no review at all.

Among the very first noneconomic rights to be considered fundamental by the Courts were the rights to acquire knowledge through education (*Meyer v. Nebraska,* 1923), and of marriage and procreation (*Skinner v. Oklahoma,* 1942). By far, however, most noneconomic fundamental rights cases have concerned familial rights and have been decided within the last twenty years. Essentially, the Court has ruled that personal choice in nearly all family matters is fundamental; any regulation restricting personal choice in family matters must be justified by a compelling state interest and must be so narrowly tailored as to effect only that interest.

Griswold v. Connecticut (1965) was the first major case to apply substantive due process strict scrutiny to state legislation regulating familial rights. The Court held unconstitutional a statute that prohibited all use of contraceptive devices and all aid and counseling in their use. The Court overturned the convictions of two Planned Parenthood administrators for counseling married couples, holding that the statute invaded privacy interests that, although not explicitly enumerated in the Bill of Rights, could be inferred from it.

> This law...operates directly on an intimate relation of husband and wife and their physician's role in one aspect of that relation...Various guarantees create zones of privacy. The right of association contained in the penumbra of the First Amendment is one, as we have seen. The Third Amendment in its prohibition against the quartering of soldiers "in any house" in time of peace without the consent of the owner is another facet of that privacy. The Fourth Amendment explicitly affirms the "right of the people to be secure in their persons, houses, papers, and effects, against unreasonable searches and seizures." The

Chief Justice Taft's Court held in **Meyer v. Nebraska** *(1923) that the right to gain knowledge through education was fundamental.*

Fifth Amendment in its Self-Incrimination Clause enables the citizen to create a zone of privacy which government may not force him to surrender to his detriment. The Ninth Amendment provides: "The enumeration in the Constitution, of certain rights, shall not be construed to deny or disparage others retained by the people."

...The present case, then, concerns a relationship lying within the zone of privacy created by several fundamental constitutional guarantees. And it concerns a law which, in forbidding the use of contraceptives rather than regulating their manufacture or sale, seeks to achieve its goals by means having a maximum destructive impact upon that relationship. Such a law cannot stand in light of the familiar principle, so often applied by this Court, that a "governmental purpose to control or prevent activities constitutionally subject to state regulation may not be achieved by means which sweep unnecessarily broadly and thereby invade the area of protected freedoms."

Eisenstadt v. Baird (1972) and *Carey v. Population Services Int'l.* (1977) made clear that *Griswold* was intended to protect the privacy interests of unmarried individuals and minors who also could not be denied access to and use of contraceptives.

Abortion. The fundamental right of privacy protected by the strict scrutiny of substantive due process was expanded in 1973 to include abortion in *Roe v. Wade*.

This right of privacy... is broad enough to encompass a woman's decision whether or not to terminate her pregnancy. The detriment that the State would impose upon the pregnant woman by denying this choice altogether is apparent. Specific and direct harm medically diagnosable even in early pregnancy may be involved. Maternity, or additional offspring, may force upon the woman a distressful life and future. Psychological harm may be imminent.

In 1965, Associate Justice Douglas (right) *wrote the Court's decision in* Griswold v. Connecticut, *the first major application of the due process clause to state regulation of familial rights.*

Mental and physical health may be taxed by child care. There is also the distress, for all concerned, associated with the unwanted child, and there is the problem of bringing a child into a family already unable, psychologically and otherwise, to care for it. In other cases, as in this one, the additional difficulties and continuing stigma of unwed motherhood may be involved. All these are factors the woman and her responsible physician necessarily will consider in consultation.

The Court in *Roe,* applying the latest scientific findings, divided pregnancy into three trimesters of three months each and held that a state may regulate a woman's right to an abortion only when there is a state interest more compelling than the woman's right to privacy and autonomy, such as the health of the mother (in the second trimester) or the life of the fetus (during the third trimester). Thus, a woman is free to choose an abortion during the first trimester with no state restrictions, but a state may regulate procedures for second-trimester abortions to protect the mother's health, and a state may prohibit third-trimester abortions where a viable fetus is present.

Since *Roe,* the Court has ruled on many controversial issues surrounding abortion. State requirements that a woman give written informed consent to her abortion are valid. The Court in *Planned Parenthood v. Danforth* (1976) held that a woman's right to privacy and autonomy protects her decision to have an abortion and thus this decision cannot be made subject to spousal or parental consents. More recently, however, several cases have held that parental consent to an abortion may be made a requirement when a minor has been found, in a judicial hearing, to be either too immature or unemancipated to make an intelligent, independent decision. The Supreme Court has ruled that states are not constitutionally compelled to fund either nontherapeutic (*Maher v. Roe,* 1977) or medically necessary (*Harris v. McRae,* 1980) abortions.

Despite *Roe* and subsequent opinions, abortion has remained a controversial and emotional issue. Anti-abortion forces counted President Reagan among their supporters, and in 1985 the Justice Department filed a brief requesting the Court to overturn *Roe.* The brief asked that the Court "return the law to the condition in which it was before that case [*Roe*] was decided" and claimed that those who wrote the 14th Amendment "would have been surprised" by *Roe.*

The Supreme Court has recently had to decide a variety of cases in which a state's interest in various aspects of social welfare has come into conflict with some aspect of

President Reagan's public support of anti-abortion sentiment created controversy and led to claims that the executive branch was attempting to influence the judicial branch of government.

family relations. With few exceptions, the Court has found freedom within the family unit to be a fundamental right, which may be restricted only by a compelling state interest. In *Moore v. City of East Cleveland* (1977), the Court held that a state cannot prohibit an extended family from living together by zoning restrictions merely to prevent overcrowding and traffic problems. *Parham v. J.R.* (1979) established the right of parents to commit their children to state mental hospitals without a hearing to protect the children, holding that children's rights are circumscribed by parental interest and responsibility. That the right to marry is fundamental was established in *Zablocki v. Redhail* (1978). There, the Court struck down a statute denying marriage licenses to parents with unfulfilled support obligations for children from previous marriages, holding that a state could find alternative means to enforce child-support short of infringing on the fundamental right of marriage.

Other aspects of privacy protected by substantive due process concern the disclosure of personal information and maintenance of autonomy in decision-making, but exceptions to such protection have been made by the Court. In *Doe v. Commonwealth's Attorney* (1976), the Supreme Court affirmed a lower court's decision upholding a sodomy law even when it was applied to consenting adults. Thus, homosexuality is not given the same protection as other aspects of family relations. Similarly, the right to engage in adultery is not a part of the right to privacy protected by substantive due process. A lower court decision condoning the discharge of two public library employees for openly committing adultery was allowed to stand in *Hollenbaugh v. Carnegie Free Library* (1978). Personal appearance may be regulated, the Court decided in *Kelley v. Johnson* (1976), where there is a strong state interest. Here, the Court found that the length of a policeman's hair may be regulated because having easily recognizable and similar appearances may aid police in protecting the public. The Supreme Court permitted the gathering of information on prescription drug users in *Whalen v. Roe* (1977), despite the legal drug users' desire for privacy, holding that the individual's interest was outweighed by the state's interest in maintaining such information, finding that no harm was inflicted upon the affected individuals since the information was kept confidential.

Procedural Due Process

In substantive due process cases, the denial of a liberty is assumed; for purposes of substantive due process, any person's interest may be a liberty. Procedural due process, however, requires that only tangible liberties or properties be afforded due process for their denial by state government. In order to determine whether process is actually due and what, in that case, the process must be, a court

must first determine which liberties and properties are entitled to due process.

Traditionally, the Court has defined the terms "liberty" and "property" quite broadly, permitting them to encompass a variety of interests and benefits, except for public and governmental benefits, which were considered to be privileges. Recently, however, the Court has recognized that much of society has become so dependent on these public benefits that they are now entitled to them by right. The term "property" has now come to include real and personal property, money, and interests acquired in specific private benefits, as well as legitimate claims to public benefits.

Goldberg v. Kelly (1971) established that welfare recipients had a constitutional right to this aid and could not be denied it without a hearing. A license to drive an automobile is also a constitutional right that cannot be revoked without a hearing (*Bell v. Burson,* 1971). This expansion of entitlements, however, has not gone so far as to include all government activities. In *Board of Regents v. Roth* (1972), the Court held that a state university is not required to hold a hearing to determine whether or not to rehire every nontenured faculty member. The right to state employment is not a constitutionally protected property right, nor is the firing of an employee necessarily a denial of his liberty to be employed. *Perry v. Sindermann* (1972), however, established that the practices of an employer may create a property interest in that employment, as when a de facto tenure program exists at a state college or university. *Bishop v. Wood* (1976) established governmental prerogative to define public benefits as liberty or property interests.

The term "liberty" has been greatly narrowed as used in the procedural due process context. Generally, the Court will defer to legislative judgment in defining liberties, but will nearly always consider any right previously recognized by state law a liberty. In *Paul v. Davis,* the Court held that no constitutionally protected liberty was infringed when police circulated a flier listing plaintiff as an "active shoplifter." There is no constitutional right to shop, the Court said, although the plaintiff's reputation may have been damaged. This holding implies that only those rights enumerated in the Constitution or previously existing within the state are liberties protected by procedural due process.

Once it is established that a right that must be protected by procedural due process has been impaired, a court will ascertain which procedural safeguards are necessary. Traditionally, a hearing was required before a state could deny an individual's interest in liberty or property, but this approach, when applied, becomes quite complicated. It entitles the parties to call witnesses, obtain counsel, request judicial review, etc. *Mathews v. Eldridge* (1976) abandoned this traditional approach in favor of a balancing test that is applied to determine whether a hearing is necessary at all, and if so, what type of procedures are necessary to ensure that due process is afforded. This new test balances the costs of providing the necessary procedures against the due process benefits they offer.

> Procedural due process imposes constraints on governmental decisions which deprive individuals of "liberty" or "property" interests within the meaning of the Due Process Clause of the Fifth or Fourteenth Amendment...This Court consistently has held that some form of hearing is required before an individual is finally deprived of a property interest...The dispute centers upon what process is due prior to the initial termination of benefits, pending review.

In *Mathews,* the Court held that disability benefits could be terminated without a prior hearing. In reaching this conclusion, the Court considered the importance of the individual interest involved, the degree to which specific procedures might safeguard that interest, and the fiscal and administrative costs to the state in providing the required procedures. This balancing approach recognizes both state and individual interests and attempts to satisfy both constitutionally.

Equal Protection

The equal protection clause of the 14th Amendment was intended to ensure that all rights created by the states are enjoyed equally by all citizens. While the immediate concern of the amendment's drafters was the protection of the recently-freed slaves, in fact, the equal protection clause prevents the creation by a state or the federal government of any classification if the purpose or effect is to deny a particular group of individuals a right enjoyed by other citizens of that state. In some cases, where a state proves that a classification is reasonably created or that it is strongly needed depending upon the class, the Court has permitted such regulations to stand.

When reviewing a state-created classification to determine whether it violates the 14th Amendment equal protection clause, the Court first examines the nature of the classification and the individual right that the law affects and uses these determinations to choose the level of scrutiny the law is to be given. Suspect classifications, such as race, which are inherently suspect, and the abridgment of fundamental rights, such as voting, are always given strict scrutiny. The state must show a compelling purpose for creating the classification, and the classification must be necessary for the achievement of this purpose, with no less-discriminatory alternatives available. Practically speaking, a state can rarely show such a compelling interest. Semisuspect classifications, such as gender, which are somewhat less suspicious than suspect classifications, and important rights, such as

education, are given intermediate scrutiny. The state must have an important purpose, and there must be a substantial relation between the creation of the classification and the state's purpose. Classifications that do not appear at all suspicious, and all other rights, including food and shelter, are subject to minimal scrutiny. The state needs only an articulated or conceivable purpose that is rationally related to the creation of the classification. Each time a class of individuals comes before a court alleging that its rights have been violated by a state, the court considers these factors and determines whether it is the state's purpose or the group's rights that are so significant that the other must be sacrificed. Although many of the classifications and rights protected by the 14th Amendment are now covered by federal statute, thus superseding the constitutional rules, many of these areas are still subject to the Protections of the 14th Amendment.

Proving Racial Discrimination. Race epitomizes the suspect classification and, in fact, was the target of the 14th Amendment. To qualify for 14th Amendment protection, however, it must be proven that a classification was created for the purpose of discriminating against that class; that is, the discrimination must be the intent of the state. A statute may be discriminatory on its face or merely applied in a discriminatory fashion. Racial discrimination was found in *Strauder v. West Virginia* (1880). Here, the Court struck down a statute allowing only whites to serve on juries, finding that the statute had no purpose other than to discriminate against blacks. Administrative discrimination, or the discriminatory application of a neutral law, was found in *Yick Wo v. Hopkins* (1886), where an ordinance prohibited the operation of laundries in wooden buildings except by special consent and only Chinese applicants were denied that consent. Although the state had a compelling purpose–safety–in keeping laundries out of wooden buildings, there was no relation between this purpose and laundries run by individuals of Chinese ancestry, thus the application of the law was discriminatory.

> [T]he facts shown establish an administration directed so exclusively against a particular class of persons as to warrant and require the conclusion, that, whatever may have been the intent of the ordinances as adopted, they are applied by the public authorities charged with their administration, and thus representing the State itself, with a mind so unequal and oppressive as to amount to a practical denial by the State of that equal protection of the laws which is secured to the petitioners, as to all other persons, by the broad and benign provisions of the Fourteenth Amendment to the Constitution of the United States. Though the law itself be fair on its face and impartial in appearance, yet, if it is applied and administered by public authority with an evil eye and an unequal hand, so as practically to make unjust and illegal discrimin-

ations between persons in similar circumstances, material to their rights, the denial of equal justice is still within the prohibition of the Constitution... No reason whatever, except the will of the supervisors, is assigned why they should not be permitted to carry on, in the accustomed manner, their harmless and useful occupation, on which they depend for a livelihood. And while this consent of the supervisors is withheld from them and from two hundred others who have also petitioned, all of whom happen to be Chinese subjects, eighty others, not Chinese subjects, are permitted to carry on the same business under similar conditions. The fact of this discrimination is admitted. No reason for it is shown, and the conclusion cannot be resisted, that no reason for it exists except hostility to the race and nationality to which the petitioners belong, and which in the eye of the law is not justified. The discrimination is, therefore, illegal, and the public administration which enforces it is a denial of the equal protection of the laws and a violation of the Forteenth Amendment of the Constitution.

Presence of a discriminatory intent must also be proven for equal protection violations. Such motive was not found in *Palmer v. Thompson* (1971) where a city chose to close its public pool rather than desegregate it, because the Court found that the city would have difficulty maintaining the pool peacefully and safely due to overcrowding and anticipated hostility between blacks and whites in the pool, which was originally designed to serve only the white community. Although this pool closing appears discriminatory in effect, the Court found a nondiscriminatory purpose. De facto discrimination may be demonstrated by a law's differential impact on minorities. In *Griggs v. Duke Power Co.* (1971), a requirement that job applicants have high school diplomas and pass intelligence tests was held to constitute de facto discrimination where these requirements were irrelevant to performance on the job. Their effect was to eliminate many otherwise qualified black applicants.

For an equal protection violation to be corrected, purposeful discrimination must be proven; discriminatory impact alone will not suffice. "Disproportionate impact is not irrelevant, but it is not the sole touchstone of an invidious racial discrimination." This rule was set forth in *Washington v. Davis* (1976), where a test of written and verbal comprehension, required for positions in a police force and failed by four times as many blacks as whites, was found not violative of the 14th Amendment. Although the result of the test was that many fewer blacks were hired, this discriminatory impact raises only a presumption of discrimination that a defendant is given the opportunity to rebut. Here, the city offered evidence of affirmative action and recruiting programs, which indicated a desire to hire minorities, thus disproving any discriminatory purpose. *Village of Arlington Heights v. Metropolitan Housing Corp.* (1977) upheld a zoning statute that kept a low-income housing project out of Arlington Heights and consequently kept many minorities from becoming residents, because the challengers of the statute failed to show that discrimination was a motivating factor in the decision to pass the law. The Court suggested a variety of evidence through which such unconstitutional motivation could be demonstrated.

Determining whether invidious discriminatory purpose was a motivating factor demands a sensitive inquiry into such circumstantial and direct evidence of intent as may be available. The impact of the official action–whether it "bears more heavily on one race than another," *Washington v. Davis, supra*, at 242–may provide an important starting point. Sometimes a clear pattern, unexplainable on grounds other than race, emerges from the effect of the state action even when the governing legislation appears neutral on its face...

The historical background of the decision is one evidentiary source, particularly if it reveals a series of official actions taken for invidious purposes...The specific sequence of events leading up to the challenged decision also may shed some light on the decisionmaker's purposes... Departures from the normal procedural sequence also might afford evidence that improper purposes are playing a role. Substantive departures too may be relevant, particularly if the factors usually considered important by the decisionmaker strongly favor a decision contrary to the one reached...

The legislative or administrative history may be highly relevant, especially where there are contemporary statements by members of the decisionmaking body, minutes of its meetings, or reports. In some extraordinary instances the members might be called to the stand at trial to testify concerning the purpose of the official action, although even then such testimony frequently will be barred by privilege.

Laws that create classifications of race and appear to have a discriminatory purpose are subject to strict scrutiny. *Korematsu v. United States* (1944) was the only case in which a racial classification passed the Court's strict scrutiny, but this case occurred during an extraordinary period of American history. The Court upheld a World War II military order confining anyone of Japanese ancestry for the safety of the United States, finding a perceived threat to national security a sufficiently compelling interest. The decision in *Korematsu* has been roundly criticized and it is doubtful that a similar law would be upheld today, as evidenced by the overturning of his conviction in federal district court in 1983. The Court overturned, as invidiously discriminatory, a law prohibiting interracial marriage in *Loving v. Virginia* (1967) because, although the law was applied equally to all races, the legislative history indicated that the true purpose was to preserve the "purity" of the white race. For a racial classification to pass strict scrutiny, it must be in further-

The Court's decision in **Korematsu v. United States,** *which legitimized the relocation and detention of Japanese-Americans during World War II, was based on the interests of national security. Korematsu's conviction was overturned in 1983.*

ance of a compelling state interest, which, obviously, "racial purity" is not.

The Brown Decisions. In 1896, in *Plessy v. Ferguson,* the Supreme Court upheld racial segregation, establishing the "separate but equal" doctrine. This doctrine lasted until 1954, when the Court ruled, in *Brown v. Board of Education,* that separate is inherently unequal. This ruling came in the context of education, where expert evidence demonstrated that segregated schools gave black students a feeling of inferiority as well as an inferior education. The rule was applied, however, everywhere that segregation existed. Putting an end to de jure segregation took years of litigation and strongly-worded Supreme Court opinions and, in fact, the full integration of public schools is yet to be achieved. In a subsequent case in

1955, also *Brown v. Board of Education* and known as Brown II, the Court ordered that desegregation be accomplished with "all deliberate speed." The Court permitted lower courts to order any remedies they found necessary to eliminate segregation where it was proven to have been deliberately created. Transfer plans, where schools were integrated but minority students were offered the option to transfer to schools where they could, again, be in the racial majority, were unconstitutional because they generally fostered segregation. Cities were not permitted to close public schools rather than integrate, as the only purpose the Court could find for this was racial discrimination. Plans providing students with the choice of which school in their district they wanted to attend were also found unconstitutional as students inevitably wound up

The efforts of Chief Justice Earl Warren, who wrote the decision, are credited for the Court's unanimous vote in **Brown v. Board of Education,** *overturning the "separate but equal" doctrine of segregation established by* **Plessy v. Ferguson** *in 1896.*

segregating themselves. The Court also permitted as a last resort such drastic remedies as busing and realignment of school districts to achieve the goal of desegregation, but only where it found that de jure segregation had occurred in that school district in the past.

Benign Racial Discrimination. Efforts to remedy past discrimination against minorities have recently resulted in a new form of discrimination that has created great controversy: benign discrimination or, more commonly, reverse discrimination. Benign racial discrimination has often been alleged in many large-scale remedial programs involving affirmative action and is generally subject to a lesser degree of scrutiny than is nonbenign discrimination because the Court has recognized that race-conscious remedies are a necessary evil to overcome the

greater evil of racial discrimination against a minority group. That governmental action need not be "color-blind," and actually cannot be color-blind, was decided in *Swann v. Charlotte-Mecklenburg Board of Education* (1971), one of the many desegregation cases.

Benign discrimination applied to reverse the effects of past discrimination in voting rights was upheld by the Supreme Court in *United Jewish Organizations v. Carey* (1977). Here, New York City voting districts were reapportioned so as to create nonwhite majorities in certain districts, increasing the chances for minority representatives to be elected. As a result, New York's Hasidic Jewish community, which had been contained within one district, was divided among two of the new, nonwhite districts.

Probably the best-known benign discrimination case is *Regents of the University of California v. Bakke* (1978), in which a white medical school applicant sued the state medical school for racial discrimination for denying him admission while accepting less-qualified minority applicants under a quota system. The school's admission procedure reserved sixteen percent of the places in its entering class for disadvantaged minority applicants, allowing lower standards for students filling those openings. The Supreme Court ruled in favor of Bakke, the white applicant, holding that race may be a factor in the admissions process, but it may not be dispositive. The same goal of remedying racial discrimination within the medical field could be achieved, according to the Court, with less discriminatory alternatives, including viewing minority status in a student as another "plus," similar to good grades or athletic ability. The quota system employed at the University of California-Davis Medical School was thus held to be unconstitutional. In *United Steel Workers v. Weber* (1979), however, the Court ruled that race-conscious remedies by private employers were permissible because the 14th Amendment prohibits only racial discrimination as practiced by the state. There, a classic quota system was used by the private employer and upheld by the Court.

In 1980, the Court committed itself to a firm decision on the constitutional use of race-conscious remedies. The Court ruled in *Fullilove v. Klutznick* (1980) that race-conscious measures may be used by the government to remedy past discrimination. The challenged statute in *Fullilove* set aside ten percent of federally-funded local public works projects for minority-owned contractors. The statute was upheld under the Court's new test for race-conscious remedies, finding them constitutional where the legislature has the power to enforce such remedies, their objective is legitimate, and the statute is rationally constructed and applied.

The Supreme Court's most recent ruling on benign racial discrimination held that valid seniority, or "last-hired-first-fired," systems outweigh race as a guide for whom to protect when an employer is forced to lay off workers. In *Firefighters Local Union No. 1784 v. Stotts* (1984), the Court found unconstitutional the laying off of white firefighters with more seniority than recently hired black firefighters whose jobs were shielded by a lower court order issued in a 1977 discrimination suit against the Fire Department. The Court stated that Title VII of the Civil Rights Act of 1964, designed to prevent employment discrimination on the basis of race or sex, "protects bona fide seniority systems, and it is inappropriate to deny an innocent employee the benefits of his seniority in order to provide a remedy in a pattern or practice suit such as this." Such a denial, which would effectually give the black firefighters retroactive seniority, is only

appropriate where "they have been actual victims of the discriminatory practice...Here, there was no finding that any of the blacks protected from layoff had been victims of discrimination."

Gender Discrimination. Discrimination on the basis of gender is currently given intermediate scrutiny; the state must have an important purpose that is closely related to the classification. In the past, however, legislation drawn to "protect" women was given minimal scrutiny, although the effect of such legislation was to limit women's rights. In *Goesaert v. Cleary* (1948), the Supreme Court upheld a statute prohibiting women from tending bar unless the bar owner was her husband or father. The Court felt that such an occupation for a woman created "moral and social problems" that could be prevented only by a male relative.

Scrutiny applied to gender classifications was gradually increased as society's perception of women modernized, and intermediate scrutiny, as applied in *Craig v. Boren* (1970), eventually became the rule. In *Craig*, an Oklahoma statute making illegal the sale of "3.2% beer" to males under twenty-one and females under eighteen was overturned by the Court for denying equal protection to males aged eighteen to twenty. Rejecting the state's statistical evidence that males in that age group are involved in more alcohol-related traffic accidents than females, the Court stated:

> Suffice to say that the showing offered by the appellees does not satisfy us that sex represents a legitimate, accurate proxy for the regulation of drinking and driving. In fact, when it is further recognized that Oklahoma's statute prohibits only the selling of 3.2% beer to young males and not their drinking the beverage once acquired (even after purchase by their 18-20 year-old female companions), the relationship between gender and traffic safety becomes far too tenuous to satisfy...[the] requirement that the gender-based difference be substantially related to achievement of the scrutiny objective.

Unlike the strict scrutiny of racial classification, statutes often do pass intermediate scrutiny and are permitted to remain in effect, despite the fact that they classify by gender. In *Geduldig v. Aiello* (1974), the Court found that a state need not cover pregnancy under its disability insurance system because such a classification is "not based on gender as such...There is no risk from which men are protected and women are not. Likewise, there is no risk from which women are protected and men are not." The Court also upheld a statutory rape law with sanctions against only men, not women, because the law was created as a deterrent to teenage pregnancy, and in this respect males and females are dissimilarly situated. The Court in *Michael M. v. Superior Court* (1981) felt that this classification was substantially related to the state's strong interest in decreasing the rate of teenage pregnancies. *Rostker v. Goldberg* (1981), a challenge to the all-male draft registration, also upheld a law that discriminated on the basis of gender. The Court gives great deference to Congress in matters of national security, and in *Rostker* the all-male registration was found to be closely related to the statute's purpose, which was to facilitate the drafting of combat troops, which by statute must also be all-male.

As with race, there are many statutes designed to remedy past discrimination against women, and these statutes often constitute benign gender discrimination. In addition to disadvantaging men, such laws often work to reinforce stereotypes of women as being weaker than men and in need of male aid; the Court has overturned many such statutes for both reasons. In *Mississippi University for Women v. Hogan* (1981), a state nursing school permitted only women to enroll for credit toward a nursing degree, and Hogan, a male who lived and worked near the school, sued for admission. The Court struck down this admissions policy on the ground that it discriminated against males, where women are not at a disadvantage in the field of nursing.

A law allowing alimony to be awarded for the benefit of women only was overturned in *Orr v. Orr* (1979) because the denial of all alimony in favor of men was not substantially related to the state's important objective of compensating women discriminated against in the workplace during marriage.

> Even if sex were a reliable proxy for need, and even if the institution of marriage did discriminate against women, these factors still would not adequately justify the salient features of [the statute]... Alabama's alleged compensatory purpose may be effectuated without placing burdens solely on husbands. Progress toward fulfilling such a purpose would not be hampered, and it would cost the state nothing more, if it were to treat men and women equally by making alimony burdens independent of sex. Thus, the gender-based distinction is gratuitous.

Laws that compensate women for past discrimination are upheld however, as in *Califano v. Webster* (1977), which permitted the granting of greater social security benefits to women because "whether from over-discrimination or from the socialization process of a male-dominated culture, the job market is inhospitable to the woman seeking any but the lowest paid jobs."

Other Issues. States may not discriminate against aliens without a compelling interest. Congress has plenary power over aliens and their admittance to the United States, leaving the states with a limited role. When the states try to increase that role, infringing on aliens' rights, strict scrutiny is often required. States have been prevented from denying welfare benefits, admission to the

bar, and civil service jobs to aliens. In *Sugarman v. Dougall* (1973), however, the Court made an exception, allowing states to deny aliens positions within the sovereign function of the state, where they may have discretionary, policy-executing power. The Court allowed, in *Foley v. Connelie* (1978), states to deny positions to aliens in state offices, and as teachers, probation officers, and state troopers.

> It would be inappropriate... to require every statutory exclusion of aliens to clear the high hurdle of "strict scrutiny" because to do so would obliterate all the distinctions between citizens and aliens, and thus depreciate the historic values of citizenship... This country entrusts many of its most important policy responsibilities to these officers, the discretionary exercise of which can often more immediately affect the lives of citizens than even the ballot of a voter or the choice of a legislature... We must examine each position in question to determine whether it involves discretionary decisionmaking, or execution of policy, which substantially affects members of the political community... Although we extend to aliens the right to education and public welfare along with the ability to earn a livelihood and engage in licensed professions, the right to govern is reserved to citizens.

The sum of the Court's opinions indicates that aliens are entitled to participate fully in the economic community but have a limited place in the political community.

Other groups subject to classification and discrimination include the indigent and those born illegitimate. The poor are generally not considered a suspect class because the level of an individual's wealth can in theory be changed. Thus, per *San Antonio Schools v. Rodriguez,* 1973), school systems supported by local property taxes are constitutional, despite the fact that students residing in wealthier communities may receive better educations than those in poorer communities. Illegitimates, however, are entitled to more protection because they were born into their class and cannot change their status of their own volition. In *Trimble v. Gordon* (1977), the Court struck down a portion of a state intestacy system that denied illegitimate children the right to be counted among their father's heirs. A state may not "attempt to influence the actions of men and women by imposing sanctions on the children born of their illegitimate relationships... Difficulties of proving paternity in some situations do not justify the total statutory disinheritance of illegitimate children whose fathers die without leaving wills."

In addition to classifications that are protected by the 14th Amendment equal protection clause, there are certain fundamental rights whose denial is subject to strict scrutiny. The right to vote, for example, is fundamental, making poll taxes and most literacy requirements unconstitutional. Access to the courts is often considered fundamental, particularly for criminal trials, but less so for civil cases. Thus, under *Griffin v. Illinois* (1956), the state cannot deny an indigent defendant a copy of his trial transcript because he cannot pay a fee, where that transcript is necessary for an effective appeal. "In criminal trials a State can no more discriminate on account of poverty than on account of religion, race, or color. Plainly the ability to pay costs in advance bears no rational relationship to a defendant's guilt or innocence and could not be used as an exercise to deprive a defendant of a fair trial." The right to travel is also fundamental and states are not permitted to institute durational residency requirements for voting privileges or welfare benefits as these would deter interstate travel.

15th Amendment

SECTION 1. The right of citizens of the United States to vote shall not be denied or abridged by the United States or by any State on account of race, color, or previous condition of servitude.

SECTION 2. The Congress shall have power to enforce this article by appropriate legislation.

When the Civil War broke out in 1861, most states either prohibited black citizens from voting or had educational and property qualifications that had to be met before the right to vote could be exercised. These qualifications effectively eliminated the possibility of black suffrage. As the population of free blacks grew, sentiments against slavery rose, but sentiments for black suffrage did not rise. States had the exclusive power to determine who could vote, therefore, blacks were not given the guarantee of equal voting privileges until sentiments regarding their suffrage changed.

The 15th Amendment, adopted in 1870, reflected the attitudinal change that eventually occurred throughout the United States. This amendment guarantees citizens the privilege to vote against any abridgment by a state or national government based upon race, color, or previous servitude. This guarantee, according to *Terry v. Adams* (1953), establishes a national policy against such discrimination, a policy applied to all elections held to determine public governmental policies or to select public officials on the national, state, or local level.

While the 15th Amendment prevents states and the

The provisions of the 14th and 15th Amendments, which were to protect and guarantee the rights of recently-freed slaves in the South, were long ignored.

federal government from giving preference to one citizen over another in the matter of voting due to race, color, or previous servitude, it does not confer a right to vote upon blacks, the Court held in *City of Mobile v. Bolden* (1980). Rather, the amendment was designed to prevent discrimination against a citizen whenever the right to vote has been granted to others (*United States v. Reese,* 1876). Thus, the citizen must wait until the state has granted the right to vote to others and has denied him the right due to his race, color, or previous servitude before he can raise a 15th Amendment claim. Under some circumstances, however, the amendment is an immediate source of the right to vote. For instance, as established by *Neal v. Delaware* (1881), when former slave-holding states failed to remove the words "white man" from their constitutional qualifications for voting after the 15th Amendment became effective, the amendment annulled the word "white" and blacks in theory were entitled to vote.

The Supreme Court declared, in *Harman v. Forssenius* (1965), that the right to vote freely for a candidate of choice is a fundamental right; it is the essence of a democratic society with a representative government. The guarantees of the 15th Amendment adopt this declaration, but apply the guarantee only to governmental action. This amendment is not a shield to private conduct, no matter how discriminatory the conduct is. Thus, a showing of state action (action by the state or one of its agents, or action under color of state law) is required for success in 15th Amendment claims.

State Action. State action is not difficult to find in the voting arena. Any official action, by a city or other governmental organization, taken to discriminate against blacks due to race, satisfies this state action requirement and is unconstitutional regardless of the actual effect of the action (*City of Richmond v. United States,* 1975). State statutes excluding blacks from participating in primary elections are plainly unconstitutional, the Court declared in *Nixon v. Herndon* (1927). Also, discrimination by state officials within the course of official duties is subject to 15th Amendment limitations, per *United States v. Raines* (1960), when it affects voting rights of others based on race or color. Additionally, state action exists where the state directs the selection of all political party officers and when primary elections are conducted by the party under state statutory authority. In this case the party is an agency of the state (*Smith v. Allwright,* 1944). Where membership in such a party is required for voting in primaries to select nominees for the general election of state offices, limiting membership to whites qualified to vote abridges the right to vote on account of race.

The right to vote in a state comes from that state. In *United States v. Cruikshank* (1876), the Court held that the right to exemption from prohibited discrimination

comes from the United States. States have broad powers to determine the conditions of suffrage. Federal rights concerning suffrage are subject to state standards where those standards are not discriminatory and do not contravene any legitimate congressional restriction. Also, state constitutions that allow citizens freedom to form political groups are not invalid if they do not forbid racial qualifications for membership.

Although the state cannot discriminate among voters on the basis of race, color, or previous servitude, it can use some types of requirements to determine who qualifies for voter registration. As established by *Lassiter v. Northampton County Board of Elections* (1959), such valid requirements include age, residence, and previous criminal record. Registration requirements are invalid if they are discriminatory on their face or in practice (*South Carolina v. Katzenbach,* 1966). The Court held in *Lane v. Wilson* (1939) that such requirements cannot inhibit the free exercise of the right to vote by blacks, even where the abstract right to vote remains unrestricted as to race. Thus, when registration is required of every nonregistered person, with failure to do so resulting in permanent loss of the right to vote for everyone except those registered in a specific year under state provisions that were invalid due to discrimination, the requirement is unconstitutional.

Literacy tests, or the requirement that a person must be able to read and write in order to vote, may be valid requirements for the exercise of voting privileges. For instance, under *Lassiter,* the requirement that a person be able to read and write any section of the state constitution in English is valid if applicable to all races. Grandfather clauses, exempting some from the literacy requirement, deny the right to vote on account of race, color, or previous servitude, violating the 15th Amendment, the Court held in *Guinn v. United States* (1915). Although fair on its face, a literacy test may be employed to discriminate; such a test is unconstitutional if the legislative setting and authority clearly indicate that the requirement exists only to make racial discrimination easy. Although a requirement to read and give a reasonable interpretation of a constitution is valid, a requirement that a person understand and explain articles of the Constitution both in their object and manner of administration is unconstitutional. The requirements exist to enable discrimination (*Davis v. Schnell,* 1949).

The Constitution protects the rights of all qualified citizens to vote in state and federal elections (*Reynolds v. Sims,* 1964). Claims of racially discriminatory vote dilution are cognizable under both the 14th and 15th Amendments. As in *Perkins v. City of West Helena* (1982), courts look at whether minority voters are denied an opportunity to participate effectively in the political process. In *Baker v. Carr* (1962), a key Court decision on voting rights, the

Associate Justice Frankfurter wrote the Court's opinion in **Gomillion v. Lightfoot,** *a 1960 decision that helped to strengthen the voting power of blacks.*

15th Amendment applies dilution of voting rights results from false tallies, refusal to count ballots from arbitrarily selected precincts, or the stuffing of ballot boxes. In addition, as the Court held in *Gomillion v. Lightfoot* (1960), claims concerning redistricting to eliminate black voting power are valid under this amendment.

Although the 14th Amendment disallows legislative apportionment and the 15th Amendment condemns racial gerrymandering (division of districts) in order to minimize the impact of racial voting, neither amendment guarantees proportional racial or ethnic representation. Section 5 of the 1965 Voting Rights Act subjects voting district reapportionment, however, to the prior approval of the U.S. attorney general or the U.S. District Court for the District of Columbia to ensure that such reapportionment "does not have the purpose and will not have the effect of denying or abridging the right to vote on account of race

or color." At-large voting systems that result in diluting racial voting power are not per se unconstitutional, but if the *intent* to discriminate can be shown to exist, such systems violate both the 14th and 15th Amendments, the Court declared in *Rogers v. Lodge* (1982).

The Supreme Court has held, in *United States v. Texas* (1966), that poll taxes do not violate the 15th Amendment, but making poll taxes a precondition to vote creates an unjustified restriction on rights under the due process clause. Also, under *Kemp v. Tucker* (1975), rejecting a registration application because the color entry was not completed does not violate the 15th Amendment. Finally, political *candidates* have rights under the 15th Amendment. According to the Supreme Court in *Hadnott v. Amos* (1969), states violate the 15th Amendment if they allow white candidates to file financial committee designations before the election but forbid black candidates to file at the same time, where filing after the election causes candidates to be disqualified from the ballot.

Enforcement. Congressional power to enforce the 15th Amendment is very broad. Two requirements must be met for valid sanctions under the amendment's enforcement power. First, the statute must punish those who restrict voting through discrimination of types required by the amendment (*United States v. Reese*, 1876). Congress cannot act generally to punish those who prevent the exercise of voting through interference, when there is no required discrimination. Second, the Court held in *James v. Bowman* (1903) that the statute must punish state action, not purely private action. If both requirements are met, the statute will not violate the 15th Amendment for being too broad.

The Supreme Court has held that congressional power under the 15th Amendment is no less broad than congressional power under the necessary and proper clause. As long as the means used are appropriate to enforce the 15th Amendment guarantees, the statute is valid. Thus, Congress can enact a statute banning voting practices having a discriminatory effect on voting, even if Section 1 of the amendment prohibits only intentional discrimination in voting (*City of Rome v. United States*, 1980).

Congress can use any rational means to carry out the limitation of the 15th Amendment; power can be exercised to the utmost extent with no limitations other than those proscribed in the Constitution. The test for appropriate power, set up by Justice Marshall, requires a legitimate end within the scope of the Constitution; using all unprohibited means plainly adapted to that end is consistent with the letter and spirit of the Constitution. If the exercised power passes this test, the statute or action will be constitutional. Section 1973 of Title 42 of the United States Code is an example of a constitutional use of the 15th Amendment enforcement power. The section allows federal perusal of state voting policies, with provisions pertaining to the suspension of eligibility requirements, review of restrictions and qualifications, and review of voting procedures.

19th Amendment

The right of citizens of the United States to vote shall not be denied or abridged by the United States or by any State on account of sex.

Congress shall have power to enforce this article by appropriate legislation.

Prior to the adoption of the 19th Amendment in 1920, after a long campaign for women's suffrage, a state could deny women the right to vote without violating the 15th Amendment. The 19th Amendment is a constitutional exercise of power with the same character and construction as the 15th Amendment, the Court held in *Leser v. Garnett* (1922). The amendment applies to both men and women, guaranteeing them the same voting rights. Like the 15th Amendment, the 19th does not give anyone the right to vote; it merely prohibits discrimination based on sex. The right to vote is left to legislative enactment by each state. Guarantees under this amendment override any inconsistent limitations on both state and federal levels (*Breedlove v. Suttles*, 1937).

The Court held in *Reynolds v. Sims* (1964) that the Constitution protects the rights of all qualified citizens to vote freely in state as well as federal elections. The 19th Amendment prohibits limitation of voting rights based upon sex but does not require states to allow women the opportunity to vote only for female candidates. Once given the right to vote, women may vote for any candidate (*Boineau v. Thornton*, 1964).

24th Amendment

SECTION 1. The right of citizens of the United States to vote in any primary or other election for President or Vice President, for electors for President or Vice President, or for Senator or Representative in Congress, shall not be denied or abridged by the United States or any State by reason of failure to pay any poll tax or other tax.

SECTION 2. The Congress shall have power to enforce this article by appropriate legislation.

The right to vote freely for a candidate of one's choice is the essence of a democratic society. Exercise of the right preserves all other fundamental rights (*Harman v. Forssenius*, 1965). The purpose of the 24th Amendment, adopted in 1964, is to guarantee the right to vote freely in *federal* elections. Neither the United States nor any individual state should impair the vested right of a registered voter to vote in a national election solely because he has failed to pay a poll tax. The states cannot impede the right to effective exercise of voting for federal officials on such grounds.

The states cannot use a poll tax to dilute votes in order to give weight to other interests or groups. Under the 24th Amendment, as the Court held in *United States v. Texas* (1966), poll tax voting requirements may not be used as a method of "purification and protection" of the ballot, if other methods exist. Otherwise, the tax would be a charge or penalty upon the exercise of a fundamental right. Such taxes can be challenged under this amendment, even though the citizen has already registered to vote and paid his poll taxes.

Landmark Cases

Landmark Cases

Abbate v. United States, 359 U.S. 187 (1959), a case dealing with the extent of 5th Amendment protection against double jeopardy. The petitioners were solicited in Chicago by a union official to dynamite telephone facilities in three states. Although the petitioners did not go through with the plan, another man who had also been approached by the union official did in fact obtain dynamite and travel to Mississippi to destroy telephone facilities there. The petitioners thereupon disclosed the plot to the Chicago police and to the telephone company. The petitioners were then indicted by an Illinois state court for violating a state statute making it a crime to conspire to injure or destroy the property of another. The petitioners pleaded guilty and were sentenced. They were subsequently indicted, tried, and convicted in a federal district court for violating a federal statute that prohibited the destruction of communications facilities "operated or controlled by the United States."

They appealed this conviction, contending that it violated their 5th Amendment rights by trying them twice for essentially the same crime. The Supreme Court held by a vote of six to three, with Chief Justice Warren and Associate Justices Black and Douglas dissenting, that the earlier conviction in state court did not bar the federal prosecution of petitioners under the double jeopardy clause of the 5th Amendment. Associate Justice Brennan, writing for the majority, ruled that although the petitioners were being prosecuted in two instances for the same act, the Court's reasoning in *United States v. Lanza* (1922) should be applied here. *Lanza* held that two sovereigns (the United States and the state of Illinois) both had constitutional authority to prohibit the same act.

Ableman v. Booth, 21 Howard 506 (1859), a case dealing with the right of state courts to issue writs of *habeas corpus* for federal prisoners. In this case, a group of Wisconsin abolitionists, with the active support of the state legislature and the state judiciary, attempted to obstruct the enforcement of the federal Fugitive Slave Law of 1850 by obtaining a court order for the release of a Wisconsin citizen who had been arrested by federal officials for harboring an escaped slave. On March 7, 1859, the Supreme Court ruled unanimously, with Chief Justice Taney writing for the Court, that the Wisconsin court's writ was an unconstitutional invasion of federal authority. Once again reaffirming the constitutionality of the Fugitive Slave Act itself, Taney emphasized the clear distinction between the spheres of jurisdiction of the states and of the federal government. If the original petitioners in this case questioned the action of certain federal officials, the proper forum for their legal action should be the federal court system.

Abrams v. United States, 250 U.S. 616 (1919), a case dealing with the power of Congress to restrict freedom of speech guaranteed by the 1st Amendment. The petitioner, Abrams, along with several others, was found guilty of violating the Espionage Act of 1917 in that he unlawfully wrote and published language "intended to incite, provoke and encourage resistance to the United States" during World War I and of conspiring to "urge, incite and advocate curtailment of production of ordnance and ammunition necessary to the prosecution of the war." Abrams subsequently appealed his conviction, contending that it violated his 1st Amendment right to free speech.

The Supreme Court upheld Abrams's conviction by a vote of seven to two, with Associate Justices Holmes and Brandeis dissenting. Associate Justice Clark, writing for the majority, reasoned that the denial of free speech in this instance was justified if the language was of a type that would tend to bring about harmful results. In a famous dissent, Justice Holmes explained that it could not be

Chief Justice William Howard Taft (right) *and Justice Oliver Wendell Holmes both dissented in* **Adkins v. Children's Hospital,** *which struck down a federal law regarding minimum wages.*

assumed that the pamphlets that the defendants had published would actually hinder the government's war effort in World War I and that the convictions should thus be overturned. Holmes contended, as he did in *Schenck v. United States* (1919), that free speech could be curtailed by the government only when there was "clear and present danger of immediate evil or an intent to bring about it." The Court grappled with this question until 1969 when, in *Brandenburg v. Ohio*, it held that the state may not bar advocacy of the use of force or violation of the law unless such advocacy "is directed to inciting or producing imminent lawless action."

Adair v. United States, 208 U.S. 161 (1908), a case dealing with the right of the federal government to prohibit compulsory nonunion pledges by employees. In 1898, Congress had enacted a law that prohibited interstate carriers from discharging employees who had joined labor unions. The petitioner, a representative of a railroad that required its employees to sign a pledge that they would not join labor unions, challenged the constitutionality of the federal law, contending that it was a violation of the freedom of contracts and of due process guaranteed by the 5th and the 14th Amendments.

On January 27, 1908, the Supreme Court decided by a vote of six to two, with Associate Justices Holmes and McKenna dissenting and Associate Justice Moody not participating, that the federal law should be struck down. Associate Justice Harlan, speaking for the majority, held that the issue of union membership was not directly connected with interstate trade and was therefore outside federal jurisdiction. In addition, Harlan termed the intention of Congress to dictate the type of contracts that private companies could offer their employees "an invasion of personal liberty as well as the right of property." This decision was one of several issued by the Fuller Court that undercut the power of organized labor.

Addyston Pipe and Steel Company v. United States, 175 U.S. 211 (1899), a case dealing with the power of the federal government to regulate the business practices of certain private businesses. The federal government obtained convictions against six companies manufacturing iron pipe that had engaged in price fixing in violation of the Sherman Antitrust Act. Since the companies were primarily engaged in manufacturing, not in commerce, they appealed the conviction, contending that their business practices were beyond the power of Congress to regulate. The Supreme Court ruled unanimously that the conviction should be sustained. Associate Justice Peckham, speaking for the Court, held that since the price fixing of the companies was a "direct restraint upon interstate commerce," those activities were held to have violated the antitrust laws. This case was a shift from the Court's reasoning in *United States v. E.C. Knight Company* (1895), in which it held that a manufacturing monopoly did not violate the antitrust laws, since "manufacturing" was not "commerce" under such laws.

Adkins v. Children's Hospital, 261 U.S. 525 (1923),

a case dealing with the right of the federal government to regulate the minimum wage of certain employees. In 1918, Congress enacted a law that established minimum wage levels for women and children employed in the District of Columbia. Subsequent to the passage of the law, a hospital and an individual challenged its constitutionality, contending that it violated their freedom of contract and right to due process guaranteed by the 5th Amendment. On April 9, 1923, the Supreme Court decided by a vote of five to three, with Chief Justice Taft, Associate Justices Holmes and Sanford dissenting, and Associate Justice Brandeis not participating, that the federal law was unconstitutional. Associate Justice Sutherland, speaking for the majority, held that the freedom to enter into unrestricted contracts was central to the American form of government. Citing the decision of the Court in *Lochner v. New York* (1905), Sutherland further ruled that regulation denied to men could not now be bestowed upon women, especially in light of the adoption of the 19th Amendment.

Ake v. Oklahoma, 53 U.S.L.W. 4179 (1985), a case dealing with the constitutional rights of indigent defendants to free psychiatric assistance if their case warrants it. In this case, an Oklahoma man, Glen Burton Ake, was arrested after a month-long crime spree during which two people were murdered. Diagnosed as a paranoid schizophrenic in the early stages of his trial, Ake was found incompetent to stand trial. After six weeks of treatment he was found competent and prosecution resumed, but Ake's request for psychiatric assistance was denied.

In a February 26, 1985, decision that overturned Ake's conviction, Associate Justice Marshall held that "a criminal trial is fundamentally unfair if the state proceeds against an indigent defendant without making sure that he has access to the raw materials integral to the building of an effective defense." Marshall concluded that on this basis and considering the fact that Ake's "future dangerousness" would be considered during sentencing, the defendant had been deprived of due process. A new trial was ordered. This eight to one ruling, with Justice Rehnquist dissenting, was a logical extension of the earlier *Gideon v. Wainright* (1963), which required states to provide free legal assistance to indigent defendants.

Alabama v. Texas, (1954), *See* United States v. California.

Alamo Foundation v. Secretary of Labor, 53 U.S.L.W. 4489 (1985), a case dealing with the responsibility of religious organizations to pay employees engaged in commercial business wages based on federal standards. The Tony and Susan Alamo Foundation, a Christian organization operating several profitable businesses, employed unpaid "associates." The foundation claimed exemption from minimum wage requirements for its workers on the basis of religious freedom guaranteed by the 1st Amendment. However, two lower courts ordered the foundation to pay the federal minimum wage to its employees.

The case was decided less than one month after deliberation began when, on April 23, 1985, the Supreme Court unanimously upheld the lower court rulings. In an opinion by Associate Justice White, the Court applied the Fair Labor Standards Act to the foundation's workers because they were involved in "ordinary commercial activities" and accepted non-cash compensation for their work. Contrary to the foundation's claim, Justice White said that the ruling in no way affected "ordinary voluntarism." He further held that since the workers were free to donate their pay to the foundation if they so desired, no interference with their religious beliefs was involved.

Alberts v. California, (1957), *See* Roth v. United States.

Alderman v. United States, 394 U.S. 165 (1969), a case dealing with the rights of defendants in criminal proceedings to examine the evidence obtained by illegal wiretaps against them. The petitioners had been convicted of transmitting to the Soviet Union information relating to the U.S. national defense. After the conviction the petitioners discovered that they had been subjected to an illegal wiretap, and they filed suit to obtain all relevant material acquired by this means, for use in their appeal. The government argued that the trial judge, after an *in-camera* examination, should turn over to the defendants only those surveillance records deemed relevant to their prosecution.

The Supreme Court ruled by a vote of eight to one,

Associate Justice Thurgood Marshall wrote the Court's opinion in **Ake v. Oklahoma**, *which extended the rights of indigent defendants established by* **Gideon v. Wainright.**

with only Associate Justice Black dissenting, that all records of illegal electronic surveillance to which any defendant has standing to object should be turned over to him without any prior judicial screening. Associate Justice White, writing for the majority, held that such a task was too complicated and complex to rely solely on the *in-camera* judgment of the trial court. White noted, however, that the disclosure should be limited to the transcripts of the petitioner's own conversations and of those that took place on his premises.

Alexander v. Holmes County Board of Education, 396 U.S. 19 (1969), a case dealing with the constitutional obligation of public school systems to eliminate racial segregation. The petitioner filed suit against a Mississippi school district, contending that its segregated conditions were a denial of the fundamental rights of the school children involved. The Supreme Court held *per curium* that such dual school systems based on race or color must be terminated at once, reasoning that continued operation of segregated schools under a standard of allowing "all deliberate speed" (*Brown v. Board of Education*, 1954) for desegregation was no longer constitutionally permissible. Therefore, it was the obligation of every school district to terminate dual school systems at once and to operate only unitary schools. The court of appeals was instructed to retain jurisdiction in order to ensure that this order was carried out.

American Communications Association, Congress of Industrial Organizations, et al. v. Douds, 339 U.S. 382 (1950), a case dealing with the constitutionality of certain loyalty oaths. In 1947, Congress passed the Taft-Hartley Act, which included a provision that all labor union officials submit affidavits that they had never been members of the Communist Party and had never advocated the violent overthrow of the government. If any official refused to do so, his or her organization would not receive the legal protection provided by the act. Several labor organizations immediately filed suit in federal court, contending that the oath requirement was a violation of the 1st Amendment protection of free speech. On May 8, 1950, the Supreme Court decided by a vote of five to one, with Associate Justice Black dissenting and Associate Justices Clark, Douglas, and Minton not participating, that the requirement for noncommunist oaths was constitutional. Chief Justice Vinson, speaking for the majority, held that the 1st Amendment protection did not apply in this case, since legitimate concerns of national security were involved. This decision was later reaffirmed by the ruling of the Court in *Dennis v. United States* (1951).

American Steel Foundries v. Trade Council, (1921), *See* Duplex Printing Press Co. v. Deering.

Apodaca v. Oregon, 406 U.S. 404 (1972), a case dealing with judicial requirements for conviction in certain state criminal trials. An Oregon statute allowed a non-unanimous verdict for conviction in non-capital criminal cases. (A vote of at least ten out of twelve jurors was necessary for the conviction.) The petitioner, Apodaca, challenged the statute, claiming that a unanimous jury verdict was required in state courts under the 6th Amendment to the Constitution. On May 22, 1972, the Supreme Court, by a vote of five to four, with Associate Justices Brennan, Marshall, Stewart, and Douglas dissenting, rejected Apodaca's contention, finding that although the 6th Amendment did require a trial by jury, unanimity was not constitutionally required. Associate Justice White wrote for the majority and Associate Justice Powell, in a concurring opinion, stated that a state trial system must adhere to "what is fundamental in jury trial" and that the Oregon statute adequately conformed to this standard even though a unanimous verdict was not required.

Argersinger v. Hamlin, 407 U.S. 25 (1972), a case dealing with the constitutional rights of defendants in state criminal trials to legal counsel. The petitioner, Argersinger, was an indigent charged under a Florida criminal statute with carrying a concealed weapon, an offense punishable by imprisonment up to six months, a $1,000 fine, or both. Argersinger was tried and convicted under this statute but was not represented by counsel at trial. He subsequently appealed his conviction on that ground. The Florida Supreme Court held that the right to counsel did not apply in this particular case since the offense was petty in nature and punishable by only six months imprisonment.

On June 12, 1972, the Supreme Court unanimously overturned Argersinger's conviction, holding that under the landmark case of *Gideon v. Wainwright* (1963), all defendants accused of a crime, whether a felony or misdemeanor, were entitled to assistance of counsel under the 6th Amendment. Associate Justice Douglas, writing for the Court, held that the nature of the crime was not to be considered in regard to this fundamental right.

Arizona v. Norris, 103 S.Ct. 3492 (1983), a case dealing with the constitutionality of certain pension plans that differentiated their benefits according to sex. A class action suit was brought by female employees of the state of Arizona challenging the constitutionality of the state's voluntary pension plan. Under that plan, the state offered its employees the option of receiving retirement benefits from any one of several companies, all of which paid women lower retirement benefits than men who had made the same contributions. Women were paid less per month because they lived longer, on average, than men, and therefore ultimately collected the same average total.

On July 6, 1983, the Supreme Court ruled by a vote of five to four, with Chief Justice Burger and Associate Justices Powell, Blackmun, and Rehnquist dissenting in part, that the plan violated Section 703(a) of Title VII of the Civil Rights Act of 1964, which forbade discrimination "against any individual with respect to...privileges of employment ...because of such individual's race, color, religion, sex or national origin." Associate Justice Marshall, writing for the majority, stated that since any woman wishing to participate in the plan would have to make greater monthly contributions than a man in order to obtain equal benefits and since men and women were not placed on an equal footing for pension plan purposes, the respondent's civil rights were held to be violated.

Ashwander v. Tennessee Valley Authority, 297 U.S. 288 (1936), a case dealing with the extent of federal power to utilize public property. Soon after the construction of the Wilson Dam as a part of the Tennessee Valley Authority (TVA) program, the TVA concluded contracts with private power companies to sell excess electricity generated by the dam. Since the sale of electric power had heretofore been exclusively in the hands of private industry, a suit was filed in federal court to cancel the government contracts and thereby overturn the entire scope of the TVA program.

On February 17, 1936, the Supreme Court decided by successive votes of eight to one and five to four, with Associate Justices Brandeis, Cardozo, McReynolds, and Roberts dissenting in part, that the sale of excess power authorized by the TVA was an exercise of the federal government's legitimate constitutional rights. Chief Justice Hughes, speaking for the majority, held that since the activities of the TVA, such as dam building and flood control, were within the federal government's power to improve means of navigation, it was also within the government's power to dispose of its rightful property as it saw fit. This decision marked one of the rare instances in which the Supreme Court sustained an economic program during the early New Deal years.

Bailey v. Drexel Furniture Co., 259 U.S. 20 (1922), a case dealing with the right of the federal government to regulate certain working conditions through its power of taxation. In 1919, after the Supreme Court had struck down the Keating-Owen Child Labor Law in *Hammer v. Dagenhart* (1918), Congress, still determined to prohibit harsh conditions of child labor, passed the Child Labor Tax Act. This act provided that any factory employing children under the age of fourteen years should be required to pay a special excise tax equivalent to 10 percent of its net profits for the year. This law also permitted representatives of the Internal Revenue Service to inspect the premises of factories and the petitioner, an IRS collector, found that the Drexel Furniture Company was liable for the child labor tax. The company paid the tax under protest and filed suit for repayment. A federal district court sustained the company's suit, and the decision was subsequently appealed.

On May 15, 1922, the Supreme Court decided by a vote of eight to one, with only Associate Justice Clarke dissenting, that the Child Labor Tax Act should be struck down. Chief Justice Taft, speaking for the majority, held that according to Article I, Section 8 of the Constitution, Congress has the right to levy taxes only to collect revenue, not to impose penalties, and that the use of taxation in this case was clearly to penalize certain employers for working conditions that they allowed. This decision was an additional attempt of the Supreme Court to restrict the "police power" of the federal government as utilized through indirect means.

Baker v. Carr, 369 U.S. 186 (1962), a case dealing with the constitutional right of the federal courts to hear challenges to legislative apportionment by the states. The Tennessee legislature had not reapportioned the electoral districts of the state since 1901, and with a shift in the population to the cities since that time, a situation resulted in which the voters in the rural districts had disproportionately greater representation than the voters in urban areas. The petitioner, a citizen of Tennessee, filed suit in federal court to challenge the existing electoral districts, contending that they violated the equal protection clause of the 14th Amendment. At issue in this case was the legal status of legislative apportionment, which the Court had previously

Supporters of organized labor were extremely critical of the Court's decision in **Bailey v. Drexel Furniture Co.**, *which held unconstitutional a federal law that sought to regulate child labor working conditions.*

The Court's decision in **Baker v. Carr**, *dealing with legislative apportionment by states, was one of the most important opinions handed down during the presidency of John F. Kennedy.*

ruled to be "political" and therefore beyond federal judicial jurisdiction in *Colegrove v. Green* (1946).

On March 26, 1962, the Supreme Court decided by a vote of six to two, with Associate Justices Frankfurter and Harlan dissenting and Associate Justice Whittaker not participating, that the federal courts had the right to hear the challenge to the Tennessee apportionment. Associate Justice Brennan, speaking for the majority, declined to deal with the question of a potential 14th Amendment violation, ruling only on the jurisdictional issue. This decision nullified the earlier ruling of the Court in *Colegrove* and was later amplified in *Wesberry v. Sanders* (1964), in which a uniform standard for legislative redistricting was proposed.

Bank of Augusta v. Earle, 13 Peters 519 (1839), a case dealing with the legal status of state-chartered corporations in other states. The state-chartered Bank of Alabama wanted to eliminate competition from any other banking institution operating in the state, and an Alabama merchant, taking up the cause of his state's bank, refused to pay a bill of exchange that had been purchased by the Bank of Augusta, Georgia. He contended that since the Bank of Augusta was chartered by Georgia, it could not legitimately operate outside that state. The Bank of Augusta then filed suit in federal court to recover payment.

Associate Justice McKinley heard the case on circuit and sustained the contention of the defendant. This decision immediately threatened to throw the nation's economy into chaos by invalidating all interstate transactions of the various state banks. The case was appealed to the Supreme Court, and Justice McKinley's decision was reversed. Chief Justice Taney, speaking for the majority, ruled that since the state of Alabama had enacted no legislation specifically prohibiting the activity of out-of-state banks, that silence must be viewed as implicit consent.

Barefoot v. Estelle, 103 S. Ct. 3383 (1983), a case dealing with guidelines for lower federal courts in handling death penalty appeals. The petitioner, Thomas A. Barefoot, was convicted in 1978 of murdering a police officer and was scheduled to be executed. He sought a last-minute stay of execution from the Supreme Court on the basis of a technically still-pending, constitutional challenge of his conviction. He had previously been through direct state court *habeas corpus* proceedings, a *habeas* proceeding in federal district court, and, finally, the U.S. Court of Appeals, which informally ruled against him. At issue in this case was the federal law regarding *habeas corpus*, which prohibits appeals to federal appeals courts with a "certificate of probable cause," issued by the federal district court, showing that the petition, even though it was denied, was not trivial.

On July 6, 1983, the Supreme Court, in an opinion written by Justice White, held by a vote of five to four that Barefoot had had a full hearing in spite of not having received a formal ruling and upheld a federal appeals court refusal to grant a stay of execution. In insisting on more stringent guidelines for consideration of petitions for writs of *habeas corpus*, the decision serves ostensibly to relieve the Supreme Court from the necessity of dealing with last-minute appeals.

Barenblatt v. United States, 360 U.S. 109 (1959), a case dealing with the constitutional rights of witnesses appearing before congressional investigating committees. The petitioner, Lloyd Barenblatt, had refused to answer questions posed to him by the House Un-American Activities Committee pertaining to his affiliation with communist organizations. Barenblatt was subsequently convicted of contempt of Congress, and he appealed that conviction, contending that his 1st Amendment rights, among others, had been violated.

On June 8, 1959, the Supreme Court decided by a vote of five to four, with Chief Justice Warren and Associate Justices Black, Brennan, and Douglas dissenting, that Barenblatt's conviction should be upheld. Associate Justice Harlan, speaking for the majority, held that since the Communist Party posed a significant danger to the nation, the congressional committee had a right to demand answers to its questions. In this and similar cases, Harlan argued, the interests of the public must be balanced against the interests of an individual's right to free expression. This decision substantially restricted the prior ruling of the Court in *Watkins v. United States (1957)*.

Barron v. Baltimore, 7 Peters 243 (1833), a case

dealing with the application of the 5th Amendment to defendants in state courts. The petitioner, a Baltimore wharf owner, had suffered financial loss from the reorganization of the harbor area by city authorities. Since his suit against the city of Baltimore had been dismissed by the Maryland state courts, he appealed to the Supreme Court on the grounds that the 5th Amendment protection against the expropriation of private property without compensation applied in this case. The Supreme Court ruled unanimously, with Chief Justice Marshall speaking for the Court, that the constitutional guarantees in the Bill of Rights were intended to apply only to actions of the federal government, not to actions of the states. This was Marshall's last major constitutional decision and, in sharp contrast to many of his previous opinions, later served as a precedent to restrict rather than to expand federal authority over the states.

Bartkus v. Illinois, 359 U.S. 121 (1959), a case dealing with the extent of 5th Amendment protection against double jeopardy. The petitioner, Bartkus, was indicted in federal court for the robbery of a federally-insured savings and loan association, a crime under both federal and Illinois law. Less than one month later, he was indicted by an Illinois grand jury for violating an Illinois robbery statute. Both indictments were based on the same action–the robbery of the savings and loan. It was also apparent that the federal authorities aided the state authorities by handing over to them all evidence they possessed in relation to the case. Bartkus was acquitted on the federal charge but was later convicted of robbery in state court and sentenced to life imprisonment. He subsequently appealed the state conviction, contending that his 5th Amendment right to avoid double jeopardy was abridged.

The Supreme Court upheld the state conviction by a vote of seven to two, with Associate Justices Black and Brennan dissenting. Associate Justice Frankfurter, writing for the majority, ruled that double jeopardy did not occur since the state prosecution was indeed a valid one, and not simply a sham or cover for, and, therefore simply another, federal prosecution. As long as there existed a separate and distinct second prosecution, Frankfurter noted, there was no 5th Amendment violation.

Beal v. Doe, 432 U.S. 438 (1977), a case dealing with the right of states to restrict the funding of certain medical abortions. The state of Pennsylvania, a participant in the federal Medicaid program, established a policy of refusing to fund nontherapeutic abortions for Medicaid recipients in the state. This policy was challenged on the grounds that it violated the terms of Pennsylvania's participation in the federal program. The Supreme Court held by a vote of six to three, with Associate Justices Brennan, Marshall, and Blackmun dissenting, that the federal Medicaid law conferred broad discretion on the states to adopt standards for determining the extent of medical assistance and that such standards needed only to be "reasonable" to be upheld.

Associate Justice Powell, writing for the majority, held that although a complete ban on abortions was unconstitutional under *Roe v. Wade* (1973), a state could refuse to fund nontherapeutic abortions and still participate in joint federal-state Medicaid assistance programs.

Betts v. Brady, 316 U.S. 299 (1942), a case dealing with the obligation of states to provide legal counsel for indigent defendants. The petitioner, a poor Maryland farmworker named Betts, was indicted for robbery and was denied a request for a court-appointed attorney as was customary only in capital cases. Pleading not guilty and speaking in his own defense, Betts was convicted of the crime and subsequently appealed his conviction to the Supreme Court, contending that his 6th Amendment right to have the assistance of counsel had been violated, a principle previously upheld by the Court in *Powell v. Alabama* (1932).

On June 1, 1942, however, the Supreme Court decided by a vote of six to three, with Associate Justices Black, Douglas, and Murphy dissenting, that Betts's conviction should be sustained. Associate Justice Roberts, speaking for the majority, held that while the states were required to appoint counsel for indigent defendants in capital cases, an extension of that requirement to all crimes would be an imposition on their resources and not necessary in most circumstances. The right to counsel was therefore, in his estimation, not one of the basic constitutional rights protected by the 14th Amendment. This decision was later reversed by the Court in *Gideon v. Wainwright* (1963).

Blum v. Stenson, 104 S. Ct. 1541 (1985), a case dealing with court-awarded attorney's fees under the Civil Rights Attorney's Fee Awards Act of 1976, which allows federal courts to award "reasonable" attorney's fees to winners of civil rights cases. In this case, New York state appealed a $119,000 fee awarded to the Legal Aid Society of New York for winning a suit on behalf of Medicaid recipients in New York. The state argued that fee awards should be made on the basis of costs incurred rather than market value. Loss of these market-value fees, however, threatened to have catastrophic effects on non-profit public interest law firms, who use these monies to finance ongoing litigation.

In a unanimous decision on March 21, 1985, written by Associate Justice Powell, the Court held that non-profit firms are entitled to compensation at the same rate as private firms. Addressing the related issue of "bonus" fees for unusually difficult and/or well-presented cases, Justice Powell reduced to $79,000 the fee awarded to the Legal Aid Society, saying they had not proved entitlement to a bonus in this case. Denying New York state's assertion that no bonuses should ever be awarded under the federal statute, Justice Powell said the bonus fees could be awarded under "extraordinary" circumstances.

Bob Jones v. United States, 461 U.S. 574 (1983), a case dealing with the constitutionality of federal tax exemptions for educational institutions that practice racial segregation. Section 501 of the Internal Revenue Code allowed a tax-exempt status to certain organizations. Among the organizations listed were corporations or foundations organized and operated exclusively for religious purposes. There was also a policy, supported by both the federal courts and the Internal Revenue Service (IRS), that prohibited a private school that operates in a racially discriminatory manner from having the benefit of this exemption. Bob Jones University, a nonprofit corporation located in Greenville, South Carolina, was an institution dedicated to the teaching and propagation of fundamentalist Christian religious beliefs. The sponsors of the university believed that the Bible forbade dating and marriage between individuals of different races, and a disciplinary rule of the university stated that no interracial dating was to be allowed between students, expulsion being the penalty for breach of the rule. The IRS, believing this rule to be racially discriminatory, revoked the tax exempt status of Bob Jones University. The university subsequently filed suit against the IRS.

On May 24, 1983, the Supreme Court upheld the IRS ruling by a vote of eight to one, with only Associate Justice Rehnquist dissenting. Chief Justice Burger, writing for the majority, ruled that the government's fundamental overriding interest in eradicating racial discrimination in education substantially outweighed whatever burden denial of tax benefits placed on Bob Jones University's exercise of religious beliefs. Although the university alleged that its practice was not discriminatory, Burger stated that discrimination on the basis of racial affiliation and association is a form of racial discrimination.

Boddie v. Connecticut, (1971), *See* United States v. Kras.

A Book Named "John Cleland's Memoirs of a Woman of Pleasure" v. Attorney General of Massachusetts, 383 U.S. 413 (1966), a case dealing with the legal standards for obscenity. The attorney general of Massachusetts brought a civil equity action to have John Cleland's book *Memoirs of a Woman of Pleasure* adjudicated obscene. A Massachusetts state trial court held the book to be obscene, therefore depriving it of protection under the 1st and 14th Amendments of the U.S. Constitution. This finding was upheld by the Massachusetts Supreme Court and appealed.

The U.S. Supreme Court reversed the Massachusetts decision, by a vote of four to three, with Associate Justices Clarke, Harlan, and White dissenting, focusing its attention upon the test for obscenity expressed in *Roth v. United States* (1957). Under *Roth*, the Supreme Court had decided that a work must be utterly without redeeming social value to be declared obscene. Associate Justice Brennan, writing for the majority, held that the Massachusetts Supreme Court had misinterpreted this standard, since it held that a book did not need to be unqualifiedly worthless before it could be deemed obscene. Brennan concluded that *Memoirs* did in fact have some literary value and could not, therefore, be deemed "obscene" under *Roth*.

Boynton v. Virginia, 364 U.S. 454 (1960), a case dealing with the constitutionality of racial segregation in interstate transportation facilities. The petitioner, Boynton, was a black law student traveling by bus from Washington, D.C., to Montgomery, Alabama. At a stop in Richmond, Virginia, he entered a restaurant in the bus terminal and seated himself in a section reserved for white customers. Ignoring the manager's request that he move to the section reserved for blacks, he was arrested, tried, and convicted in a Richmond court for unlawfully remaining on the premises of the terminal. He subsequently appealed the conviction, contending that his 14th Amendment equal protection rights had been violated.

The Supreme Court ruled by a vote of seven to two, with Associate Justices Whittaker and Clark dissenting, that Boynton's conviction should be reversed. Associate Justice Black, writing for the majority, held that the Interstate Commerce Act, which prohibited any interstate common carrier by motor vehicle (such as a bus line) from subjecting any person to unjust discrimination, had been violated and that Boynton had a right under this federal statute to remain in the portion of the restaurant designated for whites. The fact that the bus carrier had volunteered to make the terminal and the restaurant in it available to interstate passengers, Black noted, meant that the bus line had to perform the services provided by the terminal without discrimination prohibited by the Interstate Commerce Act.

Brandenburg v. Ohio, (1969), *See* Abrams v. United States.

Branzburg v. Hayes, 408 U.S. 665 (1972), a case dealing with the 1st Amendment right of journalists to withhold the identities of their sources. On November 15, 1969, the Louisville, Kentucky, *Courier-Journal* carried a story written by Branzburg, a staff reporter for the paper, which described in detail the reporter's observations of two young men synthesizing hashish from marijuana. The article, which included pictures of the individuals' hands performing this work, stated that the reporter had promised not to reveal the identity of the two hashish makers. Shortly thereafter, Branzburg was subpoenaed by a Jefferson County, Kentucky, grand jury and ordered to identify the individuals whom he had observed making the hashish. Branzburg refused to answer, claiming that the 1st Amendment of the U.S. Constitution justified this refusal. A state court did not agree and convicted Branzburg of contempt.

He subsequently appealed and on June 29, 1972, the Supreme Court upheld Branzburg's conviction by a vote of five to four, with Associate Justices Douglas, Stewart, Brennan, and Marshall dissenting. Associate Justice White, writing for the majority, held that the 1st Amendment did not create or protect the privilege of a reporter to refrain from divulging the names of the confidential sources for use

Associate Justice Charles Whittaker (**left**) *generally took a conservative position on racial segregation cases before the Court and dissented in* **Boynton v. Virginia,** *a decision concerning segregated transportation.*

in a state investigation. White, however, narrowed the scope of the decision to cases involving the reporter's privilege before state or federal grand juries. The reporter's privilege not to divulge sources to other types of courts, such as administrative courts, was not addressed.

Briscoe v. Bank of Kentucky, 11 Peters 257 (1837), a case dealing with the power of states to create and issue certain financial instruments. The petitioner in this case opposed a Kentucky law that authorized the state bank to issue bank notes, contending on the basis of the Supreme Court's decision in *Craig v. Missouri* (1830) that state-issued "bills of credit" were a violation of Article I, Section 10 of the Constitution. Since similar state bank notes had become the most common form of legal tender throughout the country, the question of their constitutionality was of the utmost economic importance. The Supreme Court, on a vote of six to one, with only Associate Justice Story dissenting, upheld the Kentucky law. Associate Justice McLean, writing the majority opinion, ruled that since the

state bank had no private stockholders and since the notes were not issued on the basis of credit obtained by the state, its notes were not unconstitutional bills of credit, but rather legitimate legal currency.

Brown v. Board of Education of Topeka, 347 U.S. 483 (1954), a case dealing with the denial of black schoolchildren admission to schools attended by white children under laws requiring or permitting segregation based on race. The complaint of the plaintiff, argued by Thurgood Marshall, later a member of the Court, centered on the denial of equal protection under the 14th Amendment.

The opinion of the Supreme Court consolidated appeals from Kansas, South Carolina, Virginia, Delaware, and the District of Columbia and held unanimously that separate was not equal and that separate educational facilities are inherently unequal. Segregation creates a feeling of inferiority, which may significantly affect a child's ability to learn. This effect is greater when it has the sanction of the government. The policy of separating the races is usually interpreted as denoting the inferiority of one of the groups. Therefore, separate educational facilities are inherently unequal and their maintenance by government authority denies equal protection under the law. In 1955, the Supreme Court reasserted its holding in *Brown* and required the school systems to desegregate "with all deliberate speed." Chief Justice Warren wrote the Court's unanimous opinion.

The *Brown* decision overturned *Plessy v. Ferguson* (1896), which had upheld the doctrine of "separate but equal" facilities for blacks and whites. One of the earliest and most important decisions of the Warren Court, it was notable for its unanimity, which had been carefully orchestrated by Chief Justice Warren. Although there was resistance to implementing *Brown*, the historic ruling had a great impact on subsequent Court decisions, civil rights legislation, and the advancement of civil rights.

Brown v. Maryland, 12 Wheaton 419 (1827), a case dealing with the power of the federal government and the states with regard to the regulation of interstate commerce. In this case, the petitioner, an importer operating in Maryland, appealed to the Supreme Court to overrule his conviction in a Maryland court for refusing to pay a state tax imposed on certain products still in their original packages, which he had brought into the state and which were still in his possession. The Supreme Court ruled by a vote of six to one, with only Associate Justice Thompson dissenting, that the Maryland law was an unconstitutional obstruction of interstate trade and therefore a violation of federal power to regulate it. Chief Justice Marshall, writing the majority opinion, used this decision as yet another opportunity to emphasize the supremacy of the Constitution and its delegated powers over state law and to validate the legitimate power of the federal government to regulate certain aspects of the economic life of the entire nation.

Buckley v. Valeo, 424 U.S. 1 (1976), a case dealing with the constitutionality of federal regulation of campaign expenditures. In 1972 and 1974, in an attempt to control the possible adverse effects of private contributions on the electoral process, Congress passed the Federal Election Campaign Act, which placed limits on the amounts that any individual or committee may contribute to a candidate, required public disclosure of certain types of contributions, established a plan for federal financing of presidential elections, and provided for the appointment of a Federal Election Commission to enforce the provisions of the statute. Sen. James Buckley of New York challenged that the limits on personal expenditure and campaign contributions and the mandatory disclosure requirement violated the 1st Amendment right to free expression and that the composition of the Federal Election Commission violated the appointments clause of Article II, Section 2 of the Constitution.

On January 31, 1976, the Supreme Court ruled on this case in four separate votes, with Associate Justice Stevens not participating. On the issue of personal expenditure by a candidate, the Court decided by a vote of seven to one, with Associate Justice White dissenting, that it was a clear violation of the 1st Amendment. On the issue of maximum contributions to campaigns, the Court decided by a vote of six to two, with Chief Justice Burger and Associate Justice Blackmun dissenting, that this provision was a legitimate means of preventing corruption in the electoral process. On the issue of federal funding for presidential elections, the Court upheld the constitutionality of the provisions by a vote of six to two, with Chief Justice Burger and Associate Justice Rehnquist dissenting. All participating justices ruled that the Federal Election Commission as provided by the act was a violation of the appointments clause of the Constitution. The effect of this complex and many-faceted decision was to establish the precedent that the federal government may regulate individual contributions to a campaign, but may not limit total expenditure.

Butchers' Benevolent Association of New Orleans v. The Crescent City Livestock Landing and Slaughterhouse Co., (1873), *See* Slaughterhouse Cases.

Calder v. Bull, 3 Dall. 386 (1798), a case dealing with the constitutional guarantee against *ex post facto* laws. In March 1793, the Hartford probate court refused to accept a will and granted the estate to the petitioners, with six months for the contesting parties to appeal the decision. After the time for appeal had run out, the Connecticut legislature passed a special resolution, which set aside the original decree of probate, and with a new hearing the will was approved. The original heirs, now the petitioners, were thereby refused the right of appeal and filed suit, claiming that the special act of the legislature was an *ex post facto* law prohibited by Article I, Section 9 of the Constitution. The Supreme Court held, by a vote of four to zero, that the constitutional protection with regard to *ex post facto* laws referred only to acts declared criminal after they had been committed. Associate Justice Chase, speaking for the Court, ruled that the case in question concerned an issue of private property and that the claim of the petitioners should be denied.

Cantwell v. Connecticut, 310 U.S. 396 (1940), a case dealing with the right of states to limit or restrict certain religious fund-raising activities. The Connecticut legislature enacted a law that required state licensing of any person who solicited in public for contributions to charitable or church funds. The petitioner, a member of the Jehovah's Witnesses, challenged the constitutionality of the statute, contending that it abridged his 1st Amendment right of the free exercise of religion.

On May 20, 1940, the Supreme Court decided unanimously that the Connecticut law was unconstitutional. Associate Justice Roberts, speaking for the Court, held that the restriction by the state of solicitation required that it make a fundamental distinction between religious and non-religious groups, a decision, the Justice argued, that state governments were not empowered to make. This decision marked the first time that the Supreme Court included the 1st Amendment protection of the free exercise of religion among the basic rights guaranteed by the privileges and immunities clause of the 14th Amendment.

Carey v. Population Services International, 431 U.S. 678 (1977), a case dealing with the authority of states to restrict the distribution of contraceptives. A New York law prohibited the distribution of contraceptives to minors under the age of sixteen. The law also prohibited the distribution of contraceptives to persons over age sixteen by anyone other than a licensed pharmacist.

The constitutionality of the statute was challenged, and the Supreme Court, by a vote of seven to two, with Chief Justice Burger and Associate Justice Rehnquist dissenting, invalidated the provisions of the law that dealt with nonprescription contraceptives. Justice Brennan, writing for the majority, relied heavily on the previous abortion cases handed down by the Supreme Court and ruled that "the decision whether or not to beget or bear a child is at the very heart of this cluster of constitutionally protected choices." When such a right as that to bear a child was at issue, regulations imposed to create a burden could be justified only by a compelling state interest, Brennan noted. If the state's interest could be justified, the regulations had to be narrowly drawn to express only that interest. The Court held that limiting distribution to licensed pharmacists was a clear burden on the individual's fundamental right to use contraceptives. The Court rejected the argument that a ban on the distribution of contraceptives to persons under age sixteen could limit early sexual behavior. Although restrictions on minors were greater than those for adults, the minors did have the fundamental right to bear a child.

Central Intelligence Agency v. Sims, 53 U.S.L.W. 4453 (1985), a case dealing with regulating public disclosure of CIA sources of information. In 1977 the Public Citizen Health Research Group and the Public Citizen Litigation Group requested the names of researchers in a CIA study of human behavior control that took place between 1953 and 1966. The public interest groups filed their request under the Freedom of Information Act; the CIA invoked the National Security Act of 1947 in refusing to disclose the researchers' names.

In its April 16, 1985, unanimous decision the Court overturned a U.S. Court of Appeals ruling, thereby granting broad discretionary powers to the CIA in withholding its sources. Chief Justice Burger wrote the majority opinion, which held that information "with respect to foreign intelligence" is exempt from disclosure under the Freedom of Information Act. All nine justices agreed that the CIA was justified in invoking the National Security Act as the basis for withholding information and that the Court of Appeals had excessively restricted the CIA's discretionary power, but they disagreed over the definition of "intelligence sources."

Associate Justices Marshall and Brennan refused to sign Chief Justice Burger's opinion, feeling that it established "an irrebuttable presumption of secrecy over an expansive array of information."

Champion v. Ames, 188 U.S. 244 (1903), a case dealing with the extent of the "police power" of the federal government. In 1895, in an attempt to discourage participation in lotteries, Congress passed the Federal Lottery Act, which prohibited the shipment of lottery tickets across state lines. The petitioner, Champion, had been convicted by that law for illegally shipping a box of lottery tickets. He appealed the conviction, contending that the law was an unconstitutional extension of federal power. At issue in this case were the limits of the interpretation of the commerce clause of the Constitution: did the federal government have the right, in the same way as state governments, to use its regulatory power to promote what it considered to be the public good?

On February 23, 1903, the Supreme Court decided by a vote of five to four, with Chief Justice Fuller and Associate Justices Brewer, Peckham, and Shiras dissenting, that Congress was within its constitutional power in the passage of the Lottery Act and that Champion's conviction should stand. Associate Justice Harlan, speaking for the majority, said that since lottery tickets were potential objects of interstate commerce they were therefore subject to federal control. He further held that the federal government could use its regulatory power to prohibit objects of interstate commerce that it deemed harmful to public health or morals. Chief Justice Fuller forcefully objected to the opinion of the majority in his dissenting opinion, regarding this open-ended expansion of federal power as extremely ill-advised. He felt that it would render the 10th Amendment meaningless and termed it "inconsistent with the views of the framers of the Constitution." The "police power" of the federal government confirmed by this decision, however, would eventually become one of its most potent tools for social and economic change.

Chandler v. Florida, 449 U.S. 560 (1981), a case dealing with the constitutionality of televised coverage of state criminal trials. The Florida legislature had enacted a law permitting the television coverage of criminal court proceedings. Chandler, a Miami police officer who had been indicted for larceny, objected to the presence of television cameras in the courtroom, but his objection was overruled, and he was subsequently convicted of the charges against him. Chandler then appealed his conviction, contending that the television coverage violated his 14th Amendment rights to due process, specifically the right to a fair trial.

On January 26, 1981, the Supreme Court decided by a vote of eight to zero, with Associate Justice Stevens not participating, that the Florida statute did not violate Chandler's due process rights and that his conviction should be upheld. Chief Justice Burger, speaking for the majority,

Chief Justice Roger Taney wrote the Court's opinion in **Charles River Bridge v. Warren Bridge,** *a decision that broadened the regulatory power of the states and moved away from the position of the Marshall Court.*

observed that the Florida statute provided the presiding judge with the discretionary power to prohibit television coverage if it seemed likely to prejudice the outcome of the trial, and in the case under consideration, the judge saw no such danger. This decision substantially affirmed the earlier ruling of the Court in *Richmond Newspapers v. Virginia* (1980), in which it held that the press may not be excluded from criminal proceedings unless the potential threat to the impartiality of the trial is specific and made public by the presiding judge.

Charles River Bridge v. Warren Bridge, 11 Peters 420 (1837), a case dealing with state-granted monopolies and the states' right of eminent domain. In 1785, the Massachusetts legislature granted a charter to the Charles River Bridge Company to construct, maintain, and collect tolls for a pedestrian crossing over the river. In 1792 the charter was extended for seventy years. In the course of time, as the traffic over the bridge and profits therefrom greatly increased, another group of investors, calling themselves the Warren Bridge Company, applied for and received a charter (1828) from the state legislature to construct a second thoroughfare. Fearing the adverse economic effects of competition, the

Charles River Bridge Company sought an injunction against the construction of the new bridge, contending that the exclusive nature of the original charter granted them by the state was an implicit part of the original contract and was, accordingly, an element that could not be legally revoked. The Massachusetts courts had denied the injunction.

The Supreme Court upheld the Massachusetts decision by a four to three vote, with Associate Justices Story, Thompson, and McLean dissenting. Chief Justice Taney, speaking for the majority, held that the state of Massachusetts did have the right to authorize the construction of the second bridge, as an exercise of its legitimate "police power," in this case, to ensure convenient and adequate bridges for its citizens. As to the question of the violation of the original contract, Taney ruled that since the text of the original charter had not specifically guaranteed its perpetual exclusivity, that right "shall not be construed to have been surrendered or diminished by the state." This decision represented a marked change from the judicial policy of the Marshall Court to protect the interests of private property and contracts toward a broader interpretation of the legitimate regulatory powers of the states.

Cherokee Nation v. Georgia, 5 Peters 1 (1831), a case dealing with the legal status of Indian territory and the legal jurisdiction of Indian claims against state governments. The petitioners in this case, representatives of the Cherokee Nation, appealed directly to the Supreme Court for protection against the state of Georgia, which had enacted legislation to evict the tribe from its lands. Although Georgia contended that the Cherokees were residents of the state and therefore subject to its laws, the petitioners maintained that since they had concluded formal treaties with the federal government, they were a "foreign state," which by Article III of the Constitution, entitled them to enter suit against the state of Georgia in the original jurisdiction of the Supreme Court. The Cherokees' problem with the state of Georgia was compounded by the election of Pres. Andrew Jackson, who supported the idea of resettling them in lands west of the Mississippi, and by the passage by Congress of a plan to implement that idea, the Indian Removal Act.

Chief Justice Marshall, speaking for the majority, held that the Cherokees were not a foreign nation and therefore not entitled to enter a suit against a state in the federal courts. Associate Justice Thompson, however, in a dissenting opinion in which he was joined by Associate Justice Story, argued that the conclusion of the treaty between the United States and the Cherokees was proof of their extraterritorial status, and he urged that their case against Georgia be taken up by the Supreme Court.

Chicago, Milwaukee & St. Paul Railway Co. v. Minnesota, 134 U.S. 418 (1890), a case dealing with the right of judicial review for private businesses regulated by state governments. At issue in this case was a Minnesota law that provided that the rulings of the state railroad commission

During the presidency of Benjamin Harrison, the Court's 1890 opinion in a Minnesota railroad regulation case narrowed the police power of the states.

with regard to freight charges within the state would be "final and conclusive." Since one of the railroads affected by this ruling was denied a review by the state supreme court, it challenged the constitutionality of the Minnesota law as a violation of its right to due process.

On March 24, 1890, the Supreme Court decided by a vote of six to three, with Associate Justices Bradley, Gray, and Lamar dissenting, that while state governments were entitled to regulate railroads operating strictly within the boundaries of their state, they must also provide for the right of judicial review. Associate Justice Blatchford, speaking for the majority, held that private companies forced to lower their rates by state action were effectively deprived of property and must have the right to appeal the rates determined for them in the courts. This ruling was seen as an additional narrowing of the "police power" doctrine of state regulation established by the Supreme Court in *Munn v. Illinois* (1877).

Chisholm v. Georgia, 2 Dall. 419 (1793), the first major opinion handed down by the Supreme Court, dealing with the basic constitutional issue of whether a state can be sued by citizens of another state. The petitioners, heirs of a former Georgia resident, Alexander Chisholm, but themselves residents of South Carolina, filed suit against the state of Georgia to collect bonds owed to Chisholm's estate, which had been confiscated by the state during the Revolutionary War. Since the limits of federal jurisdiction and state authority had not yet been fully defined, the state of Georgia believed that such a suit was an infringement of its own sovereignty and refused even to answer the claims of the petitioners, informing the Court, instead, that the federal judiciary had no jurisdiction in the case.

By a vote of four to one, with Associate Justice Iredell dissenting, the Court ruled that by Article III, Section 2 of the U.S. Constitution, citizens of one state did, in fact, have the right to sue the government of another state. The majority opinion, written by Chief Justice Jay, ordered that after the filing of a formal declaration by the plaintiffs, the state of Georgia must either appear in court to defend the suit or show cause why they could not. If Georgia continued to defy federal jurisdiction, a default judgment would be entered against the state. This opinion was seen as a potential danger to the economic survival of the states since similar suits to recover confiscated property had already been filed in Maryland, Massachusetts, New York, South Carolina, and Virginia. As a result, the 11th Amendment to the Constitution was adopted in 1798, specifically prohibiting suits by citizens of one state against the governments of another.

Citizen Publishing Company v. United States, 394 U.S. 131 (1969), a case dealing with the legality of certain business practices. In 1940, Tucson, Arizona, had only two daily newspapers, *The Citizen* and *The Star*, which were vigorous competitors. In 1936, *The Citizen* had been purchased by Small and Johnson, who made an agreement with *The Star* to fix prices, pool profits, and establish a market control. The government filed suit against the two newspapers, contending that such an action was a violation of the Sherman Antitrust Act. A lower court sustained the government's suit, and the ruling was appealed.

The Supreme Court held by a vote of eight to one, with only Associate Justice Stewart dissenting, that there was a violation of the Sherman Act, as price-fixing was illegal *per se*, and pooling of profits and an agreement not to engage in any other publishing business in the county was also covered by the act. Associate Justice Black, writing for the majority, ruled that the only real defense of the appellants was the "failing company" defense. But since there was no indication that the owners of *The Citizen* were going to sell or liquidate and since there was no evidence that the joint operating agreement was essential for the survival of *The Citizen*, the "failing company" doctrine could not be applied in a merger.

City of Akron v. Akron Center for Reproductive Health, 462 U.S. 416 (1983), a case dealing with the power of states to impose certain restrictions on the performance of medical abortions. An Akron, Ohio, ordinance required that all abortions performed after the first trimester be performed in a hospital; that physicians refrain from performing abortions on unmarried minors under the age of fifteen unless parental consent or court order was obtained; that attending physicians inform their patients of the status of their

The ruling in the **City of Akron** *case reaffirmed the Court's support of a woman's right to an abortion, but opponents of abortion such as President Reagan pressed for a constitutional amendment against the practice.*

pregnancies, including the date of possible viability and the physical and emotional complications that may result from an abortion; that physicians refrain from performing an abortion until 24 hours after the pregnant woman signs a consent form; and that physicians performing abortions ensure that fetal remains are disposed of in a "humane and sanitary manner." The constitutionality of the ordinance was challenged by three abortion clinics and a physician.

The Supreme Court, by a vote of six to three, with Associate Justices O'Connor, White, and Rehnquist dissenting, held unconstitutional the provisions of the statute dealing with performance of all second-trimester abortions in a hospital, parental consent, the 24-hour-waiting period, and the disposal of the fetal remains. Associate Justice Powell, writing for the majority, reaffirmed the earlier decision of *Roe v. Wade* (1973), in which the Court recognized that the right of privacy, grounded in the Constitution's concept of personal liberty, included a woman's right to decide whether to terminate her pregnancy.

City of Mobile v. Bolden, 446 U.S. 55 (1980), a case dealing with the constitutionality of certain municipal electoral systems. The city of Mobile, Alabama, was governed by a city commission consisting of three members who were elected at large by voters of the city. A complaint was filed on behalf of all black residents of Mobile, claiming that this at-large election system unfairly diluted the voting strength of blacks and was in violation of the 14th and 15th

Amendments. The Supreme Court ruled by a vote of seven to two, with Associate Justices White and Marshall dissenting, that the 15th Amendment claim was unfounded. Associate Justice Stewart, writing for the majority, held that the 15th Amendment required that citizens be allowed to vote without hindrance, not that certain citizens be elected. Since the Court found that blacks in Mobile could register and vote without hindrance, Stewart stated that there was no discriminatory intent to disallow minority representation, and therefore there was no violation of the 14th Amendment.

City of New York v. Miln, 11 Peters 102 (1837), a case dealing with state "police power" and its relation to federal regulation of international commerce. The issue in question in this case was the constitutionality of a New York state law that required that the captains of all vessels arriving at state ports from overseas provide harbor authorities with a list of the names, ages, birthplaces, and occupations of the arriving passengers. The defendant in this case was the agent on an arriving ship whose captain had refused to file such a report and who was subsequently fined by New York state. The agent's attorneys contended that the state law was an unconstitutional invasion of the exclusive federal right to regulate interstate and international trade. The city of New York then filed suit to collect the fine.

The Supreme Court ruled by a vote of six to one, with only Associate Justice Story dissenting, that the conviction should stand since the state law was a legitimate exercise of the state's "police power" to protect the health, prosperity, and safety of its citizens. Associate Justice Barbour, speaking for the majority, wrote that since the law was enacted to prevent the influx of indigent immigrants and not commercial goods, it did not conflict with the federal regulation of trade. This decision dramatically departed from the policy of the Marshall Court, which had consistently emphasized the primacy of federal authority in matters even indirectly involved in interstate and international commerce.

Civil Rights Cases, 109 U.S. 3 (1883), a series of related cases dealing with the constitutional right of Congress to legislate against racial discrimination by privately owned businesses. The law that was challenged in these cases was an act of Congress passed in 1875 that imposed penalties on any owner of a public establishment or conveyance who practiced racial discrimination in the conduct of his business. Although this federal law was intended to implement in practice what had been established in principle by the 13th and 14th Amendments, many northern conservatives and southerners opposed to Reconstruction saw the law as an unconstitutional infringement of personal freedom of choice.

On October 15, 1883, the Court held by an eight to one vote, with only Associate Justice Harlan dissenting, that neither the 13th nor 14th Amendment empowers the Congress to legislate in matters of racial discrimination in the private sector. Associate Justice Bradley, speaking for the majority, held that the 13th Amendment applied only to "involuntary servitude," not to discrimination and that the 14th Amendment, while prohibiting discrimination by governmental bodies, made no provisions for acts of racial discrimination by private individuals. This decision overturned the Civil Rights Act of 1875, and it was not until nearly a century later, in the 1964 case of *Heart of Atlanta Motel v. United States*, that the Court reversed its position and ruled that racial discrimination in privately owned accommodations did, in fact, come under the protection of the 13th and 14th Amendments.

Cohens v. Virginia, 6 Wheaton 264 (1821), a case dealing with the constitutional right of the federal judiciary to review and overturn the decisions of state courts in matters dealing with federal authority. Two brothers were convicted of selling District of Columbia lottery tickets in Virginia, and according to the state law by which they were tried, there could be no appeal. Appealing to the Supreme Court, they contended that since the Congress, in enacting a lottery in the District of Columbia, was acting within the Constitution, the Virginia law by which they were prosecuted was in conflict with the Constitution and therefore void.

The first question faced by the Supreme Court in this case was whether it might legitimately review the decision of the lower state court, since the case was not allowed a state appeal. The Court determined that such an appeal

Federal authority was extended during James Monroe's presidency by the Court's decision in Cohens v. Virginia, *an opinion written by Chief Justice Marshall.*

could be heard, since the maintenance of the supremacy of federal law required that the Supreme Court review all constitutional questions regardless of any restrictions imposed by state legislatures on the judicial process. Chief Justice Marshall, speaking for the Court, ruled that such an appeal was not a violation of the 11th Amendment. As to the basic issue in question, however, Marshall held that the District of Columbia lottery was intended by Congress only as a local, not a national, law, and the defendants could therefore legitimately be prosecuted for selling lottery tickets in a state where such activity was against the law. Despite the fact that this decision upheld the decision of the state court, it was an extremely important reassertion of the power of the federal judiciary to review constitutional issues in the state courts.

Coker v. Georgia, 433 U.S. 584 (1977), a case dealing with the procedural conditions under which the death sentence can be imposed in state criminal trials. The petitioner, Coker, escaped from a Georgia prison where he was serving various sentences for murder, rape, kidnapping, and aggravated assault. After his escape he committed an armed robbery and raped an adult woman. He was convicted of rape and was sentenced to death. The state argued that the aggravating circumstances of these prior convictions and his escape justified the imposition of the death penalty.

Upon appeal, on June 29, 1977, the Supreme Court ruled by a vote of seven to two, with Chief Justice Burger and Associate Justice Rehnquist dissenting, that the 8th Amendment's prohibition against cruel and inhuman punishment would be violated if the petitioner was sentenced to death for the rape of an adult woman. Associate Justice White, writing for the majority, noted that Georgia was the only state to reenact the death penalty for rape since 1972 and this was the only case out of ten in which it had been imposed by the Georgia courts. White further noted that the death penalty was disproportionate to the crime committed where no taking of life was involved, and the death penalty for rape would therefore make no measurable contribution to acceptable goals of punishment.

Colegrove v. Green, (1946), *See* Baker v. Carr.

Collector v. Day, 11 Wallace 113 (1871), a case dealing with the immunity of the salary of a state judge from the national income tax. In 1842 the Court had held in *Dobbins v. Erie County* that a state could not tax a federal officer's salary but rejected the suggestion that federal taxation might not be subject to a similar limitation. In this case the Supreme Court, by a vote of eight to one, with only Associate Justice Bradley dissenting, upheld the immunity from federal tax for state officials as well. Associate Justice Nelson, writing for the majority, relied on the concept that a state is as independent and sovereign as the federal government. The federal government employed means and instrumentalities to carry into operation the powers granted to it, Nelson noted, and for the sake of self-reliance they were exempt from a state's taxation. Since this was an adequate form of administration for the federal government, it was held that it was an adequate administration of a state government.

Committee for Public Education v. Nyquist, 413 U.S. 756 (1973), a case dealing with the constitutionality of federal assistance programs for religious school students. Three financial aid programs for nonpublic elementary and secondary schools were established by amendments to New York's education and tax laws. These programs consisted of direct money grants to qualifying schools, a tuition reimbursement plan for parents of children attending nonpublic elementary and secondary schools, and tax relief to parents failing to qualify for tuition reimbursement. The Committee for Public Education challenged these programs, contending that since 85 percent of the schools to be affected were church-affiliated, the program was in violation of the 1st Amendment separation of church and state.

The Supreme Court overturned the state statutes by a vote of six to three, with Chief Justice Burger and Associate Justices White and Rehnquist dissenting. Associate Justice Powell, writing for the majority, held that the state had to maintain a position of neutrality by not advancing or inhibiting religion. By providing income tax benefits to the parents, granting tuition reimbursements, and providing direct money grants to nonpublic (church-affiliated) schools, the state would advance the sectarian activities of religious schools, Powell stated. Therefore, since the sections of the law created the impermissible effect of advancing religion, this law was in direct violation of the constitutional requirement of separation of state and church.

Container v. Franchise Tax Board, 463 U.S. 159 (1983), a case dealing with the right of states to collect taxes from multinational companies using a formula that includes income generated in other nations. In the early 1960's, Container Corporation of America calculated its California tax returns for three years, excluding income generated by its twenty foreign subsidiaries. But California's Franchise Tax Board calculated Container's taxes on the basis of worldwide revenues. Although the corporation paid the extra taxes, it sued the Franchise Board for a refund. At issue was the constitutionality of the method of worldwide uniformity in computing corporate state taxes. Eleven states used this method. Container argued that, because foreign production costs are typically lower than in the United States, the unitary formula distorts corporate earnings, inflating revenues attributable to California and causing Container to duplicate tax payments already made to foreign host governments.

In a five to three ruling on June 27, 1983, Justice Brennan rejected Container's constitutional challenge, asserting the fairness of the worldwide apportionment formula that allows states to tax corporate revenue regardless of geographic origin. Dissenting opinion held that the California tax effectively duplicated taxes collected by foreign countries. As a result of this decision some American multinational corporations expressed determination to lobby for a states' comprehensive tax law in an effort to prevent other states from adopting the unitary tax method.

Cooley v. Board of Wardens, 12 Howard 299 (1851), a case dealing with the extent of federal jurisdiction in matters of interstate trade. The law in question was a Pennsylvania state law that required that all ships entering or leaving the port of Philadelphia engage a local pilot. The defendant, Cooley, was the agent of a ship that had failed to do so and who was subsequently fined. He filed suit in federal court to overturn his conviction on the grounds that the state law infringed on the exclusive right of the federal government to regulate interstate trade. The Supreme Court held by a vote of seven to two, with Associate Justices McLean and Wayne dissenting, that Cooley's conviction should stand. Associate Justice Curtis, writing the majority opinion, held that since an act of Congress of 1789 provided for state regulation of pilots until a uniform federal act was passed and since Congress had not acted in this matter, the Pennsylvania state law was constitutional. This decision established the right of states to regulate certain aspects of inter-

Associate Justice Davis, an early supporter of Abraham Lincoln, who appointed him to the Court, dissented in **Cummings v. Missouri,** *which held loyalty "test oaths" unconstitutional. Davis, who was criticized for his political ambitions, later resigned from the Court and was elected to the Senate.*

state commerce that were essentially local in application and effect and that were not in conflict with federal law.

Cooper v. Aaron, 358 U.S. 1 (1958), a case dealing with the constitutionality of a delay in racial desegregation of the public schools. In 1957, Arkansas's Gov. Orval Faubus called out the state militia to prevent the desegregation of the Little Rock schools as mandated by the decision of the Supreme Court in *Brown v. Board of Education* (1954), and the following year the Little Rock school board petitioned for a delay in further implementation of the desegregation plan until further challenges to *Brown* were heard. The case against the suit of the Little Rock school authorities was presented before the Supreme Court by future Associate Justice Thurgood Marshall, then serving as the director of the National Association for the Advancement of Colored People (NAACP) Legal Defense Fund.

On September 12, 1958, the Supreme Court ruled unanimously that the federal desegregation orders must be implemented immediately. Chief Justice Warren, speaking for the Court, held that state officials cannot, under any circumstances, refuse to carry out a court order based on constitutional grounds. This decision was signed by each of the nine justices and represented their determination to uphold fully their prior ruling on the unconstitutionality of racial segregation.

Craig v. Missouri, 4 Peters 410 (1830), a case dealing with the power of states to create and issue certain financial instruments. In the wake of an economic recession and several subsequent bank failures in the state, Missouri enacted a law that authorized the issuance of state loan certificates. The petitioner in this case contended that the Missouri loan certificates were a violation of Article I, Section 10 of the Constitution, which explicitly prohibited the states from issuing "bills of credit," which might flood the national economy with questionable currency. The Supreme Court sustained the petitioner's contention by a vote of four to

President Jimmy Carter's arrangements for the release of American hostages in Iran ultimately led to the Court's decision, in **Dames & Moore v. Regan***, upholding presidential authority to make such an agreement.*

three, with Chief Justice Marshall speaking for the majority and holding that the Missouri loan certificates were, in fact, technically bills of credit and therefore an unconstitutional use of state fiscal power. In a dissenting opinion, Associate Justice McLean held that since the loan certificates were not circulated and were intended only to alleviate temporary financial problems, they should not be considered a substantive violation of the constitutional ban.

Cummings v. Missouri, 4 Wallace 277 (1867), a case dealing with the constitutionality of loyalty oaths. In this case, the petitioner objected to a Missouri state law that required all clergymen, before being allowed to perform their professional duties, to swear that they were loyal citizens of the United States and had not supported the Confederacy during the Civil War. The Supreme Court ruled by a vote of five to four, with Chief Justice Chase and Associate Justices Swayne, Davis, and Miller dissenting, that such "test oaths" were unconstitutional. Associate Justice Field, writing the majority opinion, held that neither the state nor the federal government may impose the requirement of such oaths since they constitute a violation of the constitutional protection against *ex post facto* laws. This case was heard by the Supreme Court with the case of *Ex parte Garland*.

Curtis Publishing Company v. Butts, 388 U.S. 130 (1967), a case dealing with the right of public figures to recover damages in civil libel suits. The respondent, Wally Butts, the former football coach at the University of Georgia, was reported to have deliberately lost a football game against the University of Alabama. This was reported in the petitioner's magazine, *The Saturday Evening Post*. Butts subsequently received a libel judgment against the petitioner and the case was appealed.

The Supreme Court ruled by a vote of six to three, with Associate Justices Black, Douglas, and White dissenting, that a public figure who is not a public official may recover damages for a defamatory false statement if it substantially damaged his reputation. Associate Justice Harlan, writing for the majority, held that the public figure had to show that there was unreasonable conduct constituting an extreme departure from the standards of investigation and ordinary reporting. Harlan held that *The New York Times* rule regarding public officials should apply to persons who are thrust into the public light. Public figures have as ready access as public officials to mass media, both to influence policy and to counter criticism of their views and activities. Therefore, Harlan argued, *The New York Times* rule that in order to recover damages for a defamatory statement the public official must prove actual malice, also applies to public figures.

Dames & Moore v. Regan, 453 U.S. 654 (1981), a case dealing with the constitutional right of the president to nullify certain private international financial obligations. In the final days of President Carter's administration, the U.S. government concluded an agreement with the government of Iran for the release of American diplomats being held hostage. The terms of this agreement included a provision releasing all Iranian assets frozen in the United States for eventual settlement by a claims tribunal. The executive order to that effect was later implemented by President Reagan. The petitioner, a corporation that had concluded a contract with the previous government of Iran and had obtained a court-ordered attachment of Iranian assets, filed suit in federal court to prevent the secretary of the Treasury, Donald Regan, from carrying out the executive order and releasing the attached funds.

On July 2, 1981, the Supreme Court decided unanimously that the President had acted within his constitutional power. Associate Justice Rehnquist, speaking for the Court, held that even though Congress had not expressly approved the presidential action, its enactment of the International Economic Emergency Powers Act of 1977 had empowered the executive branch to suspend claims against certain foreign assets in the U.S. court system, in order to further important foreign policy objectives.

Davis v. Passman, 442 U.S. 228 (1979), a case dealing with the constitutional basis and procedure for civil suits against sex discrimination. A former staff employee filed suit against her employer, a congressman, for sex discrimination, alleging that her rights under the 5th Amendment had been violated. On June 5, 1979, the Supreme Court ruled by a vote of five to four, with Chief Justice Burger and Associate Justices Powell, Rehnquist, and Stewart dissenting, that the equal protection clause of the 5th Amendment conferred on a person a federal constitutional right to be free from gender discrimination that did not serve an important governmental goal. Associate Justice Brennan, writing for the majority, held that an injury caused by gender discrimination could be redressed by a damages remedy. The plaintiff, Brennan noted, was an appropriate party to invoke federal jurisdiction because her claim rested primarily on due process. The plaintiff, therefore, had a federal cause of action that if she should prevail on the merits of her case, would entitle her to money damages.

DeJonge v. Oregon, 299 U.S. 353 (1937), a case dealing with the right of state governments to restrict public assemblies. The Oregon legislature enacted a law that imposed criminal penalties on anyone who assisted in or even attended a meeting held by an organization that advocated the violent overthrow of the government. The petitioner, a member of such an organization, was convicted by the terms of the statute and appealed the conviction, contending that since no illegal act was actually committed or planned at the meeting, the law was an unconstitutional violation of his 1st Amendment rights.

On January 4, 1937, the Supreme Court decided by a vote of eight to zero, with Associate Justice Stone not participating, that the Oregon law should be struck down. Chief Justice Hughes, speaking for the Court, held that despite the threat of revolution that the law attempted to avert, "more imperative is the need to preserve inviolate the constitutional rights of free speech, free press, and free assembly in order to maintain the opportunity for free political discussion." This decision established the inviolability of the 1st Amendment protection of assembly against restriction by state law.

De Lima v. Bidwell, 182 U.S. 1 (1901), a case dealing with the legal status and constitutional rights of the residents of U.S. territories. After the annexation of Puerto Rico in the Spanish-American War, the representatives of several Puerto Rican sugar companies challenged the constitutionality of the imposition of import duties on their products sold within the United States. Since the island was now under American administration, they contended that they were entitled to the full protection of American law. At stake in this case, therefore, was the basic question of whether constitutional guarantees immediately apply to territories conquered or annexed by the United States.

On May 27, 1901, the Supreme Court decided by a vote of five to four, with Associate Justices Gray, McKenna, Shiras, and White dissenting, that the foreign import duties on Puerto Rican sugar should be removed. Associate Justice Brown, speaking for the slim majority, held that while the full constitutional rights of American citizenship did not automatically accrue to residents of American territories, their legal status was no longer "foreign." This case was decided on the same day as the related case of *Downes v. Bidwell* and the two together have become known as the "Insular Cases." In the latter case, however, the Court reversed itself and, by complex legalistic reasoning, determined that import duties could be applied to Puerto Rican goods.

Dennis et al. v. United States, 341 U.S. 494 (1951), a case dealing with the constitutional right of the federal government to restrict freedom of speech and assembly. In 1940, Congress passed the Smith Act, which imposed criminal penalties on anyone who taught, advocated, or encouraged the violent overthrow of government. The petitioners, Eugene Dennis and other leading members of the Communist Party of the United States, were convicted of a violation of the provisions of the law, and they subsequently appealed their convictions, contending that the law, by its vague wording, violated their 1st and 5th Amendment rights.

On June 4, 1951, the Supreme Court decided by a vote of six to two, with Associate Justices Black and Douglas

Associate Justice Sherman Minton concurred with the majority in **Dennis v. United States,** *which upheld the conviction of several Communist Party members under the "clear and present danger" doctrine.*

dissenting and Associate Justice Clark not participating, that the Smith Act was constitutional and that Dennis's conviction should stand. Chief Justice Vinson, speaking for the majority, held that the law was a legitimate exercise of federal power since the admitted teachings of the petitioners "to overthrow the government of the United States as speedily as circumstances would permit" constituted "a clear and present danger" that the government had the right to prevent.

Diamond v. Chakrabarty, 447 U.S. 303 (1980), a case dealing with the categories of patentable inventions. The respondent attempted to patent his invention of a human-made bacterium that could break down crude oil and was refused on the grounds that living organisms cannot be patented. He appealed this decision and the Supreme Court held by a five to four vote, with Associate Justices Brennan, White, Marshall, and Powell dissenting, that a live, human-made microorganism is patentable. Chief Justice Burger, writing for the majority, stated that since the respondent artificially constructed and manufactured this microorganism, he was not trying to patent a physical phenomenon but rather a manufacturing process and product. Burger further ruled that Congress does not have to authorize expressly the patentability of man-made bacterium; the patent law as it stood offered a wide scope to ensure the patentability of any type of useful invention.

Dirks v. Securities and Exchange Commission, 463 U.S. 646 (1983), a case dealing with the legal liability of stock traders who make use of private information they receive from corporate insiders. Securities analyst Raymond L. Dirks brought a scandal to light about Equity Funding Corporation after hearing about it from a former Equity officer. As a result of his warning to several clients that Equity was about to collapse, Dirks was censured by the SEC for taking advantage of his inside information and thereby violating the antifraud provisions of the securities laws. Dirks challenged the SEC in the U.S. Court of Appeals for the District of Columbia.

His long legal battle ended in victory on July 1, 1983, when the Supreme Court held six to three that he had acted properly. In an opinion written by Associate Justice Powell, the Court ruled that the SEC's rigid view of the law on insider trading threatened "to impair private initiative in uncovering violations of the law." This decision reaffirmed principles established by the Court in the 1980 *Chiarella* opinion regarding insider trading, which Justice Powell also wrote. He said that the "duty to disclose arises from the relationship between parties and not merely from one's ability to acquire information because of his position in the market." Associate Justices Blackmun, Brennan, and Marshall dissented, calling Dirk's action a "knowing and intentional violation of an insider's duty to shareholders" even though he did not act from motives of personal gain.

Dobbins v. Erie County, (1842), *See* Collector v. Day.

Doe v. McMillan, 412 U.S. 306 (1973), a case dealing with congressional immunity from civil libel suits. After the dissemination of a congressional committee report on the Washington, D.C., school system, parents of students in the system sought relief for alleged invasion of privacy. The Supreme Court ruled by a vote of five to four, with Chief Justice Burger and Associate Justices Blackmun, Rehnquist, and Stewart dissenting in part, that materials published in connection with legislative matters could create liability if they were distributed beyond the reasonable requirements of the legislative task. Associate Justice White, writing for the majority, held that while the speech and debate clause stated that congressmen shall not be questioned in any other place for any speech or debate in either house, the clause was only a partial barrier to the suits. White stated that the clause provided absolute immunity from suit for introducing the allegedly injurious material at committee hearings and for voting for publication of the committee report. The clause did not, however, provide for absolute immunity if these congressionally-approved materials were unreasonably distributed beyond the appropriate legislative purpose.

Dombrowski v. Pfister, 380 U.S. 479 (1965), a case dealing with the power of states to restrict the 1st Amendment freedom of speech guarantee. The respondents alleged that the Louisiana Subversive Activities and Communist

Control Law violated their rights of free speech under the 1st and 14th Amendments. On April 26, 1965, the Supreme Court ruled by a vote of five to two, with Associate Justices Harlan and Clark dissenting and Associate Justices Black and Stewart not participating, that the Louisiana statute, making it a felony to participate in any subversive organization as defined by the statute, was unconstitutionally broad and vague. Associate Justice Brennan, writing for the majority, noted that the statute made it a crime to fail to register as a member of a Communist front organization, and this provision was also unconstitutional because it contained the invalid presumption that any organization was a Communist front merely because it had been cited as a Communist front by the attorney general or any congressional committee without having been given an assurance of due process of notice and an opportunity to be heard.

Dooley v. United States, 182 U.S. 222 (1901), a case dealing with the legal status of Puerto Rico. The petitioner, Dooley, had paid certain duties at the port of San Juan, Puerto Rico, only under protest. These duties were collected both before and after the ratification of the peace treaty that ended the Spanish-American War. He subsequently filed suit in federal court to recover the duties. The Supreme Court held by a vote of five to four, with Associate Justices White, Gray, Shiras, and McKenna dissenting, that duties upon imports from the United States to Puerto Rico, collected by the military commander and by the president, from the time possession was taken of the island until the ratification of the peace treaty, were legally taken under the powers granted during the war. Associate Justice Brown, writing for the majority, further ruled that when the right to obtain duties for goods imported from Puerto Rico to the United States ceased, so did the right to obtain duties for goods imported from the United States to Puerto Rico.

Douglas v. California, (1963), *See* Evitts v. Lucey.

Downes v. Bidwell, 182 U.S. 222 (1901), a case dealing with the legal status and constitutional rights of the residents of U.S. territories. After the annexation of Puerto Rico in the Spanish-American War, representatives of several Puerto Rican sugar companies challenged the constitutionality of the imposition of import duties on their products sold within the United States. Since the island was now under American administration, they contended that they were no longer "foreign" and were therefore entitled to the full protection of American law. This issue was addressed broadly by the Supreme Court in the companion case of *De Lima v. Bidwell*, but at stake in *Downes* was not a question of foreign status but rather the constitutionality of a specific piece of legislation: the Foraker Act of 1900, by which Congress imposed duties on goods from Puerto Rico.

On May 27, 1901, the Supreme Court decided by a vote of five to four, with Chief Justice Fuller and Associate Justices Brewer, Harlan, and Peckham dissenting, that the Foraker Act was constitutional and that the duties it estab-

lished on Puerto Rican products were valid. Associate Justice Brown, speaking for the majority, held that although Puerto Rico was not foreign, it was still subject to the acts of Congress. In a concurring opinion, Associate Justice White introduced the concept of "incorporation," by which Congress could differentiate among various American territories and determine which legal or constitutional rights would apply to their residents.

Duncan v. Louisiana, (1968), *See* Williams v. Florida.

Duplex Printing Press Co. v. Deering, 254 U.S. 443 (1921), a case dealing with the right of the federal government to intervene in the activities of labor unions. After the passage by Congress of the Clayton Antitrust Act (1914), which exempted labor unions from prosecution under the Sherman Antitrust Act, a strike and secondary boycott were organized against the Duplex Printing Press Company. Despite the provisions of the Clayton Act, the management of the company filed suit against the labor leaders, contending that they had unlawfully conspired to obstruct the company's trade.

On January 3, 1921, the Supreme Court decided by a vote of six to three, with Associate Justices Brandeis, Clarke, and Holmes dissenting, that the claims of the Duplex Printing Company should be sustained. Associate Justice Pitney, speaking for the majority, held that the Clayton Act protected only the legal and legitimate activities of national labor unions and that a secondary boycott was clearly illegal. The decision of the Court in this case and in *American Steel Foundries v. Trade Council* (1921) effectively nullified the Clayton Antitrust Act.

Edmund v. Florida, 458 U.S. 782 (1982), a case dealing with the constitutionality of the imposition of the death sentence for certain crimes. The petitioner, Edmund, and a co-defendant were convicted of robbery and first-degree murder of two persons. The petitioner and co-defendant were both sentenced to death. The evidence showed that the petitioner was in a car when the murders took place, but since he had been found to be a constructive aider and abettor, the death sentence could be imposed under Florida law.

Edmund appealed the conviction, and the Supreme Court ruled by a vote of five to four, with Chief Justice Burger and Associate Justices O'Connor, Powell, and Rehnquist dissenting, that the imposition of the death sentence for the petitioner was unconstitutional under the 8th and 14th Amendments. Associate Justice White, writing for the majority, noted that few states had a law similar to the one at issue and that juries in those states were reluctant to sentence a person to death for a crime such as the petitioner's. The death penalty, which is uniquely severe and irrevocable, was an excessive penalty for the robber who as such does not take human life, argued White. The Court found that since the petitioner did not kill and had no intention of killing, the death penalty was excessive.

Edwards v. California, 314 U.S. 160 (1941), a case dealing with the right of states to prohibit certain classes of citizens from residence within the state. In 1940, in an attempt to deal with the growing burden of welfare assistance, the California legislature enacted a law that imposed criminal penalties on any person or corporation who knowingly brought an indigent person or persons into the state. The petitioner, Fred Edwards, had been convicted of bringing his indigent brother-in-law into the state, and he appealed that conviction, contending that not only was the state law an infringement on the exclusive jurisdiction of the federal government in matters concerning interstate commerce, but that the right to travel freely throughout the country was the right of all U.S. citizens guaranteed by the privileges and immunities clause of the 14th Amendment.

On November 24, 1941, the Supreme Court decided unanimously that the California law should be struck down. While Associate Justice Byrnes, speaking for the majority, restricted his opinion to the violation of federal jurisdiction in matters of interstate trade, Associate Justices Douglas and Frankfurter asserted that a violation of the 14th Amendment was also involved.

Eisenstadt v. Baird, 405 U.S. 438 (1972), a case dealing with the issue of whether the use of contraceptives was a matter of individual privacy. This case involved a law that made it a felony to distribute materials for prevention of conception, except by registered physicians or pharmacists, to married persons. The Supreme Court, by a vote of six to three, with Chief Justice Burger and Associate Justices Powell and Rehnquist dissenting, found no grounds for any difference that would rationally explain the different treatment accorded married and unmarried persons. Associate Justice Douglas, writing for the majority, held that since the marriage is composed of two independent individuals, each with a separate emotional and intellectual make-up, the deterrence of premarital sex cannot reasonably be regarded as the aim of the law. Therefore, Douglas noted, the law could not distinguish between married and unmarried persons when dealing with the right to purchase and use contraceptives.

Engel v. Vitale, 370 U.S. 421 (1962), a case dealing with the constitutionality of prayer in the public schools. The New York State Board of Regents had approved a nondenominational prayer for recitation each morning in the public schools. The constitutionality of that practice was subsequently challenged on the grounds that it violated the 1st Amendment prohibition against the establishment of religion.

On June 25, 1962, the Supreme Court decided by a vote of six to one, with Associate Justice Stewart dissenting and Associate Justices Frankfurter and White not participating, that prayer in the public schools, whether sectarian or nonsectarian, was unconstitutional and that the practice in the New York schools should be discontinued. Associate Justice Black, speaking for the majority, held that state governments "should stay out of the business of writing or sanctioning official prayers," leaving religion to religious organizations alone. This decision was later affirmed by the Court in *School District of Abington Township v. Schempp* (1963), in which daily Bible readings in the public schools were ruled likewise unconstitutional.

Equal Employment Opportunity Commission v. Wyoming, 460 U.S. 226 (1983), a case dealing with the power of states to impose mandatory retirement ages on certain state officials. The state of Wyoming required by law that all state game and fish wardens retire at age fifty-five. A suit was subsequently filed by the federal Equal Employment Opportunity Commission contending that the state regulation was a violation of the federal Age Discrimination in Employment Act.

The Supreme Court ruled by a vote of five to four with Chief Justice Burger and Associate Justices Powell, O'Connor, and Rehnquist dissenting, that the extension of the act to cover Wyoming state employees did not violate the state's authority to govern itself. Associate Justice Brennan, writing for the majority, found that although the forced retirement of a state game warden involved an attribute of state sovereignty, the act did not directly impair the state's ability to structure integral operations in areas of traditional governmental functions. The law required the state only to fulfill its necessity for physically prepared and occupationally qualified game wardens, Brennan noted. Therefore, the federal government's interference in the state retirement plan on behalf of the Wyoming game warden was constitutional and must be upheld.

Esteban v. Louisiana, (1873), *See* Slaughterhouse Cases.

Evitts v. Lucey, 53 U.S.L.W. 4101 (1985), a case dealing with the rights of criminal defendants to effective assistance of counsel on appeal. This seven to two decision handed down on January 21, 1985, upheld a U.S. Court of Appeals decision that Kentucky state courts had improperly dismissed Keith Lucey's appeal of a narcotics conviction. The Court of Appeals held that when Lucey's appeal was dismissed because his lawyer failed to file a necessary document, Lucey was denied his rights to effective assistance of counsel.

Associate Justice Brennan wrote the majority opinion, which was based on the 14th Amendment's right of due process and which extended an earlier decision, *Douglas v. California* (1963). This earlier case established the right of free legal assistance in the appeals process to indigent defendants. Although Lucey was not indigent and had hired his own lawyer, Justice Brennan wrote, "A party whose counsel is unable to provide effective representation is in no better position than one who has no counsel at all." Dissenting were Associate Justice Rehnquist and Chief Justice Burger, who feared this decision would further slow the process of U.S. criminal justice.

Chief Justice Chase (center) *spoke for the Court in* **Ex parte McCardle,** *which upheld the right of Congress to limit the Court's appellate jurisdiction. A different ruling could have invalidated the Reconstruction government of the former Confederate states.*

Ex parte Endo, 323 U.S. 283 (1944), a case dealing with the power of the federal government to relocate and detain certain citizens in wartime. A Japanese-American woman, whose loyalty to the United States had clearly been established, was detained in a war relocation center maintained under the relocation program. She filed suit in federal court, and the Supreme Court ruled unanimously that the petitioner was entitled to release on the grounds that there was no authority in the statutes and regulations to subject citizens to this particular detention procedure when they are considered loyal. Associate Justice Douglas, writing for the Court, did not invalidate the entire program, but did maintain that once a citizen's loyalty had been established the government had no authority to detain that citizen.

Ex parte Garland, 4 Wallace 333 (1867), a case dealing with the constitutionality of professional loyalty oaths. The petitioner opposed a federal law that required that all practicing attorneys, before being allowed to perform their professional duties, be required to swear that they were loyal citizens of the United States and had not supported the Confederacy during the Civil War. The Supreme Court ruled by a vote of five to four, with Chief Justice Chase and Associate Justices Swayne, Davis, and Miller dissenting, that the federal law was unconstitutional. Associate Justice Field, speaking for the majority, held that the imposition of such "test oaths" violated the constitutional protection against

ex post facto laws. This case was heard by the Supreme Court with *Cummings v. Missouri.*

Ex parte McCardle, 7 Wallace 506 (1869), a case dealing with the right of Congress to limit the appellate jurisdiction of the Supreme Court. In 1867, following the Supreme Court's decision in *Ex parte Milligan* (1866), Congress enacted a law by which persons unconstitutionally imprisoned might apply for a writ of *habeas corpus* in federal court and might appeal their conviction to the Supreme Court. The petitioner, William McCardle, a Mississippi newspaper editor convicted of seditious activity by military authorities, appealed in federal court for such a writ. The circuit court ruled against McCardle, but the Supreme Court agreed to hear the case on appeal. Fearing that the Supreme Court would rule against the military administration of the South and declare the federal Reconstruction Acts unconstitutional, Congress subsequently revoked many of the provisions of the 1867 law, denying the right of appeal to the Supreme Court for writs of *habeas corpus* and denying the Supreme Court jurisdiction over these cases.

The question then raised was no longer concerned with the merits of McCardle's petition but with whether Congress had the right to limit the Supreme Court's appellate jurisdiction. The Court ruled unanimously that Congress had acted within its constitutional right and that the Supreme Court therefore had no jurisdiction in this case. Chief Justice Chase, speaking for the Court, held that although the Constitution itself had granted the Supreme Court the right to hear appeals from lower courts, it was a right, according to Article III, Section 2, "with such exceptions and under such regulations as Congress shall make." According to the Chief Justice, it was not the role of the Supreme Court to examine the possible political motives of Congress in establishing such restrictions; it was the duty of the Supreme Court only to act within the limits of the jurisdiction established thereby.

Ex parte Merryman, 17 Federal Cases 9487 (1861), a circuit court ruling dealing with the right of the president to declare martial law and its effect on the civilian court system. John Merryman, a citizen of Baltimore, had been imprisoned by federal military authorities soon after the outbreak of the Civil War for anti-Union activities. Chief Justice Taney, serving on the federal circuit court, issued a writ of *habeas corpus* to the military commander of Baltimore, ordering him to bring Merryman to trial or to release him. The commander refused to comply with Chief Justice Taney's writ, contending that the declaration of martial law in Baltimore was explicitly authorized by President Lincoln and included the suspension of the privilege of the writ of *habeas corpus*.

Taney responded to his refusal by addressing a letter to the President in which he pointed out that such a suspension of constitutional privileges may be declared only by Congress and that Lincoln's action in this case was therefore unconstitutional. Lincoln and his military commander continued their refusal to comply with this ruling and the point of law was not decided by the Supreme Court until after the end of the Civil War in *Ex parte Milligan* (1866), in which the original position of Chief Justice Taney was sustained.

Ex parte Milligan, 4 Wallace 2 (1866), a case dealing with the constitutionality of martial law and military tribunals in areas where civil courts are functioning. In 1861, the Supreme Court had refused to hear the case of *Ex parte Merryman*, in which Chief Justice Taney ruled in federal circuit court that the president has no right to impose martial law and suspend the right of *habeas corpus* without the approval of Congress. After the war, however, the Supreme Court finally addressed the issue of martial law. In this case, a civilian citizen of Indiana, Lambdin P. Milligan, had been arrested by military authorities for anti-Union activities and, tried by a military tribunal, was sentenced to hang. Milligan subsequently appealed for a writ of *habeas corpus* from the federal circuit court, contending that since he was a civilian and since the federal courts in Indiana were open, the military tribunal had no jurisdiction in his case. Associate Justice Davis urged President Johnson to stay the execution of Milligan's death sentence so that the constitutional issues could be appealed to the Supreme Court.

The Court ruled unanimously in favor of Milligan's plea that in this particular instance the military tribunal lacked proper jurisidiction. On the basic constitutional issue, the Court ruled by a vote of five to four, with Chief Justice Chase and Associate Justices Miller, Swayne, and Wayne dissenting, that under no circumstances does either the president or Congress have the legal right to impose military justice on civilians outside an actual war zone. Associate Justice Davis, speaking for the majority, held that such an action violates the basic constitutional rights of every American citizen. This decision, however, was not applied to the military governments imposed in the South during Reconstruction.

Ex parte Vallandigham, 1 Wallace 243 (1866), a case dealing with the authority of the Supreme Court to review the proceedings of a military commission ordered by a U.S. Army general officer commanding a military department. The respondent was arrested and tried by a military commission on the charge of having expressed sympathy for the persons rebelling against the U.S. government and for speaking against the government in a public forum. He was sentenced by the military commission to imprisonment in a military prison. The respondent subsequently petitioned the Supreme Court to review the military court's jurisdiction, since he was a civilian, and to vacate his sentence. The Supreme Court ruled by a vote of eight to zero, with Associate Justice Miller not participating, that it had no original jurisdiction to review the proceedings of a military commission. Associate Justice Swayne, writing for the Court, held that although the Court had the power to issue a writ of *certiorari* (to review the case), it lacked jurisdiction in this case due to the military law at hand.

Ex parte Yarbrough, 110 U.S. 651 (1884), a case dealing with the jurisdiction of Congress in its enforcement of the 15th Amendment. Georgia Ku Klux Klan member Jasper Yarbrough had been convicted of violating the 1870 federal Enforcement Act for his harassment of a black citizen who had attempted to vote. The legal question at issue was whether the Congress could legitimately enact such a law under the power granted by the 15th Amendment, which itself dealt only with the right of all citizens to vote, not with the acts of other individuals towards them.

On March 3, 1884, the Court decided unanimously that the Enforcement Act of 1870 and the conviction of Yarbrough should stand. Associate Justice Miller, speaking for the Court, held that the right of the federal government to prohibit racial discrimination in all activities connected with voting was essential to the implementation of the 15th Amendment guarantees. This decision was later used as one of the precedents in *United States v. Mosley* (1915), which upheld the right of the federal government to intervene in elections in which there is suspicion of fraud or corruption.

Faretta v. California, 422 U.S. 806 (1975), a case dealing with the right of a citizen to defend himself in a criminal proceeding. The petitioner, Faretta, was charged with grand theft. He rejected the trial judge's appointment

The Court upheld the 15th Amendment, guaranteeing the right of blacks to vote, in **Ex** parte Yarbrough, *but the activities of white supremacist organizations like the Ku Klux Klan helped to deny these rights for several decades.*

of a public defender. The trial judge at first accepted this waiver of counsel but later appointed another trial judge who would not allow Faretta to represent himself.

Faretta subsequently filed suit to challenge this ruling, and the Supreme Court ruled by a vote of six to three, with Chief Justice Burger and Associate Justices Blackmun and Rehnquist dissenting, that Faretta had a constitutional right to conduct his own defense in this criminal case. Associate Justice Stewart, writing for the majority, held that the Constitution requires an intelligent, voluntary, and knowing waiver of the right to counsel and does not force a lawyer upon a defendant. Here, noted Stewart, Faretta clearly and unequivocably declared to the trial judge that he wanted to represent himself and did not want counsel. The record affirmatively showed that Faretta was literate, competent, and understanding. He was merely voluntarily exercising his informed free will. Therefore, by forcing Faretta to accept counsel under the circumstances, the trial court violated his constitutional right of self-representation.

Federal Communications Commission v. League of Women Voters, 104 S. Ct. 3106 (1984), a case dealing with the rights of public broadcasting stations that accept federal funds to engage in editorials on the air. The suit was brought in 1979 by the League of Women Voters, the Pacifica Foundation (an owner of noncommercial radio stations), and Rep. Henry Waxman to overturn a federal law prohibiting editorialization by any noncommercial station, even if it

did not receive federal funds. The Carter administration declined to defend the law, and the case was dismissed. In 1981 the law was amended to apply only to stations receiving funds from the Corporation for Public Broadcasting, established by Congress to support educational broadcasting. The original suit was revived under the Reagan administration. A federal district court ruled the law unconstitutional in 1982, and the federal government appealed to the Supreme Court.

By a vote of five to four, the Court upheld the lower court ruling, agreeing that the law violated the 1st Amendment. Justice Brennan wrote the majority opinion, in which he noted that earlier Court decisions "left room for editorial discretion," while the federal law "prohibits the broadcaster from speaking out on public issues even in a balanced and fair manner." Dissenting Justices Stevens, Rehnquist, Burger, and White based their opinions on several points made in the government's arguments, including a concern that editorial policy should not be tied in any way to federal funding.

Federal Trade Commission v. Borden Company, 383 U.S. 637 (1966), a case dealing with the power of the federal government to regulate certain business practices. The respondent produced and sold evaporated milk under its own Borden name and marketed identical milk under various private brands owned by its customers, at different prices. The Federal Trade Commission (FTC) filed suit, contending that the price differential was discriminatory and had adverse effects on competition. The FTC rejected the respondent's claim of cost justification.

The Supreme Court ruled by a vote of seven to two, with Associate Justices Stewart and Harlan dissenting, that labels do not differentiate products for the purpose of determining grade or quality under the Robinson-Patman Act, which regulated price controls, even though one label may have more customer appeal and command a higher price in the marketplace. Associate Justice White, writing for the majority, held that the FTC's rules and policies had legislative input and support and should be supported by the courts. Therefore, White noted, the Supreme Court upheld the Federal Trade Commission's policy of price-justification under these circumstances.

Federal Trade Commission v. Brown Shoe Company, 384 U.S. 316 (1966), a case dealing with the power of the federal government to regulate certain business practices. The Federal Trade Commission (FTC) found that Brown Shoe Company was in violation of Article 5 of the federal Trade Commission Act. The Brown Shoe Company used a "Franchise Stores Program," whereby retail shoe stores could buy shoes from them if the stores agreed not to buy from competitive shoe companies. The FTC concluded that the restrictive contract program was an unfair method of competition and filed suit to prohibit it.

The Supreme Court held unanimously that the FTC had the power to find such anticompetitive practices unfair. Associate Justice Black, writing for the Court, held that Brown's franchise program conflicted with the policy against contracts that removed the freedom of purchasers to buy in an open market. Therefore, Black stated, the Court supported and enforced the Federal Trade Commission's finding of unfair competitive practices and the FTC's order to the respondent to cease and desist from the use of the franchise program.

Federal Trade Commission v. Sperry and Hutchinson Company, 405 U.S. 233 (1972), a case dealing with the right of the federal government to regulate certain business practices. The Federal Trade Commission (FTC) entered a stop order against Sperry and Hutchinson on the grounds that it unfairly attempted to supress the operation of trading stamp exchanges and other redemptions of stamps.

The Supreme Court ruled by a vote of seven to zero, with Associate Justices Powell and Rehnquist not participating, that the powers of the FTC to protect consumers as well as competitors reached the area of trading stamps. Associate Justice Stewart, writing for the Court, held that the FTC was authorized to determine whether challenged practices were either unfair methods of competition or unfair or deceptive acts or practices. The Court, however, set aside the FTC's stop order, finding that Sperry and Hutchinson's conduct did not violate either the letter or the spirit of the antitrust laws. Since the FTC did not attempt to base its order on the unfairness of particular competitive practices, the Court asked

the FTC to reexamine its ruling for more substantive evidence.

Firefighters v. Stotts, 104 S. Ct. 2576 (1984), a case dealing with the propriety of a district court injunction requiring white employees to be laid off despite a city seniority system that would have mandated black employee layoffs instead. To preserve the gains blacks had made as a result of a discrimination suit filed against the Memphis, Tennessee, fire department, two lower federal courts ordered a modification of the seniority system. The firefighters' union and the city appealed this ruling to the Supreme Court.

On June 12, 1984, in a six to three decision written by Associate Justice White, the Court reversed the lower courts' rulings on the grounds that they had exceeded their authority, citing Title VII of the Civil Rights Act of 1964, which specifically protects in-place, legitimate seniority systems. In relying on the Civil Rights Act's built-in protections the Court avoided a broader stand against affirmative action employment goals and quotas, although some civil rights and women's organizations viewed the decision as a blow to the principles of affirmative action. The civil rights advocates in the case had argued for its dismissal on the grounds of being moot, because the laid-off firefighters had been recalled to work after a short time and no plans existed for future layoffs. A similar case originating in Boston had been dismissed. However, the Court noted that the Massachusetts litigants were protected by state law from being laid off again, while no such law existed in Tennessee. Dissenting Justices Blackmun, Brennan, and Marshall thought the case was moot and should be dismissed.

Flagg Brothers, Inc. v. Brooks, 436 U.S. 149 (1978), a case dealing with the extent of state action and its relation to the actions of private agents who carry it out. The respondent, Brooks, was evicted and her possessions stored by Flagg Brothers, Inc. Flagg Brothers threatened to sell Brooks's possessions when she failed to pay storage charges, and Brooks filed a complaint requesting the return of her possessions and claiming that the New York Commercial Code by which she was evicted was unconstitutional. Brooks also claimed Flagg Brothers' action was a state action because the state had authorized it by enacting the Uniform Commercial Code.

The Supreme Court ruled by a vote of five to three, with Associate Justices Marshall, Stevens, and White dissenting and Associate Justice Brennan not participating, that a warehouseman's sale of goods entrusted to him for storage did not constitute a state action because it was permitted by state law. Associate Justice Rehnquist, writing for the majority, held that since the settlement of disputes between debtors and creditors was not traditionally an exclusively public function, Flagg Brothers' actions could not be termed a state action by implying that the state delegated a power traditionally exclusively reserved to the states. While private action compelled by a state was properly attributable to the state, noted Rehnquist, mere approval by a state was insufficient. Therefore, Flagg Brothers' action was not a state action that could be judged by constitutional standards.

Fletcher v. Peck, 6 Cranch 87 (1810), a case dealing with the impairment of contracts by states. Land speculators had bribed key members of the Georgia legislature into granting large tracts of land along the Yazoo River for resale. When the corruption was revealed and the corrupt legislators were voted out of office, the new legislature revoked the land grants. The petitioner, who had purchased a tract of land from one of the original speculators with the understanding that his claim to the land was valid, but who now had his claim revoked, appealed to the Supreme Court after the Georgia courts had upheld the legislature's right to revoke the land grant.

The Supreme Court ruled unanimously that Article I, Section 10 of the Constitution prohibits the states from passing any law impairing the obligation of contracts; therefore, the original land grant issued by the Georgia legislature must stand. Chief Justice Marshall, speaking for the Court, held that, despite the fraudulent circumstances, the land grant was a valid contract between the state and the speculators that could not be amended by subsequent legislative action. This decision was the first in a series of rulings by the Marshall Court that established the right of federal intervention in state affairs through the use of the contract clause.

Fletcher v. Rhode Island, (1847), *See* License Cases.

Flood v. Kuhn, 407 U.S. 258 (1972), a case dealing with the applicability of antitrust laws to professional sports organizations. The petitioner, Curt Flood, was a professional baseball player who had been traded to another team without his prior knowledge or consent. His request to be permitted to negotiate his own contract had been denied by the baseball commissioner, and Flood consequently filed suit, challenging the constitutionality of professional baseball's "reserve clause."

The Supreme Court held by a vote of five to three, with Associate Justices Douglas, Marshall, and Brennan dissenting and with Justice Powell taking no part in the decision, that the long-standing exemption of professional baseball from antitrust laws is an established aberration and therefore the constitutionality of the reserve clause should be upheld. Associate Justice Blackmun, writing for the majority, ruled that although other professional sports are not similarly exempt, Congress had adhered to baseball. Blackmun further stated that any removal of this resulted inconsistency in sports is a matter of legislative, not judicial, resolve.

Friedman v. Schwellenbach, 330 U.S. 836 (1947), (cert. denied), a case dealing with the right of the Civil Service Commission to dismiss federal employees for alleged subversive associations. The petitioner, Friedman, was employed by the Federal Manpower Commission, but after a thorough investigation, the Civil Service Commission uncovered evidence of his membership and activities in an alleged Communist-dominated organization, and he was subsequently dismissed. Friedman later appealed this ruling, but the Supreme Court refused to review this case. The activities uncovered in the Civil Service Commission investigation created a reasonable doubt of Friedman's loyalty to the United States and therefore his dismissal did not constitute an infringement of his constitutional liberties as guaranteed by the 1st and 14th Amendments.

Frothingham v. Mellon, (1923), *See* Massachusetts v. Mellon.

Fuentes v. Shevin, 407 U.S. 67 (1972), a case dealing with the constitutionality of certain state repossession laws. Under Florida law, Fuentes's appliances were seized by the sheriff when she defaulted on the payments. The state statute authorized the seizure of goods upon default, with no notice and no opportunity to challenge the issuance of the writ of replevin. Fuentes challenged this law.

The Supreme Court ruled by a vote of four to three, with Chief Justice Burger and Associate Justices Blackmun and White dissenting and Associate Justices Powell and Rehnquist not participating, that the statute was unconstitutional since it allowed a creditor to replevy goods from a defaulting debtor without a hearing. Associate Justice Stewart, writing for the majority, held that due process required an opportunity for a hearing before a deprivation of property could take place. This right to notice and the opportunity to be heard had to be granted at a meaningful time and in a meaningful manner, Stewart noted. In order to postpone the notice requirement, the seizure had to be directly necessary to secure an important governmental or public interest, a special need had to exist for prompt action, and the state had to keep strict control over its monopoly of legitimate force. Since this statute failed to qualify under these standards, Stewart stated, it was unconstitutional.

Fullilove v. Klutznick, 448 U.S. 448 (1980), a case dealing with the constitutional right of Congress to apportion a certain percentage of federal public works funds to minority businesses. In 1977, Congress passed the Public Works Employment Act, one provision of which required that states spend at least 10 percent of the federally supplied funds with minority businesses. The petitioner, Fullilove, a non-minority businessman, filed suit against the enforcement of this act, contending that it violated his 14th Amendment equal protection rights by predicating federal and state action on racial criteria.

On July 2, 1980, the Supreme Court decided by a vote of six to three, with Associate Justices Rehnquist, Stevens, and Stewart dissenting, that the Public Works Employment Act was constitutional. Chief Justice Burger, writing for the majority, held that since it was within the power of Congress to provide funds to the states to accomplish legitimate governmental objectives, the allocation of funds to minority businesses could be seen as a reasonable means of enforcing

The Public Works Employment Act, passed during President Carter's administration in an attempt to support minority businesses, was upheld by the Court in **Fullilove v. Klutznick.**

the equal protection clause of the 14th Amendment by reversing traditional discrimination. This decision upheld the use, in certain cases, of racial criteria in government funding programs, when a past pattern of discrimination could be demonstrated.

Furman v. Georgia, Jackson v. Georgia, Branch v. Texas, 408 U.S. 238 (1972), cases dealing with the constitutionality of state death penalty statutes. The petitioners, three men convicted of murder and sentenced to death, appealed their convictions, contending that capital punishment violated their 8th Amendment protection against "cruel and unusual punishment." On June 29, 1972, the Supreme Court decided by a vote of five to four, with Chief Justice Burger and Associate Justices Blackmun, Powell, and Rehnquist dissenting, that the death penalty, as it was currently applied, was a violation of the 8th Amendment rights of the petitioners. In separate concurring opinions, the major-

ity justices held that because of the apparent arbitrariness of the imposition of the death sentence and its relatively infrequent execution, often after long delays, the use of capital punishment by state courts was unconstitutional. This decision was later effectively nullified by the ruling of the Court in the cases of *Gregg v. Georgia, Proffitt v. Florida*, and *Jurek v. Texas* (1976), in which capital punishment was ruled not to be by definition a violation of the 8th Amendment and in which judicial procedures were established for capital cases.

Garcia v. San Antonio Metropolitan Transit Authority, 53 U.S.L.W. 4101 (1985), a case dealing with the issues of federalism and states' sovereignty. In a five to four decision written by Associate Justice Blackmun, the Court ruled that the federal minimum wage regulations and hour standards apply to employees of public mass transit systems and, by extension, to other public employees as well, thereby restoring the protection of the Fair Labor Standards Act to most state workers. This decision reversed an earlier Court ruling (*National League of Cities v. Usery*, 1976), which focused on the 10th Amendment provision that reserves powers to the states that are not specifically granted to the federal government. Because of this 1976 ruling, a federal district court in Texas had ruled that San Antonio's mass transit workers were not covered by federal wage and price regulations. The federal government joined the transit workers in appealing this decision to the Supreme Court, and, after first hearing arguments in March 1984, the Court ordered new arguments in October 1984 regarding whether or not the 10th Amendment as applied in *Usery* applied in the San Antonio situation.

Rendering the Court's opinion on February 19, 1985, Associate Justice Blackmun did not deal specifically with the 10th Amendment issue but with the workability of the 1976 approach, concluding that "state sovereign interests are more properly protected by procedural safeguards inherent in the structure of the Federal system than by judicially created limitations on Federal power." Dissenting, Justice Powell asserted that this ruling "rejects almost 200 years of the understanding of the constitutional status of Federalism," an opinion shared by Associate Justices Rehnquist and O'Connor and Chief Justice Burger.

Gertz v. Robert Welch, Inc., 418 U.S. 323 (1974), a case dealing with the constitutional right of a member of the press who publishes defamatory false statements about a person who is neither a public official nor a public figure, but who is involved in a public issue, to claim a constitutional privilege against liability for injuries. The petitioner, Gertz, was an attorney for the family of a man who was murdered by a police officer. Robert Welch, publisher of *American Opinion*, printed an article concededly untrue, which discredited Gertz. Gertz sued for libel, and Welch claimed that he was protected by application of *The New York Times* rule, which held that discussion of any public issue was protected, regardless of the status of the person defamed.

The Supreme Court ruled by a vote of five to three, with Associate Justices Brennan, White, and Douglas dissenting, and Chief Justice Burger not participating, that involvement in a public issue, by itself, did not bring a private individual within the class covered by *The New York Times* rule. Associate Justice Powell, writing for the majority, held that private individuals are more deserving of recovery because their public exposure is not voluntary. Therefore, Powell stated, the rationale behind *The New York Times* rule did not extend to private individuals.

Gibbons v. Ogden, 9 Wheaton 1 (1824), a case dealing with the power of the federal government to regulate interstate commerce. Ogden, having been assigned an official monopoly by the state of New York to operate steamboats in that state's waters, sought and obtained a state court injunction against Gibbons, who was operating steamboats between New Jersey and New York. Since Gibbons was operating legally and had registered with the federal government as an interstate transport service, he appealed to the Supreme Court for removal of the New York injunction.

Speaking for the Court in a unanimous opinion, Chief Justice Marshall held that Gibbons's federal license was valid and constitutional, as a legitimate exercise of the regulation of commerce provided in Article I, Section 8 of the Constitution. The New York state law creating a commer-cial monopoly was therefore void, since it conflicted with the regulatory power of the federal government in the performance of its constitutional responsibilities, and Gibbons must be allowed to operate within the waters of New York state. This decision was of great significance for the development of a free national economy; since state laws that interfered with interstate commerce were seen as a *de facto* invasion of federal regulatory power, it would not even be necessary for a state law to be in conflict with a specific federal act to be declared void. The way was therefore cleared for the federal judiciary to intervene in all levels of commerce and to strike down state laws that were seen, even indirectly, as an obstruction of interstate trade.

Gideon v. Wainwright, 372 U.S. 335 (1963), a case involving the right to counsel in noncapital offenses. The petitioner, an indigent named Clarence Earl Gideon, was charged with a felony and, under Florida law, was not entitled to a public defender unless charged with a capital offense. Gideon conducted his own defense and was convicted, but petitioned to have his conviction declared invalid on the grounds that his constitutional right to counsel had been violated.

The Supreme Court held unanimously that the 14th Amendment's due process clause extends to state as well as federal defendants the 6th Amendment right that all persons charged with a serious crime will be guaranteed the aid of an attorney. This case overruled *Betts v. Brady* (1942) by

Justice Edward Sanford wrote the Court's opinion in **Gitlow v. New York,** *a decision that extended curbs on free speech and press beyond the "clear and present danger" test.*

requiring all states to appoint counsel for defendants who cannot afford to pay their own and demonstrated that the Court would require constitutional standards in state courts. The Court concluded, with Associate Justice Black writing the opinion, that the right to counsel is a fundamental human right, and therefore, unless a person competently and intelligently waives this right, he is entitled to have counsel appointed if he so desires but cannot afford an attorney. At a subsequent trial, with a lawyer defending him, Gideon was acquitted.

Gitlow v. New York, 268 U.S. 652 (1925), a case dealing with the right of states to limit the freedom of speech and the press. In 1902, the New York legislature enacted a law imposing criminal penalties on anyone who advocated, in word or deed, a violent overthrow of the existing government. The petitioner, Benjamin Gitlow, editor of the radical *Left Wing Manifesto*, was convicted of "criminal anarchy" by the terms of the state law. Gitlow subsequently appealed the conviction, contending that since the state could not prove that any actual harm came from his statements, the law was an unconstitutional violation of his 1st Amendment right to free speech.

On June 8, 1925, the Supreme Court decided by a vote of five to two, with Associate Justices Holmes and Brandeis dissenting, that Gitlow's conviction should stand. Associate Justice Sanford, speaking for the majority, held that the state law was not unconstitutional, since the protection of the 1st Amendment "does not deprive a state of the primary and essential right of self-preservation." This decision marked the Court's abandonment of the "clear and present danger" doctrine adopted in *Schenck v. U.S.* (1919).

Goldberg v. Kelly, 397 U.S. 254 (1970), a case dealing with the constitutional rights of welfare recipients. A qualified recipient of funds from the Aid to Families with Dependent Children program received notification of the termination of her benefits without a prior hearing, and she appealed the ruling, contending that her due process rights had been violated. The Supreme Court ruled by a vote of five to three, with Chief Justice Burger and Associate Justices Stewart and Black dissenting, that given the dependence of the recipient on the benefits for subsistence, the importance to the state that persons receive such benefits, and the absence of any emergency justifying summary procedures, due process requires that timely notice be given indicating the basis for termination. Associate Justice Brennan, writing for the majority, ruled that a hearing before an impartial examiner in which the recipient may appear personally with or without counsel to present evidence and to confront and cross-examine any adverse witnesses must be held. However, Brennan added, the state does not have to provide counsel if a person so desires but cannot afford one.

Gold Clause Cases (1935): **Norman v. Baltimore and Ohio Railroad Co.**, 294 U.S. 240; **Nortz v. United States**, 294 U.S. 317; **Perry v. United States**, 294 U.S.

330, a series of related cases dealing with the right of the federal government to regulate the value of currency and with the effect of that regulation on the obligation of contracts. In 1933, in an attempt to abolish the gold standard, Congress passed a resolution abrogating the provisions of any contract that required payment in gold. The petitioners, holders of government gold certificates and creditors who had demanded payment in gold, immediately filed suit to have the federal action overturned.

On February 18, 1935, the Supreme Court decided by a vote of five to four, with Associate Justices Butler, McReynolds, Sutherland, and Van Devanter dissenting, that the federal government had acted within its constitutional rights. Chief Justice Hughes, speaking for the slim majority in all three cases, held that, with regard to private and state contracts, the action was a justified exercise of monetary regulation. In the case of federal gold certificates, Hughes argued, the issue was slightly more complex; while the federal government had a moral obligation to fulfill its commitments, the Chief Justice ruled that he could not enforce those obligations since it was impossible to calculate the financial loss caused by the regulation in individual cases.

Goss v. Lopez, 419 U.S. 565 (1975), a case dealing with the right of school principals to suspend students for misconduct. The Supreme Court ruled by a vote of five to four, with Chief Justice Burger and Associate Justices Powell, Blackmun, and Rehnquist dissenting, that since a state confers a system of free public education to its children, a property right in that education exists. Associate Justice White, writing for the majority, held that since the suspension could impose a stigma on a child, his liberty interest is infringed. Balancing these interests against the state's interests in maintaining order and discipline within the school, White ruled that due process required that the student be furnished at least notice of the charges, an explanation of the evidence against him, and an opportunity to reply. A suspension without these qualifications is therefore unconstitutional.

Granger Cases, (1877), *See* Munn v. Illinois.

Gravel v. United States, 408 U.S. 606 (1972), a case dealing with the constitutional immunity of members of Congress regarding statements made in sessions of Congress as covered in the speech and debate clause, and whether congressional aides are accorded this same immunity. In this case Sen. Mike Gravel of Alaska had released for publication parts of the Pentagon Papers through records of a subcommittee he chaired. Gravel's aide, who had read excerpts of the papers into the subcommittee record, had helped to edit the record, and had arranged for publication, was subpoenaed to appear before a federal jury. He refused on the ground that he, as an aide to a member of Congress, was protected by the speech and debate clause.

On June 19, 1972, the Supreme Court held in a five to

four vote, with Justices Potter, Douglas, Brennan, and Marshall dissenting, that immunity did extend to congressional aides in matters of legislation. Justice White, writing for the Court, noted "The day-to-day work of such aides is so critical to the Member's performance that they must be treated as alter egos." However, the Court ruled, nonlegislative matters could be subject to grand jury testimony.

Graves v. New York ex rel. O'Keefe, 306 U.S. 466 (1939), a case dealing with the immunity of certain federal officials from state income tax. O'Keefe was a New York resident and employed by the Home Owner's Loan Corporation, which was owned and financed by the federal government. The petitioner, Graves, the New York state tax commissioner, attempted to impose a state income tax on O'Keefe.

On March 27, 1939, the Supreme Court held by a vote of eight to one, with only Associate Justice Butler dissenting, that a state can tax the income of a federal employee. Associate Justice Stone, writing for the majority, held that this corporation was a valid extension of the federal government and thus is immune from state taxes. However, if the Constitution and Congress were both silent as to federal immunity from state taxation, any immunity must be implied. Noting that the Court must consider the effect and nature of the burden on the purpose of the federal government, Stone ruled that the state income tax imposed on O'Keefe did not unconstitutionally burden the federal government. If there was any effect, it was indirect or incidental; therefore, the state tax is permissible, Stone noted.

Green v. Biddle, 8 Wheaton 1, 69 (1823), a case dealing with the authority of states to amend the conditions of land grants. Because of a large number of conflicting claims to land, the Kentucky legislature enacted a law that required that every new legal title owner to a piece of property must compensate the current occupants of that property for any improvements, before occupying the land. If compensation were not paid, the unofficial occupants were entitled to purchase the property themselves by paying the value of the property without improvements to the legal owner. The petitioners, in this case, who had purchased property in Kentucky, contended that the state law violated an agreement between Kentucky and Virginia reached in 1791, which provided that all property rights in the new state of Kentucky would be maintained on the same basis as they had been observed when that state was part of Virginia. The Supreme Court, with Associate Justice Washington writing the majority opinion, held that the Kentucky law was unconstitutional, as a violation of Article I, Section 10, of the Constitution, which prohibited the states from enacting any laws that interferred with the obligation of contracts.

Gregg v. Georgia, 428 U.S. 153 (1976), a case dealing with the constitutionality of certain state capital punishment statutes. The petitioner, Gregg, had been convicted of armed robbery and murder. He was sentenced to death during the sentencing phase of his trial under a Georgia statute that prescribed the death penalty for murder and five other crimes. Gregg subsequently appealed this sentence and challenged the Georgia law, contending that it violated his 8th Amendment protection against cruel and unusual punishment.

On July 2, 1976, the Supreme Court ruled by a vote of seven to two, with Associate Justices Brennan and Marshall dissenting, that the Georgia statute was constitutional and that Gregg's sentence should be upheld. Associate Justice Stewart, writing for the Court, held that since the jury was required to examine the relevent mitigating and aggravating circumstances in each case and that since the state supreme court automatically reviewed death sentences, there were sufficient judicial safeguards to ensure that the imposition of the death penalty would be neither arbitrary nor discriminatory, nor violate the 8th Amendment's prohibition against cruel and unusual punishment.

Griswold v. Connecticut, 381 U.S. 479 (1965), a case dealing with the constitutional right of states to prohibit the distribution and use of contraceptive devices. The Connecticut legislature had enacted a law imposing criminal penalties on any person who used a birth control device or advised another person to do so. Griswold, the executive director of the Planned Parenthood League of Connecticut, and Buxton, a professor at the Yale Medical School, were convicted by that statute of counseling married couples in birth control methods. They subsequently appealed their convictions, contending that the law violated the 14th Amendment rights of their patients. At issue in this case was the constitutional right to privacy within a marital relationship.

On June 7, 1965, the Supreme Court decided by a vote of seven to two, with Associate Justices Black and Stewart dissenting, that the Connecticut law was unconstitutional. Associate Justice Douglas, speaking for the majority, held that the state had exceeded the limits of its legitimate police power by not attempting to regulate the manufacture or sale of contraceptives, but rather by means that had "a maximum destructive impact" upon marital relationships. "Would we allow the police," Douglas asked, "to search the sacred precincts of marital bedrooms for telltale signs of the use of contraceptives?" While the majority disagreed on the constitutional basis for the right to privacy within marriage, all agreed that it was a fundamental right.

Grove City v. Bell, 104 S. Ct. 1211 (1984), a case dealing with sex discrimination laws in schools. Grove City College in Pennsylvania received no direct federal funding, but some of its students received federal tuition grants. When Grove City College refused to sign a statement regarding its compliance with the sex discrimination law, the government began proceedings to refuse the school and its students federal scholarship funding. The college and four students filed suit but an appeals court ruled that the law, Title IX of the Education Amendments of 1972, applied to the entire institution, no matter how indirectly federal funds were received.

In a six to three ruling, written by Justice White, the Court held that the sex discrimination law applied only to the departments or programs that received direct federal money. All the justices were in agreement that indirect aid, such as federal scholarships to college students, was sufficient to trigger Title IX's provision. However, Justices Brennan, Marshall, and Stevens dissented from the majority position that Title IX is "program-specific," Brennan and Marshall calling it "contrary to Congressional intent." Civil rights advocates expressed concern that this narrow interpretation of Title IX might eventually be extended to the similarly worded Title VI of the 1964 Civil Rights Act, which prohibits racial discrimination in programs that receive federal financial assistance.

Grovey v. Townsend, (1935), *See* Smith v. Allwright.

H.L. v. Matheson, 450 U.S. 398 (1981), a case dealing with the right to privacy of minors. The petitioner, an unmarried female minor living with and dependent on her parents, attempted to have an abortion. Due to a Utah statute, her parents would first have to be notified before the abortion could take place, but she filed suit to have the state law overturned, contending that it violated her right to privacy. The Supreme Court ruled by a vote of six to three, with Associate Justices Marshall, Brennan, and Blackmun dissenting, that the state statute requiring physicians treating minor girls seeking abortions to notify if possible the parents does not violate the minor's right to privacy. However, this holding was specifically limited to unemancipated minors who have failed to demonstrate maturity or who have negative relationships with their parents. Chief Justice Burger, writing for the majority, held that the statute simply requires, when possible, parental notification prior to a minor's abortion; it does not give the parents a veto power.

Hague v. Congress of Industrial Organizations, 307 U.S. 496 (1939), a case dealing with the right of municipal governments to restrict public assemblies. The city council of Jersey City, New Jersey, passed an ordinance that required public meetings and the distribution of literature by labor groups in public parks to be licensed by the police. The Congress of Industrial Organizations refused to comply with this ordinance, and its suit against the constitutionality of the ordinance was sustained in a lower court.

Mayor Frank Hague of Jersey City appealed that decision and on June 5, 1939, the Supreme Court held by a vote of five to two, with Associate Justices Butler and McReynolds dissenting and Associate Justices Frankfurter and Douglas not participating, that the municipal ordinance was unconstitutional. Chief Justice Hughes, writing one of the three concurring opinions, held that the right of public assembly was one of the inviolable rights of American citizenship. Associate Justice Roberts, in a separate opinion, stated that the ordinance was also a clear violation of the privileges and

Secretary of State Haig was named in **Haig v. Agee**. *The Court's decision upheld Haig's action in revoking the passport of Agee, a former CIA agent, in the interests of national security.*

immunities clause of the 14th Amendment, noting that the right to assemble to discuss public issues "must not, in the guise of regulation, be abridged or denied."

Haig v. Agee, 453 U.S. 280 (1981), a case dealing with the constitutional right of the secretary of State to revoke a citizen's passport on the grounds of national security. Phillip Agee, a former officer of the Central Intelligence Agency (CIA), who objected to the methods and objectives of the agency, began to divulge publicly the names of CIA operatives and various items of classified information. In order to prevent or discourage further disclosures, the Secretary of State, Alexander Haig, ordered that Agee's passport be revoked. Agee subsequently filed suit in federal court, contending that the action violated his 1st Amendment right of free speech. The district court and the court of appeals ordered that Agee's passport be restored and the Secretary of State appealed the decision.

On June 29, 1981, the Supreme Court decided by a vote of seven to two, with Associate Justices Brennan and Marshall dissenting, that Secretary of State Haig had acted within his constitutional power in revoking Agee's passport. Chief Justice Burger, speaking for the majority, held that the provisions of the Passport Act of 1926 established the right of the government to regulate the issuance of documents on the criterion of national security and that there was sufficient reason to believe that Agee's actions abroad might harm the interests of the country.

Hammer v. Dagenhart, 247 U.S. 251 (1918), a case dealing with the power of the federal government to regulate certain working conditions through its regulation of interstate trade. In 1916, Congress had passed the Keating-Owen Child Labor Law, which provided that no goods produced in factories employing children under the age of fourteen for more than eight hours per day or more than six days per week should be allowed in interstate commerce. The petitioner, the father of a child employed in a North Carolina cotton mill, filed suit against the management for violation of the Child Labor Law. The U.S. district court in which the suit was filed found the act unconstitutional because the issue was not directly concerned with interstate trade and was therefore beyond federal jurisdiction.

The ruling was subsequently appealed and on June 3, 1918, the Supreme Court decided by a vote of five to four, with Associate Justices Brandeis, Clarke, Holmes, and McKenna dissenting, that the Child Labor Law should be struck down. Associate Justice Day, speaking for the majority, held that in accordance with the decision of the Court in *United States v. E.C. Knight Co.* (1895), manufacturing was a strictly local matter and separate from interstate commerce. It was not within the jurisdiction of the federal government to regulate work conditions. This decision was later superseded by the decision of the Court in *United States v. Darby Lumber Co.*, (1941), which ruled that the federal government could impose certain labor standards on goods produced for interstate trade.

Harlow v. Fitzgerald, 457 U.S. 800 (1982), a case dealing with the liability of certain federal officials to criminal prosecution for acts committed while in office. Fitzgerald, dismissed from his job with the Department of the Air Force, filed suit against two White House aides, Harlow and Butterfield, charging them with conspiracy to violate his constitutional rights. The aides, for their part, attempted to assert that they were entitled to absolute immunity from suit.

The Supreme Court held by a vote of eight to one, with only Chief Justice Burger dissenting, that executive officials in general are normally entitled to only qualified or good-faith immunity. Associate Justice Powell, writing for the majority, held that in order for a federal official to claim absolute immunity, he must show that public policy requires it and that it extends no further than its justification warrants. Therefore, in order for a presidential aide to establish absolute immunity, he must first show that "the responsibilities of his office embraced a function so sensitive as to require a total shield from liability."

Harris v. McRae, 448 U.S. 297 (1980), a case dealing with the constitutional right of Congress to limit federal funding of abortions. In this case Congress, in its annual appropriation for Medicaid funding, included the Hyde Amendment, which severely restricted the funds available for medically approved abortions. The petitioner, McRae, a Medicaid recipient, filed suit in federal court against the Secretary of Heath, Education, and Welfare to prevent the enforcement of this funding restriction, contending that it violated her 5th Amendment equal protection and due process rights. The district court ruled in favor of McRae and the case was appealed to the Supreme Court.

On June 30, 1980, the Supreme Court decided by a vote of five to four, with Associate Justices Blackmun, Brennan, Marshall, and Stevens dissenting, that the Hyde Amendment was constitutional and that the ruling of the lower court should be reversed. Associate Justice Stewart, speaking for the majority, held that since Congress had not outlawed abortion itself, financial need alone was not sufficient to invoke constitutional protection. This decision essentially extended the earlier ruling of the Court in *Maher v. Roe* (1977), in which it held that the equal protection clause of the 14th Amendment could not be invoked to require states to fund voluntary abortions.

Hawaii Housing Authority v. Midkiff, 104 S. Ct. 2321 (1984), a case dealing with states' power of eminent domain to break up large properties and transfer ownership of the land to the tenants. A land reform program, Hawaii's Land Reform Act of 1967, was challenged by Hawaii's largest private landowner, the Bishop Estate. In 1983 a federal appeals court held that the state law was unconstitutional, but on May 30, 1984, the Supreme Court unanimously reversed this ruling. In the Court's opinion, written by Associate Justice O'Connor, a long series of Supreme Court precedents maintained the power of government to take private property for private use, in exchange for "just compensation." For the state to transfer ownership to private individuals does not in this case violate the right of eminent domain. She termed the Land Reform Act "a comprehensive and rational approach" to correct the "social and economic evil" of Hawaii's "feudal land tenure system," that satisfies the "public purposes" of the eminent domain principle.

Hawkins v. United States, (1958), *See* Trammel v. United States.

Heart of Atlanta Motel, Inc. v. United States, 379 U.S. 241 (1964), a case dealing with the right of the federal government to prohibit racial discrimination in certain privately-owned facilities. In 1964, Congress passed the Civil Rights Act, one provision of which prohibited racial discrimination or segregation in public accommodations. The petitioner, owner of an Atlanta motel that regularly refused to provide accommodation to blacks, filed suit in federal court to challenge the constitutionality of the relevant provision of the Civil Rights Act, contending that it was beyond the power of Congress to regulate such matters.

On December 14, 1964, the Supreme Court decided unanimously that the suit of Heart of Atlanta Motel should

President Johnson was a strong supporter of the Civil Rights Act of 1964, which was upheld in the **Heart of Atlanta Motel** *decision that helped to broaden minority rights.*

not be sustained. Associate Justice Clark, speaking for the Court, held that the commerce clause of the Constitution empowered Congress to regulate both commercial and non-commercial travel, and since the motel served interstate travelers, its refusal to accommodate blacks posed a potential obstruction to their freedom of movement across state lines. This decision overturned the previous ruling of the Court in the *Civil Rights Cases* (1883) and was extremely important in extending the rights of blacks and other minorities.

Helvering v. Davis, 301 U.S. 619 (1937), a case dealing with the constitutional right of the federal government to use its taxing power to achieve specific economic aims. In 1935, Congress passed the Social Security Act, which provided that the proceeds from a special tax on workers and their employers would be used to establish a mandatory federal retirement fund. Since a similar economic redistribution program, the Agricultural Adjustment Act of 1933, had been declared an unconstitutional use of federal taxation

power, a suit was filed in federal court to overturn the Social Security Act as well.

On May 24, 1937, the Supreme Court decided by a vote of seven to two, with Associate Justices Butler and McReynolds dissenting, that the suit should not be sustained. Associate Justice Cardozo, speaking for the majority, held that the object of the law, an old-age pension program, was clearly for the general welfare and therefore a legitimate use of federal power. This decision effectively reversed the Court's earlier ruling in *United States v. Butler* (1936), and it was issued on the same day as another decision upholding the constitutionality of the Social Security Act, *Steward Machine Co. v. Davis*.

Hepburn v. Griswold, 8 Wallace 603 (1870), a case dealing with the constitutional right of Congress to issue unbacked paper currency for the payment of public debts. In an effort to raise funds during the Civil War, Congress had authorized the issuance of $450,000,000 in paper money, which it declared to be legal tender for the repayment of government debts. At the time of the passage of the Legal Tender Acts, Salmon Chase, later appointed chief justice, was secretary of the Treasury and was responsible for the implementation of this federal action. After the war, there were numerous challenges to the legality of the paper money.

In this case, the issue to which the Court addressed itself was whether the legal tender could be used to repay

Justice Nathan Clifford dissented in **Hepburn v. Griswold**, *concerning the legality of paper currency, and his position was vindicated by the Court's decision a year later in* **Knox v. Lee**.

Chief Justice Stone (center) *upheld the conviction of a Japanese-American in* **Hirabayashi v. United States** *because of the extraordinary circumstances of World War II.*

government loans contracted *before* the passage of the law. The Supreme Court ruled by a vote of four to three, with Associate Justices Davis, Miller, and Swayne dissenting, that the Legal Tender Act of 1862 was unconstitutional. Chief Justice Chase, speaking for the majority, held that the act's provision for repayment of *all* government debts, even those contracted before the passage of the act, was a clear violation of the obligation of contracts. Furthermore, the same section of the Constitution made it clear that only gold or silver coin could be used for the payment of public debt.

This decision suddenly cast the legality of all paper currency into question and caused a considerable disruption throughout the new national economy based on the currency. The issue was soon reheard by the Supreme Court in *Knox v. Lee* (1871), and the previous decision was overruled.

Herndon v. Lowry, 301 U.S. 242 (1937), a case dealing with the constitutionality of certain state sedition laws. The petitioner, Herndon, was convicted of violating a Georgia law that made it unlawful for anyone to attempt to persuade another to participate in an insurrection against the organized government. He appealed the conviction, contending that it violated his 1st Amendment right to free speech.

The Supreme Court held by a vote of five to four, with Associate Justices Van Devanter, McReynolds, Sutherland, and Butler dissenting, that the state statute was too vague and too broad and should therefore be overturned. Associate Justice Roberts, writing for the majority, held that the state

needed to show more than that Herndon's words and actions might tend to incite others to insurrection at some future time. Noting that "the power of a state to abridge freedom of speech and of assembly is the exception rather than the rule," Roberts argued that in order for a statute to be constitutional, the limitation upon individual liberty must have appropriate relation to the safety of the state.

Hirabayashi v. United States, 320 U.S. 810 (1943), a case dealing with the constitutionality of wartime measures imposed on certain nationalities. Soon after the United States declared war on Japan, Congress passed a resolution that empowered the President to impose special curfews on all Japanese-Americans living on the west coast. The petitioner, himself a Japanese-American, challenged the constitutionality of this federal action, contending that the discriminatory curfew was a clear violation of his 5th Amendment rights as a citizen.

On June 21, 1943, the Supreme Court held unanimously that Hirabayashi's suit should not be sustained. Chief Justice Stone, speaking for the Court, held that the existing state of war with Japan and the dangers of domestic sabotage had created extraordinary circumstances and that the imposition of the curfew was a legitimate exercise of the war powers of the executive and legislative branches. The essence of this decision was repeated in *Korematsu v. United States* (1944), which upheld the constitutionality of the wartime relocation of Japanese-Americans.

Hishon v. King & Spalding, 104 S. Ct. 2229 (1984), a case dealing with discrimination in law firms in promotion of young lawyers to partnership. Elizabeth Hishon brought a sex discrimination suit against an Atlanta, Georgia, law firm that had rejected her for partnership, but a federal district court dismissed the suit on the grounds that a law partnership was not an employment relationship covered under Title VII of the Civil Rights Act of 1964.

On May 22, 1984, the Supreme Court unanimously overturned the district court decision, saying that the federal law does apply and that law firms may not discriminate in the promotion to partnership on the basis of sex, race, religion, or national origin. The opinion was written by Chief Justice Burger. The Court did not rule on the application of Title VII to a law firm hiring a senior lawyer from outside the firm directly into partnership. In addition, Associate Justice Powell made the point in a separate concurring opinion that the Court was not attempting to apply Title VII to cover management or relationships of law partners.

Hodel v. Virginia, 452 U.S. 264 (1981), a case dealing with the extent of federal regulating power with regard to utilization of private land. In 1977, Congress passed the Surface Mining Control and Reclamation Act, which imposed severe restrictions on the use of land for strip mining. This law was immediately challenged by several strip mine owners, who contended that Congress had exceeded its constitutional power by regulating the use of private lands.

The Supreme Court ruled unanimously that Congress had acted within its constitutional power. Associate Justice Marshall, writing for the Court, noted that surface coal mining had substantial effects on interstate commerce and the goals that Congress sought to accomplish were reasonably related to the restrictions imposed. The act did not infringe on the powers of the states guaranteed by the Constitution or the rights of the landowners. Therefore, the act and its application and enforcement were considered necessary and were not unconstitutional.

Holden v. Hardy, 169 U.S. 366 (1898), a case dealing with the right of states to establish maximum working hours for certain trades. At issue in this case was a Utah law that established an eight-hour maximum workday for miners working underground. The petitioner, a representative of one of the mining companies affected by this legislation, appealed to the Supreme Court for a ruling on the constitutionality of this law, on the grounds that it violated the company's right to due process and the freedom of contract.

On February 28, 1898, the Supreme Court decided by a vote of seven to two, with Associate Justices Brewer and Peckham dissenting, that the Utah state law was a constitutional exercise of the police power of the state. Associate Justice Brown, speaking for the majority, noted in his opinion that since "the parties do not stand on an equality," the issue of freedom of contracts was really not the central one. Where the health and safety of workers was at stake, he

Sen. William Proxmire's criticism of supposed wastefulness in government led to a lawsuit and, ultimately, to the Court's holding in **Hutchinson v. Proxmire** *that a member of Congress did not have absolute immunity from a libel suit.*

ruled, the state could legitimately claim that the imposed limits on their work was a measure intended to promote the public welfare. This decision was one of the rare instances in which the Fuller Court ruled on the side of labor against management.

Hutchinson v. Proxmire, 443 U.S. 111 (1979), a case dealing with the legal liability of certain public officials in cases of libel. Sen. William Proxmire, noted for his criticisms of what he considered wasteful government spending, attacked government agencies that funded the research of Ronald Hutchinson, a behavioral scientist. Proxmire also publicly ridiculed Hutchinson's work in a speech and in several newsletters. Hutchinson subsequently filed a libel suit against Proxmire, claiming that Proxmire's actions had caused him humiliation and had damaged his professional reputation. The district court and the court of appeals ruled against Hutchinson, on the grounds that the "speech and debate" clause of Article I, Section 6 of the Constitution protected a member of Congress from such an action. Hutchinson, however, appealed that judgment, contending that Proxmire's action was essentially outside the legislative process.

On June 26, 1979, the Supreme Court decided by a vote of seven to two, with Associate Justices Brennan and Stewart dissenting, that the judgments of the lower courts should be reversed. Chief Justice Burger, speaking for the majority, held that the speech and debate clause was never intended to offer absolute immunity to members of Congress for their public statements not directly concerned with legislative or deliberative process.

Hylton v. United States, 3 Dall. 171 (1796), the first case in which the Supreme Court was called upon to review the constitutionality of a federal law. The petitioner entered a suit in federal circuit court to contest an act passed by Congress in 1794, "laying duties upon carriages for the conveyance of persons." The petitioner suggested that the law was unconstitutional since such a tax was direct, and, according to Section II, Article I of the Constitution, it should be apportioned among the states according to population and not applied uniformly.

The Court held unanimously by a vote of three to zero, with Associate Justices Cushing, Wilson, and Ellsworth not participating, that the only direct taxes referred to in the Constitution were head taxes and land taxes and that Congress was within its constitutional power to tax carriages without differentiating among the states. Associate Justice Paterson, writing for the majority, ruled that the carriage tax was essentially an impost on consumable commodities and that the federal law should stand.

Illinois ex. rel. McCollum v. Board of Education, 333 U.S. 203 (1948), a case dealing with the constitutionality of religious instruction on public school premises. The board of education of Champaign, Illinois, established a "released time" program in which students received religious education classes in lieu of their usual studies in the school building. Although the instructors for these classes were not paid by the board of education, they were under its supervision and attendance was compulsory in the classes. The petitioner, supported by the state of Illinois, challenged the constitutionality of this program, contending that public resources and facilities were being unconstitutionally expended in the dissemination of certain religious doctrines.

On March 8, 1948, the Supreme Court held by a vote of eight to one, with only Associate Justice Reed dissenting, that the religious education program was unconstitutional. Associate Justice Black, speaking for the majority, held that the program was a clear violation of the constitutional separation of church and state. This decision was later amended by the ruling of the Court in *Zorach v. Clausen* (1952), which upheld the constitutionality of religious instruction during school hours at other locations.

Immigration and Naturalization Service v. Chadha, 462 U.S. 919 (1983), a case dealing with the right of Congress to veto immigration and deportation rulings. Chadha, a foreign national, was admitted to the United States on a student visa, and after his visa had expired, an immigration judge suspended his deportation. By the terms of the Immigration and Nationality Act, which authorized either house of Congress to invalidate the decision of the executive branch allowing a particular deportable alien to remain in the United States, the House of Representatives vetoed this suspension. Chadha subsequently challenged the constitutionality of the act.

The Supreme Court ruled by a vote of seven to two, with Associate Justices White and Rehnquist dissenting, that the congressional veto provision of the act is unconstitutional. Chief Justice Burger, writing for the majority, reasoned that this action was legislative and subject to the procedural requirements for legislative action. A one-house veto, he held, is inherently unconstitutional, and thus Congress must adhere to its own legislative procedures before it can veto a deportation suspension.

In re Debs, 158 U.S. 564 (1895), a case dealing with the right of the federal government to intervene in labor disputes. In 1894, the workers of the Pullman Car Company had gone on strike to protest the lowering of their wages by the company management. In sympathy with the Pullman workers, Eugene V. Debs, one of the leaders of the American Railway Union, ordered that the members of his organization boycott any railroad that used Pullman cars. Since nearly every railroad used them and since the railroad authorities refused to eliminate the Pullman cars from their trains, nearly all interstate railroad traffic came to a standstill. In order to forestall an indefinite disruption of railroad service,

Atty. Gen. Richard Olney presented the federal government's position in **In re Debs**, *in which the Court held that the government's intervention in the Pullman Strike was a legitimate exercise of its power.*

The majority opinion of Associate Justice Fortas in **In re Gault** *cited the 14th Amendment in helping to establish the rights of juveniles in court proceedings.*

In re Gault, 387 U.S. 1 (1967), a case dealing with the applicability of certain constitutional due process rights to defendants in juvenile court proceedings. Gerald Gault, a 15-year-old with a previous record of juvenile delinquency, was detained by police and, after summary juvenile court proceedings, was committed to the Arizona State Industrial School. Gault's parents subsequently petitioned the Arizona Supreme Court for a writ of *habeas corpus*, contending that the procedures established in the Arizona Juvenile Code violated their son's 14th Amendment due process rights. Their suit was dismissed by the state courts and the matter was appealed.

On May 15, 1967, the Supreme Court decided by a vote of seven to two, with Associate Justices Harlan and Stewart dissenting, that the Gaults' petition should be sustained. Associate Justice Fortas, speaking for the majority, held that the defendant's commitment to the State Industrial School was a clear violation of his 14th Amendment due process rights since he had been denied the right to legal counsel, had not been formally notified of charges against him, had not been informed of his right against self-incrimination, had no opportunity to confront his accusers, and had been given no right to appeal his sentence to a higher court. This decision amplified the previous ruling of the Court in *Kent v. United States* (1966) and established a precedent that many of the procedural requirements in adult courts must also be observed in juvenile court proceedings.

Insular Cases, (1901), *See* Downes v. Bidwell; DeLima v. Bidwell.

Jackson v. Metropolitan Edison Company, 419 U.S. 345 (1974), a case dealing with the legal rights of consumers of public utilities regulated by state governments. The petitioner's electric service was terminated by Metropolitan Edison Company for nonpayment. Jackson was not given any notice, a hearing, or an opportunity to pay prior to the termination. Since Metropolitan Edison was a heavily regulated private utility, using procedures permitted by state law, the petitioner filed suit, contending that his due process rights had been violated.

The Supreme Court ruled by a vote of six to three, with Associate Justices Douglas, Brennan, and Marshall dissenting, that state regulation of a private business, even if detailed and extensive, does not by itself convert private action to state action for 14th Amendment purposes. Associate Justice Rehnquist, writing for the majority, held that the state and the actual activity of the regulated entity must have a close connection and not one merely affected with a public interest. Rehnquist further noted that the state has no obligation to furnish the services provided by Metropolitan Edison. The state concededly approved the termination procedures, but not upon specific consideration. The state's approval, therefore, indicated that the procedures were permissible under state law and for these reasons Metropolitan Edison's actions could not be considered to be state actions.

the Justice Department obtained an injunction in federal court to compel Debs and other leaders of the union to lift their boycott. Debs refused to comply with the injunction and was subsequently arrested, tried, and sentenced to prison for contempt. Debs's attorneys, among whom was Clarence Darrow, appealed the conviction, petitioning the Supreme Court for a writ of *habeas corpus*, on the grounds that the federal government lacked jurisdiction in this case and that Debs therefore had been denied due process. At issue in this case was the application of the Sherman Antitrust Act, which prohibited conspiracies to obstruct interstate trade and which previously had been directed against corporations.

On May 27, 1895, the Supreme Court decided unanimously that Debs's conviction should stand. Associate Justice Brewer, speaking for the Court, held that the court injunction in this case was a legitimate exercise of the federal government's right to protect the free passage of interstate commerce and ensure the efficient delivery of the U.S. mail. This broad interpretation of interstate commerce contrasted dramatically with the narrow interpretation of the Court in *United States v. E.C. Knight Co.*, decided earlier in the year, in which the interests of management rather than organized labor were at stake. The precedent set in this case resulted in the frequent use of similar injunctions until the passage in 1932 of a federal act that prohibited their use in legitimate labor disputes.

Johnson v. Louisiana, 406 U.S. 356 (1972), a case dealing with the constitutional requirements for a verdict in state jury trials. On May 22, 1972, the Supreme Court upheld by a vote of five to four, with Associate Justices Stewart, Brennan, Douglas, and Marshall dissenting, the validity of a non-unanimous robbery conviction against due process and equal protection challenges. Associate Justice White, writing for the majority, observed that nine jurors, a substantial majority of the jury, were convinced by the evidence. Disagreement of three jurors did not alone establish reasonable doubt, White noted, particularly when such a heavy majority of the jury remained convinced of guilt. The Court perceived nothing unconstitutional or invidiously discriminatory in Louisiana's insisting that its burden of proof be carried with more jurors where more serious crimes or more severe punishments were at issue. Therefore, White concluded, a verdict that is not unanimous may give substance to the proof beyond a reasonable doubt standard.

Jones v. Alfred Mayer Co., (1968), *See* Runyon v. McCrary; Shelley v. Kraemer.

Julliard v. Greenman, 110 U.S. 421 (1884), a case dealing with the constitutionality of federal bank notes. The petitioner, Julliard, delivered to Greenman one hundred bales of cotton for the agreed price of $5,122.90 and Greenman gave Julliard a gold coin, forty cents, and two United States notes in payment. Julliard contended that these notes were not valid payment and filed suit against Greenman.

The Supreme Court held by a vote of eight to one, with only Associate Justice Field dissenting, that these notes of the United States, issued during a time of war, under acts of Congress declaring them to be legal tender for payment of debts, which were after the war reissued and paid in gold at the Treasury, could under the Constitution be legal tender in payment of Greenman's debt. Associate Justice Gray, writing for the majority, ruled that Congress has the constitutional power to make the treasury notes of the United States a legal tender in payment of private debts, in time of peace as well as in time of war.

Jurek v. Texas, (1976), *See* Furman v. Georgia, Jackson v. Georgia, Branch v. Texas.

Kaiser Aluminum Company v. Weber, 443 U.S. 193 (1979), a case dealing with the constitutionality of racial quotas in private industry. The Kaiser Aluminum Company was attempting to integrate its work force and the petitioners claimed that Kaiser's policy of reserving for blacks fifty percent of the openings in in-plant craft-training programs was racially discriminatory. The petitioner's suit was sustained by a lower federal court and Kaiser appealed.

On June 27, 1979, the Supreme Court ruled by a vote of five to two, with Chief Justice Burger and Associate Justice Rehnquist dissenting and Associate Justices Powell and Stevens not participating, that Title VII of the Civil Rights Act of 1964 did not forbid employers from adopting voluntary race-conscious affirmative-action programs to encourage minority participation in areas of the work force where they have traditionally been underrepresented. Associate Justice Brennan, writing for the majority, held that although the Civil Rights Act forbids racial discrimination in employment, the act was created to help the plight of the black worker who had traditionally been denied equal access to the work force. Therefore, voluntary affirmative action was an acceptable form of ratifying a past practice of employment discrimination.

Karcher v. Daggett, 462 U.S. 725 (1983), a case dealing with unequal distribution of population in congressional districts. The lines for New Jersey's fourteen congressional districts were redrawn in 1982, using population figures from the 1980 federal census. The state's Republican congressional representatives challenged the redistricting, asserting that the new districts deviated excessively from the ideal figure derived from dividing the 1980 population by fourteen. The Democractic leadership defined the redistricting plan as an attempt to keep some black urban neighborhoods in the same district.

In a June 22, 1983, decision the Supreme Court upheld a federal district court ruling in favor of the plaintiffs, requiring New Jersey lawmakers to come up with a new plan. The majority opinion by Associate Justice Brennan reaffirmed earlier Court rulings requiring states to aim for "precise mathematical equality" in their congressional districts. This ruling brought into question the validity of the congressional districts in at least sixteen other states. A dissenting opinion by Associate Justice White, signed by Chief Justice Burger and Associate Justices Powell and Rehnquist, decried the "sterile and mechanistic application" that "only brings the principle of 'one man, one vote' into disrepute."

Katz v. United States, 389 U.S. 347 (1967), a case dealing with the extent of 4th Amendment protection against unreasonable searches and seizures. The petitioner was convicted of transmitting wagering information by telephone on the basis of information obtained by federal agents who had attached an electronic listening device to the outside of a public telephone booth. The petitioner subsequently appealed his conviction, contending that the evidence obtained by this device should be suppressed. The government argued that the agents did not begin the surveillance until they had probable cause and then limited the surveillance to the specific purpose and area of the petitioner.

On December 18, 1967, the Supreme Court found, by a vote of eight to one, with only Associate Justice Clark dissenting, that although the agents had probable cause they should have acquired a neutral magistrate's authority before attempting the surveillance. Associate Justice Stewart, writing for the majority, ruled that the officers needed more than their reasonable expectation to find evidence. Wherever a person may be, Stewart noted, he is entitled to know that he will remain free from unreasonable searches and seizures. That protection covers not only physical trespass by an agent, but any violation of privacy that society is unwilling to accept.

Kent v. United States, (1966), *See* In re Gault.

Knox v. Lee, (1871), *See* Hepburn v. Griswold; Second Legal Tender Case.

Kolender v. Lawson, 461 U.S. 352 (1983), a case dealing with the due process clause of the 14th Amendment as it applies to vague criminal statutes. Under a California vagrancy law Edward Lawson was arrested fifteen times and convicted once for refusing to identify himself to the satisfaction of police who stopped him during his nightly strolls. Although Lawson won his case in a federal district court in Los Angeles, California appealed to the Supreme Court.

On May 2, 1983, in a seven to two opinion by Associate Justice O'Connor, the Court upheld the lower court ruling, saying that by its vagueness the California law "contains no standard" for determining what constitutes "credible and reliable identification," leaving open the possibilities for "harsh and discriminatory enforcement." Justice O'Connor said this law failed "to meet constitutional standards for definiteness and clarity." The 4th Amendment prohibiting unreasonable search and seizure was also at issue in the lower court's ruling, but the Supreme Court declined to address this issue in this case. Dissenting were Associate Justices White and Rehnquist.

Korematsu v. United States, 323 U.S. 214 (1944), a case dealing with the constitutionality of certain wartime measures applied to specific nationalities. In 1942, Congress passed a resolution empowering the president to order the relocation of all Japanese-Americans living on the West Coast to internment centers farther inland. Petitioner Fred Korematsu, a Japanese-American, challenged the constitutionality of this federal action, contending that the relocation program was a clear violation of his 5th Amendment rights.

On December 18, 1944, the Supreme Court decided by a vote of six to three, with Associate Justices Jackson, Murphy, and Roberts dissenting, that Korematsu's suit should not be sustained. Associate Justice Black, speaking for the majority, held that the existing state of war with Japan and the dangers of domestic sabotage had created extraordinary circumstances and that the relocation of Japanese-Americans was a legitimate exercise of the war powers of the executive and legislative branches. This decision confirmed the previous ruling of the Court in the case of *Hirabayashi v. United States* (1943), which upheld the constitutionality of curfews for Japanese-Americans living on the West Coast. Korematsu's conviction, called by the government an "unfortunate episode in our nation's history," was overturned by a federal district court in November 1983.

License Cases (Thurlow v. Massachusetts, Pierce v. New Hampshire, Fletcher v. Rhode Island), 5 Howard 504 (1847), three related cases dealing with the right of states to regulate the sale of certain commodities within their borders. At issue here were New England state laws restricting and licensing the importation of various intoxicating beverages from both foreign countries and other states.

Although the Supreme Court unanimously upheld the contested state laws as a legitimate exercise of the states' "police power," six of the justices filed separate opinions explaining their reasoning in this decision. Chief Justice Taney ruled that internal commerce was at issue rather than state regulation of imports. Justice Catron held that "the police power was not touched by the Constitution, but left to the states as the Constitution found it." Justice Daniel held that once imported goods had passed through customs they were open to regulation by the state. Justice Grier held that the states alone could determine which commodities posed a threat to the well-being of the community and could restrict their use and sale. Justice McLean, while reaffirming the exclusive right of the federal government to regulate interstate commerce, declared that the state laws in question were not really an obstruction of trade. Justice Woodbury upheld the state laws on the grounds that they conflicted with no treaty or federal law. The effect of this decision was to reaffirm the police power of the states in accordance with the *City of New York v. Miln* (1837) decision and to constrict the meaning of exclusive federal jurisdiction in interstate trade as established in *Brown v. Maryland* (1827).

Lochner v. New York, 198 U.S. 45 (1905), a case dealing with the legal limits of state regulation of the working conditions of certain trades. The New York legislature enacted a law that restricted the working hours of bakery employees to no more than ten hours per day and no more than sixty hours per week. The petitioner, a bakery owner who had been convicted of violating the law, appealed his conviction to the Supreme Court on the grounds that the law was an obstruction of the right of the freedom of contract guaranteed by the 14th Amendment and was an unconstitutional use of the "police power" of the state, since no particular health hazard or moral danger was at stake. At issue in this case was, therefore, how broadly the states could base their regulation of private industry.

On April 17, 1905, the Supreme Court decided by a vote of five to four, with Associate Justices Day, Harlan, Holmes, and White dissenting, that the New York law should be struck down. Associate Justice Peckham, speaking for the majority, held that while the states did have the right to establish work regulations, those regulations must be designed to alleviate a specific hazard. In the case of bakery workers, however, there was no indication that restricted hours served such a purpose. This decision served to restrict the limits of state "police power," and it was often used by the Court in the following decades to overturn state economic and labor regulations.

Loewe v. Lawler, 208 U.S. 274 (1908), also known as the Danbury Hatters' Case, a case dealing with the legality of certain actions by labor unions. The United Hatters of North America initiated a strike at the Danbury Hat Company,

The 1908 Court, in an opinion written by Chief Justice Fuller (**front, center**), *held unanimously in* **Loewe v. Lawler** *that the hatters union was liable for damages for conducting a boycott of the products of a company being struck by the union.*

owned by Dietrich Loewe and his partners. To strengthen the effect of their work action, they called for a boycott of the company's products throughout the nation. In response, Loewe and his partners successfully filed suit against the union for damages and the judgment was appealed to the Supreme Court. At issue in this case was the right of labor unions to impose secondary boycotts against the products of companies against which they were striking.

On February 3, 1908, the Supreme Court decided unanimously that the judgment against the labor union should be sustained. Chief Justice Fuller, speaking for the Court, held that the union's boycott represented a criminal conspiracy to obstruct interstate commerce by the definition of the Sherman Antitrust Act. This decision threatened to cripple the activities of national labor unions and render them liable to damage suits by private companies affected by their strikes. In 1914, however, this decision was rendered void by the passage by Congress of the Clayton Antitrust Act, which specifically exempted organized labor from criminal prosecution or civil suits for violation of antitrust laws.

Lovell v. Griffin, 303 U.S. 444 (1938), a case dealing with the right of local governments to restrict 1st Amendment freedom of speech and press. The city of Griffin, Georgia, enacted an ordinance requiring written permission from the city manager for the distribution of literature of any kind, at any time, at any place, and in any manner. The petitioner, Lovell, was convicted of violating the ordinance by distributing religious literature without a permit. He subsequently appealed his conviction, contending that the ordinance was a violation of the 1st Amendment.

On March 28, 1938, the Supreme Court ruled unanimously that a government may not prohibit all distribution of all literature without prior written approval of a government agent. Chief Justice Hughes, writing for the Court, held that the right to publish without a license was included in the freedom of the press. Hughes noted that the ordinance was overbroad because it prohibited distribution, which did not in any way interfere with proper government functions. By subjecting the person to license and censorship, this ordinance "strikes at the very foundation of the freedom of the press," wrote Hughes. The freedom of the press was not limited to newspapers or magazines and, therefore, Lovell was protected by the Constitution.

Loving v. Virginia, 388 U.S. 1 (1967), a case dealing with the right of states to prohibit miscegenation. The Virginia appellants, a black woman and a white man, were married in the District of Columbia, returned to Virginia, and were convicted of violating Virginia's ban on interracial marriages. They subsequently challenged the state law banning interracial marriages, contending that it violated the 14th Amendment.

On June 12, 1967, the Supreme Court ruled by a vote of eight to one, with only Associate Justice Roberts dissenting, that a state may not prevent marriages between persons solely because they are of different races. Chief Justice Warren, writing for the majority, rejected the notion that the mere equal application of the statute containing racial classifications was enough to remove the classifications from the 14th Amendment's prohibition of all invidious racial discriminations. The Court must consider, noted Warren, whether statutory classifications constitute arbitrary and invidious discrimination. Racial classifications are subject to the most rigid scrutiny and must be essential to the accomplishment of some permissible state objective to be permitted. Since the state of Virginia had not shown any legitimate purpose for the distinction between single-race and interracial marriages, the statute forbidding interracial marriages should not be upheld.

Lucas v. Colorado General Assembly, 377 U.S. 713 (1964), a case dealing with the constitutional standards for state legislative apportionment. The Colorado house of representatives was apportioned on the basis of population, but the senate was apportioned by population as well as other factors, such as geography, compactness, accessibility, and natural boundaries. Since the apportionment of the senate departed substantially from population-based representation, the petitioner, a resident of Colorado, filed suit for reapportionment, contending that the equal protection clause of the Constitution had been violated.

The Supreme Court ruled by a vote of six to three, with Associate Justices Clark, Harlan, and Stewart dissenting, that both houses of a bicameral state legislature must be apportioned substantially on a population basis. Chief Justice Warren, writing for the majority, held that an individual's constitutionally protected right to cast an equally-weighed vote cannot be denied if the scheme adopted fails to measure up to the requirements of the equal protection clause. Although the state had voted to approve this plan, Warren noted, a citizen cannot be denied a constitutional right simply because a majority of the people choose to do so.

Luther v. Borden, 7 Howard 1 (1849), a case dealing with the resolution of political disputes within the states by the federal government, arising from an electoral dispute within the state of Rhode Island. One of the rival factions, claiming to be the legitimately elected state government, appealed to the Supreme Court to overrule the declaration of martial law issued by the incumbent state legislature, which had invalidated the recent election results. The petitioners contended that this action necessitated intervention by the federal government as specified in Article IV, Section 4 of the Constitution, which guaranteed a republican form of government in all states.

The Court held by a vote of five to one, with Associate Justice Woodbury dissenting, that the issue was essentially a political question and should properly be addressed either to the executive or the legislative branch of the federal government. Chief Justice Taney, speaking for the majority, held that it was not the role of the judiciary to involve itself

in political disputes. Although Associate Justice Woodbury agreed with the Chief Justice's conclusion, he nevertheless believed that the declaration of martial law issued by the incumbent Rhode Island legislature was so clearly unconstitutional that the Supreme Court should declare it invalid.

McCulloch v. Maryland, 4 Wheaton 316 (1819), a case dealing with the authority of Congress, specifically, to establish a national bank and the relation of that institution to state laws. In its opposition to the creation of the federally chartered Bank of the United States, the Maryland legislature enacted a law providing that all banks operating within the state must issue their banknotes on paper bearing the tax stamp of the state. In application of that law, the state of Maryland convicted and fined McCulloch, the cashier of the Baltimore branch of the Bank of the United States, for issuing banknotes without the state's prior approval and without payment of the appropriate state tax. The constitutional questions posed by this case were whether Congress had the authority to establish a national bank and whether that bank was subject to the laws of the various states in which it operated.

The Supreme Court ruled unanimously that the Bank of the United States was a legitimate exercise of the federal power of economic regulation and as a sovereign entity it could create corporate entitites to achieve the desired regulation. Chief Justice Marshall, speaking for the Court, held that the state law in question was unconstitutional, since it impeded the workings of a branch of the federal government and therefore could not be applied to the Bank of the United States. This decision marked an important development in the role of the Supreme Court in defining the power and scope of federal authority. For the first time, the Court applied considerable latitude to the constitutional provision that Congress may enact all laws "necessary and proper" to the execution of its duties, and in so doing, paved the way for steadily increasing federal power and programs within the states.

McLaurin v. Oklahoma State Regents for Higher Education, 339 U.S. 637 (1950), a case dealing with the constitutionality of racial segregation in state-supported schools. The petitioner, McLaurin, a black student at the University of Oklahoma Law School, was denied full access to the facilities of the school because of his race and even received segregated instruction. Considering such treatment a violation of his 14th Amendment rights, he filed suit in federal court against the university authorities, and his case was subsequently presented before the Supreme Court by future Associate Justice Marshall, then serving as director of the National Association for the Advancement of Colored People (NAACP) Legal Defense Fund.

On June 5, 1950, the Supreme Court decided unanimously that McLaurin's suit should be sustained. Chief Justice Vinson, speaking for the majority, held that while no broad ruling was implied on the issue of racial segregation *per se*, segregation in this particular case was a clear violation of 14th Amendment equal protection rights. This decision was announced on the same day as the ruling in *Sweatt v. Painter*, and both cases substantially undermined the separate but equal doctrine established in *Plessy v. Ferguson* (1896).

Maher v. Roe, 432 U.S. 464 (1977), a case dealing with the constitutional obligation of a state participating in the Medicaid program to pay the expenses incident to nontherapeutic abortions for indigent women simply because it has made a policy choice to pay expenses incident to childbirth. The Supreme Court held by a vote of six to three, with Associate Justice Powell writing for the majority, that a state has no obligation under the equal protection clause to pay for a nontherapeutic abortion for an indigent woman through Medicaid. An indigent woman who desires an abortion, Powell noted, is not denied her choice; she continues to have the option of a private abortion. Associate Justices Brennan, Marshall, and Blackmun dissented.

Malloy v. Hogan, 378 U.S. 1 (1964), a case dealing with the applicability of extending the 5th Amendment guarantee against self-incrimination to state proceedings. The petitioner, Malloy, refused to testify before a state investigation of gambling operations and was sentenced to prison for contempt of court. He subsequently appealed the conviction.

On June 15, 1964, the Supreme Court ruled by a vote of five to four, with Associate Justices Clark, White, Stewart, and Harlan dissenting, that the 14th Amendment insures a person against a state invasion the same way the 5th Amendment guarantees against a federal infringement. Associate Justice Brennan, writing for the majority, held that the same standards must be used whether the claim was asserted in federal or state proceedings. It would be inconsistent with justice, Brennan noted, to have different standards used to determine the validity of a claim of privilege simply because a person is in a state rather than a federal proceeding. Therefore, the 5th Amendment right against self-incrimination can be exercised in a state proceeding.

Mapp v. Ohio, 367 U.S. 643 (1961), a case dealing with the constitutional right of state courts to allow the admission of illegally obtained evidence in state trials. In 1957, the Cleveland police entered the home of a woman suspected of complicity in a recent bombing and participation in a numbers operation. In the course of a warrantless search of the premises they discovered a quantity of obscene material and the woman, Mapp, was subsequently convicted of the violation of a state anti-obscenity law. She appealed the conviction, contending that her 4th Amendment rights had been violated. At issue in this case was the previous ruling of the Supreme Court in *Wolf v. Colorado* (1949), in which the Court ruled that while state authorities may not obtain evidence without proper warrants, the evidence thus obtained could nevertheless be admitted in state trials.

On June 19, 1961, the Supreme Court decided by a vote of five to four, with Associate Justices Frankfurter, Harlan, Stewart, and Whittaker dissenting, that Mapp's conviction should be reversed. Associate Justice Clark, speaking for the majority, held that there was no reason why state courts should not be bound by the same standards as the federal courts with regard to illegally obtained evidence, and he argued that "the ignoble shortcut to conviction left open to the State tends to destroy the entire system of restraints on which the liberties of the people rest." This decision established the "exclusionary rule" as a procedural requirement of state as well as federal trials. In this respect, the decision of the Court in this case amended its previous ruling in *Wolf*.

Marbury v. Madison, 1 Cranch 137 (1803), a case dealing with the constitutional authority of the judiciary and the expansion of its powers by Congress. The petitioner, William Marbury, was appointed justice of the peace for the District of Columbia in the last hours of the administration of Pres. John Adams but was denied his signed and sealed commission since it was mislaid in the confusion of the presidential transition and was subsequently withheld by James Madison, the new secretary of State in the Jefferson administration. Marbury filed suit in the Supreme Court for a writ of *mandamus* ordering Madison to deliver the commission forthwith. Although the Constitution did not specifically authorize the Supreme Court to issue such writs, the Judiciary Act of 1789 did.

On February 24, 1803, speaking for a unanimous Court, Chief Justice Marshall held that Marbury's commission was legal since it had been properly signed by the President and sealed by the former secretary of State (Marshall himself) and that a writ of *mandamus* should theoretically be ordered compelling the new secretary of State to deliver the commission to Marbury. However, since the Constitution had not specifically authorized the Supreme Court to issue such a writ and since the justices of the Supreme Court were sworn to uphold the Constitution alone, they were without the power to do so. This landmark decision thus indirectly yet effectively established the exclusive constitutional jurisdiction of the Supreme Court and affirmed the right and duty of the Court to review acts of Congress from the standpoint of the Constitution alone.

Martin v. Hunter's Lessee, 1 Wheaton 122 (1816), a case dealing with the right of the Supreme Court to review and overrule certain decisions of state courts. During the Revolutionary War, the Virginia legislature had passed a law confiscating the property of British loyalists, and the land of Lord Fairfax had been given to a Virginia resident named Hunter. After the war and the ratification of the treaties between the United States and Great Britain, which specifically required that loyalists be allowed to retain their property, Martin, the legal heir of Lord Fairfax, filed suit in the Virginia courts for the recovery of his property. When the Virginia court refused to abide by the terms of the treaty and

The decision of Pres. John Quincy Adams to call out the militia without congressional approval was upheld in **Martin v. Mott.**

restore the property, Martin appealed to the Supreme Court, which reversed the decision of the state court. The state then appealed the judgment of the Supreme Court, contending that it had no jurisdiction over local land matters. On March 20, 1816, the Supreme Court ruled unanimously that it did, in fact, have jurisdiction, since the Constitution had determined that Congress has the power to define the jurisdiction of the federal judiciary and that Section 25 of the Judiciary Act of 1789 provided that the Supreme Court may review the decisions of state courts where federal questions are concerned. Associate Justice Story, writing the majority opinion, held that since the central question in this case concerned the precedence of international treaties over state law, the Court had jurisdiction and the land must be restored to its rightful heir.

Martin v. Mott, 12 Wheaton 19 (1827), a case dealing with the constitutional power of the judiciary to review a presidential decision to call out the militia. In January 1827, the Supreme Court decided unanimously that such an action was not subject to judicial review and was binding on state authorities. Associate Justice Story, writing for the Court, held that since Congress had delegated the power to call out the militia to the president, this power belongs exclusively to the president and his decision is conclusive upon all other persons, including the judiciary. Therefore, Story noted, if

the president gives an order to the military, this order is binding on all citizens, and the courts have no jurisdiction in which to challenge this order.

Massachusetts v. Mellon, 262 U.S. 447 (1923), a case dealing with the right of states to challenge the constitutionality of certain federal aid programs. In 1921, Congress passed the Maternity Act, which created a voluntary state-federal program that provided financial aid to mothers and infants. Although the federal government provided only a portion of the aid, the provisions of the law required that the states follow federal guidelines in the distribution of their part of the funds and file reports to the federal government. If these conditions were not observed, the federal funds to the state would be terminated. The state of Massachusetts, in a suit against Secretary of the Treasury Mellon, challenged the constitutionality of this program, contending that the federal government had no jurisdiction over the expenditure of state funds. This challenge was coordinated with a suit filed by an individual taxpayer (*Frothingham v. Mellon,* 1923) regarding federal expenditures. At issue in the *Massachusetts* case was the legal right of a state to challenge a federal aid program.

On June 4, 1923, the Supreme Court decided unanimously that neither the state nor the individual taxpayer had the legal right to challenge the law. Associate Justice Sutherland, speaking for the Court, held that since the program was voluntary and that since neither the state nor the individual taxpayer was able to demonstrate any tangible injury or loss caused by the law, the Court was in no position to challenge the power of Congress in this matter. This decision was later used as a defense for the controversial New Deal spending programs of Pres. Franklin D. Roosevelt's administration.

Miller v. California, (1973), *See* Roth v. United States.

Minersville School District v. Gobitis, 310 U.S. 586 (1940), a case dealing with the constitutionality of compulsory pledges of allegiance in public schools. The Pennsylvania legislature enacted a law that required daily flag salutes by all public school students, and the petitioner, a member of the Jehovah's Witnesses who was the parent of a student, objected to the pledge of allegiance on religious grounds. He challenged the constitutionality of the law as a violation of his 1st Amendment rights.

On June 3, 1940, the Supreme Court held by a vote of eight to one, with only Associate Justice Stone dissenting, that the state law should be upheld. Associate Justice Frankfurter, speaking for the majority, held that in light of the impending world war, it was important for a "unifying sentiment" to be instilled in the children of the country and that for the Supreme Court to question the means by which that sentiment should be instilled "would in effect make us the school board for the country." This decision was later reversed in *West Virginia State Board of Education v. Barnette* (1943).

Minnesota Rate Cases, 230 U.S. 352 (1913), a decision dealing with the right of the federal government to regulate railroad charges within a single state. The Railroad and Warehouse Commission of Minnesota and the Minnesota legislature instituted maximum charges for railway transportation of both passengers and freight, relating to traffic exclusively between points within Minnesota. Since these rates were in conflict with federally prescribed rates, the action of the state authorities was challenged in federal court. The Supreme Court held unanimously that Congress has the constitutional power to assume regulatory control of interstate commerce, if there exists a national demand for the takeover. Associate Justice Hughes, writing for the Court, held that while Congress can control only commerce that affects more than one state, and that while the state had the authority to set rates, the rates in question were confiscatory and thus the state had superseded its constitutional limitation.

Miranda v. Arizona, 384 U.S. 436 (1966), a case dealing with the guarantee of due process for a criminal suspect and guidelines for police conduct in such matters. Ernesto Miranda, an indigent suspected of kidnapping and rape, was questioned by police and signed a confession without being advised of his rights. This confession was used in his trial and was instrumental in his conviction. Miranda appealed his conviction.

On June 13, 1966, the Supreme Court held in a five to four vote that in order to guarantee due process to a suspect in a crime, the suspect must be informed of the right to remain silent, that anything said by the suspect can be used in evidence, and that the suspect has the right to have an attorney present before any questioning can permissibly take place. Justices Clark, Harlan, Stewart, and White dissented. Chief Justice Warren wrote for the majority. The Court found that the atmosphere of a police interrogation is inherently intimidating and provokes self-incrimination. Therefore, once a suspect is in police custody anything said cannot be used in court unless the suspect is first informed of these constitutionally guaranteed rights. These requirements for handling

In **Mississippi v. Johnson,** *Andrew Johnson became the first president to be named as a defendant in a suit before the Supreme Court. The Court held that it could not prevent a president from enforcing acts of Congress.*

a suspect taken into custody have become known as the Miranda Warning. The dissenters stated that this holding would discourage all confessions.

Mississippi University for Women v. Hogan, 458 U.S. 718 (1982), a case dealing with the constitutionality of certain single-gender educational facilities. The petitioner, a man who had been refused admission to the Mississippi University for Women School of Nursing on the basis of his sex, filed suit in federal court, contending that his rights under the equal protection clause had been violated.

The Supreme Court held by a vote of five to four, with Chief Justice Burger and Associate Justices Powell, Rehnquist, and Blackmun dissenting, that in order to survive equal protection scrutiny, gender-based classifications must be substantially related to the achievement of an important governmental objective. Associate Justice O'Connor, writing for the majority, found that this classification could not be justified as compensating women for past discrimination since women normally composed a large percentage of nursing staffs in the state. This classification, O'Connor noted, actually tended to perpetuate the traditional stereotype that nursing was a woman's job. Therefore, the policy of denying qualified males admission to the nursing school of a state-supported university was unconstitutional under the 14th Amendment.

Mississippi v. Johnson, 4 Wallace 475 (1867), a case dealing with the jurisdiction of the Supreme Court over certain acts of the president. In this case, the state of Mississippi filed suit in federal court to prevent Pres. Andrew Johnson from enforcing the Reconstruction Act of 1867. According to that act of Congress, the former states of the Confederacy, having been officially abolished, would be divided into five military districts, each headed by an officer of the U.S. Army who would have the power to establish military tribunals in place of civilian courts. The petitioners in this case contended that such an act was clearly unconstitutional as established by the Supreme Court in *Ex parte Milligan* (1866). This case, however, did not address itself to the constitutionality of the Reconstruction Act, but rather to its enforcement by the president. It was the first time that the president of the United States was named as a individual defendant in a case brought before the Supreme Court, and the Court accordingly restricted its opinion to the jurisdictional question.

On April 15, 1867, the Supreme Court held unanimously that the Court lacked the legal jurisdiction to intervene in the enforcement of the Reconstruction Act. Chief Justice Chase, speaking for the Court, held that the Court cannot legally prevent the president from enforcing acts of Congress, even if those acts are clearly unconstitutional, since to do so would be to force the president to defy his constitutional responsibilities toward the legislative branch.

Missouri ex rel. Gaines v. Canada, 305 U.S. 337 (1938), a case dealing with the constitutionality of the separate but equal doctrine of racial segregation. The state of Missouri refused to allow a black student, Lloyd Gaines, to enroll in the state-supported law school, offering to provide the cost of his tuition at another institution instead. Gaines subsequently filed suit in federal court to gain admission, contending that his 14th Amendment rights had been violated by the state's action.

When the case reached the Supreme Court, Gaines's position was argued by future Associate Justice Marshall, then serving as the head of the Legal Defense Fund of the National Association for the Advancement of Colored People (NAACP). On December 12, 1938, the Supreme Court decided by a vote of seven to two, with Associate Justices Butler and McReynolds dissenting, that Gaines must be admitted to the University of Missouri Law School. Chief Justice Hughes, speaking for the majority, held that a citizen's constitutional rights accrued to him as an individual and were not a matter of race. This decision marked the Court's initial departure from the separate but equal doctrine established in *Plessy v. Ferguson* (1896).

Missouri v. Holland, 252 U.S. 416 (1920), a case dealing with the legal relationship between international treaties and the rights of state governments. Congress enacted a law for the protection of certain migratory birds, imposing fines and jail sentences against any person convicted of its violation. The constitutionality of this law was challenged in the federal courts on the grounds that it was a matter solely within the jurisdiction of state governments, and the law was overturned. Subsequent to that decision, in 1916, the United States signed a treaty with Great Britain for the protection of the same migratory species and Congress enacted the Migratory Bird Treaty Act to implement its terms. The state of Missouri challenged the constitutionality of the law, filing suit against Holland, a U.S. game warden, who had enforced the law in that state.

On April 19, 1920, the Supreme Court held by a vote of seven to two, with Associate Justices Van Devanter and Pitney dissenting, that, in light of the passage of the international treaty, the federal law was constitutional. Associate Justice Holmes, speaking for the majority, held that while under normal circumstances there is a clear boundary between state and federal jurisdiction, the implementation of duly ratified international treaties allows Congress to legislate matters otherwise relegated to state governments.

Morehead v. Tipaldo, (1936), *See* West Coast Hotel Co. v. Parrish.

Morgan v. Virginia, 328 U.S. 373 (1946), a case dealing with the constitutionality of certain state racial segregation laws. Virginia legislature had enacted a law requiring segregated seating on all public transportation, and the petitioner challenged the constitutionality of that law. His case was presented before the Supreme Court by future Associate Justice Marshall, then serving as director of the Legal Defense Fund of the National Association for the Advancement of Colored People (NAACP).

On June 3, 1941, the Supreme Court decided by a vote

of six to one, with Associate Justice Burton dissenting and Associate Justice Jackson not participating, that the Virginia law could not be applied to transportation facilities engaged in interstate trade. Associate Justice Reed, speaking for the majority, held that the commerce clause of the Constitution empowered the federal government to establish uniform standards for interstate commerce and that the requirement for racial segregation in some states but not others posed a potential disruption to the smooth operation of interstate carriers. While the Court had still not dealt with the issue of the constitutionality of racial segregation *per se*, this decision marked another major departure from the separate but equal doctrine established in the case of *Plessy v. Ferguson* (1896).

Mueller v. Allen, 463 U.S. 388 (1983), a case dealing with the constitutionality of tax deductions for education in religious schools. A Minnesota statute provided for taxpayers to deduct certain expenses incurred in providing for the education of their children, and the petitioners brought suit because certain Minnesota taxpayers were taking advantage of this tax deduction even though they were sending their children to parochial schools.

The Supreme Court held, by a vote of five to four, with Associate Justices Marshall, Brennan, Blackmun, and Stevens dissenting, that the tax deduction was not a violation of the separation of church and state doctrine. Associate Justice Rehnquist, writing for the majority, held that the deduction satisfied the elements of the *Lemon* test, namely, that the tax deduction was both secular and understandable in that it promoted the cause of education. Rehnquist also noted that the deduction did not have the primary effect of advancing the sectarian aims of the nonpublic schools, nor did it unneccessarily entangle the state in religion.

Muller v. Oregon, 208 U.S. 412 (1908), a case dealing with the right of state governments to regulate working conditions for women. In 1903 the Oregon legislature enacted a law that restricted the working hours of women in factories and commercial laundries to ten hours per day. The petitioner, the owner of a laundry in Portland, was convicted and fined of violation of the state law, and he appealed the conviction, contending that the law unconstitutionally deprived him and his employees of the freedom of contract and right to due process and was not applied equally to all workers. At issue in this case was the same question that had been addressed in *Lochner v. New York* (1905), namely, did the state have the right to regulate working conditions where no particular health or moral hazard was involved?

On February 24, 1908, the Supreme Court decided unanimously, in contrast to its holding in *Lochner*, that the Oregon law was a constitutional exercise of the state's "police power." Associate Justice Brewer, speaking for the Court, held that the regulation of women's working hours was, in fact, a matter of public health and welfare. He noted that "woman's physical structure and the performance of maternal functions place her at a disadvantage in the struggle for

Justice David Brewer wrote the Court's opinion in **Muller v. Oregon**, *which upheld an Oregon law that regulated working hours for women in factories and commercial laundries.*

subsistence," and that in this regard, regulation by the state was warranted. This decision marked a notable departure from the general tendency of the Fuller Court to rule in favor of the interests of private industry and against the regulatory power of the state. Crucial to the decision was the exhaustive brief prepared in defense of the Oregon law by associate counsel, and later Associate Justice, Louis D. Brandeis.

Munn v. Illinois, 94 U.S. 113 (1877), a case dealing with the right of states to regulate certain aspects of private industry. In 1871, the Illinois legislature, under pressure from farmers' organizations, enacted a law that set the maximum rates that could be charged by private grain elevators operating in large cities. The owners of the grain elevators subsequently filed suit in federal court, contending that the law was an infringement of the right of the federal government to regulate interstate trade and also claiming that it violated the due process provision of the 14th Amendment.

On March 1, 1877, the Supreme Court ruled by a vote of seven to two, with Associate Justices Field and Strong dissenting, that the Illinois law in question was a legitimate use of the state's police power. Chief Justice Waite, speaking for the majority, held that when private businesses perform a clearly public function, it is within the right of the states to regulate them to ensure that the public good is maintained. In that sense, the grain elevators were not the private property protected by the 14th Amendment. The

Chief Justice also ruled that since the law in question applied only to business carried on within Illinois, it did not violate the federal jurisdiction over interstate trade. This case was the most famous of the *Granger Cases*, in which the Supreme Court upheld similar regulation of agriculture-related industries in several other Midwestern states.

National Association for the Advancement of Colored People v. Alabama ex. rel. Patterson, 357 U.S. 449 (1958), a case dealing with the constitutional right of state governments to obtain the membership lists of private organizations. In 1956, in an effort to end civil rights demonstrations, the state of Alabama obtained an injunction against the activities of the National Association for the Advancement of Colored People (NAACP) on the grounds that as an outside corporation it first had to be approved by the state government before it could legally operate within the state. One of the requirements for approval was the submission of a list of all agents or members of the corporation operating within Alabama, and the NAACP refused to provide such a list. The NAACP was subsequently convicted of contempt, and it appealed that conviction, contending that the disclosure of the names of its members would violate their 14th Amendment rights.

On June 30, 1958, the Supreme Court decided unanimously that the contempt conviction should be reversed. Associate Justice Harlan, speaking for the Court, established the precedent that the freedom to associate in a private organization is one of the rights protected by the due process clause of the 14th Amendment and that the privacy of that association must be maintained in the absence of any compelling justification by government authorities.

National Collegiate Athletic Association v. Board of Regents 104 S. Ct. 2948 (1984), a case dealing with the rights of the National Collegiate Athletic Association (NCAA) to regulate the number and prices of appearances of college football teams on television. In 1981 the Universities of Oklahoma and Georgia brought this antitrust suit, arguing that the NCAA's regulation of college football on television constituted "unreasonable restraint of trade" in violation of the Sherman Antitrust Act.

On June 27, 1984, by a vote of seven to two, the Court upheld two lower federal courts that ruled in favor of the plaintiffs, calling the NCAA a "classic cartel" that "restricted rather than enhanced" intercollegiate athletics. The ruling left individual colleges free to negotiate television contracts. In the majority opinion Associate Justice Stevens characterized the NCAA's television negotiations as "naked restraint on price and output." However, the Court said the NCAA had "substantial remaining authority" to oversee the relationship between television and its member schools. In a dissenting opinion, joined by Justice Rehnquist, Justice White made the case for the NCAA's role in safeguarding amateur athletics that "most likely could not be provided in a perfectly competitive market."

National Labor Relations Board v. Friedman-Harry Marks Clothing Co., 301 U.S. 58 (1937), a case dealing with the right of the federal government to involve itself in certain labor practices in private industry. The National Labor Relations Board ordered Friedman-Harry Marks Clothing Co. to stop discharging any employees or otherwise discriminating against them because they had joined or were assisting the Amalgamated Clothing Workers of America or were otherwise engaged in union activity. The NLRB also ordered Friedman-Harry Marks to reinstate employees who had been discharged for union participation. Friedman-Harry Marks subsequently challenged the authority of the federal government to force compliance with this ruling.

The Supreme Court held by a vote of five to four, with Associate Justices McReynolds, Van Devanter, Sutherland, and Butler dissenting, that the board's orders should be enforced based on the decision in *National Labor Relations Board v. Jones & Laughlin Steel* (1937). Chief Justice Hughes, writing for the majority, noted that in *Jones* the Supreme Court held that Congress can regulate a manufacturer if the manufacturer's activity significantly affects interstate commerce. Here, Hughes applied this same rationale to a manufacturer of clothes whose factory was in Virginia but who used cloth imported from other states and sold clothes to other states.

National Labor Relations Board v. Jones & Laughlin Steel Corp., 301 U.S. 1 (1937), a case dealing with the extent of federal regulatory power over actions that affect interstate trade only indirectly. In 1935 Congress passed the National Labor Relations Act, which established a national board with power to arbitrate labor-management disputes. The Jones & Laughlin Steel Corp., having dismissed some of its employees for union activity, was ordered by the National Labor Relations Board (NLRB) to reinstate them with back pay. Jones & Laughlin refused to comply with this order, which was subsequently upheld in federal court. The ruling was then appealed on the grounds that the federal government had no jurisdiction in matters that only indirectly affected interstate commerce. At issue in this case was the interpretation of the commerce clause of the Constitution, which had been interpreted narrowly in the recent cases of *Railroad Retirement Board v. Alton Railroad Co.* and *Schechter Poultry Corp. v. United States* (1935).

On April 12, 1937, the Supreme Court decided by a vote of five to four, with Associate Justices Butler, McReynolds, Sutherland, and Van Devanter dissenting, that the National Labor Relations Act was constitutional and that the ruling of the lower court should be sustained. Chief Justice Hughes, speaking for the majority, held that since the steel industry was so intimately involved in interstate commerce, even the essentially intrastate nature of this case brought it within the purview of legitimate federal power. This decision marked a sudden change in the Court's attitude toward the economic policies of Franklin D. Roosevelt's administra-

Chief Justice Hughes wrote the Court's opinion in **NLRB v. Jones & Laughlin,** *which represented a change in the Court's hostility to New Deal programs and followed President Roosevelt's announcement of his court-packing plan.*

tion and toward a broad view of the regulatory power of the federal government.

National League of Cities v. Usery, (1976), *See* Garcia v. San Antonio Metropolitan Transit Authority.

Near v. Minnesota, 283 U.S. 697 (1931), a case dealing with the right of states to restrict the 1st Amendment freedom of the press. A Minnesota statute provided for the abatement, as a public nuisance, of any malicious, scandalous, and defamatory publication. The petitioner, Near, published a periodical that criticized law enforcement officers, and Minnesota attempted to suppress Near's publication. Near filed suit against this action, and on June 1, 1931, the Supreme Court ruled by a vote of five to four, with Associ-

ate Justices Butler, Van Devanter, McReynolds, and Sutherland dissenting, that to permit public authorities to suppress publication of scandalous matter relating to charges of official dereliction, restrained only by the publisher's ability to satisfy the judge that the charges were true, was the essence of unconstitutional censorship. Chief Justice Hughes, writing for the majority, held that freedom of the press principally meant the immunity from previous restraints or censorship. Therefore, the only permissible restraint was the deterrent effect of actions against defamatory publications arising after publication.

Nebbia v. New York, 291 U.S. 502 (1934), a case dealing with the limits of state regulatory power over private industry. In 1933, the New York legislature established the Milk Control Board, which was empowered to set minimum and maximum prices for the sale of dairy products. The petitioner, Leo Nebbia, a Rochester grocery store owner who was convicted of selling milk below the minimum price, appealed his conviction, contending that the state regulation unconstitutionally interfered with his right to sell goods on the open market.

On March 5, 1934, the Supreme Court decided by a vote of five to four, with Associate Justices Butler, McReynolds, Sutherland, and Van Devanter dissenting, that Nebbia's conviction should stand. Associate Justice Roberts, speaking for the majority, held that since the maintenance of minimum prices in the dairy industry was essential to providing an adequate market supply, the law was justified. This decision effectively altered the position of the Court established in *Munn v. Illinois* (1877), which allowed state regulation of only industry "affected with a public interest," and opened the way for far broader regulatory powers in the private sector, based on economic factors alone.

New York v. Miln, (1837), *See* City of N.Y. v. Miln.

New York v. Quarles, 104 S. Ct. 2626 (1984), a case dealing with obligations of police officers to inform a suspect in custody of his rights regarding self-incrimination. In 1980 police officers apprehended a gunman suspected of rape. When one of the officers noticed the man was wearing an empty gun holster and asked whether he had a gun, the suspect, Benjamin Quarles, replied, "The gun is over there." Quarles was arrested and charged with weapons possession, rape, and sodomy. During the trial for the weapons charge, the court ruled that Quarles's statement about the gun was inadmissible because he had not first been informed of his right to remain silent, to have a lawyer present during questioning, and to be provided with a court-appointed lawyer if he could not afford to hire one. This suspect-warning procedure had been established by *Miranda v. Arizona* (1966).

On June 12, 1984, by a vote of five to four, the Court made a "narrow exception" to the Miranda rule. In the majority opinion by Associate Justice Rehnquist, the Court held that in a situation where "overriding considerations of public safety" must prevail and quick police action is essential, the warning may be delayed. Justice Rehnquist allowed that the New York courts had applied the Miranda doctrine correctly as it stood in the Quarles case, but stated that "the need for answers to questions in a situation posing a threat to the public safety outweighs the need for the prophylactic rule protecting the Fifth Amendment's privilege against self-incrimination." A similar exception has long applied to the search warrant requirement of the 4th Amendment, in which "exigent circumstances" allow police to conduct a search without benefit of warrant. The Court thereupon reversed the lower courts' decision in *Quarles*. The dissenting opinion of Associate Justices O'Connor, Marshall, Brennan, and Stevens centered on the unnecessary blurring of the legal requirements of the Miranda rule.

New York Times v. Sullivan, 376 U.S. 254 (1964), a case dealing with the extent to which the constitutional protections for free speech and press limit a state's power to award damages in a libel action brought by a public official against critics of his official conduct. In 1960, *The New York Times* had carried a full page advertisement that included several false statements of repressive police conduct in Montgomery, Alabama. L.B. Sullivan, the city's police commissioner, sued for damages on the grounds that *The Times* had libeled him. Even though his name was not mentioned in the ad, the accusations could be read as referring to him.

On March 9, 1964, the Supreme Court found unanimously that the 1st and 14th Amendments prevent state rules that would allow a public official to recover damages for a defamatory falsehood relating to his official conduct without proof of actual malice. Associate Justice Brennan, writing for the Court, defined actual malice as "knowledge that it was false or with reckless disregard of whether it was false or not." This decision effectively established limits on libel suits by public officials and shifted the burden of proof to the plaintiff.

New York Times v. United States, United States v. Washington Post, 403 U.S. 713 (1971), a case dealing with the constitutional right of the federal government to prohibit the publication of certain material considered vital to national security. During the Vietnam War, *The New York Times* and *The Washington Post* acquired the text of a government study, popularly known as "The Pentagon Papers," that traced the history of American involvement in Vietnam. This study had been classified top secret, and when the two newspapers began to publish substantial portions of the text, the federal government filed suit to prevent further publication, contending that "national security" interests were being endangered by the newspapers' actions.

On June 30, 1971, the Supreme Court decided by a vote of six to three, with Chief Justice Burger and Associate Justices Blackmun and Harlan dissenting, that the federal government's suit should not be sustained. In an unsigned majority opinion, the Court held that any attempt by the government to restrain the freedom of the press and freedom of expression seemed by its nature to act against the guarantees of the 1st Amendment and that it was the obligation of the federal government to prove that actual harm to the nation's security would be caused by the publication in question. In the opinion of the majority, the government had failed to demonstrate such harm, and the concurring justices held that no injunction against further publication should be issued.

Nixon v. Administrator of General Services, 433 U.S. 425 (1977), a case dealing with the extent of congressional power over presidential papers. Four months after Richard M. Nixon resigned as president, Congress enacted the Presidential Recordings and Materials Preservation Act of 1974 to assure governmental custody of documents and tape recordings accumulated during the Nixon administration. Nixon subsequently challenged the law on several grounds, including the violation of separation of powers principles and of presidential privilege doctrines.

The Supreme Court held by a vote of seven to two, with Chief Justice Burger and Associate Justice Rehnquist dissenting, that the ex-president could not prevent Congress from regulating the disposition and use of presidential documents by claiming executive immunity. Associate Justice Brennan's majority opinion emphasized the narrowness of the decision (unique because of Nixon's resignation and the aftermath). The proper inquiry into whether the law was unconstitutional, Brennan suggested, focused on the extent to which the law prevents the executive branch from accomplishing its constitutionally assigned functions.

Nixon v. Fitzgerald, 457 U.S. 731 (1982), a case dealing with the legal liability of the president of the United States for a civil damages suit for actions taken while in office and within the "outside perimeter" of his official responsibility. Fitzgerald, a civilian Pentagon cost analyst, had been fired after revealing cost overruns in an Air Force transport program. Fitzgerald sued President Nixon, who settled out of court for damages claimed by Fitzgerald, but the Court agreed to rule on the issue of the immunity of presidents from such suits.

The Supreme Court held by a vote of five to four, with Associate Justices White, Blackmun, Brennan, and Marshall dissenting, that the president's unique role in the constitutional scheme demands that he be free to execute vigorously the duties of his office without the distraction of civil suits. Associate Justice Powell, writing for the majority, held that the president should be accorded absolute immunity for all action taken under any of his broad areas of constitutional authority. Other measures, including congressional oversight, impeachment, and scrutiny by the press, still exist to deter presidential misconduct, Powell also noted.

Norman v. Baltimore and Ohio Railroad Co., (1935), *See* Gold Clause Cases.

Pres. Woodrow Wilson's takeover of the nation's railroads during World War I resulted in the imposition of federal rates on intrastate carriers, an exercise of federal power upheld by the Court in **Northern Pacific Railway Co. v. North Dakota.**

Norris v. Alabama, (1935), *See* Powell v. Alabama.

Norris v. Boston, (1849), *See* Passenger Cases.

Northern Pacific Railway Co. v. North Dakota, 250 U.S. 135 (1919), a case dealing with the right of the federal government to regulate intrastate railroad rates during times of national emergency. In 1916, Congress gave the president the power, in time of war, to take control and possession of any type of transportation to carry war supplies connected with the emergency. In 1917, after U.S. entry into World War I, President Wilson, through this power, took possession and control of the railroads within the United States. When intrastate rates were adjusted to conform to federally-established interstate rates, the petitioners, directors of a private railway, challenged the action in federal court.

The Supreme Court held unanimously that the federal government had the right to establish the rates on intrastate traffic, superseding the state's previous power over the rates. Associate Justice White, writing for the Court, held that the congressional action granting the president power to control the railroads in time of war implicitly included the power to regulate intrastate rates.

Northern Securities Co. v. United States, 193 U.S. 197 (1904), a case dealing with the legal definition of an illegal business trust. The officials of two competing railroads, the Great Northern and the Northern Pacific, pooled their assets to establish a joint holding company, the Northern Securities Company. This transaction resulted in an indictment and conviction by the provision of the Sherman Antitrust Act. The representatives of the holding company subsequently appealed the conviction on the grounds that since Northern Securities was not directly concerned with the railroad business but with finances, it could not be considered a trust for the restraint of trade.

On March 14, 1904, the Supreme Court decided by a vote of five to four, with Chief Justice Fuller, and Associate Justices White, Holmes, and Peckham dissenting, that the Northern Securities Company must be dissolved. Associate Justice Harlan, speaking for the majority, held that any holding company that was established solely as an agreement between two competing businesses to eliminate competition--even if it was a purely financial instrument--was an illegal trust. This decision effectively reversed the opinion of the Court in *United States v. E.C. Knight Co.* (1895), which held that trusts must actually control trade to be illegal, and it opened the way for a more aggressive enforcement of the Sherman Antitrust Law, enforcement that the Court upheld in later decisions.

Pres. Theodore Roosevelt's influence on the Court's thinking through his appointments became apparent in **Northern Securities Co. v. United States,** *which helped define an illegal business trust and reversed the* **E.C. Knight** *decision.*

North Georgia Finishing, Inc. v. Di-Chem, 419 U.S. 601 (1975), a case dealing with procedures for garnishment of assets in pending state suits. A Georgia statute allowed plaintiffs in pending suits to be entitled to the process of garnishment. The plaintiff was required to make an affidavit before an authorized court officer or clerk to issue an attachment, stating the amount claimed to be due and explaining the reasons why he believed he would lose some or all unless process of garnishment was granted. In addition, the plaintiff was required to post bond double the amount sworn to be due. The petitioner challenged the statute, contending that its failure to provide for an early hearing violated the due process clause of the 14th Amendment.

The Supreme Court, by a vote of six to three, with Chief Justice Burger and Associate Justices Blackmun and Rehnquist dissenting, sustained the petitioner's contention. Associate Justice White, writing for the majority, held that this statute provided little safeguard for a person whose property was taken. White further noted that since there was no prior determination of the merits, a judge, not merely a clerk, should issue the writ.

Nortz v. United States, (1935), *See* Gold Clause Cases.

Ogden v. Saunders, 12 Wheaton 213 (1827), a case dealing with the constitutionality of state bankruptcy laws and their application to debts contracted between residents of different states. The Supreme Court had already dealt with the issue of state bankruptcy laws in *Sturges v. Crowninshield* (1819), ruling that while states do have the power to enact insolvency laws, those laws may not apply to debts contracted before the passage of the law, since such laws would violate the constitutional protection against the violation of contracts. In this case, the state law in question applied only to debts contracted after the passage of the law. Its difficulty, however, was that it applied to a contract between citizens of two states.

By a vote of four to three, with Chief Justice Marshall and Associate Justices Story and Duvall dissenting, the Supreme Court upheld the state insolvency law. In the first part of the decision, written by Associate Justice Washington, the majority held that the right of Congress to enact a uniform bankruptcy law as specified in Article I, Section 8 of the Constitution did not preclude state action, and since the law applied only to debts contracted after the passage of the law, the law itself had become a legitimate condition of the contract in question. As to the question of the applicability of this state law to a citizen of another state, Associate Justice Johnson, writing for the majority, held that since such a law "was incompatible with the rights of other states," it could not be held binding except on contracts between residents of the state in which it was passed.

Olmstead v. United States, 277 U.S. 438 (1928), a case dealing with the right of law enforcement agencies to employ surreptitious wiretaps in criminal investigations. The petitioner was convicted of violating the Volstead Act in his sale and distribution of alcoholic beverages largely through evidence obtained through a government wiretap of his telephone. He subsequently appealed the conviction, contending that the government wiretap violated his 4th Amendment protection against unreasonable searches and seizures.

On June 4, 1928, the Supreme Court decided by a vote of five to four, with Associate Justices Brandeis, Butler, Holmes, and Stone dissenting, that Olmstead's conviction should stand. Chief Justice Taft, speaking for the majority, held that since no actual entry into the defendant's private property was involved in the installation and use of the wiretap, it was not a violation of his constitutional rights. This was the first case in which the issue of electronic surveillance was addressed by the Supreme Court, and its position would later be modified in *Katz v. United States* (1967).

Oregon v. Elstead, 53 U.S.L.W. 4244 (1984), a case dealing with the admissibility in court of a confession made by a suspect who was not initially informed of his rights according to the Miranda rule, even though a proper warning preceded his subsequent confession. When the police went to an 18-year-old Oregon man's home and informed

In **Olmstead v. United States,** *the first wiretap case before the Court, Chief Justice Taft* (**left**) *wrote the opinion upholding a conviction based on wiretapping, while Justices Holmes* (**center**) *and Brandeis dissented.*

him that he was suspected in a burglary, he said, "Yes, I was there." The youth repeated his confession following a full reading of his Miranda rights an hour later at the station. The state appeals court reversed his conviction on the grounds that, even though it was not forced, his first confession had a coercive effect on the suspect that prompted the second confession.

The Supreme Court disagreed, holding on March 4, 1984, in a six to three decision, that an initial violation of the Miranda rule could not reasonably be held to invalidate all subsequent confessions, provided proper warnings are issued in the meantime. Writing for the majority, Associate Justice O'Connor said, "Though Miranda requires that the unwarned admission must be suppressed, the admissibility of any subsequent statement should turn . . . solely on whether it is knowingly and voluntarily made."

Disssenting were Associate Justices Brennan and Marshall, who decried the Court's "studied campaign to strip the Miranda decision piecemeal," a reference to *New York v. Quarles*, a 1984 decision allowing public safety to override the need for initial Miranda warnings. Associate Justice Stevens also dissented, fearing unnecessary confusion and weakening of 5th Amendment protections.

Oregon v. Mitchell, 400 U.S. 112 (1970), a case dealing with the constitutionality of certain federally mandated voting procedures. The respondents challenged three provisions of the 1970 amendments to the Voting Rights Act. The challenged provisions were the ban on state literacy tests, the ban on state residence requirements for voting in presidential elections, and the extension of voting rights to eighteen-year-olds.

On December 21, 1970, the Supreme Court ruled, with Chief Justice Burger and Associate Justices Harlan, Stewart, Blackmun, Brennan, and Marshall dissenting in part, that the ban on literacy tests and residence requirements should be upheld, but that the right of eighteen-year-olds to vote should be restricted to federal elections. Associate Justice Black, writing for the majority, held that Congress's power to legislate with regard to state and local elections was limited to remedial efforts concerning racial discrimination. Therefore, Congress could not require that states grant the right to vote to eighteen-year-olds in state and local elections. Subsequent to this decision, the 26th Amendment was ratified, granting voting rights in all elections to eighteen-year-olds.

Osborn v. Bank of the United States, 9 Wheaton 738 (1824), a case dealing with the right of federal agencies to file suit against state officials in federal courts. Ever since the adoption of the 11th Amendment in 1795, the established judicial precedent has been that states may not be involuntarily sued by private citizens of another state. With the establishment of the Bank of the United States, however, and the decision in *McCulloch v. Maryland* (1819), in which the Supreme Court ruled that state laws regulating its operation were unconstitutional, the question arose whether states may be liable to court action by the federal government for the illegal enforcement of unconstitutional laws.

In *Osborn* the Supreme Court held, with only Associate Justice Johnson dissenting, that the 11th Amendment did not apply to a suit filed by the Bank of the United States against a state official who attempted to enforce unconstitutional regulation of the national bank. Chief Justice Marshall, speaking for the Court, held that issues concerning the functioning of the federal government were within federal judicial jurisdiction, thereby further establishing the power of the national government to enforce the precedence of federal over state laws.

Palko v. Connecticut, 302 U.S. 319 (1937), a case dealing with the obligation of states to observe the 5th Amendment prohibition of double jeopardy in criminal trials. In this case the petitioner had been convicted of second-degree murder and sentenced to life imprisonment, but by the terms of a Connecticut statute, the prosecutor was able to appeal the conviction and obtain a new trial at which Palko was convicted of first-degree murder and sentenced to death. He subsequently appealed the second conviction, contending that the state statute and the proceedings that it permitted were a violation of his 5th Amendment rights and, by extension, of his 14th Amendment right to due process. At issue was the extent to which the Bill of Rights applied to state law.

On December 6, 1937, the Supreme Court decided by a vote of eight to one, with only Associate Justice Butler dissenting, that the state law was constitutional. Associate Justice Cardozo, speaking for the majority, held that only those provisions of the Bill of Rights that are "fundamental principles of liberty and justice" necessarily apply to the states. In this case, however, the justice found that the principles did not apply, since the law provided appeal only on a question of law.

Parker v. Davis, (1871), *See* Second Legal Tender Case.

Passenger Cases (Smith v. Turner, Norris v. Boston), 7 Howard 283 (1849), two related cases dealing with the power of states to regulate certain aspects of international trade. At issue in this case was a Massachusetts state law that imposed a head tax, intended to establish a fund for the support of indigent immigrants already arrived, on arriving foreign passengers.

The Supreme Court held by a vote of five to four, with Chief Justice Taney and Associate Justices Daniel, Nelson, and Woodbury dissenting, that the Massachusetts state law was in conflict with the exclusive federal jurisdiction over interstate and international trade and was therefore unconstitutional. This decision was a dramatic departure from the ruling of the Court in *City of New York v. Miln* (1837), which acknowledged the right of states to require the registration of arriving foreign passengers when the welfare of its citizens was at stake. Associate Justice McLean, speaking for the majority, clearly differentiated this case from the prior decision, since the state law in question imposed a tax. Taxation, unlike registration, was regulation, and therefore an impermissible action by the state.

Penn-Central Merger Cases, 389 U.S. 486 (1968), a series of cases arising from the planned merger of the Pennsylvania and New York Central railroads and from the Interstate Commerce Commission's order that certain railroads be included in the Norfolk & Western system. The Supreme Court held by a vote of eight to one, with only Associate Justice Douglas dissenting, that the Interstate Commerce Commission acted properly in regard to the Penn-Central merger. Associate Justice Fortas, writing for the majority, ruled that the merger would benefit the public and shippers, as well as the railroads and their investors, and that the rail service by the merged company would remain subject to vigorous competition from other railroads and other forms of transport. Fortas also noted that the merger, although clearly intended to protect the carriers, was in the interest of better service to the public and was not intended to restrain competion unduly.

Pennhurst v. Halderman, 104 S. Ct. 900 (1984), a case dealing with the jurisdiction of federal courts in suits against state officials and agencies. Based on the fact that federal courts have for some time been ruling on federally related state laws, a federal appeals court in Pennsylvania ordered correction of certain conditions in the Pennhurst State School and Hospital.

On January 23, 1984, the Supreme Court overturned the lower court decision, in a five to four vote that split along conservative-liberal lines in the Court. The decision does not prevent federal courts from hearing constitutional suits against states but does prohibit federal courts from issuing orders to state officials regarding state laws. This decision at least indirectly overrules precedents established by the Court regarding federal court jurisdiction. However, it relates to a 1974 Supreme Court ruling that the 11th

Amendment, which bars citizens from suing state officials in federal courts, prohibits federal courts from ordering payment of retroactive damage awards out of state treasuries. This 1984 decision further extends states' immunities by barring state law-based injunctions against state officials and extending 11th Amendment immunity to more state employees. The majority opinion was written by Associate Justice Powell. The dissenting opinion written by Associate Justice Stevens was joined by Justices Brennan, Marshall, and Blackmun.

Pennsylvania v. Nelson, 350 U.S. 497 (1956), a case dealing with the right of state governments to enact laws against seditious activity. The Pennsylvania legislature passed a law that imposed criminal penalties against any person advocating or encouraging the violent overthrow of the government, and a leader of the Communist Party of the United States was convicted of violating this statute. The Pennsylvania Supreme Court reversed that conviction on the grounds that the matter was within exclusive federal jurisdiction.

The state of Pennsylvania subsequently appealed that ruling and on April 2, 1956, the Supreme Court decided by a vote of six to three, with Associate Justices Burton, Minton, and Reed dissenting, that the ruling of the Pennsylvania Supreme Court should stand. Chief Justice Warren, speaking for the majority, held that the federal Smith Act of 1940 effectively superseded all state legislation in this matter. The effect of this decision was the nullification of many of the provisions of state anti-sedition laws.

Perez v. Ledesma, 401 U.S. 82 (1971), a case dealing with the procedural requirements for a Supreme Court review of a state law. Ledesma had been arrested and charged with displaying for sale allegedly obscene material in violation of Louisiana law. Since Ledesma claimed that the law was unconstitutional, he requested an injunction against the enforcement of the law. A three-judge court subsequently held the law constitutional but found the arrest and seizure to be invalid, thus suppressing the evidence.

The Supreme Court held by a vote of five to four, with Associate Justices Douglas, Brennan, White, and Marshall dissenting, that the three-judge court was wrong in suppressing the evidence, which stifled the pending good-faith state criminal proceeding. Associate Justice Black, writing for the majority, declared that the Supreme Court had no jurisdiction to review on direct appeal the validity of the order declaring the ordinance invalid, since it was appealable only to the court of appeals.

Perry v. United States, (1935), *See* Gold Clause Cases.

Pierce v. New Hampshire, (1847), *See* License Cases.

Plessy v. Ferguson, 163 U.S. 537 (1896), a case dealing with the right of state governments to maintain racially-segregated seating on carriers of interstate trade. The petitioner, Homer A. Plessy, a black citizen of Louisiana, was denied a seat in a railroad car designated for whites only and was arrested for refusing to leave the car when requested to do so. He subsequently appealed the conviction, contending that the Louisiana state law that established the segregated seating was a violation of his 13th and 14th Amendment rights. At issue in this case was not only the constitutionality of racial segregation but also the right of states to determine the race of citizens, since Plessy himself was of a racially mixed family.

On May 18, 1896, the Supreme Court held by a vote of eight to one, with only Associate Justice Harlan dissenting, that the "separate but equal" accommodations established by the state law did not violate the guarantees of the 13th and 14th Amendments. Associate Justice Brown, speaking for the majority, held that the 13th Amendment dealt only with the question of slavery and was therefore irrelevant to this case. With regard to the 14th Amendment, Brown ruled that it dealt only with political equality and did not apply in this social context, concluding that state segregation "neither abridges the privileges or immunities of the colored man, deprives him of his property without due process of law, nor denies him the equal protection of the laws." On the issue of the right of states to determine the race of a citizen, Brown ruled that it is within their legitimate "police power" to do so, since the constitutionality of segregation had been upheld.

Associate Justice Harlan, in his lone dissent, attacked this legalistic interpretation on the grounds that "The Constitution is color-blind, and neither knows nor tolerates classes among citizens." The "separate but equal" doctrine established by *Plessy* legitimized racial segregation and was repeatedly upheld by the Court until *Brown v. Board of Education* (1954). The Court's *Brown* decision reversed *Plessy* and inaugurated a new era in the judicial attitude toward official segregation and the civil rights of minority groups.

Plyer v. Doe, 457 U.S. 202 (1982), a case dealing with the constitutional obligation of a state to provide free public school education to all children resident within the state. The Supreme Court held by a vote of five to four that a Texas statute that denied free public education to children of illegal aliens while providing free education to children of its citizens or legally-admitted aliens violated the equal protection clause of the 14th Amendment. Chief Justice Burger and Associate Justices White, Rehnquist, and O'Connor dissented. Associate Justice Brennan, writing for the majority, held that while illegal alien children were not a "suspect class" (a class that invoked a stricter application of equal protection), they did constitute an underclass, that is, "a permanent caste" in American society. Since the state failed to show that the discrimination was justified by a substantial state interest, the statute was held to be unconstitutional.

Pollock v. Farmers' Loan and Trust Co., 157 U.S. 429, 158 U.S. 601 (1895), a case dealing with the constitutionality of a federal income tax. In 1894, Congress enacted a national tax of two percent annually on all individual

A federal income tax law, criticized on all fronts, was held invalid by the Court in **Pollock v. Farmers' Loan and Trust Co.**

On May 20, 1895, the Supreme Court held by a vote of five to four, with Associate Justices Harlan, Jackson, Brown, and White dissenting, that the federal income tax in its present form was unconstitutional. Chief Justice Fuller, speaking for the narrow majority, reiterated his earlier objections but now also held that because of the extent of its unconstitutional provisions, the entire law should be declared invalid. This decision was effectively nullified in 1913 with the adoption of the 16th Amendment, which exempted federal income taxes from the direct tax provision of the Constitution.

Powell v. Alabama, 287 U.S. 45 (1932), a case, also known as the "First Scottsboro Case," dealing with the obligation of states to provide defendants in capital cases with competent counsel. In this case eight young black men had been arrested, convicted of the rape of two white girls, and subsequently sentenced to death for that crime without

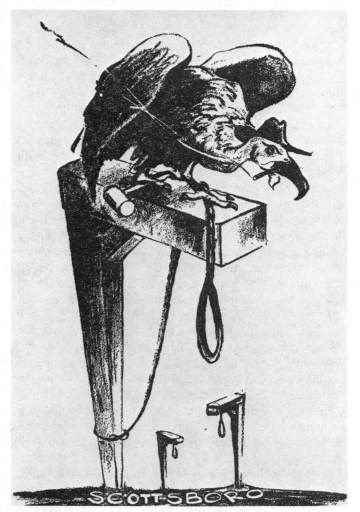

The Scottsboro case, brought before the Court in **Powell v. Alabama**, *was popularly considered an example of hostility towards blacks in Southern courts. The Court held that 14th and 16th Amendment rights had been violated during the trial and that the defendant should have had legal counsel.*

incomes exceeding $4,000. The constitutionality of this tax was immediately challenged on several grounds. The first of these was that its claim on income derived from land and private property made it a direct tax and that by Article I, Section 9 of the Constitution it must therefore be apportioned by population among the states. The second reason was that its claim on income derived from government bonds was an impermissible tax on the powers of the state. Third, the opponents of the law claimed that it unfairly differentiated among citizens by singling out those of a specific income group. In January 1895, Charles Pollock, a stockholder of the Farmers' Loan and Trust Company, filed suit in federal court to enjoin that company from complying with the new income tax law. The circuit court denied the petitioner's request, but since this was obviously a test case, it allowed a direct appeal to the Supreme Court.

After hearing the first arguments, Chief Justice Fuller, speaking for the Court on April 8, 1895, ruled that the federal act's claims on income derived from land and government bonds were impermissible. As to the claim on income derived from private property, the issue of uniformity, and the crucial question of whether the impermissible provisions invalidated the entire tax, the Chief Justice announced that the Court was evenly divided and no judgment would be rendered on those matters. The issue could not remain undecided and a rehearing was ordered in the case.

having been defended by legal counsel. The case received widespread publicity, and one of the defendants was encouraged to appeal his conviction on the grounds that the procedure employed by the court had violated his 14th Amendment right to due process.

On November 7, 1932, the Supreme Court held by a vote of seven to two, with Associate Justices Butler and McReynolds dissenting, that the conviction of the "Scottsboro Boys" should be overturned. Associate Justice Sutherland, speaking for the majority, held that not only were the defendant's 14th Amendment rights violated, but his 6th Amendment rights were violated as well. The right to be represented by counsel, Sutherland further ruled, is central to the the American judicial system and "the right to have counsel appointed, when necessary, is a logical corollary from the constitutional right..." This decision established a proper legal defense as one of the essential components of due process. In the "Second Scottsboro Case," *Norris v. Alabama*, 294 U.S. 587 (1935), the conviction of one of the defendants was invalidated because there had been racial discrimination in the grand jury's and the trial jury's selections.

Powell v. McCormack, 395 U.S. 496 (1969), a case dealing with the constitutionality of a judicial appeal of the exclusion of a duly elected member by the House of Representatives. In January 1967, the officers of the House of Representatives refused to administer the oath of office to Adam Clayton Powell, who had been reelected by the voters of the 18th New York Congressional District. Because of charges of Powell's official misconduct and misappropriation of government funds during prior service, Speaker of the House John McCormack referred the matter to a bipartisan select committee. The select committee determined that although Powell fulfilled the constitutional requirements of age, residency, and citizenship, his official misconduct and refusal to cooperate with the committee were of sufficient gravity to strip him of his congressional seat.

Speaker McCormack then ruled that a simple majority vote by the members of the House of Representatives could implement the recommendations of the committee. When the resolution passed, Powell filed suit in federal court for reinstatement and back pay, contending that the House had no constitutional right to exclude him. Powell's suit was dismissed by both the district court and the District of Columbia Circuit Court of Appeals. Future Chief Justice Burger, then serving on the court of appeals, ruled that the matter was essentially a political question, beyond the jurisdiction of the judicial branch.

On June 16, 1969, the Supreme Court decided by a vote of seven to one, with only Associate Justice Stewart dissenting, that the issue was not purely political and could be dealt with by the judiciary. Chief Justice Warren, speaking for the majority in his last important opinion, held that since Powell was constitutionally qualified for membership,

Congress could exclude him only by the two-thirds majority specified in Article I, Section 5 of the Constitution.

Prigg v. Pennsylvania, 16 Peters 539 (1842), a case dealing with the constitutionality of state fugitive slave laws. In this case a Maryland slave had escaped to Pennsylvania, and the plaintiff, Prigg, had been sent there by the slave's master to bring her back. Due to a Pennsylvania state law that prohibited the return of fugitive slaves to anyone but the slave's master, such an action constituted kidnapping, and Prigg was indicted for the crime. Accordingly, Prigg filed suit in federal court to question the constitutionality of the state law.

The Supreme Court ruled unanimously that the Pennsylvania law and all similar state laws were unconstitutional since they conflicted with the recently enacted federal Fugitive Slave Act. On another issue brought up by this case, however, the Court decided by a vote of six to three, with Justices Taney, Thompson, and Daniel dissenting, that Congress had the exclusive jurisdiction and right to enact legislation with regard to the fugitive slave question. Associate Justice Story, speaking for the majority, held that federal authorities need not obtain the permission or even the cooperation of state authorities in the return of fugitive slaves.

Prize Cases, 2 Black 635 (1863), a series of cases dealing with the right of the president to institute certain military measures without a formal declaration of war. Soon

President Lincoln's early Civil War directives were threatened by the issues in the **Prize Cases,** *but the Court upheld his legal power to establish a naval blockade.*

after the Confederate bombardment of Fort Sumter, South Carolina, in April 1861, President Lincoln ordered the blockade of southern ports. Although Congress did not sanction this order until July, the Navy quickly captured several neutral vessels carrying Confederate cargoes and claimed them to be prizes of war. Even after Congress explicitly sanctioned the blockade, it refused to acknowledge the sovereignty of the Confederacy by declaring a state of war. The owners of the captured ships therefore filed suit for the return of their property on the grounds that without congressional ratification the blockade was unconstitutional and that since no official state of war existed the cargoes were not legally enemy property subject to seizure. At stake in this case was not only the blockade, but all of Lincoln's war directives from April to July 1861.

The case was not heard until 1863, at which time the Supreme Court ruled by a vote of five to four, with Chief Justice Taney and Associate Justices Catron, Clifford, and Nelson dissenting, that President Lincoln was within his legal power to establish the blockade. Associate Justice Grier, speaking for the slim majority, noted that the action of the president must be appropriate to the threat faced by the nation at any given time and that he need not wait until Congress has officially defined a state of war that clearly already exists. As to the status of the captured cargoes, he held that all residents in areas of open rebellion can be legally considered enemies and that their property is subject to seizure as prizes of war.

Proffitt v. Florida, (1976), *See* Furman v. Georgia, Jackson v. Georgia, Branch v. Texas.

Pruneyard Shopping Center v. Robins, 447 U.S. 74 (1980), a case dealing with the right of states to protect the exercise of 1st Amendment rights on private property. The respondent, Robins, was distributing pamphlets and seeking signatures inside Pruneyard Shopping Center. The shopping center prohibited such activity and asked Robins to leave. Robins subsequently filed suit, contending that his right to free speech under the California constitution had been denied.

The Supreme Court held unanimously that a state constitution can permit free speech on privately owned, publicly available shopping centers. Associate Justice Rehnquist, writing for the majority, held that this would not deny the owner's 5th Amendment property rights or his 1st Amendment freedom of speech. Although the U.S. Constitution did not grant an individual the same rights granted by the California constitution, noted Rehnquist, states could recognize more expansive rights than those existing under the federal Constitution. The limitation of freedom of speech is only the extent to which it would infringe on another's rights. Pruneyard Shopping Center had chosen to open its property to the public and if Robins's expressions of free speech did not infringe on another person's federally insured rights then Robins was protected, Rehnquist further noted in his opinion.

The Court's decision in the **Railroad Retirement Board** *case was one of the many defeats in the 1930's of President Roosevelt's New Deal economic programs.*

Railroad Retirement Board v. Alton Railroad Co., 295 U.S. 330 (1935), a case dealing with the power of the federal government to regulate matters only indirectly concerned with interstate commerce. In 1934, Congress passed the Railroad Retirement Act, which established compulsory pension plans for all carriers engaged in interstate trade. One such railroad refused to comply with the terms of the federal law, contending that its provisions were beyond the jurisdiction of the federal government to enforce, and the Railroad Retirement Board, set up by the statute, filed suit in federal court to force compliance.

On May 6, 1935, the Supreme Court held by a vote of five to four, with Chief Justice Hughes and Associate Justices Brandeis, Cardozo, and Stone dissenting, that the Railroad Retirement Act was unconstitutional. Associate Justice Roberts, speaking for the majority, held that not only was such an act beyond the federal government's constitutional power of regulating commerce, it was also a violation of the railroad's 5th Amendment right to due process. This decision, handed down after *Schechter Poultry Corp. v. United States*, was another defeat for New Deal economic programs.

Reagan v. Farmer's Loan and Trust Co., 154 U.S. 362 (1893), a case dealing with the right of states to regulate railroad rates and procedures for appeal. In 1891 the Texas legislature created a railroad commission, granting it the power to classify and regulate rates. The act creating the commission also provided for the appointment of a three-person commission and the establishment of its bureaucratic organization. After a challenge to this statute, the Supreme Court held unanimously that the act was a valid and constitutional exercise of state sovereignty. Associate Justice Brewer, writing for the Court, stated, however, that if a person felt that the rates set by the commission were unjust, he should bring an action against the commissioners in the circuit court of Texas and not against the state of Texas.

Regan v. Wald, 53 U.S.L.W. 3270 (1984), a case dealing with presidential ability to impose restraints on travel to Cuba. In 1977, Congress passed the International Emergency Economic Powers Act limiting presidential power to impose economic embargo against a foreign country. A "grandfather clause" in that act allowed "authorities [that] were being exercised with respect to a country on July 1, 1977," to continue. President Carter had allowed travel to Cuba to resume as of March 29, 1977, and President Reagan reimposed travel restrictions in 1982. A group of people who wished to travel to Cuba challenged these restrictions, bringing suit against secretary of the Treasury Donald Regan, and a court of appeals ruled to enjoin enforcement. However, the Supreme Court granted the government's request for a stay on the grounds of "weighty concerns of foreign policy."

On June 28, 1984, the Supreme Court by a vote of five to four agreed with the government's contention that the president's "authorities" were in place even if they were not in effect on the specified date, and held that President Reagan could reimpose travel restrictions as needed. In the majority opinion, Associate Justice Rehnquist likened the travel regulations to passport restrictions that had been upheld by a 1965 Supreme Court ruling (*Zemel v. Rusk*). Dissenting with the majority's interpretation of congressional intent regarding this act were Associate Justices Blackmun, Brennan, Marshall, and Powell.

Regents of the University of California v. Bakke, 438 U.S. 265 (1978), a case dealing with the constitutionality of racial quotas in federally-funded educational institutions. The medical school of the University of California at Davis had established an admissions policy that required a sixteen percent minimum of minority students in each class. The petitioner, Bakke, was a non-minority applicant who had been denied admission, and he filed suit against the University of California, contending that because of the racial quotas less-qualified students than he had been admitted strictly on the basis of their race. This action, he contended, violated Title IV of the Civil Rights Act of 1964 as well as his equal protection rights under the 14th Amendment. At issue in this case was the constitutionality of "affirmative action" programs intended to reverse traditional racial discrimination.

On June 28, 1978, the Supreme Court held, in two separate votes of five to four, with Associate Justices Blackmun, Brennan, Marshall, and White dissenting, that Bakke's suit should be sustained. Associate Justice Powell, announcing the decision of the Court, held that the equal protection clause of the Constitution prohibits discrimination strictly on the basis of race for whatever motives. The other majority justices, however, preferred to avoid the constitutional issues and ruled that a violation of the Civil Rights Act of 1964 was the issue. This decision did not unequivocally settle the question of "affirmative action" programs and left open the possibility that such programs may be both constitutional and legal if race is only one of several elements in the selection process.

Regional Rail Reorganization Act Cases, 419 U.S. 102 (1974), a case dealing with compensation to be paid to private railroads forced to reorganize by the federal government. In 1973, Congress passed the Regional Rail Reorganization Act, which called for the reorganization of each regional railroad unless the railroad could prove it would be better able to serve the public under a plan of its own. The Penn-Central Railroad subsequently brought suit attacking the constitutionality of the act and claiming that it would suffer significant losses as a result of the reorganization.

The Supreme Court held by a vote of seven to two, with Associate Justices Douglas and Stewart dissenting, that the Penn-Central's claim could be brought under the Tucker Act, which provided for a remedy to be given to a person who brings an action against the government. Associate Justice Brennan, writing for the majority, stated that if Penn-Central's claims of unjust compensation for its railroad were justified, it was entitled to relief under the Tucker Act.

Reynolds v. Sims, 377 U.S. 533 (1964), a case dealing with the constitutional standards for state legislative apportionment. The apportionment of the Alabama legislature was based on the 1900 federal census and thus seriously discriminated against voters who lived in areas whose population had grown disproportionately in the intervening years. An Alabama resident subsequently filed suit in district court, contending that his equal protection clause rights were violated by the existing situation.

The Supreme Court held, by a vote of eight to one, with Associate Justice Harlan dissenting, that the district court's order for temporary apportionment should be affirmed. Chief Justice Warren, writing for the majority, held that the fundamental principle of representative government is one of equal representation for equal numbers of people and, therefore, votes cannot be weighed differently on the basis of where the voters happen to reside. Each state district, Warren argued, must contain as nearly an equal population as possible, and to this end, a state must apportion its legislative districts on the basis of population.

Richmond Newspapers Inc. v. Commonwealth of Virginia, 448 U.S. 555 (1980), a case dealing with the constitutional right of the press to attend criminal court proceedings. A defendant in a criminal case requested that his trial be closed to the press, contending that coverage by the media and the ensuing publicity would endanger his right to a fair trial. When the presiding judge granted that request, the petitioners, representatives of a local newspaper who had been denied access to the proceedings, subsequently filed suit, claiming that such an action by the court violated the 1st Amendment guarantees of free press. At issue in this case were the competing rights of the press to collect and disseminate information and the 6th Amendment right of a defendant to a fair trial by an impartial jury.

On July 2, 1980, the Supreme Court decided by a vote of seven to one, with Associate Justice Rehnquist dissenting and Associate Justice Powell not participating, that the suit of the Richmond newspapers should be sustained. Chief Justice Burger, speaking for the majority, acknowledged the 6th Amendment rights of defendants and the power of judges to close their courtrooms, but ruled that in this case there was no clearly demonstrable danger of publicity prejudicing the outcome of the trial. This decision established the precedent that the press must be allowed to attend court proceedings unless the reasons for the closure are specific and are made public by the presiding judge.

Roberts v. Louisiana, 431 U.S. 633 (1976), a case dealing with the constitutional procedures for the imposition of capital punishment. The petitioner, Roberts, was indicted, tried, and convicted of first-degree murder of a police officer engaged in the performance of his lawful duties. The defendant subsequently appealed this conviction, contending that the mandatory death sentence imposed in this case by Louisiana law violated the 8th and 14th Amendments. On July 2, 1976, the Supreme Court ruled, *per curiam*, with Chief Justice Burger and Associate Justices Blackmun, White, and Rehnquist dissenting, that since the Louisiana statute did not allow for consideration of particularized mitigating factors, which was essential for the capital-sentencing procedure to be constitutional, the conviction of Roberts should be overturned.

Roberts v. United States Jaycees, 104 S. Ct. 3244 (1984), a case dealing with state antidiscrimination laws as they pertain to the freedom of association in private organizations. When the national Jaycees organization attempted in 1978 to revoke the charters of the Minneapolis and St. Paul chapters because of their practice of admitting women in defiance of the national policy, the local chapters filed discrimination charges with the Minnesota Department of Human Rights. The national Jaycees lost their case in district court but won in the U.S. court of appeals. At issue was a state law prohibiting sex discrimination in places of public accommodation.

On July 3, 1984, the Supreme Court unanimously overturned the appeals court ruling. Associate Justice Brennan could find no justification for the Jaycees' claim that admitting women would prevent the achievement of their goals. The Court did not specify the extent to which this ruling applied to more traditional private clubs.

Roe v. Wade, 410 U.S. 113 (1973), a case dealing with a state's right to regulate abortions. A Texas statute that barred abortion except to save the mother's life was challenged in the courts. On January 22, 1973, the Supreme Court held by a vote of seven to two, with Associate Justices White and Rehnquist dissenting, that a woman has a "fundamental right" to privacy, founded in the 14th Amendment, and severely limited the ability of the states to control abortions. The Court also found that a fetus was not a "person" under the terms of the 14th Amendment. The majority opinion was written by Associate Justice Blackmun.

The Court's opinion held that a woman and her physician can jointly decide whether to terminate a pregnancy during the first trimester, that a state may set standards for abortions during the second trimester of pregnancy, and that only during the third trimester may the state bar all abortions except those to save the mother's life. The Court's decision in *Roe* and a companion case, *Doe v. Bolton* (1973), affected the abortion laws in forty-six states and led to changes in abortion procedures throughout the United States. The decision was vehemently attacked by anti-abortion groups and became a subject for political debate, including attempts to outlaw abortion by constitutional amendment. Subsequent court tests aimed at reversing or limiting the effect of *Roe*.

Rosenbloom v. Metromedia, 403 U.S. 29 (1971), a case dealing with the liability of the news media to a state civil libel action brought by a private individual for a defamatory falsehood reported in a news broadcast about the individual's involvement in an event of general or public interest. In this case the petitioner, after his acquittal on criminal obscenity charges, filed suit against Metromedia for libel. The respondent's radio station had broadcast news reports of the petitioner's arrest for possession of obscene material. The news reports used the terms "smut literature racket" and "girlie-book peddlers." In the libel suit the trial jury found for the petitioner, but the court of appeals reversed.

The Supreme Court ruled unanimously that the *New York Times v. Sullivan*'s knowing-or-reckless-falsity standard should apply not only to public figures, but to private citizens as well. Associate Justice Brennan, writing for the Court, held that when a matter is a subject of public or general interest, it does not become less so merely because a private individual is involved. The focus of the public is on the conduct of the participant and the effect, conduct, and significance of the conduct, and, therefore, the public has an interest in seeing that a criminal law is adequately enforced. Brennan further held that the petitioner's argument that the private individual need prove only that the publisher failed to exercise "reasonable care" cannot be reconciled with the 1st Amendment.

Rostker v. Goldberg, 453 U.S. 57 (1981), a case dealing with the constitutionality of the exclusion of women from the military draft. In an attempt to compile a list of names of potential conscripts in a time of national emergency, Congress enacted the Military Selective Service Act, one provision of which required the registration of young men. A class action suit was filed in federal court challenging the constitutionality of the registration program, on the grounds that the exemption of women from registration violated the men's 5th Amendment due process right. The district court sustained the challenge, and the federal government appealed to the Supreme Court.

On June 25, 1981, the Supreme Court held by a vote of six to three, with Associate Justices Brennan, Marshall, and White dissenting, that the Military Selective Service Act was constitutional. Associate Justice Rehnquist, speaking for the majority, held that since military tradition and policy differentiated between the potential use of men and women, the distinction in the law was not merely a discriminatory one. The purpose of the law, Rehnquist held, was to identify potential combat troops and therefore the exclusion of women, in accordance with accepted military practice, was constitutionally justified.

Roth v. United States, 354 U.S. 476 (1957), a case dealing with the legal definition of obscenity and its relation to the 1st Amendment freedom of speech. The petitioner was convicted of violating a state anti-obscenity law, and he appealed his conviction, contending that any attempt to restrict the material that he sold was a violation of his 1st Amendment rights.

On June 24, 1957, the Supreme Court held by a vote of seven to one, with Associate Justice Harlan dissenting, that Roth's conviction should be upheld. Associate Justice Brennan, speaking for the majority, held that it was within the legitimate police power of state governments to restrict or prohibit the sale of obscene materials. The definition of obscenity presented by the Court in this case was that any material that would seem to appeal primarily to "prurient interests" was obscene. This decision was announced on the same day as the companion case of *Alberts v. California*. The exclusion of obscene material from 1st Amendment protection was later reaffirmed in *Miller v. California* (1973), in which local rather than national standards became the deciding factor.

Runyon v. McCrary; Fairfax-Brewster School, Inc. v. Gonzales; Southern Independent School Association v. McCrary, 427 U.S. 160 (1976), a case dealing with racial segregation in private schools. The petitioners, Michael McCrary and Colin Gonzales, were denied admission to a private school in Arlington, Virginia, solely because of their race. Their parents filed suit against the owner of the school, Runyon, contending that his refusal to admit their children to the school was a violation of the Civil Rights Act of 1866. After an initial judgment in favor of the petitioners, Runyon appealed.

On June 25, 1976, the Supreme Court held by a vote of seven to two, with Associate Justices Rehnquist and White dissenting, that Runyon's action was a violation of the Civil Rights Act of 1866. Associate Justice Stewart, speaking for the majority, held that since Congress had the constitutional right under the 13th Amendment to legislate against racial discrimination in the making of contracts and since admission to the school in question was open to the general public, denial of admission strictly on the basis of race was illegal. This decision restricted the earlier ruling of the Court in *Jones v. Alfred Mayer Co.* (1968), limiting the application of the Civil Rights Act of 1866 to cases in which contracts were involved rather than to all cases of private racial discrimination.

Samuels v. MacKell, 401 U.S. 66 (1971), a case dealing with the judicial procedures for challenging the constitutionality of a state law. The appellants were all indicted in a New York state court on charges of criminal anarchy. They subsequently filed suit in federal district court seeking declaratory and injunctive relief against their prosecutions on the grounds that the law is unconstitutional.

The Supreme Court ruled unanimously that there was no showing by the appellants that they had suffered irreparable injury by virtue of their being prosecuted in the state courts, where they could make their constitutional contentions. Therefore, there was no basis for federal injunctive relief. Associate Justice Black, writing for the Court, held that the appellants should have been denied declaratory relief without consideration of the constitutional claims' merits. The same principles that governed the propriety of federal injunctions of state criminal proceedings, Black noted, governed the issuance of federal declaratory judgments in connection with such proceedings. The Court decided *Younger v. Harris* (1971) on similar facts.

San Antonio Independent School District v. Rodriguez, 411 U.S. 1 (1973), a case dealing with the constitutionality of certain government funding systems for the public schools. The petitioner, Rodriguez, was a resident of a predominantly poor school subdistrict in which the highest school taxes were paid. Despite the high tax rate, however, the students in this subdistrict were allocated less money per capita than were students in other, wealthier subdistricts in which the school tax rate was lower yet the total revenues were higher. Rodriguez and a number of other residents of the poorer subdistrict filed suit, contending that because of the disparity in funding for the public schools, they were denied their 14th Amendment equal protection rights. At issue in this case was the constitutionality of school funding systems based on the amount of revenue raised in each subdistrict and its possible discriminatory effect in favoring wealthier districts.

On March 21, 1973, the Supreme Court held by a vote of five to four, with Associate Justices Brennan, Douglas, Marshall, and White dissenting, that Rodriguez's suit should not be sustained. Associate Justice Powell, speaking for the majority, held that education was not one of the fundamental rights protected by the 14th Amendment and that in any

Before the Santa Clara County *decision, Chief Justice Waite held that the Court could review the case because corporations should be considered persons and were therefore entitled to 14th Amendment protection.*

case, classification by wealth was not an unconstitutional act of discrimination against a "suspect class."

Santa Clara County v. Southern Pacific Railroad Co., 118 U.S. 394 (1886), a case dealing with the legal status of private corporations and their right to constitutional protection against arbitrary acts of state governments. The background of this case was the ongoing conflict between state governments and the railroads, and the issue in question was whether state taxation of railroads, which the railroads believed was unreasonable, could be reviewed by the federal courts. Before the case was actually presented, Chief Justice Waite made a judicial ruling that would greatly affect the outcome; he held that corporations, as legitimate legal entities, should be considered to be "persons" and thereby

entitled to the protection of the 14th Amendment, which guaranteed that no "person" should be deprived of life, liberty, or property without due process of law.

In accordance with Waite's definition, the Court ruled unanimously on May 10, 1886, that the state taxation of the railroad should be subject to the scrutiny of the Supreme Court. Associate Justice Harlan, speaking for the Court, held that the railroad's tax liability was calculated on the basis of incomplete and arbitrary criteria and was therefore a violation of its constitutional rights.

Schall v. Martin, 104 S. Ct. 2403 (1984), a case dealing with the rights of state judges to keep potentially dangerous juveniles in detention centers while awaiting trial. In 1982 a federal appeals court ruled unconstitutional New

York's statute against juvenile detention, calling it "punishment without proof of guilt."

On June 4, 1984, the Supreme Court reversed that ruling, six to three. Associate Justice Rehnquist wrote the majority opinion, which was based on the belief that since juveniles "are always in some form of custody" anyway, pretrial detention is primarily a matter of transfer of custody from parent to state. Justice Rehnquist concluded that detention "serves a legitimate regulatory purpose compatible with the 'fundamental fairness' demanded by the due process clause in juvenile proceedings." Although the Court recognized that "in some circumstances detention of a juvenile would not pass constitutional muster," these cases must be reviewed individually. Dissenting Justices Marshall, Brennan, and Stevens argued against the simple "transfer of custody" assertion of the majority and against the lack of standards for determining when detention is appropriate.

Schechter Poultry Corp. v. United States, 295 U.S. 495 (1935), a case dealing with the constitutionality of the National Industrial Recovery Act of 1933. The petitioner, Schechter, who was in the poultry business in New York, was convicted for violating the act's minimum wage, maximum hour, and trade practice provisions. Ninety-six percent of the poultry marketed in New York came from other states, but Schechter sold only to local poultry dealers; his activities were all intrastate. Schechter challenged his conviction on the following points: the act unconstitutionally delegated legislative power and the application of the act to intrastate activities exceeded the commerce power.

On May 27, 1935, the Supreme Court held unanimously that Schechter's conviction should be overturned. Chief Justice Hughes, writing for the Court, held that the interstate transactions regarding poultry ended when the shipments reached Schechter's Brooklyn slaughterhouse. Since his activities were not in a current or flow of interstate commerce and did not directly "affect" interstate commerce, the hours and wages of Schechter's employees had no direct relation to interstate commmerce. In applying the "affecting commerce" rationale, Hughes insisted that "there is a necessary and well-established distinction between direct and indirect effects." Congress may therefore not extend a regulation of interstate commerce to reach intrastate activities. This decision was a major defeat for the advocates of the New Deal program who saw far-reaching federal regulation of the national economy as the most efficient means of ending the Depression.

Schenck v. United States, 249 U.S. 47 (1919), a case dealing with the extent of protection afforded by the 1st Amendment guarantees of freedom of speech. In 1917, after the outbreak of World War I, Congress passed the Espionage Act, which, among other provisions, imposed stiff penalties on anyone who offered comfort or aid to the enemy through the spoken or written word. The petitioner, Schenck, had been convicted of urging young men who had been drafted into the armed service to refuse induction. He appealed the conviction, contending that the law was a violation of his 1st Amendment rights.

On March 3, 1919, the Supreme Court ruled unanimously that Schenck's conviction should be upheld. Associate Justice Holmes, speaking for the Court, held that the 1st Amendment guarantee of the freedom of speech is not unlimited. When certain acts or words present a "clear and present danger" to the well-being of society, Holmes wrote, it is within the power of the government—it is, in fact, its obligation—to avert the threat that is thereby posed. This was the first test of the limits of the 1st Amendment protection, and the standard of a "clear and present danger" would be used frequently after World War II in the anti-communist prosecutions of the early Cold War years.

School District of Abington Township v. Schempp, 274 U.S. 203 (1963), a case dealing with compulsory prayer in the public schools. The respondents, the Schempp family, were members of the Unitarian Church and challenged local high school opening exercises involving the reading of Bible verses and the recitation of the Lord's Prayer, contending that they violated the constitutional separation of church and state.

The Supreme Court held by a vote of eight to one, with Associate Justice Stewart dissenting, that the 1st Amendment establishment clause (that the United States may not participate in the establishment of religion) prohibited state laws and practices requiring the selection and reading at the opening of the school day of verses from the Bible and the recitation of the Lord's Prayer by the students in unison. Associate Justice Clark, writing for the majority, held that in order for the statute to withstand the structures of the establishment clause there must be a secular legislative purpose and a primary effect that neither advances nor inhibits religion. The Court found that the statute that required Bible reading and prayer recitation did not withstand these requirements and therefore was unconstitutional under the establishment clause.

Scott v. Sandford, 12 Howard 299 (1857), the most important pre-Civil War case addressed by the Supreme Court dealing with the issue of slavery in the territories and with the legal status of slaves. The petitioner, a black slave named Dred Scott, was taken by his master, John Sandford, from the slave state of Missouri to the free state of Illinois and later to the territory of Wisconsin, which had been declared free according to the Missouri Compromise. Eventually Scott was brought back to Missouri by his master, but he filed suit in a Missouri court for his freedom, contending that since he had been resident in free territory, his legal status had changed. The Missouri court upheld Scott's contention and declared him to be free, but that decision was reversed in the state supreme court.

The action then moved to the federal court system as a suit between residents of different states, for Scott filed an

The Court's 1857 decision that Dred Scott was not a citizen of Missouri, while intended to settle questions about slavery, actually led to sharper disagreements and held that the Missouri Compromise was unconstitutional.

assault charge against his owner, who was a resident of the state of New York. For the case to be heard, however, Scott had to prove that he was a citizen of Missouri and the first federal judge who heard the case ruled against Scott. The case was subsequently appealed to the Supreme Court. The questions brought up by this case were of the greatest significance for the future of the institution of slavery: did a slave become free when he entered a free state? And, was a slave actually a citizen of the United States at all?

The Court announced its decision on March 7, 1857, only three days after the inauguration of Pres. James Buchanan. Each justice filed a separate opinion, yet the decision of Chief Justice Taney (from which Justices Curtis and McLean dissented) was regarded as the ruling of the Court. On the question of Scott's legal status, Taney held that according to the Constitution, "the African race were not included under the name of the citizens of a state." As to the issue of Scott's becoming free when he moved to the free state of Illinois, Taney ruled that the laws of the state in which the petitioner was currently resident, namely the slave state of Missouri, should apply. As to Scott's contention that he had been a resident of a territory in which the federal government had prohibited slavery, Taney argued that the Missouri Compromise was itself unconstitutional, since the right to own slaves had been acknowledged by the Constitution. This decision, intended to settle the legal question of

slavery, actually resulted in an even greater disagreement. It was ultimately rendered meaningless by the adoption of the 13th Amendment in 1865, which ended slavery forever, and by the adoption of the 14h Amendment in 1868, which put an end to all legal questions of whether black Americans were citizens of the United States.

Scottsboro Cases, (1932, 1935), *See* Powell v. Alabama.

Second Legal Tender Case (Knox v. Lee, Parker v. Davis), 12 Wallace 457 (1871), two related cases in which the Supreme Court reviewed its previous ruling on the unconstitutionality of federally-issued paper currency. Soon after the Court issued its decision in *Hepburn v. Griswold* (1870), U.S. Attorney General Ebenezer Hoar brought the matter before the Supreme Court again. This time, the Court held by a vote of five to four, with Chief Justice Chase and Associate Justices Clifford, Field, and Nelson dissenting, that Congress was acting within its constitutionally-derived powers in making paper currency legal tender for the payment of government debts.

Associate Justice Strong, speaking for the majority, held that the wartime issuance of paper currency was nothing less than a governmental act of self-preservation and that, accordingly, it should be considered to be protected by Article I, Section 8 of the Constitution, which gives Congress the right to enact "all laws which shall be necessary and proper." To revoke the Legal Tender Acts, Justice Strong argued, would be to throw the nation's economy into chaos, and, rebutting the various arguments brought forth in *Hepburn v. Griswold*, he ruled in favor of the laws in question. One of the crucial factors that led to the reversal of the Court's previous decision was the nomination of both Justice Strong and Justice Bradley in the interim. The fact that both nominees had clearly expressed implicit judicial support of the Legal Tender Acts led to public charges that President Grant had "packed" the court in an attempt to uphold the law.

Selective Draft Cases, 245 U.S. 366 (1918), a series of cases dealing with the power of Congress to enact legislation calling for a compulsory military draft. On January 7, 1918, the Supreme Court unanimously upheld this power, ruling that compulsory military service was neither repugnant to a free government nor in conflict with the constitutional guarantees of individual liberty. Chief Justice White, writing for the Court, held that the law granting Congress this power was enacted in order to supply an increase in the military force, which was necessary due to the existing emergency of World War I. Consequently, the Selective Draft Law was upheld as a necessary and proper method for executing powers specifically granted to Congress by the Constitution.

Shapiro v. Thompson, 394 U.S. 618 (1969), a case dealing with the constitutionality of minimum residency requirements for welfare recipients. The Thompsons had

Chief Justice White wrote the Court's opinion in the Selective Draft Cases, *which upheld the legitimacy of a compulsory draft during World War I.*

been denied welfare benefits solely because they had not been residents of Connecticut for a full year prior to their applications. They subsequently filed suit in district court, receiving a ruling that the state's denial of welfare benefits constituted an invidious discrimination denying them equal protection of the law. The state of Connecticut, represented by Shapiro, appealed this ruling to the Supreme Court, arguing that the statute preserved the fiscal integrity of state public assistance programs by discouraging the influx of poor families needing assistance.

On April 21, 1969, the Supreme Court held by a vote of seven to two, with Chief Justice Warren and Associate Justice Harlan dissenting, that a state may not create a one-year residency requirement as a condition for receiving state welfare assistance. Associate Justice Brennan, writing for the majority, held that the state's purpose was to inhibit immigration by needy persons and was constitutionally impermissible as a burden on the right to travel. The argument that the statute intended to discourage immigration of needy people seeking solely to obtain larger benefits did not justify the statute. The assertion that other administrative objectives were served by the one-year requirement did not satisfy the strict scrutiny standard, and since the state statute violated the equal protection clause, it was ruled invalid.

Shelley v. Kraemer, 334 U.S. 1 (1948), a case dealing with the constitutionality of racial discrimination in pri-

vate housing. The petitioner, Shelley, a black citizen of Missouri, purchased property in a neighborhood that excluded blacks by the terms of a restrictive covenant in all deeds. The owner of the adjoining property, Kraemer, filed suit in state court to prevent Shelley from taking possession of the property. The supreme court of Missouri ruled in favor of Kraemer, and Shelley subsequently appealed this judgment, contending that the court order that enforced the racially restrictive covenant was a "state action" in violation of his 14th Amendment rights. Shelley's case was argued before the Supreme Court by future Associate Justice Marshall, then serving as director of the National Association for the Advancement of Colored People (NAACP) Legal Defense Fund.

On May 3, 1948, the Supreme Court held by a vote of six to zero, with Associate Justices Jackson, Reed, and Rutledge not participating, that the Missouri supreme court order should be reversed. Chief Justice Vinson, speaking for the Court, held that while the restrictive covenant itself was a private action and therefore beyond government jurisdiction, it could not be enforced by the state. This decision was later extended by the ruling of the Court in *Jones v. Alfred Mayer Co.* (1968), which held that any form of racial discrimination in private housing was a violation of the 13th Amendment.

Sheppard v. Maxwell, 384 U.S. 333 (1966), a case dealing with the extent of 14th Amendment protection against prejudicial publicity in state criminal proceedings. The petitioner, Dr. Sam Sheppard, was convicted for the second-degree murder of his wife, and he subsequently applied for a federal *habeas corpus* writ, contending that the trial judge had failed to protect him sufficiently from the massive, pervasive, and prejudicial publicity that attended his prosecution.

The Supreme Court held by a vote of eight to one, with only Associate Justice Black dissenting, that the publicity did prevent Sheppard from receiving a fair trial consistent with the 14th Amendment's due process clause. Associate Justice Clark, writing for the majority, held that freedom of discussion should be given the widest range compatible with the fair and orderly administration of justice, but it must never be allowed to divert a trial from its purpose of adjudicating controversies according to legal procedures based on evidence received only in open court. Clark further ruled that identifiable prejudice to the accused need not be shown if the totality of the circumstances raises the probability of prejudice, and, in this case, the trial court failed to invoke procedures that would have guaranteed Sheppard a fair trial. The Court, for instance, could have adopted stricter rules for reporters' use of the courtroom, limited the number of reporters, and supervised their courtroom conduct. Also, the Court should have insulated the witnesses and controlled the release of leads, information, and gossip to the press by police, witnesses, and counsel.

Sipuel v. University of Oklahoma, 332 U.S. 631 (1948), a case dealing with the constitutionality of racial discrimination in certain state educational facilities. The petitioner was denied admission to the University of Oklahoma solely because she was black. Application for a writ of *mandamus* was made by the petitioner in the district court and was refused. The Oklahoma Supreme Court affirmed the district court's judgment. The Supreme Court *per curiam* reversed the rulings of the lower courts. The Court held that a person qualified to receive professional legal education offered by a state cannot be denied such education because of race. The state must provide such education for petitioner in conformity with the 14th Amendment's equal protection clause.

Slaughterhouse Cases (The Butchers' Benevolent Association of New Orleans v. The Crescent City Livestock Landing and Slaughterhouse Co., Esteben v. Louisiana), 16 Wallace 36 (1873), two related cases dealing with the right of state governments to create monopolies in private industry. In 1869 the Louisiana legislature enacted a law that authorized the operation of only one private slaughterhouse in the city of New Orleans. Since this state-sanctioned monopoly obviously deprived many of the city's butchers of employment, they filed suit in federal court for relief. Associate Justice Bradley heard this case on circuit and ruled that the state law was a violation of the spirit of the 14th Amendment, for he interpreted its "privileges and immunities" clause as protecting the right of every American citizen to pursue his chosen profession. The case was subsequently appealed to the Supreme Court and the side of the butchers was argued by former Associate Justice Campbell, who had resigned from the Court at the start of the Civil War.

On April 14, 1873, the Court held by a vote of five to four, with Chief Justice Chase and Associate Justices Bradley, Field, and Swayne dissenting, that the Louisiana legislature was not acting unconstitutionally in its enforcement of the slaughterhouse monopoly. Associate Justice Miller, speak-

*The Court's decision in the **Slaughterhouse Cases**, in which Justice Field wrote the opinion, restricted the federal government in using the 14th Amendment to overrule state actions.*

ing for the majority, held that the civil rights of U.S. citizens protected by the 14th Amendment did not include the right to engage in a particular business. Furthermore, Miller held that a particular profession could not be considered to be "property," which would be protected by the "due process" of that amendment. This was the first judicial test of the 14th Amendment, and it severely limited the extent to which the federal government could utilize it to overrule state laws.

Smith v. Allwright, 321 U.S. 649 (1944), a case dealing with the constitutionality of racial discrimination in state primary election procedures. The Democratic Party of Texas regularly excluded blacks from participation in its primary elections, which determined the various Democratic candidates for state and national office. The petitioner, a black citizen of Texas, filed suit in federal court for an injunction against this practice, contending that it effectively prevented his full participation in the electoral process. His case was presented before the Supreme Court by future Associate Justice Marshall, then serving as director of the National Association for the Advancement of Colored People (NAACP) Legal Defense Fund.

On April 3, 1944, the Supreme Court held by a vote of eight to one, with only Associate Justice Roberts dissenting, that the Texas Democrats must open their primary elections to all Democratic voters regardless of race. Associate Justice Reed, speaking for the majority, held that the discriminatory practice violated the 14th and 15th Amendment rights of the black voters in the state. This decision reversed the earlier ruling of the court in *Grovey v. Townsend* (1935).

Smith v. Turner, (1849), See Passenger Cases.

Smyth v. Ames, 169 U.S. 466 (1898), a case dealing with the legal status of private corporations and their right to due process. At issue in this case was a Nebraska state law that determined that maximum rates for railroads operating within its boundaries should be based on the present valuation of railroad property. The representatives of the railroads affected by this law argued that the rates should be based on the original cost of the property, which had subsequently dropped dramatically in a time of economic recession. Since the Nebraska law provided no right of review, the railroads appealed to the Supreme Court on the grounds that since corporations had been legally classified as "persons" by the opinion of the Court in *Santa Clara County v. Southern Pacific Railroad Co.* (1886), they were therefore deprived, in this arbitrary rate-setting, of due process of law.

On March 7, 1898, the Supreme Court decided by a vote of seven to zero, with Associate Justice McKenna and Chief Justice Fuller not participating, that the contention of the railroad should be sustained. Associate Justice Harlan, speaking for the majority, held that private corporations are entitled to a fair return on their investment and that state governments should consider this criterion in their determination of regulated rates. In the case of a dispute between a corporation and a state government, the matter, Harlan ruled,

should be resolved in the federal courts. This decision amplified the earlier rulings of the Court in *Chicago, Milwaukee, and St. Paul Railroad Co. v. Minnesota* (1890) and in *Reagan v. Farmers' Loan and Trust Co.* (1894), in restricting the power of the states to regulate private industry first set forth in *Munn v. Illinois* (1877).

Sniadach v. Family Finance Corp., 395 U.S. 337 (1969), a case dealing with the constitutional guidelines for garnishment proceedings. The respondents had instituted a garnishment action against the petitioner, Sniadach. Under the garnishment procedure in Wisconsin, the clerk of the court was empowered to issue a summons at the creditor's lawyer's request. The creditor then had ten days to serve the summons and complaint on the debtor after service on the garnishee, the employer. The wages could be unfrozen if the wage earner prevailed on the merits of the suit on the debt. The petitioner here moved that the garnishment proceedings should be dismissed for failure to meet procedural due process requirements.

The Supreme Court held by a vote of eight to one, with only Associate Justice Black dissenting, the Wisconsin's prejudgment garnishment of wages procedure violated due process. Associate Justice Douglas, writing for the majority, ruled that the procedure took property without notice and prior hearing and that it therefore violated the fundamental principles of procedural due process.

Solem v. Helm, 463 U.S. 277 (1983), a case dealing with the constitutionality of certain criminal sentences imposed by state recidivist statutes. The respondent, Helm, was convicted of writing a no-account check for $100. The ordinary maximum punishment for such a crime was five years in prison and a $5,000 fine. However, the respondent, under a South Dakota recidivist statute, was sentenced to life imprisonment without parole. This sentence was based on the fact that the respondent had six prior felony convictions.

The Supreme Court held by a vote of five to four, with Chief Justice Burger and Associate Justices White, Rehnquist, and O'Connor dissenting, that the 8th Amendment disallows sentences that are disproportionate to the crime committed. Associate Justice Powell, writing for the majority, held that in order to determine what sentence is proportionate, one had to look to other similarly situated jurisdictions and to how they sentenced the same offenders. The crime of writing a no-account check was a less serious crime, and although the petitioner could be classified a habitual felon, life imprisonment was nonetheless a severely disproportionate penalty for the crime committed.

South Carolina v. Katzenbach, 383 U.S. 301 (1966), a case dealing with the constitutionality of several provisions of the Voting Rights Act of 1965 that were directed mainly at eliminating racial discrimination. On March 7, 1966, in response to a suit brought by the state of South Carolina, the Supreme Court upheld the provisions as a

The 1881 Court, led by Chief Justice Waite, passes from the robing room to the Supreme Court Chamber. This Court upheld a federal income tax in **Springer v. United States** *because it was not a direct tax.*

proper exercise of congressional power under Section 2 of the 15th Amendment, with only Associate Justice Black dissenting in part.

Chief Justice Warren, writing for the majority, ruled that "Congress could use any rational means to effectuate the constitutional prohibition of racial discrimination in voting." The provisions of the act prescribing remedies of voting discrimination were found to be clearly legitimate responses to the problem and the specific remedies in the act were appropriate means of combatting the evil. In examining the specific remedies, the Court focused on the coverage formula for determining the localities in which literacy tests and similar voting qualifications were to be suspended for a period of five years. The areas covered by the act were found to be an appropriate target for the new remedies.

Springer v. United States, 102 U.S. 586 (1881), a case dealing with the constitutionality of a federal income tax. The petitioner, Springer, refused to pay the income tax assessed against him, and certain lands of his were seized and sold. The United States became the purchaser of the lands, received a deed, and brought ejectment against Springer. The central question was whether the tax, which was levied on the income, gains, and profits of Springer, was a direct tax.

The Supreme Court ruled unanimously that it was not a direct tax. Associate Justice Swayne, writing for the Court, held that the collector acted in good faith and it was not

improper for him to sell the lands. The state statute under which the lands were separately assessed had no application to Springer's proceedings. Swayne argued that since Congress has the power "to lay and collect taxes, duties, imposts and excises," it may, to enforce their payment, authorize the distraint and sale of either real or personal property. The owner of the property to which this is done is therefore not deprived of it without due process of the law. The duty, which the internal revenue acts provided should be assessed, collected, and paid upon gains, profits, and incomes, was an excise or duty and not a direct tax.

Standard Oil Company of New Jersey v. United States, 221 U.S. 1 (1911), a case dealing with the definition of an illegal commercial trust. The Justice Department prosecuted the Standard Oil Company for violation of the Sherman Antitrust Act, and a federal district court ruled that the company's control of the various components of the oil industry must end. Representatives of the Standard Oil Company appealed the decision, and on May 15, 1911, the Supreme Court decided by a vote of eight to one, with Associate Justice Harlan dissenting in part, that the judgment of the lower court should be sustained.

Chief Justice White, speaking for the majority, held that the management of the Standard Oil Company had clearly conspired to eliminate free competition in the oil industry, but the most significant part of his opinion dealt with the legal definition of a trust. Up to that time, the

Chief Justice White (**left**) *wrote the Court's opinion in the Standard Oil antitrust case, establishing a "rule of reason" followed in subsequent cases. He was joined in the opinion by Associate Justice McKenna* (**right**).

Sherman Antitrust Act had been interpreted unambiguously; as in *Northern Securities Co. v. United States* (1904), when *any* combination of interests that obstructed free trade was seen by the Court as a violation of the law. In this case, however, the Chief Justice argued that only those trusts, like Standard Oil, that restrict competition to an "unreasonable" degree are illegal. This subjective distinction was the reason for Justice Harlan's partial dissent in this case, in which he argued that the Supreme Court did not have the authority to make any arbitrary determinations since the Sherman Act had clearly prohibited all trusts. Despite Harlan's opposing arguments, the "rule of reason" was thereafter recognized as the central criterion for the determination of illegal business trusts.

Stanley v. Georgia, 394 U.S. 557 (1969), a case dealing with the constitutionality of state laws prohibiting the private possession of obscene materials. While searching the appellant's home for evidence of his alleged illegal gambling activities, officers found some films in his bedroom that were later examined and deemed to be obscene. The appellant was arrested, indicted, tried, and convicted for knowingly having possession of obscene material. Stanley subsequently appealed this conviction, contending that the obscenity statute was unconstitutional because it punished mere private possession of obscene matter. The Georgia Supreme Court relied on *Roth v. United States* (1957) to uphold the statute.

The Supreme Court unanimously reversed the ruling of the Georgia Supreme Court. Associate Justice Marshall, writing for the Court, held that *Roth* did not apply because it involved governmental power to prohibit or regulate certain public actions respecting obscene matter. This case, Marshall argued, involved a statute punishing mere private possession of obscene material. He further ruled that a state may not prohibit mere possession of obscene matter on the ground that it may lead to antisocial conduct, since the Constitution protects the right to receive information, regardless of its social worth. It also protects the right generally to be free from governmental intrusions into one's privacy and control of one's thoughts. Finally, a state may not proscribe such possession on the ground that it is a necessary incident to a statutory scheme prohibiting distribution of obscene material.

Steward Machine Co. v. Davis, 301 U.S. 548 (1937), a case dealing with the constitutional right of the federal government to use its taxing power to regulate interstate commerce. In 1935, Congress passed the Social Security Act, which required employers of eight or more persons to pay a federal tax based on the wages paid. An important provision of the law was that the employers whose state governments provided unemployment compensation programs that complied with federal standards would receive a tax credit. The Steward Machine Company of Alabama paid the social security tax but immediately filed suit in federal court for a refund, contending that the Social Security Act was unconstitutional since its purpose was clearly to pressure state governments to adopt federally-approved unemployment compensation plans.

On May 27, 1937, the Supreme Court decided by a vote of five to four, with Associate Justices Butler, McReynolds, Sutherland, and Van Devanter dissenting, that the suit of the Steward Machine Company should not be sustained. Associate Justice Cardozo, speaking for the majority, held that the provision of the Social Security Act in question was constitutional, since the states were in no sense coerced to act in a certain way. This decision was the first test of the constitutionality of Social Security; a second came on the same day in *Helvering v. Davis*.

Stromberg v. California, 283 U.S. 359 (1931), a case dealing with the right of states to restrict certain political demonstrations. The petitioner, Stromberg, the director of a Communist summer camp for children, was convicted of the violation of a state anti-sedition law for requiring the campers to salute a red hammer and sickle flag every morning. She subsequently appealed the conviction, contending that the state law violated her 1st Amendment right to free speech.

On May 18, 1931, the Supreme Court decided by a vote of seven to two, with Associate Justices Butler and McReynolds dissenting, that the California law was unconstitutional. Chief Justice Hughes, speaking for the majority, held that the state's prohibition against even the symbolic advocacy of a violent overthrow of the existing government was impermissibly vague, since it left to the prosecuting authorities the subjective determination of which symbols were permitted and which were not. This decision marked a shift away from the conservative tendency of the Court to uphold state anti-sedition laws, as in *Gitlow v. New York* (1925) and *Whitney v. California* (1929), and to reassert the primacy of 1st Amendment rights.

Sturges v. Crowninshield, 4 Wheaton 122 (1819), a case dealing with the constitutionality of state bankruptcy laws as they apply to the protection of the obligation of contracts. The New York legislature passed a law retroactively releasing bankrupt debtors from their financial obligations to their creditors, and the petitioner, one of the creditors, appealed to the Supreme Court, contending that the law was a violation of the protection of the obligation of contracts, as specified in Article I, Section 10 of the Constitution.

The Court held unanimously that the state law was void, but Chief Justice Marshall, speaking for the Court, held that while this particular law was invalid, states may legitimately enact insolvency laws since Congress had not yet passed a uniform bankruptcy law as explicitly authorized by Article I, Section 8 of the Constitution. This decision was later expanded by the opinion of the Court in *Ogden v. Saunders* (1827).

Sure-Tan v. National Labor Relations Board, 104 S. Ct. 2803 (1984), a case dealing with the protections of federal labor law as they relate to illegal aliens. A Chicago company, Sure-Tan Inc., asked immigration authorities to investigate the immigration status of its employees after the employees voted to unionize. As Sure-Tan was aware, almost the entire work force was composed of illegal aliens, who were thereupon arrested and given the choice of leaving the country voluntarily or being deported. A U.S. court of appeals later ruled that the workers were protected from unfair labor practices such as this anti-union action by Sure-Tan under the National Labor Relations Act.

On June 25, 1984, the Supreme Court upheld that ruling by a vote of seven to two. In a majority opinion written by Associate Justice O'Connor, the Court denied Sure-Tan's claim to have acted in accordance with the 1st Amendment's right to petition the government. O'Connor said the anti-union motivation clearly violated fair labor practices. However, the Court overturned an appeals court penalty on the company that included awards of back pay and a reinstatement of employment offer that was to remain in effect for four years for any worker who achieved legal status. Associate Justices Powell and Rehnquist dissented on the issue of federal labor laws protecting illegal aliens (in a seven to two vote) but concurred with the majority opinion regarding the reworking of appropriate remedies. Dissenting from the majority opinion of five to four on remedy were Associate Justices Brennan, Marshall, Blackmun, and Stevens.

Swann v. Charlotte-Mecklenburg Board of Education, 402 U.S. 1 (1971), a case dealing with the constitutionality of certain desegregation plans for the public schools. The petitioner, Swann, brought suit against the board of education to force desegregation. The district court ordered the board to establish a plan. When the board's plan was rejected by the court, the court adopted a plan created by a court-appointed master. *Certiorari* was granted by the Supreme Court to review the district court's implementation order.

On April 20, 1971, the Supreme Court ruled unanimously that the district courts were justified in ordering compliance with their own desegregation plans when the local school authorities fail to desegregate voluntarily. Chief Justice Burger, writing for the Court, held that the objective of the courts is to eliminate all vestiges of state-imposed segregation in public schools. The central problems involve student assignment. These are separated into four categories: racial balances or racial quotas, one-race schools, remedial altering of attendance zone, and transportation of students. A remedial plan should therefore be judged by its effectiveness.

Sweatt v. Painter, 339 U.S. 629 (1950), a case dealing with the constitutionality of racial segregation in state-supported schools. In 1946 officials of the University of Texas Law School denied admission to a black student, Herman Sweatt, on the grounds that a separate law school for blacks was soon to be established. Sweatt subsequently

In Sweatt v. Painter, *the Court held unanimously, in an opinion written by Chief Justice Vinson* (right), *that an applicant's denial of law school admission, based on race, was unconstitutional. The decision marked a departure from the "separate but equal" doctrine.*

filed suit against Theophilis Painter and the other officers of the University of Texas, contending that since his admission had been denied solely for reasons of race, his 14th Amendment guarantee of equal protection had clearly been violated. Sweatt's case was presented before the Supreme Court by future Associate Justice Marshall, then serving as director of the National Association for the Advancement of Colored People (NAACP) Legal Defense Fund.

On June 5, 1950, the Supreme Court decided unanimously that Sweatt's suit should be sustained. Chief Justice Vinson, speaking for the Court, held that in this particular case the facilities offered at the black law school were substantially inferior to those provided to whites and that Sweatt had therefore been deprived of "equal protection under law." Although Vinson refused to rule that all racial discrimination by its very nature was a violation of the 14th Amendment, this decision marked another departure from the "separate but equal" doctrine established in *Plessy v. Ferguson* (1896) and confirmed the previous ruling of the Court in a similar case, *Missouri ex rel. Gaines v. Canada* (1938).

Swift and Co. v. United States, 196 U.S. 375 (1905), a case dealing with the extent of federal jurisdiction over local commerce that affected interstate trade. Certain large meat-packing firms had managed to control the price of fresh meat in the Chicago stockyards and had been ordered by the federal court to end this practice. Representatives of the companies subsequently appealed to the Supreme Court for the removal of the injunction, contending that since the trade in live meat was a local and not an interstate matter, it was not within federal jurisdiction.

On January 20, 1905, the Supreme Court decided unanimously that the injunction against Swift and the other meat-packers should stand. Associate Justice Holmes, speaking for the Court, held that although the trust in question was local, it was a part of a larger trading operation in which the processed products would in fact become objects of interstate trade. This decision considerably broadened the limits of federal jurisdiction and established the right of the federal government to intervene in any business that was directly linked to a national trading network.

Tennessee v. Garner, 53 U.S.L.W. 4244 (1985), a case dealing with the rights of police officers to shoot unarmed fleeing felony suspects. In 1974, in a suspected burglary in Memphis, Tennessee, police officer Elton Hymon shot a 15-year-old suspect who was attempting to escape over a fence. The youth, Edward Garner, died later at the hospital. A stolen purse and $10 were found on his body. Hymon acted under a Tennessee law permitting "all the necessary means" to arrest a felony suspect. Garner's father filed a civil rights suit that received a favorable ruling by a U.S. court of appeals, which said that the statute violated the 4th Amendment's guarantee against unreasonable seizure.

This ruling was upheld by the Supreme Court on March 27, 1985, in a six to three decision, written by Associate

Justice White. The decision invalidated similar laws in nearly half the states. While Justice White stopped short of declaring Tennessee's statute unconstitutional, he required that deadly force be used only under certain conditions: if the police officer is threatened with a weapon or if the officer has good reason to believe serious physical harm has been inflicted by the suspect in the process of the crime. The Court further stipulated that "where feasible" the suspect must receive warning. Chief Justice Burger and Associate Justices O'Connor and Rehnquist dissented.

Terry v. Ohio, (1968), *See* United States v. Hensley.

Texas v. White, 7 Wallace 700 (1869), a case dealing with the post-Civil War legal status of the states of the Confederacy. In 1850, the federal government had compensated the state of Texas for certain boundary concessions with government bonds payable in 1864. By the terms of the original transaction, the state could not dispose of the bonds without the endorsement of the governor. With the outbreak of the Civil War and the secession of Texas from the Union, the regulations concerning the bonds were changed, and some of them were sold by the state government to George White. After the war, with the establishment of a new provisional government, the state of Texas filed suit against White for the return of the bonds, contending that since they did not bear the endorsement of the governor, their sale was therefore void. The questions faced by the Supreme Court in reviewing this case were (1) Was the provisional Reconstruction government of Texas entitled to make a claim in the name of the state of Texas? and (2) Did the secession of Texas from the Union end its legal status as a state and therefore disqualify it from entering a suit in federal court?

The Supreme Court held by a vote of six to three, with Associate Justices Grier, Miller, and Wayne dissenting, that states do not have a constitutional right to remove themselves from the Union, and therefore, from a legal point of view, Texas had never ceased to be a state. Chief Justice Chase, writing the majority opinion, held that all acts of the rebel government of Texas were illegal, and the provisional state goverment's appeal for the return of the bonds was sustained.

Thornhill v. Alabama, 310 U.S. 88 (1940), a case dealing with the extent of 1st Amendment protection in relation to certain state statutes. The petitioner, Thornhill, was convicted of loitering and picketing a place of business in connection with a labor dispute. He subsequently appealed his conviction, contending that the Alabama statute was a violation of 1st Amendment freedom of speech and of the press guarantees.

The Supreme Court held unanimously that freedom of speech and of the press is secured to all persons by the 14th Amendment against abridgement by the states. Associate Justice Murphy, writing for the Court, held that the courts must weigh the circumstances and appraise the substantiality of the reasons advanced in support of the challenged

Associate Justice Frank Murphy wrote the Court's opinion in Thornhill v. Alabama, *which held that free speech and press are guaranteed everyone by the 14th Amendment and that state statutes, therefore, could not abridge these rights unless there was a clear and present danger.*

regulations when abridgement of the effective exercise of these rights is claimed. Even though Thornhill's charges were framed in the words of the statute, it was not necessary to consider whether the evidence would have supported his conviction based on different and more precise charges. Freedom of speech and of press, Murphy noted, embraces at the least the liberty to discuss publicly and truthfully all matters of public concern, and the facts of a labor dispute must be regarded as within that area of free discussion. While the state may take adequate steps to preserve the peace and to protect the privacy, the lives, and the property of its people, it may not do so here where there is no "clear and present danger" of destruction of life or property or invasion of right of privacy. The Alabama statute was therefore ruled invalid.

Thurlow v. Massachusetts, (1847), *See* License Cases.

Trammel v. United States, 445 U.S. 40 (1980), a case dealing with the judicial question of the spousal privilege. The petitioner, Trammel, had been indicted along with two others for importing heroin and conspiracy to import heroin. His wife was named as a co-conspirator on his conspiracy charge. She chose to testify against him, after she was given a grant of immunity and assurances of lenient treatment. After Trammel was convicted of the charges, he appealed, contending that the admission of his wife's testimony violated the rule adopted in *Hawkins v. United States* (1958), which barred the testimony of one spouse against another unless both consent.

The Supreme Court decided unanimously that Trammel's conviction should stand. Chief Justice Burger, writing for the Court, held that in the years since *Hawkins* was decided in 1958, the trend in state law had been toward divesting the accused of the privilege to bar adverse spousal testimony, and the foundations for the privilege had long since disappeared. No longer was a woman regarded as a chattel and denied a separate legal identity. As for marital harmony, Burger noted, when one spouse is willing to testify against the other in a criminal proceeding then little is left in the way of marital harmony. The decision in *Hawkins* was not meant to foreclose whatever changes in the common-law rule may be dictated by reason and experience. An accused, therefore, may not invoke the privilege against adverse spousal testimony so as to exclude voluntary testimony of spouse.

Truax v. Corrigan, 257 U.S. 312 (1921), a case dealing with the extent of permissible labor picketing activities. In this case the owners of a restaurant refused to yield to the demands of its unionized employees. The employees went on strike and conspired to injure the owner's business by compelling the customers to go elsewhere. The employees stood outside the restaurant and threatened potential customers as they entered the building. Arizona law regulating injunctions in labor controversies enabled the employees to be immune from civil or criminal action.

The Supreme Court held by a vote of five to four, with Associate Justices Holmes, Pitney, Clarke, and Brandeis dissenting, that this law violated the 14th Amendment by depriving owners of their property without due process of law. Chief Justice Taft, writing for the majority, held that if employees of a business willfully conspire to injure their employer's business during a labor dispute they are subject to both criminal and civil actions.

Trustees of Dartmouth College v. Woodward, 4 Wheaton 518 (1819), a case dealing with the status of private corporations and the constitutional protection of the obligations of contracts. Owing to a dispute among the trustees of Dartmouth College, the New Hampshire legislature revoked the original corporate charter of the college and appointed a new board of trustees. The petitioners, the original trustees of the college, sued Woodward, the college's secretary, for the recovery of the college's seal and official documents. Having been refused reinstatement by the New Hampshire courts, they appealed for redress to the Supreme Court, where they were represented by Daniel Webster. The Court held, on a vote of five to one with Associate Justice Duvall dissenting, that the original corporate charter granted to Dartmouth before the Revolution by the British crown was a valid contract and therefore could not be amended or revoked by an action of the New Hampshire legislature, as

specified in Article I, Section 10 of the Constitution. Chief Justice Marshall, speaking for the majority, held that the state of New Hampshire, which had superseded the governmental authority of the British crown, was bound to uphold the charter and must reinstate the original trustees. The Court's decision allowed corporations significant latitude, but its effect was modified by *Charles River Bridge v. Warren Bridge* (1837).

Tyson and Bros. v. Banton, 273 U.S. 418 (1923), a case dealing with the constitutional power of state and federal governments to establish maximum prices for certain private businesses. The Supreme Court held by a vote of five to four, with Associate Justices Holmes, Brandeis, Stone, and Sanford dissenting, that the business of selling theater tickets was not so affected with a public interest that the resale price of such tickets could be regulated by law.

Associate Justice Sutherland, writing for the majority, ruled that to permit such price regulation the business must be such as to justify the conclusion that it has been devoted to a public use and its use thereby, in effect, granted to the public. The power to establish prices, noted Sutherland, does not exist for private property or business, but it exists only where the business or the property involved has become affected with a public interest. A business does not meet this criterion simply because it is a large business used by the public. Therefore, the Court found that the sale of theater tickets is not a business affected with the public interest and cannot have its prices regulated.

United States v. American Tobacco Company, 221 U.S. 106 (1911), a case dealing with the definition of an illegal commercial trust. The Justice Department prosecuted the American Tobacco Company for violation of the Sherman Antitrust Act and a federal district court ruled that the company's control of the various components of the tobacco industry must be broken up. Representatives of the American Tobacco Company appealed the decision.

On May 29, 1911, two weeks after the landmark antitrust case of *Standard Oil Company of New Jersey v. United States*, the Supreme Court revised the effect of the lower court ruling by a vote of eight to one, with only Associate Justice Harlan dissenting. Chief Justice White, speaking for the majority, held that although the activities of the American Tobacco Company had resulted in the elimination of competition, its actions had not been as "unreasonable" as those of Standard Oil. The Chief Justice ruled, therefore, that the American Tobacco Company should be reorganized rather than broken up. This was the first practical application of the "rule of reason" established in the Standard Oil case.

United States v. Banker's Trust Co., 294 U.S. 240 (1935), a case dealing with the constitutional power of Congress to issue certain types of promissory notes. In 1933, Congress passed a joint resolution regulating the issuance of gold from banking institutions. Prior to this time there had

In the American Tobacco antitrust case, the 1911 Court, led by Chief Justice White (**front, center**), *who wrote the majority opinion, applied the "rule of reason" and directed the reorganization of the trust rather than its dissolution.*

been an unusually large amount of gold taken from banks by persons who were hoarding the gold. The purpose of this joint resolution was to stop the withdrawal of gold and to stabilize the dollar. The Supreme Court held by a vote of five to four, with Associate Justices McReynolds, Van Devanter, Sutherland, and Butler dissenting, that a bond for the future payment of a stated number of dollars in gold coins of the United States is a contract for payment in money, not gold. Chief Justice Hughes, writing for the majority, ruled that Congress has the power to regulate currency and that by applying this above-stated "gold clause" Congress was within its authority to establish the most efficient monetary system for the country.

United States v. Brewster, 408 U.S. 501 (1972), a case dealing with the extent of congressional immunity from criminal prosecution. Daniel Brewster, a former U.S. senator, was convicted of accepting a bribe relating to his actions on postage rate legislation while in the Senate. He subsequently appealed his conviction, contending that his prosecution was a violation of Article I, Section 6 of the Constitution, which states that senators and representatives "shall not be questioned in any other place" for "any speech or debate in either House."

On June 29, 1972, the Supreme Court ruled by a vote of six to three, with Associate Justices Brennan, Douglas, and White dissenting, that the clause did not protect all conduct relating to the legislative process; it only "protects

against inquiry into acts that occur in the regular course of the legislative process and the motivation for those acts," stated Chief Justice Burger in the majority opinion.

United States v. Brignoni-Ponce, 422 U.S. 873 (1975), a case dealing with the legal authority of the U.S. Border Patrol to stop automobiles in areas near the Mexican border. Officers of the Border Patrol had detained a car that had crossed a fixed checkpoint because the car's occupants appeared to be of Mexican descent. In questioning the occupants it was learned that the two passengers were aliens who had entered the country illegally. All three were arrested; the respondent was charged with knowingly transporting illegal immigrants. At the respondent's trial, the motion to suppress the testimony of and about the two passengers as fruit of an illegal seizure was denied.

The case was appealed and the Supreme Court ruled unanimously that the 4th Amendment does not allow a roving patrol to stop a vehicle near the Mexican border and question its occupants about their citizenship and immigration status, when the only ground for suspicion is the apparent Mexican ancestry of the occupants. Associate Justice Powell, writing for the Court, held that to allow roving patrols broad and unlimited discretion to stop all vehicles in the border area without any reason to suspect they have violated any law would not be reasonable under the 4th Amendment. Except at the border and its functional equivalents, officers on roving patrol may stop vehicles only

Following Supreme Court decisions that invalidated the New Deal programs, including the ruling in **United States v. Butler** *that the Agricultural Adjustment Act was unconstitutional, President Roosevelt proposed enlarging the Court to overcome the influence of its conservatives. Public outcries helped mobilize opposition to the plan.*

if they are aware of specific articulable facts that reasonably warrant suspicion that the vehicle contains illegal aliens. An apparent Mexican ancestry, noted Powell, does not justify stopping all Mexican-Americans to ask if they are aliens.

United States v. Butler, 297 U.S. 1 (1936), a case dealing with the constitutional right of the federal government to use its taxing power to achieve specific economic aims. In 1933, Congress passed the Agricultural Adjustment Act, which attempted to regulate national farm production by encouraging farmers to refrain from growing certain crops. Farmers were to be rewarded with subsidies derived from a special tax on food processors. One of the potential payers of this new tax challenged the constitutionality of the law.

On January 6, 1936, the Supreme Court decided by a vote of six to three, with Associate Justices Brandeis, Cardozo, and Stone dissenting, that the Agricultural Adjustment Act was unconstitutional. Associate Justice Roberts, speaking for the majority, held that this legislation was a violation of the constitutional taxing power of the federal government since it was not really a tax but a direct transfer of funds from one segment of the population to another.

This decision was viewed as a serious defeat for the Roosevelt administration, but the substance of the Court's constitutional objections to the use of the government's taxing power to achieve certain economic objectives was effectively removed by the decision in *Helvering v. Davis* (1937), in which the Social Security Act was upheld.

United States v. California, 332 U.S. 19 (1947), a case dealing with the jurisdiction of the federal government to regulate the use of coastal tidelands. The state of California reserved to itself the right to issue licenses for the exploitation of oil resources in the tidelands off its coast. The federal government believed that it held exclusive jurisdiction over such land and its resources, and it filed suit in federal court to prevent California's licensing program. The federal government's case was presented before the Supreme Court by future Associate Justice Clark, then serving as U.S. attorney general.

On June 23, 1947, the Supreme Court decided by a vote of six to two, with Associate Justices Frankfurter and Reed dissenting and Associate Justice Jackson not participating, that the federal suit should be sustained. Associate Justice Black, speaking for the majority, held that the tidelands and the natural resources they contained, being technically beyond state boundaries, were under federal jurisdiction. This decision was later effectively superseded by the ruling of the Court in *Alabama v. Texas*, which upheld the constitutionality of a congressional act transferring control of tidelands resources to the states.

United States v. Classic, 313 U.S. 299 (1941), a case dealing with the authority of the federal government to ensure the integrity of state primary elections. The respondent, Classic, was convicted of falsifying election returns in Louisiana. His conviction was based on the federal law that made it a crime to injure, oppress, threaten, or intimidate any citizen in the exercise of any right or privilege secured to him by the Constitution. Classic appealed, and on May 26, 1941, the Supreme Court upheld Classic's conviction by a vote of four to three, with Associate Justices Douglas, Black, and Murphy dissenting.

Associate Justice Stone, writing for the majority, declared that the primary election was an integral part of the overall election procedure. The authority of Congress under Article 1, Section 4 of the Constitution to regulate elections included within it the authority to regulate primary elections, when these primaries are a vital step in the exercise by the citizens of their choice of representation in Congress. Therefore, Stone held, the federal government has the power to regulate primary elections.

United States v. Curtiss-Wright Export Corp., 299 U.S. 304 (1936), a case dealing with the constitutional right of the president to establish arms embargoes on certain countries engaged in war. In order to maintain American neutrality in a war between Bolivia and Paraguay, Congress passed a law that authorized the president to prohibit arms shipments by American companies to either of the belligerents. Curtiss-Wright violated this embargo, and the attorney general filed suit in federal court to force its compliance.

On December 21, 1936, the Supreme Court decided by a vote of seven to one, with Associate Justice McReynolds dissenting and Associate Justice Stone not participating, that both Congress and President Roosevelt had acted within their constitutional rights. Associate Justice Sutherland, speaking for the majority, held that in the field of foreign policy, the executive and legislative branches must be allowed any action not specifically denied by the Constitution. This decision was one of the rare instances in which the conservative Sutherland defended an action of the Roosevelt administration.

United States v. Darby Lumber Co., 312 U.S. 100 (1941), a case dealing with the right of the federal government to prohibit the interstate sale or shipment of certain goods. In 1938, Congress passed the Fair Labor Standards Act, which established national wage and hour standards and explicitly prohibited the interstate sale of goods manufactured under conditions that violated the labor standards. A large lumber dealer was indicted for violation of the terms of the federal law, but the indictment was dismissed in federal court on the grounds that it represented an unconstitutional extension of the federal power to regulate interstate trade. The federal government appealed this decision.

On February 3, 1941, the Supreme Court decided unanimously that the Fair Labor Standards Act should be upheld. Associate Justice Stone, speaking for the Court, held that the Constitution granted Congress the power to establish the legal framework for national commerce. Since the law was a legitimate exercise of federal authority, it was not the role of the Court to pass on the motives or wisdom of that legislative act. This decision effectively reversed the precedent set by the Court in *Hammer v. Dagenhart*.

United States v. E.C. Knight Co., 156 U.S. 1 (1895), a case dealing with the extent of federal authority to control monopolistic trade practices. The E.C. Knight Company was purchased by its competitor, the American Sugar Refining Company, thereby giving the latter company control of ninety-eight percent of the sugar refining industry in the United States. The Justice Department subsequently accused the officers of E.C. Knight of criminal conspiracy in violation of the Sherman Antitrust Act.

On January 21, 1895, the Supreme Court ruled by a vote of eight to one, with Associate Justice Harlan dissenting, that since only manufacturing, not interstate sale, was involved in this transaction, it was beyond the constitutional jurisdiction of the federal government, and the charges against the E.C. Knight Co. should therefore be dropped. Chief Justice Fuller, speaking for the majority, held that although there was no question that a manufacturing monopoly had been created, manufacturing was a local matter and federal intervention in this matter endangered nothing less than "the

The 1895 Court's decision in the E.C. Knight *sugar trust case negated much of the Sherman Antitrust Act and moved away from John Marshall's interpretation of interstate commerce. Chief Justice Fuller* (front, center) *wrote the* Knight *opinion.*

preservation of the autonomy of the states." This decision marked the high point of the Court's philosophical support of private industry. Not only did it render an important provision of the Sherman Antitrust Act virtually unenforceable, but it was also a clear rejection of the broad interpretation of interstate commerce enunciated by the Marshall Court in *Gibbons v. Ogden* (1824).

United States v. Gouveia, 104 S. Ct. 2292 (1984), a case dealing with the right-to-counsel provision of the 6th Amendment. A U.S. court of appeals overturned the conviction of six prison inmates for a murder committed in prison in California. The six had been held in a detention unit without benefit of legal counsel while the murder was under investigation. The appeals court held that the prisoners had been deprived of their right to counsel guaranteed by the 6th Amendment.

On May 29, 1984, the Supreme Court reversed the lower court's ruling by a vote of eight to one. In the Court's opinion, written by Associate Justice Rehnquist, the right to counsel applies only to "adversary judicial proceedings" like arraignment or indictment, not to prior investigations. Associate Justices Stevens and Brennan felt the right to counsel could in some cases be appropriate at an earlier stage, so although they agreed with the Court's ruling in this case,

they did not sign the majority opinion. Associate Justice Marshall dissented.

United States v. Grimaud, 220 U.S. 506 (1911), a case dealing with the authority of the executive branch to regulate the use of federal lands. The Forest Reserve Act of 1891 delegated to the secretary of Agriculture the power to make rules and regulations regarding the public use of certain federal lands. One regulation adopted by the secretary of Agriculture required prior permission for the use of federal land for grazing and provided for criminal penalties for failure to do so. The respondents, convicted of grazing sheep in the Sierra Forest Reserve without permission, appealed the conviction, contending that the regulations established by the secretary of Agriculture were an unconstitutional exercise of legislative power by the executive branch.

The Supreme Court held unanimously that the conviction should stand. Associate Justice Lamar, writing for the Court, held that Congress acted within its constitutional power in conferring power on the secretary to establish rules and regulations. The power so conferred was administrative and not legislative; therefore, it was not an unconstitutional delegation of power.

United States v. Hensley, 53 U.S.L.W. 4053 (1985), a case dealing with the rights of police officers to detain briefly

In **United States v. Hensley,** *Associate Justice O'Connor, here being sworn in by Chief Justice Burger, wrote for a unanimous Court in permitting brief stops of suspected criminals.*

persons sought for questioning by police in another jurisdiction. In this case a Kentucky man who was wanted for questioning in an armed robbery investigation in Ohio was seen in Kentucky, stopped for questioning, and found to have firearms in his car. He was convicted on federal firearms charges but his conviction was overturned by a U.S. court of appeals on the grounds that he had been subjected to unreasonable search and seizure in violation of the 4th Amendment. The Justice Department appealed this ruling to the Supreme Court.

On January 8, 1985, in an opinion written by Associate Justice O'Connor, the Court unanimously ruled to overturn the appeals court decision. Justice O'Connor observed that the Court had not established hard and fast rules regarding what are commonly referred to as "Terry stops," after *Terry v. Ohio* (1968), in which "reasonable suspicion" instead of "probable cause" became the criterion for brief investigatory stops by police. The court of appeals, in categorically prohibiting such stops, had exceeded precedents established by the Court. Justice O'Connor stressed, however, that Terry stops must be brief: that the suspect could not, for example, have been detained without a warrant until the Ohio police arrived to take him into custody if he had not committed the crime of firearms possession.

United States v. Kras, 409 U.S. 434 (1973), a case dealing with the constitutional rights of bankruptcy applicants. The respondent, Kras, filed a voluntary petition in bankruptcy. He sought discharge without payment of the fees, which were a precondition to discharge in such a proceeding. The district court found the fees to be an unconstitutional denial of 5th Amendment rights of due process and equal protection. It said that discharge in bankruptcy was a fundamental interest that could be denied only when a compelling government interest was found. The district court relied on *Boddie v. Connecticut* (1971), in which the denial to admit the plaintiffs to the courts was equated with the denial of an opportunity to be heard, a denial of due process.

The government appealed, and the Supreme Court ruled unanimously that *Boddie* was not controlling in this case. In distinguishing the two cases, Associate Justice Blackmun, writing for the Court, held that here access to courts was not the only conceivable relief available to bankrupts. Also, Kras, even though indigent, was not denied equal protection of the laws by the filing fee requirement. Blackmun stated that there was not a constitutional right to obtain discharge of one's debts in bankruptcy.

United States v. Louisiana, 339 U.S. 699 (1950), a case dealing with the legal title to offshore resources. A suit was brought against the state of Louisiana by the U.S. attorney general and thus invoked the Supreme Court's jurisdiction under Article III, Section 2, Clause 2 of the Constitution. The controversy was over who held title to the area that lay under the Gulf of Mexico beyond the low-water mark on the coast of Louisiana and outside the inland waters, the marginal sea. The United States alleged it was the owner in fee simple of this area and asked for a decree declaring this right. The United States also requested that Louisiana account for the money derived by leases to this area.

The Supreme Court held by a vote of seven to zero, with Associate Justices Jackson and Frankfurter not participating, that, following *United States v. California* (1947), the marginal sea was a national concern and that national rights were paramount in that area. Associate Justice Douglas, writing for the majority, held that since the three-mile belt off the shore was in the nation's domain, and not that of the individual states, it followed that the area extending beyond the three miles was also in the domain of the nation. It did not matter that the states had not consented to be sued by the federal government, noted Douglas, since the Court had original jurisdiction of the parties and the subject matter. Since this was a suit in equity for an injunction and accounting, Louisiana was not entitled to a jury trial. The 7th Amendment required jury trials only in actions at law.

United States v. Maine, 420 U.S. 515 (1975), a case dealing with federal jurisdiction over the offshore seabed. The federal government filed a complaint against the thirteen states bordering on the Atlantic Ocean. The United States wanted to exercise sovereign rights over the seabed and subsoil underlying the Atlantic Ocean more than three miles from the low-water mark. The states claimed right or title to this area and interfered with the rights of the United States.

The Supreme Court held by a vote of eight to zero, with Associate Justice Douglas not participating, that the sovereign rights over this area belonged in the domain of the nation rather than that of the separate states. Associate Justice White, writing for the Court, ruled that Congress had established that seabed rights beyond the three-mile limit belonged to the United States. This had been confirmed by both the Submerged Lands Act of 1953 and the later Outer Continental Shelf Lands Act of 1953, noted White.

United States v. Mosley, (1915), *See* Ex parte Yarbrough.

United States v. Nixon, 418 U.S. 683 (1974), a case dealing with the constitutional limits of executive privilege. As a result of the investigation conducted by the Watergate special prosecutor, seven officials of the Nixon administration were indicted for obstruction of justice, and the special prosecutor requested that the White House turn over certain tape recordings of conversations by the defendants for use in their trial. President Nixon refused to comply with the prosecutor's subpoena, claiming absolute executive privilege over all material requested. At issue was the apparent conflict between legitimate executive privilege and the auton-

Justice William O. Douglas (far right), who had a strong interest in environmental issues, wrote the Court's opinion in **United States v. Louisiana**, *which concerned title to offshore oil resources.*

omy of the presidency on the one hand, and the right of the judicial branch to facilitate criminal proceedings on the other. On July 24, 1974, the Supreme Court decided by a vote of eight to zero, with Associate Justice Rehnquist not participating, that the executive privilege claimed by the President was not absolute and that the tapes must be handed over to the special prosecutor. Chief Justice Burger, speaking for the majority, held that the judiciary had a legitimate right to judge the merits of claims of executive privilege. Since the subpoenaed tapes were directly relevant to an ongoing criminal prosecution, the Chief Justice ruled that the President's "generalized interest in confidentiality" was subordinate to "the fundamental demands of due process of law in the fair administration of criminal justice." This decision and the subsequent surrender of the Watergate tapes were important factors leading to the resignation of President Nixon two weeks later.

United States v. Pabst Brewing Company, 384 U.S. 546 (1966), a case dealing with the acquisition of one corporation by another when the effect would be to lessen competition substantially or to create a monopoly. In 1958, the Pabst Brewing Company acquired the Blatz Brewing Company and became the fifth largest brewer in the United States. The government filed suit based on Section 7 of the Clayton Antitrust Act, alleging that the acquisition would substantially lessen competition in the production and sale of beer. Evidence that showed that competition might be substantially lessened as a result of the merger would be enough to prove a violation of Section 7.

The Supreme Court held unanimously that the government's evidence as to the probable effect of Pabst's merger on competition was sufficient to show a violation of Section 7. Associate Justice Black, writing for the Court, held that a trend toward concentration in an industry was a highly relevant factor in deciding how substantial the anti-competitive effect of a merger might be. There was no duty for the government, noted Black, to show that the trend toward concentration was due to mergers.

United States v. Sioux Nation of Indians, 448 U.S. 371 (1980), a case dealing with American Indian claims to compensation for lands expropriated by the federal government. In 1868, under the Fort Laramie Treaty, the Sioux Nation had been awarded the Great Sioux Reservation. In 1877, Congress passed an act abrogating the Fort Laramie Treaty, taking away the rights and property given to the Sioux Indians in 1868. The Sioux brought action against the United States, alleging that the government had taken the land without just compensation. The issue had been raised as early as 1920 and had been barred by *res judicata* in 1942.

The Supreme Court held by a vote of eight to one, with only Associate Justice Rehnquist dissenting, that under a 1978 act, which allowed for review of this case without regard for *res judicata*, the Sioux were entitled to just

compensation. Justice Marshall, writing for the majority, ruled that the act was a waiver of the *res judicata* effect on the judicial decision of 1942. This waiver did not violate the doctrine of separation of powers, and the Court determined that the United States could recognize its obligation to pay a moral debt by waiving an otherwise valid defense to a legal claim.

United States v. Texas, 339 U.S. 707 (1950), a case dealing with the Supreme Court's original jurisdiction under Article III, Section 2, Clause 2 of the Constitution and put into issue the conflicting claims of the parties to oil and other products under the ocean bed below the low-water mark off the Texas shores. The state of Texas claimed both *dominium* and *imperium* in and over this area because it had had both as an independent republic.

The Supreme Court ruled by a vote of five to two, with Associate Justices Reed and Minton dissenting and Associate Justices Jackson and Clark not participating, that any claim that Texas may have had to the marginal sea was relinquished to the United States when Texas was admitted to the Union "on an equal footing with the existing States" in 1845. Associate Justice Douglas, writing for the majority, held that the "equal footing" clause of the joint resolution was designed to create parity as respects political standing and sovereignty, not to wipe out economic diversities among the states. The clause negated any implied, special limitation of any of the paramount powers of the United States in favor of a state. The "equal footing" clause prevented extension of the state into the domain of political and sovereign power of the United States in which other states had been excluded.

United States v. Topco Associates, 405 U.S. 596 (1972), a case dealing with certain types of monopolistic business practices. The United States brought an injunction action charging that Topco Associates, Inc., had violated Section 1 of the Sherman Antitrust Act. Topco was composed of twenty-three chains of supermarket retailers and two retailer-owned cooperative wholesalers. The association's basic function was to serve as a purchasing agent for its members, and no member could sell Topco-brand products outside its licensed territory. Expansion into another member's territory was permitted only with the other member's consent. So, in effect, a member had a veto power over the admission of a new member, and members could control actual or potential competition in the territorial areas in which they were concerned.

The Supreme Court held by a vote of six to one, with Chief Justice Burger dissenting and Associate Justices Powell and Rehnquist not participating, that Topco's scheme of dividing markets violated the Sherman Act because it operated to prohibit competition in Topco-brand products among retail grocery chains. Associate Justice Marshall, writing for the majority, ruled that even though the scheme was to minimize competition at the retail level, it was a horizontal restraint constituting a violation of Section 1 of the Sherman Act. Marshall further noted that Topco's limitations upon reselling at wholesale were invalid for the same reason.

United States v. Trans-Missouri Freight Association, 166 U.S. 290 (1897), a case dealing with the constitutionality of certain provisions of the Sherman Antitrust Act. In 1889 several railway companies made an agreement by which they formed themselves into an association, the Trans-Missouri Freight Association. In 1890, Congress passed the Sherman Antitrust Act to protect trade and commerce against unlawful restraints and monopolies. With the passage of the act, the association's agreement became illegal and acts done under the agreement after the act became operative were done in violation of the act.

The association challenged the constitutionality of the act, and the Supreme Court ruled by a vote of five to four, with Associate Justices White, Field, Gray, and Shiras dissenting, that a contract between railroad carriers in restraint of trade or commerce was prohibited, even when the only purpose was to affect traffic rates for the transportation of persons and property. Associate Justice Peckham, writing for the majority, held that the act's prohibitory provisions were not confined to unreasonable restraint. They applied to all contracts without exception or limitation. The dissolution of the freight association did not prevent the Court from taking the appeal and deciding the case on the merits.

United States v. U.S. District Court, 407 U.S. 297 (1972), a case dealing with the power of the president, acting through the attorney general, to authorize electronic surveillance in internal security matters without prior judicial approval. Three defendants in a criminal proceeding in U.S. District Court for the Eastern District of Michigan were charged with conspiracy to destroy government property. They moved to compel the United States to disclose certain electronic surveillance information and to have a hearing to determine whether this information had "tainted" the government's evidence. Since the Omnibus Crime Control and Safe Streets Act authorized the use of electronic surveillance, the government argued that the act recognized the president's authority to conduct warrantless surveillances for national security reasons.

The Supreme Court ruled unanimously that the act conferred no powers and was not a grant of authority to conduct warrantless national security surveillances. It was held to be merely a disclaimer of congressional intent to define presidential powers in matters affecting national security. Associate Justice Powell, writing for the Court, held that the question posed by this case was "Whether safeguards other than prior authorization by a magistrate would satisfy the 4th Amendment in a situation involving national security." If the domestic surveillances were conducted solely within the discretion of the executive branch without the detached judgment of a neutral magistrate, then the 4th Amendment's freedoms are not properly guaranteed,

Powell reasoned. Resort to appropriate warrant procedure would not frustrate the legitimate purposes of domestic security searches.

United Steelworkers of America v. Weber, 443 U.S. 193 (1979), a case dealing with the constitutionality of certain affirmative action plans to redress racial discrimination in private industry. The United Steelworkers of America had negotiated an affirmative action plan that reserved solely for blacks fifty percent of the places in a new training program. The respondent, Weber, a white employee with more seniority than some of the blacks, was denied admission to the training program, and he sued the Steelworkers, claiming a violation of Title VII of the Civil Rights Act of 1964, which prohibited all racial discrimination in admission to training programs.

The Supreme Court ruled by a vote of five to two, with Chief Justice Burger and Associate Justice Rehnquist dissenting and Associate Justices Powell and Stevens not participating, that the act left employers and unions in the private sector free to take such race-conscious steps to eliminate manifest racial imbalances in traditionally segregated job categories. Associate Justice Brennan, writing for the majority, held that the case did not involve state action so it did not involve the equal protection clause.

Veazie Bank v. Fenno, 5 Wallace 533 (1870), a case dealing with the constitutionality of a certain federal tax on state bank notes. On December 31, 1870, the Supreme Court held by a vote of six to two, with Associate Justices Nelson and Davis dissenting, that a tax imposed by the act of July 13, 1866, on the notes of state banks paid out after August 1, 1866, was constitutionally permissible. Chief Justice Chase, writing for the majority, ruled that this tax did not lay a direct tax within the meaning of the clause of the Constitution that provides "that direct taxes shall be apportioned among the several states, according to their respective numbers." Since Congress was attempting to regulate the banking industry within the United States, this tax would enable the government to know how much money the banks in each state had and thus be able to maintain a constant and reliable supply of currency for the whole country.

Wabash, St. Louis & Pacific Railway Co. v. Illinois, 118 U.S. 557 (1886), a case dealing with the right of state governments to regulate the shipping rates of interstate railroads. At issue in this case was an Illinois law that prohibited railroads from imposing discriminatory charges for freight from smaller towns without regard to distance from the ultimate point of delivery. The officials of the railroad affected by this regulation challenged the constitutionality of the law on the grounds that it was a violation of the federal right to regulate interstate commerce.

On October 25, 1886, the Supreme Court held by a vote of six to three, with Chief Justice Waite and Associate Justices Gray and Bradley dissenting, that the Illinois law was unconstitutional. Associate Justice Miller, speaking for

In **Veazie Bank v. Fenno,** *the Court held, in an opinion written by Chief Justice Chase* **(right),** *that a federal tax on state bank notes was permissible.*

the majority, held that even state regulation of an interstate carrier's transport only within the boundaries of the state was a clear obstruction of interstate trade. This decision was widely interpreted as a narrowing of the "police power" doctrine of state regulation that had been established in *Munn v. Illinois* (1877).

Walz v. Tax Commission, 397 U.S. 664 (1970), a case dealing with the constitutionality of tax exemptions for religious organizations. The petitioner, Walz, a property owner in New York, sought an injunction to prevent the New York City Tax Commission from granting property tax exemptions to religious organizations for religious properties used solely for religious worship. His contention was that the grant of exemption to church property indirectly required him to make a contribution to religious bodies and violated provisions prohibiting establishment of religion under the 1st and 14th Amendments.

The Supreme Court held by a vote of eight to one, with Associate Justice Douglas dissenting, that the tax exemption created only a minimal and remote involvement between

state and church and restricted the fiscal relationship between them and that the exemption was therefore constitutional. Chief Justice Burger, writing for the majority, held that the tax exemption was not aimed at establishing, sponsoring, or supporting religion and that its elimination would tend only to expand governmental involvement, whereas the tax exemption seemed to complement and reinforce the desired separation insulating each from the other. Also, Burger noted, two centuries of uninterrupted freedom from taxation had not given the remotest sign of leading to an established church or religion. Instead it had helped guarantee the free exercise of all forms of religious beliefs.

Ware v. Hylton, 3 Dallas 282 (1796), a case dealing with the legal relationship between international treaties and state laws. The petitioner, a British subject to whom a pre-Revolutionary War debt was owed by a resident of Virginia, sued for the payment of that debt. A Virginia law passed in 1777, however, provided that all debts owed to British subjects were to be paid to the state treasury and to be considered fulfilled.

The Supreme Court, overturning a judgment of the Virginia circuit court, held by a vote of four to zero, with Associate Justice Iredell abstaining, that international treaties take precedence over state laws and that the debt must be paid. Associate Justice Cushing, speaking for the Court, held that since a provision of the Treaty of Paris of 1783 required that all debts owed to British subjects must be repaid and that since Virginia had ratified the U.S. Constitution, which authorized the federal government to conclude treaties, the state law was effectively nullified. Athough the Court ruled in favor of the petitioner, it also suggested that the state of Virginia compensate those citizens who had paid their debts to the state treasury and who were now required to repay the original creditors.

War Prohibition Cases, 251 U.S. 146 (1919), a series of cases dealing with the authority of the federal government to prohibit the sale of alcoholic beverages during times of national emergency. Congress passed the War-Time Prohibition Act on November 21, 1918, prohibiting the sale of any distilled spirits for beverage purposes. Two cases were brought to the Court on direct appeal; they were argued on the same day and disposed of together. In the Kentucky case the plaintiff was a maker of whiskey who had whiskey stored in a distillery warehouse prior to the passage of the act. In the New York case the plaintiffs were jobbers, and the liquors were in general and special bonded warehouses.

The Supreme Court ruled unanimously that part of the war power of Congress is the power to prohibit the liquor traffic as a means of increasing war efficiency. Associate Justice Brandeis, writing for the Court, held that the exercise of the power without providing for compensation is not limited by the 5th Amendment. The act was not an appropriation of liquor for public purposes. There was a seven-month, nine-day period from the passage of the act during which liquors could be disposed of free from any government restrictions.

Watkins v. United States, 354 U.S. 178 (1957), a case dealing with the constitutional function of congressional investigations. John T. Watkins, a union official, refused to answer the questions of the House Un-American Activities Committee with regard to the supposed Communist affiliations of some of his colleagues, and he was subsequently convicted of contempt of Congress for failing to answer "any question pertinent to the question under inquiry." Watkins appealed that conviction on the grounds that the questions posed to him by the House committee had no relevance to the subject then under legislative investigation.

On June 17, 1957, the Supreme Court held by a vote of six to one, with Associate Justice Clark dissenting and Associate Justices Burton and Whittaker not participating, that Watkins's conviction should be overturned. Chief Justice Warren, speaking for the majority, held that the Constitution did not empower Congress "to expose for the sake of exposure" and noted that congressional investigating committees

have some clearly defined legislative object. Since the committee had not informed Watkins of the specific reason for their inquiry, he could not be convicted of failing to answer "pertinent questions."

Weinberger v. Wiesenfield, 420 U.S. 636 (1975), a case dealing with the constitutionality of gender-differentiated social security benefits. Federal law mandated that in the case of a deceased husband and father, social security benefits were to be payable both to the widow and to the couple's minor children in her care. However, since in the case of a deceased wife and mother benefits were payable only to the minor children and not to the widower, the law was challenged.

On March 19, 1975, the Supreme Court, by a vote of eight to zero, with Associate Justice Douglas not participating, struck down the provision, finding an unjustifiable discrimination against covered female wage earners by affording them less protection for their survivors than that provided for the survivors of male wage earners. Associate Justice Brennan, writing for the majority, held that the purpose of the benefits was to enable the surviving parent to stay at home and care for the children, and the disqualification of widowers but not widows was therefore unjustified discrimination against the children based on the gender of the surviving parent.

Wesberry v. Sanders, 376 U.S. 1 (1964), a case dealing with the constitutional standards for state legislative apportionment. The appellants, citizens and qualified voters in Georgia's 5th Congressional District, brought suit asking that Georgia's apportionment statute be declared invalid and that the governor and secretary of state be enjoined from conducting elections under it. The district was one of ten that was created in 1931, and according to the 1960 census, the population of the district was two to three times greater than that of any of the other congressional districts. The appellants alleged that they were deprived of the full benefit of their right to vote because of the failure to realign the state's congressional districts more nearly to equalize the population of each. In the district court the appellants' complaint was dismissed for "want of equity."

On February 17, 1964, the Supreme Court reversed the decision of the district court by a vote of seven to two, with Associate Justice Harlan dissenting and Associate Justice Clark dissenting in part. Associate Justice Black, writing for the majority, held that the appellants had standing to sue. As in *Baker v. Carr* (1962), which involved alleged malapportionment of seats in a state legislature, the district court had subject matter jurisdiction. The complaint, noted Black, should not have been dismissed for "want of equity." Article I, Section 2 of the Constitution provided that representatives be chosen "by the People of the several States." This meant, according to Black, that as nearly as is practicable one person's vote in a congressional election was to be worth as much as another's.

West Coast Hotel Co. v. Parrish, 300 U.S. 379 (1937), a case dealing with the right of states to enact minimum wage laws. In 1913, the Washington state legislature had enacted a law establishing minimum wage levels for women and children. A hotel chambermaid, Elsie Parrish, filed suit against her employers for the difference between the wages she actually received and the wages set by the state law. The employers subsequently challenged the constitutionality of the statute, contending that it violated their 14th Amendment rights to due process and freedom of contract.

On March 29, 1937, the Supreme Court held by a vote of five to four, with Associate Justices Butler, McReynolds, Sutherland, and Van Devanter dissenting, that the Washington law should be upheld and Parrish's suit sustained. Chief Justice Hughes, speaking for the majority, held that such a regulation was within the legitimate police power of the state to prevent "the exploiting of workers at wages so low as to be insufficient to meet the bare cost of living." This decision effectively reversed the rulings of the Court in the previous minimum wage cases of *Adkins v. Children's Hospital* (1923) and *Morehead v. Tipaldo* (1936).

West Virginia State Board of Education v. Barnette, 319 U.S. 624 (1943), a case dealing with the constitutionality of compulsory pledges of allegiance in the public schools. In 1942 the West Virginia Board of Education adopted a resolution establishing a compulsory salute to the flag by all students in the public schools. The petitioner, a member of the Jehovah's Witnesses and the parent of a student in the public schools, challenged the constitutionality of the practice, contending that it violated his religious principles and was therefore a violation of his 1st Amendment rights. His suit was upheld in federal court and the state board of education subsequently appealed the case.

On June 14, 1943, the Supreme Court decided by a vote of six to three, with Associate Justices Frankfurter, Reed, and Roberts dissenting, that the action of the West Virginia Board of Education was unconstitutional. Associate Justice Jackson, speaking for the majority, held that the issue was one not strictly of religious freedom but also of the freedom of thought and speech. The action of the board of education in ordering a compulsory flag salute, he ruled, "transcends constitutional limitations on their power and invades the sphere of intellect and spirit which it is the purpose of the First Amendment of our Constitution to reserve from all official control." This decision overruled *Minersville School District v. Gobitis* (1940).

Whitney v. California, 274 U.S. 357 (1927), a case dealing with the right of states to limit the freedom of speech and assembly. The petitioner, Charlotte Whitney, niece of former Associate Justice Field and one of the organizers of the Communist Labor Party of California, was convicted of violating that state's Criminal Syndicalism Act. That act imposed criminal penalties on anyone who joined an organization that advocated the use of violence in politi-

cal or industrial disputes. Whitney appealed the conviction, contending that the state law was an unconstitutional violation of her 1st Amendment rights.

On May 16, 1927, the Supreme Court decided unanimously that Whitney's conviction should stand. Associate Justice Sanford, speaking for the Court, held that even though no immediate danger to the state could be proved to have been instigated by the California Communist Party, the state law was justified as "all threats to the American form of government, no matter how remote, should be withstood." This decision, together with the decision of the Court in *Gitlow v. New York* (1925), represented a judicial shift away from the "clear and present danger" doctrine established in *Schenck v. United States* (1919).

Williams v. Florida, 399 U.S. 78 (1970), a case dealing with the constitutionality of six-person juries in certain state criminal proceedings. The petitioner, Williams, was convicted of robbery and appealed his conviction, contending that he should have been tried by a twelve-person jury rather than the six-person panel provided by Florida law in all but capital cases. The petitioner's counsel argued that the Supreme Court's ruling in *Duncan v. Louisiana* had made the 6th Amendment jury trial guarantee applicable to the common law jury, including its twelve-man panel.

On June 22, 1970, the Supreme Court ruled by a vote of eight to one, with Associate Jutice Douglas dissenting in part, that the Florida law permitting a six-person jury in non-capital cases should be upheld. Associate Justice White, writing for the majority, noted that the critical purpose of a jury–to be the "interposition between the accused and his accuser of the common sense judgment of a group of laymen" –did not require any particular number on the jury.

Williams v. Zbaraz, 448 U.S. 358 (1980), a case dealing with the constitutionality of legal restrictions of government funding for certain medical abortions. An Illinois statute prohibited state medical assistance payments for all abortions except when the abortion was necessary to preserve the woman's life. This prohibition was challenged and the lower court declared both the Illinois statute and the Hyde Amendment of the U.S. Congress unconstitutional. In the Hyde Amendment, Congress prohibited the use of any federal funds to reimburse the costs of abortions under the Medicaid program except under specified circumstances such as rape, incest, or the mother's life being endangered.

The Supreme Court held by a vote of five to four, with Associate Justices Brennan, Marshall, Blackmun, and Stevens dissenting, that a state participating in the Medicaid program was not obligated to pay for those necessary abortions for which federal reimbursement was unavailable under the Hyde Amendment. Associate Justice Stewart, writing for the majority, held that since the Hyde Amendment had already been found by the Court not to violate the equal protection component of the 5th Amendment, the comparable funding restrictions in the Illinois statute did not violate the equal protection clause of the 14th Amendment. Stewart further noted that since none of the parties to the original suit had challenged the validity of the Hyde Amendment, the district court lacked jurisdiction to consider its constitutionality. Even so, the Supreme Court had jurisdiction over the whole case and thus could review the other issues preserved by the appeal.

Wilson v. New, 243 U.S. 332 (1917), a case dealing with the authority of Congress to regulate the hours of work and wages of railroad employees engaged in interstate commerce. Congress had passed an act to establish an eight-hour day for employees of carriers engaged in interstate commerce. This act arose from a nationwide dispute between railroad companies and their train operatives over wages, and in this emergency, Congress assumed upon itself the power to prescribe a standard of minimum wages to be in force for a reasonable time.

The constitutionality of the action was challenged and the Supreme Court ruled by a vote of six to three, with Associate Justices Day, Pitney, and Van Devanter dissenting,

that although an emergency may not create power, it may afford reason for exerting a power already enjoyed. Chief Justice White, writing for the majority, held that this act was clearly within Congress's power under the commerce clause. The act amounted to an exertion of power of Congress to arbitrate compulsorily the dispute between the two parties. It merely illustrated the character of regulation essential for the protection of the public right.

Wolf v. Colorado, 338 U.S. 25 (1949), a case dealing with the obligation of state law enforcement officials to respect the 4th Amendment protection against unreasonable searches and seizures. Wolf, a Colorado doctor, was arrested in his office for a state crime, and at the time of his arrest police searched the premises without a warrant. The evidence that the police obtained in this search was later admitted as evidence in Wolf's trial. Wolf subsequently appealed his conviction, contending that the evidence used against him was obtained in violation of his 4th Amendment rights.

On June 27, 1949, the Supreme Court held by a vote of six to three, with Associate Justices Douglas, Murphy,

Chief Justice Taft's opinion in the **Wolff Packing** *case held that legislation could not regulate business conduct under certain circumstances and that the Industrial Court Act violated the company's 14th Amendment rights.*

and Rutledge dissenting, that Wolf's conviction should stand. Associate Justice Frankfurter, speaking for the majority, held that while the federal courts would never have admitted such evidence and while state law enforcement authorities were technically not allowed to obtain evidence without the proper warrants, no precedent existed to prohibit evidence obtained without a warrant from being used in the state courts. This decision was later overruled by the judgment of the Court in *Mapp v. Ohio* (1961), in which the exclusionary rule was extended to state court proceedings.

Wolff Packing Co. v. Court of Industrial Relations, 262 U.S. 522 (1923), a case dealing with legislative authority to abridge freedom of contract in certain circumstances. The Industrial Court Act gave the Court of Industrial Relations authority to permit an owner or employer to dissolve his business if he demonstrated that he could not continue on the terms fixed. The act declared that the preparation of human food was affected by public interest and that the legislature could regulate the business.

The constitutionality of the act was challenged, and the Supreme Court held unanimously that a declaration by the legislature that a business has become affected by a public interest was not enough to justify regulation. In writing the Court's opinion, Chief Justice Taft held that the Industrial Court Act was in conflict with the 14th Amendment in so far as it permitted the fixing of wages and deprived the owner of his property and liberty of contract without due process of law.

Woodson v. North Carolina, 42 U.S. 280 (1976), a case dealing with the constitutionality of mandatory impositions of the death penalty for the crime of first-degree murder under North Carolina law. After the Court's decision in *Furman v. Georgia* (1972), North Carolina changed its law that had provided the jury with discretion to choose whether the convicted defendant should be sentenced to death or life imprisonment in first-degree murder cases. The law was changed to make the death penalty mandatory for that crime. The petitioners, convicted of first-degree murder and given the death penalty, subsequently challenged the statute's constitutionality.

On July 2, 1976, the Supreme Court held by a vote of five to four, with Chief Justice Burger and Associate Justices White, Rehnquist, and Blackmun dissenting, that the mandatory death sentence violated the 8th and 14th Amendments. Associate Justice Stewart, writing for the majority, held that at issue here was the procedure employed by North Carolina to select persons for the unique and irreversible death penalty. The statute's failure to allow the particularized consideration of relevant aspects of each defendant's character before the imposition of the death penalty was the final reason for declaring the statute unconstitutional.

Worcester v. Georgia, 6 Peters 515 (1832), a case dealing with legal jurisdiction of state and federal law within Indian territory. The petitioner in this case, a missionary

Pres. Andrew Jackson's refusal to act on the Court's judgment in **Worcester v. Georgia** *effectively nullified the Court's attempt to establish exclusive federal authority over Indian affairs.*

who was working among the Cherokees, had been sentenced to prison for the violation of a Georgia law that restricted the activities of whites within Indian territory. The petitioner appealed to the Supreme Court for a reversal of his conviction on the grounds that the Cherokees were an autonomous nation and were not subject to Georgia laws.

Although the Supreme Court had rejected the extraterritorial claims of the Cherokees and their right to enter a suit against the state of Georgia in *Cherokee Nation v. Georgia* (1831), Chief Justice Marshall, speaking for the majority, ruled against Georgia in this case, holding that the federal government had exclusive jurisdiction over Indian affairs. Therefore, the Georgia law that required special licenses for white residents in the territory of the Cherokees was unconstitutional, and the missionary should be released. This decision, however, remained unenforced. The state of Georgia, with the tacit support of President Jackson, refused to act on the judgment, and the issue remained deadlocked.

Wyman v. James, 400 U.S. 309 (1971), a case dealing with the constitutional rights of certain welfare recipients. The respondent, James, a beneficiary of the Aid to Families with Dependent Children (AFDC) program, refused a home visit by the caseworker and received notice of the termination of her benefits. She subsequently filed suit, alleging denial of her rights guaranteed under the 1st, 3rd, 4th, 5th,

6th, 9th, 10th, and 14th Amendments and under subchapters IV and XVI of the Social Security Act.

The Supreme Court held by a vote of six to three, with Associate Justices Douglas, Marshall, and Brennan dissenting, that the home visitations provided by New York law were a reasonable administrative tool and did not violate any right guaranteed by 4th and 14th Amendments. Associate Justice Blackmun, writing for the majority, found several factors that supported the conclusion that the home visits were not unreasonable. The visits served a valid and proper administrative purpose for the dispensation of the AFDC program. James had the right to refuse the home visit, Blackmun held, but the consequence of refusal was the termination of relief benefits.

Yates v. United States, 354 U.S. 298 (1957), a case dealing with the limits of federal power to prosecute seditious activity. Several West Coast leaders of the Communist Party of the United States were convicted under the terms of the federal Smith Act of advocating the violent overthrow of the government. They subsequently appealed their convictions, contending that the law violated their 1st Amendment rights.

On June 17, 1957, the Supreme Court held by votes of six to one and four to three, with Associate Justice Clark dissenting and Associate Justices Black and Douglas dissenting in part, that the convictions should be reversed. Associate Justice Harlan, speaking for the majority, held that in the charge to the jury, the presiding judge did not emphasize the legal distinction between "advocacy of abstract doctrine and advocacy directed at promoting unlawful action." Since no such unlawful action could be proved to have resulted from the defendants' teachings, they were therefore not liable to prosecution under the terms of the act. This decision substantially restricted the enforcement of the Smith Act of 1940.

Younger v. Harris, 401 U.S. 37 (1971), a case dealing with the extent of permissible federal intervention in state courts. The respondent, Harris, had been indicted under a California criminal syndicalism law, and he sued to enjoin prosecution. The law was subsequently found unconstitutional by the district court and an injunction issued.

The Supreme Court held by a vote of eight to one, with Associate Justice Douglas dissenting, that the lower court should not have adjudicated Harris's claim because of settled doctrines against federal court interference with state court proceedings. Associate Justice Black, writing for the majority, held that where an injunction was sought against the enforcement of a state's criminal laws, federal judges could grant relief only in cases of proven harassment or prosecutions undertaken in bad faith or other extraordinary circumstances involving risk of irreparable injury. The mere fact that the state law appeared to be invalid on its face was not enough to justify federal intervention with a pending prosecution, Black noted. Even the existence of a "chilling

effect" in the area of 1st Amendment rights was not considered a significant basis, in and of itself, for prohibiting state action. However, if the law was flagrantly and patently violative of express constitutional prohibitions, then there could be a conceivable basis to prohibit state action.

Youngstown Sheet and Tube Co. v. Sawyer, 343 U.S. 579 (1952), a case dealing with the constitutional right of the president to nationalize certain industries in time of emergency. During the Korean War a labor dispute arose in the steel industry and despite the attempts by the Federal Wage Stabilization Board to resolve it, a national strike was threatened. President Truman, fearing the catastrophic effects of a steel strike during wartime, authorized the secretary of Commerce to take over the operation of the nation's steel mills. The management of one of the nationalized steel mills immediately filed suit in federal court to obtain an injunction against the seizure. The injunction was granted by the district court and then brought to the court of appeals.

Since the issue was of such crucial importance, the Supreme Court exercised its right to hear cases that had reached that judicial level and on June 2, 1952, the Supreme Court held by a vote of six to three, with Chief Justice Vinson and Associate Justices Reed and Minton dissenting, that the presidential action was unconstitutional. Associate Justice Black, speaking for the majority, held that since no federal statute empowered the president to settle labor dis-

Pres. Harry Truman's seizure of steel mills because of a labor dispute during the Korean War was held unconstitutional in **Youngstown Sheet and Tube Co. v. Sawyer.**

putes by confiscation, such an action could be taken only with prior congressional sanction.

Zablocki v. Redhail, 434 U.S. 374 (1978), a case dealing with the power of states to prohibit certain marriages. In this case Wisconsin law provided that any resident "having minor issue not in his custody and which he is under an obligation to support by any court order" could not marry without obtaining court approval. The respondent Redhail's application for a marriage license was denied because he had not obtained court permission, and he subsequently challenged the constitutionality of the statute.

The Supreme Court held by a vote of eight to one, with Associate Justice Rehnquist dissenting, that since marriage was a fundamental right, significant interference with its exercise could not be upheld unless closely tailored to effectuate sufficiently important state interests. Associate Justice Marshall, writing for the majority, held that the means used by the state to effectuate the state's interests of protecting out-of-custody children and motivating applicants to fulfill prior support obligations impinged on the right to marry. There were other available means for exacting compliance with support obligations, Marshall noted, that did not restrict the right to marry.

Zemel v. Rusk, (1965), *See* Regan v. Wald.

Zorach v. Clausen, 343 U.S. 306 (1952), a case dealing with the constitutionality of religious instruction for public school students during school hours. New York City established a "released time" program whereby it granted willing students permission to leave public school grounds during school hours in order to receive religious instruction elsewhere. No evidence of coercion on the part of school officials was found. Only those students whose parents requested their release were permitted to participate.

In a six to three decision, the Court upheld the New York program, with Associate Justice Douglas writing the majority opinion. The Court's opinion noted that although the 1st Amendment requires a separation of church and state, that separation is not absolute. Rather, it is well defined. Otherwise, there would be hostility between the state and religion, and religious groups would be unable to benefit from such basic services as fire and police protection. Since religion is an integral part of our society, the state may make provision for those citizens who desire to retreat to a religious sanctuary for worship or instruction. Justices Black, Frankfurter, and Jackson dissented separately, stating that by manipulating its compulsory education laws to help religious sects get pupils, the state had combined church and state.

Biographies
of the
Justices

Biographies of the Justices

Profiles of Each Chief Justice and Associate Justice, Arranged Alphabetically

BALDWIN, HENRY

b. January 14, 1780; member, U. S. House of Representatives (1817-1822); associate justice, U. S. Supreme Court (1830-1844); d. April 21, 1844.

Born in New Haven, Connecticut, and a graduate of Yale College (1797), Baldwin studied law in the office of Alexander Dallas. After the completion of his studies, he decided on a legal career in the west, being admitted to the Pennsylvania bar and eventually settling in Pittsburgh. In 1816, Baldwin was elected to Congress, serving three terms in the House of Representatives, during which time he became known for his outspoken defense of tariffs and protectionist trade policies. He was a strong supporter of Andrew Jackson in the national election of 1828, and with the death of Associate Justice Bushrod Washington the following year, President Jackson nominated Baldwin to the Supreme Court.

Baldwin's strong views on protectionism were an issue for debate during the deliberations in the Senate regarding his nomination, but he was confirmed with only two dissenting votes. On the Court, Baldwin gradually moved away from his early adherence to the constitutional philosophy of Chief Justice Marshall. In *United States v. Arredondo* (1832), he reaffirmed the inviolability of federal treaties with Indians in regard to public land policy.

As regards the issue of slavery, Baldwin voted with the majority in *Groves v. Slaughter* (1841), a case dealing with the Mississippi constitutional provision and law that prevented the importation of slaves into the state, as merchandise or for sale. Baldwin's opinion differed from the majority in that he viewed the prohibition as an obstruction of interstate commerce. In the same term, he was the only dissenter in *United States v. The Schooner Amistad*, in which he adopted a pro-slavery attitude, arguing that a shipload of enslaved blacks who had mutinied and taken over the slave ship that had transported them from Africa should be returned to the custody of the slave traders.

Near the end of his tenure on the Supreme Court, Baldwin's behavior became erratic, and he was eventually unable to carry out the responsibilities of his office. He died in Philadelphia in 1844.

BARBOUR, PHILIP PENDLETON

b. May 25, 1783; member, Virginia House of Delegates (1812-1814); member, U.S. House of Representatives (1814-1825, 1827-1830); federal district judge (1830-1836); associate justice, U.S. Supreme Court (1836-1841); d. February 25, 1841.

Born in Orange County, Virginia, Barbour was educated by an Episcopal clergyman and moved to Kentucky at age seventeen. Although he had already gained some legal training and had begun a private practice in Kentucky, he returned to Virginia in 1801 to spend a year at the College of William and Mary. After resuming his private practice in Virginia, he was elected to the state House of Delegates in 1812 and to the U.S. House of Representatives in 1814, eventually serving as Speaker (1821-1823). In 1825, he entered the Virginia General Court, but returned to Congress in 1827 as a defender of states' rights. In 1830, he was appointed federal judge for the district of Eastern Virginia.

With the resignation of Associate Justice Gabriel Duvall in 1836, President Jackson nominated Barbour to Duvall's seat on the Supreme Court.

On the Court, Barbour initially maintained his strong stand against the encroachment of the federal government against the sovereignty of the states. In *The City of New York v. Miln* (1837), he delivered the opinion of the Court, which held that states had the right to regulate and control the arrival of out-of-state or foreign ships, a decision that was later limited to its facts and criticized by the Court in *Henderson v. New York* (1875).

Another of Justice Barbour's important opinions, in *Charles River Bridge v. Warren Bridge* (1837), concurred with the majority opinion authored by Chief Justice Taney, in refusing to enforce against a state a claimed grant of exclusive business privilege. This was a departure from his previously uncompromising support of states' rights. Barbour ordinarily followed the position of Chief Justice Roger Taney.

Barbour was married to Frances Todd Johnson in 1804 and served on the Court until his death in Washington during the February 1841 session.

BLACK, HUGO LAFAYETTE

b. February 27, 1886; police judge, Birmingham, Alabama (1910-1911); solicitor, Jefferson County, Alabama (1914-1917); U.S. senator (1927-1937); associate justice, U.S. Supreme Court (1937-1971); d. September 25, 1971.

Born in Harlan, Alabama, to a family of modest means, Black was educated at Ashland College and studied briefly at Birmingham Medical College. The law, rather than medicine, however, proved to be Black's more serious interest, and in 1904, he enrolled in the University of Alabama Law School at Tuscaloosa. Two years later, he received his legal degree and was admitted to the Alabama bar.

After his graduation, Black established a private legal practice in Ashland, Alabama, later transferring it to Birmingham. Early in his career he developed a prominent reputation among the local legal community, in part by his successful defense of a black convict, and was appointed police judge of the city of Birmingham. In 1914, Black was elected county solicitor and in this position investigated charges of police brutality at a local jail.

With the outbreak of World War I, Black resigned his office to enlist in the Army, becoming a captain in the 81st Field Artillery. After the war, Black returned to Birmingham, where he reestablished his private legal practice. Frequently defending local workers in personal injury suits, he also served as an attorney for the local chapter of the United Mine Workers. He was married to Josephine Foster in 1921.

The most controversial chapter in Black's early career was his membership in the Birmingham chapter of the Ku Klux Klan, which he joined in 1923. Although he resigned

Hugo Black

less than two years later, it was an association that he would later regret.

Black was elected to the U.S. Senate in 1926, overcoming four other Democrats in the race to succeed Sen. Oscar Underwood. In the Senate, Black championed the causes of relief to farmers, veterans' aid, and government support of the Muscle Shoals Dam project. He was reelected in 1932 and became one of the most active supporters of the New Deal programs of the Roosevelt administration.

In 1937, after the resignation of Associate Justice William Van Devanter, President Roosevelt appointed Black to the Supreme Court. Shortly after Senate confirmation, the fact of Black's former membership in the Ku Klux Klan became public knowledge, and he felt compelled to address the nation on radio, admitting his early association and disavowing any further connection with the racist group.

Supreme Court Career. Black's subsequent Supreme Court record on civil rights issues distinguished him as one of the most liberal justices. He wrote the majority opinion in *Chambers v. Florida* (1940), overturning the murder conviction of several southern blacks who had been violently coerced by local police into confessing to the crime. He also announced the judgment for the Court in *Terry v. Adams* (1953), which held that racial discrimination in voting in party primaries was a violation of the 15th Amendment. He joined in the unanimous decision of the Court in *Brown v. Board of Education* (1954), declaring racial segregation in the public schools to be unconstitutional, and he wrote the majority opinion in *Boynton v. Virginia* (1960), which held that racial segregation in facilities for travelers violated the Interstate Commerce Act.

In contrast to his generally liberal record on civil rights, however, Black wrote the majority opinion in *Korematsu v. United States* (1944), upholding the wartime detention of Japanese-Americans as a necessary precaution in time of national emergency.

Judicial procedure and due process was another of Black's special fields of interest. He wrote the majority opinion in *Johnson v. Zerbst* (1938), establishing the important precedent that every criminal defendant in federal court is entitled to counsel according to the provisions of the 6th Amendment. He dissented in *Betts v. Brady* (1942), arguing against the Court's contention that the due process clause of the 14th Amendment does not require that states provide free legal counsel to indigent defendants. He dissented in *United States v. Rabinowitz* (1950), which restricted 4th Amendment protection against searches and seizures incident to a lawful arrest. He also voted with the minority in *Carlson v. Landon* (1952), contending that deportation proceedings for aliens were protected by the due process clause of the 4th Amendment.

Black joined the dissent in *Ullmann v. United States* (1956), arguing that witnesses who have been granted immunity do not forgo their right to avoid self-incrimination. He spoke for the Court in the landmark defendant's rights case of *Gideon v. Wainwright* (1963), overruling *Betts v. Brady* and establishing the precedent under the 14th Amendment that all persons accused of serious crimes in state courts be provided with an attorney. He also wrote the majority opinion in *Pointer v. Texas* (1965), which extended the right to confront and cross-examine prosecution witnesses in state courts. He joined the dissent in *McKeiver v. Pennsylvania* (1971), arguing that the 6th and 14th Amendments' right to a trial by jury should extend to juvenile defendants.

Black spoke for the Court in *United States v. South-Eastern Underwriters Association* (1944), expanding the regulatory power of the federal government by establishing that the insurance industry constituted interstate commerce and was therefore subject to federal regulation. This opinion suddenly called into question state regulation of insurance companies so that Congress passed a law explicitly authorizing the states to regulate.

Black maintained his support of organized labor throughout his Supreme Court career. He wrote the majority opinion in *National Labor Relations Board v. Waterman Steamship Corp.* (1940), holding that the Court of Appeals should not have substituted its judgment for that of the National Labor Relations Board. He dissented in *United Public Workers v. Mitchell* (1947), opposing restrictions on the political activities of federal government employees. He also dissented in *United States v. United Mine Workers* (1947), which upheld the contempt conviction of union

labor leader John L. Lewis. One of Black's most important opinions came in *Youngstown Sheet and Tube Co. v. Sawyer* (1952), in which he wrote the majority opinion holding that President Truman had exceeded his constitutional authority in nationalizing steel mills to head off the threat of a strike.

With regard to the relations of church and state, Black spoke for the Court in *Everson v. Board of Education of Ewing Township* (1947), which held that states may reimburse parents for the cost of transporting their children to parochial schools. He also wrote the majority opinion in *Illinois ex rel. McCollum v. Board of Education* (1948), ruling that any religious instruction on public school premises where attendance was compulsory unless excused by a parent was a violation of the 1st Amendment protection against the establishment of religion. Black's most important majority opinion on this issue came in *Engle v. Vitale* (1962), which held that voluntary prayers sponsored by the public schools are unconstitutional.

Linked to the issue of freedom of religion, in Black's philosophy, was the freedom of speech, and this became an increasingly important issue before the Court in the early years of the Cold War. Black's consistent position in defense of those considered "subversive elements" in society often brought him into ideological conflict with the majority of his colleagues on the Court.

He dissented in *American Communications Association v. Douds* (1950), which upheld a requirement of the National Labor Relations Act that all union officials produce affidavits to prove that they had never been members of the Communist Party. He voted with the minority in *Feiner v. New York* (1951), opposing the conviction of a street speaker arrested for the disturbance of the public order. He also dissented in *Garner v. Board of Public Works* (1951), opposing the Court's decision that a loyalty oath for public employees was constitutional. He dissented in *Scales v. United States* and concurred in *Noto v. United States* (1961), arguing that the 1st Amendment guarantees are violated by laws prohibiting membership in revolutionary groups. One of his last opinions came in the Pentagon Papers Case (*New York Times Co. v. United States*, 1971), in which he concurred in upholding the 1st Amendment freedom of the press against government restraint.

On the issue of obscenity, Black joined the dissent in *Roth v. United States* (1957), claiming that the publication of even "prurient" material is protected by the 1st Amendment. Taking a somewhat more conservative stand, Black dissented in *Griswold v. Connecticut* (1965), arguing that the majority had read into the Constitution rights of privacy that were not explicitly there and had thus substituted their judgment for that of the legislature in striking down a state law prohibiting the use of contraceptives.

With regard to the question of equal representation, Black dissented in *Colegrove v. Green* (1946), arguing that legislative apportionment was not a purely political question and could be legitimately reviewed by the courts. Following this philosophy, he wrote the majority opinion in *Wesberry v. Sanders* (1964), which held that congressional districts within a state must be of roughly equal population. He dissented, however, in *Harper v. Virginia State Board of Elections* (1966), which held that the imposition of a state poll tax was a violation of the 14th Amendment. He also dissented in *Gaston County v. United States* (1969), upholding the legality of a voters' literacy test. Black wrote an opinion in *Oregon v. Mitchell* (1970) upholding the constitutionality of a lowered minimum age for voting in federal elections. Throughout his judicial career Black justified his positions not on their intrinsic merits but by their conformity to what he viewed as the intentions of the drafters of the Constitution, and he consistently denounced what he saw as attempts by the Court to decide questions on the basis of the personal judgments of the justices.

After the death of his first wife, Black married Elizabeth DeMeritte in 1957. He died in Washington in 1971, shortly after his resignation from the Supreme Court.

BLACKMUN, HARRY ANDREW

b. November 12, 1908; clerk, U.S. Circuit Court of Appeals (1932-1933); judge, U.S. Circuit Court of Appeals (1959-1970); associate justice, U.S. Supreme Court (1970-   ).

Born in Nashville, Illinois, Blackmun was raised in St. Paul, Minnesota, where he was a boyhood friend of Warren Burger, with whom he would later serve on the Court. Blackmun received his undergraduate education at Harvard College (1929) and his law degree from Harvard Law School (1932). After serving as a clerk of the U.S. Court of Appeals for the 8th Circuit, Blackmun taught law at St. Paul College of Law, and in 1934, he joined a prominent Minneapolis law firm. In addition to his private practice, Blackmun also taught law at the University of Minnesota Law School (1945-1947). In 1950, he became resident counsel for the Mayo Clinic. From 1959 to 1970, Blackmun served as judge of the U.S. Court of Appeals' 8th Circuit. In 1970, after the resignation of Associate Justice Abe Fortas and the rejection of nominees Clement Haynsworth and G. Harold Carswell by the Senate, President Richard Nixon appointed Blackmun to the Supreme Court.

During the early years of his tenure on the Court, Blackmun often concurred with the opinions of his friend and fellow conservative, Chief Justice Warren Burger. Like the Chief Justice, he dissented in the Pentagon Papers Case (*New York Times Co. v. United States*, 1971), arguing that the Court should have remanded the case to determine whether the President's power to protect national security interests outweighs the 1st Amendment rights of the press. He also dissented in *Furman v. Georgia* (1972), in which he opposed the Court's abolition of state death penalty laws. Blackmun voted with the majority in *Miller v. California* (1973), which established the concept of applying local

Harry A. Blackmun

standards to determine if materials are obscene. He also joined the Court in the Nixon Tapes Case (*United States v. Nixon*, 1974), which ruled that the President did not have an absolute executive privilege to withhold evidence to be used in a criminal trial.

Blackmun's most significant majority opinion came in the landmark case of *Roe v. Wade* (1973), which struck down state anti-abortion laws on the grounds that a woman's right to privacy in this matter is protected by the 14th Amendment. He maintained this position in subsequent cases dealing with the right to abortion. In more recent years Blackmun has shown an increasingly independent attitude and has frequently joined in positions advocated by the Court's more liberal members.

BLAIR, JOHN

b. 1732; various representative and judicial positions in Virginia; associate justice, U.S. Supreme Court (1789-1796); d. August 31, 1800.

Born to a leading Virginia family (his father, John Blair, served as a member of the House of Burgesses and later as governor of Virginia), Blair was educated at the College of William and Mary and studied law in London (1755). After the completion of his studies, he returned to Virginia and became a member of the state legislature, the House of Burgesses, in 1766.

A strong supporter of the revolutionary cause in the

aftermath of the Stamp Act, Blair signed the non-importation agreement that was intended to exert economic pressure on Great Britain. In 1776, he served as a member of the state convention for the Virginia constitution and was appointed to the state's Privy Council, on which he served until 1777.

Blair's legal background distinguished him for service in the new state, and in 1780 he was appointed judge of the first state court of appeals. An ardent Federalist, he was one of the delegates from Virginia to the constitutional convention in Philadelphia and voted for the acceptance of the proposed constitution with the other delegates from his state, Washington and Madison. Later, at the Virginia constitutional convention, he actively supported ratification. In recognition of his efforts, President Washington nominated him to be one of the five original associate justices of the U.S. Supreme Court in 1789.

Even before his service on the Supreme Court, Blair was committed to the principle of judicial review. Serving as a state appellate judge, he had asserted the right of the Virginia state courts to overturn acts and resolutions of the legislature as unconstitutional in *Commonwealth of Virginia v. Caton et al.* (1782). Among his most important acts on the Supreme Court was his assertion of the impropriety of a Court serving in a non-judicial function in the Hayburn case (1792), on the basis of the separation of powers provided in the Constitution.

The pressures of serving on the southern circuit proved to be too much for him, and he resigned from the Supreme Court in 1796, retiring to his home in Williamsburg, where he died in 1800.

BLATCHFORD, SAMUEL MILFORD

b. March 9, 1820; various judicial positions in New York; associate justice, U.S. Supreme Court (1882-1893); d. July 7, 1893.

Born in New York City, the son of Richard Blatchford, a member of the New York State legislature and attorney for the Bank of England and the Bank of the United States, the younger Blatchford graduated from Columbia College in 1837 and served for several years afterward as the personal secretary of William H. Seward. He was admitted to the bar in 1842 and entered as a partner in his father's legal practice. In 1845, he left to become the law partner of Seward, maintaining his association with the former governor until 1862. In 1867, Blatchford was appointed by President Grant to be judge of the Southern District of New York, and in 1872, he was named circuit judge of the same district. With the long-awaited resignation of Associate Justice Ward Hunt in 1882, President Chester Arthur appointed Blatchford to the Supreme Court.

Throughout his service on the Court, Blatchford was known as an expert in commercial law and wrote the majority opinion in several important economic cases. In *Chicago, Milwaukee and St. Paul Railway v. Minnesota* (1890), he spoke for the Court, ruling that the judiciary has the right to review railroad tariff schedules imposed by the states because the lack of review of the reasonableness of such rates deprived the company of its property without due process of law and deprived it of equal protection of the laws. On the issue of self-incrimination, Blatchford wrote the majority opinion in *Counselman v. Hitchcock* (1892), which established the precedent that the 5th Amendment can be waived only if a party or witness is afforded absolute immunity against future prosecution for the offense to which the question relates. He joined the majority opinion in the case of *In re Neagle* (1890), which held that a federal marshal involved in a death in legitimate pursuit of his duty could not be tried by a state court.

Blatchford served on the Court until his death in Newport, Rhode Island, in 1893.

BRADLEY, JOSEPH P.

b. March 14, 1813; associate justice, U.S. Supreme Court (1870-1892); d. January 22, 1892.

Joseph P. Bradley

Born in Berne, New York, to a farming family, Bradley was educated at Rutgers University (Class of 1836) and studied law in the office of Archer Gifford in Newark, New Jersey. After being admitted to the bar in 1839, he established a lucrative private practice and married Mary Hornblower, the daughter of the chief justice of the New

Jersey Supreme Court. A specialist in commercial law, he represented the Camden and Amboy Railroad before the Supreme Court in *Milnor v. New Jersey Railroad* (1860). As a result of the Judiciary Act of 1869, the size of the Supreme Court was increased to nine, and in 1870 Bradley was nominated by President Grant to fill the vacancy caused by the death of Associate Justice John Catron in 1865.

At the time of Bradley's nomination, the Supreme Court had overturned the constitutionality of federal attempts to make treasury notes legal tender in *Hepburn v. Griswold* (1870). However, Bradley (together with William Strong, another Grant appointee) supported the constitutionality of such legislation and voted for a reconsideration of the issue in *Knox v. Lee* (1871). His opinion, concurring with the newly formed majority, reversed the previous decision.

Bradley dissented in the *Slaughterhouse Cases* (1873), in which he argued against the constitutional right of states to license monopolies and advocated a broad reading of the privileges and immunities of national citizenship protected by the 14th Amendment. Bradley was generally associated with the tendency of the Court to strike down populist and progressive economic legislation as inconsistent with the due process clause of the 14th Amendment. In the *Civil Rights Cases* (1883), however, he voted with the majority, ruling that the federal government did not have the constitutional right to legislate against private racially discriminatory conduct.

In 1877, Bradley was appointed to the Electoral Commission that resolved the controversy concerning the Hayes-Tilden presidential election. He served on the Supreme Court until his death in Washington, D.C., in 1892.

BRANDEIS, LOUIS DEMBITZ

b. November 13, 1856; associate justice, U.S. Supreme Court (1916-1939); d. October 5, 1941.

Justice Louis D. Brandeis was born in Louisville, Kentucky, the son of Austrian Jewish immigrants. Brandeis' father was a successful merchant who shipped grain and other goods along the Ohio River.

In 1872 the Brandeis family returned to Europe to visit, and young Louis was tutored in Latin and Greek in order to gain admittance to the stricter European schools. Although lacking the academic background his European contemporaries enjoyed, he entered the famous Annen-Realschule of Dresden, Germany, on a probationary basis and rose to the top of his class at the end of the first year.

After returning to the United States in 1875, Brandeis was accepted by the Harvard Law School, which was implementing the new case law approach to legal education. While in Boston, Brandeis met and developed a lasting friendship with Oliver Wendell Holmes, Jr. They often met to discuss legal theory and shared the conviction that the existing body of common law was unsuited for the complexities and changing needs of an industrial society. Both saw the injus-

Louis D. Brandeis

tices that could result when legal theory was divorced from the realities of the workplace. Together they discussed the new principle of the "living law," which incorporated both moral and legal principles, applied to social needs.

Brandeis graduated first in his class at Harvard with an overall mark of 97, the highest on record. The university had to set aside an old rule prohibiting students under twenty-one years of age to graduate in order for Brandeis, who was then still twenty, to graduate with his classmates.

Brandeis began work after graduation with a private firm of a family friend in St. Louis, Missouri. Within a year, however, he left to form his own firm in Boston with his friend and former law school roommate, Samuel D. Warren. By the end of two years, the firm of Warren and Brandeis had become notably successful. Brandeis' reputation for ability and honesty had spread over New England and beyond.

In 1883, Harvard asked Brandeis to deliver two lectures per week on the law of evidence. He was soon offered an assistant professorship for the following year. Although encouraged by his family to accept, Brandeis preferred to be an active practitioner. He enjoyed the clash of the courtroom.

As a highly successful corporate lawyer, Brandeis often represented business giants whose interests were not always in harmony with those of the public or the workers employed by them. This was a time of considerable social upheaval. Workers were unionizing to press for improved working conditions and wages, while the established institutions were interested in maintaining the status quo. Brandeis believed in free market capitalism but was against unfair monopolizing and the oppression of workers. He became active in local charities and was a member of the Civil Service Reform Association and the Boston American Citizenship Committee. He and several Boston businessmen, including Edward A. Filene, founded the Good Government Association to fight corrupt legislation and recommend just laws.

Brandeis' commitment to social causes troubled his corporate clients and many of his friends, who expected his unwavering alliance to big business and the moneyed class. He was at the same time distrusted by many liberals and union members, who felt that he changed his positions and divided his loyalties too often. Both groups were represented by Brandeis. He believed in just and fair treatment for all parties in any dispute, but his moderate positions tended to alienate the people on either side. He was often chosen as an impartial advisor or arbitrator between workers and employers or railroads and shippers and sometimes recommended resolutions that satisfied neither party. Brandeis was against bigness in any sector of the economy and saw the dangers of too much power being held by the unions as well as by the employers. He was as much against "closed shop" unions, which required all employees to join, as he was against "yellow dog" contracts, which conditioned employment upon the worker's promise not to join a union.

Brandeis insisted upon doing all of his public interest work free, so that he could follow his conscience on any particular issue rather than be tied to the demands of one party or interest.

In 1907, Brandeis argued before the U.S. Supreme Court on behalf of women laundry workers in the case of *Muller v. Oregon* (1908). The Court had previously struck down minimum hour laws in the famous case of *Lochner v. New York* (1905), holding that the state of New York's attempt to set a minimum work week for bakers was an infringement on the workers' freedom to contract for their labor. In *Muller*, Brandeis argued that the state of Oregon could pass similar legislation to protect a specific class of citizens, namely women. To impress upon the justices the need for this legislation, Brandeis compiled a lengthy statistical and factual account of the the effect long hours had on the health of women workers. He provided overwhelming proof that exhaustion from overwork caused disease, industrial accidents, and miscarriages among women. The use of such evidence in appellate advocacy was revolutionary in its day. Brandeis won a majority of the justices to his side, and the quality of his brief was praised in the Court's opinion. The brief became known as the "Brandeis brief," and today briefs of that style are often referred to as Brandeis briefs.

At this point, Brandeis' reputation had grown nationwide. He became actively involved in the 1912 campaign for president of Woodrow Wilson, who had pledged to fight the monopolies and to help laborers obtain better working conditions.

When Wilson won the election, some expected Brandeis to be named to his cabinet as attorney general. By this time, however, there was so much controversy surrounding Brandeis and his public interest activities that he was passed by. The country was therefore greatly shocked when on January 28, 1916, President Wilson nominated Brandeis to be associate justice of the Supreme Court. His appointment was bitterly opposed by some of Brandeis' oldest enemies. Many opponents centered around Senator Taft and his supporters. Taft had wanted the appointment himself and had also been hurt politically by Brandeis during his presidency. Political conservatives and representatives of big business organized an attack against Brandeis by attempting to show that Brandeis had engaged in unethical activity, was interested only in promoting himself, and was a dangerous socialist radical. People from almost every controversial case he had ever litigated appeared to testify that Brandeis was not to be trusted. A petition of fifty-five signatures of prominent Boston citizens, including Harvard's president, A. Lawrence Lowell, was submitted opposing Brandeis' appointment. The petition stated that Brandeis' reputation was not good and his temperament not appropriate for that of a Supreme Court justice. In the several weeks of hearings held regarding his appointment, however, not one charge of misconduct or unethical activity could be substantiated. After over four months of testimony, Brandeis' appointment was finally confirmed by the judiciary committee by a vote of ten to eight, and by a subsequent vote of forty-seven to twenty-two in the Senate.

Supreme Court Career. On the Court, Brandeis was to join Holmes, who after establishing his place in history as the "Great Dissenter," could now enjoy the company of a like-minded associate justice. Brandeis, in fact, was the more progressive of the two, and sometimes found himself as the lone dissenter. Even when Brandeis was not among the majority in his legal opinions, his dissents were nonetheless of great importance. They pointed to the future and were read and absorbed by younger lawyers and judges across the country. Practicing attorneys were beginning to apply his new approach of the "living law" in arguing their cases in the courts.

Justice Brandeis' first major dissent came in *New York Central Railroad v. Winfield* (1917), in which a railroad employee had sued because of injuries he received on the job. Congress had passed the Federal Employers Liability Act, and the majority of the Court held that Congress intended the act to cover completely all liability of interstate railroads in such cases, thereby pre-empting state workers' compensation statutes that also attempted to protect railroad workers. Brandeis, however, wrote in his dissent that this law was not enough and that states should have the option to pass similar laws to provide more adequately for their workers. He supported his position with a discussion of the historical inadequacy of common law protection for injured workers and the development of state worker compensation plans that did not conflict with the federal act. It was a Brandeis brief in judicial form. Other such opinions followed, the result of arduous research by Brandeis done in his workroom above his apartment in Washington, D.C.

Occasionally, Brandeis wrote for the majority, as he did in *Bunting v. Oregon* (1917), in which minimum wage laws in the state of Oregon were upheld by the Court. Felix Frankfurter of Harvard argued the case for Oregon and wrote a 400-page brief embodying a statistical analysis of the need for such protective legislation. The "Brandeis brief" had taken hold as a model for contemporary lawyers. The Brandeis brief was not without its critics, however, as the statistics used in such arguments were often seen as manipulable and unreliable. When Chief Justice White was confronted with a Brandeis brief in the case of *Adams v. Tanner* (1917), he stated, "I could compile a brief twice as thick to prove that the legal profession ought to be abolished." The majority remained suspicious of the use of such facts or the opinions of academics or other expert witnesses. Other justices would comment that such facts were interesting, but only mildly persuasive.

By the 1920's, the Progressive movement had slowed due to the general prosperity experienced by the nation. Former President Taft had been named chief justice of the Court by President Harding. Brandeis and Holmes were once again the two lone dissenters. Taft privately accused Brandeis of controlling Holmes, so often were they concurrent in their dissents. After the 1929 stock market crash, the trend was again for liberalism. Trade unions experienced a growth in strength. New justices were appointed to the Court, men who shared or were influenced by Brandeis' views. Benjamin Cardozo was appointed to replace Holmes, who at ninety was too old to continue. Taft resigned in 1930, and by 1935, Brandeis was writing for the majority.

Under the Court's new majority, the constitutionality of Franklin D. Roosevelt's New Deal legislation was generally upheld, until the National Industrial Recovery Act was passed. Under the act, the President had the power to control major aspects of interstate commerce without the approval of Congress. Brandeis regarded this as too much power to reside in one man and joined the majority in holding against Congress's attempts to delegate excessive rule-making authority to the chief executive in *Panama Refining Co. v Ryan* (1935) and *Schechter Poultry Corp. v. U.S.* (1935).

The majority of New Deal measures, however, were upheld by the Court. The die-hard conservatives were in the minority, and Chief Justice Hughes was sometimes swung over into the Brandeis camp. Many New Deal policies were almost embodiments of Brandeis-style doctrine of the control and organization of society and its larger institutions for the protection of individual rights and opportunities. Brandeis retained his disapproval for policies that threatened to spread the evils of bigness to the government itself.

By the mid-1930's, when economic recovery seemed imminent, the conservative justices regained their domination of the Court. Brandeis again became known as a dissenter, but in fact voted more often with the majority than the minority. It has been said that "His great work was done, not in opposing the Court, but in leading it."

Despite Brandeis's identity as a reformer and progressive, he was conservative in the Burkean sense of applying old, tried and true moral principles to modern times by adjusting them to the changing needs of society. He believed in non-interference with the legislative process, which in times of progressive legislation meant progressive Court opinions through the exercise of judicial restraint.

Brandeis was a Jeffersonian Democrat and favored policies that protected the independence of the individual. Any attempt at monopolization posed an unconstitutional restraint on the free enterprise system by forcing out competition from smaller businesses. Brandeis's ideal economy was based on the autonomy of the individual artisan and other self-employed citizens. Monopolies threatened this ideal by forcing men to work for others. An example of this philosophy is Brandeis's dissent in *Quaker City Cab Co. v. Pennsylvania* (1928). The case involved a state law that imposed a higher tax on intrastate cab companies owned by corporations than on those owned by individuals and partnerships. The majority struck down the law as an unconstitutional classification and a violation of the equal protection clause. Brandeis stated that the distinction between a corporation and an individual was not an unreasonable classification. The state has a right, Brandeis argued, to check the growth of corporations and their increasing power to subject labor to capital and to absorb local competition.

The 1933 case of *Liggett v. Lee* also dealt with the control of business by the state. Florida had imposed a higher sales tax on chain stores operating in more than one county. The majority held this a violation of the equal protection clause. Brandeis again dissented, stating that "business must yield to public interest." He believed that whenever ownership was separated from control, individual initiative suffered along with equality of opportunity. Brandeis was one of the first to urge businessmen to implement profit-sharing programs to increase worker incentive. By separating labor and ownership from the day-to-day operation of a business, both initiative and productivity would decline unless the worker was given a stake in the success and profitability of the business.

Brandeis's defense of individual liberty extended to the area of free speech, where he and Holmes often joined as dissenters in cases involving the right to criticize the government freely. The case of *Abrams v. United States* (1919) in which the Court upheld the convictions of anti-war activists under the Espionage Act, was the first of several in which Holmes and Brandeis were the lone dissenters. Holmes believed in the free marketplace of ideas, while Brandeis's philosophy extended to his idea of the nature of a free society. In order to change peacefully, a free democracy had to allow those unhappy with the status quo to voice their opinions. Otherwise, violent change would be encouraged by forcing divergent views underground.

Probably Brandeis's most eloquent expression of his view on the freedom of speech came in his concurring opinion in *Whitney v. California* (1927). Anita Whitney was a Communist who had been convicted under California's "criminal syndicalism" law for participating in a meeting of the Communist Labor Party Convention. The law made it a crime knowingly to become a member of any group that advocated the use of violence to effect social change. The majority of the Court upheld the law as a legitimate use of the state's police power. Because the Court could not inquire into the facts of the case to determine if Whitney's acts or statements constituted a "clear and present danger" to the state, Brandeis was forced to concur in the majority's opinion. In the process, however, he wrote as impassioned a statement for free speech as had ever been written. He stated that "Those who won our independence believed that . . . freedom to think as you will and to speak as you think are means indispensable to the discovery and spread of political truth." He further stated that "to justify suppression of free speech there must be reasonable ground to fear that serious evil will result if free speech is practiced," and that the danger apprehended must be imminent. Because Whitney had not asserted in her appeal that her actions and words did not present an imminent danger to the state, Brandeis had to uphold the conviction. The facts surrounding her prosecution were not subject to the Supreme Court's review. Nevertheless, Brandeis set a standard that was to be followed in future cases. The "clear and present danger" test later became the standard that the Court uses in deciding cases involving free speech.

Although not noticeable to the other members of the Court, Brandeis became aware in his later years on the bench that his capacity for work had started to decline. On February 13, 1939, at the age of eighty-three, Brandeis left the Court in ordinary fashion after a routine workday, never to return as a justice. That night he sent a note to the President that read: "Pursuant to the Act of March 1, 1937, I retire this day from regular active service on the Bench. Louis D. Brandeis."

Last Years. Following Brandeis's departure from the Court, he remained active in public affairs closest to his heart. He devoted much of his time to the Zionist movement and worked for the emigration of Jews in Nazi Germany to Palestine. He worked with President Roosevelt to form an organization to help both Jewish and Gentile German refugees.

Ultimately, Brandeis's strength began to fail him, and in 1940 a bout of pneumonia further debilitated him. In

October 1941 he suffered a heart attack, and on October 5, he died at the age of eighty-five in Washington, D.C. Today Brandeis's reputation continues on as one of the greatest legal minds the world has ever produced.

BRENNAN, WILLIAM JOSEPH, JR.

b. April 25, 1906; judge, New Jersey Superior Court (1949-1952); justice, New Jersey Supreme Court (1952-1956); associate justice, U.S. Supreme Court (1956-).

Born in Newark, New Jersey, son of a union organizer who later became municipal Commissioner of Safety, Brennan was educated at the Wharton School of Finance of the University of Pennsylvania, from which he received a B.S. degree in 1928. Following graduation, he entered Harvard Law School and studied under Professor Felix Frankfurter, with whom he would later serve on the Supreme Court. Brennan received his law degree from Harvard in 1931 and the next year joined the prominent Newark law firm of Pitney, Hardin & Skinner. Early in his legal career he began to specialize in labor law.

With the outbreak of World War II, Brennan enlisted in the Army and was attached to the general staff with the rank of major. After serving as legal counsel for the director of the civilian personnel division, he was named civilian labor branch chief of Army Ordnance. At the time of his demobilization in 1945, Brennan had been promoted to colonel.

Returning to his Newark law firm, Brennan resumed his career in labor law. Representing several large corporations involved in labor disputes, he spoke out for the institution of compulsory arbitration, especially in cases where work suspension affected the public good. In 1949, Brennan was appointed a judge of the New Jersey Superior Court, a position he held for three years, during which time he was assigned to the appellate division. In 1952, Gov. Alfred E. Driscoll appointed Brennan to the New Jersey Supreme Court, where he distinguished himself as a judicial innovator, implementing a system of pre-trial conferences that helped to alleviate the serious congestion on the state court dockets.

In 1956, after the resignation of Associate Justice Sherman Minton, President Eisenhower appointed Brennan, a Democrat and a liberal, to the Supreme Court. The appointment was subsequently criticized on the political grounds that the President was attempting to gain liberal votes in the upcoming election, but Brennan was confirmed by the Senate on March 19, 1957, opposed only by Sen. Joseph McCarthy, whose anti-communist investigations Brennan had previously criticized.

Supreme Court Career. Throughout his tenure on the Court, Brennan was a strong defender of 1st Amendment rights. Opposing the unlimited right of the federal government to restrict the activities of politically "subversive" elements within society, he dissented in *Barenblatt v. United States* (1959), in which he argued for the 1st Amendment rights of witnesses appearing before the House Un-American Activities Committee. He also dissented in part in *Communist Party v. Subversive Activities Control Board* (1961), which held that compulsory registration of Communist Party members did not violate their 1st Amendment rights. He took a similar minority view in *Scales v. United States* (1961), in defense of the 1st and 5th Amendment rights of revolutionary groups.

Brennan's opposition to the compulsory registration of communists was eventually accepted by the Court in *Albertson v. Subversive Activities Control Board* (1965), in which Brennan wrote the unanimous decision. He also spoke for the Court in *Keyishian v. Board of Regents* (1967), which overturned a state law requiring public school teachers to take loyalty oaths.

Brennan defended other aspects of 1st Amendment guarantees as well. He wrote the majority opinion in *NAACP v. Button* (1963), overturning state laws that prohibited the solicitation of legal businesses by public interest organizations as a violation of a 1st Amendment right of association. He also spoke for the Court in *New York Times Co. v. Sullivan* (1964), holding that the Constitution's 1st Amendment guarantees of a free press protect journalists from libel actions in most cases.

Early in his tenure, Brennan wrote the majority decision in the obscenity case of *Roth v. United States*, which held that obscene material is not protected by the free speech guarantees of the 1st Amendment. In this opinion, Brennan defined obscenity in part as that which appeals primarily to "prurient interests." He amplified on this standard in his opinion in *Jacobellis v. Ohio* (1964), holding that material must be devoid of redeeming social value in order to be classified as obscene. In *Freedman v. Maryland* (1965), his opinion established strict constitutional guidelines by which states may censor or suppress certain films. Brennan dissented in the later obscenity case of *Miller v. California* (1973), which applied "community standards" and permitted more state control in defining obscenity.

With regard to voting rights, Brennan wrote the majority opinion in *Baker v. Carr* (1962), which established for the first time federal jurisdiction over redistricting within the states. One of his most important opinions came in *Katzenbach v. Morgan* (1966), in which he held that Congress was within its constitutional power in enacting the Voting Rights Act of 1965 to enable Spanish-speaking citizens to vote even if they could not demonstrate fluency in English. He also wrote the majority opinion in *Kirkpatrick v. Preisler* (1969), holding that Missouri's congressional redistricting statute did not achieve equal representation as "nearly as practicable." He dissented, in part, however, in *Mahan v. Howell* (1973), in which the Court allowed the states greater flexibility in their plans for redistricting state legislatures.

On civil rights issues, he spoke for the Court in *Green v. County School Board* (1968), holding a "freedom of choice" plan of desegregating local schools, if it does not in fact dismantle the segregated system, is unconstitutional. Brennan also wrote the majority opinion in *Keyes v. Denver School District No. 1* (1973), holding that where there has been intentional segregation in one portion of the school district, the courts should presume that segregation in other portions was intentional as well. He joined the dissenting opinions in *Milliken v. Bradley* (1974), arguing for the propriety of judicially-ordered inter-district busing to eliminate segregation of schools.

In the case of *Regents of the University of California v. Bakke* (1978), Brennan joined Justices Blackmun, Marshall, and White in their minority view that racially-based quotas for admission to federally funded educational programs did not violate the Civil Rights Act of 1964 and were constitutional. In line with that position, Brennan spoke for the Court in *United Steel Workers of America v. Weber* (1979), upholding the legality of voluntary "affirmative action" programs designed to reduce racial discrimination in private industry.

On the issues involving criminal procedure, Brennan spoke for the Court in *Fay v. Noia* (1963), holding that a person convicted by a state court may be heard in the federal court system even if he has not exhausted all appeals within the state courts. He also wrote the majority opinion in *Malloy v. Hogan* (1964), extending the 5th Amendment protection against self-incrimination to state defendants through the due process provision of the 14th Amendment. He dissented in *Johnson v. Louisiana* and *Apodaca v. Oregon* (1972), opposing the majority decision that convictions in state jury trials need not be unanimous.

Brennan spoke for the Court in *Warden v. Hayden* (1967), upholding the right of police officers to search for supplementary evidence as well as the actual instruments of a crime. In his majority opinion in *United States v. Wade* (1967), however, he ruled that post-indictment identifications of suspects in police lineups without the presence of the suspect's attorney were inadmissible in court. He also wrote the majority opinion in *In re Winship* (1970), which required proof beyond a reasonable doubt to find that a juvenile is delinquent. He dissented in *Scott v. Illinois* (1979), which held that indigent state defendants must be provided with free legal counsel only in those cases in which conviction will result in imprisonment.

Brennan consistently supported the cause of equal rights for women before the law. He spoke for the Court in *Weinberger v. Wiesenfeld* (1975), holding that the payment of Social Security survivor's benefits only to widows and not to widowers violates the equal protection rights of working women. He also wrote the majority opinions in *Craig v. Boren* (1976), dealing with legal drinking ages, and in *Orr v. Orr* (1979), dealing with alimony. In each of these cases he held that the state laws impermissibly distinguished between the sexes.

After the retirement of Associate Justice William O.

Douglas in 1975, Brennan became the senior associate justice on the Supreme Court. In that position he continued to enunciate his relatively liberal judicial philosophy as a frequent dissenter on the more conservative Burger Court.

BREWER, DAVID JOSIAH

b. June 20, 1837; various city, county, and state judicial positions in Kansas; associate justice, Supreme Court (1889-1910); d. March 28, 1910.

David J. Brewer

Born of American missionary parents (Josiah Brewer and Emilia Field Brewer) in Smyrna (Izmir), Turkey, Brewer attended Wesleyan University in Middletown, Connecticut, for two years before transferring to Yale University, from which he graduated with honors in 1856. He then studied law for a year in the office of his uncle, Stephen J. Field, who became a Supreme Court justice in 1863. Brewer subsequently enrolled in Albany Law School, from which he graduated in 1858. He was admitted to the New York bar but soon moved to Leavenworth, Kansas, where he married Louise Landon in 1861.

Brewer's first public post was as a commissioner of the federal circuit court for the district of Kansas. He was county judge of probate and criminal courts (1862), judicial district judge (1865-1869), and city attorney of Leavenworth (1869-1870). Brewer was elected to the state supreme court in 1870 and reelected in 1876 and 1882. In

1881, when Kansas passed a prohibition amendment, Brewer defended the right of manufacturers to compensation for their confiscated property. Brewer was appointed a federal circuit court judge by President Arthur in 1884 and served until 1889, when Pres. Benjamin Harrison appointed him to succeed Justice Stanley Matthews on the U.S. Supreme Court. Brewer served on the Court with his uncle until Field's retirement in 1897.

Associate Justice Brewer was a moderate conservative who staunchly defended the right of due process, personal liberty, and property rights. He favored a strict interpretation of the Constitution, viewing with concern a drift toward federal centralization of power. He opposed the right of the federal government to impose an income tax in *Pollock v. Farmers' Loan and Trust Company* (1895). However, he stood firmly behind the power of the federal government when he wrote for a unanimous Court (*In re Debs*, 1895), denying a writ of *habeas corpus* after the arrest of labor leader Eugene Debs for refusing to obey an injunction against the Pullman strike. Brewer argued broadly for the right of the government to issue injunctions to protect interstate commerce and the U.S. mails.

Brewer dissented in *Holden v. Hardy* (1898), a case upholding the eight-hour work day for miners, and agreed with the Court in invalidating a ten-hour law for bakers in *Lochner v. New York* (1905). However, he wrote the Court's opinion upholding a ten-hour work day for women in *Muller v. Oregon* (1908), in an opinion noting the Brandeis brief and its documentary evidence. In *Reagan v. Farmers' Loan and Trust Company* (1894), Brewer argued that the due process of law entitled a carrier to a fair return on its investment. He dissented vigorously in the Chinese Exclusion cases (1889-1905), as he felt they were a denial of personal freedom. He supported woman suffrage.

From 1895 to 1898, Brewer was president of the commission created by Congress to investigate the boundary dispute between Venezuela and British Guiana. He was an anti-imperialist who favored independence for the Philippines. Brewer was a noted public speaker, an officer of the American Society of International Law, and a lecturer on American citizenship at Yale and on corporate law at Columbian University (now George Washington University).

After the death of his wife in 1898, he married Emma Minor Mott (1901) and continued to serve on the Supreme Court until his death in 1910 in Washington, D.C.

BROWN, HENRY BILLINGS

b. March 2, 1836; judicial positions in Michigan (1868-1890); associate justice, U.S. Supreme Court (1890-1906); d. September 4, 1913.

Born in South Lee, Massachusetts, the son of a wealthy local merchant, Brown was educated at Yale College (Class of 1856). After temporary study at both Yale and Harvard Law School, he moved west and was admitted to the bar in

Detroit in 1860. He served there as deputy U.S. marshal (1861-1863) and as U.S. attorney for the eastern district of Michigan (1863-1868). In 1868 he was temporarily appointed judge of the Wayne County circuit court, and in 1875 he received a presidential nomination to be federal judge of the eastern district of Michigan, a position that he held for fifteen years. In 1890, after the death of Associate Justice Samuel Miller, President Benjamin Harrison appointed Brown to the Supreme Court.

During Brown's service on the Supreme Court he rarely dissented and sought to mediate between the extreme positions of his associates. On the issue of civil rights, he wrote the majority opinion in *Plessy v. Fergusson* (1896), which upheld the constitutionality of the "separate but equal" racial segregation laws. He also spoke for the court in *Holden v. Hardy* (1898), which upheld the right of states to regulate working conditions for the health and safety of mine workers. His most notable dissent came in the case of *Pollock v. Farmers Loan and Trust Company* (1895), in which he supported the constitutionality of the first federal income tax, arguing that it need not be apportioned to the states according to population. His dissenting opinion discussed the requirement of apportionment for a direct tax upon land and its historical relevance. He stated that an indirect tax, however, could be imposed by uniformity. "Being of the opinion that a tax upon rents is an indirect tax upon land," he wrote, referring to the facts in the case at bar, "I am driven to the conclusion that the tax in question is valid." He wrote one of the separate opinions that amounted to the judgment of the Court in *Downes v. Bidwell* (1901); he argued separately that American territories have a fundamentally different legal status than do the states and that citizens of the territories do not have the constitutional rights of citizens unless an act of Congress specifically extends those rights to them.

Brown retired from the Court in 1906 at the age of seventy. He died in New York City in 1913.

BURGER, WARREN EARL

b. September 17, 1907; Assistant Attorney General (1953-1956); Judge, U.S. Court of Appeals for District of Columbia (1956-1969); chief justice, U.S. Supreme Court (1969-).

Born on a farm in Stacy, Minnesota, into a Swiss-German family, Burger began his education in public schools, worked his way through the University of Minnesota, and then studied law at night at the St. Paul (now Mitchell) College of Law. For more than twenty years Burger practiced law at the prominent firm of Boyeson, Otis, and Faricy in St. Paul and was involved in Republican politics at the state and national levels.

Court of Appeals. In 1953, Burger became an assistant attorney general under Pres. Dwight D. Eisenhower, taking charge of the civil division of the Department of

Justice. During this time Burger argued in favor of the federal government's position in *Peters v. Hobby* (1955), in which the Court held that the Civil Service Commission's Loyalty Review Board exceeded its power in barring an employee from further federal service because of unsubstantiated allegations of Communist Party membership. His careful work resulted in his nomination (1955) by Eisenhower to the U.S. Court of Appeals for the District of Columbia, to which he was confirmed in 1956. In this position Burger became known for his consistent upholding of "law and order" decisions. Burger stated his philosophy in a 1967 speech at Ripon College commencement, saying, "Governments exist chiefly to foster the rights and interests of their citizens, to protect their homes and property, their persons and their lives. If a government fails in this basic duty, it is not redeemed by providing even the most perfect system for the protection of the rights of defendants."

While Burger sat on the Court of Appeals, his decisions were primarily aimed at the exclusionary rule, which in a criminal trial disallowed evidence obtained by police using methods outside constitutional limits. His argument was not with the verdicts of most of the well-publicized criminal cases, but rather with the policy of initiating changes in procedural rules on a case-by-case basis, to which he objected vehemently. He suggested that it would be preferable to hear a case only to decide that case and leave rule making to the legislature or boards set up for rule-making purposes. An example that brought Burger attention while on the Court of Appeals was *Durham v. United States* (1954). The court's decision required acquittal on the ground of insanity if a defendant's act had resulted from mental disease or defect. Burger attempted to limit the decision, reasoning that this was an imprecise guide for judge or jury to utilize in a trial. *Frazier v. United States* (1969) saw Burger dissenting in part as the Court of Appeals extended one of the most controversial decisions of the Supreme Court under Earl Warren, *Miranda v. Arizona* (1966). Burger accepted *Miranda*'s principle of excluding from evidence confessions obtained during custodial interrogation before the defendant had been informed of his rights, but he strongly objected to further limits on police procedures and to more guidelines for protecting the defendant's 5th Amendment rights. He stated that the decision would result in procedures that "even the most alert and sophisticated lawyers and judges are taxed to follow."

During the 1960's the criminal justice opinions coming from the Court of Appeals where Burger sat were quite similar to those coming from Earl Warren's Supreme Court. Burger, however, was usually a vocal and aggressive dissenter. Sharp differences with some of his colleagues were frequent, and Burger became identified in legal circles as a strict constructionist, minimizing the rights of the criminally accused and maximizing the prosecution's tools. In one case, Burger charged his colleagues with performing the functions of the

Warren E. Burger

jury and stated, "I suggest that the kind of nit-picking appellate review exhibited by reversal of this conviction may help explain why the public is losing confidence in the administration of justice" (*Borum v. United States*, 1967). Burger's performance on the Court of Appeals showed him to be a conservative upholder of "law and order," but at the same time an activist in proposing new rules of evidence that altered conventional wisdom and protected "an ordered liberty."

Circumstances of Appointment. In 1968, Chief Justice Earl Warren told Pres. Lyndon B. Johnson that he would be resigning because of his age. Johnson then chose Abe Fortas to replace Warren. Fortas had been an associate justice since 1965, but in 1968 he faced such strong opposition that he requested that Johnson withdraw his nomination. Johnson then asked Warren to remain at his post, deciding not to nominate another candidate, which left the appointment of a chief justice to the next president, Richard M. Nixon.

On May 21, 1969, Nixon announced Warren Earl Burger as his choice for Earl Warren's replacement, with some people noting the reversal of the new nominee's name and the current Chief Justice's name, and a corresponding reversal of their legal and judicial philosophies. Burger's speeches and articles had shown Nixon that he and Burger shared a legal philosophy of "strict construction" of the Constitution. Nixon speculated that Burger on the Court might swing some of the five to four decisions of the Warren Court the

other way, making the majority view of the Court more conservative. During the presidential campaign of 1968, Nixon had frequently blamed the Warren Court for the rise in criminal activity America faced. Nixon and Burger both supported the idea of "judicial self-restraint" and hoped to influence the Supreme Court to show more deference to legislative decisions.

Burger underwent a hearing on June 3, 1969, by the Senate Judiciary Committee, a hearing in which a nonaggressive, even friendly, tone was set at the beginning. An hour and forty minutes later the committee unanimously approved the nomination. On June 9, 1969, the Senate advised and consented to the nomination, voting seventy-four to three, and Burger became the 15th Chief Justice of the United States Supreme Court, taking office on June 23, 1969. The three negative votes were in protest against the rapidity of the confirmation process. Nixon was afforded the opportunity to replace three associate justices within three years of Burger's appointment, leading some to call this the Nixon/Burger Court.

Supreme Court Opinions. Upon taking his seat as Chief Justice, Burger maintained his philosophy that policies should be determined by legislators, not judges. In matters of criminal law, the Chief Justice's votes were often interpreted as favoring limitations on defendants' rights, especially the rights established by *Miranda v. Arizona* (1966). Burger dissented in *Ashe v. Swenson* (1970), involving double jeopardy, and in *Coleman v. Alabama* (1970), involving an indigent's right to counsel at a preliminary hearing. In *Furman v. Georgia* (1972), when the Court held that capital punishment was unconstitutional as then administered, Burger strongly dissented. Burger wrote the majority opinion in *Harris v. New York* (1971), in which the Court held that confessions obtained from the accused in violation of *Miranda* could be introduced in evidence to impeach the defendant's credibility if the accused chose to take the stand in his own behalf. He wrote a vehement dissent in *Brewer v. Williams* (1977), in which the defendant's confession to the murder of a child and his subsequent conviction were reversed because of Miranda warning violations. However, he supported the decision in *Geders v. United States* (1976), which reversed the conviction of a defendant who had been denied access to his lawyer. In *United States v. Henry* (1980), Burger's opinion upheld the right of a prisoner to be protected from government attempts to elicit incriminating statements, as a violation of the right to legal counsel.

Although noted for his conservatism, Burger wrote the majority opinion in the sex discrimination case of *Reed v. Reed* (1970), which struck down an Idaho law that preferred the father over the mother as administrator of their deceased child's estate. Holding that classification by sex was an arbitrary method of reducing disputes in probate court, the Burger Court's decision was a victory for equal rights for women.

The case of *Bivens v. Six Unknown Agents* (1971) resulted in one of the Chief Justice's better known dissents. The majority upheld Bivens's claim that because federal agents illegally broke into his home without a search warrant, he was entitled to recover money damages from the government for the violation of his 4th Amendment rights. In his dissent, Burger was concerned that the decision might serve further to inhibit police in their crime supression duties, and he did not want to expand upon the rights of defendants who already could exclude from trial illegally seized evidence (*Mapp v. Ohio*, 1961). Further, Burger did not want to create the public impression that the Supreme Court was either hampering those responsible for battling crime or assisting the criminal. Burger discussed not only his opposition to the monetary damages, but his view that the exclusionary rule should be done away with if a substitute method of deterring police misconduct could be achieved. He also reprimanded the majority for exceeding the Court's judicial powers by creating an action for monetary damages based on police misconduct.

The Burger Court did not develop a consistent pattern in civil rights cases, and the Chief Justice's opinions also varied. In *Swann v. Charlotte-Mecklenburg Board of Education* (1971), the Chief Justice's opinion required Charlotte, North Carolina, to change busing and school districting policies in order to integrate the schools better. Subsequent integration decisions of the Burger Court were less favorable to the civil rights posture that had been supported by

the Warren Court. In *Milliken v. Bradley* (1974), Burger wrote the majority opinion that reversed lower court rulings that would have forced suburban and inner-city schools in metropolitan Detroit to adopt an area-wide school desegregation plan. However, in *Fullilove v. Klutznik* (1980), the Court upheld the constitutionality of a federal law providing that public works projects must allocate ten percent of federal funds received for minority businesses. The Chief Justice wrote one of the majority opinions.

In other important opinions Burger has generally been considered to share the conservative objectives of Presidents Nixon and Reagan. In the Watergate tapes case (*United States v. Nixon*, 1974), however, Burger wrote the unanimous Court's opinion requiring President Nixon to turn over tapes that had been subpoenaed by the Watergate special prosecutor. The Chief Justice has supported decisions that would lessen prohibitions against government connections with religious observances, as in *Lynch v. Donnelly* (1984), concerning a Christmas nativity scene in Pawtucket, Rhode Island. He has been supportive of federal intelligence agencies seeking to avoid public disclosure of their activities, as in *Central Intelligence Agency v. Sims* (1985).

Administrative Proposals. For Burger's entire tenure as Chief Justice his thrust has been on administrative change as opposed to change brought about through judicial opinions. A top priority was establishing methods whereby the number of cases heard and opinions written per term could be cut down drastically. Burger's "State of the Judiciary" presentation before the American Bar Association in 1984 asserted that lawyers need to monitor their behavior and bring it up to professional standards. He faulted lawyers for lax discipline, involvement in absurd lawsuits, overcharging clients, incompetence, and advertising resembling that for "mustard, cosmetics, laxatives (and) used cars." He suggested that $5,000 and $10,000 fines be levied against attorneys not behaving according to set guidelines. Additionally, Burger reiterated his plea to find out-of-court ways to settle legal disputes. Burger's ideas included studying other countries' systems for ideas applicable to the United States and assembling a rotating panel of twenty-six judges from federal circuit courts to hear cases involving issues over which the federal circuit courts had split. Burger was concerned that if the case load of the Supreme Court continued to increase, the Court would have to handle more cases without oral argument, which could lead to a decline in the thoughtful debate important to their resolution.

Chief Justice Burger has played a major role in the development and improvement of administrative programs and procedures within the federal court system. Since the late 1940's the federal judiciary has experienced a litigation explosion, which has resulted in clogged court calendars and intolerable delays in the administration of justice. The federal district courts that the Chief Justice oversees are composed of more than ninety district courts, which yearly process hundreds of thousands of criminal and civil cases. In an effort to free judges from administrative tasks and make them available for trial work, Burger created many new administrative positions in the courts, thereby reducing the time required to process individual cases. Burger also assisted in the establishment of the Institute for Court Management in 1969 and encouraged alternative methods to settle disputes such as arbitration and mediation.

Burger also served as the chairman of the U.S. Judicial Conference. This organization studies federal court practices and procedures with the intent of recommending more efficient and effective procedures. The Judicial Conference also examines areas of court policy and attempts to define standards that assure fundamental fairness and equality in the administration of justice. Burger and his fellow members of the Judicial Conference spent considerable time on such issues as sentence disparity in criminal cases, the adequacy of the trial bar, and judicial ethics.

BURTON, HAROLD HITZ

b. June 22, 1888; member, Ohio legislature (1929); mayor of Cleveland (1935-1940); U.S. senator (1941-1945); associate justice, U.S. Supreme Court (1945-1958); d. October 28, 1964.

Born in Jamaica Plain, Massachusetts, Burton was educated at Bowdoin College (Class of 1909) and received his law degree from Harvard Law School in 1912. After practicing as an attorney in Cleveland, Salt Lake City, and Boise, Idaho, he served in France during World War I. He returned to Cleveland after the war and entered politics, being elected to the state legislature in 1929. He was later elected mayor of Cleveland and served three terms in that position. In 1940 he was elected to the the U.S. Senate. In 1945, after the resignation of Associate Justice Owen Roberts, President Harry Truman appointed Burton to the Supreme Court.

During his tenure on the Court, Burton distinguished himself as both a strict constructionist and a hard-line anti-communist. He voted with the Court's minority in *Everson v. Board of Education of Ewing Township* (1947), in which he opposed the use of public funds for the transportation of students of parochial schools. He joined the majority in *American Communications Association v. Douds* (1950), in which he supported the constitutionality of the "non-communist oath" provision of the Taft-Hartley Act. In *Bailey v. Richardson* (1951), he upheld the dismissal of a government employee accused of communist allegiance, even though she had not been given the right to confront her accusers. He also joined the majority in *Dennis v. United States* (1951), which upheld the conviction of ten leaders of the Communist Party of the United States. Burton wrote the majority opinion in *Beilan v. Board of Education* (1958), which upheld the dismissal of a teacher suspected of communist sympathies who had pleaded the 5th Amendment in his refusal to answer questions about his past.

With regard to racial equality, Burton's position gradually became more liberal. He was the lone dissenter in *Morgan v. Virginia* (1946), in which he argued that it was up to Congress, not the Court, to legislate against racial segregation. However, he wrote the majority opinion in *Henderson v. United States* (1950), which held that segregation in railroad dining cars violated the Interstate Commerce Act. He joined with his associates in the landmark decision of *Brown v. Board of Education* (1954) in striking down racial segregation in public schools.

Burton retired from the Court in 1958 and died in Washington, D.C., in 1964.

BUTLER, PIERCE

b. March 17, 1866; associate justice, U.S. Supreme Court (1922-1939); d. November 16, 1939.

Pierce Butler

Born in Northfield, Minnesota, Butler was educated at Carleton College (Class of 1887) and after legal studies in St. Paul was admitted to the bar in 1888. In St. Paul, he served as assistant county attorney (1891-1893) and county attorney (1893-1897). Returning to private practice, he was elected president of the Minnesota Bar Association in 1908. In 1922, after the resignation of Associate Justice William Day, President Warren Harding appointed Butler to the Supreme Court.

During his tenure on the Court, Butler maintained a

conservative judicial philosophy and often joined in the dissenting opinions of Justices Van Devanter, McReynolds, and Sutherland in opposing federal intervention in private industry and the spread of what they considered to be subversive political philosophies. Butler wrote the majority opinion in *Burns Baking Company v. Bryan* (1924), which overturned a state law that set uniform standards for the baking industry on the grounds that it was an improper abridgement of freedom of contract. He dissented in *Stromberg v. California* (1931), which held that a statute prohibiting the public display of communist banners violated the 1st Amendment. He was also in the minority in *Near v. Minnesota* (1931), supporting the right of states to suppress "obscene, scandalous, or defamatory" publications. In the case of *Powell v. Alabama* (1932), he opposed overturning the conviction of the "Scottsboro Boys," on the grounds that the state's failure to provide the defendants with an attorney did not violate their 14th Amendment rights. Butler spoke for the Court in the case of *Morehead v. New York ex rel Tipaldo* (1936), in which the Court overturned a state law establishing minimum wages for women and children. Butler was in the minority in *National Labor Relations Board v. Jones and Laughlin Steel Corporation* (1937), arguing against the constitutional right of the federal government under the commerce clause to regulate intrastate production of goods. He also dissented in *O'Malley v. Woodrough* (1939) in which he opposed the removal of a tax exemption for the salaries of federal judges.

Butler was one of the justices whose influence President Roosevelt attempted to overcome in his "court-packing" proposal of 1937. The attempt failed, and Butler served on the Court until his death in Washington, D.C.

BYRNES, JAMES FRANCIS

b. May 2, 1879; member, U.S. House of Representatives (1911-1925); U.S. Senate (1931-1941); associate justice, U.S. Supreme Court (1941-1942); director, Office of Economic Stabilization (1942-1943); director, Office of War Mobilization (1943-1945); secretary of state (1945-1947); governor of South Carolina (1951-1955); d. April 9, 1972.

Born in Charleston, South Carolina, Byrnes was forced by economic circumstances to leave school at an early age. Working as a clerk in an attorney's office, and later as court stenographer in a South Carolina circuit court, he privately gained a legal education and was admitted to the bar in 1903. In 1908 he was elected state's attorney for the second circuit court of South Carolina and two years later was elected to the House of Representatives, where he remained until 1925, when he ran unsuccessfully for the U.S. Senate. Byrnes returned to private law practic, but was successful in his campaign for the Senate in 1930. In the Senate, he was a strong supporter of the programs of President Franklin D. Roosevelt and served as the president's legislative advisor.

In 1941, with the resignation of Associate Justice James McReynolds, President Roosevelt appointed Byrnes to the Supreme Court.

Byrnes served on the Supreme Court for a little more than a year. He wrote the majority opinion in *Edwards v. California* (1941) in which the Court struck down a state law prohibiting the entry of indigents. He joined the dissent in *Bridges v. California* (1941), which argued that a contempt conviction for publishing statements critical of a judicial decision should stand. He spoke for the Court again in *Taylor v. Georgia* (1942), which held that a state penal law requiring workers who had received advances to remain at that job until the advance was paid back violated the 13th Amendment prohibition of involuntary servitude. In *Skinner v. Oklahoma ex rel Williamson* (1942), he voted with the majority in opposing compulsory sterilization for habitual criminals. He also joined the majority in *Goldstein v. United States* (1942), which upheld the admissibility of testimony of co-conspirators who were induced to turn state's evidence after being confronted with phone messages that had been "illegally" obtained by the police.

Byrnes' short tenure on the Supreme Court proved to be just a brief interlude in an active public career. In 1942 he resigned from the Court to accept a presidential appointment as director of the Office of Economic Stabilization. A year afterwards, he became director of the Office of War Mobilization. Byrnes later served as secretary of state in the Truman administration and then governor of South Carolina. He died in Columbia, South Carolina, in 1972.

CAMPBELL, JOHN ARCHIBALD

b. June 24, 1811; various legislative and judicial positions in Alabama; associate justice, U.S. Supreme Court (1853-1861); assistant secretary of war, Confederate States of America (1862-1865); d. March 2, 1889.

Born to a prominent family in Washington, Georgia, Campbell entered Franklin College (later the University of Georgia) at age eleven, and upon his graduation in 1826, entered the U.S. Military Academy at West Point. After the death of his father, he abandoned a military career for the law, studying in the office of his uncle, John W. Campbell. In 1829, by a special act of the Georgia legislature, he was admitted to the bar at age eighteen. A year later, he moved to Montgomery, Alabama, where he embarked on a spectacular legal career. Campbell declined an appointment as associate justice of the Alabama supreme court at age twenty-four, but while pursuing his private legal practice, he served two terms in the state legislature. Having gained a national reputation for legal brilliance, he was appointed to the Supreme Court in 1853 by President Franklin Pierce to succeed Associate Justice John McKinley.

Campbell's philosophical orientation was Jeffersonian, and he consistently opposed the expansion of federal powers.

Although he personally owned no slaves, he concurred with the majority in the Dred Scott Case (*Scott v. Sandford*, 1856), which ruled that the federal government had no constitutional right to prohibit slave owners from living in the territories, nor had Congress the right to regulate which articles of property the slave owners could or could not bring with them. Therefore, slave owners could not be prohibited from entering any U.S. territory with their slaves.

Campbell opposed the secession of the southern states in 1861, but after all attempts at compromise failed, he resigned his position on the Supreme Court and was appointed assistant secretary of war in the Confederacy. At the end of the Civil War, Campbell was arrested in Richmond by federal forces. He was freed several months later at the request of his former associates on the Supreme Court, Justices Samuel Nelson and Benjamin Curtis. Upon his release, Campbell moved to New Orleans, where he began a private legal practice, appearing several times before the Supreme Court in later years. His most notable appearance was in the *Slaughterhouse Cases* (1873), in which he argued unsuccessfully for a broad interpretation of the new 14th Amendment, a position that was, in substance, later adopted. He died in Baltimore in 1889.

CARDOZO, BENJAMIN NATHAN

b. May 24, 1870; justice, New York Supreme Court (1914); associate judge, New York Court of Appeals (1914-1923); chief judge, New York Court of Appeals (1923-1932); associate justice, U.S. Supreme Court (1932-1938); d. July 9, 1938.

Born in New York City, the son of a municipal judge, Cardozo was tutored at home and entered Columbia College at age fifteen. After earning his B.A. in 1889 and his M.A. in 1890, he entered Columbia Law School and was admitted to the New York bar the following year without having received his law degree. Cardozo subsequently established a prominent reputation in the fields of corporate and commercial law, appearing frequently before the New York Court of Appeals. Named as an anti-Tammany Hall candidate, he was elected judge of the state Supreme Court (a trial court) in 1914, but resigned that position the same year to accept an appointment as associate judge of the Court of Appeals (the highest state court). He served in that position until 1923, when he was named chief judge.

Cardozo was regarded as one of the greatest legal scholars of his time; his writings include *The Nature of the Judicial Process* (1921), *The Growth of the Law* (1924), *The Paradoxes of Legal Science* (1928), and *Law and Literature* (1931). Cardozo's most significant judicial contributions were in the development of common law doctrine as a state judge.

In 1932, after the resignation of Associate Justice Oliver Wendell Holmes Jr., President Herbert Hoover appointed

Benjamin Cardozo

Cardozo to the Supreme Court. Despite his brief tenure on the Supreme Court, Cardozo compiled an impressive record of important decisions. He wrote the majority opinion in *Nixon v. Condon* (1932), which held that the exclusion of blacks from primary elections by political parties was a violation of the equal protection provision of the 14th Amendment. He wrote the majority opinion in *Baldwin v. Seelig* (1935), which held that states may not discriminate against the sale of out-of-state products. Cardozo also spoke for the Court in *Palko v. Connecticut* (1937), which denied a claim that the 14th Amendment bound states to observe the double jeopardy provision of the 5th Amendment.

A cautious supporter of the programs of the New Deal, Cardozo joined the dissent in *Railroad Retirement Board v. Alton Railroad Co.* (1935), which overturned the Railroad Retirement Act of 1934 and in *Carter v. Carter Coal Co.* (1936), which overturned the Bituminous Coal Conservation Act of 1935. He wrote the majority opinion in *Helvering v. Davis* (1937), which upheld the the constitutionality of the Social Security Act of 1935. He concurred, however, in *Schechter Poultry Corp. v. United States* (1935), which struck down certain regulations of the National Industrial Recovery Act, and joined the concurring opinion in *Ashwander v. Tennessee Valley Authority* (1936), which upheld Congress's constitutional authority to conduct business and to retain riparian rights incident to ownership of the T.V.A.

Cardozo served on the Court until his death in Port Chester, New York, in 1938.

CATRON, JOHN

b. c.1786; various judicial positions in Tennessee (1824-1837); associate justice, U.S. Supreme Court (1837-1865); d. May 30, 1865.

Little definite information has been preserved of Catron's early life and the date of his birth is only approximate. It seems that he was born in Pennsylvania and moved with his parents first to Virginia and then to Kentucky, where he lived until 1812. After serving under Andrew Jackson in the War of 1812, Catron established his permanent residence in Tennessee, studying law there and being admitted to the state bar in 1815. Soon afterwards, he began a private practice in Nashville. In 1824, Catron was elected by the legislature to become a judge of the Supreme Court of Errors and Appeals. He became its chief justice in 1831. A strong supporter of Pres. Andrew Jackson, Catron was appointed to one of the newly created associate justiceships of the Supreme Court on the last day of the Jackson administration in 1837.

Although Catron's legal education was not extensive, he played an important role on the Court in the years leading up to the Civil War. In the Dred Scott Case (*Scott v. Sandford*, 1857), he played a key part in the deliberations, concurring with the majority that Scott was a slave and not awarded any rights in the Constitution secured to citizens and that the Missouri Compromise was unconstitutional. Catron's circuit included the border states of Missouri, Kentucky, and Tennessee, and with the outbreak of the Civil War, he returned to his home state of Tennessee in an unsuccessful attempt to prevent secession. Later in the war, he returned to restore federal authority and the smooth functioning of the court system there.

Catron served on the Supreme Court until his death in Nashville in 1865. After his death, Congress legislated a reduction in the size of the Court to nine justices.

CHASE, SALMON PORTLAND

b. January 13, 1808; U.S. Senate (1849-1855, 1860-1861); governor of Ohio (1856-1860); U.S. secretary of the Treasury (1861-1864); chief justice, U.S. Supreme Court (1864-1873); d. May 7, 1873.

Born in Cornish, New Hampshire, the son of a Federalist officeholder and tavern keeper, Chase spent his early years in Keene, receiving his primary education in the local schools. After the death of his father in 1817, Chase was entrusted to his uncle, Philander Chase, then serving in Worthington, Ohio, as bishop of the Episcopal Church. In 1821, Chase enrolled in Cincinnati College, and four years later he entered Dartmouth College as a junior, earning his bachelor's degree in 1826. Another of Chase's uncles, Dudley Chase, was then serving as a U.S. senator from Vermont, and after graduation from Dartmouth, the younger Chase took advantage of the connection, moving to Washington

Salmon P. Chase

and studying law with Attorney General William Wirt.

Political Career. In 1829, Chase was admitted to the bar, and he then returned to Cincinnati, where he established a private law practice. From the very beginning of his career, Chase was deeply committed to the cause of antislavery, and in 1840 he joined the abolitionist Liberty Party. Chase later rose to national prominence in his participation in the case of *Jones v. Van Zandt* (1847), which he argued on behalf of the defendant before the Supreme Court in collaboration with his future colleague in the Senate and in the Lincoln cabinet, William Seward. Chase came before the Supreme Court again, on behalf of the plaintiff in error, in the case of *Moore v. Illinois* (1852). His attempts at demonstrating the unconstitutionality of the fugitive slave laws were once again unsuccessful, but his dedication to the abolitionist movement was acknowledged in the popular press, which derisively dubbed him "Attorney General for runaway slaves."

The creation of the Free Soil Party was a turning point in Chase's political career. In 1848, as the party's candidate, he was elected to the U.S. Senate. During his single term of office in the Senate, Chase joined forces with the militant abolitionists Charles Sumner of Massachusetts and Seward of New York, voting against the Compromise of 1850 and the Kansas-Nebraska Act.

With the formation of the Republican Party in 1854, Chase once again changed his party allegiance and became governor of Ohio in 1855. After serving two terms in that position, he decided to return to national politics, and he was elected again to the Senate in February 1860. Later in the same year, he campaigned for the Republican presidential nomination, but when the national convention reached a deadlock, he offered his support to Abraham Lincoln, virtually guaranteeing him the nomination. With the election of Lincoln in November, Chase resigned from the Senate to accept the President's appointment to become secretary of the Treasury.

After the outbreak of the Civil War, Chase's position became a crucial one for the survival of the federal government. As secretary of the Treasury he was responsible for raising funds for the conduct of the war and stabilizing the currency. This became an especially critical problem when Congress approved the Legal Tender Act in 1862. Chase was opposed to the large-scale issuance of unbacked federal banknotes, but he dutifully supervised their circulation and established a uniform national banking system.

As the war dragged on and opposition to Lincoln arose within Republican circles, relations between Chase and the President became increasingly strained. In 1864 he was persuaded to seek the presidency himself and after the renomination of Lincoln at the Republican convention, Chase resigned his post in the cabinet and returned briefly to private life.

Chief Justice. During the fall, he actively campaigned for Lincoln's reelection, and with the death of Chief Justice Roger Taney in October, President Lincoln chose to appoint his erstwhile rival as chief justice. With Lincoln's death the following April, Chase became an influential advisor to President Johnson. He helped in the formulation of Johnson's Reconstruction program and personally oversaw the reopening of the federal courts in the South.

One of the most important legal issues faced by the Supreme Court in the first two years of Chase's tenure as chief justice was the constitutionality of certain actions taken by the federal government during the Civil War. In the case of *Ex parte Milligan* (1866), the Court held invalid attempts by Congress to impose military justice on civilians in areas in which the civilian courts were still operating. Chase dissented in part, arguing that conditions of national emergency might, under specific circumstances, justify the suspension of some constitutional rights.

In the following year, in the Test Oath Cases (*Cummings v. Missouri* and *Ex parte Garland*, 1866), the Supreme Court was faced with the question of the constitutionality of compulsory oaths of allegiance for priests and clergymen and for attorneys respectively. Chase voted with the minority, arguing that no basic constitutional rights were violated by the imposition of a test of loyalty, due to the exceptional circumstances of the recently fought Civil War.

After the victory of the Radical Republicans in the 1866 congressional elections and their passage of the Reconstruction Act of 1867, the state of Mississippi filed suit in federal court to prevent Pres. Andrew Johnson from implementing the terms of the program that divided the former states of the Confederacy into five military districts, each headed by a federal military officer who would have the power to establish military tribunals in place of civilian courts. When *Mississippi v. Johnson* came before the Supreme Court in 1866, the Chief Justice spoke for a unanimous Court in holding that the case fell under the general principles that forbid judicial intervention with the exercise of executive discretion. Therefore, President Johnson could not be restrained by court order from carrying into effect the act of Congress that Mississippi alleged to be unconstitutional.

It was, in fact, an intense political struggle between Congress and the President that brought about one of Chase's most unpleasant obligations as chief justice. In 1868 he presided over the impeachment trial of President Johnson in the Senate, and although Chase was one of Johnson's strongest supporters and objected to the attempts of the Radical Republicans to use such drastic means for their own political ends, he nonetheless conducted the proceedings with admirable impartiality.

Later in the year, the Supreme Court was faced with another issue arising from the implementation of the Radical Republican Reconstruction program. William McCardle, a Mississippi newspaper editor convicted of seditious activity by military authorities, appealed for a writ of *habeas corpus*, a right that had been confirmed in the case of *Ex parte Milligan* in 1866. Congress, however, fearing that the Supreme Court would again rule against the military administration of the South and declare the federal Reconstruction Act of 1867 unconstitutional, enacted a law that took away the appellate jurisdiction of the Supreme Court in cases involving requests for writs of *habeas corpus*. Even though the statute had not been passed until after the Court had already heard arguments in *Ex parte McCardle* (1868), Chief Justice Chase, speaking for a unanimous Court, held that Congress's action was valid and the Court had no power to decide the case. Chase acknowledged that the Constitution itself had granted the Supreme Court the power to hear appeals from lower courts. But it was a power, according to Article III Section 2, "with such exceptions and under such regulations as the Congress shall make."

Perhaps the central constitutional issue of the Reconstruction era faced by the Chase Court was the legal status of the states of the former Confederacy. The case of *Texas v. White* (1868) involved a claim by the state's Reconstruction government for the return of certain bonds sold during the Civil War by the state's Confederate authorities. Chief Justice Chase, writing the majority opinion, held that all acts of the rebel government of Texas were illegal, and the provisional state government's claim for the return of the bonds should be allowed. This decision had far-reaching implications, for the Chief Justice also ruled on more general grounds that since states do not have a constitutional right to secede from the Union, the states of the Confederacy had never legally ceased to be part of the United States.

While serving as secretary of the Treasury, Chase had been instrumental in the implementation of the Legal Tender Acts of 1862 and 1863. Chase held personal doubts about the constitutionality of this action and in the post-war years, there had been numerous court challenges to the law. In *Hepburn v. Griswold* (1869), Chase, speaking for the majority, enunciated the legal basis of his opposition. He held that the acts' provision that made United States notes a legal tender in payment of all debts, public and private, was, so far as it applied to debts contracted before the passage of those acts, unwarranted by the Constitution. This decision suddenly cast into question the legality of all paper currency and caused a considerable disruption in the national economy. However, the issue was soon reheard by the Supreme Court in *Knox v. Lee* and *Parker v. Davis* (1870), also known as the Legal Tender Cases.

This time, the result was different, and the Chief Justice found himself in the minority. Also dissenting were Associate Justices Clifford, Field, and Nelson. Chase rejected the majority contention that the wartime issuance of paper currency was nothing less than a governmental act of self-preservation and that it was sanctioned by Article I, Section 8 of the Constitution, which gave Congress the right to enact "all laws which shall be necessary and proper" to carry out the other enumerated powers of Congress. One of the crucial factors that led to the reversal of the Court's previous decision was the nomination of both Justice Strong and Justice Bradley in the interim. The fact that both nominees had expressed implicit judicial support of the Legal Tender Acts led to public charges that President Grant had "packed" the court in an attempt to uphold the law.

Chase was no admirer of Grant, and throughout his tenure as chief justice, Chase had never abandoned his own presidential ambitions. Several times he had even shifted his party allegiance when such an action seemed likely to serve his political interests. In 1868, he unsuccessfully sought the Democratic presidential nomination, and in 1872, Chase was again considered for the presidency, this time by the Liberal Republicans. His health, however, was by this time declining, and Chase offered his support to Horace Greeley as the party's nominee.

One of the last important opinions issued by the Supreme Court during Chase's tenure as chief justice was in the *Slaughterhouse Cases* (*The Butchers' Benevolent Association of New Orleans v. The Crescent City Livestock Landing and Slaughterhouse Co., Esteben v. Louisiana,* 1873), dealing with the right of state governments to create monopolies in private industry. This case gave the Court its first opportunity to construe the 14th Amendment. The majority ruled that the rights protected by the 14th Amendment should be narrowly interpreted and could not be used to protect citizens' economic rights. The Chief Justice,

however, joined Justice Field's dissenting opinion, putting forward a broad definition of the "privileges and immunities," "due process," and "equal protection" guaranteed by the Amendment. This view, while initially that of a minority, came to be adopted by the Court by the turn of the century.

Less than a month after the *Slaughterhouse* decision, Chase died in his home in Washington, after a tenure on the Supreme Court of eight and a half years. He was succeeded in the office of chief justice by the nominee of President Grant, Morrison Waite.

CHASE, SAMUEL

b. April 17, 1741; member, Maryland assembly (1764-1784); delegate, Continental Congress (1774-1778, 1784-1785); delegate, Maryland Constitutional Ratification Convention (1787); chief judge, Baltimore criminal court (1788-1796); chief judge, Maryland general court (1791-1796); associate justice, U.S. Supreme Court (1796-1811); d. June 19, 1811.

Born in Somerset County, Maryland, Chase studied law in the offices of Hammond and Hall in Annapolis and was admitted to the bar in 1763. In the following year, he was elected to the Maryland Assembly and subsequently distinguished himself as a fervent supporter of American independence. In 1774 he was a member of the state Committee of Correspondence and was elected to the first Continental Congress. After being appointed to a commission to seek an alliance with Canada, he returned to Philadelphia to sign the Declaration of Independence. A later charge of war profiteering, however, resulted in the loss of his seat in the Continental Congress. He opposed the ratification of the U.S. Constitution and voted against it at the Maryland ratification convention.

Returning to private life after the Revolution, Chase established a private law practice and pursued several business interests that ultimately resulted in a declaration of bankruptcy in 1789. The previous year he had been appointed chief judge of the Baltimore criminal court. His financial difficulties did not seem to hinder Chase's legal career, for in 1791 he was appointed chief judge of the general court of Maryland. In 1796, after the resignation of Associate Justice John Blair, Pres. George Washington nominated Chase to the U.S. Supreme Court.

Chase was one of the most outspoken members of the early Court. He delivered an opinion in *Ware v. Hylton* (1796), a case that established the precedence of international treaties over state laws. He also wrote an opinion in *Calder v. Bull* (1798), a case that held that protection against *ex post facto* law applies only to criminal offenses. In *Hollingsworth v. Virginia* (1798), he argued that constitutional amendments proposed by Congress do not have to be presented to the president. In his dissenting opinion in *United States v. Worrall* (1798), Chase established the important precedent that federal courts have no common law jurisdiction in criminal cases.

Chase's volatile personality eventually led to the enmity of Thomas Jefferson and the most important event of his judicial career. Criticized for a blatantly partial charge to a jury in a treason trial, he was impeached by the House of Representatives in 1804. His trial in the Senate centered on the question of the definition of the "high crimes and misdemeanors" mentioned in the Constitution as grounds for the removal of a federal official. The Senate acquitted Chase, a majority agreeing that the Constitution referred to indictable offenses only; a precedent that shaped the subsequent history of the Court. Chase served on the Court until his death in Baltimore in 1811.

CLARK, TOM CAMPBELL

b. September 23, 1899; civil district attorney, Dallas County, Texas (1927-1932); special assistant, Department of Justice (1937-1943); assistant U.S. attorney general (1943-1945); U.S. attorney general (1945-1949); associate justice, U.S. Supreme Court (1949-1967); judge, U.S. Court of Appeals (1967-1977); director, Federal Judicial Center (1968-1970); d. June 13, 1977.

Born in Dallas, Texas, the son of a prominent local lawyer and Democratic Party functionary, Clark attended the Virginia Military Institute and, after service in the Army during World War I, graduated from the University of Texas in 1921. He received his law degree from the University of Texas Law School in 1922. After several years of private practice in his father's firm in Dallas, Clark was appointed civil district attorney, a post he held for five years. Becoming increasingly active in Democratic politics, he was appointed special assistant in the Department of Justice in the Roosevelt administration, eventually being promoted to assistant attorney general in the antitrust and criminal divisions. In 1945, President Truman appointed Clark to be attorney general. In this position, Clark was an energetic opponent of individuals and groups that he considered subversive or communist-inspired. In 1949, after the death of Associate Justice Frank Murphy, President Truman appointed Clark to the Supreme Court.

Clark's record on the Court was marked by a continued hard line in cases of individual loyalty and national security. He wrote the majority opinion in *Garner v. Board of Public Works* (1951), which upheld the constitutionality of loyalty oaths for public employees. He dissented in *Watkins v. United States* (1957), voting to uphold the contempt conviction of a witness before a congressional committee who had refused to testify about his associates' communist affiliations. He also dissented in *Yates v. United States* (1957), which reversed the conviction under the Smith Act of alleged communists.

His record on civil rights issues, however, was somewhat more liberal. He joined with all his colleagues in *Brown v. Board of Education* (1954), which held unconstitutional segregation in the public schools. He wrote the majority opinion in *Heart of Atlanta Motel v. United States* (1964), which established that Congress could prohibit discrimination in public accommodations under its authority to regulate interstate commerce.

With regard to criminal procedure, he spoke for the Court in *Mapp v. Ohio* (1961), which extended the 4th Amendment's prohibition of unreasonable search and seizure to the states through the due process clause of the 14th Amendment, and in *Ker v. California* (1963), which upheld a warrantless search incident to an arrest. He dissented in part in two important criminal procedure decisions, *Escobedo v. Illinois* (1964) and *Miranda v. Arizona* (1966).

In 1967, with the appointment of his son Ramsay to the office of attorney general in the Johnson administration, Clark resigned from the Supreme Court. After his retirement, Clark founded the Federal Judicial Center, an organization within the judiciary dedicated to the improvement of court procedures. He also continued to hear cases on various circuit courts of appeals until his death in New York City in 1977.

CLARKE, JOHN HESSIN

b. September 18, 1857; judge, U.S. district court (1914-1916); associate justice, U.S. Supreme Court (1916-1922); d. March 22, 1945.

Born in Lisbon, Ohio, Clarke was educated at Case Western Reserve University (Class of 1877), studied law in his father's office, and was admitted to the bar in 1878. In addition to his private legal practice, Clarke was active in state Democratic politics and was part owner of *The Vindicator*, a well-known Progressive newspaper in the Midwest. He was an unsuccessful candidate for the U.S. Senate in 1903, and from 1914 to 1916 he served as judge of the U.S. District Court for Northern Ohio. In 1916, after the retirement of Associate Justice Charles Evans Hughes, Pres. Woodrow Wilson appointed Clarke to the Supreme Court.

For the most part, Clarke maintained a liberal judicial philosophy during his six years on the Court. He joined in the dissent of Justices Holmes and Brandeis in *Adams v. Tanner* (1917), arguing that the states had the right to regulate the practices of private employment agencies. In *Hitchman Coal and Coke Company v. Mitchell* (1917), he also joined the dissent, opposing the Court's decision upholding an injunction to prevent union organizing. He was again in the minority in *Hammer v. Dagenhart* (1918) in which the majority of the Court struck down a congressional ban on the shipment in interstate commerce of goods produced by child labor and in *Duplex Printing Press Company v. Deering* (1921), which upheld an injunction against boycott tactics by labor unions. Clarke's was the only dissenting opinion in *Bailey v. Drexel Furniture Company* (1922), in which he again supported congressional actions to curtail child labor. On the question of the 1st Amendment guarantee of freedom of expression, Clarke dissented in *Schaefer v. United States* (1920), in which he opposed the Court's decision upholding the conviction of the officers of a German-language newspaper on the grounds that the falsity of the printed statements had not been proved. He also joined the dissent in *Truax v. Corrigan* (1921), which struck down a state statute prohibiting courts from using injunctions against peaceful picketing and boycotts in labor-management disputes.

In 1922, Clarke retired from the Supreme Court to devote full time to his interest in international affairs. He headed the campaign to secure the participation of the United States in the League of Nations, serving as president of the League of Nations Non-Partisan Association from 1922 to 1928. His later years were spent in San Diego, California, where he died in 1945.

CLIFFORD, NATHAN

b. August 18, 1803; member, Maine legislature (1831-1834); Maine attorney general (1834-1838); member, U.S. House of Representatives (1839-1843); U.S. attorney general (1846-1848); associate justice, U.S. Supreme Court (1858-1881); d. July 25, 1881.

Born in Romney, New Hampshire, the son of a local farmer, Clifford received his early education at Haverhill Academy, afterwards studying law in the office of Josiah Quincy. He was admitted to the bar in 1827 and established a private practice in Newfield, Maine. Clifford, a staunch Jacksonian Democrat, served three terms in the Maine legislature (1831-1834), eventually becoming speaker of the Assembly. In 1834 he was appointed attorney general of the state, a post from which he resigned four years later after his election to the U.S. House of Representatives. During the Polk administration, Clifford served as U.S. attorney general. With the defeat of the Democrats in 1848, he returned to his private law practice in Newfield. Nine years later, after the death of Associate Justice Benjamin Curtis, Pres. James Buchanan nominated Clifford to the Supreme Court.

Despite his New England origins, Clifford was associated with the pro-slavery wing of the Democratic Party, and throughout his tenure on the Court he consistently opposed the encroachment of federal power over the states. He joined the majority in *Ex parte Milligan* (1866), which ruled that a president may not declare martial law in an area not in open rebellion. He also joined the majority opinion written by Justice Field in *Ex parte Garland* (1867), which overturned loyalty oaths for attorneys practicing in federal courts. He joined the Chief Justice's majority opinion in the first of the Legal Tender Cases (*Hepburn v. Griswold*, 1870), arguing that Congress had no specifically defined constitutional right

to issue unsecured currency. In the reconsideration of this issue in *Knox v. Lee* (1871), he maintained his opposition. One of Clifford's last opinions on the Court was in *Ex parte Virginia* (1880), in which he joined Justice Field's dissent from the majority's conclusion that the federal government was authorized by the Constitution to intervene in state affairs to preserve the civil rights of blacks.

As senior associate justice, Clifford presided over the Court between the death of Chief Justice Chase in 1873 and the confirmation of Chief Justice Waite in 1874. During the dispute over the results of the 1876 presidential election, he presided over the Electoral Commission, arguing unsuccessfully against the cause of Rutherford B. Hayes. Clifford served on the Court until a few months before his death in Cornish, Maine, in 1881.

CURTIS, BENJAMIN ROBBINS

b. November 4, 1809; associate justice, U.S. Supreme Court (1851-1857); d. September 15, 1874.

Born in Watertown, Massachusetts, son of Benjamin Curtis III, a ship captain who was lost on one of his voyages, Curtis was educated through the efforts of his mother and graduated from Harvard College in 1829. In the following year he entered Harvard Law School but he did not complete his studies there, preferring to learn through experience as a practicing rural attorney in Northfield, Massachusetts. He returned to Boston in 1834 to join the office of Charles Pelham Curtis, whose daughter Anna he married in 1846. A friend and strong supporter of Daniel Webster, Curtis was appointed to the Supreme Court in 1851 by Pres. Millard Fillmore to succeed Associate Justice Levi Woodbury.

Curtis was only forty-one years old when he joined the Court, and he served for six years. He wrote the majority opinion in *Cooley v. Board of Wardens*, which upheld state regulation of harbors, and *Murray's Lessee v. Hoboken Land and Improvement Company* (1851), which upheld state authority to assess the costs of improvements even without full judicial trials and which gave a restricted reading to the "due process" clause of the 5th Amendment.

Curtis's most controversial action on the Court was connected with the Dred Scott Case (*Scott v. Sandford*, 1857), in which he dissented from the majority and engaged in a personal conflict with Chief Justice Roger Taney. Curtis had pointed out in his dissenting opinion that if Dred Scott were, as the majority argued, not a citizen of the United States, and therefore had no right to enter a suit, the Supreme Court would have no jurisdiction in the case. Curtis went further than mere judicial debate; he allowed his scathing attack on the Court's decision to be published in the abolitionist press. In order to head off this perceptive and logical objection, the Chief Justice secretly revised his original opinion, a practice that was a violation of standard court procedure. A bitter public argument between Curtis and Taney ensued, undermining Taney's authority and resulting in the resignation of Curtis from the Court.

Returning to private practice in Boston, Curtis argued several important cases before the Supreme Court in later life, including the Legal Tender Case (*Hepburn v. Griswold*, 1870). He also served as the chief defense counsel in the impeachment trial of Pres. Andrew Johnson in 1868. He died in Newport, Rhode Island, in 1874.

CUSHING, WILLIAM

b. March 1, 1732; associate justice, Massachusetts Bay Province Superior Court (1772-1775); associate justice, Massachusetts Superior Court (1775-1777); chief justice, Massachusetts Superior Court (1777-1780); member, Massachusetts Constitutional Convention (1779); chief justice, Massachusetts Supreme Judicial Court (1780-1789); associate justice, U.S. Supreme Court (1789-1810); d. September 13, 1810.

Born in Scituate, Massachusetts, to one of the most prominent families in colonial New England, Cushing was educated at Harvard College (Class of 1751) and studied law in the office of Jeremiah Gridley of Boston. He was admitted to the bar in 1755 and in 1760 was appointed registrar of deeds and judge of probate in Lincoln County, Maine, then a district of Massachusetts. Cushing also established a private practice there. In 1771 he was appointed to succeed his father as judge of the Massachusetts Superior Court and from 1774 became a supporter of the cause of colonial autonomy.

Cushing was chosen by the revolutionary council of the state to become associate justice of the Supreme Judicial Court in 1775, and in 1777 he became its chief justice, in which position he rendered an early anti-slavery decision and was instrumental in the suppression of Shays' Rebellion. Cushing helped to frame the Massachusetts state constitution in 1779, and in 1788 he served as vice-president of the state Constitutional Ratification Convention. In 1789, Cushing was President Washington's first nominee to be associate justice of the U.S. Supreme Court.

Cushing, a relative judicial conservative, participated in the most important cases in the early years of the Court. He concurred in *Chisolm v. Georgia* (1793), which maintained the right of a citizen of one state to sue the government of another (a decision effectively nullified by the 11th Amendment). He also voted with the majority in *Ware v. Hylton* (1796), which determined that international treaties have precedence over state laws. He wrote a separate majority opinion in both *Calder v. Bull* (1798), in which it was determined that *Ex post facto* laws applied only to common offenses, and *Fowler v. Lindsay* (1799), a case that disallowed a contest between two individuals to be brought to the Supreme Court, alleging the corresponding states as interested parties.

After the rejection of the nomination of John Rutledge as chief justice in 1795, President Washington offered the post to Cushing, who refused because of ill health. Cushing served on the Court until his death at his home in Scituate, Massachusetts, in 1810.

DANIEL, PETER VIVIAN

b. April 24, 1784; federal judge (1836-1841); associate justice, U.S. Supreme Court (1841-1860); d. May 31, 1860.

Born to a prominent Virginia family, Daniel graduated from Princeton in 1805 and studied law in the office of Edmund Randolph, attorney general and secretary of State in George Washington's administration. After being admitted to the bar in 1808, Daniel was elected to the Virginia legislature. From 1812 to 1834, he served in the Privy Council of Virginia, eventually being named the state's lieutenant governor. In 1834, Pres. Andrew Jackson offered him appointment as attorney general, which he refused. Two years later, however, he accepted a federal judgeship in the district of Virginia. With the death of Associate Justice Philip Barbour in 1841, Daniel was appointed to the Supreme Court by Pres. Martin Van Buren in the last days of his administration.

During his service on the Court, Daniel distinguished himself as a strong advocate of states' rights, particularly of the agrarian interests that characterized the South. In *Prigg v. Pennsylvania* (1842) he opposed the majority's view that the federal government's right to enact fugitive slave laws was exclusive. With regard to the issue of slavery, he concurred with the majority in the Dred Scott Case (*Scott v. Sandford*, 1857), which ruled the Missouri Compromise unconstitutional, and he held that all blacks had come to the United States as property.

Daniel was married twice; in 1809 to Lucy Nelson Randolph, the daughter of Edmund Randolph, and several years after her death to Mary Harris, in 1853. Daniel served on the Court until his death in Richmond, Virginia, in 1860.

DAVIS, DAVID

b. March 9, 1815; various legislative and judicial positions in Illinois; associate justice, U.S. Supreme Court (1862-1877); U.S. senator (1877-1883); d. June 26, 1886.

Born in Cecil County, Maryland, and educated at Kenyon College, Davis studied law in the office of Judge Henry Bishop and at Yale Law School. After his graduation from Yale in 1835, he moved west, eventually settling in Bloomington, Illinois. From 1844 to 1848, he served in the Illinois state legislature. In 1848 he was elected judge of the 8th Illinois circuit and in this capacity became a close friend of Abraham Lincoln, then a lawyer who appeared frequently in Davis's court. Davis was a strong supporter of his friend's political ambitions and was instrumental in securing the presidential nomination for Lincoln at the 1860 Republican convention. In 1861, after the death of Associate Justice

John McLean, President Lincoln appointed Davis to the Supreme Court.

Throughout his fourteen-year tenure on the Court, Davis established a reputation as a strong civil libertarian. He wrote the majority opinion in *Ex parte Milligan* (1866), which declared that neither the president nor Congress may declare martial law in any area not in open rebellion. He dissented in both *Ex parte Garland* and *Cummings v. Missouri* (1867), opposing the requirement of loyalty oaths for voters and office holders.

On economic issues, however, Davis was an advocate of federal power. He dissented in *Hepburn v. Griswold* (1870), in which he argued for the federal government's right to issue paper money as legal tender. His position in this matter was validated when the Court reversed its position in the second of the Legal Tender Cases, *Knox v. Lee* (1871). In the *Slaughter House Case* (1873), he concurred in the majority opinion reserving wide economic regulatory power to the states, notwithstanding the restrictions on state authority in the recently passed 14th Amendment.

Davis remained active in politics throughout his career. In 1872 he was nominated for president by the Labor Reform Party and during the controversy over the Hayes-Tilden presidential election of 1876, he resigned from the Supreme Court to take a seat in the U.S. Senate, which he held until 1883. He died in Bloomington, Illinois, in 1886.

David Davis

William R. Day

DAY, WILLIAM RUFUS

b. April 17, 1849; various judicial positions in Ohio; U.S. secretary of State (1898); judge, U.S. Circuit Court of Appeals (1899-1903); associate justice, U.S. Supreme Court (1903-1922); d. July 9, 1923.

Born in Ravenna, Ohio, son of Luther Day, a justice on the Ohio Supreme Court, the younger Day was educated at the University of Michigan (Class of 1870). After studies at Ravenna and at the University of Michigan Law School, he was admitted to the bar in 1872 and established a private practice in Canton, Ohio. In 1886 he was elected judge of the Court of Common Pleas. Three years later, he received a presidential appointment to become judge of a U.S. district court, but he never served in that position owing to ill health. A close friend of William McKinley, Day served briefly as secretary of State (1898), after which he was appointed (1899) judge of the United States Court of Appeals for the 6th Circuit. In 1903, after the resignation of Associate Justice George Shiras, Pres. Theodore Roosevelt appointed Day to the Supreme Court.

During his nearly twenty years on the Court, Day distinguished himself as a specialist in commercial and procedural issues. In *Dorr v. United States* (1904), he wrote the majority opinion, holding that residents of American territories are not specifically entitled to the due process provisions of the Constitution unless the territory is specifically incorporated by Congress. He rejected the "substantive due process" theory of the majority of the Court that permitted the Court to strike state regulation of working conditions as a violation of "liberty to contract" under the due process clause of the 14th Amendment. In *Lochner v. New York* (1905), he joined Associate Justice Harlan's dissent, which held that state regulation of working hours does not constitute a violation of the due process clause of the 14th Amendment. He also dissented in *Coppage v. Kansas* (1915), in which he argued that states do not violate the due process clause when they prohibit employees from reporting non-union pledges as a condition of employment. Day wrote the majority opinion in *Hammer v. Dagenhart* (1917), which held that Congress had no constitutional authority to prohibit the interstate transportation of goods manufactured by child labor.

In *Weeks v. United States* (1914), he wrote the opinion establishing the precedent that evidence obtained by illegal search and seizure may not be used in the federal courts. In *Buchanan v. Warley* (1917), he spoke for the Court in overturning city ordinances that mandated racial segregation as a violation of the 14th Amendment's protection of property rights.

Day resigned from the Court in 1922 to serve on the federal commission that adjudicated claims of American citizens against Germany arising from World War I. He died on Mackinac Island, Michigan, in the following year.

DOUGLAS, WILLIAM ORVILLE

b. October 16, 1898; professor, Yale University School of Law (1928-1934); member, Securities and Exchange Commission (1936-1937); chairman, Securities and Exchange Commission (1937-1939); associate justice, U.S. Supreme Court (1939-1975); d. January 19, 1980.

William O. Douglas

Son of a Presbyterian minister, the young Douglas lived with his parents in Minnesota and California before settling in Yakima, Washington, north of the Columbia River. When Douglas was twelve years old his father died. His mother's traditional religious and moral training would exert a profound influence on his life.

As a child Douglas suffered an outbreak of polio. His mother massaged and bathed his legs to prevent the paralysis from taking hold. After he recovered, Douglas began to take long hikes in the rugged Cascade Mountains to increase his strength. This began a life-long love of the outdoors. Throughout his career Douglas was known as a strong defender of the environment.

In 1920, Douglas graduated from Whitman College, a small liberal arts college in Washington. He majored in economics, was president of the student congress, and was elected to Phi Beta Kappa. After two years of teaching high school, Douglas was admitted to Columbia University School of Law in 1922.

Douglas earned his reputation as a maverick by hitch-hiking and hopping trains from Yakima, Washington, to New York City. Upon arrival, with fifty cents in his pocket, Douglas proceeded to take a job writing a business law course for a correspondence school. Douglas worked his way through law school and graduated second in his class. In 1924 he married his first wife, Mildred Riddle.

After graduation Douglas worked on Wall Street for two years. He tired of the eighteen-hour days and went back to Yakima, but stayed only briefly, returning to the Wall Street law firm. Douglas taught classes at Columbia University School of Law while working on Wall Street. In 1928 he left Wall Street and accepted a position as a law professor at Yale University School of Law.

Many of the bright young minds of the country joined Franklin D. Roosevelt's New Deal in the 1930's. Douglas was no exception. In 1934 he was appointed a member of the Securities and Exchange Commission and in 1937 was appointed chairman. Douglas earned a reputation as a strong commissioner and loyal New Deal member. Roosevelt rewarded Douglas's loyalty by appointing him to the Supreme Court in 1939, succeeding Justice Brandeis. At forty-one, Douglas was the second youngest judge ever appointed to the Court. He would serve until 1975, the longest term of any justice.

Early Court Years. Douglas served on the Supreme Court in the 1940's with fellow Roosevelt nominees Felix Frankfurter, Robert Jackson, Frank Murphy, and Wiley Rutledge. This Court earned a reputation as a brilliant and liberal Court. The justices, however, were not without their differences. Douglas, Black, and Murphy often opposed Frankfurter, the brilliant former Harvard professor. Douglas and Frankfurter carried on a career-long dispute over the proper role of the Court.

In his early years on the Court, Douglas voted with the majority to uphold New Deal legislation in *Wickard v. Filburn* (1942) and *United States v. Darby* (1941). He wrote the landmark decision of *Federal Power Commission v. Hope Natural Gas Co.* (1946), in which the Court ruled that the public utility rates must balance the interests of both stock owners and the public.

The wartime years were not without controversy. The federal government imposed a curfew on all persons of Japanese ancestry living on the West Coast and later placed the Japanese in camps. Douglas voted with the majority to uphold this conduct in *Hirabayashi v. United States* (1943) and *Korematsu v. United States* (1944). Each of these decisions is in contrast with Douglas's reputation as a defender of civil rights.

In *Minersville School District v. Gobitis* (1940), Douglas joined the majority to hold that a mandatory flag salute did not violate the religious freedom of the Jehovah Witnesses. This decision was overturned in *West Virginia v. Barnette* (1943). Douglas concurred, stating that the govern-ment could not impose standard religious beliefs on the public. Douglas also joined the majority in *Chaplinsky v. New Hampshire* (1943), in which the Court ruled that "fighting words" were not protected by the 1st Amendment. This decision is in contrast with his later opinions in which he strongly defended the absolute right of free speech.

Free Speech Advocate. Douglas earned his strong reputation as a defender of the 1st Amendment right of free speech in a number of important decisions. He dissented in *Dennis v. United States* (1951), in which the Court upheld the conviction of leaders of the Communist Party for conspiring and advocating the overthrow of the United States government. Douglas's dissent argued that unless there was "a clear and present danger" there could be no conviction for use of speech that advocated, but did not include, such conduct.

In two other major decisions, Douglas voted to protect the right of free speech. He wrote the majority opinion in *Terminiello v. Chicago* (1949), in which the Court reversed the conviction of a Chicago priest who was arrested for disturbing the peace after giving a loud, emotional speech. Douglas stated that the speech was protected by the 1st Amendment. He also dissented in *Beauharnais v. Illinois* (1952), in which the Court upheld the conviction of a man for using violent racial obscenities. The right of free speech, Douglas argued, could not be violated unless it was "necessary to avoid a disaster."

In the 1960's, Douglas would again write in defense of free speech. He concurred in *Brandenburg v. Ohio* (1969), in which the Court reversed the conviction of a Ku Klux Klan leader. Douglas emphasized the absolute protection of free speech by the 1st Amendment. In *Branzburg v. Hayes* (1972), Douglas dissented from a ruling that held that reporters could not withhold confidential sources from a grand jury. He argued that the ability to protect sources was important to the freedom of the press.

Other Cases. Douglas wrote two opinions in the 1950's that rejected government policies of requiring workers to sign loyalty oaths. He concurred in *Joint Anti-Facist Committee v. Mcgrath* (1951), in which the Court struck down the procedures used in the federal loyalty oath program. In *Adler v. Board of Education of City of New York* (1952), he dissented from a ruling upholding New York's loyalty oath for public school teachers.

Douglas was also a strong defender of religious freedom. In *Illinois ex rel. McCollum v. Board of Education* (1948) he concurred, holding that religious education in public schools during school hours was unconstitutional. In *Zorach v. Clauson* (1952) Douglas wrote the majority opinion in a decision that allowed students to leave school during the regular hours to attend religious instruction classes. Douglas argued that there was no establishment of religion by this activity since the courses were conducted outside the school and classes were voluntary.

In *Everson v. Board of Education* (1947) Douglas concurred, voting to uphold the public bus transportation of parochial school students, a decision he would later reject in *Engle v. Vitale* (1962). In *Engle*, he joined the majority to rule that prayer in the public schools was unconstitutional since it established religion. Douglas also dissented in *Board of Education v. Allen* (1968), which upheld a New York program of supplying textbooks to parochial schools. In *Wisconsin v. Yoder* (1972), he dissented in part, emphasizing that the rights of the children were also affected by the state's compulsory school program.

Perhaps the most significant Douglas opinion was that of *Griswold v. Connecticut* (1965), in which Douglas wrote for the majority. The Court ruled that Connecticut could not prohibit the sale of birth control devices by imposing criminal penalties on sellers and users. The *Griswold* opinion was a landmark opinion in civil rights law. Douglas wrote that the Bill of Rights protected more than the specific rights included in the Constitution. A person's right of privacy was also protected by the Bill of Rights.

Douglas also emphasized the fundamental right of privacy in *Skinner v. Oklahoma* (1942), in which he wrote for the majority in ruling a statute that required the sterilization of certain criminals unconstitutional. In *Roe v. Wade* (1973) Douglas concurred with the majority to uphold a woman's right to have an abortion.

The Vietnam War was the major political controversy of that era. The Supreme Court refused to hear challenges to many activities of the government that were connected with the Vietnam War, believing that the Court should not resolve political disputes. Douglas often dissented from these decisions. In *Holtzman v. Schlesinger* (1973), the Court refused to hear a suit challenging the bombing of Cambodia without a formal declaration of war by Congress, a decision from which Douglas dissented. In *Laird v. Tatum* (1972), Douglas also dissented from a decision not to hear a challenge to the Army's surveillance of civilians. Douglas warned that the activities were an immediate threat to the 1st Amendment rights of the civilians.

The Supreme Court refused to hear two other challenges to conduct associated with the Vietnam War. In *United States v. Richardson* (1974) the Court refused to hear a suit that challenged the withholding of the expenses of the Central Intelligence Agency from public inspection. Douglas dissented, arguing that the taxpayers had a personal stake in the controversy. In *Schlesinger v. Reservists Committee to Stop the War* (1972), the Court refused to hear a challenge to a Defense Department policy of allowing Reserve members to sit in Congress. Douglas again dissented on the grounds that the plaintiffs had a personal stake in the case.

Throughout his career on the Supreme Court Douglas frequently challenged the conduct of the government. In *Youngstown Sheet and Tube Co. v. Sawyer* (1953), the Court ruled that President Truman could not seize the steel mills to prevent a strike during the Korean War. Douglas concurred, emphasizing that this power to pass laws and condemn property belonged to Congress and not the president.

Douglas was noted for his dissents without opinion in cases that concerned the income tax laws and that were decided favorable to the Internal Revenue Service (IRS). Perhaps this was Douglas's means of disapproving the IRS policies without explaining his reasoning.

The last years of Douglas's career on the Court were spent in a struggle with Richard Nixon. He made front page news when he asserted that the chambers of the Supreme Court were bugged. He wrote a strong dissent in *Environmental Protection Agency v. Mink* (1973), in which the Court ruled that lower courts could not examine or disclose files that were marked "top secret" by the government. Douglas argued that the Freedom of Information Act required the courts to inspect the material and then release the material to the public if it was not truly top secret. This position was later adopted by Congress.

In *New York Times v. United States* (1973) the Supreme Court ruled that the press could publish the contents of the Pentagon Papers. In his last major defense of the rights of free speech and free press, Douglas concurred, arguing that these rights are absolute unless there is a grave and imminent threat to the government.

Douglas frequently has been called a "result oriented" justice who wrote for the public eye and not legal scholars. This often led to landmark decisions such as *Griswold*, but also left scholars struggling to support his decisions. His career on and off the Supreme Court reflected a life-long commitment to civil rights and the environment.

Personal Life. Perhaps no other justice was in the public eye as often as Douglas. From 1940 through 1952 people speculated that he would leave the Court and run for political office. He traveled abroad to Asia and Africa and wrote about his travels in *Of Men and Mountains* (1950) and many other works.

The postwar years were a time of change on the Supreme Court. The Roosevelt justices left the bench. Douglas also divorced his wife and was remarried, to Mercedes Davidson, in 1954. In the 1960's Douglas's personal life became the subject of controversy. He was married for a third time in 1963, to Joan Martin, and then for a fourth time in 1966, to Kathleen Heffernan. Many conservative congressmen objected to his political values and his private life. When his income from a private foundation was revealed, a move to impeach Douglas began in Congress. After an investigation by a judicial subcommittee there was no finding of wrongdoing, and the controversy subsided. In his later years he wrote two autobiographical works, *Go East, Young Man* (1974) and *The Court Years* (1980). In 1975 Douglas suffered a stroke and was forced to leave the Court. He never fully recovered and died in 1980 in Washington, D.C.

DUVALL, GABRIEL

b. December 6, 1752; U.S. congressman (1774-1796); comptroller of the U.S. Treasury (1802-1811); associate justice, U.S. Supreme Court (1811-1835); d. March 6, 1844.

Born in Prince George's County, Maryland, to a prominent Huguenot family, Duvall was appointed clerk of the Maryland Convention in 1775, while still a law student. In 1777 he was named clerk of the newly reconstituted Maryland House of Delegates and was admitted to the bar in 1778. From 1782 to 1785 he served in the State Council of Maryland. In 1786 he was elected Annapolis representative to the Maryland House of Delegates, a post that he held until 1794. In that year he was elected to the U.S. Congress, resigning in 1796 to become a judge of the Maryland Supreme Court. In 1802 he was appointed by President Jefferson to be comptroller of the Treasury. With the death of Associate Justice Samuel Chase in 1811, President Madison nominated Duvall to the Supreme Court.

Duvall distinguished himself philosophically from Chief Justice Marshall during his long service on the Supreme Court, notably dissenting from the majority in *Trustees of Dartmouth College v. Woodward* (1819). Another of his dissenting opinions was in *Mima Queen and Child v. Hepburn* (1813), in which he argued unsuccessfully that hearsay evidence should be admitted in the determination of the free status of a slave. Duvall also supported the legal status of slaves in 1829, writing for the Court in *Le Grand v. Darnall*, which held that a master's bequest of property to a slave by implication entitled the slave to freedom.

Advancing age and deafness eventually impaired Duvall's performance on the Supreme Court, and he resigned in 1835 at age 83. He died nine years later, in 1844, at "Marietta," his family estate in Maryland.

ELLSWORTH, OLIVER

b. April 29, 1745; member, Connecticut General Assembly (1773-1776); state's attorney, Hartford County (1777-1785); delegate, Continental Congress (1777-1784); member, Connecticut Council of Safety (1779); member, Connecticut Governor's Council (1780-1785; 1801-1807); judge, Connecticut Supreme Court of Errors (1785); judge, Connecticut Superior Court (1785-1789); member, Constitutional Convention (1787); U.S. senator (1789-1796); chief justice, U.S. Supreme Court (1796-1800); U.S. Commissioner to France (1799-1800); chief justice, Connecticut State Supreme Court of Appeals (1807); d. November 26, 1807.

Born in Windsor, Connecticut, into a prominent local family, Ellsworth received his preparatory education at home from the Reverend Joseph Bellamy and was enrolled as a student at Yale College in 1762. Two years later, after a somewhat mysterious and sudden departure from Yale, he resumed his studies at Princeton, where he received a B.A. degree in 1766. After his graduation from college, Ellsworth apparently was persuaded by his father to pursue a religious career. Returning to his home in Windsor, he began what were to be short-lived theological studies with the Reverend John Smalley of neighboring New Britain; in the following year, 1768, Ellsworth began to study law.

Admitted to the bar in 1771, Ellsworth at first had considerable difficulty in earning a living at his chosen profession. In 1772 he married Abigail Wolcott of East Windsor and supplemented their meager income by farming some land he had been given by his father. With Ellsworth's appointment to the Connecticut General Assembly, however, the reputation of his private law practice greatly improved. Moving his residence and his practice to Hartford in 1775, he became one of the most sought-after attorneys in the state, eventually amassing a personal fortune through successful business investments and real estate.

With the outbreak of the Revolution, Ellsworth was named to a state committee that supervised and audited Connecticut's expenditures during the course of the war. In 1777 he was named a delegate to the Continental Congress, in which he served for seven years. In acknowledgement of his legal background, he was appointed to the committees on Marine Affairs, Board of Treasury, and Appeals, in which he had to arbitrate the conflicting wartime claims of various states. In many ways the Committee on Appeals was a forerunner of the Supreme Court, and Ellsworth's service on it, especially in cases dealing with Admiralty Law, laid the foundation for his later judicial philosophy regarding the relationship of the judiciary to the authority of the states. During the same period he also served as the state's attorney of Hartford County, as a member of the Connecticut Council of Safety, which controlled the state's military affairs, and as a member of the Governor's Council.

In 1784, Ellsworth resigned from the Continental Congress and resumed his private law practice, although he continued to serve on the state Governor's Council. When that body became a state court of appeals in 1785, Ellsworth served on it as judge. Later in the same year, he resigned that position to accept a nomination as judge of the newly-created state superior court.

National Prominence. Ellsworth was selected as one of his state's three delegates to the Constitutional Convention in Philadelphia in 1787, and he played an important role in the adoption of the "Connecticut Compromise," which reconciled the power of the larger states with demand for equal representation by the small states by establishing two branches of the national legislature, the Senate and the House of Representatives. He is also credited with suggesting "United States" as the official name of the new nation. In the Connecticut state ratification convention the following year, Ellsworth was instrumental in obtaining the Constitution's adoption by his home state. One of his most persuasive reasons for urging its acceptance was the role that he foresaw that the federal judiciary would play. "If the United States go beyond their powers," Ellsworth argued, "if they make a law which the Constitution does not authorize, it is void; and the judicial power, the national judges, who, to secure their impartiality, are to be made independent, will declare it void."

As a result of the elections of 1788, Ellsworth was chosen by the state legislature to represent Connecticut in the U.S. Senate. There he emerged as one of the early Senate leaders, helping to establish its rules of procedure, to organize the diplomatic service, to deal with the problems of national finance, and to establish the structure of the federal judiciary, through his co-authorship of the Judiciary Act of 1789.

This act established that the Supreme Court would have six justices and hold semi-annual sessions. On the lowest level of the federal judiciary, a district court with a resident judge would be set up in each state, and for appeals from those district courts, three judicial circuits were to be established, each circuit court meeting semi-annually in each of its states, presided over by two supreme court justices and the appropriate district judge. The circuit courts would, in addition, have original jurisdiction in international cases and in cases between citizens of different states. With the passage of this act in September 1789, the federal union could at last begin to function.

In 1796, after the resignation of John Jay, the Supreme Court's first chief justice, and the refusal of the Senate to confirm the nomination of John Rutledge, Pres. George Washington appointed Ellsworth to that post on March 3, 1796. The following day, he was confirmed by the Senate by a vote of 21 to 1 and took his place at the head of the Supreme Court.

Chief Justice. Ellsworth's tenure as chief justice was brief, lasting less than four years. Since few cases were argued before the Supreme Court itself, the primary work of a justice—even a chief justice—lay in the circuit courts. Nonetheless Ellsworth wrote some important opinions in his first session on the Supreme Court. Two, in particular, concerned the admiralty issues that he had first dealt with in the Committee of Appeals in the Continental Congress. In *United States v. La Vengeance* (1796), he and the other justices considerably extended the maritime authority of the federal government not only to acts committed on the high seas but to those on inland waters as well. In the case of *Moodie v. The Ship Phoebe Ann* (1796), Ellsworth spoke for the Court in affirming the precedence of international treaties over other national laws. A similar ruling came in *Ware v. Hylton* (1796), in which Ellsworth concurred with the majority in overriding a state law that contradicted the peace treaty of 1783 with Great Britain.

One of Ellsworth's most important rulings for the future direction of the Supreme Court came in *Wiscart v. Dauchy* (1796). Reviewing a case that had been adjudicated in circuit court in favor of the plaintiff and brought before the Supreme Court by the defendants on appeal rather than writ of error, Ellsworth established the essential distinction between the two procedures, observing that an appeal

subjects "the facts as well as the law to review and retrial" whereas a writ of error "removes nothing for re-examination but the law." Accordingly, Ellsworth ruled that the circuit court judgment should stand, since the Supreme Court was empowered by Congress to rule only on questions of law.

In the midst of Ellsworth's tenure as chief justice, relations between the United States and France had become strained in the aftermath of the French Revolution, and in 1799, Ellsworth accepted the commission of Pres. John Adams to negotiate with the government of Napoleon to avert an impending war. The commission succeeded in that limited goal, but failed in an attempt to extract French reparations for seized American vessels, and, in addition, Ellsworth's health was seriously affected by the rigors of the transatlantic journey. While still overseas, he conveyed his resignation as chief justice to President Adams.

Returning to Windsor, Connecticut, Ellsworth accepted an appointment to the Governor's Council and was named the first chief justice of the state Supreme Court of Appeals in 1807. By that time his health had declined even further, and he died at his home in Windsor later in the same year.

FIELD, STEPHEN JOHNSON

b. November 4, 1816; member, California legislature (1850-1851); justice, California Supreme Court (1857-1863); associate justice, U.S. Supreme Court (1863-1897); d. April 9, 1899.

Stephen Field

Born in Haddam, Connecticut, Field spent his later teenage years in the Near East with his missionary sister (later mother of Associate Justice David Brewer), returning to the United States in 1833 to attend Williams College. After graduation in 1837, Field studied law in the office of his brother David Dudley Field, the great codifier and law reformer. (A third brother, Cyrus Field, was famous for his role in the laying of the first transatlantic telegraph cable.) Stephen was admitted to the New York bar in 1841. In 1849, at the time of the Gold Rush, Field moved to California and embarked on a tumultuous law practice in Marysville. In 1850 he was elected to the legislature, where he was instrumental in drafting the civil and criminal codes of the new state. He was elected to the state supreme court in 1857. In 1863, with the creation of a new Supreme Court justiceship and federal circuit for the Far West, Pres. Abraham Lincoln appointed Field, a war Democrat, to the Supreme Court.

Field was an eloquent opponent of the intervention of government in economic affairs. He wrote the majority opinion in *Ex parte Garland* (1866), which ruled against the administration of loyalty oaths. He also spoke for the Court in *Paul v. Virginia* (1869), which determined that the issuing of a policy of insurance is not a transaction of commerce within the meaning of the clause in the Constitution delegating the regulation of interstate commerce to Congress and therefore regulation of such transactions should be left to the individual states. Field dissented in the second Legal Tender Cases (*Knox v. Lee* and *Parker v. Davis*, 1870), in which he argued against the right of the federal government to issue unsecured currency. He also dissented in the *Slaughterhouse Cases* (1873), in which he opposed the right of the state to grant official monopolies. Field also wrote the dissenting opinion in *Munn v. Illinois* (1877), opposing the right of state governments to regulate rates charged by private businesses. In the *Sinking Fund Cases* (1879), he dissented again, condemning the congressional requirement that railroads set aside twenty-five percent of their net earnings to ensure payment of their debts.

With regard to judicial immunity, Field wrote the majority opinion in *Bradley v. Fisher* (1871), which established the precedent that judges of courts of record of superior or general jurisdiction are not liable to civil actions for their judicial acts, even when such acts are in excess of their jurisdiction and are alleged to have been done maliciously or corruptly. Another important precedent in this area resulted from one of the most notable and colorful incidents of Field's career. In 1888, Field had charged David S. Terry, a lawyer who appeared before him in circuit court, with contempt, and Terry threatened to murder Field if he appeared again in California. Undaunted by the threat but prepared for it, Field returned to California the following year with a deputy marshal who shot and killed Terry when he approached them on a train. The resulting murder charge against the marshal, David Neagle, was set aside in *In re Neagle* (1889), which ruled that federal officers may not be prosecuted for acts committed in pursuance of their official duties.

Field, disabled by advancing age, resigned from the Court in 1897. He had served on the Court longer than any other justice up to that time. He believed that the Constitution was properly used as a shield against government actions that interfered with private property and individual economic choice. This conservative philosophy engrafted on the 14th Amendment was extremely influential and dominated constitutional law for decades. As its most cogent expositor, Field left a critically important impression on the Court. He died in Washington, D.C., in 1899.

FORTAS, ABE

b. June 19, 1910; assistant director, Securities and Exchange Commission (1938-1939); counsel, Public Works Administration (1939-1941); undersecretary, Department of the Interior (1942-1946); advisor, U.S. delegation to the United Nations (1945-1946); associate justice, U.S. Supreme Court (1965-1969); d. April 5, 1982.

Born in Memphis, Tennessee, and educated at Southwestern College (Class of 1930), Fortas studied at the Yale Law School, where he was chosen editor of the *Yale Law Journal*. After graduating at the top of his class in 1933, Fortas was appointed assistant professor of law and remained at Yale until 1937. He had become involved in the programs of the Roosevelt administration and eventually left Yale to become assistant director of the public utilities section of the Securities and Exchange Commission under his former professor and later colleague on the Court, William O. Douglas. In 1939 he joined the Public Works Administration as general counsel, and later joined the Department of the Interior, where he became undersecretary in 1942. Fortas also served as advisor to the U.S. delegation to the United Nations. Returning to private practice in 1946, Fortas became a well-known civil rights advocate, appearing before the Supreme Court in *Gideon v. Wainwright* (1963), which established the right of all indigent criminal defendants to free legal counsel. Fortas had long been a supporter and advisor to Lyndon Johnson, and in 1965, after the resignation of Associate Justice Arthur Goldberg, President Johnson appointed Fortas to the Supreme Court.

During his brief tenure on the Court, Fortas retained a strong interest in civil rights. He voted with the majority in *Miranda v. Arizona* (1966), which established that all criminal suspects must be informed of their constitutional rights against self-incrimination before being taken into custody. Fortas dissented in *Fortson v. Morris* (1966), denying the power of the malapportioned Georgia legislature to select a governor in the event that no candidate had received a popular majority in the general election. He wrote the majority opinion in *In re Gault* (1967), which established juvenile defendants' due process rights, such as the right to counsel, and protection against self-incrimination. He also spoke for the Court in *Tinker v. Des Moines Independent School District* (1969), upholding the 1st Amendment right of school pupils to engage in non-disruptive political protests.

In 1968, with the retirement of Chief Justice Earl Warren, President Johnson nominated Fortas to the position of chief justice. Considerable conservative opposition arose in the Senate, and Johnson was forced to withdraw the nomination. In 1969, Fortas's reputation was further damaged by the disclosure that he had accepted money from a foundation established by an indicted stock manipulator. Although no criminal wrongdoing was established, the public outcry that the disclosure aroused forced Fortas to resign from the Supreme Court, the first time that a justice had ever left the bench under the shadow of unethical conduct. After his retirement, Fortas returned to his private practice in Washington, D.C., where he died in 1982.

FRANKFURTER, FELIX

b. November 15, 1882; War Department (1910-1914); chairman, War Labor Policies Board (1918); associate justice, U.S. Supreme Court (1939-1962); d. February 22, 1965.

Felix Frankfurter

Born in Vienna, Austria, the third son of six children, his family came to the United States and settled in New York City when he was twelve years old. Felix had not, at the time, heard one word of English; it has been said, however, that he learned the language within six weeks. Felix told a humorous story of his returning home one day and saying to his mother, "This man Laundry must be very rich, he has stores all over town."

Felix's two older brothers immediately went to work to help support the family, while Felix and his brother Paul were sent to public school, P.S. 25. New York City offered a stimulating intellectual climate for the boys, and within two years of arriving in New York, Felix was ready for high school. Frankfurter entered City College, which offered a program combining high school and college in five years. He became vice president of the senior class, assistant editor of a college magazine, and a member of the chess club and the debating society. He graduated third in his class at the age of nineteen.

Upon graduation in 1902, Frankfurter went to work for the newly formed New York City Tenement House Department. He started going to New York Law School at night, switched over to New York University Law School, and ended up applying to Harvard Law School in the same year. Harvard imbued Frankfurter with a deep sense of commitment to law and the search for truth. He graduated first in his class.

Early Career. Frankfurter's first position upon graduation was with the New York firm of Hornblower, Byrne, Miller, and Potter. He did not stay long, leaving as soon as he had an offer to join the United States Attorney's office. This was to be the beginning of a long-term relationship with U.S. Attorney Henry L. Stimson, who became Frankfurter's close friend and mentor. Frankfurter was to become Stimson's personal assistant in several working situations. With Stimson, he worked on important litigation and became familiar with the leading political figures of that time. He worked in both the Theodore Roosevelt and Taft administrations under Stimson in the War Department. In 1911 he became Law Officer of the Bureau of Insular Affairs and argued cases before the Supreme Court, which enabled him to develop a closer relationship with both Justice Brandeis and Justice Holmes. They represented the cutting edge of the Progressive movement in law, a philosophy he began to identify with more and more.

When the famous split in the Republican Party took place between Roosevelt and Taft, Frankfurter chose to stay with Stimson under the more conservative Taft, even though ideologically he identified more with Roosevelt. When Taft was defeated, he stayed temporarily under Woodrow Wilson's administration, but soon left to accept an associate professorship at Harvard Law School. There he intended to develop further the ideal of modern sociological jurisprudence and legal realism begun by Brandeis and Holmes.

Frankfurter believed in the use of experts to form public policy, but also had faith that the public was educable as to the solutions.

In 1916, Frankfurter changed his party affiliation to work with President Wilson. The Republicans had lost their identity with Progressivism once Roosevelt had defected. During this time Frankfurter also became a trustee of the *New Republic* magazine and wrote several articles for it.

During 1917, Frankfurter became secretary and counsel to the President's Mediation Commission and settled labor disputes. While serving in that capacity, he developed an undeserved reputation as a radical for his defense of unpopular public figures. Frankfurter, on the other hand, saw himself as an impartial investigator and expert fighting against the public's misinformed "passion."

Frankfurter accepted the chairmanship of the War Labor Policies Board in the Labor Department in the following year. There he developed his ability to handle disputes to an even greater extent, convincing the president of United States Steel to adopt an eight-hour work day. Frankfurter also confirmed his commitment to the enforcement of civil liberties while investigating cases in which the states had used illegal means to attack labor organizers. His investigations sometimes led to a favorable outcome for the defendants in politically volatile cases. His reputation for defending unpopular causes would be furthered by his later support of the defense in the famous Sacco-Vanzetti case.

Sacco and Vanzetti were two immigrant Italians who had been convicted of murder stemming from an armed robbery of a payroll wagon in Braintree, Massachusetts. To heighten the public's already impassioned hatred against foreigners, it was brought out that the men were anarchists who had avoided the military draft of World War I.

Frankfurter's attention was drawn to the case when he found that certain evidence used to convict the defendants was false and was nevertheless knowingly used by the prosecution. Frankfurter became actively involved in a citizens' group organized to direct and fund Sacco and Vanzetti's defense. He wrote a blistering article, published in *The Atlantic Monthly*, criticizing the obvious mistakes and prejudice of the presiding trial judge and the general unfairness of the proceedings as a whole. This directed even more hostility toward Frankfurter from some of Boston's most prominent citizens, but increased public awareness of the injustices of the case, while lending the defense more legitimacy by being associated with Frankfurter's name.

Although Frankfurter was not successful in saving Sacco and Vanzetti from execution, the experience deepened his commitment to the legal system as an instrument of reason to combat prejudice and hatred.

During the New Deal years of the 1930's, Frankfurter played a dominant role in shaping policy and advising Pres. Franklin D. Roosevelt, although he never actually held an official post. His professional history was consistently in keeping with his tendency to work best behind the scenes. When Roosevelt offered him the post of solicitor general, he turned it down. This, unfortunately for the administration, struck a blow against the New Deal, which needed the help of the ablest legal minds of the time in order to defend its policies in the federal courts. Frankfurter was a proponent of a mixed Brandeis/Keynes formula to fight the Depression, a formula that attacked corporate and financial bigness through progressive taxation and massive government spending to employ workers.

Frankfurter soon developed a reputation as a placement officer for the New Deal by securing jobs for many former Harvard Law School students and clerks for Holmes and Brandeis in the federal government. Most of these positions were in the new Agricultural Adjustment Administration, but Frankfurter's actual ability to secure such positions was often greatly exaggerated by his enemies.

Frankfurter was instrumental in constructing the new Securities Act, which had come under considerable attack from Wall Street giants and members of the House and Senate alike for its initial vagueness and heavy-handedness against corporate officers for violations of reporting regulations for stock transfers. The passage of the bill was a major victory for the New Deal, which placed much of the blame for the Depression and the general panic following the stock market crash on the securities industry.

In 1933, and at the height of Frankfurter's influence and success, he accepted the highly honored Eastman Professorship at Oxford University in England. This move illustrates Frankfurter's love of ideas over politics, but resulted in a constructive acquaintance with John Maynard Keynes, the English economist whose ideas about the money supply were later to be used in Roosevelt's administration. Frankfurter was an unabashed Anglophile, and his time in England allowed him to indulge in his admiration for the English judicial system and other cultural institutions.

Supreme Court. When Benjamin Cardozo's death in 1939 left a vacancy on the Supreme Court, Roosevelt appointed Frankfurter to take his place. During Frankfurter's tenure on the bench, which lasted until 1962, he surprised many of his supporters and friends by adhering to the conservative philosophy of judicial restraint. This often placed him on the side of the Court's conservatives and disappointed those who expected him to be the libertarian leader he had always been as a private citizen. Frankfurter merely saw significant differences between the roles of legislator and judge. His restraint often furthered the interests of liberalism in the New Deal era, when much progressive social legislation was being struck down by the Supreme Court.

Underlying Frankfurter's adoption of the self-restraint doctrine was his belief in the democratic political process. The "reasonable" policy decisions of popularly elected officials, in Frankfurter's opinion, should not be interfered with by the courts.

Frankfurter's use of judicial restraint would often place him on the opposite side of liberals, however, as in *Minersville School District v. Gobitis* in 1939. Frankfurter wrote the majority opinion, which upheld a state statute requiring school children to salute the flag. The statute was challenged by Jehovah's Witnesses as a violation of their right to the free exercise of their religion. Although later overruled, the case is an extreme example of judicial deference to legislative judgment. Frankfurter also inflamed many liberals with his opinion in the *Meadowmoor Dairies* (1941) case. Frankfurter, again writing for the majority, held that picketing "in a context of violence" loses its "appeal to reason" and upheld state power to enjoin picketing after prolonged violence in a labor dispute.

Frankfurter was soon to be at the center of a split within the Court, as evidenced by the case of *Jones v. Opelika* (1941). *Jones* and *Gobitis* were decisions against the same religious minority. Three dissenters found the *Jones* case simply a logical extension of the principles upon which *Gobitis* rested. Justices Black, Douglas, and Murphy stated in their opinion that they had changed their minds about their votes in *Gobitis*. The majority in *Jones* nevertheless upheld a municipality's right to levy a tax on the sale of religious literature by Jehovah's Witnesses.

Another major dispute centered on the applicability of the Bill of Rights to the states by way of the 14th Amendment. Although Frankfurter did not adhere to the theory of incorporation, a minority of Justices Black, Douglas, and Murphy began a campaign to make the entire Bill of Rights so applied.

Frankfurter favored a more flexible due process approach first set forth by Justice Cardozo in *Palko v. Connecticut* (1937). Both Cardozo and Frankfurter believed in a more selective incorporation of the Bill of Rights. The problem was in deciding on a standard with which to decide what rights guaranteed by the first eight amendments were so fundamental that a denial by a state would constitute a violation of due process. Cardozo held in *Palko* that the "double jeopardy" rule, which prevents federal prosecutors from trying a defendant twice for the the same offense, does not apply to the states.

In *Adamson v. California* (1947), Frankfurter also indicated that some, but not all, of the rights contained in the Bill of Rights were to be applied to the states. Frankfurter stated that the 14th Amendment held the individual states to "those canons of decency and fairness which express the notions of justice of English-speaking peoples even toward those charged with the most heinous offenses." Although he admitted that this standard of justice did not contain an objective formula, he would hold all judges to the limits of accepted notions of justice and to withhold their personal biases. He wrote a concurring

opinion in *Adamson* upholding a state law allowing the prosecution to comment on the failure of the defendant to testify at his own trial.

In later cases, Frankfurter spoke of rights basic to a "free society" and those "implicit in the concept of ordered liberty." He further stated that defining due process involved a gradual process of "inclusion and exclusion of certain rights into the 14th Amendment. In *Wolf v. Colorado* (1949) he wrote the majority opinion, which held that the federal exclusionary rule barring the use of evidence obtained by illegal search and seizure was not applicable to the states, thereby upholding a state court conviction secured by the introduction of evidence illegally obtained. Three years later in *Rochin v. California* (1952) Frankfurter wrote the majority opinion reversing a state court conviction based on evidence obtained by pumping the stomach of a suspect. Frankfurter condemned the behavior of the police as conduct that "shocks the conscience." He insisted that state law enforcement officials "respect certain decencies of civilized conduct." He compared the case with those involving forced confessions. Although he maintained that judges should not rely on their personal notions of fairness and decency, such vague standards of conscience, decency, and civilized conduct seemed impossible to apply without an individual judge injecting his own values. A more objective standard was needed. Black remained a strong critic of Frankfurter's approach, stating in his concurrence in *Rochin* that "faithful adherence to the specific guarantees in the Bill of Rights insures a more permanent protection of individual liberty than that which can be afforded by the nebulous standards stated by the majority."

Frankfurter's approach to the question of due process indeed created much confusion among the Supreme Court justices themselves, let alone the rest of the country's state courts. In *Irvine v. California* (1954), the Court upheld a state court conviction in which evidence had been obtained by breaking into the suspect's home and planting electronic surveillance microphones in the bedroom. The judgment of the Court was partially based on its decision in *Rochin*, which implied to them that there must be some element of physical coercion involved in order to prevent the use of such evidence. Frankfurter dissented, stating that the majority misunderstood his opinion in *Rochin* by placing emphasis on the physical aspect of the intrusion. He maintained that the conduct of the police here was an equally offensive violation of the suspect's rights as that in *Rochin* and definitely went beyond a mere illegal search and seizure as that in *Wolf*.

The result of this series of cases was that "ordinary" violations of 4th Amendment rights would not prevent the introduction of evidence so obtained, whereas "additional aggravating conduct" would render such evidence inadmissible.

Finally, in 1961, in *Mapp v. Ohio*, the Court held that

all state searches violating 4th Amendment rights are inadmissible in state courts of law. The majority thereby lent some certainty to an increasingly foggy area of the law. Frankfurter joined in the dissent, however, as it was a direct overruling of his prior opinion in *Wolf*. Black had won a major battle, as *Mapp* specifically incorporated the 4th Amendment and made the exclusionary rule applicable to all state cases.

Frankfurter's liberalism was tempered by his fervent patriotism, resulting in decisions such as *Gobitis* produced. He joined a bitter dissent in the case of *Schneiderman v. United States* (1943), in which the majority voted to reverse a state's revocation of a Communist Party member's citizenship. When *Gobitis* was overruled in 1943 in *West Virginia State Board of Education v. Barnette*, Frankfurter wrote the dissent, restating his commitment to restraint where a legislature chooses a reasonable means to achieve a legitimate end. Frankfurter also emphasized his effort at repressing his own personal biases in order to maintain the proper judicial disinterestedness.

Although Frankfurter failed to become the undisputed leader of the Court, as he and many others had expected, he nevertheless left his mark. In his later years on the Court, he was somewhat less strict in his application of judicial restraint. When called upon to rule on issues touching his most valued ideal of fundamental due process in criminal cases, he was more apt to rely on more subjective standards for review. He struck down police conduct he regarded as "shocking" to his "conscience," thereby ignoring the objective standard of review of which he so often wrote.

Frankfurter was recognized by his peers as one of the greatest minds ever to sit on the Supreme Court, but at the same time he became an enigma because of his seemingly contradictory behavior once appointed. Frankfurter resigned in 1962 and died three years later in Washington, D.C.

FULLER, MELVILLE WESTON

b. February 11, 1833; delegate, Illinois Constitutional Convention (1862); member, Illinois legislature (1863-1864); chief justice, U.S. Supreme Court (1888-1910); member, American delegation to the Venezuela-British Guiana Boundary Commission tribunal (1899); member, Permanent Court of Arbitration at the Hague (1900-1910); d. July 4, 1910.

Born in Augusta, Maine, and raised in the home of his maternal grandfather, Nathan Weston, a former chief justice of the Maine Supreme Court, Fuller was educated at Bowdoin College (Class of 1853). After graduation, he spent a year studying law at the law office of an uncle in Bangor and later attended Harvard Law School for only six months. He was admitted to the Maine bar in 1855. Fuller established a private practice in Augusta and became involved in local politics there, serving as member and later president of the city common council, as well as city solicitor. In addition to his legal and political duties, Fuller also worked briefly as an editor on the *Augusta Age*, a prominent Democratic newspaper in the state. In this position he developed a bitter political rivalry with James G. Blaine, editor of the *Kennebec Journal*, whom Fuller would help to defeat in the presidential election of 1884.

In 1856, Fuller moved to Chicago and established a private law practice there. Two years later, he married Calista Reynolds of Chicago. During the early years of his Chicago practice, Fuller had limited financial success, and he supplemented his law career with continued involvement in journalism and political affairs. In Illinois Democratic politics, Fuller found a philosophical ally in Stephen Douglas, who, like Fuller, believed that slavery was an issue to be decided by individual states. Their political alliance developed, and in 1858 Fuller played an important role in Douglas's successful campaign for a U.S. Senate seat against Abraham Lincoln.

Fuller continued his support of Douglas against Lincoln in the presidential election of 1860. During the Civil War, Fuller supported the Union side, although his philosophical differences with the Lincoln administration often made his support little more than lukewarm. In 1861 he was elected a delegate to the Illinois Constitutional Convention, and in 1863 he won a seat in the state legislature, where he spoke out against the Lincoln administration and its Emancipation Proclamation.

In 1866, two years after the death of his first wife, Fuller married Ellen Coolbaugh, daughter of the president of the Union National Bank, the largest bank in Chicago, and his fortunes as a practicing attorney rose. In addition to representing Union National, he argued cases for several large Chicago businesses and railroads and appeared before the U.S. Supreme Court for the first time in 1872. In one of his most publicized cases, he defended Charles Edward Cheney, a prominent local Episcopal leader, before a church tribunal on charges of ecclesiastical disobedience. This required a great familiarity with the tenets of canon law. He also became involved in conflicting claims of state and local government, defending the right of the city of Chicago to its shorefront property and against street railway companies that had been given long-term monopolies by the state.

Fuller attended every Democratic National Convention between 1864 and 1884, and in the latter year was an active supporter of the candidacy of Grover Cleveland against Fuller's former rival, James G. Blaine. Shortly after Cleveland's inauguration, Fuller was first offered an appointment as chairman of the Civil Service Commission and then as solicitor general, both of which he declined.

In April 1888, however, after the death of Chief Justice Morrison Waite, President Cleveland nominated Fuller to succeed him, and this was an honor that he could not refuse. The confirmation battle in the Senate was especially bitter,

Melville Fuller

and the Senate acted only after a long delay. The Republican majority voiced objections to Fuller's legal connections to large corporations and suspected him of questionable loyalty during the Civil War. These objections were finally overcome and in August, Fuller, who had never held either a judicial or a federal office, was finally confirmed as Chief Justice by a Senate vote of 41 to 20.

Chief Justice. During his tenure as chief justice, Fuller led the Court through a series of important decisions for the future judicial history of the United States. The Fuller Court was characterized by its steadfast conservatism, reflecting a similar trend in American political life. The advances in civil rights promised by the 13th and 14th Amendments were, for the most part, turned back, and states' rights and the rights of big business were important themes. Although Fuller's tenure was lengthy and he wrote more than 800 majority opinions, he was not regarded, except officially, as a judicial leader. The most that can be said is that his conservative philosophy generally reflected the tenor of his Court.

At the start of Fuller's tenure the power of state and federal governments to regulate private business was sharply restricted by the Court. He joined the majority in *Chicago, Milwaukee, and St. Paul Railroad v. Minnesota* (1890), which held that courts had the right to review the reasonableness of state tariff schedules. He also voted with the majority in *Reagan v. Farmers' Loan and Trust Co.* (1894) and *Smyth v. Ames* (1898), which affirmed the authority of courts to review the reasonableness of rates established by state commissions empowered to do so. In *Smyth* the Court looked at the rates "as an entirety" to determine whether the rates were so unreasonably low as to amount to a seizure of the railroad company's property without just compensation, in violation of the 14th Amendment.

In two cases Fuller expressed a preference for limiting the original jurisdiction of the Supreme Court. He dissented in *United States v. Texas* (1892), opposing the determination that the Supreme Court has original jurisdiction over all cases in which the United States is a party. He wrote the majority opinion in *California v. Southern Pacific Co.* (1895), holding that the Supreme Court cannot claim original jurisdiction in cases brought by states against a citizen of another state or their own citizens.

He wrote the majority opinion in the case of *United States v. E.C. Knight Co.* (1895), the first Supreme Court test of the Sherman Antitrust Act. His opinion concluded that a holding company that controlled the refining of 98 percent of the sugar in the country was not an illegal trust as defined by federal law. In *Knight* the Court construed the act as having no application to manufacturing as opposed to trading activities. Any broader construction, the Court implied, would place the act in constitutional jeopardy since it would then regulate activities not directly connected to interstate commerce and, therefore, beyond the constitutional reach of Congress. This narrow definition was later revised. One such decision was in *Northern Securities Co.*

v. United States (1904), in which Fuller dissented from such an expansion, arguing that a holding company that combined the assets of two competing railroads was not in itself a restraint of interstate trade.

Fuller also spoke for the Court in the landmark income tax case of *Pollock v. Farmers' Loan and Trust Co.* (1895), which held invalid a flat rate federal income tax of two percent on all incomes over $4,000. The Chief Justice's opinion held that since, among other sources, the tax was collected on income from land, it was a direct tax as defined by the Constitution and therefore void because not apportioned according to representation. The decision of the Court in this case led to the subsequent passage of the 16th Amendment in 1913, explicitly empowering Congress to enact a federal income tax.

In addition to the issues of monopolies and interstate commerce that had begun to be addressed during the years of the Waite Court, Fuller had to deal with the increasing questions of foreign immigration and the role of organized labor in national economic affairs. He dissented in *Fong Yue Ting v. United States* (1893), arguing that Chinese laborers could not be deported without due process of law. There were limits to Fuller's sympathy, however; in *United States v. Wong Kim Ark* (1898), he dissented, opposing an interpretation of the 14th Amendment that concluded that all children born in the United States to unnaturalized alien parents are citizens of the United States and that children born outside of the United States to parents who were U.S. citizens are not themselves citizens until and unless naturalized.

With regard to economic concerns, Fuller distinguished himself as a relative conservative, more inclined to support the rights of private property and individual economic freedom than to allow the interference of the government in the "public good." He joined the majority in *Lochner v. New York* (1905), which overturned state laws regulating the length of working hours. He wrote the majority opinion in *Loewe v. Lawlor* (1908), which ruled on an attempt by a combination of labor organizations and its members to compel a manufacturer (whose goods were sold almost entirely in other states) to unionize his shops. The Court held that the boycott of his goods, preventing their sale in states other than his own in an effort to force him to comply with their demands, was a combination of restraint of trade or commerce within the Antitrust Act. This decision later led to the Clayton Antitrust Act of 1914, which exempted labor unions from prosecution under the original Sherman Antitrust Act.

With the reelection of Grover Cleveland in 1892, Chief Justice Fuller was offered the position of secretary of State in the new administration. Despite his own feelings, he declined the appointment, believing that if he were to accept it, he would downgrade the prestige of the Supreme Court in the public perception.

In addition to his duties on the Court, Fuller maintained many other civic responsibilities, including his service as regent of the Smithsonian Institution and as trustee of his alma mater, Bowdoin College. In 1899 he accepted a presidential appointment as member of the American delegation to the Venezuela-British Guiana Boundary Commission tribunal, and from 1900, served as a member of the Permanent Court of Arbitration at the Hague.

Fuller served on the Supreme Court until his death in 1910 at his summer residence in Sorrento, Maine.

GOLDBERG, ARTHUR JOSEPH

b. August 8, 1908; secretary of Labor (1961-1962); associate justice, U.S. Supreme Court (1962-1965); U.S. ambassador to the United Nations (1965-1968).

Born in Chicago, the son of Russian immigrant parents, Goldberg was educated at Northwestern University, where he received a law degree in 1929. Entering a Chicago law firm, he specialized in labor law, representing several unions in major strike negotiations. After service during World War II in the Office of Strategic Services (OSS), he was appointed general counsel of the Congress of Industrial Organizations and was instrumental in its merger with the American Federation of Labor. He was named secretary of Labor in the Kennedy administration, and in 1962, with the resignation of Associate Justice Felix Frankfurter, President Kennedy appointed Goldberg to the Supreme Court.

Goldberg's appointment shifted the balance of the Court to a liberal judicial position. He concurred in *School District of Abington v. Schempp* (1963), striking down a state law authorizing daily religious exercises in the public schools. He wrote the majority opinion in *Murphy v. Waterfront Commission of New York Harbor* (1964), which held that a witness who had been granted immunity in one jurisdiction could not be compelled to testify if his testimony would tend to incriminate him under the laws of another jurisdiction. Goldberg also spoke for the Court in the landmark decision of *Escobedo v. Illinois* (1964), which held that confessions obtained from suspects in custody who had not been advised of their right to remain silent and who had been denied their right to consult with counsel were inadmissible in court.

Goldberg concurred in the landmark civil rights case *Heart of Atlanta Motel v. United States* (1964), which held that Congress had the power under the commerce clause to prohibit discrimination in public accommodations in the Civil Rights Act of 1964. He wrote the majority opinion in *Aptheker v. Secretary of State* (1964), which held that membership in the Communist Party should not be the basis for denial of a passport. In *Jacobellis v. Ohio* (1964), he voted with the majority to overturn the obscenity conviction of a movie theater owner. He also concurred in *Pointer v. Texas* (1965), which held that the 6th Amendment right to confront and cross-examine witnesses was applicable to criminal defendants in state courts under the due process clause of the 14th Amendment. In *United Mine Workers v. Pennington* (1965), he dissented from the majority opinion, arguing that courts should not use antitrust laws to interfere with union activity involving mandatory subjects of collective bargaining.

In 1965, Goldberg resigned from the Court to accept President Johnson's appointment as U.S. ambassador to the United Nations. He served in that position until 1968, when he returned to private law practice in New York City. After an unsuccessful campaign for the governorship of New York in 1970, Goldberg transferred his law practice to Washington, D.C., where he also served as a professor of law at American University.

GRAY, HORACE

b. March 24, 1828; associate justice, Massachusetts supreme judicial court (1864-1873); Massachusetts chief justice (1873-1881); associate justice, U.S. Supreme Court (1881-1902); d. September 15, 1902.

Horace Gray

Born in Boston to an aristocratic New England family and educated at Harvard College (Class of 1845), Gray completed his law studies at Harvard Law School and was admitted to the bar in 1851. In 1854, he was appointed

reporter of decisions in the Massachusetts supreme judicial court, supervising the publication of sixteen volumes of the court's decisions. During the Civil War, Governor John Andrew nominated Gray to be an associate justice of that court (1864) and he subsequently became its chief justice (1873). In 1881, after the resignation of Associate Justice Nathan Clifford, Pres. Chester Arthur nominated Gray to the Supreme Court.

Throughout his tenure on the Court, Gray maintained an independent judicial temperament and in the later years of his service was the leader of a group that often differed with the opinions of Chief Justice Fuller. He disagreed with the majority in two of the Virginia Coupon Cases (*Mayre v. Parsons* and *Poindexter v. Greenhow*, 1885) in which he argued that the suits could not be maintained because they were in substance and effect suits against a state (Virginia), which are prohibited by the 11th Amendment. In *Antoni v. Greenhow* (1883), however, he concurred with the majority in the decision that states may change procedure connected with the remedy of the rights of holders of bond issues so long as the remedy furnished is substantially equivalent to that which existed at the time of sale and thus the obligation of the contract with the state is not impaired.

In the case of *Bowman v. Chicago and North Western Railroad* (1888), Gray again dissented, arguing that restrictions on the shipment and importation of alcoholic beverages were within the constitutional "police powers" of the states. In another important railroad decision, *Chicago, Minneapolis and St. Paul Railroad v. Minnesota* (1890), Gray joined the dissent, arguing that the courts do not have a right to review state tariff schedules unless the charge set exceeds a fixed maximum.

Gray was a bachelor until late in life when, in 1889, he married Jane Matthews, daughter of Associate Justice Stanley Matthews. Gray served on the Court until shortly before his death in 1902 in Washington, D.C.

GRIER, ROBERT COOPER

b. March 5, 1794; various judicial positions in Pennsylvania; associate justice, U.S. Supreme Court (1846-1870); d. September 26, 1870.

Born in Cumberland County, Pennsylvania, the son of a Presbyterian minister who had become the principal of a private academy in Northumberland, Grier received his early education from his father. After graduation from Dickinson College in 1812, he succeeded him as the principal of the Northumberland Academy. Privately pursuing his interest in law, Grier was admitted to the bar in 1817 and decided to leave his teaching position to establish a law practice in Bloomsburg and Danville. In 1829 he married Isabella Rose, the daughter of wealthy Scottish immigrants, with whom he established a residence near Williamsport. He served as judge of the Allegheny district court from 1833 to 1846. In

1846, two years after the death of Associate Justice Henry Baldwin, Grier was appointed to the Supreme Court by Pres. James Polk.

Politically, Grier was a Democrat, but he maintained a strong pro-Union position in the years leading up to the Civil War. He concurred in the majority opinion in the Dred Scott Case (*Scott v. Sandford*, 1857), which declared the Missouri Compromise unconstitutional. His premature disclosure of that decision to President-elect Buchanan caused considerable controversy.

In the Reconstruction period, Grier was an opponent of the unrestricted growth of federal power. In *Ex parte McCardle* (1869), dealing with the constitutionality of martial law in the occupied Southern states, he privately protested against the Court's refusal to hear the appeal on the grounds of lack of jurisdiction. Grier's inability to arrive at a decision regarding the constitutionality of federally issued legal tender in the case of *Hepburn v. Griswold* (1870) led his associates on the bench to urge him to resign and make way for a younger man.

Grier's health deteriorated seriously as the result of a stroke he suffered in 1867. He acceded to the request of the other justices and resigned from the Court in February 1870. He died in Philadelphia several months later.

HARLAN, JOHN MARSHALL

b. June 1, 1833; judge, Franklin County court (1858); Kentucky attorney general (1863-1867); member, Louisiana Reconstruction Commission (1877); associate justice, U.S. Supreme Court (1877-1911); U.S. representative, Bering Sea Tribunal of Arbitration (1893); d. October 14, 1911.

Born in Boyle County, Kentucky, he was named after the great chief justice by his father, James Harlan, who served as a U.S. congressman, state attorney general, and federal attorney. The younger Harlan was educated at Centre College in Danville (Class of 1850) and studied briefly after his graduation at the law school of Transylvania University in Lexington. Harlan completed his law studies in the office of his father in Frankfort and was admitted to the bar in 1853. He married Malvina Shanklin in 1856.

After several years of private practice, Harlan was appointed judge of the Franklin County Court. He served in this position for only one year, resigning to run for the U.S. Congress as a candidate of the Whig and "Know-Nothing" parties. His campaign was unsuccessful, but Harlan remained active in Kentucky politics, serving as a state presidential elector in 1860, pledged to the Constitutional Union Party. In 1861 he transferred his residence to Louisville, where he established a law practice in partnership with W.F. Bullock.

As a slaveowner and conservative, Harlan had opposed the candidacy of Lincoln in 1860, but with the outbreak of the Civil War he remained loyal to the Union side. In 1861 he enlisted in the 10th Kentucky Volunteer Infantry, rising to

John Marshall Harlan

the rank of colonel by 1863, when he resigned from active service. In the same year, he was elected attorney general of Kentucky, and his political career resumed. Throughout the rest of the war, he continued his outspoken criticism of the Lincoln administration and publicly opposed the adoption of the 13th Amendment, as an infringement of the sovereignty of the states. He did, however, free his own slaves before the end of the war. In 1864 he actively supported George B. McClellan's unsuccessful campaign for the presidency.

Soon after the end of the war, Harlan resigned from his office of attorney general and resumed his private law practice. In 1871 he was the unsuccessful Republican candidate for governor and in the following year was considered as a possible vice-presidential candidate to run with President Grant. In 1875 he ran again for governor and was again defeated in the general election. The following year, Harlan headed the Kentucky delegation to the Republican national convention and was instrumental in the nomination of Rutherford B. Hayes.

Shortly after his inauguration, President Hayes appointed Harlan to serve on a federal Reconstruction commission in Louisiana, whose objective was to arbitrate the disputed state election of 1876, to reorganize the state government, and to determine whether federal troops stationed there since the end of the Civil War could be withdrawn. Harlan's service on the commission proved to be valuable, and late in 1877, after the resignation of Associate Justice David Davis, President Hayes appointed Harlan to the Supreme Court.

Supreme Court. Harlan began his Supreme Court tenure at a time when the limits of federal power were being determined in the courts and when the judicial implications of Reconstruction and the wartime constitutional amendments had not been resolved. On many of these important issues, Harlan's judicial philosophy diverged from that of his colleagues, and over his more than thirty years of service, he gained a reputation for his frequent dissenting opinions.

Despite his early opposition to the 13th and 14th Amendments and the various Reconstruction measures of the federal government, Harlan became a strong defender of civil rights during his tenure on the Supreme Court. He wrote the majority opinion in *Neal v. Delaware* (1881), overturning a state constitutional provision that restricted jury service to whites. He dissented in the *Civil Rights Cases* (1883), which held that the 13th and 14th Amendments do not give the federal government authority to intervene to prevent racial discrimination by private individuals.

Harlan was also in the minority in *Louisville, New Orleans, and Texas Railway Co. v. Mississippi* (1890), arguing that state-required racially segregated accommodations on public transport were an interference of interstate trade. In this case, the statute provided for "separate but equal" accommodations for white and black passengers. Justice Harlan opined that this regulation was one of intrastate commerce and therefore void. The most eloquent defense of this philosophy came in Harlan's dissenting opinion in *Plessy v. Ferguson* (1896), in which he argued in a lone dissent that state laws requiring "separate but equal" facilities in transportation but not in commerce denied equal protection under the law. "Our Constitution is color-blind," wrote Harlan, "And neither knows nor tolerates classes among citizens. In respect of civil rights, all citizens are equal before the law." A similar position on this issue was finally sustained and accepted by the Supreme Court in *Brown v. Board of Education* (1954).

With regard to the constitutional rights of individuals, Harlan dissented in *Hurtado v. California* (1884), contending that a grand jury indictment was an essential component of the judicial process when a person is required to answer for a capital offense in a state prosecution. He dissented again in *Maxwell v. Dow* (1900), contending that the 14th Amendment guarantee of due process requires that all citizens accused of serious crimes be tried before a full jury of twelve members. He was also in the minority in the Insular Case *Downes v. Bidwell* (1901), arguing that the protection of the Bill of Rights should be conferred on residents of all American territories. His *Downes* dissent emphasized that Puerto Rico was a part of the United States subject to all duties, imports, and excises that were uniform throughout the states, even though the island was a territory and not a state. He maintained this position in his lone dissent in

Hawaii v. Mankichi (1904), which was a stern warning against the dangers of colonialism for the American system.

Harlan was of the opinion that the federal and state governments should be granted wide authority to legislate for the public good. He wrote the majority opinion in *Mugler v. Kansas* (1887), which upheld state prohibition laws, and in *Hennington v. Georgia* (1896), which upheld a state law prohibiting the operation of railroads on Sunday. He dissented in *Interstate Commerce Commission v. Alabama Midland Railroad Co.* (1897), unsuccessfully supporting the right of the federal agency to regulate interstate railroad rates. He wrote the majority opinion in *Champion v. Ames* (1903), in which the Court upheld a federal law prohibiting the interstate shipment of lottery tickets. In this case the Court recognized that the federal government's commerce power included the right to legislate to uphold public morality. He dissented in *Lochner v. New York* (1905), arguing for the right of states to set limits on working hours.

There were limits on state jurisdiction, however, and Harlan was a believer in the ultimate supremacy of the federal government. He wrote the majority opinion in *United States v. Texas* (1892), ruling that the Supreme Court of the United States has original jurisdiction of a suit brought by the United States against a state, or brought by a state against another, to determine a state boundary. He dissented in the income tax case of *Pollock v. Farmers' Loan and Trust Co.* (1895) on the grounds that he felt the taxing powers of the federal government were being infringed.

Harlan was a strong defender of free competition in private industry and dissented in *United States v. E.C. Knight Co.* (1895), arguing that any monopoly was a clear infringement of the freedom of trade and within the prohibition of the federal anti-trust law. He wrote an opinion in which three justices joined, which was concurred with by a separate opinion in *Northern Securities Co. v. United States* (1904). The Court ruled that a holding company formed to combine the assets of two competing railroads was a blatant restraint of trade. Among Harlan's last opinions were two notable dissents on this same issue of the restriction of trade in violation of the Sherman Act. In *Standard Oil Company of New Jersey v. United States* and *United States v. American Tobacco Co.* (1911), Harlan concurred with the Court's decision that the oil and tobacco trusts must be dismantled but dissented in the revised legal interpretation that only "unreasonable" combinations violate federal laws against the restraint of trade.

In addition to his Supreme Court service, Harlan taught constitutional law at Columbian (later George Washington) University from 1889 to 1910. In 1892 he accepted a presidential appointment as U.S. representative to the Bering Sea Tribunal of Arbitration, called to negotiate an international agreement with Great Britain over jurisdiction in that area.

Harlan served on the Supreme Court until his death in Washington, D.C., after a brief illness in 1911. His grandson, also named John Marshall Harlan, later served as an associate justice on the Supreme Court.

HARLAN, JOHN MARSHALL

b. May 20, 1899; chief counsel, New York Crime Commission (1951-1953); judge, U.S. Court of Appeals (1954-1955); associate justice, U.S. Supreme Court (1955-1971); d. December 29, 1971.

Born in Chicago, the son of a prominent local family and grandson and namesake of Associate Justice John Marshall Harlan, Harlan was educated at Princeton (Class of 1920) and subsequently studied as a Rhodes scholar at Oxford, where he received a law degree in 1923. On his return to the United States, he continued his law education at the New York Law School and was admitted to the bar in 1925. He then served as chief of the prohibition section of the office of the U.S. Attorney for Southern New York (1925-1927). In 1928 he was appointed special assistant state attorney general. Harlan entered private practice in 1930. After service in the Army Air Force during World War II, he resumed his private corporate practice and served as chief counsel for the New York State Crime Commission from 1951 to 1953. In 1954 he was appointed judge of the U.S. Court of Appeals for the 2nd Circuit. In the same year, after the death of Associate Justice Robert Jackson, Pres. Dwight D. Eisenhower appointed Harlan to the Court.

Supreme Court. During his tenure on the Court, Harlan proved to be of a relatively conservative philosophy and took a hard line against what he considered to be politically subversive elements in society. He dissented in *Slochower v. Board of Education of New York City* (1956), arguing that the dismissal without notice or hearing of public employees who claimed the 5th Amendment privilege against self-incrimination was not a violation of the due process guarantee of the 14th Amendment. He also joined the dissent in *Kent v. Dulles* (1958), which held that the secretary of State could not withhold the passports of citizens suspected of communist beliefs or associations. He wrote the majority opinion in *Barenblatt v. United States* (1959), which held that Congress could call witnesses suspected of subversive affiliations without violating their 1st Amendment rights. He joined the majority in *Communist Party v. Subversive Activities Control Board* (1961), which upheld the Subversive Activities Control Act of 1950, requiring the registration of members of the U.S. Communist Party.

With regard to equal rights and civil rights issues, Harlan spoke for the Court in *NAACP v. Alabama ex. rel. Patterson* (1958), which established the right of political groups to withhold their membership lists from governmental authorities. He dissented in *Reynolds v. Sims* (1964), which held that malapportioned state legislative districts violated the equal protection clause of the 14th Amendment. Harlan dissented in *Malloy v. Hogan* (1964), which applied

the 14th Amendment to ensure protection against self-incrimination for state criminal defendants. He also dissented in the landmark cases of *Escobedo v. Illinois* (1964) and *Miranda v. Arizona* (1966), opposing what he considered an unreasonable restriction on police procedures.

Due to his failing health, Harlan retired from the Court in 1971. He died later in the year in Washington, D.C.

HOLMES, OLIVER WENDELL JR.

b. March 8, 1841; associate justice, Massachusetts Supreme Judicial Court (1882-1899); chief justice, Massachusetts Supreme Judicial Court (1899-1902); associate justice, U.S. Supreme Court (1902-1932); d. March 6, 1935.

Born on March 8, 1841, in Boston, Oliver Wendell Holmes, Jr., had the family background and social life of an intellectual aristocrat, which served to expose him to the best minds of the era. Further, his background provided him with opportunity to pursue art and philosophy. His father was a wealthy physician with such diverse interests that he found it impossible to practice medicine, and instead Oliver Wendell Holmes, Sr., concentrated his attention on literature and poetry. His mother, Amelia Jackson, was the daughter of Judge Jackson, who had retired from the Massachusetts Supreme Judicial Court.

Following a family tradition, Holmes received his education at Harvard College, graduating in 1861. In his yearbook he was nominated as class poet. At this point in his life Holmes was seriously considering a career in writing, and examples of his work reflect potential for literary success. However, the outbreak of the Civil War interrupted his fledgling literary career. Holmes was a dedicated soldier, and after initial army training was commissioned as a first lieutenant in the Twentieth Massachusetts Infantry. Holmes and his regiment saw action in several of the bloodiest battles of the war. Holmes was wounded three times; on one such occasion his father, after receiving word of his son's having been wounded at Antietam, traveled to Maryland to find him. Dr. Holmes wrote of this arduous task in the *Atlantic Monthly*, describing the anxiety and pain of his search and his final success when he found his son on a train of wounded moving from the South to Philadelphia. Holmes's courage and military abilities brought him promotion to the rank of lieutenant colonel before his discharge in 1864. His combat experience had a great effect on his outlook on life and on his perceptions of men and the political and economic world in which they struggle.

Early Legal Career. At the conclusion of his military service, Holmes resumed his literary career and also entered Harvard Law School, from which he graduated in June 1866. Holmes was an outstanding legal scholar, who demonstrated an early mastery of expression of the complex and difficult theories of law and justice. It is not known why Holmes enrolled in the law school while desiring a career in

Oliver Wendell Holmes Jr.

literature; however, the matter of earning a living may have turned his attention to more practical affairs. In 1867 Holmes signed the roll of Attorneys of the Commonwealth of Massachusetts and joined a local law firm for a three-year apprenticeship.

Holmes did not enjoy lawyering as a profession and soon found diverse methods to combine law with his love for literature and philosophy. During this period of his life he worked very hard to distinguish himself as a legal scholar and found great opportunity to do so in assuming the editorship of the *American Law Journal*. Also, at this time Holmes sought and received an appointment as a lecturer at the Harvard Law School. He now had a new, and to him more exciting, profession in legal teaching, scholarship, and writing, a profession that he could embrace fully and pursue with confidence. Holmes could never accept the view of the law as a business enterprise. To him that view was a distortion of a largely intellectual and philosophical exercise. The capstone of this period of his scholarly career was the publication of his book *The Common Law* in 1881, which led to an appointment as professor at Harvard Law School. This publication was a great success and well received by legal scholars and served to usher in a new and ambitious analysis of tired and traditional legal theories. The success of his ideas created more than academic opportunity, and after only one semester as professor at Harvard Law School, he was offered a seat on the Supreme Judicial Court of

Massachusetts. Had Holmes remained a law professor there is little doubt that he would have distinguished himself among legal scholars, but the opportunity to sit as a judge resulted in a departure from the classroom.

Supreme Court Years. Holmes had a strong desire to shape the law and viewed a judicial appointment as the perfect opportunity to accomplish that end. He served on the Massachusetts Supreme Judicial Court until 1902, and for his last three years was its chief justice. In 1902, Justice Horace Gray retired from the U.S. Supreme Court, and Holmes was ultimately selected to fill the vacancy. During his tenure on the Supreme Court, Holmes participated in the decisions of many major cases. Whether he wrote the opinion for the Court or his own concurring or dissenting opinion, all of his writing is characterized by a penetrating, analytical style, reflecting great ability and learning. Holmes could simplify the complexities of the issues before him and demonstrated recognition of the economic and political realities of his time, as well as concern for the public need.

His dissent in *Lochner v. New York* (1905) became a classic. This case concerned the constitutionality of a New York state law that limited employment for bakery workers to sixty hours per week and to ten hours per day. The challenge was based on a claim that the law denied liberty to contract to the employer without due process of law. In deciding this issue the Court divided 5-4, with the majority opinion invalidating the New York law. Three of the dissenting justices joined in a dissenting opinion, but Holmes wrote his own dissent. Holmes denounced the majority for invoking the Constitution to foist its own conservative economic philosophy on the political branches. He denied that the Court had the authority to stand between the legislature and whatever social or economic approach it chose.

The Northern Securities case (*Northern Securities Company v. United States*, 1904) was viewed by Pres. Theodore Roosevelt as the most important case to come before the Court during his presidency. The case involved the power and size of industry and the meaning of the restraint of trade provisions of the Sherman Act. The view of industry was that a merger by several major business conglomerates of their various railroad interests would "enlarge commerce," not restrain it. Roosevelt's view was that if business got too big, "bust it," as a threat to competition, thereby avoiding a monopoly. Regarding this matter, President Roosevelt had been relying on the votes of certain justices to support his position. Ultimately the government won, but a jubilant Roosevelt had to contend with a 5-4 vote, a vote in which to his surprise Holmes entered his dissent against the government's position.

In 1916, Congress passed laws to keep goods made by children out of interstate commerce. The father of three working children decided to test these new laws on the practical basis of his need for his children's income and on the legal basis of their work being "the production of manufactured goods" and having "nothing whatsoever" to do with the interstate commerce that Congress was authorized to regulate (*Hammer v. Dagenhart*, 1918). Although these laws were struck down by the Court, Holmes, who found the practice of child labor abhorrent, entered a strong dissent, claiming that the courts should not outlaw the rules that Congress created to eliminate such harsh and unconscionable practices and expressing a broad view of commerce. Later, in 1941, the Court overturned its earlier position on the child labor issue, and in doing so relied on the views of Holmes as expressed in his previous dissent.

Schenck v. United States (1919) was based on legislation passed by Congress shortly after the United States entered into World War I. These laws were designed to punish attempts to discourage men from enlistment in the military and attempts to promote insubordination by military men against their commanders. Charles Schenck and others who were all Socialists wrote and delivered a leaflet to men who were drafted into military service. This document compared the draft to slavery and declared the draft illegal under the 13th Amendment. This activity was clearly designed to be harmful and disruptive to U.S. efforts in the war. When the case came before the Supreme Court, Holmes wrote the decision, stating that "in many places and in ordinary times" the Socialists would be within their rights, but the acts in question created a "clear and present danger" and ultimately threatened the very core of American unity

and military efforts against a determined enemy. Such a danger could constitutionally be prohibited.

Holmes had a long association with Louis Brandeis, who had been the youngest graduate of the Harvard Law School. Brandeis and Holmes met on many occasions to discuss their theories of law and justice, and over the years their paths crossed many times. It was Brandeis who argued the case of *Muller v. Oregon* (1908) before the Supreme Court, and who in that case for the first time presented the Court with not only legal, but also medical and sociological, information to consider in making its deliberations. Later, they met again in Washington when Brandeis was appointed to the Supreme Court. Holmes had long felt that his fellow justices on the Court did not fully appreciate his work and that often his efforts were not recognized for full value. With the arrival of Brandeis, Holmes felt the presence of a friendly spirit with whom he could continue to share his view.

In *Abrams v. United States* (1919), Brandeis joined Holmes in dissent when the Court decided a case brought under the Sedition Act. The case was sparked when, as a reaction to the United States sending troops into Russia following the Russian Revolution, several people scattered leaflets from the roof of a building. The leaflets called for a general strike on the part of all workers in retaliation for the presence of U.S. troops on Russian soil. However, under these circumstances Holmes and Brandeis could not find the "clear and present danger" that Holmes had found in *Schenck*. The acts of the accused, even in light of existing world and political concerns, were unlikely to cause any serious harm. When the parties involved received long prison terms of up to twenty years, Holmes was deeply disturbed over how his country could respond to such acts with such a harsh penalty. Holmes was aware that similar acts occurring in other countries would result in jail terms of only a few months at most and viewed the decision of the Court as an embarrassment and a shame to the nation. For Holmes the greater danger was in the persecution of opinion and in the supression of a "free traffic in ideas."

Moore v. Dempsey (1923) dealt with the right to a fair trial. The case was based on an attack against black sharecroppers by whites, at a time when the sharecroppers were meeting to discuss hiring a lawyer to bring to court their claim that they were being cheated by their landlords. After a series of incidents, one white man was killed, and five blacks were arrested and accused of his murder. The situation became so explosive that the Army had to be called in by the government to establish control. Mob influence and fear permeated the trial and resulted in an easy conviction based upon questionable evidence. The case was appealed to the Supreme Court, and its action ultimately resulted in the release of all five of the accused. Holmes, in writing the opinion, stated that such trials were inherently unfair. In his view, law and logic, not public passions, should control legal proceedings.

It was cases such as these that earned Holmes his sobriquet, the "Great Dissenter." Although others on the Court dissented more often, no one dissented with more skill and finesse than Holmes. Perhaps his greatest tribute is in the number of cases decided after his service on the Court that reversed earlier Court rulings and then adopted the dissenting opinion of Holmes as the new majority position of the Court. Holmes retired from the Court in 1932. He died in 1935 in Washington, D.C., and received a soldier's burial, as infantrymen fired a volley of shots for each wound Holmes had received in the Civil War.

Holmes's jurisprudence had a profound influence on constitutional law and law in general. He embraced a deep skepticism and was partly responsible for the decline of the idea that law could be a real but abstract set of rules that were somehow independent of the people who legislated, enforced, and judged. He was a man of great contrasts and even contradictions, combining patriotism with cynicism and pessimism with an unshakable commitment to reason.

HUGHES, CHARLES EVANS

b. April 11, 1862; governor of New York (1907-1910); associate justice, U.S. Supreme Court (1910-1916); Republican presidential candidate (1916); secretary of State (1921-1925); member, Permanent Court of Arbitration, The Hague (1926-1930); member, Permanent Court of International Justice (1928-1930); chief justice, U.S. Supreme Court (1930-1941); d. August 27, 1948.

Charles Evans Hughes

Born in Glens Falls, New York, Hughes was the only son of an itinerant Baptist preacher and a school teacher. After completing a rigorous, self-designed course of home study entitled the "Charles Evans Hughes plan of study" Hughes entered Madison College (now Colgate University) to become a Baptist preacher. He was fourteen years old. After two years, Hughes transferred to Brown University, where he graduated third in his class in 1881. At Brown his desire to preach was replaced by a desire to practice law. Unable to afford law school immediately after graduation, Hughes taught Greek, Latin, and math at a private boys' school and clerked for the law firm of Chamberlin, Carter and Hornblower for a year. Hughes entered law school in 1882 and graduated with highest honors in 1884. After passing the bar he rejoined the firm of Chamberlin, Carter and Hornblower. There he stayed until 1905, taking a three-year hiatus from 1891 to accept a professorship at Cornell Law School. During this period he also married Antoinette Carter, daughter of one of the partners.

Hughes's career reached a turning point in 1905. At that time he accepted an appointment to act as special counsel for the Stevens Gas Commission and the Armstrong Insurance Commission. Both committees were set up by the New York legislature and were dedicated to uncovering fraud in the areas of utilities and insurance, respectively. Because Hughes possessed a great aptitude for math, he was able to assimilate the complicated technical data involved in these investigations. This ability enabled him to identify and expose corruption in the utility company investigation and in the insurance industry. He won local and national acclaim through his work in these investigations. As the Republican gubernatorial candidate in 1906 he easily defeated the Democratic nominee, William Randolph Hearst.

During the two terms Hughes served as governor his most notable achievement came with the passage of a bill that prohibited race-track gambling. He was also instrumental in establishing a system of commissions whose purpose was to regulate utility rates and in passing a workmen's compensation act. His less successful efforts were in regulating child labor and instituting a new system of direct primaries to replace the old system of nominating candidates for public office.

Associate Justice and Statesman. Justice Brewer of the Supreme Court died in 1910, and Pres. William Howard Taft nominated Hughes to take his place. Hughes took his oath on October 10, 1910, and served until June 10, 1916. During that period Hughes's major decisions were in the areas of civil rights, states' rights, and congressional power under the commerce clause.

Hughes was known as a liberal during this period. This reputation must have been based on his opinions in civil rights cases such as *Bailey v. Alabama* (1911) in which, speaking for the majority, Hughes struck down a statute that imposed criminal sanctions on an employee who failed to perform a labor contract but had accepted payment in advance. That statute made failure to perform evidence that the employee intended to defraud his employer. Hughes found this to be such a powerful weapon in the hands of the employer that it would force an employee into a position of involuntary servitude in violation of the 13th Amendment. Three years later Hughes authored another majority opinion in *McCabe v. Atchison, Topeka, & Santa Fe Railroad* (1914) in which the Court invalidated a state law that permitted intrastate railroads to provide sleeping and dining cars for whites and not for blacks. This law fell because it denied citizens equal protection under the law. In yet another civil rights case, *Truax v. Raich* (1915), Hughes voided an Arizona law that limited the percentage of aliens who could be employed in the state on equal protection grounds. The statute also encroached on the exclusive federal power to regulate the movement of aliens, because people could not live where they could not work.

In most cases Hughes championed the cause of minority members and the indigent, but one case in which he did not was *Miller v. Wilson* (1915). In that case, he and the rest of the Court upheld a California law that limited the number of hours a woman could work because this was a valid exercise of the power of the state to preserve the public interest. Women had a social duty to bear children, and limiting the number of hours a woman could work was seen as a way to protect their health.

In addition to civil rights, Hughes had a great concern for states' rights. In 1913 two utility cases came before the Court, and Hughes dissented in both: *Grand Trunk Western Railroad v. South Bend* (1913) and *Owensboro v. Cumberland Telephone and Telegraph* (1913). In the former, the majority held that a city had no power to repeal part of a grant made to a railroad company to lay track even though the railroad had failed to exercise its right for forty years. In the latter, the Court declared that a city could not exact compensation twenty years after it had granted a telephone company the right to install telephone poles and wires on its streets. Clearly, Hughes objected to the denial of a state's power to regulate utilities.

Prominent among the Associate Justice's opinions were two addressing the power of Congress under the commerce clause. In the *Minnesota Rate Cases* (1913), Hughes spoke for the Court in declaring that Congress did have the power to regulate some purely intrastate railroads because they were so intertwined with interstate transport. One year later, in *Houston, East & West Texas Railway Co. v. United States* (1914), also known as the Shreveport Case, Hughes further declared that under this same power the Interstate Commerce Commission could order intrastate carriers to raise their rates to a level consistent with those of interstate railroads. The underlying rationale was that intrastate rates affected interstate commerce. The Shreveport Doctrine, born from this case, later found application in many other areas of commerce.

In 1916, Hughes left the Supreme Court to run for president on the Republican ticket. After losing, he returned to private practice until 1921, when Pres. Warren Harding appointed him secretary of State. He held this position until 1925. In 1926 he became a member of the Permanent Court of Arbitration, The Hague, and in 1928 he first sat on the Permanent Court of International Justice. Both of these positions continued until 1930, when he was nominated as chief justice of the Supreme Court by Pres. Herbert Hoover. On February 24, 1930, Hughes took his seat.

Chief Justice. During his second term on the Court, some of Hughes's most memorable decisions came in the areas of civil liberties and civil rights. He exhibited a particular concern for the rights associated with the 1st Amendment. Writing for the majority in *Stromberg v. California* (1931), the Chief Justice struck down a statute that prohibited a display of a red flag "as a sign, symbol, or emblem of opposition to organized government." Although symbolic, such a display qualified as political speech and was therefore guarded by the 1st Amendment. Six years later Hughes, in his *DeJonge v. Oregon* (1937) opinion, expanded the meaning of speech to include the right to assemble.

Hughes's high regard for freedom of the press was illustrated by his opinion in *Near v. Minnesota* (1931), in which he voided a statute that sought to enjoin an anti-Semitic publication because it violated the 1st Amendment by censoring the press. Hughes also guarded the freedom of religion. In *United States v. Macintosh* (1931) he was the sole dissenter from a majority opinion that denied citizenship to a Baptist preacher from Canada because he refused to bear arms.

Toward the end of his service, Hughes took part in two decisions that forwarded the civil rights of blacks. The first was *Missouri ex. rel. Gaines v. Canada* (1938), in which Hughes wrote for the majority, demanding that a state provide a black person with the same opportunity it gave to a white in obtaining a legal education within the state. Failure to do so was a violation of the equal protection clause. One year later Hughes joined the majority in *Lane v. Wilson* (1939) in declaring an Oklahoma statute unconstitutional under the 15th Amendment, which bans racial discrimination in voting. That statute exempted all those voters registered in 1914 from re-registering and established a registration period of only fourteen days for all those not registered in 1914, when only whites voted.

In addition to these cases, Hughes also upheld the right of employees to picket peacefully in labor disputes in *Senn v. Tile Layers Union* (1939), *Hague v. CIO* (1939), *Thornhill v. Alabama* (1940), and *Carlson v. California* (1940). But his most controversial decisions came in the field of economics.

President Roosevelt took office in 1933 and immediately started to introduce legislation aimed at effecting economic recovery. At first this New Deal legislation was upheld by the Supreme Court. In *Home Building and Loan*

Association v. Blaisdell (1934), Hughes recognized the emergency state of the nation and upheld a state mortgage moratorium law. Later that year the Court also sustained a state law that regulated milk prices in *Nebbia v. New York* (1934), holding that this regulation was a reasonable way for a state to promote the public welfare. It appeared that this type of legislation would always be upheld by the Court, but the situation soon changed. Between 1935 and 1936 the Court invalidated a good portion of the New Deal legislation.

The Court first invalidated a provision of the National Industrial Recovery Act (NIRA) in *Panama Refining Co. v. Ryan* (1935), in which the Chief Justice stated that the president did not have the authority to keep oil, which was produced in violation of state regulation, out of the stream of interstate commerce. Then the Court struck down the Railroad Retirement Act of 1934 in *Railroad Retirement Board v. Alton Railroad Co.* (1935) when Congress attempted to establish a comprehensive pension plan for railroad employees. Speaking through the Chief Justice, the Court said that this act was outside the scope of interstate commerce and thus not within the power of Congress. In *Schechter Poultry Corp. v. United States* (1935) Hughes spoke for a unanimous Court in voiding another section of the NIRA, one that authorized the president to approve "fair competition" codes in certain industries. This was intrastate commerce and, in any event, Congress had no authority to delegate power to the president in this area.

The final blows against New Deal legislation came in 1936. In *United States v. Butler* the Court struck down the Agricultural Adjustment Act of 1933 as an unconstitutional use of the spending and taxing powers of Congress. That act allowed Congress to tax certain food producers and use that tax to pay farmers who would reduce their volume of production. The Court also said that agriculture was outside the scope of federal authority. Following the *Butler* case came *Carter v. Carter Coal* (1936), in which the Bituminous Coal Conservation Act of 1935 fell under Justice Sutherland's majority opinion. That act sought to regulate the working conditions of miners and the price of coal. Again, the mining of coal was not within federal power to regulate because it was only the step preceding commerce.

Believing that the destruction of his legislation was due to the advanced age of most of the judges (four of them were at least seventy), President Roosevelt proposed in 1937 a court packing plan, which provided that a new younger justice would be appointed for every seated justice over seventy. Although this plan never passed, its introduction was followed by a major reversal in the Court's decisions. From 1937 the New Deal legislation largely withstood judicial review.

National Labor Relations Board v. Jones & Laughlin Steel Corp. (1937) was the first subsequent decision to uphold New Deal legislation. There Hughes's opinion sustained the National Labor Relations Act of 1935, which authorized Congress to regulate intrastate matters such as labor-management disputes because they directly affected interstate commerce. One month later, in *Steward Machine Co. v. Davis* (1937), Hughes joined the majority in holding that Congress could encourage participation in a federal unemployment compensation program by awarding employers a tax credit for doing so, because employment affected commerce. Finally, the *Helvering v. Davis* (1937) decision upheld the constitutionality of a provision of the Social Security Act of 1935 enabling Congress to tax employees and employers and then pay that money to retired employees. It directly overruled *Butler*, decided only two years earlier.

After 1937, Hughes continued to write opinions in the area of civil rights. Among those opinions were *Lovell v. Griffin* (1938), which protected a citizen's 1st Amendment right to distribute handbills on a public street, and *Cox v. New Hampshire* (1941), which allowed a state to regulate by law the time, place, and manner of a parade as long as that law was narrowly drawn and applied in a nondiscriminatory manner. Hughes also joined with the majority in affirming the plenary power of Congress in the area of interstate commerce in such cases as *Mulford v. Smith* (1939), in which the Court allowed Congress to regulate tobacco warehouses to enforce production quotas; *United States v. Darby* (1941), in which the Court protected Congress's right to regulate wages and hours; and *Edwards v. California* (1941), in which Hughes wrote the Court opinion that struck down a state statute that imposed criminal sanctions on any person who knowingly brought an indigent nonresident into the state. In that opinion the Court enunciated a "right to travel" for the first time.

Hughes remained active on the Court until his retirement as Chief Justice on June 2, 1941. He died at his summer home on Cape Cod at Osterville, Massachusetts, on August 17. 1948.

HUNT, WARD

b. June 14, 1810; various legislative, executive, and judicial positions in New York; associate justice, U.S. Supreme Court (1873-1882); d. March 24, 1886.

Born in Utica, New York, the son of Montgomery Hunt and Elizabeth Stringham Hunt, Ward Hunt graduated from Union College (Class of 1828) and studied law with Judge Gould in Litchfield, Connecticut, and later in the office of Judge Hiram Denio of Utica. After his admission to the bar in 1831, Hunt became a partner in the private legal practice of Judge Denio. He later served in the New York state legislature (1838-1840) and as mayor of the city of Utica (1844). Politically, Hunt was an abolitionist and was one of the founders of the Republican Party in New York. In 1865, he was elected judge of the state court of appeals, later becoming its chief judge. In December 1872, after the resignation of Associate Justice Samuel Nelson, Hunt was appointed to the Supreme Court by Pres. Ulysses S. Grant; he took his seat on the Court in January 1873.

Hunt's role on the Court was not influential, since his active service lasted only four years. The most important of his opinions occurred in the *Slaughterhouse Cases* (1873), in which he concurred with the majority, upholding the constitutional right of states to license commercial monopolies. In *Reading Railroad v. Pennsylvania* (1873), he joined Justice Miller's dissent, along with Justice Field, arguing that state taxes levied on goods in transit were not a restriction of interstate commerce and that by no device could a state compel citizens of other states to pay a tax for the privilege of having their goods transported through that state by ordinary channels of commerce. The dissenting opinion considered such tactics a restriction by a state imposed in order to place on others the burden of supporting its own government "as was done in the days of the helpless Confederation." Hunt's most important constitutional opinion came in his dissent in *United States v. Reese* (1876), in which he supported criminal penalties for public officials who restricted voting rights in a case that involved the denial of the right to vote on account of race or color.

In 1879, Hunt suffered a severe stroke, and for the next three years he was unable to carry out his judicial responsibilities. He finally resigned from the Court in 1882 after Congress passed a special act providing him with a full pension. Hunt was married twice; to Mary Ann Savage in 1837, and, after her death, to Maria Taylor in 1853. He died in Washington, D.C., in 1886.

IREDELL, JAMES

b. October 5, 1751; various commercial, legal, and judicial positions in North Carolina; associate justice, U.S. Supreme Court (1790-1799); d. October 20, 1799.

The son of an English family engaged in the maritime trade, James Iredell was sent to America in 1768 at age seventeen to work as comptroller of customs at Edenton, North Carolina, and to supervise the interests of his uncle's business there. Law was Iredell's personal interest, and while working in the customs house, he simultaneously pursued legal studies at the office of Samuel Johnston, being licensed to practice in 1771 and marrying Johnston's sister Hannah in 1773. In the following year, 1774, he was appointed collector of the port of Edenton.

Iredell adopted a pro-American stand at the outbreak of the Revolution and in 1776 resigned from his port duties to pursue his legal career. He was subsequently named one of the commissioners to revise the laws of the state of North Carolina, and he took special interest in the organization of the state court system. Serving briefly as a superior court judge (1777), he was later named attorney general of the state (1779-1781).

During the debate over the adoption of the proposed Constitution of the United States, Iredell eloquently advocated its ratification both in published articles and at the state convention in 1788. His strong support for the Federalist position brought him to the attention of President Washington, who nominated him to become an associate justice of the Supreme Court in 1790, after the withdrawal of an original nominee, Robert Harrison of Maryland.

Iredell was a staunch Federalist who defended the independence of the Court by asserting the impropriety of a Court serving in a nonjudicial capacity in the Hayburn case (1792) and in his opinion on *Calder v. Bull* (1798), in which he indicated his belief that the courts were empowered to disregard legislation in conflict with the Constitution. He also spoke out strongly for the principle of states' rights, for which he wrote the only dissenting opinion in *Chisholm v. Georgia* (1793), arguing that the sovereignty of the states could not be compromised by private suits brought against them in federal courts. His opinion in this case was confirmed with the adoption of the 11th Amendment, which provided immunity for the states against such actions.

Iredell opposed the requirement that Supreme Court justices also serve on the circuit courts, and the strain of the constant traveling apparently weakened his health. He died at age forty-eight, in his home in Edenton, while carrying out his duties in the southern circuit.

JACKSON, HOWELL EDMUNDS

b. April 8, 1832; U.S. senator (1881-1886); judge, U.S. Circuit Court (1886-1891); judge, U.S. Circuit Court of Appeals (1891-1893); associate justice, U.S. Supreme Court (1893-1895); d. August 8, 1895.

Howell E. Jackson

Born in Paris, Tennessee, and educated at West Tennessee College (Class of 1849), Jackson later attended the University of Virginia (1851-1852) and Cumberland University (1856). He studied law in Lebanon, Tennessee, and was admitted to the bar in 1856, afterwards establishing a private practice in Memphis. At the outbreak of the Civil War, Jackson opposed secession, but when his state left the Union, he served in the Confederacy as receiver of sequestered property in West Tennessee.

After the war, Jackson resumed his private law practice. In 1877, he was appointed judge of the state court of arbitration and in 1880, he was elected to the state legislature. In the following year, he was elected as a compromise candidate to the U.S. Senate. He resigned from the Senate in 1886 to accept a presidential appointment as judge of the 6th circuit. Five years later, he was appointed judge of the newly-created circuit court of appeals in Cincinnati. In 1893, after the death of Associate Justice Lucius Lamar, Pres. Benjamin Harrison appointed Jackson to the Supreme Court.

Only a year after his confirmation, Jackson was stricken with a severe case of tuberculosis, and this illness caused his absence from the Court during most of his brief tenure. One of his few contributions to the Court was in the income tax case of *Pollock v. Farmers' Loan and Trust Company* (1895), in which he joined the dissent, arguing for the constitutionality of a federal income tax. During the deliberations, however, he suggested that federal taxation of Supreme Court justices' salaries would be unconstitutional. Shortly after this case was decided, Jackson died at his home near Nashville.

JACKSON, ROBERT HOUGHWOUT

b. February 13, 1892; general counsel, Bureau of Internal Revenue (1934-1936); special counsel, Securities and Exchange Commission (1935); assistant U.S. attorney general (1936-1938); U.S. solicitor general (1938-1939); U.S. attorney general (1940-1941); associate justice, U.S. Supreme Court (1941-1954); chief U. S. prosecutor, Nuremberg war crimes trial (1945-1946); d. October 9, 1954.

Born in Spring Creek, Pennsylvania, and raised in Jamestown, New York, Jackson entered Albany Law School at age eighteen, and although he completed his course of study in only one year, he was not admitted to the bar until 1913, when he became twenty-one. Establishing a private law practice in Jamestown, Jackson served in various municipal capacities and became the director of a local bank. After turning down an appointment to the state Public Service Commission, he was appointed by Pres. Franklin D. Roosevelt to be general counsel for the Bureau of Internal Revenue and also served as special counsel for the Securities and Exchange Commission. Jackson later became the most prominent legal defender of the New Deal programs as head of the Antitrust Division of the Department of Justice, solicitor general, and attorney general. In 1941,

Robert H. Jackson

after Associate Justice Harlan F. Stone became chief justice, President Roosevelt appointed Jackson to the Court.

Despite his liberal background, Jackson distinguished himself during his tenure on the Court as a strict interpreter of the protections extended by the Bill of Rights and the 14th Amendment. He dissented in *Murdock v. Pennsylvania* (1943), which held that the state may not impose a tax on the sale of religious literature. He also wrote the minority opinion in *West Virginia State Board of Education v. Barnette* (1943), in which the Court held unconstitutional the requirement of flag salutes in the public schools as an interference with the free exercise of religion. He was the lone dissenter in *Smith v. Allwright* (1944), contending that exclusion of blacks from voting in party primaries was prohibited in the 15th Amendment. In *Korematsu v. United States* (1944) he opposed the wartime internment of Japanese-Americans.

On economic issues, Jackson wrote the majority opinion in *Wickard v. Filburn* (1942), in which the Court broadly interpreted the right of the federal government to regulate the production of commodities in interstate commerce. He concurred in *Youngstown Sheet and Tube Co. v. Sawyer* (1952), which held that President Truman had exceeded his constitutional authority in nationalizing the steel mills, without the consent of Congress, to prevent a strike.

In 1945, President Truman appointed Jackson to the International Military Tribunal, and he served as chief prosecutor at the trials at Nuremberg of the Nazi leaders. In 1946, after the conclusion of the war crimes trials, Jackson resumed his duties on the Supreme Court, on which he served until his death in Washington, D.C., in 1954.

JAY, JOHN

b. December 12, 1745; member, New York Committee of Correspondence (1774); member, Continental Congress (1774-1775, 1777); New York chief justice (1777-1778); president, Continental Congress (1778-1779); joint commissioner to Paris Peace Conference (1782-1783); U.S. secretary of foreign affairs (1784-1789); chief justice, U.S. Supreme Court (1789-1795); ambassador to Great Britain (1794-1795); governor of New York (1795-1801); d. May 17, 1829.

John Jay

Born in New York City, John Jay was descended on both his maternal and paternal sides from prominent colonial families. His mother, the former Mary Van Cortlandt, was the daughter of Jacobus Van Cortlandt, one of New York's most powerful Dutch citizens. His father, Peter Jay, was the son of Augustus Jay, a Huguenot merchant who had established an enormously successful import-export and retail trade.

John Jay received his early education from his mother and private tutors. At age fourteen, he was admitted to Kings College (later Columbia University), where he became particularly interested in foreign affairs. He gradua-

ted in 1764 and immediately embarked on a career in the law. He was accepted as a clerk in the office of Benjamin Kissam, a well-known New York City attorney, where he spent four years gaining his formal legal training. Soon after his admission to the bar in 1768, Jay established a private legal practice, entering into a partnership with Robert Livingston and continuing his professional relationship with Kissam. Jay was soon recognized as one of the most promising young lawyers in New York, and in 1774, he married Sarah Van Brugh Livingston, the youngest daughter of William Livingston, subsequently governor of New Jersey during the Revolution.

Early in his professional career, Jay also began to devote considerable time to public service. In 1773, he was named the secretary of the Royal Boundary Commission, which had been established to settle a territorial dispute between New York and New Jersey. Jay's participation in the long, complex, and ultimately successful negotiations proved to be a formative experience for his later diplomatic work. On several subsequent occasions he would suggest the establishment of similar mixed commissions for the arbitration of international disputes.

In the increasing political turbulence of the mid-1770's, Jay's commitment to public service gradually overshadowed his private professional life. In 1774, he became a member of the New York Committee of Correspondence, and he gradually accepted the necessity of a complete break with Great Britain. Jay was later selected as one of the delegates from New York to the First and Second Continental Congresses.

National Leader. At the time of the Declaration of Independence, Jay was in New York, where he had also become actively involved in the formulation of the new state constitution. In 1777 he was appointed the first chief justice of the state supreme court and was thereby given the responsibility of implementing the new state constitution. In the following year, Jay also returned to the Continental Congress and was elected its president, then the nation's highest civilian office.

As the Revolutionary War entered a critical phase, Jay's public responsibilities continued to expand. In 1779, he was appointed minister plenipotentiary to Spain with the assignment of obtaining official recognition and monetary support for the United States from Spain. Even though Jay's mission proved to be only partially successful, he nonetheless distinguished himself as an able negotiator, and in 1782, Benjamin Franklin sought Jay's assistance in formulating the terms of a treaty with Great Britain to end the Revolutionary War.

From the outset, Jay held a hardline negotiating position at the Paris Peace Conference. He insisted that the American representatives be recognized by their British counterparts as the ministers of a sovereign state, not merely as spokesmen for the rebellious British colonies. Despite the fears of his fellow American negotiators, Benjamin Franklin and John Adams, that this precondition might endanger the negotiations, Jay remained firm and the British grudgingly accepted his point, thereby tacitly recognizing the sovereignty of the new nation before real negotiations began.

After the successful conclusion of the Treaty of Paris in 1783, Jay decided to return to America and resume his private law career. On his arrival in New York, however, he found that he had been elected secretary for Foreign Affairs by the Continental Congress, an office crucial to the establishment of a secure position for the United States in the community of nations. In this office, Jay was fully occupied for the next five years, particularly in diplomatic wrangling with Great Britain over the enforcement of the Treaty of Paris. The most serious problems with the enforcement of the treaty were Great Britain's refusal to evacuate its garrisons in the Northwest and their disruption of American shipping and impressment of American seamen. The British, for their part, contended that the Americans had not complied with their agreement to facilitate the payment of prewar debts owned to Loyalists and British subjects.

Spain also proved a source of concern in early U.S. foreign policy, for the Spanish still held portions of the lower Mississippi and prevented the free flow of American shipping down the river. Jay was able to reach an agreement with Spain ceding the use of the river for twenty-five years, but the members of the Continental Congress, fearing the dangerous precedent that might be set by such a cession, refused to ratify the pact. It became clear to Jay, as a result of this repudiation, than an effective U.S. foreign policy could be established only with a stronger, more centralized form of government.

In 1787, as the delegates to the Constitutional Convention convened in Philadelphia to debate and formulate a new and stronger federal system for the United States, Jay emerged as a strong advocate of the federalist plan. After the convention, he joined with Alexander Hamilton and James Madison in the writing and publication of the Federalist Papers, contributing five essays on the necessity for a coherent, unified foreign policy for the new nation as provided in the proposed constitution. In the following year, Jay was instrumental in obtaining the positive vote in New York for ratification.

Supreme Court Service. After the first national election, Jay became one of President-elect George Washington's most influential advisors, and although he declined appointment as secretary of State, he freely offered his diplomatic expertise and experience in the organization of the Department of State. Washington was anxious for Jay to play an important role in the new government and prevailed upon Jay to accept nomination as the first chief justice. On September 24, 1789, the same day that President Washington signed the Judiciary Act, which established the organization of the nation's court system, Jay's nomination was made public. It was confirmed by a voice vote in the Senate only two days later.

It was not until February 1, 1790, however, that the first session of the Supreme Court was officially convened. As chief justice, Jay presided over the opening session in the Royal Exchange Building in New York City, with only Associate Justices William Cushing and James Wilson in attendance. Since no cases were pending before the Court, Jay adjourned the first session ten days later and began his duties in the circuit court, hearing cases in New York and New England.

Since the Supreme Court and the rest of the federal judiciary were new and untested institutions, it was up to Jay as the first chief justice to lay down both the procedural framework for their later activity and the extent and nature of their authority. One of the first constitutional questions posed was whether the Supreme Court could issue an advisory opinion without first being confronted with a proper case. In November 1790, Treasury Secretary Alexander Hamilton wrote to Jay requesting that he denounce a resolution passed by the Virginia legislature condemning federal assumption of state debts. Jay refused, and he later also refused a request by President Washington for the justices of the Supreme Court to offer advice on foreign affairs.

In 1791, Jay was confronted with two important constitutional questions. The first of these concerned the legitimate function of the federal judiciary. Congress had enacted a law that required that while on circuit the justices of the Supreme Court review and approve applications by disabled veterans for federal pensions. Jay spoke for a unanimous New York circuit court in rejecting this law, since Congress was empowered by the Constitution only to assign purely judicial functions to the courts. This issue again came before the Supreme Court in the following year in the *Hayburn* case, and although it was resolved without decision, Jay's initial ruling established an approach that would be utilized by Chief Justice Marshall in the landmark case of *Marbury v. Madison* (1803), explicitly establishing the power of the Court to declare invalid an unconstitutional act of Congress.

The second constitutional issue Jay confronted in 1791 was the priority of international treaties over state law. The case in which this issue arose was heard on the circuit court and dealt with a Connecticut law that authorized state courts to require the payment of interest on the prewar debts owed to British subjects. The circuit court overturned this law on the grounds that it was incompatible with the terms of the Treaty of Paris, which Jay himself had helped to formulate.

In 1792, Jay and his colleagues on the circuit court established another important precedent, dealing with the compatibility of state law with the Constitution. The facts in *Champion and Dickason v. Casey* were that the Rhode Island legislature had enacted a special law extending a specific debtor's obligations for a period of three years. Jay overturned this state law on the grounds that it violated Article I,

Section 10 of the Constitution, prohibiting states from enacting any laws that impaired the obligation of contracts.

It was not until 1793 that the Supreme Court was confronted with its first significant case, *Chisholm v. Georgia*, a case dealing with the basic constitutional issue of whether a state can be sued by citizens of another state. The petitioners, heirs of former Georgia resident Alexander Chisholm, but themselves residents of South Carolina, filed suit against the state of Georgia to collect bonds owed to Chisholm's estate that had been confiscated by the state during the Revolutionary War. Although Article III, Section 2 of the Constitution explicitly empowered the federal judiciary to hear suits between states and citizens of other states, the practical boundary between federal jurisdiction and state authority had not yet been fully defined, and the state of Georgia believed that such a suit was an infringement of its own sovereignty.

When the case was brought before the Supreme Court, the legal representatives of the government of Georgia refused even to answer the claims of the petitioners, informing the Court, instead, that the federal judiciary had no jurisdiction in the case. On February 18, 1793, the Supreme Court decided by a vote of 4-1, with only Associate Justice James Iredell dissenting, that the suit of the petitioners should be sustained. Chief Justice Jay's majority opinion provided, beyond the points of law involved, his own conception of the guiding philosophical principles of the Constitution and of the American system of government.

The right of citizens to sue other states in federal court was a wise principle of government, Jay wrote, "because it leaves not even the most obscure and friendless citizen without means of obtaining justice from a neighboring state; because it obviates occasions of quarrels between states on account of the claims of their respective citizens; because it recognizes and strongly rests on this great moral truth, that justice is the same whether due from one man or a million, or from a million to one man; . . . and, because it brings into action and enforces this great and glorious principle, that the people are the sovereign of this country, and consequently that fellow citizens and joint sovereigns cannot be degraded by appearing with each other in their own courts to have their controversies determined."

The Georgia officials were unpersuaded by Jay's reasoning and sentiments. The Supreme Court opinion was seen as a potential danger to the economic survival of the states since similar suits to recover confiscated property had already been filed in Maryland, Massachusetts, New York, South Carolina, and Virginia. The Georgia legislature therefore joined with the legislatures of the other interested states to circumvent the precedent established in *Chisholm v. Georgia*, drafting a constitutional amendment that explicitly prohibited the federal judiciary from hearing similar suits. This amendment, the 11th, was ratified and became part of the Constitution in 1798.

In 1794, the Supreme Court was once again involved with a case, *Georgia v. Brailsford*, concerning the state of Georgia and the claims of an outside creditor. Brailsford, a British subject, filed suit in circuit court to collect a prewar debt owed to him by a private citizen of Georgia. The state of Georgia, instead of resisting the suit, this time sought to become involved directly, claiming that since it had confiscated the debt, it should be a party to the suit. The chief Justice granted Georgia's request and convened a special jury to rule on the case, and even though the final judgement was in Brailsford's favor, Jay's action in this case served to restore confidence in the legal standing of the states before the federal judiciary.

In the same year, the Supreme Court was called upon to deal with a case that had important implications for the nation's foreign policy and international law. The political background of *Glass v. The Sloop Betsey* (1794) was the outbreak of war between France and Great Britain and the desire of President Washington that the United States remain neutral in that conflict.

The facts were that in 1793, a French privateer operating off the eastern coast of the United States captured a neutral Swedish vessel, *The Betsey*, bringing it into Baltimore as a prize. A Maryland merchant, Alexander Glass, who owned part of the ship's cargo, petitioned the federal district court to act as an admiralty court and adjudicate his claim against the French privateer. The French consul, however, contended that according to international law, he alone had the jurisdiction to rule on Glass's claim. The U.S. district court agreed with the consul and claimed that it had no jurisdiction in the case. Since that decision threatened to undercut American neutrality and call into question U.S. sovereignty with regard to maritime law, the issue of jurisdiction was appealed to the Supreme Court.

In a unanimous decision, the Supreme Court ruled that the district court did, in fact, have jurisdiction in this case. Chief Justice Jay, speaking for the Court, handed down an unequivocal defense of American sovereignty from a judicial standpoint. "No foreign power," wrote Jay in his opinion, "can of right institute, or erect, any court of judicature of any kind, within the jurisdiction of the United States, but such only as may be warranted by, and be in pursuance of treaties . . . ."

In the spring of 1794, Jay temporarily left his judicial duties to accept a presidential diplomatic mission to Great Britain. The differences over the enforcement of the Treaty of Paris remained unresolved and the continued presence of British troops in the Northwest garrisons and the impressment of American seamen into the British Navy threatened to bring on renewed warfare between the two countries. Jay conducted extensive negotiations with Lord Grenville over the issues in question and succeeded in negotiating an agreement that at least temporarily diffused Anglo-American tensions. The agreement, which came to be known as Jay's

Treaty, provided for British evacuation of the Northwest garrisons and the resolution of territorial and financial claims by special bipartisan commissions. Jay was unable, however, to convince the British to end their impressment of American seamen or to allow unrestricted American trade with the West Indies. Since it was clear that this was the best compromise that could be obtained at the time, the Senate ratified the agreement, despite widespread public protests and demonstrations.

In addition to his judicial and diplomatic responsibilities, Jay also maintained an active interest in domestic politics while chief justice. In 1792, he had been encouraged by the leaders of New York's Federalist Party to run for governor against incumbent George Clinton. The campaign proved to be unsuccessful, not only because Jay refused to involve himself in active politicking, but also because the Clinton-backed Board of Election Canvassers unfairly disallowed many Federalist ballots.

Later Life. In 1795, however, Jay's political fortunes changed dramatically. His Federalist allies had again put forth his name for governor during his absence in England, and on his return he unexpectedly found that he had been elected. In light of this unsought victory and because he had begun to tire of the travel and time required by his circuit court duties, Jay resigned as chief justice to become governor of New York. To succeed him as chief justice, President Washington nominated former Associate Justice John Rutledge. When Rutledge's nomination was rejected by the Senate, Associate Justice Oliver Ellsworth was nominated and confirmed as chief justice.

Jay served as governor of New York for the next six years. Among his most significant achievements were the revision of the New York criminal code, the establishment of a model penitentiary program, and the adoption of an antislavery law. During the presidential election of 1800, when the Federalist control of the executive branch seemed in danger, Alexander Hamilton appealed to him to alter the accepted method of selecting the state's presidential electors to ensure a Federalist victory. Jay refused, contending that even the interests of his party could not compel him to undertake what he considered to be an abuse of gubernatorial power.

Later in the same year, outgoing Pres. John Adams offered Jay an opportunity to become chief justice of the Supreme Court again. Although his nomination had already been confirmed by the Senate, Jay had decided to retire from public life, and he declined the office. As a result of Jay's decision, Pres. John Adams subsequently appointed John Marshall as chief justice.

In the years that followed his retirement, Jay spent most of his time on his estate in Bedford, New York, where he lived, for the most part, as a gentleman farmer. After the death of his wife in 1802, his only participation in public affairs was his outspoken public opposition to the War of 1812 and his eloquent condemnation of slavery at the time of the Missouri Compromise in 1820. His main interest in his later years was the Episcopal Church.

At the time of his death in Bedford in 1829, Jay was the last surviving member of the First Continental Congress and was respectfully regarded as one of the most influential figures in the early history of the United States. He was buried in the Jay family cemetery in Rye, New York, and was survived by two sons and five daughters.

JOHNSON, THOMAS

b. November 4, 1732; various legislative and judicial positions in Maryland; associate justice, U.S. Supreme Court (1791-1793); d. October 26, 1819.

Born in Calvert County, Maryland, the son of Thomas Johnson and Dorcas Sedgwick Johnson, the younger Thomas was educated at home and later sent to Annapolis to work as a registry clerk at the Land Office. Gaining a law education at the office of Stephen Bordley, he became a member of the Provincial Assembly in 1762.

Johnson was later one of the most outspoken opponents of the Stamp Act and was named a delegate to the Maryland convention in 1774 and a Maryland representative to the Continental Congress in 1775 and 1776. He formally nominated George Washington to become commander-in-chief of the Continental Army. During the Revolution, he served as brigadier general of the Maryland militia and became the first governor of the state (1777-1779).

After working on behalf of the ratification of the U.S. Constitution at the Maryland convention, he was appointed chief judge of the Maryland General Court (1790). In 1791, after the resignation of Associate Justice John Rutledge, President Washington nominated Johnson to Rutledge's seat on the Supreme Court.

Johnson's service on the Court was brief and uneventful. In 1791, he accepted appointment to the board of commissioners planning the national capital. In 1793, he resigned from the Supreme Court, whose circuit court duties he found particularly burdensome. After his retirement, he declined nomination to become secretary of State (1795) and remained a private citizen until his death in Frederick, Maryland, in 1819.

JOHNSON, WILLIAM

b. December 17, 1771; various legislative and judicial positions in South Carolina; associate justice, U.S. Supreme Court (1804-1834); d. August 4, 1834.

Born in Charleston, South Carolina, the son of Sarah Nightingale Johnson and William Johnson, a well-known revolutionary activist, he was educated at Princeton (Class of 1790) and studied law under Charles Cotesworth Pickney, being admitted to the bar in 1793. He was married to Sarah

Bennet in 1794. Johnson served in the lower house of the South Carolina legislature from 1794 to 1798. In 1798, he was elected judge of the court of common pleas. He was, politically, a Democratic-Republican, and with the resignation of Alfred Moore from the Supreme Court in 1804, Pres. Thomas Jefferson nominated Johnson.

During his long service on the Court, Johnson distinguished himself as a critic of Chief Justice John Marshall. Among his more important opinions was his dissent in *Craig v. Missouri* (1830), in which he argued, against the majority, that states have the right to offer certain types of temporary bills of credit, or loans. In general, however, despite his Democratic-Republican background, he leaned toward the nationalist position, concurring with the majority in *Gibbons v. Ogden* (1824), which held that the federal government has the right to regulate navigation and that such regulation superseded contrary state laws. In *Ogden v. Sanders* (1827), however, which upheld the constitutionality of state bankruptcy laws, he was in the majority while Chief Justice Marshall was in the minority.

In circuit court, Johnson maintained his opinion that the federal government has the right to control interstate commerce, in particular the commerce in slaves, and this position proved so unpopular in his native state that he was forced to move to Pennsylvania in 1833. He served on the Court until his death in Brooklyn, New York, in 1834.

LAMAR, JOSEPH RUCKER

b. October 14, 1857; associate justice, Georgia Supreme Court (1903-1905); associate justice, U.S. Supreme Court (1911-1916); d. January 2, 1916.

Born in Elbert County, Georgia, the son of a prominent minister, Lamar graduated from Bethany College in 1877 and received his law degree from Washington and Lee University in 1878. In 1880, he established a private law practice in Augusta, Georgia, and served in the Georgia legislature from 1886 to 1889. He was appointed to a commission to revise the civil laws of Georgia in 1893, and from 1903 to 1905, he served as associate justice of the state supreme court. After his return to private practice in 1906, Lamar gained national prominence by arguing successfully before the Supreme Court the case of *Central of Georgia Railway Company v. Wright* (1907), in which he won a reversal of the state method of taxation of railroads on the grounds that the states did not provide the taxpayer with due process of law. In 1911, after Associate Justice Edward White became chief justice, Pres. William Howard Taft appointed Lamar to the Supreme Court.

Lamar's service on the Court was brief, but he rendered several important decisions during his tenure. He wrote the majority opinion in *Gompers v. Bucks Stove and Range Company* (1911), in which the Court overturned the contempt conviction of the labor leader Samuel Gompers and established the distinctions between civil and criminal contempt. He dissented in *German Alliance Insurance Company v. Lewis* (1914), in which he argued that a state did not have the right to regulate insurance rates as those rates did not immediately affect the public good. He concurred in *McCabe v. Atchison, Topeka and Santa Fe Railroad* (1914), where the constitutionality of the principle of "separate but equal" segregation laws was upheld. He dissented in *United States v. Mosely* (1915), in which he opposed federal intervention in state elections, even in the case of accusations of election fraud or corruption. In *United States v. Midwest Oil Company* (1915), he wrote the majority opinion, establishing the precedent that the federal government may restrict the exploitation of natural resources by private companies.

At the end of his career, Lamar was appointed by President Wilson to serve on an international mediation commission between the United States and Argentina, Brazil, and Chile. He served on the Supreme Court until his death in Washington, D.C., in 1916.

LAMAR, LUCIUS QUINTUS CINCINNATUS

b. September 17, 1825; member, U.S. House of Representatives (1857-1860, 1873-1877); various diplomatic and judicial positions in the Confederacy; U.S. senator (1877-1885); secretary of the interior (1885-1888); associate justice, U.S. Supreme Court (1888-1893); d. January 23, 1893.

Born in Putnam County, Georgia, Lamar was educated at Emory College (Class of 1845) and studied law in the office of Judge Absalom Chappell in Macon. He was admitted to the bar in 1847 and two years later established a private law practice in Oxford, Mississippi. Entering politics as a Democrat, Lamar was elected to Congress in 1857, serving until the outbreak of the Civil War. After brief active service with the Confederate Army in Virginia, he was appointed Confederate commissioner to Russia, and later, judge-advocate of the Third Corps of the Army of Northern Virginia. After the war, he taught law at the University of Mississippi and was elected to Congress again in 1872. He became known as a voice of moderation in the South during the Reconstruction period and was elected to the U.S. Senate in 1876. In 1885, Pres. Grover Cleveland appointed him secretary of the Interior, and three years later, after the death of Associate Justice William Woods, Lamar was appointed to the Supreme Court.

Lamar's service in the Confederacy created considerable opposition to his confirmation, and throughout his relatively brief service on the Court he maintained his support of states' rights. In the case of *Chicago, Milwaukee and St. Paul Railroad v. Minnesota* (1890), he dissented from the majority, arguing that the federal judiciary should not have broad power to review state regulation of freight tariff schedules. In *In re Neagle* (1890), he again differed with the majority opinion in his belief that state courts do have the constitutional right to prosecute federal officials for murder, even if such an act were committed in legitimate pursuit of their duty. Also consistent with his judicial philosophy was his dissent in *United States v. Texas* (1892), in which he argued that the federal judiciary does not have original jurisdiction in every case in which the United States is a party.

Lamar was married twice: in 1847, to Virginia Longstreet and, after her death, to Henrietta Holt in 1887. Lamar served on the Court for five years until his death in Macon, Georgia, in 1893.

LIVINGSTON, HENRY BROCKHOLST

b. November 25, 1757; judge, New York Supreme Court (1802-1807); associate justice, U.S. Supreme Court (1806-1823); d. March 18, 1823.

Born in New York City, the son of William Livingston, a former governor of New Jersey, and Susannah French, he graduated from Princeton in 1774 and served as a captain in the Continental Army during the Revolution. After service abroad as private secretary to his brother-in-law John Jay, later U.S. chief justice, Livingston studied law in the office of Peter Yates in Albany and was admitted to the New York bar in 1783. Politically, he broke with the Federalists and, as a supporter of Jefferson, became a Democratic-Republican. In 1802, he was appointed to the Supreme Court of New York, and in 1806, with the death of Associate Justice William Paterson, Livingston was appointed to the Supreme Court by President Jefferson.

As a member of the Marshall Court, Livingston's Republican ideological orientation gradually shifted toward the prevailing nationalism of his associates. He concurred with the majority in *United States v. Coolidge* (1816), which reaffirmed the decision in *United States v. Hudson* (1812) that there could be no federal common law jurisdiction in criminal cases, and in *Trustees of Dartmouth College v. Woodward* (1819), which defended the legal status of private corporations.

On the circuit, Livingston was known as an expert in commercial and maritime law. His most notable circuit decisions were related to the enforcement of the Embargo Act (1807), in which he defended the act's constitutionality, while arguing that its violation could not be classified as treason, if the object was private gain.

Livingston was married three times. Besides his duties in the Supreme Court and on the circuit, he was a founding member of the New-York Historical Society, a trustee of the New York Society Library, and a strong advocate of the establishment of a public school system in New York. He served on the Supreme Court until his death in Washington, D.C., in 1823.

LURTON, HORACE HARMON

b. February 26, 1844; judge, Tennessee Supreme Court (1886-1893); judge, U.S. Circuit Court (1893-1909); associate justice, U.S. Supreme Court (1909-1914); d. July 12, 1914.

Born in Newport, Kentucky, Lurton was educated by private tutors and attended the University of Chicago until his studies were interrupted by the outbreak of the Civil War. In 1861, he returned to his home state and enlisted in the Confederate Army, and during his active service he was captured by Union forces. After the war, he began law studies at the Cumberland University Law School and was admitted to the bar in 1867. Establishing a private practice in Clarksville, Tennessee, Lurton was appointed to the Tennessee Supreme Court (1886), eventually becoming its chief justice in 1893. In that same year, he received a presidential appointment to become judge of the U.S. Court of Appeals for the 6th Circuit. In this position, Lurton became a close associate of William Howard Taft, who was the presiding judge of that circuit, and in 1910, after the death of Associate Justice Rufus Peckham, President Taft appointed Lurton to the Supreme Court.

Lurton was sixty-six years old when his nomination was confirmed, and his tenure on the Court was relatively brief. He joined Justice Holmes's dissent in *Bailey v. Alabama* (1911), in which the Court invalidated as a violation of the 13th Amendment's prohibition of slavery a state law that held that nonperformance of a contract was *prima facie* evidence of prior intent to defraud and therefore could be punished by forced service. He wrote the majority opinion in *Coyle v. Smith* (1911), in which the Court held that Congress may not intervene in the purely internal affairs of states as a condition of their admission to the Union. He maintained his support of the rights of the states in his minority opinion in the *Shreveport Rate Case* (1914), which held that Congress has the authority under the commerce clause to regulate rail tariffs within states.

Lurton distinguished himself throughout his long judicial career as a legal scholar, and he served as professor of law at Vanderbilt University Law School from 1898 to 1910. He served on the Supreme Court until his death in Atlantic City, New Jersey, in 1914.

McKENNA, JOSEPH

b. August 10, 1843; member, U.S. House of Representatives (1885-1892); judge, 9th U.S. Circuit Court (1892-1897); U.S. attorney general (1897); associate justice, U.S. Supreme Court (1898-1925); d. November 21, 1926.

Born in Philadelphia and raised in Benecia, California, McKenna was educated at the Benecia Collegiate Academy. After deciding against a career in the Catholic priesthood, he studied law and was admitted to the bar in 1865. He entered politics as a Republican and served as Solano County district attorney (1866-1870) and as a representative in the state legislature (1875-1876). He later served four terms in the U.S. House of Representatives, resigning in 1892 to become judge of the 9th U.S. Circuit Court. Pres. William McKinley named him attorney general in 1897, but he served in that position for only a few months. In 1898, after

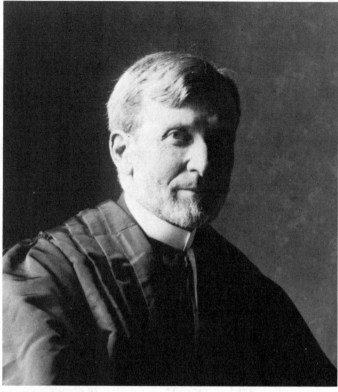

Joseph McKenna

the death of Associate Justice Stephen Field, McKenna was appointed to the Supreme Court.

McKenna's nomination aroused considerable controversy on the grounds that he had been closely associated with conservative California railroad interests, but during his tenure he displayed a liberal judicial temperament. He dissented in *Adair v. United States* (1908), arguing that Congress should have the right to prohibit firing of railroad employees for union membership. In his dissent in *Adams v. Tanner* (1917), he again took the side of employees, supporting the right of states to regulate the practices of employment agencies. McKenna spoke for the Court in *Bunting v. Oregon* (1917), upholding the right of states to regulate working hours of women. In *Hammer v. Dagenhart* (1918), he joined with Justices Brandeis and Clark in Holmes's dissent against the Court's invalidation of federal legislation against child labor.

On the issue of judicial procedure, McKenna dissented in *Pettibone v. Nichols* (1906), in which he was the only member of the Court to argue that a federal court has broad power to order the release of a person held by state authorities if the person's arrest was improper. In another action arising out of this case, *Moyer v. Peabody* (1909), McKenna concurred with the majority that a state governor has the power to abrogate normal judicial procedure during a time of emergency.

McKenna resigned from the Court in 1925 and died in Washington, D.C., the following year.

McKINLEY, JOHN

b. May 1, 1780; member, U.S. House of Representatives (1833-1835); U.S. senator (1826-1831, 1837); associate justice, U.S. Supreme Court (1837-1852); d. July 19, 1852.

Born in Culpeper County, Virginia, McKinley spent his boyhood in Kentucky, where he studied law and was admitted to the bar, establishing a private practice in Frankfort. In 1818, he moved to Huntsville, Alabama, where he entered politics and was elected representative of Lauderdale County in the state legislature two years later. A loyal Jacksonian Democrat, McKinley was elected to the U.S. Senate in 1826. With his defeat for reelection in 1831, he returned to the state legislature, later being elected for a single term to the U.S. House of Representatives. In 1837, McKinley was elected again to the U.S. Senate, but before he could take his seat, he was nominated by Pres. Martin Van Buren to one of the two associate justiceships of the Supreme Court established by the Judiciary Act of 1837.

McKinley's most notable vote during his relatively brief tenure on the Court occurred in *Groves v. Slaughter* (1841). In this case he dissented from the majority, stating that although a Mississippi law barring the importation of out-of-state slaves was constitutional as the Court ruled, any debts incurred by the purchase of such slaves should be considered void.

McKinley was married twice; to Juliana Bryan and, after her death, to Elizabeth Armistead. In his later years, McKinley suffered increasingly poor health. He served on the Court until his death in Louisville, Kentucky, in 1852.

McLEAN, JOHN

b. March 11, 1785; member, U.S. House of Representatives (1813-1816); judge, Ohio Supreme Court (1816-1822); U.S. postmaster general (1823-1829); associate justice, U.S. Supreme Court (1829-1861); d. April 4, 1861.

Born in Morris County, New Jersey, McLean was the son of Irish immigrants who moved to the western frontier, eventually settling permanently in Warren County, Ohio. He received little formal education and at age eighteen was indentured for two years to the clerk of the Hamilton County Court in Cincinnati. During that period, McLean studied law with Arthur St. Clair and was admitted to the bar in 1807. After his marriage to Rebecca Edwards, he established his residence in Lebanon, Ohio, and founded a weekly newspaper there. In 1812, he was elected to the U.S. Congress from Cincinnati, resigning that office in 1816 to serve as a judge on the Ohio Supreme Court. After brief service as commissioner of the United States Land Office, he was appointed in 1823 by Pres. James Monroe to be postmaster general and was reappointed to that position by Pres. John Quincy Adams. In 1829, after the death of Associate Justice Robert Trimble, McLean was appointed by Pres. Andrew Jackson to the Supreme Court.

McLean's long career on the Court was characterized

by his scrupulous dedication to his duties both in Washington and on the circuit assigned to him, which included Tennessee, Kentucky, and Ohio. He was an outspoken opponent of slavery, arguing in *Groves v. Slaughter* (1841) that states had the right to regulate slave trade and thereby restrict trade in slaves. His most important opinion on this subject, in which he wrote one of the two dissenting opinions, concerned the Dred Scott Case (*Scott v. Sandford*, 1857), in which he argued that not only was it within the power of Congress to prohibit slavery by establishing territorial governments, but that the institution of slavery itself was contrary to moral principles and maintained only by the force of local laws.

McLean consistently defended his right to participate in national political affairs despite his position on the bench and was actively considered for the presidential nomination of the Free-Soil Anti-Slavery Party in 1848 and by the Republicans in 1856 and 1860. He served on the Supreme Court until his death in Cincinnati in 1861.

McREYNOLDS, JAMES CLARK

b. February 3, 1862; various federal judicial positions; U.S. attorney general (1913-1914); associate justice, U.S. Supreme Court (1914-1941); d. August 24, 1946.

Born in Elkton, Tennessee, McReynolds was educated at Vanderbilt University (Class of 1882) and received his law training at the University of Virginia. He was admitted to the Tennessee bar in 1884 and established a successful private practice in Nashville. From 1903 to 1907, he served as assistant U.S. attorney general, and during the Wilson administration, he was appointed to the cabinet as attorney general. In 1914, after the death of Associate Justice Horace Lurton, Pres. Woodrow Wilson appointed McReynolds to the Supreme Court.

Throughout his long tenure on the Court, McReynolds distinguished himself as an extreme conservative and as a steadfast opponent of federal intervention in economic affairs. He dissented in *Bunting v. Oregon* (1917), in which he opposed state regulation of working hours, and he also opposed the majority ruling in *Wilson v. New* (1917), which permitted Congress to impose temporary labor settlements to prevent strikes. McReynolds was an equally strong supporter of individual rights and the rights of states. He wrote the majority opinion in *Newberry v. United States* (1921), in which he argued against federal intervention in state primary elections. He also spoke for the Court in *Pierce v. Society of Sisters* (1922), in which the Court overturned an even more sweeping state law that was aimed at the abolition of nonpublic schools. He dissented in *Carroll v. United States* (1925), in which he opposed an extension of the right of police officers to make searches without a warrant.

McReynolds was one of a number of justices who consistently opposed the social programs of the New Deal. The court-packing scheme (1937) of President Roosevelt was intended in part to overcome the decisions of this group. As President Roosevelt made more appointments to the Court, McReynolds found himself more frequently in dissent. In his dissent in *Norman v. Baltimore and Ohio Railroad* (1935), one of the Gold Clause Cases, he violently attacked congressional abrogation of the requirement that currency be redeemable in gold. He also dissented in *National Labor Relations Board v. Jones & Laughlin Steel Company* (1937), in which the Court recognized a considerably broader power in the federal government to intervene in labor issues. His was the only dissenting voice in *Ashwander v. Tennessee Valley Authority* (1936), in which he attacked the Congress's constitutional authority to operate the federal project as a business.

McReynolds retired from the Supreme Court in 1941 and died in Washington, D.C., in 1946.

MARSHALL, JOHN

b. September 24, 1755; U.S. minister to France (1797-1798); member, U.S. House of Representatives (1799-1800); U.S. secretary of State (1800-1801); chief justice, U.S. Supreme Court (1801-1835); d. July 6, 1835.

John Marshall

Students of American constitutional history generally agree that John Marshall was the greatest judge to serve on the U.S. Supreme Court. Many of Marshall's contemporaries as well as many of his successors on the Court concur.

Pres. John Adams, who appointed Marshall as chief justice in 1801, claimed the appointment was "the proudest act of my life." Justice Oliver Wendell Holmes, considered by some to be Marshall's equal as a Supreme Court justice, also felt that Marshall was the preeminent judge in American constitutional law. He wrote that "if American law were to be represented by a single figure, sceptic and worshiper alike would agree that the figure could be one alone, and that one, John Marshall."

Marshall's early life hardly foreshadowed a career as a great judge. He was born in 1755 in Prince William (later Faquier) County, Virginia. He received a very meager education during his youth in rural Virginia. In 1775, he began his service in the Continental Army, which lasted intermittently until 1780. Upon completion of his military service, he turned to the law. Between May and July 1780 he attended George Wythe's law lectures at the College of William and Mary. He supplemented Wythe's lectures by maintaining a commonplace book in which he copied large sections of Matthew Bacon's *New Abridgement of Law, Virginia Acts of Assembly* (1769). With this training in law, he was admitted to the bar of Faquier County in August 1780.

Typical of young lawyers in the new republic, Marshall was active in state and local politics. He served in the Virginia House of Delegates (1782-1785, 1787-1790, 1795-1796) and as a member of the Virginia Executive Council (1782-1784). As an increasingly prominent member of the Federalist Party of Virginia, Marshall had opportunities to serve the national government. But the demands of a growing law practice and a heavy financial burden from land speculation ventures prevented him from accepting any of the numerous offers of government positions. Finally, in June 1797, he accepted an offer to become minister to France. Among the reasons for accepting the diplomatic post was the prospect of substantial financial reward. The mission to France gave Marshall much of what he desired. A grateful Congress eventually gave him almost $20,000 for his services, and as a loyal member of the Federalist Party he could expect even more prestigious posts.

In 1800, Pres. John Adams reorganized his cabinet and prevailed on Marshall to accept the post of secretary of State. Later that same year, Chief Justice Oliver Ellsworth informed Adams of his decision to resign. In the aftermath of the Jeffersonian victory in the election of 1800, it became increasingly important to Adams to replace Ellsworth with a loyal Federalist. Initially, Adams offered the position to John Jay, the first chief justice, but after a long delay Jay declined. Much sentiment existed for Adams to elevate Associate Justice William Paterson of New Jersey to the chief justiceship. Despite substantial support for Paterson, Adams saw little advantage in appointing him. On January 20, 1801, he nominated John Marshall to succeed Ellsworth. The Senate quickly confirmed Marshall, and he took the oath on February 4, 1801. For the last month of the Adams presidency, Marshall served as both secretary of State and chief justice. Thus, through a combination of partisan loyalty, fortuitous circumstance, and confidence in his abilities, John Marshall became chief justice of the United States. During the next thirty-four years he would become the most important influence upon American constitutional law in all of American history.

Marshall and the American Judicial Tradition. The branch of government over which Marshall presided in 1801 was in a state of crisis. The federal judiciary was clearly not the equal of the legislative and executive branches. The problems of the judicial branch were greatest at the highest level. During the first twelve years of its existence, the Supreme Court suffered from weak leadership as well as uncertainty over its role in the constitutional system. Justices usually wrote separate opinions, which often revealed the existence of significant differences of opinion, especially on the question of whether or not the Supreme Court could invalidate congressional legislation. Furthermore, some federal judges became increasingly involved in partisan politics as they abandoned judicial impartiality and played major roles in the enforcement of the Alien and Sedition Acts of 1798. Finally, the Supreme Court's influence was severely restricted by a light case load. During the years from 1789 to 1801, the Court decided only fifty-five cases, and the most notable one, *Chisholm v. Georgia* (1793), was invalidated by the 11th Amendment in 1798.

In 1801, the position of the judiciary was placed in further jeopardy by continued partisan conflict. The new president, Thomas Jefferson, publicly hoped to heal the nation's partisan wounds, but privately intended to bring the judiciary under the control of the executive branch. In September 1801, he wrote Chancellor Robert Livingston of New York: "I join you in taking shame for the depravity of our judges." While the Jeffersonians viewed the judiciary in political terms, few understood the importance of an independent judiciary better than John Marshall. In the crucible of political controversy Marshall forged the basic elements of the American judicial tradition that preserved the independence of the judiciary in the American system of government. As G. Edward White has written, that tradition comprises a "distinctive blend of independence, sensitivity to political currents and appearance of impartiality."

A number of matters concerned the Jeffersonians. First of all, the Judiciary Act of 1801 had expanded the jurisdiction of the federal courts of first instance and threatened, as the Jeffersonians saw it, to create a truly uniform judicial system. The centralizing influence that such a development would create was more than the Jeffersonians could tolerate. Secondly, the new judgeships created under the 1801 act, while bringing about needed reform, had been filled entirely by Federalists. After considerable deliberation, Jefferson and his advisors decided that the 1801 act lay beyond redemption. In March 1802, they won their first victory in their assault on the judiciary by repealing the 1801 Judiciary Act. The effect of the repeal was to revive the structure of the judiciary outlined in the Judiciary Act of 1789.

Repeal of the 1801 Judiciary Act asserted congressional control over the lower federal courts. The next step in Jefferson's attack on the judiciary was to subordinate the judicial branch to the executive branch through the impeachment process. In 1804, District Judge John Pickering of New Hampshire was impeached and removed from office after his trial in the Senate. Pickering's removal actually had less to do with partisan politics than his obvious incompetence. He clearly suffered from both alcoholism and insanity. The following year, the Jeffersonian-controlled Congress impeached Associate Justice Samuel Chase of Maryland. Chase's vigorous enforcement of the Sedition Act of 1798 had inflamed partisan passions more than the actions of any other judge. It was assumed that his removal would lead to executive dominance of the judiciary. At his trial, some stalwart Jeffersonians had second thoughts, and the attempted removal failed.

Marshall's first real opportunity to outline his approach to the art of judging came in *Marbury v. Madison* (1803). The case has acquired lasting significance because it contains the first clear statement of the principle of judicial review by the Supreme Court. That principle was well known in Anglo-American jurisprudence in the seventeenth and eighteenth centuries, but the reach of judicial review had not been established in American constitutional law. The clarity with which Marshall enunciated the principle and the fact that the Supreme Court invalidated a section of a statute passed by Congress explain *Marbury*'s importance. In 1958, in a landmark segregation decision, the Supreme Court reaffirmed the place of *Marbury* when it wrote that "this decision [*Marbury*] declared the basic principle that the Federal judiciary is supreme in the exposition of the law of the Constitution, and that principle has ever since been respected by this Court and the Country as a permanent and indispensible feature of our constitutional system."

The case of *Marbury v. Madison* arose when the new secretary of State, James Madison, refused to deliver William Marbury's commission of appointment as one of forty-two new justices of the peace for the District of Columbia. The new positions had been created by the outgoing Federalist-controlled Congress for strictly partisan reasons. With the expiration of Adams's term at midnight on March 3, 1801, the commissions of appointment had been signed and the official seal affixed, but at least four had not yet been delivered. It fell to the new secretary of State to deliver the commissions, but Pres. Thomas Jefferson ordered Madison not to deliver them.

In December 1801, Marbury applied to the Supreme Court for a writ of *mandamus*. This writ commanded a public official to perform some task he was authorized by statute to carry out. Authority for the Supreme Court to issue such a writ rested not in the Constitution, but on Section 13 of the Judiciary Act of 1789. That section of the 1789 law authorized the Supreme Court to issue writs of *mandamus* as part of its original jurisdiction. Because of the political controversy that surrounded this case and other problems involving the Jeffersonians and the federal judiciary, a final decision was delayed for more than a year.

In late February 1803, Marshall read his opinion for a unanimous Court. He found that Marbury was entitled to his commission since the appointment was complete with the president's signature. The secretary of State's failure to deliver the commission left Marbury with no choice but to seek a court order compelling delivery. For Marshall, the only remaining question was whether the Judiciary Act of 1789 could properly authorize the Supreme Court to issue such a writ. At this point, Marshall found a conflict between the language of the Constitution and the authority of Congress. While Marbury was entitled to his commission and the writ of *mandamus* was a proper remedy, the Supreme Court was powerless to aid him. Congress had unconstitutionally expanded the original jurisdiction of the Supreme Court. The original jurisdiction was limited by the language of Article III of the Constitution.

By ruling in this manner, Marshall avoided a major conflict between the executive and judicial branches and firmly established the principle of judicial review in American constitutional law. As Herbert Johnson has written, "*Marbury v. Madison* stands as one of the most artful utilizations of judicial power in the history of the Supreme Court."

Four years later the treason trial of Aaron Burr put Marshall's assertion of judicial independence to a severe test. Aaron Burr's political career lay in ruins after his duel with Alexander Hamilton in 1804. In 1806, he led a motley group of soldiers of fortune in an attempt either to take Mexico for the United States or to detach the southwestern territories from the United States. Whatever the goal, President Jefferson and others publicly pronounced Burr guilty of treason well before he was brought to trial. Burr was finally arrested, formally charged with treason, and brought to Richmond, Virginia, for trial. As judge for the U.S. Circuit Court for Virginia, Marshall presided over the seven-month trial, which began in March 1807. He was determined not to let Jefferson use charges of treason for political purposes. After protracted legal proceedings, a Jeffersonian-Republican dominated jury found Burr not guilty. Marshall has been accused of allowing his personal dislike of Jefferson needlessly to politicize the trial, but in reality he "vindicated the integrity of the judiciary on behalf of individual rights and fair criminal procedure."

Federal Supremacy. As chief justice, Marshall built a body of nationalistic constitutional law intended to assure the supremacy of the national government when conflicts between national and state authority arose and to protect private property. His arguments relied heavily on the contract and commerce clauses of the Constitution as he fashioned them into effective instruments for limited state action. The process began with the contract clause, as Marshall used the constitutional provision prohibiting impairment of contracts to limit state legislative action, foster the growth of corporations, and define the limits of state bankruptcy laws. *Fletcher v. Peck* (1810) was the first of the contract clause cases as well as the first Supreme Court opinion to invalidate a state law as being contrary to the Constitution. In 1795, the Georgia legislature sold some 35 million acres of land to four land companies. Shortly after the sale it became clear that numerous Georgia legislators had been bribed. The following year most of the corrupt legislators had been defeated, and the new legislature revoked the land sale. Between these two legislative acts, considerable amounts of land had been sold to third parties on a legitimate basis. With the revocation of the sale by the legislature, numerous third parties lost their recently purchased land. When the Georgia courts upheld the revocation, the case was appealed to the Supreme Court.

Marshall held that the grant to the original land companies took the form of a contract between the state of Georgia and the recipients of the grant. Regardless of the circumstances, the land speculators held clear title to the land. To permit the subsequent legislature to revoke the original grant would violate the constitutional provision preventing impairment of contracts.

Marshall took a similar approach to the contract clause in the celebrated case of *Dartmouth College v. Woodward* (1819). The New Hampshire legislature had revoked the original royal charter of Dartmouth College and had appointed a new board of trustees. The New Hampshire courts upheld the legislature, and the original trustees appealed to the Supreme Court. Daniel Webster represented his alma mater in one of his most emotional appearances before the Supreme Court.

Marshall's opinion invalidated the New Hampshire legislative action. He argued that the original royal charter constituted a contractual arrangement between the British Crown, the benefactors of the college, and the trustees of the institution. The state of New Hampshire succeeded to the place of the Crown with the American Revolution, but the essential obligations remained unchanged. The charter was a contract within the meaning of the Constitution. Therefore the act of the New Hampshire legislature revoking the original charter was an unconstitutional impairment of a contract.

As noted by numerous scholars, the Dartmouth College case stands as the high-water mark in Marshall's expansion of the contract clause. For a time the doctrine protected all corporate charters from legislative alteration. In the aftermath of the case, it became common for newly-granted corporate charters to contain a clause reserving the right of the state to amend the charter at any time.

Two weeks after the Dartmouth College case, Marshall handed down the last great contract clause opinion of the 1819 term. *Sturges v. Crowninshield* (1819) dealt with the constitutionality of state bankruptcy legislation. Before 1841, the only congressional legislation in this area was a very limited bankruptcy law in effect between 1801 and 1803. In the absence of congressional action, state legislatures enacted bankruptcy laws of various sorts. In 1811, New York passed a bankruptcy statute that relieved insolvent debtors of obligations contracted before the law was passed. Shortly before passage of the New York law, Richard Crowninshield had borrowed money from Josiah Sturges. After the bankruptcy law was enacted, Crowninshield sought a discharge from his obligation under the law's provisions. In 1816, Sturges, after finding no relief in New York courts, filed suit in federal court, claiming that the New York law impaired the obligation of contract. The challenge to the New York law reached the Supreme Court during the economic turmoil caused by the Panic of 1819. In response to popular demands for debtor relief, many state legislatures had enacted bankruptcy laws that clearly disadvantaged creditors. For this reason the case acquired more attention than might have been expected.

In his opinion, Marshall dealt with two major issues: first, whether states could enact bankruptcy laws given the constitutional provision granting that power to Congress; and, second, whether the New York statute violated the contract clause. He argued that state government might properly enact bankruptcy legislation only in the absence of congressional action. As to the second issue, Marshall argued that the transaction between Crowninshield and Sturges clearly constituted a contract, and since the New York law relieved the debtor of his obligation, the law stood in conflict with the contract clause. While not stating the issue with great clarity, what the Supreme Court did in *Sturges* was to attack the retroactive feature of the New York law. In *Ogden v. Saunders* (1827) the Court upheld a bankruptcy law that discharged insolvent debtors from obligations entered into after the law was passed.

Federal Activism. The expansion of the contract clause was an essential feature of Marshall's judicial nationalism. Of greater importance, however, were the opinions in *McCulloch v. Maryland* (1819) and *Gibbons v. Ogden* (1824), which provided the constitutional basis for an activist federal government. The case of *McCulloch v. Maryland* was the third of the great cases of the 1819 term, considered by some to be the most significant term in the Court's history. *McCulloch* reached the Supreme Court on appeal from Maryland when the state of Maryland attempted to tax the Baltimore branch of the Second Bank of the United States. The cashier of the bank, McCulloch, had been held liable by Maryland courts for the taxes due under state law. The participation of some of the greatest lawyers in the country heightened interest in this case. Daniel Webster and

William Pinkney represented the bank, while Luther Martin and Joseph Hopkinson represented Maryland.

The first question Marshall addressed was whether or not Congress had the authority to charter a bank. He began with an analysis of the nature of the Union, relying heavily on a doctrine of national sovereignty. While the power of the national government was limited to specific areas, it was "supreme within its spheres of action." Pursuing a Hamiltonian doctrine of broad construction, he found that chartering a bank fell within that sphere. Congress possessed that authority from the "necessary and proper" clause of Article I of the Constitution.

The second question Marshall took up was whether the state of Maryland could tax the branch bank. He again invoked the principle of national sovereignty. He argued that when a state law conflicted with national law, the state must give way. Since the bank was a "lawful instrument of federal authority," the state's attempt to inhibit its functions by taxation was unconstitutional. *McCulloch* had the very important consequence of giving judicial sanction to a "loose construction" of the Constitution. Such an interpretation freed Congress from many of the strictures that a literal reading of the Constitution would have imposed.

While *McCulloch* greatly expanded the possible arena of federal activity through the "necessary and proper" clause, *Gibbons v. Ogden* contributed to the same development through a broad interpretation of the commerce clause. The case had its origins in the practice of many states of granting exclusive economic rights to encourage economic development. Beginning shortly after independence, several states granted exclusive rights to steam navigation in their navigable waters to encourage the development of the steamboat. The exclusive grants were of little consequence until 1807, when the joint venture of Robert Livingston and Robert Fulton led to the development of the first successful steamboat. Showing great foresight, Livingston had secured a short-lived monopoly over steam navigation in New York waters from the New York legislature in 1798 and received a thirty-year renewal in 1808. Livingston and Fulton envisioned a series of exclusive grants that would allow them to monopolize steamboat trade on numerous inland waterways, but especially on the Ohio and Mississippi rivers. In 1811, they received an eighteen-year grant from Orleans Territory, but all other states refused their requests. The New York monopoly withstood numerous legal challenges, but the Orleans Territory grant was dissolved in 1812.

Among those who challenged the New York grant was former New Jersey Governor Aaron Ogden. In 1815, he abandoned his legal challenge and purchased a license to operate a steamboat in New York and New Jersey waters with Livingston's heirs. He formed a brief partnership with Thomas Gibbons, which dissolved in 1818. Gibbons continued to operate his steamboat in New York waters despite the fact that he had no authorization from New York to do so. In 1820, a New York court granted an injunction against Gibbons. Gibbons then appealed to the U.S. Supreme Court, claiming a right to operate under the federal Coastal Licensing Act of 1793.

The case attracted a great deal of attention because of the issues at stake and the personalities involved. Daniel Webster and Attorney General William Wirt represented Gibbons, while New York Attorney General Thomas Oakley and the flamboyant Thomas Addis Emmet appeared for Ogden. In early February 1824, five full days were devoted to oral arguments. A month later, on March 2, 1824, Marshall handed down his opinion.

The primary question Marshall faced was whether a state can grant exclusive rights to navigate its waters. He held that the New York statute that granted the monopoly was void, because Congress had been granted authority to regulate commerce by the Constitution and had exercised that authority by passing the federal Coastal Licensing Act of 1793. He held back from arguing that the commerce clause granted an exclusive power to Congress, preferring the ground of selective exclusivity. There were some areas where states could enact regulatory legislation, but Marshall preferred to call these police powers. He further intimated that the national government could enter these areas as well if the national interest demanded it. *Gibbons v. Ogden* was an extremely popular opinion since it struck down a monopoly and assured that no state could monopolize navigation of its interstate waterways. The lasting significance of *Gibbons*, though, lies in the very broad definition of commerce that Marshall developed. That broad definition has provided the constitutional basis for the growth of the modern activist state. Marshall argued that commerce was more than traffic; it was intercourse, and it was regulated by the rules for carrying on intercourse. From this broad definition the constitutionality of diverse government functions from regulating various types of commercial activity to enforcing the Civil Rights Act of 1964 have rested. Much of the lasting significance of Marshall's judicial career rests on *Gibbons*.

State Court Decisions. The last area where Marshall's opinions contributed to an assertion of federal supremacy concerned the review of decisions of state courts. In *Cohens v. Virginia* (1821), Marshall confronted an attempt by the state of Virginia to prevent or restrict appeals from its courts to the Supreme Court. Ostensibly, the controversy over Supreme Court review of state court final decisions had been settled in favor of the Supreme Court in *Martin v. Hunter's Lessee* (1816). But Virginia Chief Justice Spencer Roane defied the Supreme Court by refusing to conform to the Supreme Court opinion. As a result, the impact of Supreme Court review of state court decisions remained uncertain. Should the states prevail, an important, perhaps essential, pillar of federal supremacy would be lost. *Cohens v. Virginia* arose when two brothers, who were residents of

Washington, D.C., were charged with illegally selling District of Columbia lottery tickets in Norfolk, Virginia. Virginia had enacted a law that forbade the sale of out-of-state lottery tickets in Virginia. The Cohen brothers were convicted and fined $100. They attempted to appeal, claiming they were acting under a federal law (the District of Columbia lottery law), which should take precedence over Virginia law. They found, however, that Virginia had also enacted a statute that prevented appeals from convictions such as the one they faced. Since they had raised a "federal question" at trial, they appealed to the Supreme Court.

The issue Marshall faced was whether or not the Supreme Court had the authority to review a decision of a state court that was not the highest court in the state. If states could block Supreme Court review in the manner of Virginia, the supremacy clause with respect to judicial review would be at the discretion of state legislatures. Marshall argued that the Supreme Court had the authority to review all state judicial proceedings that arose under the Constitution and laws or treaties of the United States. He held that such review was essential if a uniform interpretation of the Constitution was to prevail. Only in this way could the Supreme Court perform its responsibility of protecting the supremacy of the federal union. Marshall also denied that the 11th Amendment prevented such appeals, claiming that the amendment was intended only to keep the states from being sued.

Once Marshall asserted that the Supreme Court had jurisdiction, he turned to the actual conviction. He was as artful in *Cohens* as he had been in *Marbury*. The District of Columbia lottery law was a mere local regulation and did not protect the Cohens from Virginia law. In ruling as he did in *Cohens*, Marshall preserved one of the most important sources of federal supremacy from an attack by the states.

The Closing Years. The 1824 term proved to be the high point of Marshall's assertion of federal supremacy. During the next few years he found that he had to accommodate some of his most cherished views to the reality of a new era in American public life. The most difficult aspect of the new reality was a dramatic increase in states' rights sentiments. Changes in the composition of the Supreme Court also affected what the Chief Justice could do, since he no longer dominated the Court as he once had. In 1827 the Court upheld a state bankruptcy law in *Ogden v. Saunders*. This time the Court dealt with issues that had been avoided in the earlier *Sturges v. Crowninshield* (1819). Most importantly, Justice Willian Johnson argued that congressional jurisdiction over bankruptcy was not exclusive. Marshall rejected both Johnson's attack on the contract clause and the exclusiveness of congressional authority when he filed his only dissent in a constitutional law case. Three years later, in *Providence Bank v. Billings* (1830), Marshall modified the Dartmouth College doctrine by holding that Rhode Island could tax a bank unless the bank's charter expressly prohibited such taxation.

The commerce clause also underwent some modification in Marshall's later years on the Court. In *Willson v. Blackbird Marsh Creek Company* (1829), Marshall upheld a Delaware law that allowed the construction of a dam on a navigable river. A vessel owned by Willson had broken through the dam. The company sued for damages, won in state court, and Willson appealed to the Supreme Court, claiming *Gibbons* controlled the case. Marshall ignored the coasting act he had relied upon in *Gibbons* and held that the Delaware law was a proper exercise of a state's police power since the company drained a swamp, improved property values, and enhanced public health.

Marshall's final compromise with his highly nationalistic views came in *Barron v. The Mayor and City Council of Baltimore* (1833). Acting under the authority of a state law, the city of Baltimore had diverted the flow of water in such a way as to reduce the usefulness of a wharf owned by John Barron. Barron sued for damages, claiming that the city's action constituted a taking without just compensation, thereby violating a provision of the 5th Amendment. The issue for the Court was whether or not the Bill of Rights acted as a limitation on the states. Simply put, Marshall found no controversy. The Bill of Rights acted as a limitation upon the national government *only*.

Marshall also suffered his most ignominious defeat toward the close of his brilliant career. The problem involved the status of the Cherokee Indians, and by implication all Indians east of the Mississippi. By treaty, the federal government had attempted to guarantee the Cherokees their land, much of which lay in the state of Georgia. But by 1830, the government formally adopted a policy of removing all eastern tribes to the unoccupied land west of the Mississippi River. Numerous friends of the Cherokees initiated lawsuits against various aspects of state and federal Indian policy. In two instances, Marshall had an opportunity to express the views of the Supreme Court on the matter. In *Cherokee Nation v. Georgia* (1831), he argued that Indian tribes could not be considered as separate nations or states, but were certainly under the protection of the United States rather than any individual state. Marshall's equivocation failed to defuse the problem. The following year, in *Worcester v. Georgia* (1832), Marshall forcefully defended the Cherokees' right to hold their lands against the state of Georgia. But the state ignored the decision, and President Jackson did nothing to enforce it. The Cherokees marched westward along the "Trail of Tears," and the Supreme Court stood humiliated. This seems to have been one occasion when Marshall chose to pursue principle no matter what the cost. By the time of the Cherokee cases he had come to believe the Indians were a "helpless people depending on our magnanimity and justice for the preservation of their existence." Marshall's personal views reflected in constitutional law did nothing to allay the final removal of all of the eastern tribes.

After 1831, a combination of factors took a heavy toll

on Marshall. The death of his beloved wife Polly, fear of growing sectional antagonisms, and old age all made life increasingly difficult. At the close of the 1835 term the seventy-nine-year-old Chief Justice was injured in a stage coach accident. He sought medical treatment in Philadelphia, where he died on July 6, 1835. During his remarkable career he wrote 547 of the 1,111 opinions handed down by the Supreme Court. Through the force of his personality, his deliberate style, and his intellectual qualities he dominated the Supreme Court as no other chief justice has done since. He molded the federal judiciary into a co-equal branch of government and produced a body of constitutional law that assured that the Constitution was the supreme law of the land. As Justice Joseph Story noted at the opening of the 1836 term, his "life was its own best eulogy."

MARSHALL, THURGOOD

b. July 2, 1908; judge, U.S. Court of Appeals, 2nd circuit (1961-1965); U.S. solicitor general (1965-1967); associate justice, U.S. Supreme Court (1967-).

Thurgood Marshall

Born in Baltimore, Maryland, the son of a primary school teacher and the great-grandson of a slave, Marshall was educated at Lincoln University in Pennsylvania (Class of 1930) and received his training in law at Howard University Law School, graduating first in his class in 1933. Soon after his admission to the bar, he established a private law practice in Baltimore and began to pursue an active career in civil rights cases.

After representing the Baltimore branch of the National Association for the Advancement of Colored People (NAACP) in several court cases, Marshall was named special counsel for that organization in 1938. In 1940, he was named head of the NAACP Legal Defense and Education Fund. In this position, Marshall gained a national reputation as one of the most prominent civil rights attorneys in the country, frequently appearing before the Supreme Court.

Early Career. Among the landmark cases argued by Marshall were *Smith v. Allwright* (1944), in which he convinced the Supreme Court that racially restricted state primary elections were a violation of black citizens' voting rights, and *Morgan v. Virginia* (1946), in which the Court held unconstitutional Virginia laws requiring racially segregated seating on interstate transportation. *Sweatt v. Painter* (1950) resulted in the first steps toward racial integration at Southern state universities, while in *Shelley v. Kraemer* (1948) the Court found a violation of the 14th Amendment when a state court enforced racial discrimination in the private housing sector.

Marshall's most famous case before the Court was *Brown v. Board of Education* (1954), in which the unanimous Court decided that the "separate but equal" doctrine of racial segregation established by the Court in *Plessy v. Ferguson* (1896) was a violation of black public school students' 14th Amendment rights. In the following year he again appeared before the Supreme Court to argue *Lucy v. Adams* (1955), a case that resulted in the admission of the first black student to the University of Alabama. Marshall also appeared in *Cooper v. Aaron* (1958), which reinstated a permanent injunction requiring the immediate desegregation of the Little Rock, Arkansas, public schools. He also successfully defended the constitutional rights of black sit-in protesters in *Garner v. Louisiana* (1961).

Despite the protests of Southern senators, Pres. John F. Kennedy appointed Marshall to the U.S. Court of Appeals in the fall of 1961. Four years later, in the Johnson administration, the political climate of the country had begun to change, and Marshall accepted a presidential appointment to become U.S. solicitor general, the first time that a black person had been named to that post. Serving in this position, he successfully argued for the constitutionality of the Voting Rights Act of 1965 before the Supreme Court in *South Carolina v. Katzenbach* (1966). He also successfully argued that the federal government could criminally prosecute a sheriff and his co-conspirators who, with racial motivation, murdered three black men (*United States v. Price*, 1966).

Supreme Court. In 1967, after the resignation of Associate Justice Tom C. Clark, President Johnson nominated Marshall to the Supreme Court, noting that the appointment of the first black to serve on the Supreme Court was "the right thing to do, the right time to do it, the right man, and the right place." The nomination aroused bitter opposition from Sen. Strom Thurmond and other Southern senators, but he was confirmed by the full Senate on August 30, 1967, on a sixty-nine to eleven vote.

Early in his tenure, Marshall generally concurred with the liberal judicial position of the Warren Court. After Warren's retirement, however, with the more conservative orientation of the Burger Court, Marshall dissented more frequently, and, together with Associate Justice William Brennan, often enunciated the remaining liberal views on the Court.

On the Supreme Court, Marshall maintained his strong support of efforts to end racial discrimination, including segregation in the public schools. He joined the unanimous Court in *Green v. County School Board* (1968), which held that a school district's plan to desegregate by permitting students to choose which school to attend is unconstitutional unless the school board proves that the plan "promises meaningful and immediate progress toward disestablishing state-approved segregation." He joined the dissenting opinions in *Moose Lodge No. 107 v. Irvis* (1972), which argued that in granting a liquor license to a private club that excluded blacks, there was sufficient state action behind the discrimination to violate the 14th Amendment. He joined the opinion of the Court in *Keyes v. Denver School District No. 1* (1973), which held that where plaintiffs have established that state officials intentionally segregated a portion of the school system, courts should presume that segregation of the rest of the school system was also intentional unless the school board can prove otherwise.

One of his most significant dissenting opinions came in *San Antonio Independent School District v. Rodriguez* (1973), in which he argued that education is a fundamental right and that the unequal system of funding public schools from local property taxes discriminates on the basis of wealth in violation of the equal protection clause of the 14th Amendment. He also dissented from the result in *Regents of the University of California v. Bakke* (1978), in which he argued that the use of racial quotas by state universities to remedy the effects of past discrimination did not violate the 14th Amendment.

Marshall also remained an outspoken advocate of expanded voting rights. He concurred in part and dissented in part in *Oregon v. Mitchell* (1970), agreeing with the Court that Congress had the power to lower the voting age in federal elections to 18, but dissenting from the majority's decision that Congress did not have the power to lower the age in state and local elections. He wrote the majority opinion in *Dunn v. Blumstein* (1972), holding that state durational residency requirements for voting violated the equal protection clause of the 14th Amendment. He joined Justice Brennan's opinion, concurring in part and dissenting in part, in *Mahan v. Howell* (1973), which held that the equal protection clause allows states more flexibility in state legislative redistricting than in congressional redistricting.

In regard to criminal procedure, Marshall wrote the majority opinion in *Benton v. Maryland* (1969), holding that the 5th Amendment protection against double jeopardy should be extended to defendants in state as well as federal courts. To this extent, the decision overturned the Court's prior decision in *Palko v. Connecticut* (1937). He was the lone dissenter in *Williams v. Florida* (1969), which held that six-member juries in state courts did not violate the criminal defendant's right to trial by jury. He also voted with the minority in *McKeiver v. Pennsylvania* (1971), supporting the right of juvenile defendants to a jury trial. He dissented again in *Johnson v. Louisiana* and *Apodaca v. Oregon* (1972), opposing the Court's decision that state jury convictions that are not unanimous do not violate the defendant's due process right requiring guilt to be proved beyond a reasonable doubt.

Marshall also joined Justice Brennan's dissenting opinion in *Scott v. Illinois* (1979), arguing that states should provide indigent defendants with legal counsel not only in cases where the defendant is actually sentenced to prison, but also in every case where the criminal statute authorizes a prison sentence. He concurred with the majority in *Furman v. Georgia* (1972), which held unconstitutional state capital punishment statutes and dissented in *Jurek v. Texas* (1976), in which the Court determined that capital punishment is not *per se* a violation of the 8th Amendment prohibition against cruel and unusual punishment and attempted to set down standards for the sentencing process in capital crimes.

On the conflict between obscenity and 1st Amendment rights, Marshall wrote the majority opinion in *Stanley v. Georgia* (1969), holding unconstitutional state laws that made the private possession of obscene materials a criminal offense. He joined the dissenting opinion in the landmark obscenity case of *Miller v. California* (1973), which established that juries had significant discretion to determine what is obscene in light of "community standards" and thus without 1st Amendment protection. The 1st Amendment right of free speech was also the central element in Marshall's majority opinion in *Amalgamated Food Employees Union v. Logan Valley Plaza* (1968), which held that strikers must be allowed to picket even on private property if that property is ordinarily open to the public. This decision was later overruled over Marshall's dissent.

Marshall joined the majority opinion in the landmark case of *Roe v. Wade* (1973), which held unconstitutional state anti-abortion laws. He dissented, however, in *Harris v. McRae* (1980), arguing that the restriction of Medicaid funding for abortions violates the equal protection rights of indigent women. He voted with the majority in *Taylor v. Louisiana* (1975), which struck down state jury selection procedures exempting women from jury duty as a violation of the 6th Amendment. Marshall dissented in *Rostker v. Goldberg* (1981), arguing that the exclusion of women from the requirement of registration for the military draft violates the right to equal protection of the laws.

In regard to environmental issues, Marshall spoke for the Court in both *Hodel v. Indiana* and *Hodel v. Virginia Surface Mining and Reclamation Association* (1981), holding that federal strip mining reclamation requirements did not infringe on the powers reserved to the states by the 10th Amendment and were a legitimate exercise of the constitutional power of Congress to regulate interstate commerce.

MATTHEWS, STANLEY

b. July 21, 1824; various legislative and judicial positions in Ohio; U.S. senator (1877-1879); associate justice, U.S. Supreme Court (1881-1889); d. March 22, 1889.

Stanley Matthews

Born in Cincinnati, Ohio, the son of the president of Woodward College, Matthews was educated at Kenyon College (Class of 1840) and studied law in Cincinnati. In 1842, he moved to Tennessee and was admitted to the bar, later establishing a private practice in Columbia. A supporter of James Polk, Matthews edited the weekly *Tennessee Democrat* in 1843 and after his return to Ohio the following year, he edited the *Cincinnati Morning Herald*. In 1848, he was elected clerk of the Ohio House of Representatives. He later served in the Ohio Senate (1855-1857) and as U.S. attorney for the southern district of Ohio (1858-1861). In 1863, after active service in the 23rd Ohio Infantry and 51st Ohio Volunteers, Matthews served as judge of the Cincinnati superior court, resigning two years later to pursue his private law practice. In 1881, after the resignation of Associate Justice Noah Swayne, Matthews was nominated to the Supreme Court by Pres. James Garfield.

Matthews's nomination to the Court in 1881 was actually his second; in 1880, his nomination by President Hayes had been rejected by the Senate on the grounds that Matthews's former railroad and corporate clients might exert undue influence on his judicial decisions. His subsequent nomination was confirmed by a majority of only one vote.

During his eight-year tenure on the Court, Matthews ruled on several important commercial and economic issues. In *Yick Wo v. Hopkins* (1886) he wrote the Court's opinion holding that a city licensing scheme that was administered in a racially discriminatory way was unconstitutional. He wrote the majority opinion in *Bowman v. Chicago and North Western Railway Company* (1888), in which the Court overturned a state law prohibiting the shipment of alcoholic beverages as a restriction of interstate trade. His most important constitutional decision came in the case of *Hurtado v. California* (1888), which held that states may charge private citizens with crimes without the prior indictment of a grand jury. His opinion was one of the Court's most important discussions of the meaning of "due process of law."

Matthews served on the Court until his death in Washington, D.C., in 1889.

MILLER, SAMUEL FREEMAN

b. April 5, 1816; associate justice, U.S. Supreme Court (1862-1890); d. October 13, 1890.

Born in Richmond, Kentucky, and having received a medical degree from Transylvania University in 1838, Miller began a law career relatively late in life. While practicing medicine in Barborville, Kentucky, he studied law in his spare time and was admitted to the bar in 1847, at age thirty-one. As an opponent of slavery, he moved his family to Keokuk, Iowa, in 1850, becoming a partner in a local law firm. After the Dred Scott decision (*Scott v. Sandford*, 1857), Miller became active in the Iowa Republican Party and was a candidate for governor in 1861. In 1862, Miller was appointed to the Supreme Court by Pres. Abraham Lincoln to fill the vacancy left by the resignation of Associate Justice John Campbell of Alabama.

Miller's career on the Court was long and influential. He was described by Chief Justice Salmon P. Chase as "beyond question the dominant personality" on the Court in his steadfast support of individual rights against vested interests. In the Reconstruction period he was a strong advocate of federal power. He wrote the dissenting opinion in *Ex parte Garland* (1867), in which Chief Justice Chase, Justices Swayne and Davis joined, supporting the requirement of loyalty oaths for lawyers, teachers, and ministers during the period immediately following the Civil War. Justice Miller wrote the dissent in *Hepburn v. Griswold* (1870) and was joined by Justices Swayne and Davis, arguing the right

Samuel Miller

of the federal government to issue unsecured currency. His position in this matter was adopted by the Court in an opinion written by Justice Strong in the second of the Legal Tender Cases, *Knox v. Lee* (1871). In *Ex parte Milligan* (1866), he agreed that the president does not have the right to declare martial law in areas not in open rebellion, but joined the partial dissent, which sought to maintain the right of Congress to do so "in time of public danger." Miller also voted with the majority in *Watson v. Jones* (1872), which limited the degree of interference of civil courts in controversies concerning property rights of religious societies. The Court stated three propositions, one of which a court must refer to in order to decide a case with this type of issue. Where the property rights in question depend on the doctrine, discipline, ecclesiastical law, role or custom, or church government, the court will consider a decision by the highest tribunal within that organization to be conclusive.

The most notable opinion in Miller's tenure on the bench occurred in the *Slaughterhouse Cases* (1873), which was argued before the Court by the man that Miller succeeded, John Campbell. Miller wrote the majority opinion, which upheld the right of states to grant monopolies to corporations, arguing that the inevitable economic discrimination this caused did not violate the "privileges or immunities" clause of the 14th Amendment.

In 1877, Miller served on the Electoral Commission, which resolved the controversy surrounding the presidential election of 1876. He remained active in Republican politics and was considered several times for the chief justiceship.

Miller served on the Court until his death in Washington, D.C., in 1890.

MINTON, SHERMAN

b. October 20, 1890; member, Indiana Public Service Commission (1933-1934); U.S. senator (1935-1941); judge, U.S. circuit court of appeals (1941-1949); associate justice, U.S. Supreme Court (1949-1956); d. April 9, 1965.

Sherman Minton

Born in Georgetown, Indiana, Minton was educated at Indiana University (Class of 1915) and received his law degree from Yale Law School in 1917. After brief private practice in New Albany, Indiana, he served as an Army captain in World War I, eventually returning to New Albany after the war to resume his professional career. In 1933, Minton accepted an appointment to the Indiana Public Service Commission, and in 1934 he was elected to the U.S. Senate. As a senator, he supported Roosevelt's unsuccessful "court-packing" plan of 1937. Defeated for reelection to the Senate, Minton was appointed judge of the U.S. Court of Appeals for the 7th Circuit. In 1949, after the death of Associate Justice Wiley Rutledge, Pres. Harry Truman appointed Minton to the Supreme Court.

While Minton maintained his liberal stand on labor issues, he proved to be a relatively hard-line anticommunist and conservative with regard to civil rights. He wrote the majority opinion in *United States v. Rabinowitz* (1950), which held that a warrantless search by police of the immediate area of an arrest is not a violation of the defendant's 4th Amendment rights. He dissented in *Teamsters Union v. Hanke* (1950), which upheld an injunction issued to a private employer to prevent union picketing at his place of business. In *Bailey v. Richardson* (1951), he voted to uphold the constitutionality of the dismissal of a federal employee accused of communist associations even though she had not been allowed to confront her accusers. He concurred in *Dennis v. United States* (1951), which upheld the conviction of several prominent leaders of the American Communist Party on the grounds that their activities presented a "clear and present danger" to the government of the United States. He joined the dissent in *Youngstown Sheet and Tube Company v. Sawyer* (1952), which held that the president did not have the constitutional authority to seize and operate industries vital to national security in times of labor unrest. He was the only dissenter in *Terry v. Adams* (1953), in which he voted to uphold the legality of a state primary process held by an exclusively white club, which, effectively, chose the nominee of the Democratic Party. Despite this opinion, Minton joined with all the other justices in the landmark case of *Brown v. Board of Education* (1954), which overturned state segregation laws in the public schools.

Minton's health declined in the later years of his tenure, and he resigned from the Supreme Court in 1956. He died in New Albany, Indiana, in 1965.

MOODY, WILLIAM HENRY

b. December 23, 1853; various judicial positions in Massachusetts; member, U.S. House of Representatives (1895-1902); U.S. secretary of the Navy (1902-1904); U.S. attorney general (1904-1906); associate justice, U.S. Supreme Court (1906-1910); d. July 2, 1917.

Born in Newbury, Massachusetts, Moody was educated at Phillips Academy and Harvard College (Class of 1876). He studied law at the Harvard Law School and in the office of Richard Dana and was admitted to the bar in 1878. Establishing a private practice in Haverhill, Massachusetts, Moody served as the city solicitor for two years (1888-1890). In 1890, he was appointed district attorney for the eastern district of Massachusetts, and he took part in the prosecution of the Lizzie Borden case. He was elected to the U.S. Congress in 1895 and in 1902 he was appointed secretary of the Navy in the Roosevelt administration. He later became attorney general, in which capacity he successfully argued the landmark antitrust case of *Swift and Company v. United States* (1905) before the Supreme Court. In 1906, after the resignation of Associate Justice Henry Brown, Pres. Theodore Roosevelt appointed Moody to the Supreme Court.

Moody's tenure on the Court was short, but he participated in several important constitutional decisions. He wrote the majority opinion in *Twining v. New Jersey* (1908), which held that the 5th Amendment constitutional protection against self-incrimination does not extend to state defendants under the 14th Amendment. His most important dissent came in the *Employers' Liability Cases* (1908), which held that Congress had gone beyond its power under the commerce clause in enacting the Federal Employers' Liability Act of 1906.

Ill health forced Moody's resignation from the Court in 1910. He died in Haverhill, Massachusetts, in 1917.

MOORE, ALFRED

b. May 21, 1755; attorney general of North Carolina (1782-1791); various legislative and judicial positions in North Carolina; associate justice, U.S. Supreme Court (1799-1804); d. October 15, 1810.

The son of Judge Maurice Moore and Ann Grange Moore, Alfred was born in New Hanover County, North Carolina, and educated in Boston. After studying law with his father and being admitted to the bar in 1775, he was married to Susanna Eagles. During the Revolution, he served in the 1st North Carolina Continental Regiment and, later, as a colonel of the militia. In 1782, he was elected attorney general of the state of North Carolina. He resigned from that post in 1791, due to his opposition to the creation of the conflicting office of solicitor general. The following year he was elected to the state House of Commons. In 1795, he was defeated in the General Assembly for election to the U.S. Senate.

President Adams nominated Moore to be a commissioner to negotiate a treaty with the Cherokee Nations in 1798, and in the same year he was elected by the General Assembly to be judge of superior court. With the death of fellow North Carolinian James Iredell in 1799, President Adams nominated Moore to become associate justice of the Supreme Court.

Moore served on the Court for only five years. His most notable opinion came in *Bas v. Tingy* (1800), in which he held that a national state of war (in this case with France) superseded the pursuit of private business dealings. In *Stuart v. Laird* (1803), all justices sitting agreed that the practice of and acquiescence in the Supreme Court justices also serving as circuit judges, commencing with the organization of the judicial system, was legal.

Among Moore's private interests was the State University of North Carolina, which he strongly supported and for which he served as a trustee (1789-1807). He resigned from the Supreme Court in 1804 and died in Bladen County, North Carolina, in 1810.

MURPHY, FRANK

b. April 13, 1890; mayor of Detroit (1930-1933); governor general of the Philippines (1933-1935); governor of Michigan (1937-1938); U.S. attorney general (1939-1940); associate justice, U.S. Supreme Court (1940-1949); d. July 19, 1949.

Born in Harbor Beach, Michigan, Murphy was educated at the University of Michigan (Class of 1912), from which he also received a law degree in 1914. After active service in World War I, he continued his law education at Lincoln's Inn in London and Trinity College in Dublin before returning to Detroit to establish a private law practice. In 1919, he was appointed assistant U.S. attorney for eastern Michigan, and he later served as judge of the recorder's court (1923-1930) and mayor of Detroit (1930-1933). In 1933, he was appointed by President Roosevelt to serve as governor general of the Philippines. Returning to the United States in 1936, he was elected governor of Michigan and served for one term. When he was defeated for reelection, Murphy was appointed attorney general in the Roosevelt administration and became known for his active enforcement of civil rights cases. In 1940, after the death of Associate Justice Pierce Butler, President Roosevelt appointed Murphy to the Supreme Court.

During his tenure on the Court, Murphy continued his strong commitment to the cause of civil liberties in clear contrast to the arch-conservative Butler, whom he had succeeded. Murphy wrote the majority opinion in *Thornhill v. Alabama* (1940), which held that peaceful picketing by labor unions is protected by the 1st Amendment. He joined the dissent in *Betts v. Brady* (1942), which argued unsuccessfully that the 6th and 14th Amendments require states to provide defendants with attorneys even if they cannot afford them. Murphy concurred in *West Virginia State Board of Education v. Barnette* (1943), which held that the 1st Amendment prohibited compulsory pledges of allegiance in the schools. He spoke for the Court in *Schneiderman v. United States* (1943), in which the Court held that the government must show by clear and convincing evidence that the defendant was not attached to the United States Constitution in order to revoke his naturalized citizenship. One of Murphy's most significant dissenting opinions came in *Korematsu v. United States* (1944), in which he spoke out against the wartime internment of Japanese-Americans. He again dissented in *United States v. United Mine Workers* (1947), which upheld the contempt conviction of union leader John L. Lewis.

Murphy served on the Supreme Court until his death in Detroit in 1949.

NELSON, SAMUEL

b. November 10, 1792; associate justice, New York Supreme Court (1831-1837); chief justice, New York Supreme Court (1837-1845); associate justice, U.S. Supreme Court (1845-1872); d. December 13, 1873.

The son of Scotch-Irish immigrants, Nelson was born in Hebron, New York, and received his early education at Washington Academy and Granville Academy. After graduating from Middlebury College in 1813, he studied law in the office of Savage & Woods and was admitted to the bar in 1817. In 1820, Nelson served as postmaster of Cortland,

New York, and as a presidential elector for James Monroe. Three years later, he was appointed judge of the sixth state circuit, serving in that position until 1831, when he was appointed to the state supreme court as an associate justice. From 1837 to 1845, he served as chief justice of that court. In 1845, more than a year after the death of Associate Justice Smith Thompson, Nelson was appointed to the Supreme Court by Pres. John Tyler.

Nelson's long service on the Court was characterized by his expertise in commercial, maritime, and international law. He played an important part in the Dred Scott Case (*Scott v. Sandford*, 1857), in which he wrote the opinion that was originally to have been that of the Court, dismissing the case as being outside its jurisdiction. In the final opinion of the Court in this case, he concurred with the majority, declaring the Missouri Compromise to be unconstitutional.

During the Civil War, Nelson remained a loyal Democrat, urging conciliation with the Southern states and opposing the unilateral growth in the powers of the executive branch and the military. In *Ex parte Milligan* (1866), he agreed that the president has no constitutional right to declare martial law in an area not in open rebellion. Nelson voted with the majority in *Hepburn v. Griswold* (1869), declaring the issuance of unsecured currency by the federal government during the Civil War to be unconstitutional. In 1871, when the Court voted to overturn this decision in *Knox v. Lee*, Nelson remained in opposition and dissented.

After the war, as an expert in maritime law, Nelson served as one of the commissioners to settle the Alabama claims (1871). The demands of this assignment and failing health forced him to resign from the Court in 1872. He died in Cooperstown, New York, in 1873.

O'CONNOR, SANDRA DAY

b. March 26, 1930; Arizona assistant attorney general (1965-1969); member, Arizona senate (1969-1975); judge, county superior court (1974-1979); judge, Arizona court of appeals (1979-1981); associate justice, U.S. Supreme Court (1981-).

Born in El Paso, Texas, and raised on a ranch in Arizona, O'Connor was educated at Stanford University (Class of 1950) and in 1952 received her law degree from Stanford University Law School, where she was a classmate of William Rehnquist, who was later her associate on the Supreme Court. Finding it impossible as a woman to find a suitable position in several West Coast law firms, O'Connor served as a deputy county attorney in San Mateo, California (1952-1953). After service in Germany as a civilian lawyer in the U.S. Army Quartermaster Corps (1953-1956), she returned to the United States and established a private practice in Maryvale, Arizona. There she served on several county and state commissions and became active in the

Sandra Day O'Connor

Republican Party. In 1965, she was appointed assistant attorney general for Arizona, and in 1969 she was named by the governor to fill a vacancy in the state senate. She was later reelected to the senate and became its majority leader in 1972. In 1974, she was elected judge of the Maricopa County Superior Court and served in that position until 1979, when she was named to the Arizona court of appeals.

In 1981, after the resignation of Associate Justice Potter Stewart, Pres. Ronald Reagan fulfilled one of his campaign promises by appointing O'Connor to be the first woman justice in the history of the Supreme Court. In her confirmation hearings, O'Connor elaborated on her relatively conservative judicial philosophy, and her early decisions on the Court maintained this orientation, except in some cases concerning defendants' rights.

She wrote the majority opinion in *Rose v. Lundy* (1982), which held that all claims by prison inmates must be reviewed by state courts before a writ of *habeas corpus* can be submitted to a federal court. In *Tibbs v. Florida* (1982), which upheld double jeopardy (being tried more than once for the same crime), she wrote for the Court that when the "weight of the evidence" rationale is used, a retrial is possible. *Arizona v. Rumsey* (1984), for which she also wrote the majority opinion, held that if the death penalty had not been imposed during initial sentencing, it could not be imposed during a retrial. O'Connor joined the dissent in *New York v. Quarles* (1984), which limited the Miranda warning by ruling that when public safety is compromised,

police do not have to advise a suspected criminal of his or her rights. The next year, however, her opinion in *United States v. Hensley* (1985) supported a broadening of the warrantless stop and frisk laws of the 1960's *(Terry v. Ohio)*. *Terry* had permitted stopping a person only on "reasonable suspicion" that a crime was about to be committed, while *Hensley* also allows a stop on the suspicion of previous crimes.

Regarding job discrimination, she spoke for the Court in the majority opinion in *Ford v. Equal Employment Opportunity Commission* (1982), which allowed an employer to lessen liability in a job discrimination suit by making a job offer to the employee initiating the suit. Even if the job offer is not accepted, the employer is no longer liable for back pay to the employee. In *Equal Employment Opportunity Commission v. Wyoming* (1983), a case that declared state and local public employees covered by a federal law that banned job discriminations because of age, O'Connor joined the dissent. In 1983, in *Akron v. Akron Center*, she was responsible for writing the dissenting opinion against the Court's opinion that upheld *Roe v. Wade*, a 1973 decision that approved abortion with restriction for women in the first three months of pregnancy.

She concurred with the Court in *Grove City College v. Ball* (1984), which held that Title IX (Educational Amendments, 1972) could be enforced only on those programs receiving federal aid, not on whole schools because some of the students individually received federal aid. She voted with the majority in *Lynch et al. v. Donnelly et al.* (1984), which declared the use of public funds for Christmas crèches or Nativity scenes reminders of an "historical religious event" and therefore constitutional.

PATERSON, WILLIAM

b. December 24, 1745; attorney general of New Jersey (1776-1783); United States senator (1789-1790); governor of New Jersey (1790-1793); associate justice, U.S. Supreme Court (1793-1806); d. September 9, 1806.

Born in County Antrim, Ireland, the son of Richard and Mary Paterson, who settled in New Jersey in 1750, Paterson was educated at Princeton (Class of 1763) and studied law in the office of Richard Stockton, being admitted to the bar in 1769. In 1775, he served as a delegate to the New Jersey provincial congress and in 1776 as member of the state constitutional convention. He was also named attorney general. Paterson was elected to the Continental Congress in 1780, but declined the office.

In 1787, he was a delegate to the federal constitutional convention at Philadelphia and introduced the New Jersey Plan, by which he proposed that the states be represented equally in a unicameral legislature. Paterson was one of the signers of the proposed Constitution and worked for its ratification. In 1789, he was elected to the U.S. Senate and in 1790, on the death of William Livingston, was chosen to succeed him as governor. With the resignation of Thomas Johnson from the Supreme Court in 1793, President Washington nominated Paterson to become an associate justice.

Paterson's contribution to the history of the federal judiciary began during his service in the Senate. As a leading member of the Judiciary Committee, he co-authored the Judiciary Act of 1789 with Sen. Oliver Ellsworth, who later became chief justice. An important provision of this act implied the right of the Supreme Court to judge the constitutionality of all legislation. While governor of New Jersey, Paterson directed the codification of the state's laws and court procedures.

On the Supreme Court, Paterson was a strong nationalist, active in the prosecution of cases under the Sedition Laws. His most important opinion, *Vanhorne's Lessee v. Dorrance* (1794), was issued in circuit court and was one of the first to defend the right of the federal courts to declare state laws unconstitutional. In 1801, with the death of Chief Justice Oliver Ellsworth, the Hamiltonian Federalists urged Paterson's promotion to that post, but President Adams appointed John Marshall.

Paterson was married twice; in 1779, to Cornelia Bell and, after her death, in 1785 to Euphemia White. He served on the court until his death in Albany, New York, in September 1806. Paterson, New Jersey, is named after him.

PECKHAM, RUFUS WHEELER JR.

b. November 8, 1838; various judicial positions in New York; associate justice, U.S. Supreme Court (1895-1909); d. October 24, 1909.

Born in Albany, New York, the son of Rufus Peckham Sr., later a justice of the New York Supreme Court, the younger Peckham was educated at Albany Boys' Academy and Union College and studied law in his father's office, the firm of Peckham & Tremain in Albany. He was admitted to the bar in 1859 and began to practice in his father's firm. Peckham served as district attorney of Albany County from 1869 to 1872 and as corporation counsel of the city of Albany from 1881 to 1883. In 1883, he was elected a justice of the New York Supreme Court and then, three years later, judge of the New York Court of Appeals, the state's highest court. In 1895, after the death of Associate Justice Howell Jackson, Pres. Grover Cleveland appointed Peckham to the Supreme Court.

During his nearly fifteen-year tenure on the Court, Peckham distinguished himself as an extreme conservative and an active proponent of aggressive judicial enforcement of what he took to be federal constitutional rights. He wrote the majority opinion in *Allgeyer v. Louisiana* (1897), in which he argued that the 14th Amendment guarantees the right of citizens to make contracts without unreasonable interference by state regulation. He dissented in *Holden v. Hardy* (1898), a case that held setting maximum work hours of mine workers to be a valid exercise of a state's police power. His position was later supported in the famous case of *Lochner v. New York* (1905), for which he wrote the majority opinion. This case is now widely criticized as an example of improper judicial intrusion into legislative decisions on matters of social welfare. He also spoke for the Court in *Maxwell v. Dow* (1900), which overturned the requirement of twelve-person juries in state courts.

In one of the Insular Cases (*Downes v. Bidwell*, 1901), Peckham dissented because of his belief that the constitutional status of the residents of unincorporated American territories was not a matter that should be determined by Congress alone. One of Peckham's last opinions, *Ex parte Young* (1908), established the precedent that the federal judiciary may enjoin the enforcement of a state law if its constitutionality is in question.

Peckham served on the Court until his death at Altamont, New York, in 1909.

PITNEY, MAHLON

b. February 5, 1858; various legislative and judicial positions in New Jersey; member, U.S. House of Representatives (1895-1899); associate justice, U.S. Supreme Court (1912-1922); d. December 9, 1924.

Born in Morristown, New Jersey, and educated at Princeton (Class of 1879), Pitney studied law in the office of his father and was admitted to the bar in 1885. Politically, Pitney identified himself with the Republican Party, and he served two terms in the U.S. House of Representatives. In 1899, he returned to his home state and was elected to the New Jersey Senate, becoming its president in 1901. In the same year he was appointed to the state supreme court, a position in which he served until 1908, when he was nominated to become chancellor of the state, a post that his father had once held. In 1912, after the death of Associate Justice John Harlan, Pres. William Taft appointed Pitney to the Supreme Court.

During his eleven years on the Court, Pitney distinguished himself as a conservative and as an opponent of the unrestricted growth of labor unions. He wrote the majority opinion in *Coppage v. Kansas* (1915), in which the Court struck down a state law prohibiting employment contracts that called for workers to sign a pledge that they would not join a labor union. This decision was further defined in his majority opinions in *Hitchman Coal and Coke Company v. Mitchell* (1917), and *Eagle Glass and Manufacturing Company v. Rowe* (1917), which held that if a majority of workers had signed nonunion pledges, their employer could obtain a court injunction barring further union organizing activities, which interfered with that arrangement, at his place of business. He spoke for the Court in *Duplex Printing Press Company v. Deering* (1921), which invoked the antitrust laws to uphold the right of employers to obtain injunctions against union boycotts.

In regard to the intervention of the federal government into the private sector, Pitney dissented in the *Shreveport*

Rate Case (1914), in which he opposed any congressional regulation of intrastate rail tariffs. In *Eisner v. Macomber* (1920), the Court held that the federal government did not have the right to tax stock dividends. His most significant majority opinion occurred in *Mountain Timber Company v. Washington* (1917), in which the Court upheld the constitutionality of state workmen's compensation laws.

After suffering a severe stroke in 1922, Pitney resigned from the Court and died in Washington, D.C., in 1924.

POWELL, LEWIS FRANKLIN JR.

b. September 19, 1907; member, Richmond Board of Education (1952-1969); president, Virginia Board of Education (1968-1969); associate justice, U.S. Supreme Court (1971-).

Lewis F. Powell, Jr.

Born in Suffolk, Virginia, Powell was educated at Washington and Lee University, receiving his B.A. in 1929 and his law degree in 1931. In the following year, he received a master of laws degree from Harvard Law School. After being admitted to the bar, Powell joined a prominent Richmond law firm to which he returned after active service in World War II. He also entered public service as a member of the Richmond Board of Education during the period of its peaceful desegregation. In 1968, he was appointed president of the Virginia State Board of Education. Powell also gained a national reputation in legal circles as president of the American Bar Association (1964-1965) and president of the American College of Trial Lawyers (1968-1969). In

1971, with the resignation of Associate Justice Hugo Black, Pres. Richard Nixon appointed Powell to the Supreme Court.

Although Powell had no previous judicial experience before his appointment to the Court, his previous bar positions had made his conservative philosophy well known. He wrote the majority opinion in *Kastigar v. United States* (1972), which restricted the interpretation of the 5th Amendment self-incrimination guarantees. He dissented in *Furman v. Georgia* (1972), opposing the Court's blanket ruling against state capital punishment laws. This position was further elaborated in Powell's opinion in *Profitt v. Florida* (1976), in which he argued that the death penalty is not, in and of itself, "cruel and unusual punishment," and that Florida's death sentencing procedures were not arbitrary and capricious.

Powell voted with the Court in *United States v. Nixon* (1974), which held that executive privilege did not justify withholding the "Watergate tapes" from use in a criminal trial. He also spoke for the Court in *First National Bank of Boston v. Bellotti* (1978), which held unconstitutional a state law barring corporations from contributing funds to support a referendum issue in which its commercial interests are not directly involved.

Powell cast the deciding vote in *Regents of University of California v. Bakke* (1978). His opinion, which was therefore critical to the outcome, was not joined by any other justice. He argued that the use of racial quotas in admission to public universities was involved but that it might be permissible to take into account the need for racial diversity by some other less rigorous means. He consistently voted against judical requirements of mandatory busing as a means of desegregation of the public schools. Powell has been viewed as a moderate on the Court, preferring specific analyses of individual cases to the creation and application of more sweeping, less flexible rules.

REED, STANLEY FORMAN

b. December 31, 1884; member, Kentucky General Assembly (1912-1916); general counsel, Federal Farm Board (1929-1932); general counsel, Reconstruction Finance Corporation (1932-1935); U.S. solicitor general (1935-1938); associate justice, U.S. Supreme Court (1938-1957); d. April 2, 1980.

Born in Maysville, Kentucky, Reed was educated at Kentucky Wesleyan College, from which he graduated in 1902, and at Yale University, where he received a second B.A. degree in 1906. He studied law at the University of Virginia, Columbia University, and the Sorbonne and was admitted to the Kentucky bar in 1910. After establishing a private practice in Maysville, he was elected to the state legislature. During World War I he served in the Army in the intelligence branch.

Reed's first position in the federal government came in 1929, when he accepted a presidential appointment to serve as general counsel for the Federal Farm Board. He remained

Stanley Reed

in Washington at the start of the Roosevelt administration, serving as general counsel to the Reconstruction Finance Corporation. Reed proved to be an active supporter of the programs of the New Deal, and he was successful in his defense of the Tennessee Valley Authority before the Supreme Court (*Ashwander v. Tennessee Valley Authority*, 1936) as U.S. solicitor general. In 1938, after the resignation of Associate Justice George Sutherland, President Roosevelt appointed Reed to the Supreme Court.

During his long service on the Court, Reed remained a philosophical supporter of federal intervention in social and economic affairs. He wrote the majority opinion in *United States v. Rock Royal Cooperative* (1939), which upheld the authority of the federal government to control and regulate the price of milk. He spoke for the Court in *United States v. Appalachian Electric Power Co.* (1940), establishing wide congressional authority over hydroelectric power and inland navigation. His majority opinion in *Gray v. Powell* (1941) upheld an administrative interpretation of the Bituminous Coal Act of 1937 that determined who was a "producer" of coal under the act.

In the field of civil rights, Reed wrote the majority opinion in the landmark civil rights case of *Smith v. Allwright* (1944), in which the Court held that political parties, as essential components of the electoral process, are required by the equal protection clause of the 14th Amendment to allow minority groups to participate in their primaries. He also spoke for the Court in *Morgan v. Virginia* (1946),

which prohibited segregated seating in interstate transportation. In *Brown v. Board of Education* (1954), he joined with all of his colleagues in declaring public school segregation unconstitutional.

On labor issues, Reed balanced the right of the workers against the public order. He dissented in *Milk Wagon Drivers Union v. Meadowmoor Dairies* (1941), which upheld an injunction against a labor union's picketing, where the controversy had been attended by acts of violence. However, in *United Public Workers v. Mitchell* (1947), he wrote the majority opinion, which upheld laws limiting the political activity of federal employees. He joined the dissent in *Youngstown Sheet and Tube Co. v. Sawyer* (1952), which held that President Truman did not have the authority to nationalize essential industries to prevent a strike.

Reed resigned from the Supreme Court in 1957. In retirement, he served briefly on President Eisenhower's Civil Rights Commission and continued to hear cases in the District of Columbia Court of Claims and Court of Appeals. He died in Huntington, New York, in 1980.

REHNQUIST, WILLIAM HUBBS

b. October 1, 1924; assistant U.S. attorney general (1969-1971); associate justice, U.S. Supreme Court (1971-   ).

Born in Milwaukee, Wisconsin, Rehnquist was educated at Stanford University (Class of 1948) and received a master's degree in political science from Harvard in 1950

William H. Rehnquist

and a law degree from Stanford Law School in 1952. After serving as clerk to Supreme Court Justice Robert Jackson, Rehnquist established a private law practice in Phoenix, Arizona, in 1953. There he became active in the conservative wing of the Republican Party, and with the election of Richard Nixon in 1968, Rehnquist received a presidential appointment to serve as assistant attorney general in the Office of Legal Counsel of the Justice Department. In 1971, with the resignation of Associate Justice John Harlan, President Nixon appointed Rehnquist to the Supreme Court.

Although he had no prior judicial experience, his conservative background was well known. He dissented in *Furman v. Georgia* (1972), in which he argued that the death penalty is not cruel and unusual punishment. He also dissented in *Roe v. Wade* (1973), arguing that the Constitution contains no "privacy" right to an abortion. Rehnquist also joined the dissent in *Keyes v. Denver School District No. 1* (1973), arguing that the gerrymandering of some school attendance zones should not give rise to the presumption that *de jure* intentional segregation was occurring throughout the entire school district. Because of his prior association with the Nixon administration, Rehnquist did not participate in the Watergate Tapes Case (*United States v. Nixon*, 1974).

Rehnquist spoke for the Court in *Edelman v. Jordan* (1974), which held unconstitutional the district court judgment requiring a state to spend public funds to pay retroactive benefits to welfare recipients. This decision, however, was significantly narrowed in *Fitzpatrick v. Bitzer* (1976), for which Rehnquist also wrote the opinion for the Court. He joined the dissent in *Davis v. Passman* (1979), which upheld the right to sue congressmen for money damages for the violation of 5th Amendment rights. He also dissented in *United Steelworkers of America v. Weber* (1979), where he held that a company's affirmative action program violated the Civil Rights Act of 1964. Rehnquist joined a similar argument in *University of California Regents v. Bakke* (1978), which invalidated (with no majority opinion) certain types of racial quotas in state educational institutions.

In *Rostker v. Goldberg* (1981), Rehnquist wrote the majority opinion upholding the constitutionality of a law excluding women from registering for the draft. He also spoke for the Court in *Dames & Moore v. Regan* (1981), which upheld the right of Pres. Jimmy Carter to release frozen Iranian assets as part of an agreement for the safe return of the American hostages from Teheran. He wrote for the Court in *New York v. Quarles* (1984), a five to four decision that permitted an exception to the rights of criminal suspects established by *Miranda v. Arizona* (1966). His decision in *Hunter v. Underwood* (1985) was based on the equal protection section of the 14th Amendment. The decision struck down an Alabama constitutional clause barring those convicted of numerous petty crimes, including moral turpitude, from voting. Rehnquist held that racial discrimination had been the motivation for Alabama instituting the provision in 1901 and that it was therefore unconstitutional.

ROBERTS, OWEN JOSEPHUS

b. May 2, 1875; assistant district attorney, Philadelphia (1901-1904); special deputy U.S. attorney general, Pennsylvania (1918); special U.S. attorney (1924-1930); associate justice, U.S. Supreme Court (1930-1945); chairman, Pearl Harbor Inquiry Board (1941-1942); d. May 17, 1955.

Born in Philadelphia, Roberts graduated from the University of Pennsylvania (Class of 1895) and then from its law school, being admitted to the bar in 1898. From 1898 to 1918 he served on the faculty of the law school, during which time he also served as an assistant district attorney in Philadelphia and as a deputy U.S. attorney general in the prosecution of espionage cases during World War I. During the Coolidge administration, Roberts was appointed special prosecutor in cases connected with the "Teapot Dome" scandal, and he was personally responsible for the conviction of former Interior Secretary Albert Fall. In 1930, after the death of Associate Justice Edward Sanford and the rejection by the Senate of the nomination of John J. Parker, Pres. Herbert Hoover appointed Roberts to the Supreme Court.

During the early years of his tenure on the Court, Roberts distinguished himself as a judicial conservative, opposing the ideological direction of the New Deal. He wrote the majority opinion in *Railroad Retirement Board v.*

Owen J. Roberts

Alton Railroad Co. (1935), which struck down the Railroad Retirement Act of 1934. In *United States v. Butler* (1936), Roberts wrote the majority opinion that overturned the Agricultural Adjustment Act of 1933. However, he joined the concurring opinion in *Ashwander v. Tennessee Valley Authority* (1936), which upheld the constitutionality of Congress's exercise of power over the TVA.

In matters of interstate commerce, Roberts showed a more liberal viewpoint. He wrote the majority opinion in *Nebbia v. New York* (1934), which upheld the right of states to regulate private business in the interests of the public. In *Mulford v. Smith* (1939), Roberts upheld the constitutionality of tobacco supply and marketing quotas under the Agricultural Adjustment Act of 1938.

Roberts's record on civil rights was mixed. He spoke for the Court in *Grovey v. Townsend* (1935), which held that since political parties are private organizations, the equal protection clause of the 14th Amendment could not be invoked to force them to accept minority members. In *Herndon v. Lowry* (1937), however, his majority opinion overturned the conviction of a black political activist on the grounds that the activist did not pose a "clear and present danger" to the government of the United States. He joined the dissent in *Korematsu v. United States* (1944), opposing the wartime internment of Japanese-Americans.

In 1941, Roberts was appointed by President Roosevelt to head a commission that investigated the preparedness of the military at the time of Pearl Harbor. Roberts resigned

from the Supreme Court in 1945 and served as the dean of the University of Pennsylvania Law School from 1948 to 1951. He died in Chester Springs, Pennsylvania, in 1955.

RUTLEDGE, JOHN

b. September 1739; member, Continental Congress (1774-1776, 1782-1783); president, South Carolina General Assembly (1776-1778); governor of South Carolina (1779-1782); member, Constitutional Convention (1787); associate justice, U.S. Supreme Court (1789-1791); chief justice, South Carolina Supreme Court (1791-1795); chief justice pro tem, U.S. Supreme Court (1795); member, South Carolina Assembly (1798-1799); d. June 21, 1800.

John Rutledge

Born in Charleston, South Carolina, Rutledge received his early education from his father and later studied law at the Inns of Court in London, being admitted to the bar in 1760. After returning to Charleston, he was elected to the provincial Commons House, in which he served until the outbreak of the Revolutionary War. Rutledge was active in the Stamp Act Congress of 1765 and was elected to the First Continental Congress in 1774. He was also instrumental in the drafting of the South Carolina constitution and was elected the first president of the state General Assembly in 1776. He was elected governor in 1779 and struggled through the following three years of battles and British occupation of the state. Following the evacuation of the British, Rutledge was elected to the U.S. Congress. He was later elected to represent his state in the Constitutional Convention of 1787.

During the convention's debate on the manner of government, Rutledge distinguished himself as a conservative, urging that wealth be a criterion for voting rights and that the president be elected by the Congress rather than directly by the people. In 1789, Pres. George Washington appointed Rutledge to become one of the first associate justices of the U.S. Supreme Court; Rutledge at first accepted this appointment, but he never attended any sessions in Washington and resigned two years later to become chief justice of the South Carolina Supreme Court.

In June 1795, Rutledge wrote to President Washington, suggesting himself as a suitable replacement for Chief Justice John Jay, who was about to retire. Washington accepted the suggestion and placed Rutledge's name in nomination, and although Rutledge actually served as chief justice for one term, his increasingly erratic behavior and apparent insanity persuaded the Senate finally to reject his nomination in December 1795.

Following his rejection by the Senate, Rutledge became a virtual recluse and died in Charleston in 1800.

RUTLEDGE, WILEY BLOUNT JR.

b. July 20, 1894; judge, U.S. district court of appeals (1939-1943); associate justice, U.S. Supreme Court (1943-1949); d. September 10, 1949.

Born in Cloverport, Kentucky, Rutledge was educated at Maryville College and at the University of Wisconsin (Class of 1914) and spent several years after his graduation as a teacher. He received his law education at the University of Colorado and was admitted to the bar in 1922. After a short period of private practice, Rutledge began to teach law on the graduate level, serving as an associate professor of law at the University of Colorado (1924-1926), professor and later dean of the law school at Washington University (1926-1935), and at the State University of Iowa (1935-1939). In 1939, he accepted a presidential appointment to become judge of the federal Court of Appeals in Washington, D.C. In 1943, with the resignation of Associate Justice James Byrnes, Pres. Franklin Roosevelt appointed Rutledge to the Supreme Court.

Rutledge distinguished himself as a liberal during his six-year tenure on the Court. He voted with the majority in *West Virginia State Board of Education v. Barnette* (1943), which struck down a state law requiring every student in the public schools to pledge allegiance to the flag. He also concurred in *Schneiderman v. United States* (1943), which held that alleged communist affiliations are not sufficient grounds for revocation of naturalized citizenship. He dissented in *In re Yamashita* (1946), in which he sharply criticized the judicial procedure in a war crimes trial that resulted in the execution of the defendant. He joined the majority in *Morgan v. Virginia* (1946), one of the first important rulings against racial segregation in the South. He dissented in *Everson v. Board of Education of Ewing Township* (1947), opposing the expenditure of public funds for the transportation of students in parochial schools. He was also in the minority in *United States v. United Mine Workers* (1947), in which the Court upheld the contempt conviction of union leader John L. Lewis. One of his last opinions came in a dissent in *Wolf v. Colorado* (1949), in which the majority held that although evidence obtained in violation of the 4th Amendment is inadmissible in federal courts, the defendant is not denied due process if it is admitted in state courts.

Rutledge served on the Court until his death in York, Maine, in 1949.

SANFORD, EDWARD TERRY

b. July 23, 1865; assistant U.S. attorney general (1907-1908); judge, U.S. district court (1908-1923); associate justice, U.S. Supreme Court (1923-1930); d. March 8, 1930.

Born in Knoxville, Tennessee, Sanford was educated at the University of Tennessee (Class of 1883) and received his law training at Harvard Law School. He was admitted to the bar in 1888 and established a private practice in Knoxville in 1890. In 1907, he was appointed assistant attorney general by Pres. Theodore Roosevelt and then served as a U.S. district court judge from 1908 to 1923. In 1923, after the resignation of Associate Justice Mahlon Pitney, Pres. Warren Harding appointed Sanford to the Supreme Court.

In his seven-year tenure on the Court, Sanford distinguished himself as a liberal in economic matters although his position was more uncertain with regard to civil rights. He joined the dissent in *Adkins v. Children's Hospital* (1923), in which he argued unsuccessfully for the right of the District of Columbia to impose minimum wage standards. He also sided with the minority in *Tyson & Brother v. Banton* (1927), arguing that the states had the right to regulate the sale of theater tickets by ticket brokers.

Sanford wrote the majority opinion in *Gitlow v. New York* (1925), which established the precedent that the freedom of expression established by the 1st Amendment protects against state interference as well as federal interference. In *Corrigan v. Buckley* (1926), he wrote the majority opinion, which held that civil rights protected by the 5th and 14th Amendments do not apply where there has been no governmental interference with those rights, but only private interference. In *Whitney v. California* (1927), he spoke for the Court in upholding a state law that prohibited public declarations of support for violent revolution. He dissented in *United States v. Schwimmer* (1929), however, which upheld the denial of naturalized citizenship to an applicant

Edward Terry Sanford

who declared that she would not, as required, bear arms in defense of the country.

Sanford served on the Supreme Court until his death in Washington, D.C., in 1930.

SHIRAS, GEORGE JR.

b. January 26, 1832; associate justice, U.S. Supreme Court (1892-1903); d. August 2, 1924.

Born in Pittsburgh, Pennsylvania, and educated at Ohio University and Yale College (Class of 1853), Shiras began his law studies at Yale Law School and completed them in the office of Judge Hopewell Hepburn of Pittsburgh. He was admitted to the bar in 1855 and after brief private practice in Iowa, returned to Pittsburgh to become the legal partner of Judge Hepburn. In this capacity, Shiras was involved as an attorney for the growing railroad, coal, steel, and iron industries in western Pennsylvania. Shiras's interest in partisan politics was slight and in 1882, he declined nomination by the Pennsylvania legislature to the U.S. Senate. In 1888, he served as a presidential elector. Four years later, after the death of Associate Justice Joseph Bradley, Pres. Benjamin Harrison appointed Shiras to the Supreme Court.

Although Shiras's nomination to the Court was initially opposed in the Senate on the grounds that his previous industrial clients would exercise undue influence upon his rulings, he was confirmed unanimously. His most notable opinion on the Court occurred early in his tenure in the income tax case of *Pollock v. Farmers Loan & Trust Company* (1895). After initially supporting the constitutionality of a federal income tax, Shiras changed his vote and thereby created the majority, which overturned the statute. He joined the dissent in *DeLima v. Bidwell* (1901), in which he argued unsuccessfully that full constitutional rights should be extended to the residents of American territories. Another of his minority opinions occurred in *Champion v. Ames* (1903), in which he opposed federal restrictions on the interstate shipment of lottery tickets as restrictive of commerce.

Shiras retired from the Court in 1903 at the age of seventy-one. He died in Pittsburgh in 1924.

STEVENS, JOHN PAUL

b. April 20, 1920; various federal legislative and judicial positions; judge, U.S. circuit court of appeals (1970-1975); associate justice, U.S. Supreme Court (1975-).

Born in Chicago, the son of a wealthy local family, Stevens was educated at the University of Chicago (Class of 1941). After service during World War II as a naval intelligence officer, he attended Northwestern University Law School, graduating first in his class and receiving a law degree in 1947. From 1947 to 1948, he served as clerk to Supreme Court Justice Wiley Rutledge. Stevens entered private practice in Chicago in 1948 and became an authority on antitrust law. For this reason, he was appointed associate

John P. Stevens

counsel of a House subcommittee investigating monopolies (1951-1952) and later a member of a federal commission that studied antitrust laws (1953-1955). Stevens also taught law at Northwestern University Law School (1953) and at the University of Chicago Law School (1954-1955). In 1970, he accepted a presidential appointment to become judge of the U.S. Court of Appeals for the 7th Circuit. In 1975, after the resignation of Associate Justice William O. Douglas, Pres. Gerald Ford appointed Stevens to the Supreme Court.

During his tenure on the Court, Stevens distinguished himself by an eclectic and unpredictable jurisprudence. He dissented in *National League of Cities v. Usery* (1976), arguing that Congress does have the power, under the commerce clause of Article I of the Constitution, to impose minimum wage standards for employees of municipal and state governments. He wrote the majority opinion in *Jurek v. Texas* (1976), which held that the death penalty is not by definition "cruel and unusual punishment" and that the sentencing procedures for capital crimes in Texas were not so arbitrary as to violate the 8th and 14th Amendments. Further elaborating on this issue, Stevens spoke for the Court in *Roberts v. Louisiana* (1976), which held that the death penalty cannot be mandatory for certain classes of crimes.

Stevens dissented in *Marshall v. Barlows Inc.* (1978), arguing that warrantless inspections by the Occupational Safety and Health Administration (OSHA) did not violate the 4th Amendment. He also joined with Justice Rehnquist's opinion, concurring in part and dissenting in part, in *Butz v. Economou* (1978), which argued for absolute immunity from civil liability for federal officials acting in the course of their duties. He concurred in part and dissented in part in *University of California Regents v. Bakke* (1978), arguing that because the Civil Rights Act of 1964 prohibited denying Bakke admission to medical school because of his race, the Court need not have considered the constitutionality of the university's entire special admissions program. In *Fullilove v. Klutznick* (1980) he dissented, arguing that the requirement that 10% of federal funds used in public works projects must go toward contracts for minority businesses violates the 5th Amendment.

STEWART, POTTER

b. January 23, 1915; member, Cincinnati City Council (1950-1953); vice-mayor, Cincinnati (1952-1953); judge, U.S. Court of Appeals (1954-1958); associate justice, U.S. Supreme Court (1958-1981); d. December 7, 1985.

Potter Stewart

Born in Jackson, Michigan, Stewart was educated at Yale College (Class of 1937) and received his law degree from Yale Law School in 1941. Soon after establishing a private law practice in New York City, he enlisted in the Navy for service during World War II. In 1947, he moved to Cincinnati, where his father had been elected mayor, and became personally involved in municipal politics, serving on the city council and eventually in the capacity of vice-mayor. In 1954, Stewart received a presidential appointment to become judge of the U.S. District Court of Appeals for the 6th Circuit, and during the subsequent years of the Eisenhower administration, he also served on the committee for the White House Conference on Education and on the Committee for Court Administration for the Judicial Conference of the United States. In 1958, after the resignation of Associate Justice Harold Burton, President Eisenhower appointed Stewart to the Supreme Court.

During his tenure on the Court, Stewart was particularly interested in criminal procedure. He wrote the majority opinion in *Elkins v. United States* (1960), which prohibited the use in federal criminal trials of evidence illegally obtained by state authorities. He also joined the dissent in the landmark defendants' rights cases of *Escobedo v. Illinois* (1964) and *Miranda v. Arizona* (1966), which he judged to be an unjustified restriction on police procedure. He also dissented in *In re Gault* (1967), opposing the introduction of due process rights in juvenile courts. He wrote the majority opinion in *Katz v. United States* (1967), which prohibited unauthorized wiretaps where the defendant has a reasonable expectation of privacy as a violation of the 4th Amendment protection against unreasonable searches and seizures. He also wrote the majority opinion in *Chimel v. California* (1969), which restricted the extent of warrantless searches police could make at the time of a suspect's arrest. In *Coolidge v. New Hampshire* (1971), Stewart, again speaking for the Court, further restricted the right of police to obtain evidence without a search warrant issued by a neutral and detached magistrate.

Stewart wrote the majority decision in the important civil rights case of *Jones v. Alfred H. Mayer Co.* (1968), which construed the 1870 civil rights statute to prohibit private racial discrimination in the sale or leasing of property as well as discrimination under the guise of state law. He also spoke for the Court in *Hills v. Gautreaux* (1976), which held that where federal agencies had deliberately located public housing to avoid integrating white neighborhoods, the lower court order to remedy the situation could affect construction plans beyond the limits of the city where the discrimination occurred. He dissented, however, in *Fullilove v. Klutznick* (1980), in which he opposed the use of quotas to correct the effects of racial discrimination against minority businesses.

Stewart frequently was seen as a moderate between liberal and conservative camps and his vote was often decisive in Court judgments. Stewart retired from the Supreme Court in 1981 and died in Hanover, N.H.

STONE, HARLAN FISKE

b. October 11, 1872; U.S. attorney general (1924-1925); associate justice, U.S. Supreme Court (1925-1941); chief justice, U.S. Supreme Court (1941-1946); d. April 22, 1946.

Born in Chesterfield, New Hampshire, to a local farming family, Stone originally intended to pursue a career in agronomy and studied briefly at the Massachusetts Agricultural School before transferring to Amherst College and beginning premedical studies. At Amherst, Stone's career plans changed again, with an increasing interest in the law. It was also at Amherst that Stone gained the friendship of Calvin Coolidge, the man who would later appoint him to the Supreme Court.

After graduation from Amherst in 1894 and a year of teaching high school science, Stone began his law studies at the Columbia University Law School, receiving his degree and being admitted to the New York bar in 1898. The following year, he joined the prominent Wall Street law firm of Sullivan & Cromwell and was also appointed to the faculty of the Columbia Law School. In 1899 he also married, to Agnes Harvey. He served as dean of the Columbia Law School from 1910 to 1923. In 1915, Stone published a series of his Columbia lectures under the title *Law and Its Administration*.

In 1924, in the wake of the "Teapot Dome" scandal and the widespread corruption of the Harding administration, Stone was appointed attorney general by his old college friend, Pres. Calvin Coolidge. In this position, Stone reorganized the Federal Bureau of Investigation and suggested the appointment of J. Edgar Hoover as its director. In the following year, after the resignation of Associate Justice Joseph McKenna, President Coolidge appointed Stone to the Supreme Court.

Associate Justice. During his long tenure on the Court, Stone distinguished himself as an advocate of judicial restraint, believing that the personal attitudes of the justices toward specific legislation should not affect their judgment of its constitutionality. During the early years of the Roosevelt administration, in particular, when the various programs of the New Deal were subjected to exacting judicial scrutiny, Stone dissented on many of the Court's opinions, often in the company of Justices Holmes, Brandeis, and later Cardozo.

One of Stone's early notable opinions, however, came in a case dealing with the rights of the accused. He joined in the dissent in *Olmstead v. United States* (1928), arguing that surreptitious police wiretaps were a violation of the Constitution's 4th Amendment guarantee against unreasonable searches and seizures.

Throughout his career, Stone was especially concerned with electoral procedures and voting rights. On the same issue several years later, Stone wrote the majority opinion in *United States v. Classic* (1941), which determined that the federal government has the right to regulate state primary elections for nominees to Congress when they are an essential component of the voting process in federal elections.

After the passage of the early New Deal programs, the social and economic intervention of the federal government came under repeated judicial attack. Stone dissented in

Harlan Fiske Stone

Railroad Retirement Board v. Alton Railroad Co. (1935), arguing that the pension plan for railroad workers established by the Railroad Retirement Act was constitutional, despite the conclusion of the majority that such a program had nothing to do with the regulation of interstate commerce and therefore went beyond the power of Congress to enact. He dissented in *United States v. Butler* (1936), arguing that the majority had relied on personal opposition to the Agricultural Adjustment Act of 1933 instead of on more objective constitutional standards.

Stone maintained this position with regard to the regulation of working conditions in *Morehead v. New York ex rel. Tipaldo* (1936), in which he dissented from the holding that whatever the effectiveness of state minimum wage laws in promoting the public good, they were a violation of the due process provision of the 14th Amendment. This decision was overruled only a year later. In the same year he joined Justice Cardozo's dissent in *Carter v. Carter Coal Co.* (1936), arguing that the Bituminous Coal Conservation Act of 1935, which instituted compulsory wage and hour standards in the mining industry, was unconstitutional. He joined the concurring opinion in *Ashwander v. Tennessee Valley Authority* (1936), which upheld the constitutional authority of Congress to establish the TVA.

Notwithstanding his belief in judicial restraint, Stone insisted that certain rights granted by the 1st Amendment must be considered to be basic and strictly protected. He wrote a separate concurring opinion in *Hague v. Congress of Industrial Organizations* (1939), which upheld an order enjoining municipal officers from interfering with the right of labor unions to assemble peaceably.

This same note was clearly enunciated by Stone in his lone dissent in *Minersville School District v. Gobitis* (1940), which held that the 1st Amendment rights of religious groups had not been violated by compulsory "pledges of allegiance" in the public schools. This position was later accepted by a majority of the Court in *West Virginia State Board of Education v. Barnette* (1943).

In regard to the right of the federal government to regulate interstate commerce, Stone wrote the majority opinion in *United States v. Darby Lumber Co.* (1941), which held that the Congress has the power to prohibit interstate trade in products manufactured under conditions that failed to meet certain minimum wage and hour standards. This overruled the previous decision of the Court in *Hammer v. Dagenhart* (1918), which had held that federal jurisdiction applied only to the sale and distribution, not to the manufacture, of products transported across state lines.

Chief Justice. In 1941, after the resignation of Chief Justice Charles Evans Hughes, President Roosevelt appointed Stone to succeed Hughes as chief justice, marking only the second time in Supreme Court history that a sitting associate justice had been elevated to the position of leadership on the Court.

During World War II, the Stone Court was called upon to rule on several issues brought about by the extraordinary conditions of war. He wrote the majority opinion in *Ex parte Quirin* (1942), establishing that the president could appoint a military commission to try enemy saboteurs and that they did not have to be tried by a civilian jury. He spoke for the Court in *Hirabayashi v. United States* (1943), upholding the right of the federal government to impose a curfew on Japanese-Americans living on the West Coast. Stone also wrote the majority opinion in *Yakus v. United States* (1944), upholding the constitutionality of the Emergency Price Control Act of 1942. In *In re Yamashita* (1946), Stone's majority opinion supported the jurisdiction of an American military court that had sentenced a Japanese general to death for war crimes.

With the gradual change of the composition of the Court during the later years of the Roosevelt administration, the majority shifted to a much more liberal philosophy with regard to social and economic legislation and individual rights. In the role of chief justice, Stone found himself often in the minority. He joined the dissent in *United States v. South-Eastern Underwriters Association* (1944), which held that the insurance industry was subject to federal legislation. He also joined dissents in *Thomas v. Collins* (1945) and in *Marsh v. Alabama* (1946), cases that were based on a strict reading of the constitutional guarantee of freedom of speech.

Stone's last opinion came in *Girouard v. United States* (1946), which held that a resident alien who was a pacifist for religious reasons should not be denied American citizenship for refusing to acknowledge his obligation to bear arms in the country's defense. Stone had previously joined the dissent on Court decisions that had affirmed a similar denial of citizenship, but in this case, he altered his position. Although the Court now overturned the previous decisions, Stone dissented, holding that because Congress had not significantly altered the law since the earlier decisions, it was not the responsibility of the Court to legislate what the Congress had not intended to do. Stone served on the Court until his death in Washington, D.C., in 1946.

STORY, JOSEPH

b. September 18, 1779; speaker, Massachusetts House of Representatives (1811); member, U.S. House of Representatives (1808-1809); associate justice, U.S. Supreme Court (1811-1845); d. September 10, 1845.

Born in Marblehead, Massachusetts, the son of a physician and revolutionary activist who had taken part in the Boston Tea Party, Story received his early education at Marblehead Academy. In the autumn of 1794, at age fifteen, as a result of a fight with a classmate, he was forced to leave that institution and complete his preparation for college by himself. Within six months, he not only finished his preparatory studies, but also mastered the course work of the first semester of the college freshman year. In recognition of that achievement, he was admitted to Harvard College in the winter of 1795.

Throughout his college career, Story remained an

Joseph Story

exceptionally hard-working student, graduating second in his class in 1798. Soon afterward he began his law studies in the busy office of Congressman Samuel Sewall of Marblehead, and there his studies were again left largely to his own initiative. When Sewall accepted appointment as a judge, Story transferred his law apprenticeship to the office of Samuel Putnam in nearby Salem. Finally admitted to the bar in 1801, Story established a private law practice in Salem and in 1804, married Mary Oliver, a local minister's daughter, who died the following year.

Despite the fact that he was an active Republican in a largely Federalist state, Story was elected to the Massachusetts legislature in 1805. He served in that body until his election to the U.S. House of Representatives in 1808, the year in which he took his second wife, Sarah Wetmore, daughter of a local judge. Story's career in Congress proved to be short and unhappy; he resigned after a single term, owing to his supposed party disloyalty in his opposition to President Jefferson's embargo on foreign trade. Returning to Massachusetts and the state legislature, Story was elected speaker of the House in 1811.

In the same year, after the death of Associate Justice William Cushing, Pres. James Madison offered the position to Levi Lincoln of Massachusetts, former attorney general in the administration of Thomas Jefferson. Lincoln, however, declined the appointment even after confirmation by the Senate. Next, Madison appointed Alexander Wolcott of Connecticut, but this appointment was rejected by the Senate on the grounds that Wolcott was professionally unqualified for the position. Madison then offered the appointment to John Quincy Adams, who was serving as U.S. minister in Russia, but Adams declined the appointment as well. Finally, on the recommendation of a Massachusetts congressman, Madison offered the associate justiceship to Story. Story had his own reservations about the size of a Supreme Court justice's salary, but he accepted the nomination and thereby became, at age thirty-two, the youngest person ever appointed to the Supreme Court.

Supreme Court. Soon after his appointment to the bench, Story became occupied with the large number of privateering cases that flooded into the courts of his circuit following the outbreak of the War of 1812. In one of the most important of these circuit cases, *De Lovio v. Boit* (1815), he affirmed a wide federal jurisdiction over matters of admiralty law. In fact, admiralty law was to become one of Story's special fields of expertise. Later, on the Supreme Court itself, Story issued several important admiralty decisions. For example, in *The Thomas Jefferson* (1825), for which he wrote the Court's unanimous opinion, it was established that the maritime and admiralty jurisdiction of the federal courts does not extend beyond the sea or tidal waters. In *United States v. Schooner Amistad* (1841) he held that a boatload of black slaves who had killed the crew and brought the ship into an American port should be repatriated as freemen to Africa, despite the claim of the Spanish owners of the ship.

During the first part of Story's tenure on the Supreme Court, Chief Justice John Marshall was the dominating judicial influence. In Story, Marshall found a true soulmate who shared his jurisprudence and his nationalist view of the federal system. But Story was more than a mere clone of Marshall. He wrote the majority opinion in the landmark case of *Martin v. Hunter's Lessee* (1816), in which he upheld the 25th section of the Judiciary Act of 1789 and established the principle that the Supreme Court should be the final arbiter of all cases dealing with constitutional issues, federal laws, and international treaties, even if they originated in state or local courts.

This decision provided one of the most important judicial precedents used in three 1819 landmark cases. In *Dartmouth College v. Woodward* and *Sturges v. Crowninshield*, Marshall applied the contracts clause to protect private interests against certain regulations by the state. In *McCulloch v. Maryland* the Chief Justice pronounced a sweepingly liberal definition of the powers of Congress and a correspondingly broad restriction on the power of states to interfere with federally sanctioned activity.

Story held firm to this judicial position, joining Marshall in dissenting in the case of *Ogden v. Saunders* (1827), in which the Court upheld the right of states to pass limited insolvency laws that could cancel certain debts. In the dissenting opinion, Marshall opined that even limited insol-

vency laws enacted by the states were an infringement on the spirit of the Constitution in this matter. Story wrote the unanimous opinion in *Martin v. Mott* (1827), in which the Court held that it was within the president's constitutional power to call out the militia without being subject to the agreement of the states affected or to judicial review.

When Chief Justice Marshall died in 1835, Story was regarded by some as the most qualified successor to the post. Unfortunately for Story, Pres. Andrew Jackson did not agree. Story had opposed the President (and it was one of the rare times he had opposed Marshall as well) in *Cherokee Nation v. Georgia* (1831), in which Story concurred with Justice Thompson's dissent in which he argued that the Cherokees were indeed a foreign state within the meaning of the Constitution and were entitled to judicial redress. Story also opposed Jackson by defending the Bank of the United States. Consequently, Jackson, having once called Story "the most dangerous man in America," passed over the associate justice from Massachusetts without comment and nominated Roger B. Taney of Maryland to become the new chief justice.

After the appointment of Taney, Story joined the dissenting opinions more frequently. He was the lone dissenter in *New York v. Miln* (1837), arguing that the registration of passengers arriving in U.S. ports was beyond the legitimate police power of the states' government and was an unconstitutional interference with the exclusive right of Congress to regulate commerce. He also joined the dissent in *Briscoe v. Bank of the Commonwealth of Kentucky* (1837), opposing the issuance of bills of credit by a state bank.

One of the most important of Story's minority opinions also came in 1837 in *Charles River Bridge v. Warren Bridge*, a case with considerable implications for the relations between government and private industry. The facts in the case were that the state of Massachusetts had granted an apparent monopoly to the Charles River Bridge Company for pedestrian traffic, but the Massachusetts legislature subsequently authorized the construction of a second bridge, the Warren bridge. Story unsuccessfully argued that the original contract had been violated, that the act of the legislature granting the Warren bridge a charter impaired the obligation of the prior contract and grant to the Charles River Bridge Company and that therefore it was void. The majority of the Court, however, ruled that the state franchise of the bridge did not grant an exclusive privilege and should charters for property in lines of travel be interpreted to carry out implied contracts, the state would be forced to stop all improvements in railroads and canals until the claims of old turnpike corporations could be settled.

Toward the end of his tenure on the Court, Story devoted himself increasingly to the question of slavery. In addition to his dramatic decision in the *Amistad* case, he spoke for the Court in *Prigg v. Pennsylvania* (1842), in which the Court overturned a state law regarding the return of escaped slaves to their owners in other states, ruling that legislation on fugitives from labor was exclusively the jurisdiction of Congress. One of Story's most important opinions came in *Swift v. Tyson* (1842), in which he spoke for the Court in claiming the right of the federal judiciary to rule on commercial cases without consideration of any applicable state law.

In 1829, Story accepted a professorship of law at Harvard and was instrumental in the early development of the Harvard Law School. Because it was his custom to deliver no formal lectures to his students, Story began to write and edit a series of legal textbooks known as his *Commentaries*, which were published between 1832 and 1845. These works became standard authorities both in the United States and in England. Story's activities as a law professor and legal scholar were as significant for the development of American law as was his service on the Court. In both he exerted a towering influence on the future scope of the legal profession. Story had intended to resign from the Supreme Court at the end of the 1845 session, but he died in Cambridge, Massachusetts, before that session had ended, still involved in the work of his circuit court.

STRONG, WILLIAM

b. May 6, 1808; member, U.S. House of Representatives (1847-1851); judge, Pennsylvania Supreme Court (1857-1868); associate justice, U.S. Supreme Court (1870-1880); d. August 19, 1895.

William Strong

Born in Somers, Connecticut, and educated at Yale College (Class of 1828), Strong worked as a teacher before he began his law studies at Yale Law School. He was admitted to the Pennsylvania bar in 1832 and soon afterward established a private practice in Reading. He served two terms as a Democrat in Congress and was later elected to the Pennsylvania Supreme Court. In 1870, after the resignation of Associate Justice Robert Grier, Strong was appointed to the Supreme Court by Pres. Ulysses S. Grant.

Strong was embroiled in a controversy at the very beginning of his tenure on the Court. The constitutionality of federally issued legal tender had been overturned by the Supreme Court in *Hepburn v. Griswold* (1870), but public opinion urged a reconsideration. Strong had upheld the right of the federal government to issue paper money on the Pennsylvania bench, and on the Supreme Court, he wrote the majority opinion in the second of the Legal Tender Cases, *Knox v. Lee* (1871), which reversed the Court's earlier decision. In the *Slaughterhouse Cases* (1873), he concurred with the majority, upholding the right of states to license monopolies when such was necessary and proper to effect a purpose that had in view the public good. Regarding the issue of civil rights for blacks during the Reconstruction period, Strong wrote the majority opinion in *Strauder v. West Virginia* and *Ex parte Virginia* (1880), which confirmed the right of all citizens to serve on juries. These cases focused on the rights of black defendants to have black people as members of their jury. The Court held that under the 14th Amendment no citizen could be denied equal protection of the laws nor deprived of life, liberty, or property without due process. Therefore, black defendants were entitled to have black jurors decide their fate as white defendants were entitled to white jurors. Further, citizens could not be disqualified from service on the basis of race, color, or previous servitude.

Strong served on the Electoral Commission that resolved the controversy over the Hayes-Tilden presidential election of 1876. He retired from the Court in 1880 and taught law at Columbian University (later George Washington University) in Washington, D.C., until his death in 1895.

SUTHERLAND, GEORGE

b. March 25, 1862; senator, Utah legislature (1896-1900); member, U.S. House of Representatives (1901-1903); U.S. senator (1905-1917); associate justice, U.S. Supreme Court (1922-1938); d. July 18, 1942.

Born in Buckinghamshire, England, Sutherland spent his boyhood in Springville, Utah, where his parents had immigrated in 1864. After attending Brigham Young University and the University of Michigan Law School, he was admitted to the bar in 1883 and established a private practice in Provo, Utah. Sutherland served two terms in the Utah legislature and a single term in the U.S. House of Representatives. In 1904, he was elected to the U.S. Senate. After his defeat for reelection in 1916, Sutherland served as the presi-

George Sutherland

dent of the American Bar Association (1916-1917) and as an advisor to Pres. Warren Harding. In 1922, after the resignation of Associate Justice John Clarke, President Harding appointed Sutherland to the Supreme Court.

Sutherland was a staunch conservative, and he often joined the dissenting position of Justice James McReynolds in opposing the intervention of the federal government in the political affairs of states and economic affairs of private business. He joined the dissent with McReynolds in *Moore v. Dempsey* (1923), which overturned the conviction of Southern blacks tried under an atmosphere of mob violence. He wrote the majority opinion in *Adkins v. Children's Hospital* (1923), which struck down minimum wage laws for the District of Columbia. He also spoke for the majority in *Bedford Cut Stone Company v. Journeymen Stone Cutters' Association* (1927), which upheld a court injunction granted to a private employer against boycott tactics by unionized laborers. He joined the dissent in *Meyer v. Nebraska* (1923), which overturned a xenophobic state law prohibiting the teaching of foreign languages in private schools, and he also joined the dissent in *Near v. Minnesota* (1931), which supported the constitutionality of government suppression of "obscene, defamatory, and scandalous" periodicals. He dissented in *Home Building and Loan Company v. Blaisdell* (1934), which upheld a state statute that postponed foreclosure proceedings because of the severe economic effects of the Depression. One of Sutherland's most effective attacks on the policies of the New Deal came in *Carter v. Carter Coal Company* (1936), which held that regulation of the coal industry prescribed by the Bituminous Coal Conservation Act of 1935 was unconstitutional.

Sutherland remained a constant opponent of the social programs of the Roosevelt administration and retired from the Court in 1938, after President Roosevelt's attempt to alter the judicial balance of the Court by adding more justices had failed. Sutherland died in Stockbridge, Massachusetts, in 1942.

SWAYNE, NOAH HAYNES

b. December 7, 1804; various legislative and judicial positions in Ohio; associate justice, U.S. Supreme Court (1862-1881); d. June 8, 1884.

Educated at a Quaker academy near his home in Frederick County, Virginia, and originially intending to become a physician, Swayne eventually chose a law career, studying in the office of John Scott and Francis Brooks, and was admitted to the bar in 1823. After the completion of his studies, Swayne, a life-long opponent of slavery, moved to Ohio, where he established a private law practice and was appointed state prosecutor in 1826. He later served in the state legislature (1829) and was appointed U.S. attorney for the district of Ohio by Pres. Andrew Jackson, serving in this position for nine years (1830-1838). He later resumed his private law practice in Columbus, participating in several fugitive slave cases. A year after the death of Associate Justice Peter Daniel in 1860, Swayne was appointed to the Supreme Court by Pres. Abraham Lincoln.

At the time of his appointment, Swayne had no judicial

Noah Swayne

experience, but he had the support of the governor of Ohio and the entire Ohio congressional delegation. During his tenure on the Court, he proved to be a moderate, balancing the rights of individuals and states with the responsibilities of the federal government. In *Ex parte Milligan* (1866), he concurred with the majority that a president may not declare martial law in areas not in open rebellion, although he joined Chief Justice Salmon P. Chase in his partial dissent, which argued that Congress had a right to suspend civil trials in "time of public danger." In the Legal Tender Cases (*Hepburn v. Griswold*, 1870, and *Knox v. Lee*, 1871), he voted to uphold the constitutionality of the federal government's right to issue unsecured currency, in *Hepburn v. Griswold* being in the minority and in *Knox v. Lee* in the majority. In the *Slaughterhouse Cases* (1873), Swayne dissented, opposing the right of a state government to license a monopoly. Justice Swayne believed that such a legislative creation abridged the privileges and immunities of the plaintiff, depriving them of liberty or property without due process of law as well as denying them equal protection of the laws of the state.

Swayne retired from the Supreme Court in 1881 at age seventy-six. He died in New York City three years later.

TAFT, WILLIAM HOWARD

b. September 15, 1857; judge, Ohio Superior Court (1887-1890); U.S. solicitor general (1890-1891); judge,

U.S. Circuit Court (1892-1900); president, Philippine Commission (1900-1901); governor, Philippine Islands (1901-1904); U.S. secretary of War (1904-1908); president of the United States (1909-1913); joint chairman, National War Labor Board (1918-1919); chief justice, U.S. Supreme Court (1921-1930); d. March 8, 1930.

Born in Cincinnati, Ohio, Taft was descended on both his paternal and maternal sides from prominent New England families, with longstanding involvement in law and public service. His father, Alphonso Taft, served as a judge on the Cincinnati Superior Court, as secretary of War in the Grant administration, and was later appointed U.S. ambassador to Austria and Russia during the administration of Pres. Chester A. Arthur. From an early age, the younger Taft showed an interest in law and politics and distinguished himself as an excellent student. He graduated at the head of his class at Cincinnati's Woodward High School and entered Yale University in 1874.

After graduation from Yale four years later, being honored as class salutatorian, Taft returned to Ohio and enrolled in the University of Cincinnati Law School. In addition to his law studies, he pursued journalistic interests, working part-time as a law reporter for the *Cincinnati Commercial*. With his admission to the Ohio bar in 1880, Taft followed the political tradition of his family and became actively involved in the state Republican Party.

His participation in the local elections of 1881 gained him appointment as assistant county attorney, and in the following year, at age twenty-five, he was named collector of internal revenue for Cincinnati. After only a few months in this position, however, he resigned in a bitter personal protest over the system of political patronage.

Taft was married to Helen Herron in 1886, and she proved to be an important advisor and confidante in the course of his later career. In 1887, he accepted an appointment by Ohio Governor Joseph Foraker to become judge of the Ohio Superior Court. Taft served in that position for the next three years and during that time, he set his sights on an even higher judicial post. In 1889, there was a vacancy on the Supreme Court due to the death of Associate Justice Stanley Matthews, and Taft's name was put forth as a possible nominee. Taft did not receive the nomination, but his future lay in Washington nonetheless. In 1890, Pres. Benjamin Harrison appointed Taft to the office of solicitor general, and in that position he became familiar with the workings of the federal judiciary, successfully arguing sixteen cases before the Supreme Court.

Taft's tenure as solicitor general was brief, for after only two years he accepted another presidential appointment to become judge of the U.S. District Court for the 6th Circuit. Among the major issues Taft faced on the federal bench were increasingly strained relations between organized labor and management. In general, Taft opposed attempts by union organizers to interfere with the operations

William Howard Taft

of companies threatened by strikes. At the same time, however, he aggressively upheld the terms of the Sherman Antitrust Act, and one of his most important decisions in this area was upheld by the Supreme Court in *Addyston Pipe and Steel Co. v. United States* (1899).

Following the Spanish American War, Taft resigned from the bench to accept a diplomatic assignment from Pres. William McKinley. American military occupation of the Philippine Islands was to be replaced by civilian government, and Taft was appointed president of the Philippine Commission and in the following year, governor of the Philippines. Despite his earlier desire for a Supreme Court appointment, Taft chose to remain on the islands rather than succeed retiring Justice George Shiras in 1903. In 1904, however, Taft agreed to return to Washington to become secretary of War in the cabinet of Pres. Theodore Roosevelt.

In that capacity, Taft became a valued presidential advisor, personally supervising the early phases of the construction of the Panama Canal. When President Roosevelt announced his intention not to run for reelection, Taft's name was immediately put forth. Despite his initial hesitation, Taft received the President's endorsement and the nomination of the Republican Party, and he soundly defeated the Democratic candidate, William Jennings Bryan, in the national election of 1908.

President. During Taft's four years in office, he had the opportunity to fill several vacancies on the Supreme Court. In addition to the appointment of Associate Justices Horace Lurton, Charles Evans Hughes, Willis Van Devanter, Joseph Lamar, and Mahlon Pitney, he elevated Associate Justice Edward Douglas White to the chief justiceship, the post that Taft had long coveted for himself.

As Taft's administration continued, considerable opposition to his policies arose within his own Republican Party. Former President Roosevelt's initial support for his successor gradually gave way to unconcealed hostility and a decision to contest the 1912 presidential election. Although Taft received the Republican nomination, Roosevelt's candidacy at the head of the Bull Moose Party disastrously splintered the Republican vote. In the November election, Taft was resoundingly defeated; he received only eight electoral votes.

Following the inauguration of Woodrow Wilson, Taft accepted an appointment as Kent Professor of Constitutional Law at Yale University Law School. He continued to hope for a Supreme Court appointment and in the meantime served as the president of the American Bar Association. In that capacity he vigorously opposed the nomination of Associate Justice Louis Brandeis in 1916. During World War I, Taft was appointed chairman of the National War Labor Board, and after the armistice, he campaigned for American participation in the League of Nations.

Chief Justice. With the election of Republican Warren Harding in 1920, Taft's Supreme Court ambitions were finally realized. In 1921, with the death of Chief Justice Edward White, whom Taft himself had appointed eleven years before, President Harding appointed Taft to succeed him on the Supreme Court. Taft's nomination was confirmed by the Senate on the same day that it was proposed by the President, and with that confirmation, Taft became the only man in American history ever to hold the highest office in both the executive and judicial branches.

During his tenure as chief justice, Taft's most important contributions to the development of the federal judiciary lay in the realm of administrative reorganization. The court system that Taft headed had become swamped with an unprecedented number of cases, and some means of coordination among judges was clearly necessary if the federal courts were to carry out their constitutional responsibilities effectively. To that end, the Chief Justice helped in the formulation of two important pieces of federal legislation: the Judiciary Act of 1922, which enabled federal judges to reform court procedures, and the Judiciary Act of 1925, which gave the Supreme Court greater control over the number and nature of cases it was required to hear.

In judicial philosophy, Taft distinguished himself as a staunch conservative, and in his first major opinion, in *Truax v. Corrigan* (1921), he demonstrated his longstanding opposition to the militant activities of labor unions. At issue in this case was the right of state governments to prohibit injunctions by management against picketing and boycotts by striking employees. The Chief Justice held that such a law was unconstitutional as it violated the 14th Amendment due process rights of the management in not protecting their access and use of their property.

Chief Justice Taft also held a restrictive view of the constitutional right of the federal government to use its taxing power to achieve social aims. He made this clear in his majority opinion in *Bailey v. Drexel Furniture Co.* (1922), the child labor tax case in which the Supreme Court overturned the Federal Revenue Act of 1919. The object of that legislation was to discourage child labor in mines and factories by imposing a 10 percent tax on the profits of companies that refused to comply with federal guidelines. Upholding the precedent of the Court established in *Hammer v. Dagenhart* (1918), Taft characterized the law as an attempt "to coerce people of a state to act as Congress wishes them to act in respect of a matter completely the business of a state government under the federal Constitution."

In *Adkins v. Children's Hospital* (1923), however, Taft wrote a dissenting opinion that supported another attempt by Congress to enact social legislation, rather than viewing the case statute, as did the majority, as an effort to limit the freedom of contract between employer and employee. Associate Justices Holmes and Sanford also dissented, arguing for the constitutionality of minimum wages for women and children working in the District of Columbia. Another of Taft's decisions that reinforced federal authority came in *J.W. Hampton and Co. v. United States* (1928), in which he wrote the opinion of the Court that upheld the right of Congress to enact protective tariff laws, both as a means of raising revenue and as a protective measure for the economy of the nation.

With regard to the powers of law enforcement agencies in their attempts to enforce Prohibition, Taft wrote the majority opinion in *Carroll v. United States* (1925). In this case he upheld the constitutionality of warrantless searches of automobiles by federal authorities if there was reasonable suspicion of criminal activity. In a similar issue, Taft established a precedent with even greater significance; in *Olmstead v. United States* (1928), he held that police wiretaps were not a violation of the 4th Amendment protection from unreasonable searches and seizures, since a suspect's property was not physically violated by such acts. That decision was later reversed by *Katz v. United States* (1967).

Having himself served as president, Taft was especially sensitive to the rights and responsibilities of the executive branch. In *Ex parte Grossman* (1925), he upheld the presidential power to issue pardons, and in *Myers v. United States* (1926), a decision that Taft considered one of the most important in his tenure as chief justice, he held that Congress may not require its consent in presidential dismissal of certain federal appointees.

On the issue of judicial procedure, Taft's most important opinion came in *Tumey v. Ohio* (1927), in which the petitioner appealed a fine levied by a judge who was also the city's mayor. Writing for a unanimous Court, Taft held that since a portion of the fine was allocated to the city treasury, the judge had a personal interest in the outcome of the trial. Taft therefore ruled that this violated the defendant's 14th Amendment due process rights to an impartial judge and that states should henceforth observe this constitutional requirement in their appointments to judicial posts.

Taft relished his role as chief justice, which he cherished even more than the presidency as the crowning achievement of his long career. After serving less than nine years on the Supreme Court, Taft resigned from the bench in 1930 at age seventy-three because of ill health. He was succeeded in the office of chief justice by Charles Evans Hughes, one of his own Supreme Court appointees. Taft died a few months later at his home in Washington, D.C., and was buried in Arlington National Cemetery.

TANEY, ROGER BROOKE

b. March 17, 1777; member, Maryland House of Delegates (1799-1800); member, Maryland Senate (1816-1821); attorney general, Maryland (1827-1831); U.S. attorney general (1831-1833); U.S. secretary of the Treasury (1833-1834); chief justice, U.S. Supreme Court (1836-1864); d. October 12, 1864.

Born in Calvert County, Maryland, Taney was the second son of a prominent local Catholic family. His father, Michael Taney, was a prosperous tobacco grower and his mother, Monica Brooke Taney, was descended from an aris-

Roger B. Taney

tocratic family that had arrived in Maryland in 1650. Taney's early years were spent on the family plantation, where he received his primary education in the local schools. At age fifteen, he entered Dickinson College in Pennsylvania, from which he graduated in 1795 at the head of his class.

Choosing a career in the law, Taney studied in the office of Judge Jeremiah Townley Chase of Annapolis, who served on the Maryland General Court. He remained there for three years, being admitted to the bar in 1799. In addition to his legal aspirations, Taney also sought a career in politics, and soon after leaving Judge Chase's office, he returned to his native Calvert County, where he gained the support of the local planters and was elected to the Maryland House of Delegates as a Federalist representative.

Taney's first period of public service, however, was brief. In the overwhelming victory of the Jeffersonian Republicans in the 1800 national elections, he was defeated for reelection to the House of Delegates. In the following year, he moved to Frederick, where he established a private law practice. Despite his unsuccessful attempt to regain a seat in the Maryland House of Delegates in 1803, Taney became a prominent member of the local legal community. In 1806, he married Francis Scott Key's sister Anne Key, with whom he had seven children.

Taney continued to participate actively in the affairs of the Maryland Federalist Party, and he eventually became one of its leaders. In 1812, when the question of war with Great Britain caused considerable controversy within the party, Taney emerged as the spokesman for a minority that actively supported the American participation in the hostilities. After the end of the war, Taney was elected to the Maryland senate in 1816.

Among his most important concerns during his single five-year term in the state senate were banking and economic regulation. In addition to serving as a director of the Frederick County Bank, he sought to decentralize the availability of credit by helping to found a bank for farmers at Hagerstown and sponsored legislation in the senate to prevent the devaluation of state bank notes. In sharp contrast to his later opposition, Taney was a supporter of the Bank of the United States at this stage in his career, and he voted against the bill that imposed a state tax on the operations of that institution. The law was later declared unconstitutional in *McCulloch v. Maryland* (1819).

After the end of his senate term in 1821, Taney moved from Frederick to Baltimore and resumed his private law career. His experience in economic and banking issues was extremely valuable, and he served as counsel for the Union Bank of Maryland in its legal wranglings with the Bank of the United States. Taney's views with regard to this institution were clearly changing; revelations of mismanagement and illegal practices at the Baltimore branch had transformed his earlier support to increasing antagonism.

The dissolution of the Federalist Party also affected Taney's political future, and he became an outspoken supporter of Andrew Jackson in his unsuccessful bid for the presidency in 1824. That support was the beginning of a longstanding political alliance, and in the 1828 election Taney agreed to serve as the chairman of the Jackson Central Committee for Maryland.

In 1827, Taney left his private practice in Baltimore to become state attorney general, an office that he held for the next five years. With the election of Andrew Jackson in 1828, Taney's political involvement in the Democratic Party intensified. Becoming one of the President's most trusted advisors, he was appointed U.S. attorney general in 1831.

Soon after his arrival in Washington, Taney was involved once again with a controversy concerning the Bank of the United States. At issue in the Congress was a new law revising its charter and granting it far broader economic power than it had previously possessed. While other members of the Jackson cabinet urged the President not to oppose the new charter, Taney urged him to use his veto power to overrule Congress and was instrumental in the drafting of Jackson's historic veto message.

That action marked the beginning of a political war, for 1832 was an election year, and the officers of the bank, headed by its president, Nicholas Biddle, made every effort to secure the defeat of Jackson. After their efforts proved unsuccessful, the newly reelected President was determined to destroy his political enemies and their bank. The most effective means of achieving this objective was the withdrawal of all federal funds from the bank. When Jackson's Treasury secretary, William Duane, refused to implement this drastic action, Jackson promptly dismissed him and appointed Taney in his place.

Once the withdrawal was effected, Taney quickly established a procedure for the deposit of government funds in selected state banks. One of these "pet banks" was the Union Bank of Maryland, and since Taney had previously served as its counsel, he was inevitably accused of conflict of interest. Opposition to the President's action among the supporters of the Bank of the United States grew more intense, reaching a climax in Taney's Treasury confirmation hearings before the Senate. Taney's nomination was defeated, and he was replaced as secretary of the Treasury by future Supreme Court Justice Levi Woodbury.

For the time being, Taney returned to Maryland and retired from public life. In 1835, however, after the resignation of Associate Justice Gabriel Duvall, President Jackson nominated Taney to succeed him on the Supreme Court. Emotions were still running high in the aftermath of the Bank of the United States controversy, and the Senate indefinitely postponed consideration of the nomination, thereby effectively defeating it. Jackson, however, was determined that Taney should return to public life, and later that year, after the death of Chief Justice John Marshall, Jackson nominated Taney to the Supreme Court as chief justice.

Early Decisions. The nomination did not come before the Senate until the following March, and since there had been changes in the makeup of the Senate, Taney was confirmed on March 16 by a vote of twenty-nine to fifteen. Initially, there were apprehensions that Taney's close association with the Jackson administration would make him something less than a completely impartial chief justice, and, in fact, three of the cases in which he participated in the first year of his tenure seemed to indicate a basic change from the philosophy of the Marshall Court.

The judicial legacy of John Marshall was one of strict limitation of state power insofar as it impinged on the sanctity of contracts. Taney's first majority opinion as chief justice, in *Charles River Bridge v. Warren River Bridge* (1837), introduced a certain flexibility in the Court's attitude toward such state legislation. The facts in the case were that the Massachusetts legislature had granted a charter in 1785 to the Charles River Bridge Company to construct and maintain a pedestrian crossing over the river, but several decades later, as the traffic over the bridge increased, another group of investors, the Warren Bridge Company, received permission from the state to construct a second thoroughfare. The Charles River Bridge Company sought an injunction against the construction of the new bridge, contending that exclusivity was an implicit feature of its original charter, and since the charter constituted a contract, it could not be violated by the state.

Chief Justice Taney's opinion in this case emphasized the duty of the state to ensure convenient and adequate bridges for its citizens. The original charter ought not, therefore, to be interpreted so as to restrict the actions of subsequent legislatures. So interpreted, there was no violation of the charter by the second bridge and thus no constitutional violation. While this decision recognized that a state charter was a legal contract, it also upheld the ability of states to utilize charters for promoting public welfare.

Soon after the *Charles River Bridge* decision, the Taney Court faced the question of the limits of federal authority to regulate commerce in *New York v. Miln* (1837). In upholding a state regulation requiring all ship captains arriving from foreign ports to present a passenger list to the local harbor authorities, the majority clearly demonstrated a belief that the commerce clause of the Constitution did not grant exclusive jurisdiction over such matters to Congess. Despite the lone dissent of Associate Justice William Story, who had been Marshall's close philosophical ally, the Taney Court ruled that states could legitimately intervene in interstate or international commercial activity if the intervention was a legitimate exercise of the state's "police power."

The last of the precedent-setting cases of the 1837 session was *Briscoe v. Commonwealth Bank of Kentucky*, and in its ruling, the Court in an opinion written by Justice McLean once again sharply diverged from the philosophy of the Marshall years. At issue in this case was the right of state banks to issue their own bank notes; in a previous case, *Craig v. Missouri* (1830), Chief Justice Marshall had written the majority opinion, ruling that such an action was a violation of Article I, Section 10 of the Constitution, prohibiting the states from issuing bills of credit. The difference in the ruling of the Taney Court, however, was its conclusion that a state bank was not the state itself. The state's role was in exercising its power to incorporate banks that could issue these notes. Since the issuance of bank notes was a natural function of banking, the majority of the Court upheld its constitutionality.

Although Taney appeared to be a strong supporter of the power of state governments in these early decisions, his majority opinion in the case of *Bank of Augusta v. Earle* (1839) defined the limits of state power with regard to outside corporations. In this case the state-chartered Bank of Alabama wanted to eliminate competition from any other banking institution operating in the state, and an Alabama merchant took up the cause of his state's bank and refused to pay a bill of exchange that had been purchased by the Bank of Augusta, Georgia. He contended that since the Bank of Augusta was chartered by Georgia, it could not legitimately operate outside of that state.

The issue, therefore, was one of utmost importance to the economic development of the country: could corporations chartered in one state legally operate in another state without the legal sanction of that state? Chief Justice Taney, speaking for the majority, managed to reconcile the rights of both the states and the corporations. He held that since the state of Alabama had enacted no legislation specifically prohibiting the activity of out-of-state banks, that silence must be viewed as implicit consent. Taney recognized, however, the rights of the state to enact specific legislation against the activities of outside corporations.

During the first decade of Taney's tenure as chief justice, the Supreme Court underwent dramatic changes in organization and personnel. Shortly before the end of the Jackson administration, Congress expanded the Court's membership to nine, and in addition to the two newly-created justiceships, four more associate justices were appointed during the next eight years. In 1844, Congress extended the length of the Court's annual sessions and its own procedures for filing motions and for hearing cases were regularized.

In the late 1840's, the Taney Court once again faced the question of the relative limits of state and federal uniformity in interstate and international commerce, but the judicial conclusion that it reached was far from clear. In the *License Cases* (1847), the Court upheld the right of states to regulate the sale and distribution of imported liquor within their boundaries. The Chief Justice, in a separate opinion, concluded that the issue was not state regulation of imports, but rather of internal commerce. The effect of this decision was to reaffirm the police power of the states in accordance with the Court's previous ruling in *New York v. Miln* (1837).

The *Passenger Cases* (1849) presented an even more difficult problem, and the Chief Justice was in the minority when the Court's ruling was announced. At issue in this case was a Massachusetts state law that imposed a head tax on arriving foreign passengers, intended to establish a fund for the support of indigent immigrants already arrived. While the Court had approved certain state regulation of immigration in *Miln*, it now rejected the imposition of a tax. Taney, however, argued that since the tax was not intended merely to produce revenue but to prevent pauperism and guard citizens against the introduction of disease, it was within the state's legitimate "police power." Further, Taney contended that the power of the state to tax vehicles or instruments of commerce was not explicitly prohibited merely by the affirmative grant of power to the federal government, as were duties on imports and tonnage, and that the *Passenger Cases*, therefore, abridged and might lead to serious impairment of the taxing power of the states.

The controversial issue of the political intervention of the federal government in the political affairs of the states was another problem that the Court faced in the 1849 term. In *Luther v. Borden*, arising from a constitutional dispute within the state of Rhode Island, the outcome of a claimed trespass action turned on which of two rival factions was the legitimate state government. One side invoked Article IV, Section 4 of the Constitution, which guaranteed a republican form of government in all states. The Supreme Court, in an opinion authored by Taney, recognized the significance of that guarantee, yet classified the Rhode Island dispute as a subject that the Constitution treats as essentially political in its nature and that therefore could not be settled in a judicial proceeding. However, the Court held that the issue could be addressed either to Congress, which had the power under the Constitution to recognize a state government, or to the president, who, by act of Congress, was vested with the power to recognize one side as the true government.

The Question of Slavery. Slavery was by far the most explosive issue faced by the nation during Taney's tenure as chief justice. His first ruling with regard to interstate commerce in slaves came in *Groves v. Slaughter* (1841), in which he concurred with the majority in upholding the validity of a contract given in Mississippi for the purchase of slaves in that state, in direct opposition to a Mississippi constitutional prohibition against the importation of slaves into that state as merchandise or for sale. A far more important case was that of *Prigg v. Pennsylvania* (1842), in which the Court overturned a state law that restricted the methods by which slave owners could apprehend fugitive slaves. The Court held that the power of legislation in relation to fugitives from labor was exclusively in the national legislature and that the rights of slave owners to reclaim slaves was derived from the Constitution. Justice Story delivered the opinion of the Court, which reaffirmed the constitutionality of the federal Fugitive Slave Act and held that it was the responsibility of state governments to protect the "private property" of slave owners from other states. The Chief Justice concurred with the majority but disagreed with the holding that the right to legislation on fugitives from labor was exclusively in the federal government. Taney said that the state should be allowed "to protect the master, when he is endeavouring to seize a fugitive from his service . . . provided the state law is not in conflict with the remedy provided by Congress."

These early cases, however, did not attempt to rule on the basic philosophical problem of involuntary servitude or, even more pressing, the legal status of slaves in states that had abolished slavery. Throughout his career, Taney had always been opposed to the institution of slavery and had freed the slaves that he had inherited from his father's estate. He favored resettlement of American blacks in Africa and became a member of the Colonization Society, which was dedicated to that goal. At the same time, however, Taney opposed any attempt by the nonslave states to interfere with slavery in states where it was established by law.

This latter issue inevitably became a matter of bitter sectional controversy, and it was faced by the Taney Court in *Strader v. Graham* (1851). In this case, the owner of two fugitive slaves sued a riverboat captain from whose vessel the slaves had escaped. The proceedings were instituted in Kentucky, under whose laws the slave owner could recover the value of his slaves. The captain contended that the slaves became free the moment they entered Ohio, a free state, and that they were, therefore, freemen when received on board his boat. Prior to their return to Kentucky and eventual escape, the slaves, who were musicians, had traveled to Ohio many times to perform, with the consent of the slave owner. The Kentucky court held, in accordance with Kentucky law, that the men were slaves and that the owner was entitled to recover their value from the captain of the boat. The decree was affirmed by the Court of Appeals for Kentucky and brought by writ of error to the Supreme Court. The Chief Justice delivered the opinion of the Court, dismissing the case for lack of jurisdiction, holding that the states had undoubted right to determine the status of persons within their territory and that the Constitution in no sense controlled the states in this realm. Thus, for the time being, it seemed that a solution had been found to the problem of the status of slaves: it would be determined by the laws of their home state.

Six years later, in the Dred Scott Decision (*Scott v. Sandford*, 1857), the issue was raised once again with consequences of tremendous significance for the future course of American history. In this case the petitioner, a slave named Dred Scott, was taken by his master, John Sandford, from the slave state of Missouri to the free state of Illinois and later to the territory of Wisconsin, which had been declared free according to the Missouri Compromise. Eventually, Scott was brought back to Missouri by his master, but he filed suit in a Missouri court for his freedom, contending that since he had been resident in a free territory, his legal status had changed. After various complex lower court procedures, the case was finally appealed to the Supreme Court. While the Chief Justice had intended to dismiss Scott's suit summarily, on the basis of *Strader v. Graham*, the determination of Associate Justices McLean and Curtis to use the case to uphold the federal right to prohibit slavery in the territories forced the Court to confront the basic constitutional issues of slave status and whether the Missouri Compromise, which was a federal prohibition against slavery as a prerequisite to admission to the Union of certain territories, violated the due process clause of the 5th Amendment of the Constitution.

The Court announced its decision on March 7, 1857, only three days after the inauguration of Pres. James Buchanan. Each justice filed a separate opinion, yet the decision of Chief Justice Taney (from which Associate Justices Curtis and McLean dissented) has received the most attention. On the question of Scott's legal status, Taney held that a slave is not a citizen of the United States within the meaning of the Constitution. The framers of that document had not intended enslaved persons to be included because they were not regarded as members of the states nor numbered among its "people or citizens." Conservatively, the special rights and immunities guaranteed to citizens do *not* apply. Further, not being citizens, slaves are not entitled to

sue in that character in a court; therefore, the lower court had no jurisdiction in the suit with such a party.

As to the issue of Scott's becoming free when he moved to the free state of Illinois, Taney decided that the laws of the state in which the petitioner was currently resident, namely the slave state of Missouri, should apply. As to Scott's contention that he had been a resident of a territory in which the federal government had prohibited slavery, Taney argued that the Missouri Compromise was itself unconstitutional, since the Constitution had acknowledged the sanctity of private property, and the prohibition of slavery in the territories would violate the due process rights of slave owners who wished to settle there.

This decision, intended to settle the legal question of slavery, actually resulted in even greater disagreement. Abolitionists were outraged by the Court's overturning of the Missouri Compromise, and the issue arose with even greater intensity in *Ableman v. Booth* (1859). In this case, a group of Wisconsin abolitionists attempted to obstruct the enforcement of the federal Fugitive Slave Act of 1850 by obtaining a state court order for the release of a Wisconsin citizen who had been arrested by federal officials for harboring an escaped slave.

The Supreme Court ruled unanimously, with Chief Justice Taney writing the majority opinion, that the Wisconsin court's writ was an unconstitutional invasion of federal authority; that the process of a state court or judge has no authority beyond the limits of the sovereignty that confers the power; and that the writ of *habeas corpus* issued had no authority within the limits of authority assigned by the Constitution of the United States. Once again reaffirming the constitutionality of the Fugitive Slave Act itself, Taney emphasized the distinction between the spheres of jurisdiction of the states and of the federal government.

By 1860, the positions of the Northern states and the Southern states had hardened, and there was no longer any possibility of compromise. The last years of Taney's tenure as chief justice were, therefore, concerned with the issues arising from the extraordinary conditions of civil war.

Civil War Decisions. Taney had great personal regrets over the secession of the Southern states, and he believed that the Union should not be preserved by force. The nation's greatest resource, Taney believed, was the Constitution, and he was determined that the constitutional rights of all citizens must be upheld, even at a time of national crisis. Soon after the oubreak of the hostilities, he faced this issue on the circuit court in a case that resulted from the imposition of martial law by President Lincoln in the Chief Justice's home state of Maryland.

The case, *Ex parte Merryman* (1861), dealt with the right of the president to impose military justice on persons not directly involved in the hostilities. John Merryman, a citizen of Baltimore, had been imprisoned by federal military authorities soon after the outbreak of the Civil War for anti-Union activities. Chief Justice Taney, sitting as the federal circuit court, issued a writ of *habeas corpus* to the military commander of Baltimore, ordering him to bring Merryman to trial or to release him. The commander refused to comply with Chief Justice Taney's writ, and Taney responded to this refusal by addressing a letter to the President in which he pointed out that such a suspension of constitutional privileges may be declared only by Congress. Lincoln and his military commanders nevertheless continued their refusal to comply with the ruling. It was only after the end of the Civil War and after Taney's death that the reasoning of his opinion was upheld by the Supreme Court in the similar case of *Ex parte Milligan* (1866).

The Chief Justice was roundly criticized for his opposition to many of the wartime measures of the Lincoln administration. In the last year of his tenure, he joined Justice Nelson's dissenting opinion in the *Prize Cases* (1862). In that case, the Supreme Court ruled that the President was within his legal power to establish a blockade of Southern ports and to seize cargoes when there is an actual state of war and that such actual state of war may exist without any formal declaration of it by either party.

Taney never lived to see a reconciliation between the states and the final resolution of the various legal and moral issues that had precipitated the Civil War. He died in Washington, D.C., in the autumn of 1864 at the age of eighty-seven, to be succeeded in the office of chief justice by Lincoln's secretary of the Treasury, Salmon P. Chase.

THOMPSON, SMITH

b. January 17, 1768; associate justice, New York Supreme Court (1802-1814); chief justice, New York Supreme Court (1814-1818); secretary of the Navy (1819-1823); associate justice, U.S. Supreme Court (1823-1843); d. December 18, 1843.

Born in Amenia, New York, Thompson graduated from Princeton in 1788 and then studied law in the office of James Kent in Poughkeepsie, being admitted to the bar in 1792. In 1794, he married Sarah Livingston and in 1800 was elected to the New York state legislature. Two years later, he was appointed associate justice of the New York Supreme Court. In 1814, he was named chief justice of that court. After serving as secretary of the Navy in the Monroe administration, he was nominated by President Monroe to fill the vacancy on the Supreme Court created by the death of Associate Justice Henry B. Livingston in 1823.

Thompson's career in the Supreme Court was distinguished by his advocacy of states' rights and his consistent opposition to the nationalism of Chief Justice John Marshall. Among his most important dissenting opinions were *Brown v. Maryland* (1827), in which he argued against the majority that the states had a right to tax direct imports intended for domestic trade within the state, and *Craig v. Missouri* (1830), in which he argued that states had the right to issue their own special and limited bills of credit. In his dissent in *Cherokee Nation v. Georgia* (1831), he argued that the Cherokee nation was a sovereign state within the meaning of the Constitution, and that, therefore, the Supreme Court had jurisdiction over a case that that foreign state brought against one of the United States.

In *Kendall v. United States* (1838), Thompson wrote the majority opinion, in which he held, against the position of President Jackson, that the federal judiciary could issue a writ of *mandamus* commanding an officer of the executive branch to perform a ministerial duty necessary to the completion of an individual right arising under the laws of the United States. With regard to the issue of slavery, Thompson voted with the majority in *Groves v. Slaughter* (1841), which validated the sale of slaves in Mississippi despite a Mississippi state constitutional prohibition, and he argued to uphold the controversial Fugitive Slave Act in *Prigg v. Pennsylvania* (1842).

Thompson was a lifelong political activist, and his service on the Court did not put an end to his political activities. In 1828, he waged an unsuccessful campaign for the governorship of New York and received bitter criticism for not having resigned his position on the Supreme Court to do so. He served on the Court until his death in Poughkeepsie, New York, in 1843.

TODD, THOMAS

b. January 23, 1765; various judicial and legislative positions in Kentucky; associate justice, U.S. Supreme Court (1807-1826); d. February 7, 1826.

Born in King and Queen County, Virginia, Todd was left an orphan at age eleven but managed to acquire an elementary education. He served as a soldier in the Revolution, afterwards moving to Danville, Kentucky, to study law with his mother's cousin, Judge Harry Innes. He was admitted to the Kentucky bar in 1786. After a brief period in private practice, Todd was appointed clerk of the federal circuit court in the district of Kentucky, and after 1792, he was appointed clerk of the Kentucky state Court of Appeals, eventually becoming its chief justice in 1806. In the following year, Todd was nominated by President Jefferson to be the first Supreme Court associate justice from the newly-created western circuit, comprising the states of Ohio, Kentucky, and Tennessee.

Because of the distance of his circuit from Washington, Todd was often absent from the deliberations of the Supreme Court, and few of his opinions are preserved. In most cases he supported the constitutional interpretations of Chief Justice Marshall, despite the fact that he was an appointee of President Jefferson.

Todd was married twice; in 1788 to Elizabeth Harris and, after her death in 1811, to Lucy Payne, the sister of Dolley Madison. Todd served on the Supreme Court until his death in Frankfort, Kentucky, in 1826.

TRIMBLE, ROBERT

b. November 17, 1776; various legislative and judicial positions in Kentucky; associate justice, U.S. Supreme Court (1826-1828); d. August 25, 1828.

Born in Augusta County, Virginia, Trimble moved at an early age with his parents to Clark County, Kentucky, and spent his boyhood on the western frontier. Trimble received his formal education at Bourbon Academy in Bourbon County and at Kentucky Academy in Woodford County. He studied law in the offices of George Nicholas and James Brown and was admitted to the Kentucky bar in 1800, establishing his residence in Paris, Kentucky. After brief service in the state legislature, he was nominated judge of the court of appeals in 1807, a post from which he resigned in 1809 to return to his private law practice, although he agreed to serve as district attorney from 1813 to 1817. From 1817 to 1826, he served as a federal judge in the district of Kentucky. With the death of fellow Kentuckian Thomas Todd in 1826, Trimble was nominated by Pres. John Quincy Adams to be associate justice of the Supreme Court.

Trimble served on the Court for only two years, but during his tenure he consistently upheld the supremacy of federal over state laws, despite his Jeffersonian political orientation. His most notable disagreement with the position of Chief Justice John Marshall occurred in *Ogden v. Saunders* (1827), in which Trimble argued with the majority that state bankruptcy laws could be deemed valid to bar actions against debtors who obtained a certificate of discharge for debts contracted after the enactment of those laws. However, a discharge of debt under one state's laws cannot be pleaded in barring an action brought by a citizen from any state other than that where the discharge was obtained. Trimble died at his home in Paris, Kentucky, in 1828 at age 51.

VAN DEVANTER, WILLIS

b. April 17, 1859; various judicial and legislative positions in the territory of Wyoming; judge, U.S. circuit court (1903-1910); associate justice, U.S. Supreme Court (1910-1937); d. February 8, 1941.

Born in Marion, Indiana, the son of a local attorney, Van Devanter was educated at De Pauw University (Class of 1878) and studied law at the Cincinnati Law School. After being admitted to the bar in 1881, he worked for a time in his father's office and in 1884 established his own private practice in Cheyenne, Wyoming. Van Devanter served as the Cheyenne city attorney (1887-1888) and was elected to the territorial legislature (1888). In 1888, he received a presidential appointment to be chief justice of the territorial supreme court, a position that he held until the admission of Wyoming to the Union in 1890. Van Devanter was active in Republican Party politics and served as the state party chair-

Willis Van Devanter

man from 1892 to 1894. In 1897 he became an assistant U.S. attorney general and in 1903 was named judge of the U.S. Court of Appeals for the 8th Circuit. In 1910, after the resignation of Associate Justice William Moody, President Taft appointed Van Devanter to the Supreme Court.

In his long tenure on the Court, Van Devanter distinguished himself as an extreme conservative in judicial philosophy. He dissented in *Bunting v. Oregon* (1917), which upheld state regulation of working hours, and in the Rent Law Cases (*Block v. Hirsch* and *Marcus Brown Holding Co. v. Feldman*, 1921), in which the Court upheld a District of Columbia rent control law. He wrote the controversial majority opinion in *Evans v. Gore* (1920), which determined that the salaries of federal judges could not be subject to income tax. He joined the dissent in *Near v. Minnesota* (1931), which held that "The Newspaper Gag Law," authorizing the suppression of obscene or defamatory periodicals, violated the 1st and 14th Amendments. He also wrote the majority opinion in *New York Central v. Winfield* (1917), which overturned state support for workers disabled in railroad accidents on the grounds that the Federal Employer's Liability Act exclusively regulated the issue.

Van Devanter had planned to retire from his judicial position in 1932, but the election of Franklin Delano Roosevelt as president convinced him that his conservative voice was needed on the Supreme Court, and he remained on the bench until 1937. He died in Washington, D.C., in 1941.

VINSON, FREDERICK MOORE

b. January 22, 1890; member, U.S. House of Representatives (1924-1929, 1931-1938); judge, U.S. Court of Appeals (1938-1943); chief judge, U.S. Emergency Court of Appeals (1942-1943); director, Office of Economic Stabilization (1943-1945); Federal Loan Administrator (1945); director, Office of War Mobilization and Reconversion (1945); U.S. secretary of the Treasury (1945-1946); chief justice, U.S. Supreme Court (1946-1953); d. September 8, 1953.

Frederick M. Vinson

Born in Louisa, Kentucky, the son of the county jailer, Vinson was educated at Kentucky Normal College and later at Centre College of Kentucky, where he excelled in athletics and graduated at the head of his class in 1909. He immediately began his law studies at the same institution. After receiving his law degree in 1911 and refusing an offer to play professional baseball, he established a private law practice in Louisa.

Early in his career, Vinson became active in local Democratic Party politics and was appointed city attorney of Louisa in 1913. After active service in World War I, Vinson resumed his law practice and was appointed commonwealth attorney for the 32nd Kentucky judicial district. He served in that position for two years, until his appointment in 1924 to fill a vacant congressional seat. In the House of Representatives, Vinson distinguished himself as a specialist in economic matters, becoming a member of the Ways and Means

Committee and supporting a thorough reform of the federal tax codes. Although he was defeated in a reelection campaign in 1928, he was returned to the House in 1930 and was reelected for three more terms.

In 1938, Vinson resigned his seat in the House of Representatives to accept a presidential appointment as judge of the U.S. Court of Appeals for the District of Columbia. With the onset of World War II, he also served as chief judge of the U.S. Emergency Court of Appeals, where he reviewed hundreds of price control orders that had been determined according to the Emergency Price Control Act.

Vinson resigned from the bench in 1943 to accept an appointment by President Roosevelt as the director of the Office of Economic Stabilization. Immediately after the war, President Truman named Vinson federal loan administrator and, subsequently, director of the Office of War Mobilization and Reconversion. In July 1945, Vinson resigned that position to accept a place in the Truman cabinet as secretary of the Treasury.

Chief Justice. In 1946, after the death of Chief Justice Harlan Stone, President Truman appointed Vinson to be the new chief justice. He was confirmed by the Senate on June 20, 1946.

Although Vinson's tenure as chief justice lasted only seven years, he distinguished himself as a defender of the propriety of far-reaching federal intervention in economic and social matters. He believed that the Court should grant the legislative and executive branches the fullest range of their power within limits set down by the Constitution. In one of his first major decisions, Vinson spoke for the Court in *United States v. United Mine Workers* (1947), upholding both the civil and criminal contempt convictions of union leader John L. Lewis, who had refused to call off a strike by his organization in violation of a court order.

Five years later, Vinson issued another opinion that again demonstrated his belief that the federal government had wide powers to preserve the economic well-being of the country. He joined the dissent in *Youngstown Sheet and Tube Co. v. Sawyer* (1952), arguing that the president was within his constitutional authority to nationalize the steel industry at a time of national emergency [the Korean War] to prevent an impending strike.

In regard to the perceived threat of communist infiltration and subversion in the early Cold War years, Vinson tended to view government loyalty oaths and investigations of subversive groups as a legitimate function of national security. He spoke for the Court in *American Communications Association v. Douds* (1950), which upheld the right of the federal government to compel union leaders to file affidavits denying any association with the Communist Party. The Court held that such a requirement was not a violation of the 1st Amendment protection of free speech, but rather a legitimate safeguard of national security. He also wrote the majority opinion in *Dennis v. United States* (1951), upholding the provision of the Smith Act of 1940, which issued criminal penalties for teaching communist theory and advocating the violent overthrow of the government.

Vinson joined the dissent, however, in *Joint Anti-Fascist Refugee Committee v. McGrath* (1951), in which the Court held invalid the distribution by the attorney general of a list of "subversive organizations." He wrote the majority opinion, however, in *Stack v. Boyle* (1951), which held that the excessive bail imposed on twelve American communist leaders was a violation of their 8th Amendment rights.

Civil Rights and Liberties. Vinson wrote the majority opinion in the civil rights case of *Shelley v. Kraemer* (1948), which, although admitting that racial discrimination in housing by private individuals was not a violation of the 14th Amendment, ruled that state courts may not affirmatively enforce such discrimination. Vinson also spoke for the Court in *Sweatt v. Painter* (1950), which held that a state may not deny admission to a state law school to a black student, although there was a separate state law school for black students. He also wrote the majority opinion in *McLaurin v. Oklahoma State Regents* (1950), expanding his attack on the "separate but equal" doctrine and holding that a black student may not be segregated in the use of facilities of the state university that he or she attends. These opinions paved the way for the eventual end to government-sponsored segregation in education in *Brown v. Board of Education* (1954), which was heard by the Court at the end of Vinson's tenure but not decided until after his death.

With regard to civil liberties, he dissented in *Terminiello v. Chicago* (1949), which held that a municipal breach-of-peace law was a violation of the 1st Amendment right of free speech. Vinson also wrote the majority opinion in *Kunz v. New York* (1951), which held that a municipal ordinance barring public prayer meetings without a permit was a violation of the 1st and 14th Amendments. There was a limit to freedom of speech, however, and Vinson outlined his distinction in his majority opinion in *Feiner v. New York* (1951), which upheld the conviction of a speaker who had ignored repeated police requests that he stop in light of an impending disturbance.

Vinson was a consistent advocate of the right of police to conduct what they considered to be reasonable searches of suspects' persons and property. He wrote the majority opinion in *Harris v. United States* (1947), which held that a warrantless search may be valid if it is connected with an arrest. He dissented in *Trupiano v. United States* (1948), which reviewed the circumstances under which police must obtain warrants before conducting a search.

One of Vinson's last opinions came in the controversial and emotion-ridden case of *Rosenberg v. United States* (1953), an appeal of the death sentences of Julius and Ethel Rosenberg, who had been convicted of transmitting American nuclear secrets to the Soviet Union. Despite the repeated refusal of the Court to hear an appeal in the Rosenberg case,

Associate Justice William O. Douglas granted a last-minute stay of execution. The following day, Chief Justice Vinson called a special session of the Court in which it lifted the stay of execution on the grounds that the legal objections to the Rosenbergs' death sentence were not significant enough to merit further litigation. Later on the same day, the Rosenbergs were executed at Sing Sing Prison in New York.

Even after his appointment to the Supreme Court, Vinson remained a close and valued advisor to President Truman. Truman, in fact, later urged Vinson to seek the Democratic presidential nomination in 1952. Vinson was married once, to Roberta Dixson in 1923. He served as chief justice until his death in Washington, D.C., in 1953.

WAITE, MORRISON REMICK

b. November 29, 1816; member, Ohio House of Representatives (1850-1852); counsel, U.S. delegation to the Geneva Arbitration (1871); president, Ohio Constitutional Convention (1873-1874); chief justice, U.S. Supreme Court (1874-1888); d. March 23, 1888.

Morrison R. Waite

Born in Lyme, Connecticut, the son of Henry Matson Waite, a local judge and later chief justice of the Connecticut Supreme Court, the younger Waite was educated at Yale College (Class of 1837). After graduation, he left his native New England and began law studies in the office of Samuel

Young in Maumee City, near Toledo, Ohio, in 1838. The following year, Waite was admitted to the bar and joined the law firm as a partner. In 1840, he married Amelia Warner, a second cousin from Connecticut.

During his early years of law practice, Waite became a specialist in financial and real estate issues, often arguing cases before the Ohio Supreme Court. Politically active in local Whig politics, Waite served one term in the Ohio legislature, ran two unsuccessful campaigns for a seat in Congress, and helped to organize the Ohio Republican Party in 1856. Meanwhile he maintained his lucrative private law practice in Toledo, representing Ohio railroad interests. He declined an appointment to the state supreme court in 1863.

A strong supporter of the Union cause during the Civil War, Waite was appointed by President Grant in 1871 to serve as counsel to the American delegation to the Geneva Arbitration Conference, called to settle wartime claims of the United States against Great Britain in the *Alabama* case. At the conference, Waite played an important role in the formulation of the written indictment of the British government for its aid to the Confederate side. With the final award of $15,500,000 in compensation for the United States, Waite won national attention and praise.

Chief Justice. Returning to Ohio, Waite was elected president of the Ohio Constitutional Convention of 1873. It was during that convention that Waite learned of his unexpected nomination to the Supreme Court by President Grant, to succeed the late Chief Justice Salmon P. Chase. Waite's nomination was completely unexpected as he had no judicial experience and had never even argued a case before the Supreme Court. President Grant had previously put forth three other nominations: political boss Roscoe Conkling of New York; his own attorney general, George Williams of Oregon; and Caleb Cushing of Massachusetts. All either declined or were withdrawn in the face of inevitable Senate rejection before Grant settled on Waite.

Waite took the bench at an extremely critical period in the history of the Court and of the country at large. The 13th and 14th Amendments and the Radical Reconstruction legislation had yet to be tested, and the expansion of the railroads and large corporations were to pose significant challenges for the formulation of the legal history of the United States.

Civil Rights Issues. From the very start of his tenure as chief justice, Waite made it clear that he opposed direct federal intervention to enforce civil rights in the Southern states. Waite believed that the states alone possessed the right to qualify voters and that the federal government had no jurisdiction to intervene with that process. He wrote the majority opinion in *Minor v. Happersett* (1875), which upheld a state law prohibiting women's suffrage. That case was decided under the 14th Amendment, which had recently been adopted. The Court held that the 14th Amendment did not encompass voting rights, since this right was not necessarily one of the privileges and immunities of citizenship

prior to the adoption of the amendment, nor did this amendment create that right in citizens. Therefore, although all women were citizens if they were born of citizen parents, this did not, in and of itself, provide to them the vote.

He also wrote the majority opinion in *United States v. Reese* (1876), which overturned two sections of the Civil Rights Act of 1870, on the grounds that these sections, not being confined in their operation to unlawful discrimination on account of race, color, or previous servitude, were beyond the limit of the 15th Amendment and unauthorized. Therefore, the Court held that Congress had not provided by "appropriate legislation" for the punishment of an inspector of a municipal election for refusing to receive and count at such election the vote of a black citizen of the United States. Waite also spoke for the Court in *United States v. Cruikshank* (1876), in which the Court held that the alleged violence, oppression, and intimidation used by state officials in preventing blacks from peaceably assembling and voting and in hindering the free exercise of their protected rights could not definitely be proved because the allegations were not specific. The Court explained that the rules of pleading in a criminal case charging conspiracy require certainty and precision in order to find people guilty, and because the allegations did not inform the accused of the exact nature of the offense charged, as is constitutionally required, the indictment was not good nor sufficient in law. The decision of the majority in *The Civil Rights Cases* (1883) made it clear that in order to bring a case under the 14th Amendment, there must be state action; private action does not fall under that constitutional prohibition. This decision, in which Waite concurred, effectively overturned the Civil Rights Act of 1875.

Sovereignty of the States. In the same way that his judicial philosophy in civil rights issues left considerable power in the hands of the states, Waite also believed that the states should be allowed to regulate certain businesses for the public good. In *Munn v. Illinois* (1877), he wrote the opinion in which the Court upheld the constitutional right of states to regulate private businesses in which the public had an interest and, in this case, the rates charged by public grain elevators and warehouses. In fact, Waite considered the "police power" of the state to be so much a responsibility that he held in *Stone v. Mississippi* (1880), a case involving a twenty-five-year state charter to a lottery company, that the state could under no circumstances issue a contract that absolved it of any possibility of interference. "All agree," he wrote, "that the legislature cannot bargain away the police power of a state." He held the same position in regard to the railroads, dissenting in *Wabash, St. Louis, and Pacific Railroad Co. v. Illinois* (1886), in opposition to the ruling that states could not regulate interstate rail rates and that such statutes are void even as to the part of such transmission that may be within the state. He spoke for the Court, however, in *Peik v. Chicago and Northwestern Railroad Co.* (1877), which affirmed the conditions under which states had the right to regulate rail rates.

Up to the time of Waite's tenure, the operative Supreme Court decision with regard to state interference in the operation of private corporations was the Dartmouth College Case (*Dartmouth College v. Woodward*, 1816). In *Ruggles v. Illinois* (1883), Chief Justice Waite delivered the opinion under which the Court decided that states have an indirect means of regulating corporate by-laws, that is, the by-laws were restricted to those that were not repugnant to the laws of the states. Therefore, the amendment to the charter of a railroad company in Illinois did not release the company from restrictions upon the amount of rates contained in general and special statutes of the state. Waite wrote the majority opinion in *Spring Valley Water Works v. Schottler* (1884), ruling that state government even had the right to regulate the manner in which gas and water companies' and other state-granted monopolies' rates were set. In *Schottler* the prices were set by local municipal authorities.

Perhaps Waite's most important opinion in this area came in *Stone v. Farmer's Loan and Trust Company* (1886), in which the Court determined that the states have wide power of regulation of railroads. In *Stone*, a Mississippi statute that created a commission and charged it with the duty of supervising railroads was held to be within the limits of state authority. In this way the state could act upon the reasonableness of the tolls and charges fixed and regulated.

By the same token, Waite was a strong supporter of the wide interpretation of the legitimate police powers and sovereignty of the states. In *Louisiana v. Jumel* (1882), the Court protected the political power of the state to control the money in the state treasury and held that no state statute or judicial decision authorized a suit against Louisiana in its own courts nor could Louisiana be sued in the courts of the United States by a citizen of another state under the 11th Amendment. In the same year, he dissented in *United States v. Lee*, joining the opinion that argued that a suit against federal officers was an impermissible suit against the United States itself, since the United States is exempt from suit without consent, as is each sovereign.

The regulation of interstate commerce was also becoming a very important matter in the years of the Waite Court, and Waite held to the position that while states had an almost unlimited right to regulate businesses operating exclusively within their boundaries, businesses that operated in several states were beyond their jurisdiction. In *Hall v. De Cuir* (1878), he wrote the opinion for the Court that overturned a state law prohibiting discrimination on interstate transport as an interference in the power of Congress to act in this matter. And Waite considerably widened the definition of interstate commerce itself in *Pensacola Telegraph Co. v. Western Union Co.* (1878), when he wrote the opinion for the Court that held that it is not only the right, but the duty, of Congress to take care that intercourse among the states and the transmission of intelligence are not obstructed or unnecessarily encumbered by state legislation.

With regard to individual rights granted by the Constitution, Waite issued several important opinions that closely defined the limits of the Bill of Rights. In *Reynolds v. United States* (1878), a case testing the federal legislation against polygamy in the territories, the Court held in an opinion written by the Chief Justice that the freedom of religion protection extended only to religious beliefs and that a person's religious belief cannot be accepted as justification for committing an overt act made criminal by the law. In *Hurtado v. California* (1884), the Court ruled, with Waite joining the majority, that the 14th Amendment protection of due process did not necessarily require an indictment by a grand jury in a prosecution by a state for murder; that prosecutions for felonies by information are not illegal by virtue of the due process clause of the 14th Amendment.

Throughout his career on the Supreme Court, Waite consistently refused to become involved in political issues. He refused consideration for the Republican presidential nomination in 1876, and in the following year he declined a place on the Electoral Commission, which decided the outcome of that race. Waite served as chief justice until his death in 1888 in Washington, D.C., after a short illness.

WARREN, EARL

b. March 19, 1891; deputy city attorney, Oakland, California (1919-1920); deputy district attorney, Alameda County (1920-1925); district attorney, Alameda County (1925-1939); California attorney general (1939-1943); governor of California (1943-1953); chief justice, U.S. Supreme Court (1953-1969); d. July 9, 1974.

Born in Los Angeles, the son of a Norwegian-born railway worker, Warren was raised in Bakersfield and educated at the University of California at Berkeley, where he received his bachelor's degree in 1912 and his doctorate in jurisprudence in 1914. After his admission to the California bar, he established a private law practice in San Francisco and Oakland. During World War I, he served as an infantry lieutenant in the Army.

After the war, Warren chose to leave his law practice to seek a career in public life. Serving first as the clerk of a state legislative committee in 1919, he later worked in various capacities in the local, county, and state judiciary. As an active member of the California Republican Party, he established a reputation as an aggressive prosecutor, intent on fighting governmental corruption, and he was elected state attorney general in 1938.

In that position, Warren forcefully spoke out against what he identified as subversive elements in society and gained the staunch support of his party's conservative wing. As Warren's reputation in political circles grew, he was urged to seek higher office and was the successful Republican candidate for governor of California in 1942.

During his first year in office, Governor Warren main-

Earl Warren

tained his long-standing law-and-order philosophy, opposing, among other liberal issues, the return of Japanese-Americans who had been relocated at the beginning of World War II. In three successive terms of office, however, Warren's political philosophy began to shift to the left. He established a system of public defenders in the California court system and proposed a state public health insurance plan.

With a much broader base of political support, Warren became active in national Republican politics and accepted the party's vice-presidential nomination in 1948. Running with Thomas Dewey in the hard-fought campaign against the incumbent Harry Truman, Warren suffered the only electoral defeat of his entire political career. Returning to Sacramento, he resumed his gubernatorial responsibilities, and after an unsuccessful bid for the Republican presidential nomination (won by Eisenhower) in 1952, he finally announced his decision not to seek a fourth term as California's governor in 1953.

The sudden death of Chief Justice Fred Vinson at approximately the same time prompted Pres. Dwight D. Eisenhower to appoint Warren to succeed Vinson on the Supreme Court. Warren's nomination was not opposed, and he was confirmed by a voice vote of the Senate on March 1, 1954. It was assumed by most observers at the time that Warren would bring to the office a generally conservative judicial philosophy; in contrast to those expectations, however, Warren's assumption of the office of chief justice initiated one of the most active and controversial periods in the history of the Court.

The Chief Justice and the Court. The common belief that a chief justice directly influences the decisions of the Supreme Court over which he presides is both realistic and inaccurate. While it is true that the U.S. Supreme Court popularly bears the name of the chief justice then sitting, the office of chief justice itself presents few opportunities for shaping the decisions of the Court as a whole. While the chief justice presides at oral argument, any associate justice may question the advocates. The chief justice, when he is a member of the majority, assigns the job of opinion-writing, but when he is in the minority, assignments are made by the majority's senior associate justice.

A chief justice with a reputation for substantial scholarship or a long tradition of meritorious judicial service might well influence his less-accomplished fellows on the Court, but Earl Warren, whose legal career was overshadowed by his political achievements, was neither of these. Further, he was appointed to head a court whose membership included three gifted and cantankerous appointees of Franklin D. Roosevelt: Hugo Black, liberal and self-styled 1st Amendment literalist; William O. Douglas, New Deal architect, former Securities and Exchange Commission chairman, and Yale law professor; and Felix Frankfurter, Harvard law professor and American Civil Liberties Union founder, a man by general agreement considered to be the most influential law teacher of his generation. Frankfurter had grown conservative as an associate justice and had become the leader of a conservative trio of justices comprising himself, Harold Burton, and Stanley Reed. More moderate, or at least less predictable in their opinions, were Justices Tom Clark, Robert Jackson, and Sherman Minton, who was to retire in 1956 and be succeeded by William Brennan.

For either critics or admirers to credit Earl Warren with an intellectual or political domination over so diverse and mature a set of justices is hardly credible. On the contrary, each member of the Warren Court, seventeen in the fifteen-year history of that Court, found himself inundated by waves of requested redress for widely-perceived postwar sociological grievances. In dealing with the specific issues and points of law, each justice developed his own philosophical viewpoint. Judicial positions gradually coalesced, and the Warren Court, the Chief Justice leading, often following, occasionally foot-dragging in dissent, began to restructure American society.

The Segregation Decisions. Chief Justice Warren's most important judicial opinion, and one of the most important ever promulgated by any justice, was written for a unanimous Court in *Brown v. Board of Education* (1954). Relying in large part on the belief that governmentally-required racial segregation in public schools produced ineradicable feelings of racial inferiority on the part of members of the stigmatized race, the opinion overturned *Plessy v. Ferguson* (1896), which had permitted such segregation where the segregated facilities "were substantially equal." In the course of overturning *Plessy*, Warren included observations about the influence history might properly have on this and other interpretations of the equal protection clause of the 14th Amendment:

> In approaching this problem, we cannot turn the clock back to when the Amendment was adopted, or even to 1896 when *Plessy v. Ferguson* was written. We must consider public education in the light of its full development and its present place in American life throughout the Nation. Only in this way can it be determined if segregation in public schools deprives these plaintiffs of the equal protection of the laws.

This approach to history and, consequently, to precedent was to prove prophetic. Much of the constitutional jurisprudence of the Warren Court was characterized by strong unwillingness to be limited to the contexts and practices of the past. The *Brown* opinion, however, was remarkable for a third reason; in addition to its substantive result and its relegation of history to a diminished role in constitutional interpretation, the opinion was unanimous. Here Warren, at the very outset of his career as chief justice, was able to bring about a rare unanimity of expression on this most controversial of issues, racial segregation, and to prevent the all-but-unpersuadable members of the Court from filing separate concurrences, or even dissents. Two concurrences had been written, by Justices Frankfurter and Jackson, but were abandoned by their authors, largely at the behest of Chief Justice Warren. It is probable that a partial price for this unanimity of expression was the unusual step of separating remedy, or implementation, from an opinion on the question of law itself. One year later, in *Brown v. Board of Education* (1955), the Court asked for reargument regarding compliance. The second case came to be known as *Brown II*. Warren, again for a unanimous Court, ordered desegregation of the public schools "with all deliberate speed," a standard for desegregation performance that was to leave the nation's school system largely unchanged at the end of his career as chief justice.

The last of Warren's segregation opinions occurred in 1967, again the expression of a unanimous Court. In *Loving v. Virginia* (1967), a Virginia state law prohibiting interracial marriage was held to violate the 14th Amendment. No public outcry followed this decision, in contrast to the *Brown* decisions of the previous decade. The illegality of governmental racial classification for any invidious purpose was by then well established, and the civil rights movement had long since turned its attention to the redress of perceived private social and economic harms.

A discussion of Earl Warren's racial decisions must also consider his support for Franklin Roosevelt's Executive Order 9066, promulgated in February 1942, when Warren was California attorney general, and in effect during Warren's first term as California governor. This order authorized the relocation of West Coast Japanese-Americans to barracks in desert regions of the American West. While support for this relocation was an understandable response to the national and particularly California trauma that followed Pearl Harbor, the Supreme Court upheld the order in *Korematsu v. United States* in 1944. The patently racial nature of the classification (no German- or Italian-Americans were relocated) and Warren's unnecessarily vehement support for it hardly suggest that he would later write the unanimous opinions in *Brown v. Board of Education* and *Loving v. Virginia*.

Warren's support for Executive Order 9066, which he later deeply regretted, illustrates two things that characterized Warren throughout his public life: first, his celebrated and often criticized growth or change in office, and second, the professional background that initially separated him from his colleagues on the Court. Preeminently a politician, Governor Warren had been highly respected by members of both parties for his political acumen and for his undeniable energy in office. His racial segregation decisions, indeed his decisions in general, exhibit the politician's best gifts: sensitivity to needed change and a willingness to use the governmental instruments at hand to effect the changes. This predisposition for action was quickly to characterize the Warren Court itself.

Reapportionment Decisions. Unlike the segregation cases, which involved the early overruling of some precedents (*Plessy v. Ferguson*) and the extension of others (*Sweatt v. Painter*, 1950), the reapportionment decisions came late (*Baker v. Carr*, 1962) and literally were unprecedented to the Warren Court. The decisions were unprecedented because the federal judiciary had traditionally held voter complaints about legislative malapportionment outside the competencies of the federal courts to redress. Two reasons were offered for this stance: first, that claims were outside the jurisdiction of the federal courts, and second, that even if the claims were inside federal jurisdiction, they were not "justiciable" because redress for malapportionment was by implication a prerogative of the legislative branch.

Thus, a very limited view of federal court jurisdiction, the so-called "political question" doctrine, and the expanding American population had worked together by the late 1960's to produce congressional and state legislative districts so different in population that many congressmen or state legislators represented two or even three times as many voters as others. Not suprisingly, state legislatures and even the federal Congress, populated as they were by the direct or indirect beneficiaries of this malapportionment, showed predictable reluctance to upset the status quo by periodic reapportionment. Further, and perhaps most importantly, there were no accepted guidelines for the drafting of new district boundaries. Since no legislative seat would be safe if all district lines were to be redrawn, the consequence was that as malapportionment grew, so did legislative reluctance to address it.

This reluctance to consider malapportionment cases was swept away by the Court's decision in *Baker v. Carr* (1962). Justice Brennan, speaking for a majority that included Chief Justice Warren, found voter-sponsored reapportionment cases within the jurisdiction of the federal courts and also found that voters were proper parties to bring such cases. Furthermore, he ruled that the issues were "justiciable" within the scope of the now much-reduced "political question" doctrine. The *Baker* majority did not, however, indicate what constitutional doctrine required proper apportionment of legislative districts, thus setting the stage for the appearance, two years later, of Chief Justice Warren's majority opinion in *Reynolds v. Sims* (1964): "We hold that, as a basic constitutional standard, the Equal Protection Clause [of the 14th Amendment] requires that the seats in both houses of a bicameral state legislature must be apportioned on a population basis." Responding directly to the widespread view that states, basing their practices on the federal Senate model, should have at least one division of their house apportioned along county lines, Warren reasoned: "Considerations of area alone provide an insufficient justification for deviation from the equal-population principle. Again, people, not land or trees or pastures, vote."

As had occurred following the segregation decisions of the preceding decade, the Warren Court's reapportionment decisions produced powerful responses. The House of Representatives passed a bill that attacked the *Reynolds* decision and, more significantly, Illinois Sen. Everett Dirkson proposed a constitutional amendment allowing states to retain their now unconstitutionally apportioned districts. Both attempts were narrowly defeated in the Senate.

Once again, Warren's record as a California politician offered no clue to the position he would so emphatically espouse as chief justice. In 1948, Governor Warren had defended California malapportionment even though Los Angeles, with a population numbering in the millions, was given no more representation in the California Senate than California counties with populations of less than 50,000. Commenting after his retirement on this apparent paradox, Warren observed: "In California . . . [it] simply was a matter of political expediency. But I saw the situation in a different light on the Court. There, you have a different responsibility to the entire country."

Unlike the Eisenhower administration in the 1950's, when its support for the segregation decisions was somewhat measured, the Kennedy-Johnson administration wholeheartedly embraced the reapportionment decisions of the 1960's. *Gray v. Sanders* (1963), which held unconstitutional Georgia's county unit primary system, was itself successfully argued by Attorney General Robert Kennedy. Another significant difference was that the apportionment decisions, although bitterly opposed initially, found a much more rapid acceptance by legislators than did the segregation decisions of the preceding decade. While the 1968 presidential campaign was replete with criticism of the Chief Justice and his colleagues, hostility to the reapportionment decisions themselves was notably absent, and legislative compliance to them was largely complete.

Church-State Relations. As he had with the subjects of segregation and reapportionment, Warren wrote the initial opinions on church-state relations himself. Here, however, he was less successful in conveying his message. The essential formulation necessary to harmonious yet independent relations between church and state seemed to elude him, and as if in recognition of the unsatisfactory nature of his work, he began to assign majority opinions on these cases to other justices.

Two clauses in the 1st Amendment control the church-state relationship: first, the free exercise clause, which purports to bar governmental interference with the free exercise of religion, and second, the establishment clause, which prohibits governmental establishment of religion. Warren's majority opinions in four cases decided on May 29, 1961, dealt with both establishment and free exercise-based objections to Sunday closing laws.

In *McGowan v. Maryland* (1961), and *Two Guys from Harrison-Allentown, Inc. v. McGinley* (1961), employees of two large discount department stores had been convicted of selling merchandise on Sunday in violation of Maryland and Pennsylvania law respectively. Neither appellants argued infringement of their religious liberty, but only that they had suffered economic injury because they were required to close on Sunday. Their argument that the equal protection clause of the 14th Amendment prevented the state from exempting certain commodities (drugs, gasoline, refreshments, etc.) from the closing requirement was rejected on the basis of well-understood 14th Amendment precedents. Finally, Warren considered the contention that Sunday closing laws themselves constituted an establishment of religion and concluded that most of them were of a secular rather than of a religious character. Therefore, he did not think that they bore a relationship to the establishment of religion and held that the states could enact such laws.

The questions presented by *Braunfeld v. Brown* (1961) and *Gallagher v. Crown Kosher Super Market* (1961) were more difficult. Both cases involved objections by Orthodox Jews to a closing requirement and to the dilemma that the requirement created for them. If they closed on Sunday, as the state required, they would lose a day of business to their non-Sabbatarian competitors, for their Orthodox religion required them to close their businesses on Saturday as well. This, they argued, prohibited the free exercise of their religion; they were forced either to lose business or to violate a tenet of their faith. Here Warren wrote for a plurality consisting only of himself and Justices Clark, Black, and Whittaker; concurrences were written by Justices Harlan and Frankfurter. After careful examination of the relevant free exercise precedents, Warren concluded not that they should be overruled, but rather that they were inapplicable, commenting in *Braunfeld* that "the law's effect does not inconvenience all members of the Orthodox Jewish faith but only those who believe it necessary to work on Sunday." Braunfeld's argument that the secular purposes of the statute could be achieved and his religious objections accommodated if the state were to allow Sabbatarians to substitute their day of rest for Sunday was also rejected by Warren.

Two years later *Braunfeld*'s authority as a precedent was deeply undercut by *Sherbert v. Verner* (1963). In that case, South Carolina had refused unemployment compensation to a Seventh Day Adventist who was unable to obtain employment because he refused to work on Saturday, his Sabbath. He argued that the unemployment compensation law discriminated against workers with religious objections to Saturday work. Justice Brennan, who had dissented in *Braunfeld*, wrote the majority opinion in *Sherbert*, reasoning that the state was required to show "a compelling interest" before it could restrain religious liberty and made clear that this standard was applicable to both direct (*Reynolds*) and indirect (*Braunfeld*) restraints. *Braunfeld*, however, was not overruled, although its authority appeared highly questionable after *Sherbert*. Justice Warren silently joined but did not lead the *Sherbert* majority.

Warren also joined the majority in two controversial establishment clause cases that prohibited prayer and Bible-reading in the public schools: *Engel v. Vitale* (1962), and *School District of Abington Township v. Schempp* (1963). Warren was himself a sincerely religious man, and he expressed in his *Memoirs* the motives for his votes in these cases, believing that they were not suggested by the opinions themselves:

> We also were heavily attacked by many people, particularly legislators, when we declared compulsory prayers in the public schools to be unconstitutional. I vividly remember one bold newspaper headline saying "Court outlaws God." Many religious denominations in the same spirit condemned the Court . . . Scores of Constitutional Amendments and legislative bills were proposed in the Congress to circumvent the decision but were later abandoned when the public came to recognize that the ruling was not an irreligious one. Rather it tried to maintain the separation of church and state guaranteed by the First Amendment.

Criminal Procedure. Two policies appear to have motivated Chief Justice Warren and the Warren Court in their dramatic alteration of the law of criminal procedure. There was a desire to bring state and federal criminal justice systems into greater procedural congruity, and there was also a wish to eradicate or at least greatly minimize disparate treatment of rich and poor within both systems.

At the outset of Warren's tenure as chief justice, the federal criminal justice system provided protections for the accused that were largely unavailable in comparable state prosecutions: indigent defendants were provided with counsel (*Brown v. Mississippi*, 1936); evidence produced by searches and seizures in violation of the 4th Amendment were excluded from trials (*Weeks v. United States*, 1914); and confessions produced by coercion and/or delay in bring-

ing the accused before a judicial official were inadmissible (*McNabb v. United States*, 1943). These protections either did not apply to state defendants, or they were applied in such a restricted manner as to attenuate the protection. The 4th Amendment prohibition against unreasonable search and seizure, for example, applied to state prosecutions, but not to the admissibility of illegally obtained evidence (*Wolf v. Colorado*, 1949).

Warren's first decision in criminal procedure occurred during his first term in office. In *Irvine v. California* (1954), Patrick Irvine, a Long Beach bookmaker, had been convicted on the basis of evidence produced by a microphone illegally planted in his bedroom by Long Beach police officers. Irvine's only hope of avoiding a term in jail turned on the applicability to his case of either *Wolf v. Colorado*, which would deem the evidence inadmissible, or *Rochin v. California* (1952), holding the evidence obtained by a police-compelled stomach-pumping inadmissible in Rochin's trial for narcotics violation. Warren, voting to break the four-four deadlock, refused to extend *Rochin*'s "assault of the body" exclusionary rule to the evidence produced by the illegally-planted *Irvine* microphone.

During the 1956-1957 term, however, Warren was no longer willing to exonerate law enforcement practices he felt to be unconscionable and unconstitutional. In *Breithaupt v. Abram* (1957), a case much like *Rochin*, he dissented with Justices Black and Douglas, arguing that a state conviction of manslaughter could not be based on evidence of intoxication established by a blood test taken while the defendant was unconscious following an automobile collision. In *In re Groban* (1957), with Justices Douglas and Brennan he joined a dissent by Justice Black, arguing that the state could not compel a person to appear alone before a law enforcement officer and give testimony against his will. In *Grunewald v. United States* (1957), he joined a concurring opinion by Justice Black and Justices Douglas and Brennan, objecting to the majority view that a court could draw inference about lack of honesty from a defendant's use of the privilege against self-incrimination.

The late 1950's and early 1960's thus found the Chief Justice repeatedly teamed with Justices Black, Douglas, and Brennan, dissenting in matters dealing with criminal procedure. When on occasion they were joined by Justice Clark, or, as in *Griffin v. Illinois* (1956), by Justice Frankfurter, dramatic changes were worked in the law. *Griffin* invalidated state statutes requiring filing and transcript fees from indigent defendants wishing to appeal their convictions–a major cause of indigent defendant failure to appeal. Warren, however, did not write either the dissenting or the rare majority opinions with which he agreed.

The Black-Douglas-Brennan-Warren criminal procedure wing of the Court received increasing support from every justice appointed after 1957. Potter Stewart, Eisenhower's last appointee, replaced Burton in 1958; Byron

White replaced Whittaker in 1962; Arthur Goldberg replaced Frankfurter in 1962; Abe Fortas replaced Goldberg in 1965; and Thurgood Marshall replaced Clark in 1967. It was during the tenure of these men that the great changes in the American criminal justice system were accomplished. The mechanism utilized was the judicial "incorporation" of selected segments from the Bill of Rights (the first eight amendments) into the 14th Amendment, since this allowed amendments originally limiting the activities only of the federal government to be applied to the states.

Mapp v. Ohio (1961), for instance, applied the 4th Amendment to the states and held illegally seized evidence inadmissible in state criminal proceedings. The 5th Amendment privilege against self-incrimination was applied to the states by *Malloy v. Hogan* (1964). The 6th Amendment provisions guaranteeing right to counsel, confrontation of witness, speedy trial, and jury trial were incorporated in *Gideon v. Wainwright* (1963), *Pointer v. Texas* (1965), *Klopfer v. North Carolina* (1967), and *Duncan v. Louisiana* (1968), respectively. The cruel and unusual punishment limitations of the 8th Amendment were incorporated in *Robinson v. California* (1962). Warren joined the majority in all these cases, but wrote only *Klopfer*, an incorporation opinion in which he briefly explored Anglo-American roots of the 6th Amendment's speedy trial guarantee.

Warren's great opinion in this area came, as *Reynolds* had followed *Baker v. Carr*, in an attempt to clarify and extend a controversial recent precedent. The recent precedent this time was the celebrated case of *Escobedo v. Illinois* (1964). Escobedo had been arrested and interrogated about the fatal shooting of his brother-in-law, and although he had repeatedly asked to see his lawyer and although his lawyer, also present at the police station, had asked to see Escobedo, the police refused for hours to bring the two together, allowing a conference only after Escobedo had made incriminating statements to the police about the killing.

Justice Goldberg, writing for a majority that included Chief Justice Warren, had little difficulty overturning Escobedo's conviction. "When [law enforcement] . . . shifts from investigatory to accusatory–when its focus is on the accused and its purpose is to elicit a confession–our adversary system begins to operate, and, under the circumstances here, the accused must be permitted to consult with his lawyer." After the *Escobedo* decision, questions quickly arose as to the scope of police duty to warn or inform suspects of their right to counsel.

This decision set the stage for the Court's ruling in *Miranda v. Arizona* (1966). Miranda was arrested at his home, taken to a Phoenix police station, and identified by a complaining witness. He was then moved to an interrogation room and questioned by two police officers. Miranda was not informed that he had a right to have an attorney present and two hours of questioning produced a written confession signed by Miranda and containing a paragraph that stated that the confession was voluntary and made "with full knowledge of my legal rights, understanding any statement I make may be used against me." He was convicted of kidnapping and rape, receiving two sentences of from twenty to thirty years' imprisonment, to run concurrently.

The Chief Justice, speaking for a five-man majority, reversed Miranda's conviction and created the famed "Miranda warning," which included the opinion that:

> . . . when an individual is taken into custody or otherwise deprived of his freedom by the authorities in any significant way and is subject to questioning, the privilege against self-incrimination is jeopardized. Procedural safeguards must be employed to protect the privilege, and unless other fully effective means are adopted to notify the person of his rights of silence and to assure that the exercise of the right will be scrupulously honored, the following measures are required. He must be warned prior to any questioning that he has the right to remain silent, that anything he says can be used against him in a court of law, that he has the right to the presence of an attorney, and that if he cannot afford an attorney one will be appointed for him prior to any questioning if he so desires. Opportunity to exercise these rights must be afforded to him throughout the interrogation. After such warnings have been given, and such opportunity afforded him, the individual may knowingly and intelligently waive these rights and agree to answer questions or make a statement. But unless and until such warnings and waiver are demonstrated by the prosecution at trial, no evidence obtained as a result of interrogation can be used against him . . .

Again, Warren's background as an anti-racketeering California district attorney and the generally strong anti-crime positions that he took in that office do not suggest the pro-defense posture of his years as chief justice. Warren's *Memoirs*, however, reveal his deeper insights into the sociopolitical concerns of *Miranda*. He felt that the attacks on *Miranda* were unwarranted and that "there was really nothing new . . . except to require police and prosecutors to advise the poor, the ignorant, and the unwary of a basic constitutional right in a manner which had been followed by the Federal Bureau of Investigation procedures . . . ."

Obscenity Issues. Like reapportionment, constitutional limitations on the ability of state and federal governments to regulate obscene or pornographic materials were nonexistent prior to the Warren Court's attempt to provide them in *Roth v. United States* (1957). Roth had been convicted under a federal statute that prohibited the mailing of obscene, lewd, lascivious, filthy, or indecent material and made knowing attempts to mail such items a crime. Justice Brennan, speaking for the majority of five, found obscene materials outside the protection of the 1st and 14th Amendments and thereby made a precise definition of obscenity central to subsequent litigation. He ruled that the statute in question was constitutionally sound and that the federal regulation of obscene materials was proper. Chief Justice Warren concurred, but he expressed reservations about the breadth of the majority opinion, which he believed might permit limitation of legitimate expression. He wanted to limit the decision to the facts because the "line dividing the salacious or pornographic from literature or science is not straight and unwavering."

Few observations have been more accurate, yet the Warren Court subsequently struggled mightily, but never successfully (or popularly), with a definition of obscene material. By 1964, however, Warren had accepted the *Roth* test of obscenity: that obscene material is that which "to the average person, applying contemporary community standards . . . appeals to prurient interest." When acknowledging his acceptance of this test (as in *Jacobellis v. Ohio*, 1964), however, Warren argued that the community standards were local and strongly suggested that the Supreme Court could avoid the pitfalls of censorship by merely examining trial records to determine whether sufficient evidence existed to prove that the constitutional test was satisfied.

Two years later, in *A Book Named "John Cleland's Memoirs of a Woman of Pleasure" v. Attorney General of Massachusetts* (1966), Warren joined Justices Fortas and Brennan in a Brennan-authored opinion that added a new element to the *Roth* test of obscenity, that the work be "utterly without redeeming social value." Although greatly influential in the lower courts, this test never proved acceptable to a majority of the Warren Court.

Conclusion. In addition to his judicial responsibilities, Warren accepted the request of Pres. Lyndon Johnson in 1963 to head a special commission to investigate the assassination of Pres. John F. Kennedy. The report of the Warren Commission, as it came to be known, received widespread criticism for its apparent eagerness to demonstrate that Lee Harvey Oswald, the alleged assassin, had acted alone and was not involved in any wider conspiracy.

In 1969, after fifteen years of service, Warren resigned from the Supreme Court. He was succeeded by Warren Burger, who was appointed by Pres. Richard Nixon. Within a year of Warren's retirement, the philosophical outlook of the Court had already begun to shift to the right, but the contribution of the Warren years had left an indelible mark. Warren's leadership had accelerated the Court's self-conscious evolution into a body that actively defended and defined civil liberties rather than merely elucidating specific points of law.

Warren's contribution to this change in the governmental role of the Supreme Court, however, did not appear to have been the product of any serious personal debate. The chief justice left such political and philosophical concerns to those on the Court most interested in them, notably Justices Frankfurter and Black. Instead, he seems to have asked in each case to come before the Court, "What is the proper result?" To that end, Warren devoted the final years of his life to a reform of the American judicial system, working

with one of his former colleagues, retired Justice Tom C. Clark, on the recommendations of a public foundation, the Federal Judicial Center. He lived in Washington, D.C., after his retirement and died there in 1974.

WASHINGTON, BUSHROD

b. June 5, 1762; various legislative and legal positions in Virginia; associate justice, U.S. Supreme Court (1798-1829); d. November 26, 1829.

The nephew of George Washington and the son of John and Hannah Bushrod Washington, Bushrod Washington was born in Westmoreland County, Virginia, and educated at the College of William and Mary (Class of 1778). After service in the Continental Army during the Revolution, Washington studied law in the office of James Wilson (later one of the original associate justices of the Supreme Court) and was elected to the Virginia House of Delegates in 1787. In 1788, he was elected to the Virginia State Convention, at which he strongly supported ratification of the Constitution. Upon the death of James Wilson in 1798, Washington was nominated by President Adams to the Supreme Court.

During his tenure on the Court, Washington was closely associated with Chief Justice John Marshall and rarely dissented from the Chief Justice's opinions. One of Washington's most important opinions, in *Green v. Biddle* (1823), established the Supreme Court's power to overrule a state law on the grounds that it impaired the obligation of a valid contract. In *Terret v. Taylor* (1815), the five justices present ruled that church lands must be considered private property beyond the control of the state. His most significant dissent from the majority of the Court was in *Mason v. Haile* (1827), in which he argued unsuccessfully that a state cannot retroactively abolish imprisonment for debt.

He was married to Julia Ann Blackburn in 1785. After the death of Martha Washington, George Washington's widow, in 1802, Bushrod inherited Mount Vernon, which became his home until his death in 1829.

WAYNE, JAMES MOORE

b. c.1790; various legislative and judicial positions in Georgia; member, U.S. House of Representatives (1829-1835); associate justice, U.S. Supreme Court (1835-1867); d. July 5, 1867.

The son of a British army officer who had emigrated to South Carolina before the Revolution and eventually settled in Savannah, Georgia, Wayne was educated by a private tutor and entered Princeton at age fourteen. After his graduation in 1808, he returned to Savannah and studied law with John Y. Noel; he later moved to New Haven, Connecticut, and continued his law studies with Judge Chauncy there. In 1810, he was admitted to the Georgia bar and began private practice in Savannah. After service in the War of 1812, he was elected to the Georgia House of Representatives

(1815-1816) and served afterward as the mayor of Savannah (1817-1819). In 1822 he was nominated as a judge of the Georgia superior court. He began the first of three terms in the U.S. House of Representatives in 1829. Wayne was a strong supporter of the Jackson administration, and in 1835, with the death of Associate Justice William Johnson, President Jackson appointed Wayne to the Supreme Court.

Wayne's tenure on the Court was characterized by his attempt to achieve a compromise on the issue of slavery and by his support for the preservation of the Union, despite pressure from fellow Southerners. In the Dred Scott Case (*Scott v. Sandford*, 1857), he concurred with the majority that Congress did not have the authority, under any of the powers granted it by the Constitution, to abolish slavery in the territories of the United States and that the Missouri Compromise therefore was unconstitutional and void.

With the outbreak of the Civil War, Wayne opposed the secession of his home state and continued to serve on the Supreme Court. His last important opinion came in *Ex parte Milligan* (1866), in which he agreed with the majority that the president had no constitutional right to deny any of the safeguards of civil liberty to citizens not connected with the military service and never resident in a state in rebellion. Wayne served on the Court until his death in Washington, D.C., in 1867.

WHITE, BYRON RAYMOND

b. June 8, 1917; clerk to the chief justice, U.S. Supreme Court (1946-1947); deputy U.S. attorney general (1961-1962); associate justice, U.S. Supreme Court (1962-).

Born in Fort Collins, Colorado, White was educated at the University of Colorado (Class of 1938), where he received national recognition as an All-American football player and earned his nickname "Whizzer." He played professional football for one season after his graduation and then studied at Oxford as a Rhodes scholar. In 1940, he entered the Yale Law School and played two more seasons in the National Football League. During World War II he served in the Navy, returning to Yale after the war to earn his law degree in 1946. In 1947, he served as clerk to Chief Justice Fred Vinson and subsequently established a private law practice in Denver. A strong supporter and friend of Pres. John F. Kennedy, White was appointed deputy attorney general in 1961. In 1962, with the resignation of Associate Justice Charles Whittaker, President Kennedy appointed White to the Supreme Court.

Despite his liberal political background, White proved to be a relative conservative on the court. He joined the dissent in *Malloy v. Hogan* (1964), which extended the privilege against self-incrimination to criminal defendants in state courts. He joined the dissenting opinion in *Aptheker v. Secretary of State* (1964), arguing that the Court should not have invalidated a statute that withheld passports from citi-

Byron R. White

zens who were members of the Communist Party. Significantly, White also dissented in the landmark criminal defendants' rights cases of *Escobedo v. Illinois* (1964) and *Miranda v. Arizona* (1966).

One of White's particular areas of interest was the role of the jury in criminal procedure. He wrote the majority opinion in *Duncan v. Louisiana* (1968), which held that the due process clause of the 14th Amendment entitles defendants accused of serious crimes in state courts to receive a jury trial. He also wrote the majority opinion in *Williams v. Florida* (1970), which upheld the constitutionality of six-person juries in state criminal cases. He spoke for the Court in *Taylor v. Louisiana* (1975), which held unconstitutional state jury selection procedures excluding women from service on juries.

In civil rights issues, White joined the dissenting opinion in *Jones v. Alfred H. Mayer Co.* (1968), arguing that the 1870 civil rights statute prohibiting racial discrimination in leasing and selling property should not apply to purely private discrimination, but only to discrimination occurring under color of state law. He wrote the majority opinion in *Washington v. Davis* (1976), holding that while the equal protection components of the 5th and 14th Amendments prohibit intentional, invidious discrimination, they do not extend protection to groups that are unintentionally affected by a racially neutral policy. He voted with the justices in *Regents of the University of California v. Bakke* (1977), who held that racial quotas in state universities to overcome the effects of past discrimination do not violate the equal protection clause. He also spoke for the Court in *Columbus Board of Education v. Penick* (1979), which upheld the lower court's finding that the school system had an intentionally segregated school system, which must be dismantled.

WHITE, EDWARD DOUGLASS JR.

b. November 3, 1845; member, Louisiana Senate (1874); justice, Louisiana Supreme Court (1878-1880); U.S. senator (1891-1894); associate justice, U.S. Supreme Court (1894-1911); chief justice, U.S. Supreme Court (1911-1921); d. May 19, 1921.

Edward D. White, Jr.

Born in Lafourche Parish, Louisiana, the son of Edward Douglass White, a former judge, congressman, and governor of Louisiana, the younger White was raised on the family's sugar plantation. After the death of his father, he was educated at Mount St. Mary's College in Maryland, the Jesuit College in New Orleans, and Georgetown College in Washington, D.C. With the outbreak of the Civil War and the secession of his native state from the Union, White left college and enlisted in the Confederate Army, serving as an *aide de camp*. In 1863, at age eighteen, he was taken prisoner by Union forces after the fall of Port Huston. He was released later in the year and remained in Louisiana throughout the rest of the war.

In 1865, White began his law studies in the New Orleans office of Attorney Edward Bermudez and at the same time became a student at the University of Louisiana (later Tulane) Law School. He was admitted to the bar in 1868. It was White's intention to follow the tradition established by his father and to enter public life. After establishing a private law practice in New Orleans, he became involved in Democratic Party politics in the state.

An ardent opponent of the Reconstruction policies of the federal government, White was elected to the Louisiana senate in 1874. Two years after the victory of the anti-Reconstruction forces in the disputed state election of 1876, White was appointed a justice of the Louisiana Supreme Court at age thirty-three. His tenure in this position was brief, however; the election of a rival Democractic faction and the adoption of a new state constitution in 1880 with a new age minimum for state judges forced White to resign from the bench.

For almost a decade, White pursued his private law practice, while also remaining active in political affairs. In the election of 1888, there were charges of corruption in the state lottery, and, as a result of his active support of the victorious anti-lottery faction, White was elected by the legislature to the U.S. Senate in 1891.

Appointment to the Court. In 1893, Associate Justice Samuel Blatchford died, and Pres. Grover Cleveland intended to follow tradition in the appointment of a successor to the seat that had been occupied by a New Yorker since 1806. There was another tradition, however, that of "senatorial courtesy," which required that every judicial appointment gain the tacit approval of the senators of the candidate's state. One of the New York senators, David B. Hill, was a bitter political rival of President Cleveland, and he rejected both of Cleveland's New York nominations, William Hornblower and Wheeler Peckham (whose younger brother Rufus would be appointed associate justice the following year). President Cleveland thereafter abandoned any attempt to placate his rival and selected not a New Yorker, but a Louisianan, Sen. Edward White, for the Supreme Court.

White was confirmed as associate justice on February 19, 1894. The regional tradition was broken, and it would not be the last tradition to fall in White's long Supreme Court tenure. In 1910, after the sudden death of Chief Justice Melville Fuller, Pres. William Howard Taft appointed White to succeed Fuller. This was the first time in Supreme Court history that an associate justice was appointed and confirmed as chief justice.

Economic Regulation Issues. At the time of White's appointment as associate justice, the Supreme Court was faced with growing pressure from two main groups in American society. The industrialization of the country had created radical new economic conditions and both organized labor and organized management were anxious for the Court to intervene on their behalf.

Throughout his twenty-seven years on the Court, White was repeatedly called upon to deal with the increasingly important economic issues surrounding corporate combinations and their effect on free trade. In *United States v. E.C. Knight and Co.* (1895), he joined the majority in effectively subverting the intention of the Sherman Antitrust Act. In this decision the Court determined that a corporation that controlled 98 percent of the sugar manufactured in the United States was not in violation of the federal law, because Congress did not have the authority under the commerce clause to intervene in the manufacture of products, only in their interstate sale. Nine years later White joined the dissent in *Northern Securities Co. v. United States* (1904), which broadened the definition of a trust to include holding companies.

It was only after he became chief justice, however, that White laid down the judicial definition of a trust that is still used in the courts. Speaking for the Court in *Standard Oil Co. v. United States* (1911), he established the "rule of reason" as a criterion for illegality and defined illegal trusts as only those that restrain trade to an unreasonable degree. He used substantially the same arguments in the companion case of *United States v. American Tobacco Co.* (1911), which led to the reorganization, but not to the dissolution, of the tobacco trust.

It is significant that White joined the dissent in the landmark income tax case of *Pollock v. Farmers' Loan and Trust Co.* (1895). In this case the majority overturned the federal income tax law of 1894, which had prescribed a flat 2 percent tax on all incomes of more than $4,000 a year. The majority of the justices ruled that since some of the revenue collected by this tax came from the income derived from land, it was therefore a direct tax as defined by the Constitution and could be apportioned among the states only according to population, not by individuals. White opposed this attack on the revenue gathering power of the federal government, and his position was later validated by the passage of the 16th Amendment in 1913. White wrote the majority opinion in *Brushaber v. Union Pacific Railroad Co.* (1916), which upheld the income tax law and overturned the previous decision of the Court.

White's position with regard to federal regulation of commerce was also subject to change. He concurred in the Lottery Case (*Champion v. Ames*, 1903), which upheld congressional authority under the commerce clause to prohibit the shipment of lottery tickets through the mails. He wrote the majority opinion in *McCray v. United States* (1904), which considerably expanded the power of the federal government by upholding a law that allowed it to use its taxing power for the public good. He wrote the majority opinion in *Clark Distilling Co. v. Western Maryland Railway* (1917), which held that states may prohibit the entry of alcoholic beverages without burdening interstate commerce. However, he joined the majority in *Hammer v. Dagenhart* (1918), which overturned a federal law prohibiting the interstate shipment of goods made with child labor because it was beyond Congress's power under the commerce clause.

Social Issues. In the Insular Cases (1901), White joined the dissent in *DeLima v. Bidwell*, arguing against the Court's contention that products from American territories should not be subject to import tariffs. White concurred in *Downes v. Bidwell*, which held that constitutional guarantees are not automatically extended to residents of American territories. White believed that there was an essential legal distinction between "incorporated" and "unincorporated" territories, and this was a concept accepted by the Court in *Dorr v. United States* (1904).

White's judicial philosophy with regard to social legislation and the "police power" of state and federal governments changed during the course of his Supreme Court career. He joined Justice Harlan's dissent in *Lochner v. New York* (1905), which argued that the state's police power enables it to regulate the length of working hours for women, but he opposed a similar universal standard for men in his dissent in *Bunting v. Oregon* (1917). While he joined the Court in upholding a New York state workman's compensation law in *New York Central Railroad Co. v. White* (1917), he joined the dissent in *Mountain Timber Co. v. Washington* (1917), which upheld a slightly different version of the same program in Washington state.

In White's most important civil rights decision, he spoke for the Court in *Guinn v. United States* (1915), which held unconstitutional a "grandfather clause" in the Oklahoma constitution that exempted all voters whose ancestors voted prior to 1866 from a literacy test, since it unfairly tended to restrict the voting population to those voting before the adoption of the 15th Amendment. Therefore, the law was obviously intended to make difficult the enfranchisement of the black population of the state. White also wrote the majority opinion in the *Selective Draft Law Cases* (1918), which held that the constitutional authority of Congress to raise armies in the national defense does not violate the 13th Amendments's protection against involuntary servitude or other constitutional guarantees of liberty.

White was married in 1894, the year of his appointment to the Supreme Court, to Leita Kent. He served on the Court until his death in Washington, D.C., in 1921.

WHITTAKER, CHARLES EVANS

b. February 22, 1901; judge, U.S. District Court (1954-1956); judge, U.S. Circuit Court of Appeals (1956-1957); associate justice, U.S. Supreme Court (1957-1962); d. November 26, 1973.

Born in Troy, Kansas, the son of a local farmer, Whittaker left high school before graduation, but was nevertheless admitted to the University of Kansas City (Missouri) Law School at age nineteen. After passing the bar in 1923, he joined a Kansas City law firm, eventually becoming a full partner and being elected president of the Missouri Bar Association. In 1954, he was appointed judge of the U.S. District Court for western Missouri and in 1956, he became judge of the U.S. Court of Appeals for the 8th Circuit. With the resignation of Associate Justice Stanley Reed in 1957, President Eisenhower appointed Whittaker to Reed's seat on the Supreme Court.

During his five-year tenure on the Court, Whittaker distinguished himself as a relative conservative with regard to civil liberties, and he frequently cast the deciding vote in a number of important cases. He voted with the majority in *Gore v. United States* (1958), which upheld the imposition of multiple sentences for a single narcotics conviction. Whittaker joined the dissenting opinion in *Kent v. Dulles* (1958), which argued that the secretary of State has the right to withhold passports when an applicant refused to file an affidavit regarding Communist Party membership. He also joined the dissent in *Boynton v. Virginia* (1960), which held that racial segregation on interstate bus routes violated the Interstate Commerce Act. In *Gomillion v. Lightfoot* (1960), however, he concurred with the majority in striking down a state redistricting law that effectively denied voting rights to blacks. He spoke for the majority in *McNeal v. Culver* (1961), which held that the due process rights of the defendant had been violated because he had been incapable of representing himself and had been denied legal counsel. He also wrote the majority opinion in *Chapman v. United States* (1961), which reversed a federal conviction on the grounds that the warrantless search of the defendant's apartment violated the 4th Amendment although the police officers had the consent of the defendant's landlord.

Plagued by failing health, Whittaker resigned from the Court in 1962. He died in Kansas City, Kansas, in 1973.

WILSON, JAMES

b. September 14, 1742; delegate, Continental Congress (1775-1777, 1783, 1785-1787); delegate, Constitutional Convention (1787); delegate, Pennsylvania Constitutional Ratification Convention (1787); associate justice, U.S. Supreme Court (1789-1798); d. August 21, 1798.

Born in Fifeshire, Scotland, Wilson attended the University of St. Andrews, the University of Glasgow, and the University of Edinburgh before immigrating to America in 1766. In the following year, he began to study law in the office of John Dickinson and was admitted to the bar in 1767. In 1774, he was appointed to the local committee of correspondence and elected to the first provincial conference. An eloquent opponent of parliamentary authority over the American colonies, Wilson was elected to the Second Continental Congress in 1775. Becoming gradually more conservative, he bitterly opposed the adoption of the Pennsylvania state constitution in 1776 and was stripped of his seat in the Continental Congress in 1777.

Establishing his residence in Philadelphia, Wilson turned his interest increasingly toward private business interests, investing heavily in land. In 1787, he was a delegate to the Constitutional Convention in Philadelphia and signed the final draft of the Constitution. He was also instrumental in the formulation of the revised Pennsylvania state constitution of 1790. In 1789, Pres. George Washington nominated Wilson to become one of the first associate justices of the U.S. Supreme Court.

Wilson's first important decision on the Court was not, strictly speaking, a judicial one. In the First Hayburn Case (1792), his refusal to serve as a federal pension commissioner established the right of a Supreme Court justice to declare an act of Congress unconstitutional. In *Hylton v. United States* (1796), he concurred with the majority in upholding the principle of judicial review by deciding the constitutionality of a U.S. tax on carriages for the conveyance of persons. Wilson's most important opinion came in *Chisholm v. Georgia* (1793), in which he supported the right of private citizens of one state to sue the government of another (a decision effectively nullified by the 11th Amendment).

Even after being appointed to the Supreme Court, Wilson continued the large-scale land speculations that would eventually ruin his public career. When his investments proved disastrous, he was forced to flee from Pennsylvania to New Jersey, where he was finally captured and jailed by his creditors. He served on the Court until his death in 1798 at Edenton, North Carolina.

WOODBURY, LEVI

b. December 22, 1789; various legislative and judicial positions in New Hampshire; governor of New Hampshire (1823-1824); U.S. senator (1825-1831, 1841-1845); secretary of the Navy (1831-1834); secretary of the Treasury (1834-1841); associate justice, U.S. Supreme Court (1846-1851); d. September 4, 1851.

Born in Francetown, New Hampshire, and educated at Atkinson Academy and Dartmouth College (Class of 1809), Woodbury studied law with Judge Jeremiah Smith and was admitted to the bar in 1812. An ardent supporter of Pres. James Madison, he entered politics and served as clerk of the New Hampshire state senate in 1816. In the following year, he was appointed by Gov. William Plumer to be associate justice of the state superior court. From 1823 to 1824, he was governor of New Hamsphire. After his defeat for reelection in 1824, he entered the state legislature briefly before serving a single term in the U.S. Senate. He served as secretary of the Navy in the Jackson administration and as secretary of the Treasury under both President Jackson and President Van Buren. With the election of John Tyler, Woodbury returned to the U.S. Senate. In 1846, after the death of Associate Justice Joseph Story, Woodbury was appointed to the Supreme Court by Pres. James Polk.

Although Woodbury served on the Supreme Court less than six years, he was an active participant in the constitutional debates that came before the Court during his tenure, often disagreeing with the opinions of the majority of his associates. He joined the dissent in *Luther v. Borden* (1849), arguing that although the judiciary has no constitutional authority to act on political issues the Court could decide whether the statute establishing martial law over the state, under which the defendants sought to justify their acts, was constitutional. Another of his dissenting opinions was in the Passenger Cases (1849), in which he was not convinced that the levy of a head tax on arriving aliens was not a legitimate right of the states. In the earlier case of *Jones v. Van Zandt* (1847), Woodbury wrote the majority opinion, upholding the Fugitive Slave Act of 1793.

Woodbury remained active in national politics after his appointment to the Supreme Court and was seriously considered for the Democratic presidential nomination in 1848. He was also a life-long advocate of free public schools and cultural activities for the general public. He served on the Supreme Court until his death in Portsmouth, New Hampshire, in 1851.

WOODS, WILLIAM BURNHAM

b. August 3, 1824; various executive and legislative positions in Ohio and Alabama; judge, U.S. Circuit Court (1869-1880); associate justice, U.S. Supreme Court (1880-1887); d. May 14, 1887.

Born in Newark, Ohio, to a farming family, Woods attended Western Reserve College and graduated from Yale in 1845. He studied law in the office of S.D. King of Newark, Ohio, and was admitted to the bar in 1847. Entering politics as a Democrat, Woods was elected mayor of Newark (1857) and later to the Ohio legislature (1858),

where he became speaker of the house. At first an opponent of Lincoln, Woods was a strong supporter of the Union during the Civil War. In 1862, he enlisted in the 76th Ohio Infantry and saw active service throughout the war. At the time of his retirement from military service in 1866, he had risen to the rank of brigadier general. After the war, Woods settled in Alabama, where he served in the Reconstruction government of the state. In 1869, he was appointed U.S. circuit judge for the 5th Judicial Circuit by President Grant and subsequently moved his residence to Atlanta. In 1880, after the retirement of Associate Justice William Strong, Woods was appointed to his seat on the Supreme Court by Pres. Rutherford B. Hayes.

Woods's appointment to the Court was occasioned by the lack of a Southern justice, and during his Court tenure, Woods actively participated in the civil rights decisions that undermined the effect of Reconstruction. He wrote the majority opinion in *United States v. Harris* (1883), which ruled that the Civil Rights Enforcement Act, or Anti-Klan Act, of 1870 was unconstitutional, as the civil rights provisions of the 14th Amendment applied only to states, not to individuals. In *United States v. Lee* (1882), a suit involving Arlington Cemetery land owned for ten years by the U.S. government, he joined the dissenting position, arguing that the federal government cannot be sued without consent and that the judgment rendered by the Court without authority was therefore erroneous. Woods also helped overturn the original decision in the *Slaughterhouse Cases* (1873) by voting with the majority in *Butcher's Association v. Crescent City Company* (1884), which ruled that subsequent state legislatures may alter or cancel previous monopoly licenses.

Woods served on the Court until his death in Washington, D.C., in 1887.

Appendixes

CHIEF JUSTICES: ALPHABETICAL LISTING

| Name | Life Dates | | Tenure as Chief Justice |
	Born	Died	
Burger, Warren Earl	Sept. 17, 1907		June 23, 1969–
Chase, Salmon Portland	Jan. 13, 1808	May 7, 1873	Dec. 6, 1864–May 7, 1873
Ellsworth, Oliver	April 29, 1745	Nov. 26, 1807	Mar. 4, 1796–Sept. 30, 1800
Fuller, Melville Weston	Feb. 11, 1833	July 4, 1910	July 20, 1888–July 4, 1910
Hughes, Charles Evans	April 11, 1862	Aug. 27, 1948	*Feb. 24, 1930–June 2, 1941
Jay, John	Dec. 12, 1745	May 17, 1829	Sept. 26, 1789–June 29, 1795
Marshall, John	Sept. 24, 1755	July 6, 1835	Feb. 4, 1801–July 6, 1835
Rutledge, John	Sept. 1739	June 21, 1800	*pro tem 1795
Stone, Harlan Fiske	Oct. 11, 1872	April 22, 1946	*June 27, 1941–April 22, 1946
Taft, William Howard	Sept. 15, 1857	March 8, 1930	June 30, 1921–Feb. 3, 1930
Taney, Roger Brooke	March 17, 1777	Oct. 12, 1864	March 16, 1836–Oct. 12, 1864
Vinson, Frederick Moore	Jan. 22, 1890	Sept. 8, 1953	June 10, 1946–Sept. 8, 1953
Waite, Morrison Remick	Nov. 29, 1816	March 23, 1888	Jan. 21, 1874–March 23, 1888
Warren, Earl	March 19, 1891	July 9, 1974	March 1, 1954–June 23, 1969
White, Edward D.	Nov. 3, 1845	May 19, 1921	*Dec. 12, 1910–May 19, 1921

*Also served as Associate Justice

ASSOCIATE JUSTICES: ALPHABETICAL LISTING

| Name | Life Dates | | Supreme Court Tenure |
	Born	Died	
Baldwin, Henry	Jan. 14, 1780	April 21, 1844	Jan. 6, 1830–April 21, 1844
Barbour, Philip Pendleton	May 25, 1783	Feb. 25, 1841	March 15, 1836–Feb. 25, 1841
Black, Hugo Lafayette	Feb. 27, 1886	Sept. 25, 1971	Aug. 17, 1937–Sept. 17, 1971
Blackmun, Harry Andrew	Nov. 12, 1908		May 12, 1970–
Blair, John	1732	Aug. 31, 1800	Sept. 26, 1789–Jan. 27, 1796
Blatchford, Samuel Milford	March 9, 1820	July 7, 1893	March 27, 1882–July 7, 1893
Bradley, Joseph P.	March 14, 1813	Jan. 22, 1892	March 21, 1870–Jan. 22, 1892
Brandeis, Louis Dembitz	Nov. 13, 1856	Oct. 5, 1941	June 1, 1916–Feb. 13, 1939
Brennan, William Joseph, Jr.	April 25, 1906		March 19, 1957–
Brewer, David Josiah	June 20, 1837	March 28, 1910	Dec. 18, 1889–March 28, 1910
Brown, Henry Billings	March 2, 1836	Sept. 4, 1913	Dec. 29, 1890–May 28, 1906
Burton, Harold Hitz	June 22, 1888	Oct. 28, 1964	Sept. 19, 1945–Oct. 13, 1958
Butler, Pierce	March 17, 1866	Nov. 16, 1939	Dec. 21, 1922–Nov. 16, 1939
Byrnes, James Francis	May 2, 1879	April 9, 1972	June 12, 1941–Oct. 3, 1942
Campbell, John Archibald	June 24, 1811	March 2, 1889	March 25, 1853–April 26, 1861
Cardozo, Benjamin Nathan	May 24, 1870	July 9, 1938	Feb. 24, 1932–July 9, 1938
Catron, John	c. 1786	May 30, 1865	March 8, 1837–May 30, 1865
Chase, Samuel	April 17, 1741	June 19, 1811	Jan. 27, 1796–June 19, 1811
Clark, Tom Campbell	Sept. 23, 1899	June 13, 1977	Aug. 18, 1949–June 12, 1967
Clarke, John Hessin	Sept. 18, 1857	March 22, 1945	July 24, 1916–Sept. 1, 1922
Clifford, Nathan	Aug. 18, 1803	July 25, 1881	Jan. 12, 1858–July 25, 1881
Curtis, Benjamin Robbins	Nov. 4, 1809	Sept. 15, 1874	Dec. 29, 1851–Sept. 30, 1857
Cushing, William	March 1, 1732	Sept. 13, 1810	Sept. 26, 1789–Sept. 13, 1810
Daniel, Peter Vivian	April 24, 1784	May 31, 1860	March 2, 1841–May 31, 1860
Davis, David	March 9, 1815	June 26, 1886	Dec. 8, 1862–March 7, 1877
Day, William Rufus	April 17, 1849	July 9, 1923	Feb. 23, 1903–Nov. 13, 1922
Douglas, William Orville	Oct. 16, 1898	Jan. 19, 1980	April 4, 1939–Nov. 12, 1975
Duvall, Gabriel	Dec. 6, 1752	March 6, 1844	Nov. 18, 1811–Jan. 10, 1835

| Name | Life Dates | | Supreme Court Tenure |
	Born	Died	
Field, Stephen Johnson	Nov. 4, 1816	April 9, 1899	March 10, 1863–Dec. 1, 1897
Fortas, Abe	June 19, 1910	April 5, 1982	Aug. 11, 1965–May 15, 1969
Frankfurter, Felix	Nov. 15, 1882	Feb. 22, 1965	Jan. 17, 1939–Aug. 28, 1962
Goldberg, Arthur Joseph	Aug. 8, 1908		Sept. 25, 1962–July 25, 1965
Gray, Horace	March 24, 1828	Sept. 15, 1902	Dec. 20, 1881–July 9, 1902
Grier, Robert Cooper	March 5, 1794	Sept. 26, 1870	Aug. 4, 1846–Jan. 31, 1870
Harlan, John Marshall	June 1, 1833	Oct. 14, 1911	Nov. 29, 1877–Oct. 14, 1911
Harlan, John Marshall	May 20, 1899	Dec. 29, 1971	March 16, 1955–Sept. 23, 1971
Holmes, Oliver Wendell, Jr.	March 8, 1841	March 6, 1935	Dec. 4, 1902–Jan. 12, 1932
Hughes, Charles Evans	April 11, 1862	Aug. 27, 1948	*May 2, 1910–June 10, 1916
Hunt, Ward	June 14, 1810	March 24, 1886	Jan. 9, 1873–Jan. 7, 1882
Iredell, James	Oct. 5, 1751	Oct. 20, 1799	Feb. 10, 1790–Oct. 20, 1799
Jackson, Howell Edmunds	April 8, 1832	Aug. 8, 1895	Feb. 18, 1893–Aug. 8, 1895
Jackson, Robert Houghwout	Feb. 13, 1892	Oct. 9, 1954	July 7, 1941–Oct. 9, 1954
Johnson, Thomas	Nov. 4, 1732	Oct. 26, 1819	Nov. 7, 1791–Jan. 16, 1793
Johnson, William	Dec. 17, 1771	Aug. 4, 1834	March 24, 1804–Aug. 4, 1834
Lamar, Joseph Rucker	Oct. 14, 1857	Jan. 2, 1916	Jan. 3, 1911–Jan. 2, 1916
Lamar, Lucius Quintus Cincinnatus	Sept. 17, 1825	Jan. 23, 1893	Jan. 16, 1888–Jan. 23, 1893
Livingston, Henry Brockholst	Nov. 25, 1757	March 18, 1823	Dec. 17, 1806–March 18, 1823
Lurton, Horace Harmon	Feb. 26, 1844	July 12, 1914	Dec. 20, 1909–July 12, 1914
McKenna, Joseph	Aug. 10, 1843	Nov. 21, 1926	Jan. 21, 1898–Jan. 25, 1925
McKinley, John	May 1, 1780	July 19, 1852	Sept. 25, 1837–July 19, 1852
McLean, John	March 11, 1785	April 4, 1861	March 7, 1829–April 4, 1861
McReynolds, James Clark	Feb. 3, 1862	Aug. 24, 1946	Aug. 29, 1914–Feb. 1, 1941
Marshall, Thurgood	July 2, 1908		Aug. 30, 1967–
Matthews, Stanley	July 21, 1824	March 22, 1889	May 12, 1881–March 22, 1889
Miller, Samuel Freeman	April 5, 1816	Oct. 13, 1890	July 16, 1862–Oct. 13, 1890
Minton, Sherman	Oct. 20, 1890	April 9, 1965	Oct. 4, 1949–Oct. 15, 1956
Moody, William Henry	Dec. 23, 1853	July 2, 1917	Dec. 12, 1906–Nov. 10, 1910
Moore, Alfred	May 21, 1755	Oct. 15, 1810	Dec. 10, 1799–Jan. 26, 1804
Murphy, Frank	April 13, 1890	July 19, 1949	Jan. 15, 1940–July 19, 1949
Nelson, Samuel	Nov. 10, 1792	Dec. 13, 1873	Feb. 14, 1845–Nov. 28, 1872
O'Connor, Sandra Day	March 26, 1930		Sept. 21, 1981–
Paterson, William	Dec. 24, 1745	Sept. 9, 1806	March 4, 1793–Sept. 9, 1806
Peckham, Rufus Wheeler, Jr.	Nov. 8, 1838	Oct. 24, 1909	Dec. 9, 1895–Oct. 24, 1909
Pitney, Mahlon	Feb. 5, 1858	Dec. 9, 1924	March 13, 1912–Dec. 31, 1922
Powell, Lewis Franklin, Jr.	Sept. 19, 1907		Dec. 6, 1971–
Reed, Stanley Forman	Dec. 31, 1884	April 2, 1980	Jan. 25, 1938–Feb. 25, 1957
Rehnquist, William Hubbs	Oct. 1, 1924		Dec. 10, 1971–
Roberts, Owen Josephus	May 2, 1875	May 17, 1955	May 20, 1930–July 31, 1945
Rutledge, John	Sept. 1739	June 21, 1800	*Sept. 26, 1789–March 5, 1791

*Also served as Chief Justice

Name	Life Dates Born	Died	Supreme Court Tenure
Rutledge, Wiley Blount, Jr.	July 20, 1894	Sept. 10, 1949	Feb. 8, 1943–Sept. 10, 1949
Sanford, Edward Terry	July 23, 1865	March 8, 1930	Jan. 29, 1923–March 8, 1930
Shiras, George, Jr.	Jan. 26, 1832	Aug. 2, 1924	July 26, 1892–Feb. 23, 1903
Stevens, John Paul	April 20, 1920		Dec. 17, 1975–
Stewart, Potter	Jan. 23, 1915	Dec. 7, 1985	May 5, 1959–July 3, 1981
Stone, Harlan Fiske	Oct. 11, 1872	April 22, 1946	*Jan. 5, 1925–June 27, 1941
Story, Joseph	Sept. 18, 1779	Sept. 10, 1845	Nov. 18, 1811–Sept. 10, 1845
Strong, William	May 6, 1808	Aug. 19, 1895	Feb. 18, 1870–Dec. 14, 1880
Sutherland, George	March 25, 1862	July 18, 1942	Sept. 5, 1922–Jan. 17, 1938
Swayne, Noah Haynes	Dec. 7, 1804	June 8, 1884	Jan. 24, 1862–Jan. 25, 1881
Thompson, Smith	Jan. 17, 1768	Dec. 18, 1843	Dec. 19, 1823–Dec. 18, 1843
Todd, Thomas	Jan. 23, 1765	Feb. 7, 1826	March 3, 1807–Feb. 7, 1826
Trimble, Robert	Nov. 17, 1776	Aug. 25, 1828	May 9, 1826–Aug. 25, 1828
Van Devanter, Willis	April 17, 1859	Feb. 8, 1941	Dec. 15, 1910–June 2, 1937
Washington, Bushrod	June 5, 1762	Nov. 26, 1829	Dec. 20, 1798–Nov. 26, 1829
Wayne, James Moore	c. 1790	July 5, 1867	Jan. 9, 1835–July 5, 1867
White, Byron Raymond	June 8, 1917		April 11, 1962–
White, Edward D.	Nov. 3, 1845	May 19, 1921	*Feb. 19, 1894–Dec. 12, 1910
Whittaker, Charles Evans	Feb. 22, 1901	Nov. 26, 1973	March 19, 1957–March 29, 1962
Wilson, James	Sept. 14, 1742	Aug. 21, 1798	Sept. 26, 1789–Aug. 21, 1798
Woodbury, Levi	Dec. 22, 1789	Sept. 4, 1851	Jan. 3, 1846–Sept. 4, 1851
Woods, William Burnham	Aug. 3, 1824	May 14, 1887	Dec. 21, 1880–May 14, 1887

*Also served as Chief Justice

CHIEF JUSTICES: CHRONOLOGICAL LISTING

Name	Biography Page	Life Dates		State	College	Law School
		Born	Died			
Jay, John	302	12/12/1745	5/17/1829	New York	King's Col. (Columbia)	
*Rutledge, John	326	9/1739	6/21/1800	S. Carolina		Inns of Court, London
Ellsworth, Oliver	282	4/29/1745	11/26/1807	Connecticut	Princeton, Yale	
Marshall, John	309	9/24/1755	7/6/1835	Virginia		Wm. & Mary
Taney, Roger Brooke	338	3/17/1777	10/12/1864	Maryland	Dickinson College	
Chase, Salmon Portland	272	1/13/1808	5/7/1873	Ohio	Cincinnati College, Dartmouth	
Waite, Morrison Remick	346	11/29/1816	3/23/1888	Connecticut	Yale	
Fuller, Melville Weston	288	2/11/1833	7/4/1910	Illinois	Bowdoin	Harvard Law School

Appointment		Reason for Leaving		Years Served	Landmark Decisions
President	Confirmed	Died	Resigned		
Washington	9/26/1789		1795	6	Champion & Dickason v. Casey Chisholm v. Georgia Georgia v. Brailsford Glass v. The Sloop Betsey
Washington	pro tem 1795			1	
Washington	3/4/1796		1800	4	United States v. La Vengeance Moodie v. The Ship Phoebe Ann Ware v. Hylton Wiscart v. Dauchy
Adams	2/4/1801	1835		34	Marbury v. Madison Fletcher v. Peck Trustees of Dartmouth College v. Woodward Sturges v. Crowninshield Ogden v. Saunders McCulloch v. Maryland Gibbons v. Ogden Martin v. Hunter's Lessee
Jackson	3/16/1836	1864		28	Charles River Bridge v. Warren River Bridge City of New York v. Miln License Cases Passenger Cases Prigg v. Pennsylvania Scott v. Sandford Ex parte Merryman
Lincoln	12/6/1864	1873		8	Ex parte Milligan Ex parte Garland Ex parte McCardle Texas v. White Hepburn v. Griswold Knox v. Lee Slaughterhouse Cases
Grant	1/1/1874	1888		14	Minor v. Happersett United States v. Reese United States v. Cruikshank Munn v. Illinois Peik v. Chicago & Northwestern Railroad Co. Stone v. Farmer's Loan & Trust Co. Hall v. DeCuir Pensacola Telegraph Co. v. Western Union Co.
Cleveland	7/20/1888	1910		22	United States v. Texas California v. Southern Pacific Co. United States v. E. C. Knight Co. Pollock v. Farmer's Loan and Trust Co. United States v. Wong Kim Ark Loewe v. Lawlor

Name	Biography Page	Life Dates		State	College	Law School
		Born	Died			
*White, Edward Douglass, Jr.	356	11/3/1845	5/19/1921	Louisiana	Mt. St. Mary's, Georgetown	
Taft, William Howard	336	9/15/1857	3/8/1930	Ohio	Yale	U. of Cincinnati Law School
*Hughes, Charles Evans	297	4/11/1862	8/27/1948	New York	Madison (Colgate), Brown	Columbia U. Law School
*Stone, Harlan Fiske	330	10/11/1872	4/22/1946	New York	Amherst, Columbia	Columbia U. Law School
Vinson, Frederick Moore	345	1/22/1890	9/8/1953	Kentucky	Centre Col.	Centre Col.
Warren, Earl	348	3/19/1891	7/9/1974	California	U. of Calif.	U. of Calif.
Burger, Warren Earl	266	9/17/1907		Minnesota	U. of Minn.	St. Paul Col. of Law (now Mitchell)

*Also served as Associate Justice

Appointment		Reason for Leaving		Years Served	Landmark Decisions
President	Confirmed	Died	Resigned		
Taft	12/12/1910	1921		10	Standard Oil Co. v. United States Brushaber v. Union Pacific Railroad Co. Clark Distilling Co. v. Western Maryland Railway Hammer v. Dagenhart Guinn v. United States Selective Draft Law Cases
Harding	6/30/1921		1930	8	Truax v. Corrigan Bailey v. Drexel Furniture Co. Adkins v. Children's Hospital J. W. Hampton & Co. v. United States Carroll v. United States Olmstead v. United States Ex parte Grossman Tumey v. Ohio
Hoover	2/24/1930		1941	11	Stromberg v. California DeJonge v. Oregon Near v. Minnesota Missouri ex. rel. Gaines v. Canada Schechter Poultry Corp. v. United States National Labor Relations Board v. Jones & Laughlin Lovell v. Griffin Edwards v. California
Roosevelt	6/27/1941	1946		5	Ex parte Quirin Hirabayashi v. United States Yakus v. United States In re Yamashita Girouard v. United States
Truman	6/10/1946	1953		7	United States v. United Mine Workers American Communications Association v. Douds Shelly v. Kraemer Sweatt v. Painter Kunz v. New York Harris v. United States Rosenberg v. United States
Eisenhower	3/1/1954		1969	15	Brown v. Board of Education Loving v. Virginia Reynolds v. Sims McGowan v. Maryland Miranda v. Arizona Roth v. United States
Nixon	6/23/1969				Furman v. Georgia Harris v. New York Brewer v. Williams United States v. Henry Reed v. Reed Bivens v. Six Unknown Agents Swann v. Charlotte-Mecklenburg Board of Education Milliken v. Bradley Fullilove v. Klutznik United States v. Nixon

ASSOCIATE JUSTICES: CHRONOLOGICAL LISTING

Name	Biography Page	Life Dates		State	College	Law School
		Born	Died			
Rutledge, John	326	9/1739	6/21/1800	S. Carolina		Inns of Court, London
Cushing, William	277	3/1/1732	9/13/1810	Mass.	Harvard	private study
Wilson, James	358	9/14/1742	8/21/1798	Penn.	St. Andrews, Scotland	private study
Blair, John	258	1732	8/31/1800	Virginia	Wm. & Mary	Inns of Court, London
Iredell, James	300	10/5/1751	10/20/1799	N. Carolina		private study
Johnson, Thomas	305	11/4/1732	10/26/1819	Maryland		private study
Paterson, William	321	12/24/1745	9/9/1806	New Jersey	Princeton	private study
Chase, Samuel	274	4/17/1741	6/19/1811	Maryland		private study
Washington, Bushrod	354	6/5/1762	11/26/1829	Virginia	Wm. & Mary	private study
Moore, Alfred	319	5/21/1755	10/15/1810	N. Carolina		private study
Johnson, William	305	12/17/1771	8/4/1834	S. Carolina	Princeton	private study
Livingston, Henry Brockholst	307	11/25/1757	3/18/1823	New York	Princeton, Harvard	private study
Todd, Thomas	343	1/23/1765	2/7/1826	Kentucky		private study
Story, Joseph	332	9/18/1779	9/10/1845	Mass.	Harvard	private study
Duvall, Gabriel	282	12/6/1752	3/6/1844	Maryland		
Thompson, Smith	343	1/17/1768	12/18/1843	New York	Princeton	private study

Appointment		Reason for Leaving Date			Years Served	Chief Justice(s)	Landmark Decisions
President	Date	Chief Justice	Died	Resigned			
Washington	9/26/1789			1791	1	Jay	
Washington	9/26/1789		1810		21	Jay Ellsworth Marshall	Calder v. Bull Fowler v. Lindsay
Washington	9/26/1789		1798		9	Jay Ellsworth	Chisholm v. Georgia Hylton v. United States
Washington	9/26/1789			1796	6	Jay	Hayburn Case Georgia v. Brailsford Chisholm v. Georgia
Washington	2/10/1790		1799		9	Jay Ellsworth	Chisholm v. Georgia Ware v. Hylton Calder v. Bull
Washington	11/7/1791			1793	1	Jay	Georgia v. Brailsford
Washington	3/4/1793		1806		13	Jay Ellsworth Marshall	Vanhorne's Lessee v. Dorrance
Washington	1/27/1796		1811		15	Ellsworth Marshall	Calder v. Bull Ware v. Hylton United States v. Worrall
Adams	12/20/1798		1829		31	Ellsworth Marshall	Green v. Biddle Mason v. Haile
Adams	12/10/1799			1804	5	Ellsworth Marshall	Bas v. Tingy Stuart v. Laird
Jefferson	3/24/1804		1834		30	Marshall	Craig v. Missouri Gibbons v. Ogden Ogden v. Sanders
Jefferson	12/17/1806		1823		16	Marshall	United States v. Coolidge Trustees of Dartmouth Col. v. Woodward
Jefferson	3/3/1807		1826		19	Marshall	
Madison	11/18/1811		1845		34	Marshall Taney	Martin v. Hunter's Lessee United States v. Schooner Amistad Prigg v. Pennsylvania Swift v. Tyson
Madison	11/18/1811			1835	23	Marshall	Trustees of Dartmouth Col. v. Woodward Mima Queen & Child v. Hepburn LeGrand v. Darnall
Monroe	12/19/1823		1843		20	Marshall Taney	Kendall v. United States Brown v. Maryland Craig v. Missouri Groves v. Slaughter

Name	Biography Page	Life Dates		State	College	Law School
		Born	**Died**			
Trimble, Robert	344	11/17/1776	8/25/1828	Kentucky	Bourbon & Kentucky Academies	private study
McLean, John	308	3/11/1785	4/4/1861	Ohio		private study
Baldwin, Henry	255	1/14/1780	4/21/1844	Penn.	Yale	private study
Wayne, James Moore	354	c. 1790	7/5/1867	Georgia	Princeton	private study
Barbour, Philip Pendleton	255	5/25/1783	2/25/1841	Virginia	Wm. & Mary	private study
Catron, John	272	c. 1786	5/30/1865	Tennessee		private study
McKinley, John	308	5/1/1780	7/19/1852	Alabama		private study
Daniel, Peter Vivian	277	4/24/1784	5/31/1860	Virginia	Princeton	private study
Nelson, Samuel	320	11/10/1792	12/13/1873	New York	Middlebury	private study
Woodbury, Levi	358	12/22/1789	9/4/1851	New Hampshire	Dartmouth	Tapping Reeve Law School
Grier, Robert Cooper	291	3/5/1794	9/26/1870	Penn.	Dickinson	private study
Curtis, Benjamin R.	276	11/4/1809	9/15/1874	Mass.	Harvard	Harvard Law School
Campbell, John Archibald	270	6/24/1811	3/2/1889	Alabama	Franklin U., U.S. Military Academy	private study
Clifford, Nathan	276	8/18/1803	7/25/1881	Maine	Haverhill	private study
Swayne, Noah Haynes	335	12/7/1804	6/8/1884	Ohio	Quaker Academy	private study
Miller, Samuel Freeman	317	4/5/1816	10/13/1890	Iowa	Transylvania U.	private study
Davis, David	277	3/9/1815	6/26/1886	Illinois	Kenyon	Yale Law School
Field, Stephen Johnson	283	11/4/1816	4/9/1899	California	Williams	private study
Strong, William	334	5/6/1808	8/19/1895	Penn.	Yale	Yale Law School
Bradley, Joseph P.	259	3/14/1813	1/22/1892	New Jersey	Rutgers	private study
Hunt, Ward	299	6/14/1810	3/24/1886	New York	Union Col.	private study

Appointment		Reason for Leaving Date			Years Served	Chief Justice(s)	Landmark Decisions
President	Date	Chief Justice	Died	Resigned			
J. Q. Adams	5/9/1826		1828		2	Marshall	Ogden v. Saunders
Jackson	3/7/1829		1861		32	Marshall Taney	Groves v. Slaughter Scott v. Sandford
Jackson	1/6/1830		1844		14	Marshall	United States v. Arredondo Groves v. Slaughter United States v. Schooner Amistad
Jackson	1/9/1835		1867		32	Marshall Taney Chase	Scott v. Sandford Ex parte Milligan
Jackson	3/15/1836		1841		5	Taney	City of N.Y. v. Miln Charles River Bridge v. Warren River Bridge
Jackson	3/8/1837		1865		28	Taney Chase	Scott v. Sandford
Van Buren	9/25/1837		1852		15	Taney	Groves v. Slaughter
Van Buren	3/2/1841		1860		19	Taney	Prigg v. Pennsylvania Scott v. Sandford
Tyler	2/14/1845			1872	27	Taney Chase	Scott v. Sandford Ex parte Milligan Hepburn v. Griswold Knox v. Lee
Polk	1/3/1846		1851		5	Taney	Waring v. Clarke Luther v. Borden Passenger Cases Jones v. Van Zandt
Polk	8/4/1846			1870	23	Taney	Scott v. Sandford Ex parte McCardle
Fillmore	12/29/1851			1857	6	Taney	Cooley v. Bd. of Wardens Murray's Lessee v. Hoboken Land & Improvement Co. Scott v. Sandford
Pierce	3/25/1853			1861	8	Taney	Scott v. Sandford
Buchanan	1/12/1858		1881		23	Taney Chase Waite	Ex parte Milligan Ex parte Garland Hepburn v. Griswold Ex parte Virginia
Lincoln	1/24/1862			1881	19	Taney Chase Waite	Ex parte Milligan Hepburn v. Griswold Knox v. Lee Slaughterhouse Cases
Lincoln	7/16/1862		1890		28	Taney Chase Waite Fuller	Ex parte Garland Hepburn v. Griswold Slaughterhouse Cases
Lincoln	12/1/1862			1877	14	Taney Chase Waite	Hepburn v. Griswold Slaughterhouse Cases
Lincoln	3/10/1863			1897	34	Taney Chase Waite Fuller	Ex parte Garland Paul v. Virginia Munn v. Illinois Bradley v. Fisher
Grant	2/18/1870			1880	10	Chase Waite	Knox v. Lee Strauder v. W. Va. Ex parte Virginia
Grant	3/21/1870		1892		22	Chase Waite Fuller	Knox v. Lee Slaughterhouse Cases Civil Rights Cases
Grant	1/9/1873			1882		Chase Waite	Slaughterhouse Cases United States v. Reese Reading RR v. Penn.

Name	Biography Page	Life Dates		State	College	Law School
		Born	**Died**			
Harlan, John Marshall	292	6/1/1833	10/14/1911	Kentucky	Centre Col.	Transylvania U.
Woods, William Burnham	359	8/3/1824	5/14/1887	Georgia	W. Reserve, Yale	private study
Matthews, Stanley	317	7/21/1824	3/22/1889	Ohio	Kenyon	private study
Gray, Horace	291	3/24/1828	9/15/1902	Mass.	Harvard	Harvard Law School
Blatchford, Samuel Milford	259	3/9/1820	7/7/1893	New York	Columbia	
Lamar, Lucius Quintus Cincinnatus	306	9/17/1825	1/23/1893	Miss.	Emory	private study
Brewer, David Josiah	265	6/20/1837	3/28/1910	Kansas	Wesleyan, Yale	Albany Law School
Brown, Henry Billings	265	3/2/1836	9/4/1913	Michigan	Yale	Yale Law School, Harvard Law School
Shiras, George, Jr.	328	1/26/1832	8/2/1924	Penn.	Ohio U., Yale	Yale Law School
Jackson, Howell Edmunds	300	4/8/1832	8/8/1895	Tennessee	W. Tenn. Col., U. of Va., Cumberland	private study
White, Edward D.	356	11/3/1845	5/19/1921	Louisiana	Mt. St. Mary's, Georgetown	private study
Peckham, Rufus Wheeler, Jr.	322	11/8/1838	10/24/1909	New York	Union	private study
McKenna, Joseph	307	8/10/1843	11/21/1926	California	Collegiate Institute	
Holmes, Oliver Wendell, Jr.	294	3/8/1841	3/6/1935	Mass.	Harvard	Harvard Law School
Day, William Rufus	279	4/17/1849	7/9/1923	Ohio	U. of Michigan	U. of Michigan Law School
Moody, William Henry	319	12/23/1853	7/2/1917	Mass.	Harvard	Harvard Law School
Lurton, Horace Harmon	307	2/26/1844	7/12/1914	Tennessee	U. of Chicago	Cumberland U. Law School

Appointment		Reason for Leaving Date			Years Served	Chief Justice(s)	Landmark Decisions
President	Date	Chief Justice	Died	Resigned			
Hayes	10/29/1877		1911		34	Waite Fuller White	Plessy v. Ferguson Hennington v. Georgia Champion v. Ames United States v. Texas Northern Securities Co. v. United States
Hayes	12/21/1880		1887		6	Waite	United States v. Harris Presser v. Illinois United States v. Lee
Garfield	5/12/1881		1889		8	Waite Fuller	Bowman v. Chicago & N.W. Railway Co. Hurtado v. California Yick Wo v. Hopkins
Arthur	12/20/1881			1902	20	Waite Fuller	Mayre v. Parsons Poindexter v. Greenhow Bowman v. Chicago & N.W. Railway Co. Chicago, Milwaukee & St. Paul RR v. Minn.
Arthur	3/27/1882		1893		11	Waite Fuller	Chicago, Milwaukee & St. Paul RR v. Minn. Counselman v. Hitchcock In re Neagle
Cleveland	1/16/1888		1893		5	Waite Fuller	Chicago, Milwaukee & St. Paul RR v. Minn. In re Neagle United States v. Texas
Harrison	12/18/1889		1910		20	Fuller	Reagan v. Farmers Loan & Trust Co. Kansas v. Colorado Muller v. Oregon In re Debs
Harrison	12/29/1890			1906	16	Fuller	Pollock v. Farmers Loan & Trust Co. Plessy v. Fergusson Downes v. Bidwell Holden v. Hardy
Harrison	7/26/1892			1903	10	Fuller	Pollock v. Farmers Loan & Trust Co.
Harrison	2/18/1893		1895		2	Fuller	Pollock v. Farmers Loan & Trust Co.
Cleveland	2/19/1894	1910			17	Fuller	United States v. E. C. Knight Co. Adair v. United States
Cleveland	12/9/1895		1909		14	Fuller	Lochner v. New York Allgeyer v. Louisiana Maxwell v. Dow Ex parte Young
McKinley	1/21/1898			1925	26	Fuller White Taft	Adair v. United States Adams v. Tanner Bunting v. Oregon Pettibone v. Nichols
T. Roosevelt	12/4/1902			1932	29	Fuller White Taft Hughes	Northern Securities Co. v. United States Schenck v. United States Missouri v. Holland Lochner v. New York Abrams v. United States Hammer v. Dagenhart Moore v. Dempsey
T. Roosevelt	2/23/1903			1922	19	Fuller White Taft	Hammer v. Dagenhart Dorr v. United States Lochner v. New York Coppage v. Kansas Weeks v. United States Buchanan v. Warley
T. Roosevelt	12/12/1906			1910	3	Fuller	Twining v. New Jersey Employers' Liability Cases
Taft	12/20/1909		1914		4	Fuller White	Coyle v. Smith Shreveport Rate Case

Name	Biography Page	Life Dates		State	College	Law School
		Born	Died			
Hughes, Charles Evans	297	4/11/1862	8/27/1948	New York	Colgate, Brown	Columbia U. Law School
Van Devanter, Willis	344	4/17/1859	2/8/1941	Wyoming	DePauw U.	U. of Cincinnati Law School
Lamar, Joseph Rucker	306	10/14/1857	1/2/1916	Georgia	U. of Georgia, Bethany	Washington & Lee U.
Pitney, Mahlon	322	2/5/1858	12/9/1924	New Jersey	Princeton	private study
McReynolds, James Clark	309	2/3/1862	8/24/1946	Tennessee	Vanderbilt	U. of Va. Law School
Brandeis, Louis Dembitz	260	11/13/1856	10/5/1941	Mass.	Annen-Real-Schule, Dresden, Germany	Harvard Law School
Clarke, John Hessin	275	9/18/1857	3/22/1945	Ohio	Case W. Reserve	private study
Sutherland, George	334	3/25/1862	7/18/1942	Utah	Brigham Young U.	U. of Michigan Law School
Butler, Pierce	269	3/17/1866	11/16/1939	Minnesota	Carleton	private study
Sanford, Edward Terry	327	7/23/1865	3/8/1930	Tennessee	U. of Tenn.	Harvard Law School
Stone, Harlan Fiske	330	10/11/1872	4/22/1946	New York	Amherst	Columbia U. Law School
Roberts, Owen Josephus	325	5/2/1875	5/17/1955	Penn.	U. of Penn.	U. of Penn. Law School
Cardozo, Benjamin Nathan	271	5/24/1870	7/9/1938	New York	Columbia	Columbia U. Law School

Appointment		Reason for Leaving Date			Years Served	Chief Justice(s)	Landmark Decisions
President	Date	Chief Justice	Died	Resigned			
Taft	5/2/1910			1916	6	Fuller White	Bailey v. Alabama McCabe v. Atchison, Topeka & Santa Fe RR Minnesota Rate Cases Owensboro v. Cumberland Tel. & Tel.
Taft	12/15/1910			1937	26	White Taft Hughes	Evans v. Gore New York Central v. Winfield Bunting v. Oregon Near v. Minnesota
Taft	1/3/1911		1916		5	White	Gompers v. Bucks Stove & Range Co. United States v. Midwest Oil Co. United States v. Mosely
Taft	3/13/1912			1922	11	White Taft	Hitchman Coal & Coke Co. v. Mitchell Duplex Printing Press Co. v. Dearing Coppage v. Kansas Mntn. Timber Co. v. Washington
Wilson	8/29/1914			1941	26	White Taft Hughes	Newberry v. United States Pierce v. Soc. of Sisters Norman v. B&O RR Ashwander v. T.V.A.
Wilson	6/1/1916			1939	23	White Taft Hughes	Muller v. Oregon Pierce v. United States Olmstead v. United States NY Cen. RR v. Winfield Bunting v. Oregon Liggett v. Lee Abrams v. United States Whitney v. California
Wilson	7/24/1916			1922	6	White Taft	United States v. Doremus Bunting v. Oregon Stafford v. Wallace Wilson v. New Adams v. Tanner Schaeffer v. United States
Harding	9/5/1922			1938	15	Taft Hughes	Adkins v. Children's Hosp. Bedford Cut Stone Co. v. Journeymen Stone Cutters' Assoc. Carter v. Carter Coal Co. Near v. Minnesota Moore v. Dempsey
Harding	12/21/1922		1939		17	Taft Hughes	Burns Baking Co. v. Bryan Morehead v. New York ex rel Tipaldo Stromberg v. California Powell v. Alabama
Harding	1/29/1923		1930		7	Taft	Gitlow v. New York Corrigan v. Buckley Whitney v. California United States v. Schwimmer
Coolidge	1/5/1925	1941			16	Taft Hughes	United States v. Classic Hague v. CIO Minersville School Dist. v. Gobitis U.S. v. Darby Lumber Co.
Hoover	5/20/1930			1945	15	Hughes Stone	RR Retirement Board v. Alton RR United States v. Butler Nebbia v. New York Grove v. Townsend Herndon v. Lowry
Hoover	2/24/1932		1938		6	Hughes	Great N. RR Co. v. Sunburst Oil & Refining Co. Nixon v. Condon Baldwin v. Seelig Palko v. Conn. Helvering v. Davis

Name	Biography Page	Life Dates		State	College	Law School
		Born	**Died**			
Black, Hugo Lafayette	256	2/27/1886	9/25/1971	Alabama	Ashland Birmingham Medical College	U. of Ala. Law School
Reed, Stanley Forman	323	12/31/1884	4/2/1980	Kentucky	Kentucky Wesleyan, Yale	U. of Va., Columbia, Sorbonne
Frankfurter, Felix	285	11/15/1882	2/22/1965	New York	CCNY	Harvard Law School
Douglas, William Orville	279	10/16/1898	1/19/1980	Washington	Whitman	Columbia U. Law School
Murphy, Frank	319	4/13/1890	7/19/1949	Michigan	U. of Michigan	U. of Mich. Law School, Lincoln's Inn, London, Trinity Col., Dublin,
Byrnes, James Francis	270	5/2/1879	4/9/1972	S. Carolina		private study
Jackson, Robert Houghwout	301	2/13/1892	10/9/1954	New York		Albany Law School
Rutledge, Wiley Blount, Jr.	327	7/20/1894	9/10/1949	Iowa	Maryville, U. of Wisconsin	U. of Colorado Law School
Burton, Harold Hitz	269	6/22/1888	10/28/1964	Ohio	Bowdoin	Harvard Law School
Clark, Tom Campbell	275	9/23/1899	6/13/1977	Texas	Va. Mil. Inst., U. of Texas	U. of Texas Law School
Minton, Sherman	318	10/20/1890	4/9/1965	Indiana	Indiana U.	Yale Law School
Harlan, John Marshall	294	5/20/1899	12/29/1971	New York	Princeton, Oxford	New York Law School

Appointment		Reason for Leaving Date			Years Served	Chief Justice(s)	Landmark Decisions
President	Date	Chief Justice	Died	Resigned			
F. D. Roosevelt	8/17/1937			1971	34	Hughes Stone Vinson Warren Burger	Chambers v. Florida Boynton v. Virginia Korematsu v. United States Gideon v. Wainwright Pointer v. Texas Youngstown Sheet & Tube Co. v. Sawyer N.Y. Times Co. v. United States Wesberry v. Sanders
F. D. Roosevelt	1/25/1938			1957	19	Hughes Stone Vinson Warren	United States v. Rock Royal Coop. United States v. Appalachian Elec. Power Co. Gray v. Powell Smith v. Allwright Morgan v. Virginia United Pub. Wrkrs. v. Mitchell
F. D. Roosevelt	1/17/1939			1962	23	Hughes Stone Vinson Warren	Minersville School Dist. v. Gobitis Meadowmoor Dairies Adamson v. California Wolf v. Colorado Rochin v. California Dennis v. United States Baker v. Carr
F. D. Roosevelt	4/4/1939			1975	36	Hughes Stone Vinson Warren Burger	Terminiello v. Chicago Brandenburg v. Ohio McCollum v. Bd. of Educ. Zorach v. Clauson Griswold v. Conn. Skinner v. Oklahoma Roe v. Wade N.Y. Times Co. v. United States Environmental Protection Agency v. Mink
F. D. Roosevelt	1/15/1940		1949		9	Hughes Stone Vinson	Thornhill v. Alabama W. Va. St. Bd. of Educ. v. Barnette Schneiderman v. United States Korematsu v. United States United States v. United Mine Workers
F. D. Roosevelt	6/12/1941			1942	1	Stone	Edwards v. California Taylor v. Georgia Goldstein v. United States
F. D. Roosevelt	7/7/1941		1954		13	Stone Vinson Warren	Murdock v. Pennsylvania W. Va. St. Bd. of Educ. v. Barnette Smith v. Allwright Wickard v. Filburn Youngstown Sheet & Tube Co. v. Sawyer
F. D. Roosevelt	2/8/1943		1949		6	Stone Vinson	W. Va. St. Bd. of Educ. v. Barnette Schneiderman v. United States In re Yamashita Morgan v. Virginia Wolf v. Colorado
Truman	9/19/1945			1958	13	Stone Vinson Warren	Beilan v. Bd. of Educ. Henderson v. United States Morgan v. Virginia
Truman	8/18/1949			1967	18	Vinson Warren	Brown v. Bd. of Educ. Baker v. Carr Mapp v. Ohio School Dist. of Abington v. Schempp Heart of Atlanta Motel v. United States Garner v. Bd. of Pub. Works Ker v. California
Truman	10/4/1949			1956	7	Vinson Warren	United States v. Rabinowitz Dennis v. United States Terry v. Adams
Eisenhower	3/16/1955			1971	16	Warren Burger	Yates v. United States Barenblatt v. United States Baker v. Carr Miranda v. Arizona NAACP v. Ala. ex. rel. Patterson Escobedo v. Illinois

Name	Biography Page	Life Dates		State	College	Law School
		Born	Died			
Brennan, William Joseph, Jr.	263	4/25/1906		New Jersey	U. of Penn.	Harvard Law School
Whittaker, Charles Evans	357	2/22/1901	11/26/1973	Missouri		U. of Kansas Law School
Stewart, Potter	329	1/23/1915	12/7/85	Ohio	Yale	Yale Law School
White, Byron Raymond	355	6/8/1917		Colorado	U. of Colorado, Oxford	Yale Law School
Goldberg, Arthur Joseph	290	8/8/1908		Illinois	Northwestern U.	Northwestern U. Law School
Fortas, Abe	284	6/19/1910	4/5/1982	Tennessee	Southwestern Col.	Yale Law School
Marshall, Thurgood	315	6/2/1908		New York	Lincoln U.	Howard U. Law School
Blackmun, Harry Andrew	258	11/12/1908		Minnesota	Harvard	Harvard Law School
Powell, Lewis Franklin, Jr.	323	9/19/1907		Virginia	Washington & Lee	Harvard Law School, Wash. & Lee U. Law School
Rehnquist, William Hubbs	324	10/1/1924		Arizona	Stanford, Harvard	Stanford Law School
Stevens, John Paul	328	4/20/1920		Illinois	U. of Chicago	Northwestern U. Law School
O'Connor, Sandra Day	321	3/26/1930		Arizona	Stanford	Stanford Law School

Appointment		Reason for Leaving			Years Served	Chief Justice(s)	Landmark Decisions
President	Date	Chief Justice	Died	Resigned			
Eisenhower	3/19/1957					Warren Burger	Barenblatt v. United States NAACP v. Button N.Y. Times Co. v. Sullivan Baker v. Carr United Steel Wrkrs of Amer. v. Weber Malloy v. Hogan Weinberger v. Wiesenfeld Orr v. Orr
Eisenhower	3/19/1957			1962	5	Warren	Gomillion v. Lightfoot McNeal v. Culver Chapman v. United States Kent v. Dulles Boynton v. Virginia
Eisenhower	5/5/1959			1981	23	Warren Burger	Elkins v. United States Katz v. United States Chimel v. California Coolidge v. New Hampshire Jones v. Alfred H. Mayer Co. Hills v. Gautreaux Escobedo v. Illinois Miranda v. Arizona
Kennedy	4/11/1962					Warren Burger	Duncan v. Louisiana Williams v. Florida Taylor v. Louisiana Washington v. Davis Columbus Bd. of Ed. v. Penick
Kennedy	9/25/1962			1965	3	Warren	Murphy v. Waterfront Comm. of N.Y. Harbor Escobedo v. Illinois Aptheker v. Sec. of State United Mine Workers v. Pennington
Johnson	8/11/1965			1969	4	Warren	Gideon v. Wainwright In re Gault Tinker v. Des Moines Ind. School Dist.
Johnson	8/30/1967					Warren Burger	Smith v. Allwright Dunn v. Blumstein Benton v. Maryland Stanley v. Georgia Amalgamated Food Employees Union v. Logan Val. Plaza Reg. of U. of Calif. v. Bakke Brown v. Bd. of Education
Nixon	5/12/1970					Burger	Roe v. Wade N.Y. Times Co. v. United States Furman v. Georgia Miller v. California United States v. Nixon
Nixon	12/6/1971					Burger	Kastigar v. United States Profitt v. Florida First Nat'l Bank of Boston v. Bellotti Reg. of U. of Calif. v. Bakke
Nixon	12/10/1971					Burger	Edelman v. Jordan Fitzpatrick v. Bitzer Rostker v. Goldberg Dames & Moore v. Regan New York v. Quarles Hunter v. Underwood
Ford	12/17/1975					Burger	Jurek v. Texas Roberts v. Louisiana Marshall v. Barlows Inc. Fullilove v. Klutznick
Reagan	9/21/1981					Burger	Rose v. Lundy Tibbs v. Florida Arizona v. Rumsey United States v. Hensley Ford v. EEOC Akron v. Akron Center

SITTING COURTS

The chart below shows the periods of time during which a group of justices sat together on the Supreme Court. The Chief Justices (denoted by an *) are listed first, with the Associate Justices following in order of descending seniority. Frequently, more than one court is listed in a single year, reflecting the gap in time between the resignation or death of a justice and the confirmation of his replacement.

Years	Members
1789–1790	John Jay*
	John Rutledge
	William Cushing
	James Wilson
	John Blair
1790–1791	John Jay*
	John Rutledge
	William Cushing
	James Wilson
	John Blair
	James Iredell
1791–1793	John Jay*
	William Cushing
	James Wilson
	John Blair
	James Iredell
	Thomas Johnson
1793–1795	John Jay*
	William Cushing
	James Wilson
	John Blair
	James Iredell
	William Paterson

Years	Members
1795–1796	John Rutledge* (pro tem)
	William Cushing
	James Wilson
	John Blair
	James Iredell
	William Paterson
1796–1798	Oliver Ellsworth*
	William Cushing
	James Wilson
	James Iredell
	William Paterson
	Samuel Chase
1798–1799	Oliver Ellsworth*
	William Cushing
	James Iredell
	William Paterson
	Samuel Chase
	Bushrod Washington
1799–1800	Oliver Ellsworth*
	William Cushing
	William Paterson
	Samuel Chase
	Bushrod Washington
	Alfred Moore

Years	Members	Years	Members
1801–1804	John Marshall* William Cushing William Paterson Samuel Chase Bushrod Washington Alfred Moore	1823	John Marshall* Bushrod Washington William Johnson Thomas Todd Joseph Story Gabriel Duvall
1804–1806	John Marshall* William Cushing William Paterson Samuel Chase Bushrod Washington William Johnson	1823–1826	John Marshall* Bushrod Washington William Johnson Thomas Todd Joseph Story Gabriel Duvall Smith Thompson
1806–1807	John Marshall* William Cushing Samuel Chase Bushrod Washington William Johnson Henry Brockholst Livingston	1826–1828	John Marshall* Bushrod Washington William Johnson Joseph Story Gabriel Duvall Smith Thompson Robert Trimble
1807–1810	John Marshall* William Cushing Samuel Chase Bushrod Washington William Johnson Henry Brockholst Livingston Thomas Todd	1828–1829	John Marshall* Bushrod Washington William Johnson Joseph Story Gabriel Duvall Smith Thompson
1810–1811	John Marshall* Samuel Chase Bushrod Washington William Johnson Henry Brockholst Livingston Thomas Todd	1829	John Marshall* Bushrod Washington William Johnson Joseph Story Gabriel Duvall Smith Thompson John McLean
1811	John Marshall* Bushrod Washington William Johnson Henry Brockholst Livingston Thomas Todd	1830–1834	John Marshall* William Johnson Joseph Story Gabriel Duvall Smith Thompson John McLean Henry Baldwin
1811–1823	John Marshall* Bushrod Washington William Johnson Henry Brockholst Livingston Thomas Todd Joseph Story Gabriel Duvall	1835	John Marshall* Joseph Story Gabriel Duvall Smith Thompson John McLean Henry Baldwin James Moore Wayne

Years	Members	Years	Members
1835–1836	Joseph Story Gabriel Duvall Smith Thompson John McLean Henry Baldwin James Moore Wayne	1844–1845	Roger Brooke Taney* Joseph Story John McLean James Moore Wayne John Catron John McKinley Peter Vivian Daniel
1836–1837	Roger Brooke Taney* Joseph Story Smith Thompson John McLean Henry Baldwin James Moore Wayne Philip Pendleton Barbour	1845–1846	Roger Brooke Taney* John McLean James Moore Wayne John Catron John McKinley Peter Vivian Daniel Samuel Nelson
1837	Roger Brooke Taney* Joseph Story Smith Thompson John McLean Henry Baldwin James Moore Wayne Philip Pendleton Barbour John Catron	1846	Roger Brooke Taney* John McLean James Moore Wayne John Catron John McKinley Peter Vivian Daniel Samuel Nelson Levi Woodbury
1837–1841	Roger Brooke Taney* Joseph Story Smith Thompson John McLean Henry Baldwin James Moore Wayne Philip Pendleton Barbour John Catron John McKinley	1846–1851	Roger Brooke Taney* John McLean James Moore Wayne John Catron John McKinley Peter Vivian Daniel Samuel Nelson Levi Woodbury Robert Cooper Grier
1841–1843	Roger Brooke Taney* Joseph Story Smith Thompson John McLean Henry Baldwin James Moore Wayne John Catron John McKinley Peter Vivian Daniel	1851	Roger Brooke Taney* John McLean James Moore Wayne John Catron John McKinley Peter Vivian Daniel Samuel Nelson Robert Cooper Grier
1843–1844	Roger Brooke Taney* Joseph Story John McLean Henry Baldwin James Moore Wayne John Catron John McKinley Peter Vivian Daniel	1851–1853	Roger Brooke Taney* John McLean James Moore Wayne John Catron John McKinley Peter Vivian Daniel Samuel Nelson Robert Cooper Grier Benjamin Robbins Curtis

Years	Members	Years	Members
1853–1857	Roger Brooke Taney* John McLean James Moore Wayne John Catron Peter Vivian Daniel Samuel Nelson Robert Cooper Grier Benjamin Robbins Curtis John Archibald Campbell	1862–1863	Roger Brooke Taney* James Moore Wayne John Catron Samuel Nelson Robert Cooper Grier Nathan Clifford Noah Haynes Swayne Samuel Freeman Miller David Davis
1857–1858	Roger Brooke Taney* John McLean James Moore Wayne John Catron Peter Vivian Daniel Samuel Nelson Robert Cooper Grier John Archibald Campbell	1863–1864	Roger Brooke Taney* James Moore Wayne John Catron Samuel Nelson Robert Cooper Grier Nathan Clifford Noah Haynes Swayne Samuel Freeman Miller David Davis Stephen Johnson Field
1858–1860	Roger Brooke Taney* John McLean James Moore Wayne John Catron Peter Vivian Daniel Samuel Nelson Robert Cooper Grier John Archibald Campbell Nathan Clifford	1864–1865	Salmon Portland Chase* James Moore Wayne John Catron Samuel Nelson Robert Cooper Grier Nathan Clifford Noah Haynes Swayne Samuel Freeman Miller David Davis Stephen Johnson Field
1860–1861	Roger Brooke Taney* John McLean James Moore Wayne John Catron Samuel Nelson Robert Cooper Grier John Archibald Campbell Nathan Clifford	1865–1867	Salmon Portland Chase* James Moore Wayne Samuel Nelson Robert Cooper Grier Nathan Clifford Noah Haynes Swayne Samuel Freeman Miller David Davis Stephen Johnson Field
1862	Roger Brooke Taney* James Moore Wayne John Catron Samuel Nelson Robert Cooper Grier Nathan Clifford	1867–1870	Salmon Portland Chase* Samuel Nelson Robert Cooper Grier Nathan Clifford Noah Haynes Swayne Samuel Freeman Miller David Davis Stephen Johnson Field
1862	Roger Brooke Taney* James Moore Wayne John Catron Samuel Nelson Robert Cooper Grier Nathan Clifford Noah Haynes Swayne		

Years	Members	Years	Members
1870	Salmon Portland Chase* Samuel Nelson Nathan Clifford Noah Haynes Swayne Samuel Freeman Miller David Davis Stephen Johnson Field	1874–1877 *(Continued)*	William Strong Joseph P. Bradley Ward Hunt
1870	Salmon Portland Chase* Samuel Nelson Nathan Clifford Noah Haynes Swayne Samuel Freeman Miller David Davis Stephen Johnson Field William Strong	1877	Morrison Remick Waite* Nathan Clifford Noah Haynes Swayne Samuel Freeman Miller Stephen Johnson Field William Strong Joseph P. Bradley Ward Hunt
1870–1872	Salmon Portland Chase* Samuel Nelson Nathan Clifford Noah Haynes Swayne Samuel Freeman Miller David Davis Stephen Johnson Field William Strong Joseph P. Bradley	1877–1880	Morrison Remick Waite* Nathan Clifford Noah Haynes Swayne Samuel Freeman Miller Stephen Johnson Field William Strong Joseph P. Bradley Ward Hunt John Marshall Harlan
1872–1873	Salmon Portland Chase* Nathan Clifford Noah Haynes Swayne Samuel Freeman Miller David Davis Stephen Johnson Field William Strong Joseph P. Bradley	1880–1881	Morrison Remick Waite* Nathan Clifford Noah Haynes Swayne Samuel Freeman Miller Stephen Johnson Field Joseph P. Bradley Ward Hunt John Marshall Harlan William Burnham Woods
1873–1874	Salmon Portland Chase* Nathan Clifford Noah Haynes Swayne Samuel Freeman Miller David Davis Stephen Johnson Field William Strong Joseph P. Bradley Ward Hunt	1881	Morrison Remick Waite* Nathan Clifford Samuel Freeman Miller Stephen Johnson Field Joseph P. Bradley Ward Hunt John Marshall Harlan William Burnham Woods
1874–1877	Morrison Remick Waite* Nathan Clifford Noah Haynes Swayne Samuel Freeman Miller David Davis Stephen Johnson Field	1881	Morrison Remick Waite* Nathan Clifford Samuel Freeman Miller Stephen Johnson Field Joseph P. Bradley Ward Hunt John Marshall Harlan William Burnham Woods Stanley Matthews

Years	Members	Years	Members
1881	Morrison Remick Waite* Samuel Freeman Miller Stephen Johnson Field Joseph P. Bradley Ward Hunt John Marshall Harlan William Burnham Woods Stanley Matthews	1888 *(Continued)*	Stanley Matthews Horace Gray Samuel Milford Blatchford Lucius Quintus Cincinnatus Lamar
		1888	Samuel Freeman Miller Stephen Johnson Field Joseph P. Bradley John Marshall Harlan Stanley Matthews Horace Gray Samuel Milford Blatchford Lucius Quintus Cincinnatus Lamar
1881–1882	Morrison Remick Waite* Samuel Freeman Miller Stephen Johnson Field Joseph P. Bradley Ward Hunt John Marshall Harlan William Burnham Woods Stanley Matthews Horace Gray	1888–1889	Melville Weston Fuller* Samuel Freeman Miller Stephen Johnson Field Joseph P. Bradley John Marshall Harlan Stanley Matthews Horace Gray Samuel Milford Blatchford Lucius Quintus Cincinnatus Lamar
1882	Morrison Remick Waite* Samuel Freeman Miller Stephen Johnson Field Joseph P. Bradley John Marshall Harlan William Burnham Woods Stanley Matthews Horace Gray	1889	Melville Weston Fuller* Samuel Freeman Miller Stephen Johnson Field Joseph P. Bradley John Marshall Harlan Horace Gray Samuel Milford Blatchford Lucius Quintus Cincinnatus Lamar
1882–1887	Morrison Remick Waite* Samuel Freeman Miller Stephen Johnson Field Joseph P. Bradley John Marshall Harlan William Burnham Woods Stanley Matthews Horace Gray Samuel Milford Blatchford	1889–1890	Melville Weston Fuller* Samuel Freeman Miller Stephen Johnson Field Joseph P. Bradley John Marshall Harlan Horace Gray Samuel Milford Blatchford Lucius Quintus Cincinnatus Lamar David Josiah Brewer
1887–1888	Morrison Remick Waite* Samuel Freeman Miller Stephen Johnson Field Joseph P. Bradley John Marshall Harlan Stanley Matthews Horace Gray Samuel Milford Blatchford	1890	Melville Weston Fuller* Stephen Johnson Field Joseph P. Bradley John Marshall Harlan Horace Gray Samuel Milford Blatchford Lucius Quintus Cincinnatus Lamar David Josiah Brewer
1888	Morrison Remick Waite* Samuel Freeman Miller Stephen Johnson Field Joseph P. Bradley John Marshall Harlan		

Years	Members	Years	Members
1890–1892	Melville Weston Fuller* Stephen Johnson Field Joseph P. Bradley John Marshall Harlan Horace Gray Samuel Milford Blatchford Lucius Quintus Cincinnatus Lamar David Josiah Brewer Henry Billings Brown	1894–1895 *(Continued)*	David Josiah Brewer Henry Billings Brown George Shiras, Jr. Howell Edmunds Jackson Edward Douglass White, Jr.
1892	Melville Weston Fuller* Stephen Johnson Field John Marshall Harlan Horace Gray Samuel Milford Blatchford Lucius Quintus Cincinnatus Lamar David Josiah Brewer Henry Billings Brown	1895	Melville Weston Fuller* Stephen Johnson Field John Marshall Harlan Horace Gray David Josiah Brewer Henry Billings Brown George Shiras, Jr. Edward Douglass White, Jr.
1892–1893	Melville Weston Fuller* Stephen Johnson Field John Marshall Harlan Horace Gray Samuel Milford Blatchford Lucius Quintus Cincinnatus Lamar David Josiah Brewer Henry Billings Brown George Shiras, Jr.	1895–1897	Melville Weston Fuller* Stephen Johnson Field John Marshall Harlan Horace Gray David Josiah Brewer Henry Billings Brown George Shiras, Jr. Edward Douglass White, Jr. Rufus Wheeler Peckham, Jr.
1893	Melville Weston Fuller* Stephen Johnson Field John Marshall Harlan Horace Gray Samuel Milford Blatchford David Josiah Brewer Henry Billings Brown George Shiras, Jr. Howell Edmunds Jackson	1897–1898	Melville Weston Fuller* John Marshall Harlan Horace Gray David Josiah Brewer Henry Billings Brown George Shiras, Jr. Edward Douglass White, Jr. Rufus Wheeler Peckham, Jr.
1893–1894	Melville Weston Fuller* Stephen Johnson Field John Marshall Harlan Horace Gray David Josiah Brewer Henry Billings Brown George Shiras, Jr. Howell Edmunds Jackson	1898–1902	Melville Weston Fuller* John Marshall Harlan Horace Gray David Josiah Brewer Henry Billings Brown George Shiras, Jr. Edward Douglass White, Jr. Rufus Wheeler Peckham, Jr. Joseph McKenna
1894–1895	Melville Weston Fuller* Stephen Johnson Field John Marshall Harlan Horace Gray	1902	Melville Weston Fuller* John Marshall Harlan David Josiah Brewer Henry Billings Brown George Shiras, Jr. Edward Douglass White, Jr. Rufus Wheeler Peckham, Jr. Joseph McKenna

Years	Members
1902–1903	Melville Weston Fuller*
	John Marshall Harlan
	David Josiah Brewer
	Henry Billings Brown
	George Shiras, Jr.
	Edward Douglass White, Jr.
	Rufus Wheeler Peckham, Jr.
	Joseph McKenna
	Oliver Wendell Holmes, Jr.
1903–1906	Melville Weston Fuller*
	John Marshall Harlan
	David Josiah Brewer
	Henry Billings Brown
	Edward Douglass White, Jr.
	Rufus Wheeler Peckham, Jr.
	Joseph McKenna
	Oliver Wendell Holmes, Jr.
	William Rufus Day
1906	Melville Weston Fuller*
	John Marshall Harlan
	David Josiah Brewer
	Edward Douglass White, Jr.
	Rufus Wheeler Peckham, Jr.
	Joseph McKenna
	Oliver Wendell Holmes, Jr.
	William Rufus Day
1906–1909	Melville Weston Fuller*
	John Marshall Harlan
	David Josiah Brewer
	Edward Douglass White, Jr.
	Rufus Wheeler Peckham, Jr.
	Joseph McKenna
	Oliver Wendell Holmes, Jr.
	William Rufus Day
	William Henry Moody
1909	Melville Weston Fuller*
	John Marshall Harlan
	David Josiah Brewer
	Edward Douglass White, Jr.
	Joseph McKenna
	Oliver Wendell Holmes, Jr.
	William Rufus Day
	William Henry Moody
1909–1910	Melville Weston Fuller*
	John Marshall Harlan
	David Josiah Brewer
	Edward Douglass White, Jr.

Years	Members
1909–1910 *(Continued)*	Joseph McKenna
	Oliver Wendell Holmes, Jr.
	William Rufus Day
	William Henry Moody
	Horace Harmon Lurton
1910	Melville Weston Fuller*
	John Marshall Harlan
	Edward Douglass White, Jr.
	Joseph McKenna
	Oliver Wendell Holmes, Jr.
	William Rufus Day
	William Henry Moody
	Horace Harmon Lurton
1910	Melville Weston Fuller*
	John Marshall Harlan
	Edward Douglass White, Jr.
	Joseph McKenna
	Oliver Wendell Holmes, Jr.
	William Rufus Day
	William Henry Moody
	Horace Harmon Lurton
	Charles Evans Hughes
1910	John Marshall Harlan
	Edward Douglass White, Jr.
	Joseph McKenna
	Oliver Wendell Holmes, Jr.
	William Rufus Day
	William Henry Moody
	Horace Harmon Lurton
	Charles Evans Hughes
1910	John Marshall Harlan
	Edward Douglass White, Jr.
	Joseph McKenna
	Oliver Wendell Holmes, Jr.
	William Rufus Day
	Horace Harmon Lurton
	Charles Evans Hughes
	Willis Van Devanter
1910–1911	Edward Douglass White, Jr.*
	John Marshall Harlan
	Joseph McKenna
	Oliver Wendell Holmes, Jr.
	William Rufus Day
	Horace Harmon Lurton
	Charles Evans Hughes
	Willis Van Devanter

Years	Members
1911	Edward Douglass White, Jr.*
	John Marshall Harlan
	Joseph McKenna
	Oliver Wendell Holmes, Jr.
	William Rufus Day
	Horace Harmon Lurton
	Charles Evans Hughes
	Willis Van Devanter
	Joseph Rucker Lamar
1911–1912	Edward Douglass White, Jr.*
	Joseph McKenna
	Oliver Wendell Holmes, Jr.
	William Rufus Day
	Horace Harmon Lurton
	Charles Evans Hughes
	Willis Van Devanter
	Joseph Rucker Lamar
1912–1914	Edward Douglass White, Jr.*
	Joseph McKenna
	Oliver Wendell Holmes, Jr.
	William Rufus Day
	Horace Harmon Lurton
	Charles Evans Hughes
	Willis Van Devanter
	Joseph Rucker Lamar
	Mahlon Pitney
1914–1916	Edward Douglass White, Jr.*
	Joseph McKenna
	Oliver Wendell Holmes, Jr.
	William Rufus Day
	Charles Evans Hughes
	Willis Van Devanter
	Joseph Rucker Lamar
	Mahlon Pitney
	James Clark McReynolds
1916	Edward Douglass White, Jr.*
	Joseph McKenna
	Oliver Wendell Holmes, Jr.
	William Rufus Day
	Charles Evans Hughes
	Willis Van Devanter
	Mahlon Pitney
	James Clark McReynolds
1916	Edward Douglass White, Jr.*
	Joseph McKenna
	Oliver Wendell Holmes, Jr.
	William Rufus Day
	Charles Evans Hughes

Years	Members
1916 *(Continued)*	Willis Van Devanter
	Mahlon Pitney
	James Clark McReynolds
	Louis Dembitz Brandeis
1916–1921	Edward Douglass White, Jr.*
	Joseph McKenna
	Oliver Wendell Holmes, Jr.
	William Rufus Day
	Willis Van Devanter
	Mahlon Pitney
	James Clark McReynolds
	Louis Dembitz Brandeis
	John Hessin Clarke
1921–1922	William Howard Taft*
	Joseph McKenna
	Oliver Wendell Holmes, Jr.
	William Rufus Day
	Willis Van Devanter
	Mahlon Pitney
	James Clark McReynolds
	Louis Dembitz Brandeis
	John Hessin Clarke
1922	William Howard Taft*
	Joseph McKenna
	Oliver Wendell Holmes, Jr.
	William Rufus Day
	Willis Van Devanter
	Mahlon Pitney
	James Clark McReynolds
	Louis Dembitz Brandeis
	George Sutherland
1922	William Howard Taft*
	Joseph McKenna
	Oliver Wendell Holmes, Jr.
	Willis Van Devanter
	Mahlon Pitney
	James Clark McReynolds
	Louis Dembitz Brandeis
	George Sutherland
1922–1923	William Howard Taft*
	Joseph McKenna
	Oliver Wendell Holmes, Jr.
	Willis Van Devanter
	James Clark McReynolds
	Louis Dembitz Brandeis
	George Sutherland
	Pierce Butler

Years	Members	Years	Members
1923–1925	William Howard Taft* Joseph McKenna Oliver Wendell Holmes, Jr. Willis Van Devanter James Clark McReynolds Louis Dembitz Brandeis George Sutherland Pierce Butler Edward Terry Sanford	1932–1937 *(Continued)*	Pierce Butler Harlan Fiske Stone Owen Josephus Roberts Benjamin Nathan Cardozo
1925–1930	William Howard Taft* Oliver Wendell Holmes, Jr. Willis Van Devanter James Clark McReynolds Louis Dembitz Brandeis George Sutherland Pierce Butler Edward Terry Sanford Harlan Fiske Stone	1937–1938	Charles Evans Hughes* James Clark McReynolds Louis Dembitz Brandeis George Sutherland Pierce Butler Harlan Fiske Stone Owen Josephus Roberts Benjamin Nathan Cardozo Hugo Lafayette Black
1930	Charles Evans Hughes* Oliver Wendell Holmes, Jr. Willis Van Devanter James Clark McReynolds Louis Dembitz Brandeis George Sutherland Pierce Butler Harlan Fiske Stone	1938	Charles Evans Hughes* James Clark McReynolds Louis Dembitz Brandeis Pierce Butler Harlan Fiske Stone Owen Josephus Roberts Benjamin Nathan Cardozo Hugo Lafayette Black Stanley Forman Reed
1930–1932	Charles Evans Hughes* Oliver Wendell Holmes, Jr. Willis Van Devanter James Clark McReynolds Louis Dembitz Brandeis George Sutherland Pierce Butler Harlan Fiske Stone Owen Josephus Roberts	1938–1939	Charles Evans Hughes* James Clark McReynolds Louis Dembitz Brandeis Pierce Butler Harlan Fiske Stone Owen Josephus Roberts Hugo Lafayette Black Stanley Forman Reed
1932	Charles Evans Hughes* Willis Van Devanter James Clark McReynolds Louis Dembitz Brandeis George Sutherland Pierce Butler Harlan Fiske Stone Owen Josephus Roberts	1939	Charles Evans Hughes* James Clark McReynolds Louis Dembitz Brandeis Pierce Butler Harlan Fiske Stone Owen Josephus Roberts Hugo Lafayette Black Stanley Forman Reed Felix Frankfurter
1932–1937	Charles Evans Hughes* Willis Van Devanter James Clark McReynolds Louis Dembitz Brandeis George Sutherland	1939	Charles Evans Hughes* James Clark McReynolds Pierce Butler Harlan Fiske Stone Owen Josephus Roberts Hugo Lafayette Black Stanley Forman Reed

Years	Members	Years	Members
1939 *(Continued)*	Felix Frankfurter William Orville Douglas	1943–1945	Harlan Fiske Stone* Owen Josephus Roberts Hugo Lafayette Black Stanley Forman Reed Felix Frankfurter William Orville Douglas Frank Murphy Robert Houghwout Jackson Wiley Blount Rutledge, Jr.
1939–1940	Charles Evans Hughes* James Clark McReynolds Harlan Fiske Stone Owen Josephus Roberts Hugo Lafayette Black Stanley Forman Reed Felix Frankfurter William Orville Douglas	1945–1946	Harlan Fiske Stone* Hugo Lafayette Black Stanley Forman Reed Felix Frankfurter William Orville Douglas Frank Murphy Robert Houghwout Jackson Wiley Blount Rutledge, Jr. Harold Hitz Burton
1940–1941	Charles Evans Hughes* James Clark McReynolds Harlan Fiske Stone Owen Josephus Roberts Hugo Lafayette Black Stanley Forman Reed Felix Frankfurter William Orville Douglas Frank Murphy	1946–1949	Frederick Moore Vinson* Hugo Lafayette Black Stanley Forman Reed Felix Frankfurter William Orville Douglas Frank Murphy Robert Houghwout Jackson Wiley Blount Rutledge, Jr. Harold Hitz Burton
1941	Charles Evans Hughes* Harlan Fiske Stone Owen Josephus Roberts Hugo Lafayette Black Stanley Forman Reed Felix Frankfurter William Orville Douglas Frank Murphy	1949–1953	Frederick Moore Vinson* Hugo Lafayette Black Stanley Forman Reed Felix Frankfurter William Orville Douglas Robert Houghwout Jackson Harold Hitz Burton Tom Campbell Clark Sherman Minton
1941–1942	Harlan Fiske Stone* Owen Josephus Roberts Hugo Lafayette Black Stanley Forman Reed Felix Frankfurter William Orville Douglas Frank Murphy James Francis Byrnes Robert Houghwout Jackson	1953–1954	Hugo Lafayette Black Stanley Forman Reed Felix Frankfurter William Orville Douglas Robert Houghwout Jackson Harold Hitz Burton Tom Campbell Clark Sherman Minton
1942–1943	Harlan Fiske Stone* Owen Josephus Roberts Hugo Lafayette Black Stanley Forman Reed Felix Frankfurter William Orville Douglas Frank Murphy Robert Houghwout Jackson		

Years	Members	Years	Members
1954–1955	Earl Warren* Hugo Lafayette Black Stanley Forman Reed Felix Frankfurter William Orville Douglas Harold Hitz Burton Tom Campbell Clark Sherman Minton	1959–1962 (*Continued*)	John Marshall Harlan William Joseph Brennan, Jr. Charles Evans Whittaker Potter Stewart
1955–1956	Earl Warren* Hugo Lafayette Black Stanley Forman Reed Felix Frankfurter William Orville Douglas Harold Hitz Burton Tom Campbell Clark Sherman Minton John Marshall Harlan	1962	Earl Warren* Hugo Lafayette Black Felix Frankfurter William Orville Douglas Tom Campbell Clark John Marshall Harlan William Joseph Brennan, Jr. Potter Stewart Byron Raymond White
1956–1957	Earl Warren* Hugo Lafayette Black Stanley Forman Reed Felix Frankfurter William Orville Douglas Harold Hitz Burton Tom Campbell Clark John Marshall Harlan	1962–1965	Earl Warren* Hugo Lafayette Black William Orville Douglas Tom Campbell Clark John Marshall Harlan William Joseph Brennan, Jr. Potter Stewart Byron Raymond White Arthur Joseph Goldberg
1957–1958	Earl Warren* Hugo Lafayette Black Felix Frankfurter William Orville Douglas Harold Hitz Burton Tom Campbell Clark John Marshall Harlan William Joseph Brennan, Jr. Charles Evans Whittaker	1965–1967	Earl Warren* Hugo Lafayette Black William Orville Douglas Tom Campbell Clark John Marshall Harlan William Joseph Brennan, Jr. Potter Stewart Byron Raymond White Abe Fortas
1958–1959	Earl Warren* Hugo Lafayette Black Felix Frankfurter William Orville Douglas Tom Campbell Clark John Marshall Harlan William Joseph Brennan, Jr. Charles Evans Whittaker	1967–1969	Earl Warren* Hugo Lafayette Black William Orville Douglas John Marshall Harlan William Joseph Brennan, Jr. Potter Stewart Byron Raymond White Abe Fortas Thurgood Marshall
1959–1962	Earl Warren* Hugo Lafayette Black Felix Frankfurter William Orville Douglas Tom Campbell Clark	1969–1970	Warren Earl Burger* Hugo Lafayette Black William Orville Douglas John Marshall Harlan William Joseph Brennan, Jr.

Years	Members	Years	Members
1969–1970 *(Continued)*	Potter Stewart Byron Raymond White Thurgood Marshall	1975–1981	Warren Earl Burger* William Joseph Brennan, Jr. Potter Stewart Byron Raymond White Thurgood Marshall Harry Andrew Blackmun Lewis Franklin Powell, Jr. William Hubbs Rehnquist John Paul Stevens
1970–1971	Warren Earl Burger* Hugo Lafayette Black William Orville Douglas John Marshall Harlan William Joseph Brennan, Jr. Potter Stewart Byron Raymond White Thurgood Marshall Harry Andrew Blackmun	1981–	Warren Earl Burger* William Joseph Brennan, Jr. Byron Raymond White Thurgood Marshall Harry Andrew Blackmun Lewis Franklin Powell, Jr. William Hubbs Rehnquist John Paul Stevens Sandra Day O'Connor
1971–1975	Warren Earl Burger* William Orville Douglas William Joseph Brennan, Jr. Potter Stewart Byron Raymond White Thurgood Marshall Harry Andrew Blackmun Lewis Franklin Powell, Jr. William Hubbs Rehnquist		

LANDMARK CASES: CHRONOLOGICAL LISTING

The table below of key Supreme Court decisions, arranged chronologically, shows the year of the decision, its title, its category, and the predominant point at issue. The category designations are correlated with the main text chapters in which these broad constitutional questions are examined: Category I: The Constitutional Powers of the Branches of the Federal Government; Category II: Division of Power: The Federal Government and the States; Category III: Individual Rights. The cases are described more fully in the Landmark Cases section.

Year	Case	Category	Issue
1793	Chisholm v. Georgia, 2 Dall. 419	II:	right of citizen to sue government of another state
1796	Hylton v. United States, 3 Dall. 171	II:	Congressional power to tax
	Ware v. Hylton, 3 Dallas 282	II:	international treaties take precedence over state laws
1798	Calder v. Bull, 3 Dall. 386	III:	Constitutional protection of *ex post facto* laws refers only to acts after they have been committed
1803	Marbury v. Madison, 1 Cranch 137	I:	affirmed right and duty of Supreme Court to review acts of Congress from standpoint of Constitution alone
1810	Fletcher v. Peck, 6 Cranch 87	II:	federal government may intervene in state affairs through use of contract clause
1816	Martin v. Hunter's Lessee, 1 Wheaton 122	II:	Supreme Court may review state court decisions
1819	Sturges v. Crowninshield, 4 Wheaton 122	II:	struck down New York state law that released bankrupt debtors from obligations to creditors

Year	Case	Category	Issue
1819 *(Continued)*			
	Trustees of Dartmouth College v. Woodward, 4 Wheaton 518	II:	charter, valid when issued, cannot be amended or revoked by state
	McCulloch v. Maryland, 4 Wheaton 316	II:	state laws cannot restrict national bank
1821	Cohens v. Virginia, 6 Wheaton 264	II:	Supreme Court reviews all constitutional questions despite state restrictions
1823	Green v. Biddle, 8 Wheaton 1, 69	II:	Constitution prohibits states from enacting any laws that interfere with obligations of contracts
1824	Osborn v. Bank of the United States, 9 Wheaton 738	II:	federal agencies can file suit against state officials in federal courts
	Gibbons v. Ogden, 9 Wheaton 1	II:	paved the way for federal intervention when conflict with state law
1827	Martin v. Mott, 12 Wheaton 19	I:	executive branch has exclusive power to call out militia
	Brown v. Maryland, 12 Wheaton 419	II:	supremacy of Constitution over state law in interstate trade
	Ogden v. Saunders, 12 Wheaton 213	II:	upheld state insolvency law
1830	Craig v. Missouri, 4 Peters 410	II:	states cannot issue "bills of credit"
1831	Cherokee Nation v. Georgia, 5 Peters 1	II:	Cherokees, not a foreign nation within state, not entitled to enter suit against another state
1832	Worcester v. Georgia, 6 Peters 515	II:	federal government has jurisdiction over Indian affairs
1833	Barron v. Baltimore, 7 Peters 243	II:	constitutional guarantees in Bill of Rights apply only to actions of federal government
1837	Briscoe v. Bank of Kentucky, 11 Peters 257	II:	state banks can issue bank notes
	Charles River Bridge v. Warren Bridge, 11 Peters 420	II:	broadened interpretation of legitimate regulatory power of states
	City of New York v. Miln, 11 Peters 102	II:	certain state laws, to protect the health, prosperity, and safety of its citizens, do not conflict with federal control of interstate commerce
1839	Bank of Augusta v. Earle, 13 Peters 519	II:	state-chartered corporations are legal in other states
1842	Prigg v. Pennsylvania, 16 Peters 539	II:	Fugitive Slave Act superseded any state law
1847	License Cases, 5 Howard 504	II:	upheld state liquor laws as legitimate exercise of states' "police power"

Year	Case	Category	Issue
1849	Luther v. Borden, 7 Howard 1	I:	judiciary should not enter political disputes
	Passenger Cases, 7 Howard 283	II:	states cannot regulate international trade
1851	Cooley v. Board of Wardens, 12 Howard 299	II:	states have the right to regulate certain aspects of interstate commerce
1857	Scott v. Sandford, 12 Howard 299	III:	blacks are not citizens (invalidated by 13th and 14th amendments)
1859	Ableman v. Booth, 21 Howard 506	II:	state courts may issue writs of *habeas corpus* for federal prisoners
1861	Ex parte Merryman, 17 Federal Cases 9487	I:	unsolved case concerning right of President to impose martial law; also regarding issuance of *habeas corpus* writ. (Solved in *Ex parte Milligan*)
1863	Prize Cases, 2 Black 635	I:	President need not wait for approval of Congress to declare war where war clearly exists
1866	Ex parte Milligan, 4 Wallace 2	I:	President cannot impose martial law on civilians outside a war zone
	Ex parte Vallandigham, 1 Wallace 243	I:	Supreme Court lacks jurisdiction to review military court decision
1867	Mississippi v. Johnson, 4 Wallace 475	I:	Supreme Court could not intervene in enforcement by the President of the Reconstruction Act, even though Act was unconstitutional
	Cummings v. Missouri, 4 Wallace 277	III:	loyalty ("test") oaths are unconstitutional
	Ex parte Garland, 4 Wallace 333	III:	federal loyalty oath is unconstitutional
1869	Ex parte McCardle, 7 Wallace 506	I:	Congress has the right to limit the appellate jurisdiction of the Supreme Court
	Texas v. White, 7 Wallace 700	II:	since illegal to secede, all Confederacy states remained US states; therefore all acts by "rebels" were illegal
1870	Hepburn v. Griswold, 8 Wallace 603	I:	struck down Legal Tender Act of 1862 as a violation of obligation of contracts
	Veazie Bank v. Fenno, 5 Wallace 533	II:	tax imposed on notes of state banks was permissible because it was not a direct tax
1871	Collector v. Day, 11 Wallace 113	II:	state officials are immune from federal income tax
	Second Legal Tender Case, 12 Wallace 457	I:	paper currency is legal tender for payment of government debts

Year	Case	Category	Issue
1873	Slaughterhouse Cases, 16 Wallace 36	III:	state can enforce a monopoly in private business; civil rights of U.S. citizens does not include the right to engage in a particular business
1877	Munn v. Illinois, 94 U.S. 113	II:	states can regulate certain aspects of private industry
1881	Springer v. United States, 102 U.S. 586	I:	Congress has the power to set and collect taxes and duties and may authorize sale of property to enforce payment
1883	Civil Rights Cases, 109 U.S. 3	I:	Congress may not legislate in matters of racial discrimination in the private sector
1884	Ex parte Yarbrough, 110 U.S. 651	III:	racial discrimination prohibited in all activities connected with voting
	Juilliard v. Greenman, 110 U.S. 421	I:	Congress is empowered to make U.S. Treasury notes legal tender during war and peace
1886	Santa Clara County v. Southern Pacific Railroad Co., 118 U.S. 394	II:	state taxation of the railroad should be the subject of the scrutiny of the Supreme Court
	Wabash, St. Louis & Pacific Railway Co. v. Illinois, 118 U.S. 557	II:	state cannot regulate interstate commerce
1890	Chicago, Milwaukee & St. Paul Railway Co. v. Minnesota, 134 U.S. 418	II:	state governments can regulate intrastate railroads, but must also provide judicial review
1893	Reagan v. Farmer's Loan and Trust Co., 154 U.S. 362	II:	upheld a Texas railroad commission to classify and regulate rates as valid exercise of state sovereignty
1895	In re Debs, 158 U.S. 564	II:	upheld Sherman Antitrust Act
	Pollock v. Farmers' Loan and Trust Co., 157 U.S. 429, 158 U.S. 601	I:	federal income tax in present form is unconstitutional
	United States v. E.C. Knight Co., 156 U.S. 1	II:	local manufacturing is beyond the jurisdiction of federal intervention
1896	Plessy v. Ferguson, 163 U.S. 537	III:	separate but equal doctrine does not violate the 13th and 14th amendments
1897	United States v. Trans-Missouri Freight Association, 166 U.S. 290	II:	contract between railway carriers in restraint of trade or commerce is prohibited
1898	Holden v. Hardy, 169 U.S. 366	II:	states have the right to set certain maximum working hours for certain trades
	Smyth v. Ames, 169 U.S. 466	II:	private corporations are entitled to fair return on investment, and state governments should consider this in determination of regulated rates

Year	Case	Category	Issue
1899	Addyston Pipe and Steel Company v. United States, 175 U.S. 211	II:	federal government has right to regulate practices of certain private businesses
1901	De Lima v. Bidwell, 182 U.S. 1 (Insular Case)	II:	U.S. territories are not foreign; struck down import duties on Puerto Rican sugar
	Dooley v. United States, 182 U.S. 222 (Insular Case)	II:	duties on goods from Puerto Rico to U.S. and from U.S. to Puerto Rico ceased
	Downes v. Bidwell, 182 U.S. 222	II:	Foraker Act is constitutional, and duties established by it on Puerto Rico are valid
1903	Champion v. Ames, 188 U.S. 244	I:	Congress has right to pass Lottery Act and to regulate it
1904	Northern Securities Co. v. United States, 193 U.S. 197	II:	any company formed by two companies to eliminate competition is illegal and must be dissolved
1905	Lochner v. New York, 198 U.S. 45	II:	struck down state law regulating working conditions of certain trades; regulations can be made only to eliminate certain hazards
	Swift and Co. v. United States, 196 U.S. 375	II:	upheld injunction against local meat packers; they are part of larger process and are therefore considered part of interstate commerce
1908	Adair v. United States, 208 U.S. 161	III:	federal government does not have right to prohibit compulsory non-union pledges by employees
	Loewe v. Lawler, 208 U.S. 274 (Danbury Hatters' Case)	III:	secondary boycotts by labor unions are illegal
	Muller v. Oregon, 208 U.S. 412	II:	state can regulate working conditions for women
1911	Standard Oil Company of New Jersey v. United States, 221 U.S. 1	III:	definition of illegal trust ("those corporations that restrict competition to an 'unreasonable' degree")
	United States v. American Tobacco Company, 221 U.S. 106	III:	since actions had not been "unreasonable" as defined in *Standard Oil*, in eliminating competition, there was no need to break up company
	United States v. Grimaud, 220 U.S. 506	I:	Congress has right to confer administrative power on the Secretary of Agriculture to establish rules and regulations on the use of federal lands
1913	Minnesota Rate Cases, 230 U.S. 352	I:	Congress has constitutional power to assume regulatory control of interstate commerce

Year	Case	Category	Issue
1917	Wilson v. New, 243 U.S. 332	I:	Congress has power to arbitrate nationwide dispute (railroads and train operatives)
1918	Hammer v. Dagenhart, 247 U.S. 251	III:	struck down Child Labor Law (1916)
	Selective Draft Cases, 245 U.S. 366	III:	upheld compulsory military draft
1919	Abrams v. United States, 250 U.S. 616	I:	Congress has power to restrict freedom of speech in certain cases
	Northern Pacific Railway Co. v. North Dakota, 250 U.S. 135	II:	federal government can regulate intrastate railroad rates during times of national emergency
	Schenck v. United States, 249 U.S. 47	III:	upheld Espionage Act and ruled that "clear and present danger" does not violate the 1st Amendment
	War Prohibition Cases, 251 U.S. 146	I:	upheld War-Time Prohibition Act (1918)
1920	Missouri v. Holland, 252 U.S. 416	II:	implementation of duly ratified international treaties allows Congress to legislate matters otherwise relegated to the states
1921	Duplex Printing Press Co. v. Deering, 254 U.S. 443	III:	nullified Clayton Antitrust Act
	Truax v. Corrigan, 257 U.S. 312	III:	denying an employer of property by willfully conspiring to injure business during a labor dispute is illegal
1922	Bailey v. Drexel Furniture Co., 259 U.S. 20	II:	struck down Child Labor Tax Act; restricted "police power" of federal government
1923	Adkins v. Children's Hospital, 261 U.S. 525	III:	federal government does not have right to regulate minimum wage of certain employees
	Massachusetts v. Mellon, 262 U.S. 447	II:	neither state nor individual has legal right to challenge certain federal laws
	Tyson and Bros. v. Banton, 273 U.S. 418	II:	resale price of theater tickets cannot be regulated by law because they are not so affected with a public interest
	Wolff Packing Co. v. Court of Industrial Relations, 262 U.S. 522	III:	Industrial Court Act conflicts with 14th Amendment because it permits fixing of wages and deprives owner of property and liberty of contract
1925	Gitlow v. New York, 268 U.S. 652	III:	upheld state law on subversive statements—ruled it did not violate the 1st Amendment and that state has right to self-preservation
1927	Whitney v. California, 274 U.S. 357	III:	upheld California's Criminal Syndicalism Act, which made it unlawful to join an organization that advocated violence in political and industrial disputes

Year	Case	Category	Issue
1928	Olmstead v. United States, 277 U.S. 438	III:	wiretapping is legal since actual entry does not take place
1931	Near v. Minnesota, 283 U.S. 697	III:	defined freedom of the press as immunity from previous restraints and censorship
	Stromberg v. California, 283 U.S. 359	II:	struck down California anti-sedition law
1932	Powell v. Alabama, 287 U.S. 45	III:	state obligated to provide competent counsel for capital case defendants
1934	Nebbia v. New York, 291 U.S. 502	II:	justified state law in setting minimum prices in the dairy industry
1935	Gold Clause Cases	II:	upheld right of federal government to abolish gold standard and to thus abrogate provisions of contracts that required payment in gold
	Railroad Retirement Board v. Alton Railroad Co., 295 U.S. 330	II:	Railroad Retirement Act is unconstitutional
	Schechter Poultry Corp. v. United States, 295 U.S. 495	I:	Congress may not extend a regulation of interstate commerce to intrastate commerce
	United States v. Banker's Trust Co., 294 U.S. 240	I:	Congress can establish the most efficient monetary system for the country
1936	Ashwander v. Tennessee Valley Authority, 297 U.S. 288	II:	federal government has the right to exercise authority over the sale of excess electricity
	United States v. Butler, 297 U.S. 1	I:	struck down Agricultural Adjustment Act of 1933 as a violation of constitutional taxing power
	United States v. Curtiss-Wright Export Corp., 299 U.S. 304	I:	the President has the right to establish arms embargoes on certain countries engaged in war
1937	DeJonge v. Oregon, 299 U.S. 353	III:	struck down Oregon law making it unlawful to assemble for purpose of advocating violent overthrow of the government
	Helvering v. Davis, 301 U.S. 619	I:	Social Security Act is a legitimate use of the federal power to tax
	Herndon v. Lowry, 301 U.S. 242	II:	declared Georgia law (making it unlawful to try to persuade another to participate in insurrection) too vague
	National Labor Relations Board v. Jones & Laughlin Steel Corp., 301 U.S. 1	II:	upheld National Labor Relations Act
	Palko v. Connecticut, 302 U.S. 319	III:	upheld law permitting appeal of conviction and resentencing
	Steward Machine Co. v. Davis, 301 U.S. 548	II:	upheld Social Security Act
	West Coast Hotel Co. v. Parrish, 300 U.S. 379	II:	state minimum wage law is constitutional

Year	Case	Category	Issue
1938	Lovell v. Griffin, 303 U.S. 444	III:	upheld person's right to publish and distribute without a license
	Missouri ex. rel. Gaines v. Canada, 305 U.S. 337	III:	separate but equal theory not constitutional; state universities must admit students regardless of race
1939	Graves v. New York ex. rel. O'Keefe, 306 U.S. 466	II:	state can tax income of federal employee
	Hague v. Congress of Industrial Organizations, 307 U.S. 496	III:	right of public assembly is an inviolable right
1940	Cantwell v. Connecticut, 310 U.S. 396	III:	upheld free exercise of religion; struck down state law requiring state licensing for soliciting charitable or church funds
	Minersville School District v. Gobitis, 310 U.S. 586	III:	upheld state law requiring pledge of allegiance in school
	Thornhill v. Alabama, 310 U.S. 88	III:	freedom of press and speech is secured to all persons against abridgement by the states
1941	Edwards v. California, 314 U.S. 160	II:	struck down state law making it criminal offense to bring indigent into state knowingly
	United States v. Darby Lumber Co., 312 U.S. 100	II:	upheld Fair Labor Standards Act
	United States v. Classic, 313 U.S. 299	II:	federal government has power to regulate primary elections
1942	Betts v. Brady, 316 U.S. 299	III:	states obliged to provide legal counsel for indigent defendants
1943	Hirabayashi v. United States, 320 U.S. 810	III:	curfew for Japanese-Americans during World War II legitimate because extraordinary circumstances were created by the war
	West Virginia State Board of Education v. Barnette, 319 U.S. 624	III:	struck down compulsory pledge of allegiance in schools
1944	Ex parte Endo, 323 U.S. 283	III:	once a citizen's loyalty has been established, that citizen cannot be detained in a war location center
	Korematsu v. United States, 323 U.S. 214	III:	relocation of Japanese-Americans during World War II justified by extraordinary circumstances
	Smith v. Allwright, 321 U.S. 649	III:	primaries open to all in the party regardless of race
1946	Morgan v. Virginia, 328 U.S. 373	II:	state law cannot be applied to interstate transportation facilities; segregation on interstate transportation illegal

Year	Case	Category	Issue
1947	Friedman v. Schwellenbach, 330 U.S. 836	III:	Civil Service Commission has right to dismiss employees for alleged subversive associations
	United States v. California, 332 U.S. 19	II:	tidelands and their natural resources are under federal jurisdiction
1948	Illinois ex. rel. McCollum v. Board of Education, 333 U.S. 203	III:	religious classes on public premises are unconstitutional
	Shelley v. Kraemer, 334 U.S. 1	II:	a restrictive covenant is a private action and beyond government jurisdiction; it cannot be enforced by the state
	Sipuel v. University of Oklahoma, 332 U.S. 631	III:	state education system cannot deny a person professional legal education because of race
1949	Wolf v. Colorado, 338 U.S. 25	III:	evidence obtained with a warrant can be used in state courts
1950	American Communications Association, Congress of Industrial Organizations, et al. v. Douds, 339 U.S. 382	III:	requirement for non-Communist oaths is constitutional
	McLaurin v. Oklahoma State Regents for Higher Education, 339 U.S. 637	II:	segregation in state supported schools is a clear violation of the 14th Amendment
	Sweatt v. Painter, 339 U.S. 629	III:	unequal facilities for blacks and whites deprives blacks of equal protection under the law
	United States v. Louisiana, 339 U.S. 699	II:	the marginal sea (beyond the 3-mile limit) is national property
	United States v. Texas, 339 U.S. 707	II:	whatever claims Texas may have had to the marginal sea were relinquished when Texas became a state
1951	Dennis et al. v. United States, 341 U.S. 494	III:	upheld Smith Act; conviction of Communist Party members stood as "clear and present danger"
1952	Youngstown Sheet and Tube Co. v. Sawyer, 343 U.S. 579	I:	presidential nationalization of steel mills during Korean War was unconstitutional
	Zorach v. Clausen, 343 U.S. 306	III:	public school children can leave school for religious instruction; separation of church and state is not absolute, but is well-defined
1954	Brown v. Board of Education of Topeka, 347 U.S. 483	III:	separate is not equal, denies equal protection of 14th Amendment; segregated educational facilities are inherently unequal
1956	Pennsylvania v. Nelson, 350 U.S. 497	II:	Smith Act (1940) supersedes all state legislation regarding sedition

Year	Case	Category	Issue
1957	Roth v. United States, 354 U.S. 476	III:	defines obscenity as "any material that would seem to appeal primarily to 'prurient interests'"
	Watkins v. United States, 354 U.S. 178	III:	Congressional hearing committees must inform those questioned of the specific reason for the inquiry
	Yates v. United States, 354 U.S. 298	III:	restricted enforcement of Smith Act (1940)
1958	National Association for the Advancement of Colored People v. Alabama ex. rel. Patterson, 357 U.S. 449	III:	freedom to associate in a private organization is guaranteed by the 14th Amendment
	Cooper v. Aaron, 358 U.S. 1	II:	federal desegregation orders must be implemented immediately by the states
1959	Abbate v. United States, 359 U.S. 187	III:	5th Amendment protects against double jeopardy
	Barenblatt v. United States, 360 U.S. 109	III:	Communist Party poses such a significant danger to the nation that an individual's right to free expression can be suppressed
	Bartkus v. Illinois, 359 U.S. 121	III:	a separate and distinct second prosecution for the same crime does not constitute double jeopardy
1960	Boynton v. Virginia, 364 U.S. 454	II:	segregation involving interstate commerce is illegal
1961	Mapp v. Ohio, 367 U.S. 643	II:	established "exclusionary rule" as procedural requirement of state as well as federal trials
1962	Baker v. Carr, 369 U.S. 186	II:	federal courts have right to hear challenges to reapportionment by the states
	Engel v. Vitale, 370 U.S. 421	III:	prayer in schools is unconstitutional
1963	Gideon v. Wainwright, 372 U.S. 335	II:	due process of law extends to state as well as to federal defendants, in this case, right to counsel
	School District of Abington Township v. Schempp, 274 U.S. 203	III:	prohibited laws and practices involving Bible readings and prayers in public schools
1964	Heart of Atlanta Motel, Inc. v. United States, 379 U.S. 241	II:	motel serving interstate travelers subject to provisions of Civil Rights Act of 1964
	Lucas v. Colorado General Assembly, 377 U.S. 713	II:	both houses of bicameral legislature must be apportioned substantially on basis of population
	Malloy v. Hogan, 378 U.S. 1	II:	5th Amendment right against self-incrimination can be exercised in a state proceeding

Year	Case	Category	Issue
1964 *(Continued)*	New York Times v. Sullivan, 376 U.S. 254	II:	states cannot make rules that would allow public official to recover damages for defamatory falsehood relating to official conduct without proof of actual malice
	Reynolds v. Sims, 377 U.S. 533	II:	a state must apportion its legislative districts on the basis of population
	Wesberry v. Sanders, 376 U.S. 1	II:	a state must apportion its legislative districts on the basis of population
1965	Dombrowski v. Pfister, 380 U.S. 479	II:	struck down state statute that made it a felony to participate in subversive organizations as too broad and vague
	Griswold v. Connecticut, 381 U.S. 479	III:	struck down Connecticut law regarding distribution and use of contraceptives
1966	A Book Named "John Cleland's Memoirs of a Woman of Pleasure" v. Attorney General of Massachusetts, 383 U.S. 413	III:	a work that has some redeeming social value cannot be banned as obscene
	Federal Trade Commission v. Brown Shoe Company, 384 U.S. 316	II:	struck down unfair competitive practices
	Federal Trade Commission v. Borden Company, 383 U.S. 637	II:	upheld Federal Trade Commission's policies and rule and, in particular, the policy of price-justification
	Miranda v. Arizona, 384 U.S. 436	III:	a suspect must be informed of his rights
	Sheppard v. Maxwell, 384 U.S. 333	III:	due process clause violated if defendant prevented from receiving a fair trial due to publicity
	South Carolina v. Katzenbach, 383 U.S. 301	II:	upheld Voting Rights Act of 1965; remedies to implement act were legal
	United States v. Pabst Brewing Company, 384 U.S. 546	III:	trend toward concentration in an industry showed violation of antitrust laws
1967	Curtis Publishing Company v. Butts, 388 U.S. 130	III:	recovery of damages for defamatory statements applies to public figures as well as public officials
	In re Gault, 387 U.S. 1	III:	Arizona Juvenile Code violated due process clause
	Katz v. United States, 389 U.S. 347	I:	4th Amendment protection from unreasonable searches and seizures
	Loving v. Virginia, 388 U.S. 1	II:	state cannot prevent marriages based on race
1968	Penn-Central Merger Cases, 389 U.S. 486	II:	merger permissible if in the better interest of the public

Year	Case	Category	Issue
1969	Alexander v. Holmes County Board of Education, 396 U.S. 19	III:	public school systems obliged to eliminate segregation
	Alderman v. United States, 394 U.S. 165	III:	defendants have the right to obtain materials gathered by illegal wiretaps
	Citizen Publishing Company v. United States, 394 U.S. 131	III:	price-fixing is illegal and in violation of Sherman Antitrust Act
	Powell v. McCormack, 395 U.S. 496	I:	a member of the House, duly elected, may be excluded from the House only by a ⅔ majority
	Shapiro v. Thompson, 394 U.S. 618	II:	the state cannot create a one-year residency requirement as a condition for receiving welfare
	Sniadach v. Family Finance Corp., 395 U.S. 337	II:	established constitutional guidelines for garnishment
	Stanley v. Georgia, 394 U.S. 557	III:	private prossession of obscene matter is not unconstitutional
1970	Goldberg v. Kelly, 397 U.S. 254	III:	due process of law; welfare benefits cannot be terminated without timely notice and a hearing
	Oregon v. Mitchell, 400 U.S. 112	III:	upheld ban on literacy tests and residence requirements as prerequisite for voting in presidential elections; restricted 18-year-old vote to federal elections
	Walz v. Tax Commission, 397 U.S. 664	III:	tax exemption for religious institutions is constitutional
	Williams v. Florida, 399 U.S. 78	III:	6-person jury allowed in non-capital cases
1971	New York Times v. United States; United States v. Washington Post, 403 U.S. 713	III:	any attempt by government to restrain freedom of press and of expression is unconstitutional
	Perez v. Ledesma, 401 U.S. 82	I:	established procedural requirements for Supreme Court review of a state law
	Rosenbloom v. Metromedia, 403 U.S. 29	III:	regarding libel suits, private individuals are subject to the same standards as public officials in matters of public interest
	Samuals v. MacKell, 401 U.S. 66	II:	the same principles that govern propriety of federal injunctions of state criminal proceedings govern issuance of federal declaratory judgments in connection with such proceedings
	Swann v. Charlotte-Mecklenburg Board of Education, 402 U.S. 1	II:	district courts can order compliance with their own desegregation plans when local school authorities fail to desegregate voluntarily
	Wyman v. James, 400 U.S. 309	III:	home visits to welfare recipients not unreasonable or violation of 4th and 14th amendments

Year	Case	Category	Issue
1971 *(Continued)*	Younger v. Harris, 401 U.S. 37	II:	federal judge can grant injunction against enforcement of state's criminal laws only in cases of proven harassment or prosecutions in bad faith or other extraordinary circumstances
1972	Argersinger v. Hamlin, 407 U.S. 25	III:	all defendants accused of crime have right to counsel under the 6th Amendment
	Apodaca v. Oregon, 406 U.S. 404	III:	unanimity not required in non-capital criminal trials by jury
	Branzburg v. Hayes, 408 U.S. 665	III:	reporters' sources before state or federal juries are not protected by the 1st Amendment
	Eisenstadt v. Baird, 405 U.S. 438	III:	law cannot distinguish between married and unmarried people when dealing with right to purchase contraceptives
	Federal Trade Commission v. Sperry and Hutchinson Company, 405 U.S. 233	III:	FTC has power to protect consumers as well as competitors
	Furman v. Georgia, Jackson v. Georgia, Branch v. Texas, 408 U.S. 238	II:	use of capital punishment by state courts is unconstitutional
	Fuentes v. Shevin, 407 U.S. 67	III:	court must hold hearing before deprivation of property can take place
	Flood v. Kuhn, 407 U.S. 258	III:	reserve clause in professional baseball is constitutional
	Gravel v. United States, 408 U.S. 606	I:	immunity does not extend to congressional aides in matters of legislation
	Johnson v. Louisiana, 406 U.S. 356	III:	a non-unanimous verdict may give substance to proof beyond a reasonable doubt standard
	United States v. Brewster, 408 U.S. 501	I:	immunity clause only covers legislators in regular course of duties pertaining to legislative matters
	United States v. Topco Associates, 405 U.S. 596	III:	company's scheme of dividing markets and prohibiting competition violated Sherman Antitrust Act
	United States v. U.S. District Court, 407 U.S. 297	I:	Omnibus Crime Control and Safe Streets Act confers no powers to conduct warrantless national security surveillances
1973	Committee for Public Education v. Nyquist, 413 U.S. 756	II:	struck down state laws regarding aid to private education
	Doe v. McMillan, 412 U.S. 306	I:	congressional immunity from civil libel suits is not absolute
	Roe v. Wade, 410 U.S. 113	III:	women have the right to privacy and should be able to have an abortion

Year	Case	Category	Issue
1973 *(Continued)*			
	San Antonio Independent School District v. Rodriguez, 411 U.S. 1	III:	education is not one of the fundamental rights covered under the 14th Amendment
	United States v. Kras, 409 U.S. 434	III:	bankruptcy court fees are constitutional since courts are not the only conceivable relief available to bankrupts
1974	Gertz v. Robert Welch, Inc., 418 U.S. 323	III:	private individuals may be sued for libel
	Jackson v. Metropolitan Edison Company, 419 U.S. 345	III:	state regulation of private business does not by itself convert private action to state action for 14th Amendment purposes
	Regional Rail Reorganization Act Cases, 419 U.S. 102	III:	Penn-Central's claims of unjust compensation for its railroad were justified and relief was given under the Tucker Act
	United States v. Nixon, 418 U.S. 683	I:	executive privilege is not absolute; the tapes must be delivered to the special prosecutor
1975	Faretta v. California, 422 U.S. 806	III:	defendant has right to defend self in criminal proceedings
	Goss v. Lopez, 419 U.S. 565	III:	suspension from school without due process is unconstitutional
	North Georgia Finishing, Inc. v. DiChem, 419 U.S. 601	III:	established garnishment procedures
	United States v. Brignoni-Ponce, 422 U.S. 873	III:	border patrols may not stop vehicles unless specific facts for suspicion are evident
	United States v. Maine, 420 U.S. 515	II:	seabed rights (beyond 3-mile limit) are national
	Weinberger v. Weisenfield, 420 U.S. 636	III:	deceased wife and mother benefits are payable to husband and children
1976	Buckley v. Valeo, 424 U.S. 1	III:	federal government may regulate individual contributions to a political campaign, but may not limit total expenditure
	Gregg v. Georgia, 428 U.S. 153	III:	upheld Georgia capital punishment law
	Runyon v. McCrary, Fairfax-Brewster School, Inc. v. Gonzales, Southern Independent School Association v. McCrary, 427 U.S. 160	III:	denial of admission to private school strictly on the basis of race is unconstitutional
	Roberts v. Louisiana, 431 U.S. 633	II:	struck down state law that did not allow for mitigating factors in capital punishment sentencing
	Woodson v. North Carolina, 42 U.S. 280	III:	mandatory death sentence violates the 8th and 14th amendments

Year	Case	Category	Issue
1977	Beal v. Doe, 432 U.S. 438	II:	state can refuse to fund nontherapeutic abortions and still participate in joint, federal-state Medicaid assistance program
	Carey v. Population Services International, 431 U.S. 678	II:	states cannot restrict distribution of contraceptives
	Coker v. Georgia, 433 U.S. 584	III:	death penalty disproportionate to the crime, in this case rape
	Maher v. Roe, 432 U.S. 464	II:	state has no obligation to pay for nontherapeutic abortion for indigent women through Medicaid
	Nixon v. Administrator of General Services, 433 U.S. 425	I:	ex-president cannot claim immunity from congressional disposition and use of presidential documents
1978	Flagg Brothers, Inc. v. Brooks, 436 U.S. 149	II:	sale of stored, unclaimed goods by warehouseman is not a state action just because a state law has directed warehouse to store goods
	Regents of the University of California v. Bakke, 438 U.S. 265	III:	struck down discrimination against majority group members on basis of race
	Zablocki v. Redhail, 434 U.S. 374	III:	marriage is a fundamental right, not to be interfered in by the state unless state interests are affected
1979	Davis v. Passman, 442 U.S. 228	III:	established procedure for sex discrimination cases
	Hutchinson v. Proxmire, 443 U.S. 111	I:	member of Congress is not protected from libel not directly concerned with legislative or deliberative process
	Kaiser Aluminum Company v. Weber, 443 U.S. 193	III:	voluntary affirmative action is acceptable to ratify past practice of employment discrimination
	United Steelworkers of America v. Weber, 443 U.S. 193	III:	equal protection clause does not apply when company makes own rules to implement affirmative action programs, because state action is not involved
1980	City of Mobile v. Bolden, 446 U.S. 55	III:	election of city council members by voters at large does not violate 14th and 15th amendments
	Diamond v. Chakrabarty, 447 U.S. 303	III:	live, human-made microorganism is patentable
	Fullilove v. Klutznick, 448 U.S. 448	III:	upheld Public Works Employment Act
	Harris v. McRae, 448 U.S. 297	III:	upheld Hyde Amendment—states are not necessarily required to fund abortions
	Pruneyard Shopping Center v. Robins, 447 U.S. 74	III:	free speech is permitted on private property that is publicly available

Year	Case	Category	Issue
1980 *(Continued)*			
	Richmond Newspapers Inc. v. Commonwealth of Virginia, 448 U.S. 555	III:	closing a court trial to the press must demonstrate prejudice in outcome of the trial
	Trammel v. United States, 445 U.S. 40	III:	spouse can testify against spouse because women have a separate legal identity
	United States v. Sioux Nation of Indians, 448 U.S. 371	III:	Sioux Indians are entitled to compensation for lands and rights taken away in 1868
	Williams v. Zbaraz, 448 U.S. 358	II:	a state participating in Medicaid program is not obligated to pay for those necessary abortions not covered for federal reimbursement under the Hyde Amendment
1981	Chandler v. Florida, 449 U.S. 560	III:	TV cameras cannot be excluded from a trial unless the judge feels they will affect the outcome of the trial
	Dames & Moore v. Regan, 453 U.S. 654	I:	executive branch has power to suspend claims against certain foreign assets in U.S. courts
	Haig v. Agee, 453 U.S. 280	I:	upheld Passport Act of 1926—the government can regulate issuance of documents on criterion of national security
	H. L. v. Matheson, 450 U.S. 398	III:	parental notification, when possible, prior to a minor's abortion is not invasion of privacy
	Hodel v. Virginia, 452 U.S. 264	II:	strip mining restrictions are legitimate
	Rostker v. Goldberg, 453 U.S. 57	III:	upheld Military Selective Service Act— differentiation between men and women is not a discriminatory issue
1982	Edmund v. Florida, 458 U.S. 782	III:	death penalty is excessive for one who has not taken a human life
	Harlow v. Fitzgerald, 457 U.S. 800	I:	federal officials are entitled to qualified or good faith immunity
	Mississippi University for Women v. Hogan, 458 U.S. 718	III:	denial of qualified males to the nursing school of a state-supported university is unconstitutional
	Nixon v. Fitzgerald, 457 U.S. 731	I:	President has absolute immunity for all action taken under any of his broad areas of constitutional authority
	Plyer v. Doe, 457 U.S. 202	III:	state is obliged to provide free public education to all children
1983	Arizona v. Norris, 103 S. Ct. 3492	III:	upheld ban on discrimination in employment on account of race, color, religion, sex, or nationality
	Barefoot v. Estelle, 103 S. Ct. 3383	II:	established guidelines for lower federal courts to handle death penalty appeals

Year	Case	Category	Issue
1983 *(Continued)*			
	Bob Jones v. United States, 461 U.S. 574	III:	organizations, usually tax-exempt, that practice racial discrimination are not entitled to tax exemption
	City of Akron v. Akron Center for Reproductive Health, 462 U.S. 416	III:	reconfirmed woman's right to terminate pregnancy
	Container v. Franchise Tax Board, 463 U.S. 159	II:	states have the right to tax multinational companies, including income generated from other nations
	Dirks v. Securities and Exchange Commission, 463 U.S. 646	III:	stock traders are not liable legally for private information obtained from corporate insiders
	Equal Employment Opportunity Commission v. Wyoming, 460 U.S. 226	II:	upheld Age Discrimination in Employment Act and held that federal interference did not violate state's authority to govern itself
	Immigration and Naturalization Service v. Chadha, 462 U.S. 919	I:	one-house veto stipulation of the Immigration and Nationality Act is unconstitutional
	Karcher v. Daggett, 462 U.S. 725	II:	upheld equality in congressional districts
	Kolender v. Lawson, 461 U.S. 352	III:	struck down California vagrancy law as being too vague
	Mueller v. Allen, 463 U.S. 388	III:	certain tax deductions for education in religious schools are constitutional
	Solem v. Helm, 463 U.S. 277	III:	8th Amendment disallows sentences disproportionate to crimes committed
1984	Federal Communications Commission v. League of Women Voters, 104 S. Ct. 3106	III:	struck down law that prohibited editorialization by noncommercial broadcasting systems
	Firefighters v. Stotts, 104 S. Ct. 2576	III:	protects in-place, legitimate seniority systems
	Grove City v. Bell, 104 S. Ct. 1211	III:	sex discrimination law in colleges is applied to departments or programs receiving direct aid, not to whole school
	Hawaii Housing Authority v. Midkiff, 104 S. Ct. 2321	II:	eminent domain: state has power to break up large properties and transfer ownership of land to tenants
	Hishon v. King & Spalding, 104 S. Ct. 2229	III:	law firms may not discriminate in promotion to partnership on basis of sex, race, religion, or nationality
	National Collegiate Athletic Association v. Board of Regents, 104 S. Ct. 2948	III:	NCAA cannot regulate number and prices of appearances of college football teams on TV
	New York v. Quarles, 104 S. Ct. 2626	III:	Miranda warning may be "delayed" in cases of public safety and need for quick police action
	Oregon v. Elstead, 53 U.S.L.W. 4244	III:	initial violation of Miranda rule does not invalidate subsequent confessions when proper warnings are given

Year	Case	Category	Issue
1984 *(Continued)*	Pennhurst v. Halderman, 104 S. Ct. 900	II:	federal courts cannot issue orders to state officials regarding state laws
	Regan v. Wald, 53 U.S.L.W. 3270	I:	struck down grandfather clause of the International Emergency Economic Powers Act (1977)
	Roberts v. United States Jaycees, 104 S. Ct. 3244	III:	Jaycees must admit women to their organization
	Schall v. Martin, 104 S. Ct. 2403	III:	pretrial detention of juveniles serves a legitimate purpose and is constitutional
	Sure-Tan v. National Labor Relations Board, 104 S. Ct. 2803	III:	anti-union motivation involving illegal aliens is illegal
	United States v. Gouveia, 104 S. Ct. 2292	III:	right to counsel applies only to "adversary judicial proceedings" (arraignment/indictment) not to prior investigations
1985	Ake v. Oklahoma, 53 U.S.L.W. 4179	III:	indigent defendants have the right to free psychiatric assistance if warranted
	Alamo Foundation v. Secretary of Labor, 53 U.S.L.W. 4489	III:	religious organizations must pay employees engaged in commercial business wages that are based on federal standards
	Blum v. Stenson, 104 S. Ct. 1541	III:	non-profit legal firms are entitled to compensation at the same rate as private firms
	Central Intelligence Agency v. Sims, 53 U.S.L.W. 4453	III:	information about foreign intelligence is exempt from disclosure under the Freedom of Information Act
	Evitts v. Lucey, 53 U.S.L.W. 4101	III:	if a lawyer is not effective, then a client has been denied his 14th Amendment rights to effective counsel
	Garcia v. San Antonio Metropolitan Transit Authority, 53 U.S.L.W. 4101	III:	federal minimum wage regulations and hour standards apply to public employees
	Tennessee v. Garner, 53 U.S.L.W. 4244	III:	deadly force by police officers should be used only if suspect threatens with weapon or if physical harm has been done during crime
	United States v. Hensley, 53 U.S.L.W. 4053	III:	established rules for brief detention by police

The
Constitution
of the
United States

We the People of the United States, in Order to form a more perfect Union, establish Justice, insure domestic Tranquility, provide for the common defence, promote the general Welfare, and secure the Blessings of Liberty to ourselves and our Posterity, do ordain and establish this Constitution for the United States of America.

ARTICLE I.

SECTION 1. All legislative Powers herein granted shall be vested in a Congress of the United States, which shall consist of a Senate and House of Representatives.

SECTION 2. The House of Representatives shall be composed of Members chosen every second Year by the People of the several States, and the Electors in each State shall have the Qualifications requisite for Electors of the most numerous Branch of the State Legislature.

No Person shall be a Representative who shall not have attained to the Age of twenty five Years, and been seven Years a Citizen of the United States, and who shall not, when elected, be an Inhabitant of that State in which he shall be chosen.

Representatives and direct Taxes shall be apportioned among the several States which may be included within this Union, according to their respective Numbers, which shall be determined by adding to the whole Number of free Persons, including those bound to Service for a Term of Years, and excluding Indians not taxed, three fifths of all other Persons. The actual Enumeration shall be made within three Years after the first Meeting of the Congress of the United States, and within every subsequent Term of ten Years, in such Manner as they shall by Law direct. The Number of Representatives shall not exceed one for every thirty Thousand, but each State shall have at Least one Representative; and until such enumeration shall be made, the State of New Hampshire shall be entitled to chuse three, Massachusetts eight, Rhode-Island and Providence Plantations one, Connecticut five, New-York six, New Jersey four, Pennsylvania eight, Delaware one, Maryland six, Virginia ten, North Carolina five, South Carolina five, and Georgia three.

When vacancies happen in the Representation from any State, the Executive Authority thereof shall issue Writs of Election to fill such Vacancies.

The House of Representatives shall chuse their Speaker and other Officers; and shall have the sole Power of Impeachment.

SECTION 3. The Senate of the United States shall be composed of two Senators from each State, chosen by the

Legislature thereof, for six Years; and each Senator shall have one Vote.

Immediately after they shall be assembled in Consequence of the first Election, they shall be divided as equally as may be into three Classes. The Seats of the Senators of the first Class shall be vacated at the Expiration of the second Year, of the second Class at the Expiration of the fourth Year, and of the third Class at the Expiration of the sixth Year, so that one third may be chosen every second Year; and if Vacancies happen by Resignation, or otherwise, during the Recess of the Legislature of any State, the Executive thereof may make temporary Appointments until the next Meeting of the Legislature, which shall then fill such Vacancies.

No Person shall be a Senator who shall not have attained to the Age of thirty Years, and been nine Years a Citizen of the United States, and who shall not, when elected, be an Inhabitant of that State for which he shall be chosen.

The Vice President of the United States shall be President of the Senate, but shall have no Vote, unless they be equally divided.

The Senate shall chuse their other Officers, and also a President pro tempore, in the Absence of the Vice President, or when he shall exercise the Office of President of the United States.

The Senate shall have the sole Power to try all Impeachments. When sitting for that Purpose, they shall be on Oath or Affirmation. When the President of the United States is tried, the Chief Justice shall preside: And no Person shall be convicted without the Concurrence of two thirds of the Members present.

Judgment in Cases of Impeachment shall not extend further than to removal from Office, and disqualification to hold and enjoy any Office of honor, Trust or Profit under the United States: but the Party convicted shall nevertheless be liable and subject to Indictment, Trial, Judgment and Punishment, according to Law.

SECTION 4. The Times, Places and Manner of holding Elections for Senators and Representatives, shall be prescribed in each State by the Legislature thereof; but the Congress may at any time by Law make or alter such Regulations, except as to the Places of chusing Senators.

The Congress shall assemble at least once in every Year, and such Meeting shall be on the first Monday in December, unless they shall by Law appoint a different Day.

SECTION 5. Each House shall be the Judge of the Elections, Returns and Qualifications of its own Members, and a Majority of each shall constitute a Quorum to do Business; but a smaller Number may adjourn from day to day, and may be authorized to compel the Attendance of absent Members, in such Manner, and under such Penalties as each House may provide.

Each House may determine the Rules of its Proceedings, punish its Members for disorderly Behaviour, and, with the Concurrence of two thirds, expel a Member.

Each House shall keep a Journal of its Proceedings, and from time to time publish the same, excepting such Parts as may in their Judgment require Secrecy; and the Yeas and Nays of the Members of either House on any question shall, at the Desire of one fifth of those Present, be entered on the Journal.

Neither House, during the Session of Congress, shall, without the Consent of the other, adjourn for more than three days, nor to any other Place than that in which the two Houses shall be sitting.

SECTION 6. The Senators and Representatives shall receive a Compensation for their Services, to be ascertained by Law, and paid out of the Treasury of the United States. They shall in all Cases, except Treason, Felony and Breach of the Peace, be privileged from Arrest during their Attendance at the Session of their respective Houses, and in going to and returning from the same; and for any Speech or Debate in either House, they shall not be questioned in any other Place.

No Senator or Representative shall, during the Time for which he was elected, be appointed to any civil Office under the Authority of the United States, which shall have been created, or the Emoluments whereof shall have been encreased during such time; and no Person holding any Office under the United States, shall be a Member of either House during his Continuance in Office.

SECTION 7. All Bills for raising Revenue shall originate in the House of Representatives; but the Senate may propose or concur with amendments as on other Bills.

Every Bill which shall have passed the House of Representatives and the Senate, shall, before it become a Law, be presented to the President of the United States; If he approve he shall sign it, but if not he shall return it, with his Objections to that House in which it shall have originated, who shall enter the Objections at large on their Journal, and proceed to reconsider it. If after such Reconsideration two thirds of that House shall agree to pass the Bill, it shall be sent, together with the Objections, to the other House, by which it shall likewise be reconsidered, and if approved by two thirds of that House, it shall become a Law. But in all such Cases the Votes of both Houses shall be determined by Yeas and Nays, and the Names of the Persons voting for and against the Bill shall be entered on the Journal of each House respectively. If any Bill shall not be returned by the President within ten Days (Sundays excepted) after it shall have been presented to him, the Same shall be a Law, in like Manner as if he had signed it, unless the Congess by their Adjournment prevent its Return, in which Case it shall not be a Law.

Every Order, Resolution, or Vote to which the Concurrence of the Senate and House of Representatives may be necessary (except on a question of Adjournment) shall be presented to the President of the United States; and before the Same shall take Effect, shall be approved by him, or being disapproved by him, shall be repassed by two thirds of the Senate and House of Representatives, according to the Rules and Limitations prescribed in the Case of a Bill.

SECTION 8. The Congress shall have Power To lay and collect Taxes, Duties, Imposts and Excises, to pay the Debts and provide for the common Defence and general Welfare of the United States; but all Duties, Imposts and Excises shall be uniform throughout the United States;

To Borrow Money on the credit of the United States;

To regulate Commerce with foreign Nations, and among the several States, and with the Indian Tribes;

To establish an uniform Rule of Naturalization, and uniform Laws on the subject of Bankruptcies throughout the United States;

To coin Money, regulate the Value thereof, and of foreign Coin, and fix the Standard of Weights and Measures;

To provide for the Punishment of counterfeiting the Securities and current Coin of the United States;

To establish Post Offices and post Roads;

To promote the Progress of Science and useful Arts, by securing for limited Times to Authors and Inventors the exclusive Right to their respective Writings and Discoveries;

To constitute Tribunals inferior to the supreme Court;

To define and punish Piracies and Felonies committed on the high Seas, and Offences against the Law of Nations;

To declare War, grant Letters of Marque and Reprisal, and make Rules concerning Captures on Land and Water;

To raise and support Armies, but no Appropriation of Money to that Use shall be for a longer Term than two Years;

To provide and maintain a Navy;

To make Rules for the Government and Regulation of the land and naval Forces;

To provide for calling forth the Militia to execute the Laws of the Union, suppress Insurrections and repel Invasions;

To provide for organizing, arming, and disciplining the Militia, and for governing such Part of them as may be employed in the Service of the United States, reserving to the States respectively, the Appointment of the Officers, and the Authority of training the Militia according to the discipline prescribed by Congress;

To exercise exclusive Legislation in all Cases whatsoever, over such District (not exceeding ten Miles square) as may, by Cession of Particular States, and the Acceptance of Congress, become the Seat of the Government of the United States, and to exercise like Authority over all Places purchsed by the Consent of the Legislature of the State in which the Same shall be for the Erection of Forts, Magazines, Arsenals, dock-Yards, and other needful Buildings;—And

To make all Laws which shall be necessary and proper for carrying into Execution the foregoing Powers, and all other Powers vested by this Constitution in the Government of the United States, or in any Department or Officer thereof.

SECTION 9. The Migration or Importation of such Persons as any of the States now existing shall think proper to admit, shall not be prohibited by the Congress prior to the Year one thousand eight hundred and eight, but a Tax or duty may be imposed on such Importation, not exceeding ten dollars for each Person.

The Privilege of the Writ of Habeas Corpus shall not be suspended, unless when in Cases of Rebellion or Invasion the public Safety may require it.

No Bill of Attainder or ex post facto Law shall be passed.

No Capitation, or other direct, Tax shall be laid, unless in Proportion to the Census or Enumeration herein before directed to be taken.

No Tax or Duty shall be laid on Articles exported from any State.

No Preference shall be given by any Regulation of Commerce or Revenue to the Ports of one State over those of another; nor shall Vessels bound to, or from, one State, be obliged to enter, clear, or pay Duties in another.

No Money shall be drawn from the Treasury, but in Consequence of Appropriations made by Law; and a regular Statement and Account of the Receipts and Expenditures of all public Money shall be published from time to time.

No Title of Nobility shall be granted by the United States: And no Person holding any Office of Profit or Trust under them, shall, without the Consent of Congress, accept any present, Emolument, Office, or Title, of any kind whatever, from any King, Prince, or foreign State.

SECTION 10. No State shall enter into any Treaty, Alliance, or Confederation; grant Letters of Marque and Reprisal; coin Money; emit Bills of Credit; make any Thing but gold and silver Coin a Tender in Payment of Debts; pass any Bill of Attainder, ex post facto Law, or Law impairing the Obligation of Contracts, or grant any Title of Nobility.

No State shall, without the Consent of the Congress,

lay any Imposts or Duties on Imports or Exports, except what may be absolutely necessary for executing its inspection Laws: and the net Produce of all Duties and Imposts, laid by any State on Imports or Exports, shall be for the Use of the Treasury of the United States; and all such Laws shall be subject to the Revision and Controul of the Congress.

No State shall, without the Consent of Congress, lay any Duty of Tonnage, keep Troops, or Ships of War in time of Peace, enter into any Agreement or Compact with another State, or with a foreign Power, or engage in War, unless actually invaded, or in such imminent Danger as will not admit of delay.

ARTICLE II.

SECTION 1. The executive Power shall be vested in a President of the United States of America. He shall hold his Office during the Term of four Years, and, together with the Vice President, chosen for the same term, be elected, as follows

Each State shall appoint, in such Manner as the Legislature thereof may direct, a Number of Electors, equal to the whole Number of Senators and Representatives to which the State may be entitled in the Congress: but no Senator or Representative, or Person holding an Office of Trust or Profit under the United States, shall be appointed an Elector.

The Electors shall meet in their respective States, and vote by Ballot for two Persons, of whom one at least shall not be an Inhabitant of the same State with themselves. And they shall make a List of all the Persons voted for, and of the Number of Votes for each; which List they shall sign and certify, and transmit sealed to the Seat of the Government of the United States, directed to the President of the Senate. The President of the Senate shall, in the Presence of the Senate and House of Representatives, open all the Certificates, and the Votes shall then be counted. The Person having the greatest Number of Votes shall be the President, if such Number be a Majority of the whole Number of Electors appointed; and if there be more than one who have such Majority, and have an equal Number of Votes, then the House of Representatives shall immediately chuse by Ballot one of them for President: and if no Person have a Majority, then from the five highest on the List the said House shall in like Manner chuse the President. But in chusing the President, the Votes shall be taken by States, the Representation from each State having one Vote; a quorum for this Purpose shall consist of a Member or Members from two thirds of the States, and a Majority of all the States shall be necessary to a Choice. In every Case, after the Choice of the President, the Person having the greatest Number of Votes of the Electors shall be the Vice President. But if there should remain two or more who have equal Votes, the Senate shall chuse from them by Ballot the Vice President.

The Congress may determine the Time of chusing the Electors, and the Day on which they shall give their Votes; which Day shall be the same throughout the United States.

No Person except a natural born Citizen, or a Citizen of the United States, at the time of the Adoption of this Constitution, shall be eligible to the Office of President; neither shall any Person be eligible to that Office who shall not have attained to the Age of thirty five Years, and been fourteen Years a Resident within the United States.

In Case of the Removal of the President from Office, or of his Death, Resignation, or Inability to discharge the Powers and Duties of the said Office, the Same shall devolve on the Vice President, and the Congress may by Law provide for the Case of Removal, Death, Resignation or Inability, both of the President and Vice President, declaring what Officer shall then act as President, and such Officer shall act accordingly, until the Disability be removed, or a President shall be elected.

The President shall, at stated Times, receive for his Services, a Compensation, which shall neither be encreased nor diminished during the Period for which he shall have been elected, and he shall not receive within that Period any other Emolument from the United States, or any of them.

Before he enter on the Execution of his Office, he shall take the following Oath or Affirmation:—"I do solemnly swear (or affirm) that I will faithfully execute the Office of President of the United States, and will to the best of my Ability, preserve, protect and defend the Constitution of the United States."

SECTION 2. The President shall be Commander in Chief of the Army and Navy of the United States, and of the Militia of the several States, when called into the actual Service of the United States; he may require the Opinion in writing, of the principal Officer in each of the executive Departments, upon any Subject relating to the Duties of their respective Offices, and he shall have Power to grant Reprieves and Pardons for Offences against the United States, except in Cases of Impeachment.

He shall have Power, by and with the Advice and Consent of the Senate, to make Treaties, provided two thirds of the Senators present concur; and he shall nominate, and by and with the Advice and Consent of the Senate; shall appoint Ambassadors, other public Ministers and Consuls, Judges of the supreme Court, and all other Officers of the United States, whose Appointments are not herein otherwise provided for, and which shall be established by Law: but the Congress may by Law vest the Appointment of such inferior Officers, as they think proper, in the President alone, in the Courts of Law, or in the Heads of Departments.

The President shall have Power to fill up all Vacancies that may happen during the Recess of the Senate, by granting Commissions which shall expire at the End of their next Session.

SECTION 3. He shall from time to time give to the Congress Information of the State of the Union, and recommend to their Consideration such Measures as he shall judge necessary and expedient; he may, on extraordinary Occasions, convene both Houses, or either of them, and in Case of Disagreement between them, with Respect to the Time of Adjournment, he may adjourn them to such Time as he shall think proper; he shall receive Ambassadors and other public Ministers; he shall take care that the Laws be faithfully executed, and shall Commission all the Officers of the United States.

SECTION 4. The President, Vice President and all civil Officers of the United States, shall be removed from Office on Impeachment for, and Conviction of, Treason, Bribery, or other High Crimes and Misdemeanors.

ARTICLE III.

SECTION 1. The judicial Power of the United States, shall be vested in one supreme Court, and in such inferior Courts as the Congress may from time to time ordain and establish. The Judges, both of the supreme and inferior Courts, shall hold their Offices during good Behaviour, and shall, at stated Times, receive for their Services a Compensation, which shall not be diminished during their Continuance in Office.

SECTION 2. The judicial Power shall extend to all Cases, in Law and Equity, arising under this Constitution, the Laws of the United States, and Treaties made, or which shall be made, under their Authority;—to all Cases affecting Ambassadors, other public Ministers and Consuls;—to all Cases of admiralty and maritime Jurisdiction;—to Controversies to which the United States shall be a Party;—to Controversies between two or more States;—between a State and Citizens of another State;—between Citizens of different States;—between Citizens of the same State claiming Lands under Grants of different States, and between a State, or the Citizens thereof, and foreign States, Citizens or Subjects.

In all Cases affecting Ambassadors, other public Ministers and Consuls, and those in which a State shall be Party, the supreme Court shall have original Jurisdiction. In all the other Cases before mentioned, the supreme Court shall have appellate Jurisdiction, both as to Law and

Fact, with such Exceptions, and under such Regulations as the Congress shall make.

The Trial of all Crimes, except in Cases of Impeachment, shall be by Jury; and such Trial shall be held in the State where the said Crimes shall have been committed; but when not committed within any State, the Trial shall be at such a Place or Places as the Congress may by Law have directed.

SECTION 3. Treason against the United States, shall consist only in levying War against them, or in adhering to their Enemies, giving them Aid and Comfort. No Person shall be convicted of Treason unless on the Testimony of two Witnesses to the same overt Act, or on Confession in open Court.

The Congress shall have Power to declare the Punishment of Treason, but no Attainder of Treason shall work Corruption of Blood, or Forfeiture except during the Life of the Person attained.

ARTICLE IV.

SECTION 1. Full Faith and Credit shall be given in each State to the public Acts, Records, and judicial Proceedings of every other State. And the Congress may by general Laws prescribe the Manner in which such Acts, Records and Proceedings shall be proved, and the Effect thereof.

SECTION 2. The Citizens of each State shall be entitled to all Privileges and Immunities of Citizens in the several States.

A Person charged in any State with Treason, Felony, or other Crime, who shall flee from Justice, and be found in another State, shall on Demand of the executive Authority of the State from which he fled, be delivered up, to be removed to the State having Jurisdiction of the Crime.

No Person held to Service or Labour in one State, under the Laws thereof, escaping into another, shall, in Consequence of any Law or Regulation therein, be discharged from such Service or Labour, but shall be delivered up on Claim of the Party to whom such Service or Labour may be due.

SECTION 3. New States may be admitted by the Congress into this Union; but no new State shall be formed or erected within the Jurisdiction of any other State; nor any State be formed by the Junction of two or more States, or Parts of States, without the Consent of the Legislatures of the States concerned as well as of the Congress.

The Congress shall have Power to dispose of and make all needful Rules and Regulations respecting the Territory or other Property belonging to the United States; and nothing in this Constitution shall be so construed as to Prejudice any Claims of the United States, or of any particular State.

SECTION 4. The United States shall guarantee to every State in this Union a Republican Form of Government, and shall protect each of them against Invasion; and on Application of the Legislature, or of the Executive (when the Legislature cannot be convened) against domestic Violence.

ARTICLE V.

The Congress, whenever two thirds of both Houses shall deem it necessary, shall propose Amendments to this Constitution, or, on the Application of the Legislatures of two thirds of the several States, shall call a Convention for proposing Amendments, which, in either Case, shall be valid to all Intents and Purposes, as Part of this Constitution, when ratified by the Legislatures of three fourths of the several States, or by Conventions in three fourths thereof, as the one or the other Mode of Ratification may be proposed by the Congress; Provided that no Amendment which may be made prior to the Year One thousand eight hundred and eight shall in any Manner affect the first and fourth Clauses in the Ninth Section of the first Article; and that no State, without its Consent, shall be deprived of its equal Suffrage in the Senate.

ARTICLE VI.

All Debts contracted and Engagements entered into, before the Adoption of this Constitution, shall be as valid against the United States under this Constitution, as under the Confederation.

This Constitution, and the Laws of the United States which shall be made in Pursuance thereof; and all Treaties made, or which shall be made, under the Authority of the United States, shall be the supreme Law of the Land; and the Judges in every State shall be bound thereby, any Thing in the Constitution or Laws of any State to the Contrary notwithstanding.

The Senators and Representatives before mentioned, and the Members of the several State Legislatures, and all executive and judicial Officers, both of the United States and of the several States, shall be bound by Oath or Affirmation, to support this Constitution; but no religious Test shall ever be required as a Qualification to any Office or public Trust under the United States.

ARTICLE VII.

The Ratification of the Conventions of nine States, shall be sufficient for the Establishment of this Constitution between the States so ratifying the Same. Done in Convention by the Unanimous Consent of the States present the Seventeenth Day of September in the Year of our Lord one thousand seven hundred and Eighty seven and the Independence of the United States of America the Twelfth IN WITNESS WHEREOF We have hereunto subscribed our Names,

New Hampshire	John Langdon
	Nicholas Gilman
Massachusetts	Nathaniel Gorham
	Rufus King
Connecticut	Wm. Saml. Johnson
	Roger Sherman
New York	Alexander Hamilton
New Jersey	Wil.: Livingston
	David Brearley.
	Wm. Paterson.
	Jona: Dayton
Pennsylvania	B Franklin
	Thomas Mifflin
	Robt Morris
	Geo. Clymer
	Thos. FitzSimons
	Jared Ingersoll
	James Wilson
	Gouv Morris
Delaware	Geo: Read
	Gunning Bedford jun
	John Dickinson
	Richard Bassett
	Jaco: Broom
Maryland	James McHenry
	Dan of St Thos. Jenifer
	Danl Carroll
Virginia	John Blair—
	James Madison Jr.
North Carolina	Wm. Blount
	Richd. Dobbs Spaight.
	Hu Williamson
South Carolina	J. Rutledge
	Charles Cotesworth Pinckney
	Charles Pinckney
	Pierce Butler.
Georgia	William Few
	Abr Baldwin

In Convention Monday, September 17th 1787.
Present
The States of
New Hampshire, Massachusetts, Connecticut, Mr. Hamilton from New York, New Jersey, Pennsylvania, Delaware, Maryland, Virginia, North Carolina, South Carolina and Georgia.

Resolved,

That the preceeding Constitution be laid before the United States in Congress assembled, and that it is the Opinion of this Convention, that it should afterwards be submitted to a Convention of Delegates, chosen in each State by the People thereof, under the recommendation of its Legislature, for their Assent and Ratification; and that each Convention assenting to, and ratifying the Same, should give Notice thereof to the United States in Congress assembled. Resolved, That it is the Opinion of this Convention, that as soon as the Conventions of nine States shall have ratified this Constitution, the United States in Congress assembled should fix a Day on which the Electors should assemble to vote for the President, and the Time and Place for commencing Proceedings under this Constitution. That after such Publication the Electors should be appointed, and the Senators and Representatives elected: That the Electors should meet on the Day fixed for the Election of the President, and should transmit their Votes certified, signed, sealed and directed, as the Constitution requires, to the Secretary of the United States in Congress assembled, that the Senators and representatives should convene at the Time and Place assigned; that the Senators should appoint a President of the Senate, for the sole Purpose of receiving, opening and counting the Votes for President; and that after he shall be chosen, the Congress, together with the President, should, without Delay, proceed to execute this Constitution.

By the Unanimous Order of the Convention

Go. Washington—Presidt.

W. Jackson Secretary.

AMENDMENT I.

Congress shall make no law respecting an establishment of religion, or prohibiting the free exercise thereof; or abridging the freedom of speech, or of the press; or the right of the people peaceably to assemble, and to petition the Government for a redress of grievances.

AMENDMENT II.

A well regulated Militia, being necessary to the security of a free State, the right of the people to keep and bear Arms, shall not be infringed.

AMENDMENT III.

No Soldier shall, in time of peace, be quartered in any house, without the consent of the Owner, nor in time of war, but in a manner to be prescribed by law.

AMENDMENT IV.

The right of the people to be secure in their persons, houses, papers, and effects, against unreasonable searches and seizures, shall not be violated, and no Warrants shall issue, but upon probable cause, supported by Oath or affirmation, and particularly describing the place to be searched, and the persons or things to be seized.

AMENDMENT V.

No person shall be held to answer for a capital, or otherwise infamous crime, unless on a presentment or indictment of a Grand Jury, except in cases arising in the land or naval forces, or in the Militia, when in actual service in time of War or public danger; nor shall any person be subject for the same offence to be twice put in jeopardy of life or limb; nor shall be compelled in any criminal case to be a witness against himself, nor be deprived of life, liberty, or property, without due process of law; nor shall private property be taken for public use, without just compensation.

AMENDMENT VI.

In all criminal prosecutions, the accused shall enjoy the right to a speedy and public trial, by an impartial jury of the State and district wherein the crime shall have been committed, which district shall have been previously ascertained by law, and to be informed of the nature and cause of the accusation; to be confronted with the witnesses against him; to have compulsory process for obtaining witnesses in his favor, and to have the Assistance of Counsel for his defence.

AMENDMENT VII.

In Suits at common law, where the value in controversy shall exceed twenty dollars, the right of trial by jury shall be preserved, and no fact tried by a jury, shall be otherwise reexamined in any Court of the United States, than according to the rules of the common law.

AMENDMENT VIII.

Excessive bail shall not be required, nor excessive fines imposed, nor cruel and unusual punishment inflicted.

AMENDMENT IX.

The enumeration in the Constitution, of certain rights, shall not be construed to deny or disparage others retained by the people.

AMENDMENT X.

The powers not delegated to the United States by the Constitution, nor prohibited by it to the States, are reserved to the States respectively, or to the people.

AMENDMENT XI.
(Adopted Jan. 8, 1798)

The Judicial power of the United States shall not be construed to extend to any suit in law or equity, commenced or prosecuted against one of the United States by Citizens of another State, or by Citizens or Subjects of any Foreign State.

AMENDMENT XII.
(Adopted September 25, 1804)

The Electors shall meet in their respective states and vote by ballot for President and Vice-President, one of whom, at least, shall not be an inhabitant of the same state with themselves; they shall name in their ballots the person voted for as President, and in distinct ballots the person voted for as Vice-President, and they shall make distinct lists of all persons voted for as President, and of all persons voted for as Vice-President, and of the number of votes for each, which lists they shall sign and certify, and transmit sealed to the seat of the government of the United States, directed to the President of the Senate;—The President of the Senate shall, in presence of the Senate and House of Representatives, open all the certificates and the votes shall then be counted;—The person having the greatest number of votes for President, shall be the President, if such number be a majority of the whole number of Electors appointed; and if no person have such majority, then from the persons having the highest numbers not exceeding three on the list of those voted for as President, the House of Representatives shall choose immediately, by ballot, the President. But in choosing the President, the votes shall be taken by states, the representation from each state having one vote; a quorum for this purpose shall consist of a member or members from two-thirds of the states, and a majority of all the states shall be necessary to a choice. And if the House of Representatives shall not choose a President whenever the right of choice shall devolve upon them, before the fourth day of March next following, then the Vice-President shall act as President, as in the case of the death or other constitutional disability of the President.—The person having the greatest number of votes as Vice-President, shall be the Vice-President, if such number be a majority of the whole number of Electors appointed, and if no person have a majority, then from the two highest numbers on the list, the Senate shall choose the Vice-President; a quorum for the purpose shall consist of two-thirds of the whole number of Senators, and a majority of the whole number shall be necessary to a choice. But no person constitutionally ineligible to the office of President shall be eligible to that of Vice-President of the United States.

AMENDMENT XIII.
(Adopted Dec. 18, 1865)

SECTION 1. Neither slavery nor involuntary servitude, except as a punishment for crime whereof the party shall have been duly convicted, shall exist within the United States, or any place subject to their jurisdiction.

SECTION 2. Congress shall have power to enforce this article by appropriate legislation.

AMENDMENT XIV.
(Adopted July 28, 1868)

SECTION 1. All persons born or naturalized in the United States and subject to the jurisdiction thereof, are citizens of the United States and of the State wherein they reside. No State shall make or enforce any law which shall abridge the privileges or immunities of citizens of the United States; nor shall any State deprive any person of life, liberty, or property, without due process of law; nor deny to any person within its jurisdiction the equal protection of the laws.

SECTION 2. Representatives shall be apportioned among the several States according to their respective numbers, counting the whole number of persons in each State, excluding Indians not taxed. But when the right to vote at any election for the choice of electors for President and Vice-President of the United States, Representatives in Congress, the Executive and Judicial officers of a State, or the members of the Legislature thereof, is denied to any of the male inhabitants of such State, being twenty-one years of age, and citizens of the United States, or in any way abridged, except for participation in rebellion, or other crime, the basis of representation therein shall be reduced in the proportion which the number of such male citizens shall bear to the whole number of male citizens twenty-one years of age in such State.

SECTION 3. No person shall be a Senator or Representative in Congress, or elector of President and Vice-President, or hold any office, civil or military, under the United States, or under any State, who, having previously taken an oath, as a member of Congress, or as an officer of the United States, or as a member of any State legislature, or as an executive or judicial officer of any State, to support the Constitution of the United States, shall have engaged in insurrection or rebellion against the same, or given aid or comfort to the enemies thereof. But Congress may by a vote of two-thirds of each House, remove such disability.

SECTION 4. The validity of the public debt of the United States, authorized by law, including debts incurred for payment of pensions and bounties for services in suppressing insurrection or rebellion, shall not be questioned. But neither the United States nor any State shall assume or pay any debt or obligation incurred in aid of insurrection or rebellion against the United States, or any claim for the loss or emancipation of any slave; but all such debts, obligations and claims shall be held illegal and void.

SECTION 5. The Congress shall have power to enforce, by appropriate legislation, the provisions of this article.

AMENDMENT XV.
(Adopted March 30, 1870)

SECTION 1. The right of citizens of the United States to vote shall not be denied or abridged by the United States or by any State on account of race, color, or previous condition of servitude.

SECTION 2. The Congress shall have power to enforce this article by appropriate legislation.

AMENDMENT XVI.
(Adopted Feb. 25, 1913)

The Congress shall have power to lay and collect taxes on incomes, from whatever source derived, without apportionment among the several States, and without regard to any census or enumeration.

AMENDMENT XVII.
(Adopted May 13, 1913)

The Senate of the United States shall be composed of two Senators from each State, elected by the people thereof, for six years; and each Senator shall have one vote. The electors in each State shall have the qualifications requisite for electors of the most numerous branch of the State legislatures.

When vacancies happen in the representation of any State in the Senate, the executive authority of such State shall issue writs of election to fill such vacancies: su-Providedea, That the legislature of any State may empower the executive thereof to make temporary appointments until the people fill the vacancies by election as the legislature may direct.

This amendment shall not be so construed as to affect the election or term of any Senator chosen before it becomes valid as part of the Constitution.

AMENDMENT XVIII.
(Adopted Jan. 29, 1919)

SECTION 1. After one year from ratification of this article the manufacture, sale, or transportation of intoxicating liquors within, the importation thereof into, or the exportation thereof from the United States and all territory subject to the jurisdiction thereof for beverage purposes is hereby prohibited.

SECTION 2. The Congress and the several States shall have concurrent power to enforce this article by appropriate legislation.

SECTION 3. This article shall be inoperative unless it shall have been ratified as an amendment to the Constitution by the legislatures of the several States, as provided in the Constitution, within seven years from the date of the submission hereof to the States by the Congress.

AMENDMENT XIX.
(Adopted Aug. 26, 1920)

The right of citizens of the United States to vote shall not be denied or abridged by the United States or by any State on account of sex.

Congress shall have power to enforce this article by appropriate legislation.

AMENDMENT XX.
(Adopted Feb. 6, 1933)

SECTION 1. The terms of the President and Vice President shall end at noon on the 20th day of January, and the terms of Senators and Representatives at noon on the 3d day of January, of the years in which such terms would have ended if this article had not been ratified; and the terms of their successors shall then begin.

SECTION 2. The Congress shall assemble at least once in every year, and such meeting shall begin at noon on the 3d day of January, unless they shall by law appoint a different day.

SECTION 3. If, at the time fixed for the beginning of the term of the President, the President elect shall have died, the Vice President elect shall become President. If a President shall not have been chosen before the time fixed for the beginning of his term, or if the President elect shall have failed to qualify, then the Vice President elect shall act as President until a President shall have qualified; and the Congress may by law provide for the case wherein neither a President elect nor a Vice President elect shall have qualified, declaring who shall then act as President, or the manner in which one who is to act shall be selected, and such person shall act accordingly until a President or Vice President shall have qualified.

SECTION 4. The Congress may by law provide for the case of the death of any of the persons from whom the House of Representatives may choose a President whenever the right of choice shall have devolved upon them, and for the case of the death of any of the persons from whom the Senate may choose a Vice President whenever the right of choice shall have devolved upon them.

SECTION 5. Sections 1 and 2 shall take effect on the 15th day of October following the ratification of this article.

SECTION 6. This article shall be inoperative unless it shall have been ratified as an amendment to the Constitution by the legislatures of three-fourths of the several States within seven years from the date of its submission.

AMENDMENT XXI.
(Adopted Dec. 5, 1933)

SECTION 1. The eighteenth article of amendment to the Constitution of the United States is hereby repealed.

SECTION 2. The transportation or importation into any State, Territory, or possession of the United States for delivery or use therein of intoxicating liquors, in violation of the laws thereof, is hereby prohibited.

SECTION 3. This article shall be inoperative unless it shall have been ratified as an amendment to the Constitution by conventions in the several States, as provided in the Constitution, within seven years from the date of the submission hereof to the States by the Congress.

AMENDMENT XXII.
(Adopted Feb. 27, 1951)

SECTION 1. No person shall be elected to the office of the President more than twice, and no person who has held the office of President, or acted as President, for more than two years of a term to which some other person was elected President shall be elected to the office of the President more than once. But this Article shall not apply to any person holding the office of President when this Article was proposed by the Congress, and shall not prevent any person who may be holding the office of President, or acting as President, during the term within which this Article

becomes operative from holding the office of President or acting as President during the remainder of such term.

SECTION 2. This Article shall be inoperative unless it shall have been ratified as an amendment to the Constitution by the legislatures of three-fourths of the several States within seven years from the date of its submission to the States by the Congress.

AMENDMENT XXIII.
(Adopted Mar. 29, 1961)

SECTION 1. The District constituting the seat of Government of the United States shall appoint in such manner as the Congress may direct:

A number of electors of President and Vice President equal to the whole number of Senators and Representatives in Congress to which the District would be entitled if it were a State, but in no event more than the least populous State; they shall be in addition to those appointed by the States, but they shall be considered, for the purposes of the election of President and Vice President, to be electors appointed by a State; and they shall meet in the District and perform such duties as provided by the twelfth article of amendment.

SECTION 2. The Congress shall have power to enforce this article by appropriate legislation.

AMENDMENT XXIV.
(Adopted Jan. 23, 1964)

SECTION 1. The right of citizens of the United States to vote in any primary or other election for President or Vice President, for electors for President or Vice President, or for Senator or Representative in Congress, shall not be denied or abridged by the United States or any State by reason of failure to pay any poll tax or other tax.

SECTION 2. The Congress shall have the power to enforce this article by appropriate legislation.

AMENDMENT XXV.
(Adopted Feb. 10, 1967)

SECTION 1. In case of the removal of the President from office or of his death or resignation, the Vice President shall become President.

SECTION 2. Whenever there is a vacancy in the office of the Vice President, the President shall nominate a Vice President who shall take the office upon confirmation by a majority vote of both houses of Congress.

SECTION 3. Whenever the President transmits to the President pro tempore of the Senate and the Speaker of the House of Representatives his written declaration that he is unable to discharge the powers and duties of his office, and until he transmits to them a written declaration to the contrary, such powers and duties shall be discharged by the Vice President as Acting President.

SECTION 4. Whenever the Vice President and a majority of either the principal officers of the executive departments or of such other body as Congress may by law provide, transmit to the President pro tempore of the Senate and the Speaker of the House of Representatives their written declaration that the President is unable to discharge the powers and duties of his office, the Vice President shall immediately assume the powers and duties of the office as Acting President.

Thereafter, when the President transmits to the President pro tempore of the Senate and the Speaker of the House of Representatives his written declaration that no inability exists, he shall resume the powers and duties of his office unless the Vice President and a majority of either the principal officers of the executive departments or of such other body as Congress may by law provide, transmit within four days to the President pro tempore of the Senate and the Speaker of the House of Representatives their written declaration that the President is unable to discharge the powers and duties of his office. Thereupon Congress shall decide the issue, assembling within forty-eight hours for that purpose if not in session. If the Congress, within twenty-one days after receipt of the latter written declaration, or, if Congress is not in session, within twenty-one days after Congress is required to assemble, determines by two-thirds vote of both houses that the President is unable to discharge the powers and duties of his office, the Vice President shall continue to discharge the same as Acting President; otherwise, the President shall resume the powers and duties of his office.

AMENDMENT XXVI.
(Adopted June 30, 1971)

SECTION 1. The right of citizens of the United States, who are 18 years of age or older, to vote shall not be denied or abridged by the United States or by any state on account of age.

SECTION 2. The Congress shall have power to enforce this article by appropriate legislation.

Bibliography

The Court

Abraham, Henry J., *Freedom and the Court: Civil Rights and Liberties in the United States* (New York, 1982).

—, *Justices and Presidents: A Political History of Appointments to the Supreme Court* (New York, 1985).

Agresto, John, *The Supreme Court and Constitutional Democracy* (Ithaca, NY, 1984).

Baker, Liva, *Miranda: Crime, Law and Politics* (New York, 1985).

Baldwin, S. W., *Two Centuries Growth in American Law, 1701–1901* (New York, 1901).

Barnes, Catherine A., *Men of the Supreme Court: Profiles of the Justices* (New York, 1978).

Bartee, Alice F., *Cases Lost, Causes Won: The Supreme Court and the Judicial Process* (New York, 1984).

Berger, Raoul, *Death Penalties: The Supreme Court's Obstacle Course* (Cambridge, MA, 1982).

Bickel, Alexander M., *The Least Dangerous Branch* (Indianapolis, IN, 1962).

Bickel, Alexander M., and Schmidt, Benno C., Jr., *History of the Supreme Court of the United States: The Judiciary and Responsible Government* (New York, 1984).

Cahn, Edmond, ed., *Supreme Court and Supreme Law* (Bloomington, IN, 1954).

Clayton, James M., *The Making of Justice: The Supreme Court in Action* (New York, 1964).

Currie, David P., *The Constitution in the Supreme Court: The First Hundred Years, 1789–1888* (Chicago, 1985).

Dunham, Allison, and Kurland, Philip B., eds., *Mr. Justice* (Chicago, 1964).

Epstein, Lee, *Conservatives in Court* (Knoxville, TN, 1985).

Fairman, Charles, *History of the Supreme Court of the United States: Reconstruction and Reunion* (New York, 1986).

Freund, Paul A., ed., *History of the Supreme Court of the United States* (New York, 1971).

Friedman, Leon, and Israel, Fred, eds., *The Justices of the United States Supreme Court 1789–1969: Their Lives and Major Opinions* (New York, 1969).

Galloway, John, ed., *The Supreme Court and the Rights of the Accused* (New York, 1973).

Haines, Charles Groves, *The Role of the Supreme Court in American Government and Politics: 1789–1835* (Berkeley, CA, 1944).

Halpern, Stephen C., and Lamb, Charles M., *Supreme Court Activism and Restraint* (Lexington, MA, 1982).

Harrell, Mary Ann, *Equal Justice Under the Law: The Supreme Court in American Life* (Washington, D.C., 1975).

Holzer, Henry M., *Sweet Land of Liberty? The Supreme Court and Individual Rights* (Costa Mesa, CA, 1983).

Kelley, Wayne, ed., *The Supreme Court and Its Work* (Washington, D.C., 1981).

Kluger, Richard, *Simple Justice: The History of Brown v. Board of Education and Black America's Struggle for Equality* (New York, 1975).

Konvitz, Milton R., *Expanding Liberties: Freedom's Gains in Postwar America* (New York, 1966).

Kurland, Philip, and Casper, Gerhard, eds., *Landmark Briefs and Arguments of the Supreme Court of the United States: Constitutional Law* (Arlington, VA, 1977).

Kutler, Stanley I., *Judicial Power and Reconstruction Politics* (Chicago, 1968).

Lermack, Paul, *Rights on Trial: The Supreme Court and the Criminal Law* (Millwood, NY, 1983).

Lewis, William D., ed., *Great American Lawyers* (Philadelphia, 1909).

McCloskey, Robert Green, *The American Supreme Court* (Chicago, 1960).

—, *The Modern Supreme Court* (Cambridge, MA, 1972).

McCune, Wesley, *The Nine Young Men* (New York, 1947).

Marcus, Maeva, and Perry, James R., eds., *The Documentary History of the Supreme Court of the United States* (New York, 1985).

Mason, Alpheus Thomas, *The Supreme Court from Taft to Burger* (Baton Rouge, LA, 1979).

—, *The Supreme Court from Taft to Warren* (Baton Rouge, LA, 1958).

Mason, Alpheus Thomas, and Beaney, William M., *The Supreme Court in a Free Society* (Englewood Cliffs, NJ, 1959).

Mendelson, Wallace, *Supreme Court Statecraft: The Rule of Law and Men* (Ames, IA, 1985).

Menez, Joseph F., *Decision Making in the Supreme Court of the United States: A Political and Behavioral View* (Lanham, MD, 1984).

Murphy, Walter F., *Congress and the Court: A Case Study in the American Political Process* (Chicago, 1962).

Newmyer, R. Kent, *The Supreme Court Under Marshall and Taney* (Arlington Heights, IL, 1969).

Paul, Arnold M., *Conservative Crisis and the Rule of Law* (Ithaca, NY, 1960).

Perry, Michael J., *The Constitution, The Courts and Human Rights: An Inquiry into the Legitimacy of Constitutional Policymaking by the Judiciary* (New Haven, 1984).

Pollack, Louis H., ed., *The Constitution and the Supreme Court: A Documentary History* (Cleveland, 1966).

Pritchett, C. Herman, *Congress versus the Supreme Court: 1957–1960* (Minneapolis, 1961).

—, *The Roosevelt Court: A Study in Judicial Politics and Values, 1937–1947* (New York, 1948).

Rodell, Fred, *Nine Men: A Political History of the Supreme Court from 1790 to 1955* (New York, 1955).

Schlesinger, Steven R., *The United States Supreme Court: Fact, Evidence and Law* (Lanham, MD, 1983).

Schwartz, Bernard, *A Basic History of the U.S. Supreme Court* (Princeton, 1968).

—, *The Supreme Court: Constitutional Revolution in Retrospect* (New York, 1957).

Silver, David M., *Lincoln's Supreme Court* (Urbana, IL, 1956).

Sutherland, Ernest, *The Story of the Supreme Court* (Indianapolis, IN, 1936).

Umbreit, Kenneth Bernard, *Our Eleven Chief Justices* (New York, 1938).

Warren, Charles, *The Supreme Court in United States History* (Boston, 1926).

Wasby, S. L., *The Supreme Court in the Federal Judicial System* (New York, 1984).

Westin, Alan, ed., *An Autobiography of the Supreme Court: Off-the-Bench Commentary by the Justices* (New York, 1963).

—, *The Supreme Court: Views from Inside* (New York, 1961).

Wilkinson, J. Harvie, *From Brown to Bakke: The Supreme Court and School Integration 1954–1978* (New York, 1979).

Witt, Elder, ed., *Guide to the U.S. Supreme Court* (Washington, D.C., 1979).

Woodward, Bob, and Armstrong, Scott, *The Brethren: Inside the Supreme Court* (New York, 1979).

The Justices

BLACK, HUGO LAFAYETTE

Ball, Howard, *The Vision and the Dream of Justice Hugo L. Black* (University, AL, 1975).

Black, Hugo, *A Constitutional Faith* (New York, 1969).

Black, Hugo, Jr., *My Father: A Remembrance* (New York, 1975).

Dilliard, Irving, ed., *One Man's Stand for Freedom* (New York, 1963).

Dunne, Gerald T., *Hugo Black and the Judicial Revolution* (New York, 1977).

Frank, John P., *Mr. Justice Black* (New York, 1949).

Hamilton, Virginia Van Der Veer, *Hugo Black: The Alabama Years* (Baton Rouge, LA, 1972).

Mendelson, Wallace, *Justices Black and Frankfurter: Conflict in the Court* (Chicago, 1966).

Strickland, Stephen, ed., *Hugo Black and the Supreme Court* (Indianapolis, IN, 1967).

Williams, Charlotte, *Hugo L. Black* (Baltimore, 1950).

BRANDEIS, LOUIS DEMBITZ

Bickel, A. M., *The Unpublished Opinions of Mr. Justice Brandeis: The Supreme Court at Work* (Cambridge, MA, 1957).

Konefsky, Samuel J., *The Legacy of Holmes and Brandeis* (New York, 1956).

Lief, A., ed., *The Social and Economic Views of Mr. Justice Brandeis* (New York, 1930).
Mason, Alpheus Thomas, *Brandeis: A Free Man's Life* (New York, 1946).
—, *Brandeis: Lawyer and Judge in the Modern State* (Princeton, 1933).
Murphy, Bruce A., *The Brandeis-Frankfurter Connection: The Secret Political Activities of Two Supreme Court Justices* (New York, 1982).

BRENNAN, WILLIAM JOSEPH, JR.
Friedman, Stephen J., ed., *An Affair with Freedom: Justice William J. Brennan, Jr.* (New York, 1967).

BROWN, HENRY BILLINGS
Kent, Charles A., *Memoir of Henry Billings Brown* (New York, 1915).

BURGER, WARREN EARL
Blasi, Vincent, ed., *The Burger Court: The Counter-Revolution That Wasn't* (New Haven, 1983).
Galloway, John, ed., *Criminal Justice and the Burger Court* (New York, 1978).
Lee, Francis, G., *Neither Conservative Nor Liberal: The Burger Court on Civil Rights and Civil Liberties* (Melbourne, FL, 1983).
Pfeffer, Leo, *Religion, State and the Burger Court* (Buffalo, NY, 1985).

BURTON, HAROLD HITZ
Berry, Mary, *Stability, Security and Continuity: Mr. Justice Burton and Decision-Making in the Supreme Court 1945–1958* (Westport, CT, 1978).

BUTLER, PIERCE
Danielski, David J., *A Supreme Court Justice is Appointed* (New York, 1964).

BYRNES, JAMES FRANCIS
Byrnes, James F., *All in One Lifetime* (New York, 1958).

CAMPBELL, JOHN ARCHIBALD
Connor, Henry G., *John Archibald Campbell* (Cambridge, MA, 1920).

CARDOZO, BENJAMIN NATHAN
Cardozo, Benjamin N., *The Nature of the Judicial Process* (New Haven, 1921).
Hellman, George S., *Benjamin N. Cardozo* (New York, 1940).
Levy, Beryl H., *Cardozo and Frontiers of Legal Thinking* (New York, 1938).
Pollard, Joseph P., *Mr. Justice Cardozo* (New York, 1935).

CHASE, SALMON PORTLAND
Belden, Thomas, and Belden, Marva, *So Fell the Angels* (Boston, 1956).
Donald, David, *Inside Lincoln's Cabinet* (New York, 1954).

CLARKE, JOHN HESSIN
Warner, Hoyt, L., *Mr. Justice Clarke* (Cleveland, 1959).

CLIFFORD, NATHAN
Clifford, Philip Q., *Nathan Clifford, Democrat* (New York, 1922).

DANIEL, PETER VIVIAN
Frank, John P., *Justice Daniel Dissenting: A Biography of Peter V. Daniel* (Cambridge, MA, 1964).

DAVIS, DAVID
King, Willard L., *Lincoln's Manager: David Davis* (Cambridge, MA, 1960).

DAY, WILLIAM RUFUS
McLean, Joseph E., *William Rufus Day: Supreme Court Justice from Ohio* (Baltimore, 1946).

DOUGLAS, WILLIAM ORVILLE
Countryman, Vern, *The Douglas Opinions* (New York, 1977).
—, *The Judicial Record of Justice William O. Douglas* (Cambridge, MA, 1974).
—, *William O. Douglas of the Supreme Court: A Selection of His Opinions* (New York, 1959).
Douglas, William O., *The Court Years 1939–1975: The Autobiography of William O. Douglas* (New York, 1980).
—, *Go East Young Man: The Early Years* (New York, 1974).
Simon, James, *Independent Journey: The Life of William O. Douglas* (New York, 1980).

ELLSWORTH, OLIVER
Brown, William G., *The Life of Oliver Ellsworth* (New York, 1905).

FIELD, STEPHEN JOHNSON
Swisher, Carl B., *Stephen J. Field: Craftsman of the Law* (Washington, D.C., 1930).

FORTAS, ABE
Fortas, Abe, *Concerning Dissent and Civil Disobedience* (New York, 1968).
Lewis, Anthony, *Gideon's Trumpet* (New York, 1964).
Shogan, Robert, *A Question of Judgment: The Fortas Case and the Struggle for the Supreme Court* (Indianapolis, IN, 1972).

FRANKFURTER, FELIX
Baker, Liva, *Felix Frankfurter* (New York, 1969).
Frankfurter, Felix, *Felix Frankfurter Reminisces* (New York, 1962).
—, *Of Law and Life and Other Things that Matter* (Cambridge, MA, 1965).
—, *Of Law and Men* (New York, 1956).
—, *Law and Politics* (New York, 1939).
Frankfurter, Felix, and Landis, James M., *The Business of the Supreme Court: A Study in the Federal Judicial System* (New York, 1927).
Freedman, Ralph, ed., *Roosevelt and Frankfurter: Their Correspondence 1928–1945* (Boston, 1968).
Hirsch, H. N., *The Enigma of Felix Frankfurter* (New York, 1981).
Kurland, Philip B., *Felix Frankfurter on the Supreme Court: Extrajudicial Essays on the Court and the Constitution* (Cambridge, MA, 1970).
—, *Mr. Justice Frankfurter and the Constitution* (Chicago, 1971).
Lash, Joseph P., *From the Diaries of Felix Frankfurter* (New York, 1975).
Mendelson, Wallace, ed., *Felix Frankfurter: The Judge* (New York, 1964).
—, *Felix Frankfurter: A Tribute* (New York, 1964).
—, *Justices Black and Frankfurter: Conflict in the Court* (Chicago, 1966).
Murphy, Bruce A., *The Brandeis-Frankfurter Connection: The Secret Political Activities of Two Supreme Court Justices* (New York, 1982).
Parrish, Michael E., *Felix Frankfurter and His Times: The Reform Years* (New York, 1982).
Thomas, Helen S., *Felix Frankfurter: Scholar on the Bench* (Baltimore, 1960).

FULLER, MELVILLE WESTON
King, Willard L., *Melville Weston Fuller* (New York, 1950).

GOLDBERG, ARTHUR JOSEPH
Goldberg, Arthur J., *AFL-CIO: Labor United* (New York, 1956).
—, *Equal Justice: The Warren Era in the Supreme Court* (New York, 1971).
Moynihan, Daniel P., *The Defenses of Freedom: The Public Papers of Arthur J. Goldberg* (New York, 1966).

HOLMES, OLIVER WENDELL, JR.

Biddle, Francis, *Justice Holmes, Natural Law and the Supreme Court* (New York, 1961).
Bowen, Catherine Drinker, *Yankee from Olympus* (Boston, 1944).
Frankfurter, Felix, *Mr. Justice Holmes and the Supreme Court* (Cambridge, MA, 1961).
Holmes, Oliver Wendell, *The Common Law* (Boston, 1961 rev.).
Howe, Mark DeWolfe, *Justice Oliver Wendell Holmes: The Shaping Years, 1841–1870; The Proving Years, 1870–1882* (Cambridge, MA, 1957–1962).
Konefsky, Samuel J., *The Legacy of Holmes and Brandeis* (New York, 1956).

HUGHES, CHARLES EVANS

Glad, Betty, *Charles Evans Hughes and the Illusions of Innocence* (Urbana, IL, 1966).
Hendel, Samuel, *Charles Evans Hughes and the Supreme Court* (New York, 1951).
Hughes, Charles Evans, *Supreme Court of the United States: Its Foundations, Methods and Achievements, an Interpretation* (New York, 1928).
Perkins, Dexter, *Charles Evans Hughes and American Democratic Statesmanship* (Boston, 1956).
Pusey, Merlo J., *Charles Evans Hughes* (New York, 1951).
Wesser, Robert F., *Charles Evans Hughes: Politics and Reform in New York, 1905–1910* (Ithaca, NY, 1967).

JACKSON, ROBERT HOUGHWOUT

Desmond, Charles S., *Mr. Justice Jackson* (New York, 1969).
Gerhart, Eugene C., *America's Advocate: Robert H. Jackson* (Indianapolis, IN 1958).
—, *Lawyer's Judge: Supreme Court Justice Jackson* (Albany, NY, 1961).
Jackson, Robert H., *Full Faith and Credit: The Lawyer's Clause of the Constitution* (New York, 1945).
—, *The Struggle for Judicial Supremacy: A Study of a Crisis in American Power Politics* (New York, 1947).
—, *The Supreme Court in the American System of Government* (Cambridge, MA, 1955).

JAY, JOHN

Monaghan, Frank, *John Jay* (New York, 1935).

JOHNSON, WILLIAM

Morgan, Donald G., *Justice William Johnson, the First Dissenter: The Career and Constitutional Philosophy of a Jeffersonian Judge* (Columbia, SC, 1954).

LAMAR, JOSEPH RUCKER

Lamar, Claudia Pendleton, *The Life of Joseph Rucker Lamar* (New York, 1926).

LAMAR, LUCIUS QUINTUS CINCINNATUS

Cate, W. A., *Lucius Q. C. Lamar, Secession and Reunion* (Chapel Hill, NC, 1935).
Mayes, Edward, *Lucius Q. C. Lamar, His Life, Times and Speeches* (Nashville, TN, 1896).

McKENNA, JOSEPH

McDevitt, Brother Matthew, *Joseph McKenna: Associate Justice of the United States* (Washington, D.C., 1946).

McLEAN, JOHN

Weisenberger, Francis P., *The Life of John McLean: A Politician on the United States Supreme Court* (Columbus, OH, 1937).

MARSHALL, JOHN

Beveridge, Albert J., *The Life of John Marshall* (Boston, 1916–1919).
Haskins, George L., *The Foundations of Power: John Marshall, 1801–1815* (New York, 1981).
Jones, W. Melville, *Chief Justice John Marshall: A Reappraisal* (Ithaca, NY, 1966).
Servies, James A., *A Bibliography of John Marshall* (Washington, D.C., 1956).

MARSHALL, THURGOOD
Bland, Randall W., *Private Pressure on Public Law: The Legal Career of Justice Thurgood Marshall* (Port Washington, NY, 1973).

MILLER, SAMUEL FREEMAN
Fairman, Charles, *Mr. Justice Miller and the Supreme Court, 1862–1890* (Cambridge, MA, repr. 1966).
Gregory, Charles, *Samuel Freeman Miller* (Iowa City, IA, 1907).

MURPHY, FRANK
Fine, Sidney, *Frank Murphy: The Detroit Years* (Ann Arbor, MI, 1975).
Howard, J. Woodford, *Mr. Justice Murphy: A Political Biography* (Princeton, 1968).
Norris, Harold, *Mr. Justice Murphy and the Bill of Rights* (Dobbs Ferry, NY, 1965).

POWELL, LEWIS FRANKLIN, JR.
Wilkinson, J. Harvie, *Serving Justice: A Supreme Court Clerk's View* (New York, 1974).

REED, STANLEY FORMAN
O'Brien, F. William, *Justice Reed and the First Amendment* (Washington, D.C., 1958).

RUTLEDGE, JOHN
Barry, Richard, *Mr. Rutledge of South Carolina* (New York, 1942).

RUTLEDGE, WILEY BLOUNT, JR.
Harper, V. Fowler, *Justice Rutledge and the Bright Constellation* (Indianapolis, IN, 1965).

SHIRAS, GEORGE, JR.
Shiras, George III, and Shiras, Winfield, *Justice George Shiras, Jr. of Pittsburgh* (Pittsburgh, 1953).

STONE, HARLAN FISKE
Konefsky, Samuel J., *Chief Justice Stone and the Supreme Court* (New York, 1945).
Mason, Alpheus Thomas, *Harlan Fiske Stone: Pillar of the Law* (New York, 1956).

STORY, JOSEPH
Newmyer, R. Kent, *Supreme Court Justice Joseph Story: Statesman of the Old Republic* (Chapel Hill, NC, 1985).
Schwartz, Mortimer D., and Hogan, John C., *Joseph Story* (New York, 1959).
Story, Joseph, *Miscellaneous Writings* (Boston, 1852).
Story, W. W., *Life and Letters of Joseph Story* (Boston, 1851).

SUTHERLAND, GEORGE
Paschal, Joel, *Mr. Justice Sutherland* (Princeton, 1951).

TAFT, WILLIAM HOWARD
McHale, F., *President and Chief Justice: The Life and Public Services of William Howard Taft* (Philadelphia, 1931).
Mason, Alpheus Thomas, *William Howard Taft: Chief Justice* (New York, 1964).
Pringle, H. F., *The Life and Times of William Howard Taft* (New York, 1939).
Taft, William Howard, *The Anti-Trust Act and the Supreme Court* (New York, 1914).

TANEY, ROGER BROOKE
Lewis, Walker, *Without Fear or Favor: A Biography of Chief Justice Roger Brooke Taney* (Boston, 1965).

Smith, Charles W., Jr., *Roger B. Taney: Jacksonian Jurist* (Chapel Hill, NC, 1936).
Swisher, Carl Brent, *Roger B. Taney* (New York, 1935).

VINSON, FREDERICK MOORE
Pritchett, C. Herman, *Civil Liberties and the Vinson Court* (Chicago, 1954).

WAITE, MORRISON REMICK
Magrath, C. Peter, *Morrison R. Waite: The Triumph of Character* (New York, 1963).
Trimble, Bruce R., *Chief Justice Waite: Defender of the Public Interest* (Princeton, 1938).

WARREN, EARL
Christman, Henry H., *The Public Papers of Chief Justice Earl Warren* (New York, 1966).
Frank, John P., and Karsh, Yousuf, *The Warren Court* (New York, 1964).
Huston, Luther, *Pathway to Judgment: A Study of Earl Warren* (Philadelphia, 1966).
Katcher, Leo, *Earl Warren: A Political Biography* (New York, 1967).
Kurland, Gerald, *The Supreme Court Under Warren* (Charlottesville, NY, 1973).
Levy, Leonard W., ed., *The Supreme Court Under Earl Warren* (New York, 1972).
Pollack, Jack Harrison, *Earl Warren: The Judge Who Changed America* (Englewood Cliffs, NJ, 1979).
Schwartz, Bernard, *Super Chief: Earl Warren and His Supreme Court—A Judicial Biography* (New York, 1983).
—, *Unpublished Opinions of the Warren Court* (New York, 1985).
Warren Earl, *The Memoirs of Earl Warren* (New York, 1977).
Weaver, John D., *Warren: The Man, The Court, The Era* (Boston, 1967).
White, G. Edmund, *Earl Warren: A Public Life* (New York, 1982).

WAYNE, JAMES MOORE
Lawrence, Alexander A., *James Moore Wayne, Southern Unionist* (Chapel Hill, NC, 1943).

WHITE, EDWARD DOUGLASS, JR.
Klinkhamer, Sister Marie Carolyn, *Edward Douglass White, Chief Justice of the United States* (Washington, D.C., 1943).

WILSON, JAMES
Smith, C. P., *James Wilson, Founding Father: 1742–1798* (Chapel Hill, NC, 1956).

Acknowledgments and Credits

Acknowledgments

Numerous people made significant contributions to the reference guide. The editors are particularly indebted to the advisors: Richard S. Kay of the School of Law, University of Connecticut; Robert C. Khayat of the School of Law, University of Mississippi; and James W. Zirkle of the Marshall-Wythe School of Law, College of William and Mary. The advisors were most generous with their time and were always available to offer suggestions that greatly improved the book. Richard S. Kay was especially helpful during the initial structuring and outlining stages and also reviewed many of the biographies. In addition, he reviewed the first draft of the Division of Power: The Federal Government and the States section. Robert C. Khayat helped to shape and review the Landmark Cases section and also reviewed The Constitutional Powers of the Branches of the Federal Government. James W. Zirkle provided essential guidance on the Individual Rights section and prepared the section on The Role of the Court. Rubi Finkelstein wrote the section on The Constitutional Powers of the Branches of the Federal Government and made a major contribution to the following section, Division of Power: The Federal Government and the States. Joyce Phipps also helped with this latter section. The Individual Rights section was written by Deborah A. Bosworth and Caryn L. Zimmerman, with the help of Paul D. Bain and David A. Sattler. Amy Ravitz prepared the outlines for the second and third sections.

Diane Hamilton of Washington, D.C., used her extensive knowledge of collections in the capital to help shape the types of illustrations chosen for the book. She also proved indefatigable in her efforts to obtain the illustrations ultimately selected.

Neil Asher Silberman played a key role in planning the structure of both the biographies of the justices and the landmark cases. He also wrote a number of the biographies and landmark case descriptions. Robert J. Haws of the University of Mississippi wrote the biography of John Marshall, while William B. Shaw of the University of Mississippi prepared the biography of Earl Warren. Other writers who contributed biographies and/or landmark cases included: Jessica L. Braus, Susan Braus, Thomas J. Farrell, Joseph Hammer, Mary T. Henderson, Elizabeth Milton, Cynthia Moreland, Lindsay P. Rand, Amy Ravitz, and Christy Townley-Mann.

Suzanne Stone Burke and Elizabeth J. Jewell acted as assistant editors. Rebecca Lyon did the copyediting and proofreading, while Carol B. Dudley prepared the general index. Diane B. Surprenant was editorial assistant.

Credits

Jacket (front) Diane Hamilton
Jacket (back) Library of Congress
12, 13, 15, 16, 17, 18, 19, 20, 21, 22, 23, 25, 26, 27 Library of Congress
28, 29 National Archives
30, 31, 32, 33 Library of Congress
34, 35, 36, 37, 38 National Archives
40, 41, 42, 48, 50, 52 Library of Congress
54 National Archives (National Park Service)
55, 58, 59, 60, 61, 64, 67 Library of Congress
68 National Archives
69 Library of Congress
71 U.S. Senate
72 National Archives
73, 78, 80, 81, 82, 83, 84, 85, 86, 87, 88 Library of Congress
89 National Archives (U.S. Office of War Information)
90, 91, 92, 93 Library of Congress
96 National Archives
98 Library of Congress
101, 106 National Archives
113, 114, 117, 118, 119, 120, 121, 122, 123 Library of Congress
124, 125 National Archives
127 Supreme Court Historical Society
128, 129, 130, 134 Library of Congress
139, 141 National Archives
144, 146, 149, 150 Library of Congress
151 (top) National Archives
151 (bottom) Karl Schumacher, The White House
155, 156 National Archives
159, 161, 166 Library of Congress
167 National Archives
169, 170 Library of Congress
173 National Archives
176, 177 Library of Congress

178 Michael Evans, The White House
179, 181 Library of Congress
182 The White House
184 National Archives
187, 189 Library of Congress
192 The White House
193 Library of Congress
196 Department of State
198 (top) The White House
198 (bottom), 199 Library of Congress
200 U.S. Senate
201 Library of Congress
202 National Archives
205, 208, 209, 211, 213, 215, 216, 217, 220, 221, 222, 226, 228, 229 Library of Congress
230 California Historical Society Library
232, 233 Library of Congress
235, 236 National Archives
238, 239, 241 Library of Congress
242 The White House
243 National Archives
246, 249, 250 Library of Congress
251 Harry S. Truman Library (U.S. Army)
256, 258, 259, 260, 265, 267, 269, 271, 272, 278, 279, 283, 285, 289, 291, 292, 295, 297, 300 Library of Congress
301 National Archives
302, 308, 309, 315, 317, 318 (left) Library of Congress
318 (right) National Archives
321 The White House
323 Library of Congress
324 National Archives
325 Library of Congress
326 (left) National Archives
326 (right), 328, 329, 331, 332, 334, 335, 336, 337, 339, 344, 345, 346, 349, 355, 356 Library of Congress

Index